Potentials of
Childhood

Potentials of Childhood

Volume I. A Historical View of Early Experience

William Fowler
Tufts University

LexingtonBooks
D.C. Heath and Company
Lexington, Massachusetts
Toronto

Library of Congress Cataloging in Publication Data

Fowler, William, 1921-
  Potentials of childhood.

  Vol. 2 written in collaboration with Karen Ogston and others.
  Includes bibliographical references and index.
  Contents: v. 1. A historical view of early experience—v. 2. Studies in
early developmental learning.
  1. Ability in children. 2. Cognition in children. 3. Learning.
4. Education, Preschool. I. Title.
BF723.A25F68   1983   155.4   80-8839
ISBN 0-669-04387-7 (v. 1)
ISBN 0-669-06433-5 (v. 2)
ISBN 0-669-06432-7 (2-vol. set)

Copyright © 1983 by D.C. Heath and Company

Second printing, September 1984

Published simultaneously in Canada

Printed in the United States of America on acid-free paper

International Standard Book Number: 0-669-04387-7

Library of Congress Catalog Card Number: 80-8839

To Neva

Contents

Figures and Tables

Preface

How important is early experience to cognitive development? This question has plagued sages, scholars, and ordinary people from the earliest times, provoking controversy as early as Plato and the Greeks, and more recently with the advent of Freud's theories, the research on perceptual deprivation, institutionalization in infancy, early learning, and the early-intervention studies of the 1960s. The problem is embedded in the nature- versus- nurture issue, which Hebb and Hunt in their different ways helped to transform, Hebb in hypothesizing about the neurological bases for early experience and Hunt in burying the ghosts of preformationism and predeterminism and developing a cognitive structural basis for early developmental learning from Piaget. In the past few years the trend has been to downplay the importance of early experience, the Clarkes in England, among others, marshaling evidence to demonstrate the reversibility of the effects of early deprivation. Yet too many problems remain for the issue to be discarded or solved quite so soon.

The purpose of these two volumes is to review the experimental evidence on early stimulation with a view toward formulating the problem in different terms. The aim is to establish a developmental perspective to evaluate studies on early experience and a paradigm for research on developmental stimulation. Except for the substantial body of literature on nursery-school and day-care attendance and the early-intervention studies on children from impoverished backgrounds, much of the research on early learning consists of short-term training studies, which generally lose sight of competence as integral to an organism and a history. Learning is a cumulative, developmental phenomenon, rooted in ecology and powered by experience. It is a process in which children, developing according to their biological capacity and the type and quality of stimulation, gradually acquire concepts and rules that form a cognitive system for understanding and manipulating the world. According to this framework, the work described here is an attempt to determine the degree of importance of the early periods of developmental stimulation and what dimensions of stimulation affect the process. The objective is to contribute toward the establishment of a conception of and an approach to research on developmental learning as a necessary basis for studying the experiential roots of cognitive process and the development of competence. Early experience is germane to so many fields and facets of early education, child care, and child development that the book has been prepared to reach an extended audience. The language is free of jargon and narrow technical concepts, and the book encompasses a number of broad issues relevant to human development and society.

The work consists of two volumes. Volume I is a historical survey and critical analysis of perspectives and research on early education and early experience; volume II is a series of studies on early developmental learning following a strategy developed over the course of these and other studies. The first four chapters of volume I present concepts and review literature on cultural and group bases for the origins of competence (chapter 1), formulate differences in socialization practices between folk and large-scale societies (chapter 2), review the history of approaches to early education (chapter 3), and review classical studies illustrating the problems and limitations of historical approaches to the study of early stimulation and development (chapter 4). Chapter 5 is an overview of the dimensions and concept areas of the developmental stimulation process; following which collected evidence on early developmental stimulation is reviewed in the last four chapters (6-9).

The first chapter of volume II introduces the strategy that has guided the research of the author and his students in the collected studies. This is followed by a detailed summary and analysis of earlier studies on early reading, general cognitive, motor and language stimulation (chapters 2 and 3). Reports on four recent doctoral dissertations encompassing research on early stimulation of language, motor skills, reading, and problem solving constitute the next four chapters (4-7). The final chapter (8) synthesizes the major findings and themes of the entire book.

None of the literature reviews is exhaustive. The body of material that bears on early stimulation, particularly the literature on early intervention, is too vast, redundant, and scattered to consider reviewing in all its ramifications. The major objectives have been to report studies that document the evidence and point up the processes and limitations of designs and strategies. For some of the same reasons, most of the literature reviewed has been confined to studies on developmentally oriented, experimental stimulation, with a generous inclusion of case-study literature (including my own), wherever the approach has been sufficiently analytic and systematic. Thus correlation studies, which do not provide the same type of evidence and are particularly elusive with regard to pegging developmental spans and dimensions, studies on early perceptual deprivation, and studies on the neurological bases of stimulation and learning have all been largely excluded. Although both deprivation and neurology are obviously of first importance, the focus here has been on the cumulative effects of stimulation, not its absence, and on the cognitive and behavioral effects, not the underlying neurological changes that are presumed to occur with stimulation. Although the effects of cognitive stimulation on social and emotional development are mentioned here and there, no attempt has been made to discuss the emerging body of studies on cognitive stimulation in the social sphere.

Too many mentors and colleagues have contributed toward the development of the ideas in this work to list them all by name. I would simply like to mention Myrtle McGraw, one of the pioneers, and Joe Hunt, one of the founders of the field of early learning and cognitive development; both have long been a special inspiration to me. Marilyn Torrey and Nancy Caudle are owed a special debt for their tireless efforts and skills in deciphering and transcribing my convoluted scrawls. As for my collaborators contributing to volume II and other students who have worked with me in the past, they know best what research on early developmental stimulation means in pain and tribulation.

Potentials of
Childhood

1 The Cultural and Ecological Basis for the Socialization of Competence

Human competence[1] is extremely variable. Mental ability ranges from the barest coping of the retarded to the extraordinary brilliance of the genius, from IQ scores well below 50 to 200 or more, though it is estimated that less than 0.26 percent of the U.S. population falls below 50 or rises above 150 IQ (Newland 1976). Because the distribution of IQ test scores approximates the normal curve, nearly 70 percent of the U.S. population clusters in a relatively narrow average IQ range between 85 and 115. The lowest levels mean difficulty in tying shoe laces and tending to toilet needs, to say nothing of reading and writing or even speaking in connected discourse. Very high IQ levels embrace such skills as the ability to engage in several complex tasks concurrently, retain vast amounts of information, learn many languages easily, solve intricate problems with dispatch, and develop original formulas, codes, logical systems, and theories. Most striking are the contrasts between the concrete thinking, virtual absence of memory, slowness in learning, crudeness of accomplishment, and dullness of curiosity at the lower levels and the abstract thinking, vicelike memory, rapidity of learning, marvels of accomplishment, and endless curiosity at the upper levels.

Competence Variation

Valid though they may be in outline, the foregoing descriptions of the extremes of ability are merely stereotypes, neither of which exactly describes either the very dull or the very bright. Except for persons organically retarded, either by brain damage or specific genetic defect, few individuals function pervasively at such low levels, and, at the other end of the scale, rarely is such an array of superior skills combined in one person. Variations in human competence are as extensive by type as they are by complexity (levels). Thus an individual of otherwise limited skills may be an accomplished weaver, a craft that involves much fine-motor dexterity, painstaking perceptual following of intricate designs, and subtle skills for matching color hues and shades. Memory deficiency in daily events or current affairs in another individual, such as a collector, may contrast with a bewildering competence to recognize endless small differences between postage stamps or vehicle models. At the upper reaches, originality in theoretical physics may well be accompanied by awkwardness in writing skills, as it was in the Danish scientist Nils Bohr, a Nobel Prize winner and founder of the Institute of Theoretical Physics at Copenhagen (Rozenthal 1968). Michael Faraday resorted to spatial representation to construct the first models of electromagnetic field theory because of his limited mathematical skills (Hoffman 1963), and Einstein used visual and visual-motor signs and images to work out mental problems in physics rather than words, which came only later and with difficulty for him (Ghiselin 1955).

Variation in competency appears to be the rule. Variation within individuals is at least as great as variation between individuals. The single IQ score, designed to reflect *g*, or general intelligence, in fact masks differences in skill patterns from individual to individual. Historically constructed to measure *g* through discarding items that did not correlate highly with one another (Meyers and Dingman 1960), ability tests have come to take account of differences in types of skills, beginning with Thurstone's (1944) measures of primary mental abilities (verbal, numerical, reasoning, perceptual speed, and spatial), expanding with the Wechsler ten-sub scale series for measuring intelligence (1951, 1974), and later such efforts as the Meeker (1969) templates to tease out specific skill differences buried in the Stanford-Binet (1960). Thus several individuals with identical IQ scores are likely to display quite different combinations of strengths and weaknesses in memory, numerical, verbal, spatial-reasoning, divergent-thinking, and other skills. One of the most widespread manifestations of the differentiation of abilities that the single IQ test score masks is the consistency with which individuals tend to cluster in two groups, the verbally skilled and the mathematically skilled, which are also patterned by sex (Anastasi 1958; Beckman 1968; Dye and Very 1972). The correlation between such factors among college students in one study reached only .23 (Garrett 1938). Most mental tests also fail to take account of a variety of specialized competencies, such as music, art, dance, athletics, and technical knowledge in special fields (Anastasi 1958; Wilson 1953).

One of the by-products of the *g* approach to measuring abilities is a curious anomaly in Cox's (1926) classic study of the historically brilliant: generally recognized individuals of the stature of Copernicus, "The Founder of Modern Astronomy," (p. 230). Cervantes (author of the great Spanish classic, *Don Quixote*), and philosopher John Locke, "One of the Most Influential Thinkers of Modern Times" (p.328) were retrospectively assigned IQ values as low as 105, 105, and 125, and no higher than 130, 110, and 130, respectively, compared to more or less equally (but certainly no more) eminent and complex geniuses like Grotius, Macaulay, and Bentham, whose IQs were minimally estimated as 185, 170, and 170, respectively. Although some of the discrepancy was a function of the relative sparseness of reliable information on their life histories, the tendency to downplay the individual's own works as criteria reflects the narrowness of the generalist IQ approach to the assessment of abilities. Other extraordinarily skilled and creative figures such as Rembrandt, Bach, and even Leonardo da Vinci (*the Renaissance man*), suffered similar fates, having to get along with IQs evaluated as no more than 110, 125, and 135, respectively, no doubt in part because their main work was in the arts, where skills not included in IQ measures count more (though this is hardly true of the engineering brilliance of Leonardo).

Even more indicative of the limitations of IQ measures and the concept of generalized intelligence are the extremes in unevenness among competencies reported for the idiot savant, in whom extraordinarily rapid and complex mental calculating skills may be combined with an IQ of 50 (Anastasi 1958; Duckett 1977). Similarly stark contrasts have been observed among individuals able to sing an extensive repertoire of tunes or paint complex pictures, yet virtually without speech and other common skills. Abilities may be patterned in many ways and to many degrees.

A burgeoning variety of models and measures pay recognition to the basic diversity of human abilities. Most are empirically and intuitively derived without a great deal of conceptual integration, either in terms of mental structures or developmental processes (Fowler 1980a). Many of the recent ability measures, such as the McCarthy Scales (1972) or the Woodcock-Johnson Psycho-Education Battery (1977), measure a host of cognitive abilities organized into categories (despite the lack of developed theory), thus bringing together in single instruments batteries to assess the diversity of human competencies. Various verbal, quantitative, memory, reasoning, and perceptual and motor factors are combined in this way and, in the case of the Woodcock-Johnson battery, extended to embrace assessment of aptitude, achievement, and interest in school subjects (reading, language, and math). The most comprehensive approach to multiple-ability assessment is Guilford's (1967) so-called structure of intellect, which postulates the existence of as many as 120 different cognitive ability factors, each composed of combinations of three basic cognitive dimensions, operations (evaluation, memory), products (units, classes), and content (figural, symbolic). One of the more promising exceptions to this traditional empirical trend in test construction is the measure based on Piagetian theory, such as various measures of conservation (Green, Ford, and Flamer 1971) and the infant scales designed by Uzgiris and Hunt (1975). The latter have dissected Piaget's unimodel sensorimotor scheme into six distinct ordinal scales of development.

Besides their weakness in theory, few of the common ability measures make any provision for assessing skills in the arts or athletics or indeed for measuring skill differences in any content areas of knowledge, which may in fact account for a great many individual differences. A model of cognitive structures and developmental processes that grapples with the total range of human competencies is presented in a later chapter.

Sources of Competence Variation

Differences between Social Groups

Human development occurs under diverse conditions that influence the type and complexity of abilities attained. Within any large-scale, hierarchically organized society, children grow up in different social classes, receive different amounts and types of formal schooling, live in country or city, and are members of different ethnic groups and subcultures that follow different practices. Among the different groups mean IQ scores typically vary by as much as 20 or more points on most standardized tests, particularly those with heavy verbal components (Anastasi 1958; Hess 1970). But IQ tests obscure many other ability differences between groups. Even recognizing that IQ tests furnish useful summary information on verbally weighted academic skills, traditional tests are widely considered to be biased against different subcultural or ethnic groups, particularly among the poorer, less-educated strata of society (Ginsberg 1972; Horowitz and Paden 1973). Thus the pattern of higher IQ scores for advantaged children over disadvantaged children (those from various poor, less-educated, minority and rural groups) fails to take account of adaptive coping skills, oral language skills, and the specialized, community-related skills and knowledge typically found in different combinations among the various groups.

Until recent decades the IQ scores of rural children regularly averaged around 10 points below the scores of urban children. The lower level has been attributed to the poor educational facilities, poor school attendance resulting from the heavy demands of agricultural work patterns, and the sparseness of cultural amenities in rural communities (Anastasi 1958). Urban- versus- rural-differences have been widely reported in Canada (Burnett, Beach, and Sullivan 1963) and in various European countries (Klineberg 1931) and other areas as well (for Ceylon see Straus 1954), except in Great Britain, where urban-rural differences in schooling and cultural facilities are small (Anastasi 1958). No one doubts, however, that children on the traditional family farm grew up learning a significant body of competencies that would baffle their urban counterparts. We have only to list a few of the many clusters of skills associated with tending animals (feeding, milking, breeding, slaughtering, harnessing, and harness repair), growing crops (preparing fields, planting, weeding, harvesting, rotating crops), pruning trees, repairing tools, and gathering fuel (cutting and hauling logs, chopping wood, sharpening saws and axes) to appreciate the extensive sets of competencies, whether on American family farms or in traditional European peasant communities (Beers 1937; Sorokin, Zimmerman, Galpin 1931; Williams 1925). Differences in both general IQ and specific patterns have gradually disappeared with advances in agricultural technology, the growth of rural transportation, communication, and school systems, and the massive migrations to the city in all countries. Children remaining in farming areas still acquire special skills not in the repertoire of the urban or suburban child, although the rural skills are now more technologically dependent than those of the past (chain saws, tractors, milking machines).

An interesting illustration from a Third World country points up still other skills that rural children may acquire, even as they usually lag on IQ type measures. Kagan (1974) reports that unschooled children from rural Kenya sorted pictures of animals by what is usually considered a method of abstract classification (domestic versus wild), whereas urban, schooled children from Nairobi sorted by visible features (color) (Fjellman 1971). There are many combinations of similarities and differences. In a study of unschooled black children in rural Virginia, conservation-of-quantity scores followed general norms but children were not able to solve class-inclusion problems prior to age 11 (Sigel and Mermelstein 1965). The same unevenness in differences has been found across many studies showing general ability deficits associated with lack of schooling in different countries, although the amount of contact with industrial modes of thinking appears to be a factor as well (Dasen 1972). Children from isolated fishing communities and mountain communities, British canal-boat families, and Gypsy communities have historically shown the same depressed IQ test patterns (Anastasi 1958; Gordon 1923). The levels for all these culturally isolated groups have generally averaged around 10 or more IQ points below the 100 IQ norms on most tests, but declines typically increased markedly with age up to adulthood, often falling as much as 40 to 50 points below norms. While the reasons are similar in terms of lack of schooling and access to the cultural amenities associated with literacy in urban life, each group tended to foster its own combination of competencies. Thus fishing life generated knowledge of the lore of fish habitat and feeding patterns, the local techniques developed over generations for catching fish, and many specialized skills for building, maintaining, and handling fishing boats (Nemec 1972; Mowatt and DeVisser 1968). Gypsy children learned the care of animals and vehicles, how to follow migratory route signs, and metalworking and other construction crafts (Clébert 1967); mountain children acquired various hunting, farming, and woodsman's skills (Hirsch 1928; Raine 1924; White 1937); and canal-boat children learned how to steer and navigate, how to tend and manage the animals that pulled the barges, and how to handle, load, and maintain barges and cargo (Al-Issa 1970; Gordon 1923; Hadfield 1968). The discrepancy between the diverse patterns of highly refined and functional competencies in these subcultures and the grossly depressed general IQ scores, reflecting abstract verbal skills (especially at the older age levels—Anastasi 1958) that have served no purpose in these communities in times past, points up both the narrowness of mental tests as measures of intelligence and the great variability of human competencies.

Competencies also vary considerably among the many ethnic subcultural groups that abound in countries and hierarchical societies of almost any size. In addition to the usual large social-class differences in mental-test scores, Lesser and his associates (Lesser, Fifer, and Clark 1965) found significant pattern variations among four U.S. cultural groups (Chinese, Jews, blacks, and Puerto Ricans) on scales assessing four different mental abilities (verbal, reasoning, numerical, and spatial), thus revealing important competence differences among groups that would have remained unknown had only a general-ability (IQ) test been used. Jews and Chinese were both much higher than the other two groups in nearly all skills, blacks being slightly higher than Chinese on verbal skills. Jews were much higher than any other group in verbal skills, the Chinese highest in spatial skills. Differences among group profiles were substantial and many of the mean differences between group pairs on the individual scales were significant. Substantially the same pattern of profile differences among the same cultures was obtained in a replication study in Boston (Stodolsky and Lesser 1967).

Corroborative data on the exceptional verbal skills of Jewish children can be found in many sources (Anastasi 1958). Verbal ability and scholarship have a long tradition among Middle European and East European Jews (Zborowski 1949). Among Terman's (1925) famous one thousand gifted children, at least 10.5 percent were Jews, twice the percentage (5 percent) in the population of California schoolchildren from which the sample was drawn. The critierion was the verbally loaded IQ test. In one study of twenty-eight children from the rare level of 170 IQ, twenty-three (82 percent) came from Jewish homes (Sheldon 1954). Children from the Sephardic Jewish cultures of the Middle East have been found to score significantly below Jewish children from European backgrounds, however (Smilansky and Smilansky, 1968), as much as 17 points on the most verbally loaded tests (Gross 1967). Unlike the verbal intellectual values of Jews of European origin, Sephardic Jews immigrated from feudally based cultures that place few premiums on verbal achievement and scholarship.

Much has been made of the intellectual deficits of poor black children from the U.S. urban ghettoes or rural South, who typically score from 10 to 20 or more IQ points below suburban counterparts in the white middle class (Anastasi 1958; Hess 1970; Horowitz and Paden 1973; Kennedy 1969). Deficiencies in cognition, language, attention, motivation, and the gamut of possible skills have been implicated at one time or another (Bereiter and Engelmann 1966; Bloom, Davis, and Hess, 1965; Riessman 1962). More penetrating researches have revealed differential strengths in black children's profiles that contradict the earlier stereotype. The now classic study of Hess and Shipman (1965) pointed up dramatically what had long been evident, that the major differences were linked to social class and educational levels. In the Lesser et al. investigation (1965) highly significant differences appeared between mean scores of children from the middle class and lower class on all scales in every cultural group. The differences were greater between middle-class and lower-class blacks, moreover, than between the classes of any other cultural group.

But the accumulated research on poor black children's cognitive development shows considerable differentiation and relative strengths as well. In Lesser et al.'s 1965 cultural profiles, lower class blacks performed better than lower class Puerto Ricans on verbal and reasoning skills, significantly so on the verbal scales, while the trend was reversed on numerical and spatial skills. Aside from the now widely known contribution of motivational and task factors to performance on standardized IQ and similarly verbally loaded and administered mental tests, item content itself often reflects cultural bias against poor black (and other lower class) children. A comparison of two samples of information test items from two IQ tests, one the widely used Wechsler series, the other a test devised by Dove specifically for poor urban blacks is instructive in this regard (Kagan 1974:116):

Wechsler Test	Dove's Test
1. Who wrote *Hamlet*?	1. In C.C. Ryder what does C.C. stand for?
2. Who wrote the *Iliad*?	2. What is a gashead?
3. What is the Koran?	3. What is Willy May's last name?
4. What does *audacious* mean?	4. What does "handkerchief head" mean?
5. What does *plagiarize* mean?	5. Whom did "Stagger Lee" kill in the famous blues legend?

It is evident that experiences quite outside the mainstream culture may socialize abilities in quite different ways.

The supposed social-class deficit in language conceptualized by Bernstein (1962; see also Hess 1970) as the product of a restricted code marked by grammatical barrenness, limited vocabulary, and failure to take account of the listener's frame of reference and knowledge, also turns out to be overstated. Labov (1972) conducted a systematic linguistic and cultural analysis of black vernacular in urban centers across the nation, drawing on his own and others' observations of black youth in the inner cities. Although using a variety of different grammatical forms (contraction or deletion of copula, multiple negation, and a varying phonology and vocabulary), black vernacular is a variant of standard English with equal complexity and richness of thought processes. Labov goes on to record the restricted verbal performance of inner city black children in formal school and other similar middle-class institutional settings compared with the rich, varied, and imaginative flow of speech they display with peers in their own milieu or in open-ended situations where trust has been established with researchers. The extensive use of metaphor and imagery in common speech and the pattern of reproduction of traditional oral poetry and tales (the dozens, sounding, and signifying), often making considerable use of ritual insult and improvisation, disclose a complexity and richness of culture and thought that belie the steretype of cultural deprivation and deficit (Abrahams 1970; Labov 1972).

The effects of dialect are well illustrated in a study by Baratz (1969), in which poor urban blacks performed better on a sentence-repetition task structured in black vernacular syntax than did lower-middle-class white children, but significantly less well when standard English was employed. Osser, Wang, and Zaid (1969) report that much of the problem of black children in comprehension and speech imitation is incurred because of the problem of decoding and encoding in standard English.

Notwithstanding the strengths that appear when assessed in situ, in the local dialect and on information specific to the indigenous community and culture, it is evident that these strengths do not compensate for a relative lack of development in many poor black and other minority group children of certain generalized verbal and abstract competencies, which are the primary currency in our complex industrialized society. As we shall see, strengths found among virtually all less formally educated and relatively poor groups from many cultural and racial backgrounds in their originally adaptive practical and oral language skills, which are the residue of their folk histories, do not compensate for competence development in the decontextualized abstractions of industrial society (Cole and Bruner 1972).

Cross-cultural Differences

Study of abilities in quite different cultures began with the concept of general intelligence and IQ testing (Anastasi 1958; Wober 1974). Since the study of abilities and mental processes did not begin until this century, after the planet had been thoroughly divided into countries and colonies controlled and influenced by the technologically advanced societies, we can only speak of cultures as more or less separated from mainstream societies.

The difference in cultural boundedness between the subcultures studied by Lesser and his associates (1965) and those located in isolated reservations or even in the bush of thinly populated regions in Africa, remote (at least at the time) from the urban industrial centers of Europe and America, is often more a distinction of degree than of kind. The pattern of folk culture-urban society differences as measured by the early IQ measures was much the same as for subcultural-versus-mainstream differences within industrial societies.

Gaps between different cultures are generally greatest on tests most heavily loaded with abstract verbal concepts (Anastasi 1958; Cole et al. 1971; Luria 1976; Vernon 1969), but differences also are often great on various performance tests, presumably reflecting problems with the concept and procedures of formal test taking, individual achievement motivation, abstract puzzle solving, unfamiliar materials, and arbitrary speed requirements largely alien to members of various folk cultures (Anastasi 1958; Cole and Bruner 1972; Glick 1975; Klineberg 1935; Pepitone 1980; Porteus 1931).

The picture is not all one-sided, however. In Ceylon village children in rural areas, which retain many features of the original folk culture, score much lower than American norms on all tests but score slightly better on language than on performance measures, a pattern considerably at variance from the usual performance advantage found in rural areas of technologically advanced societies (Straus 1954). At the university level this traditional verbal strength combines with a stress on verbal scholarship and rejection of manual tasks in the highly stratified class and caste system to result in verbal scores greatly in excess of American university students' levels despite performance scores much below.

Similar discrepancies can be found on performance measures. Thus many folk-cultural groups score somewhat lower on various scales of this type, Navaho Indian children for example (Leighton and Kluckhohn 1947) averaging around 20 IQ points lower, African and Indian children in South Africa 15 points lower (Lloyd and Pidgeon 1961), and Canadian Indian and Eskimo children (MacArthur 1968; Turner and Penfold 1952; Vernon 1969; Wiltshire and Gray 1969) and Ugandan children (Vernon 1969) to similar degrees. In a number of Native American tribes in the western United States (Hopi, Sioux, Zuni) Havighurst and Hilkevitch (1944), however, found that Hopi children scored *above* (by as much as 10 to 15 mean points) the norms for U.S. children on the Grace Arthur Point Performance Scale, and *all* tribes scored consistently higher than U.S. children on the Goodenough Draw-a-Man test (Havighurst, Gunther, and Pratt 1946). Thompson and Joseph (1944) attribute the Hopi advantage to the cultural complexity of their social organization and symbol systems. The performance advantage in drawing appears to be at least partly the result of cultural emphasis on graphic arts for males among the Hopi (Dennis 1942) and similar tribes

(Havighurst, Gunther, and Pratt 1946). Mean scores for boys run considerably higher, while mean scores for girls run slightly lower than U.S. norms.

Another interesting reversal of the trend toward depressed performance scores appears in the investigations of DuBois (1939) and Porteus (1931). The former constructed and standardized a Draw-a-Horse test on Pueblo Indian children on which the mean score of a sample of U.S. white children was only 74. On a specially devised test of foot-tracking skills, at which Porteus found Australian aborigines typically excelled, aborigines scored at about the same level as middle-class white high school students in Hawaii, despite the aborigines' lack of familiarity with photographs. Members of folk cultures, who lack experience with drawings and photographs and thus knowledge of the rules of perspective, have been found in several studies to encounter difficulty in interpreting content and in perceiving images three dimensionally (Deregowski 1980; Duncan, Gourlay, and Hudson 1973; Hudson 1960; Ives and Gardner 1980; Segall, Campbell, and Herskovits 1966). In contrast to the high scores of Hopi children on the Draw-a-Man test of Goodenough and their inflated scores on an ecologically relevant Draw-a-Horse test, illiterate Bedouins in the Syrian desert, whose exposure to photographs and representational drawings (their own art is geometric) is limited, scored only around 50 IQ on human-figure-drawing measures, drawing mainly stick figures (Dennis 1960).

This variation among cultures in patterns of ability persists apparently even among individuals residing as a subculture for more than a generation in large urban areas of a complex society dominated by a majority culture, as the data of Lesser and his associates (1965) shows. Such persistence was reported earlier by Porteus (1939) in pattern differences among different subcultural groups in Hawaii. He found Japanese were more skilled than Chinese on performance and mechanical aptitude tests, but patterns were reversed on the more verbal, Binet-type tests and in auditory memory span. Similarly Darsie (1926) found that Japanese children in mainland United States significantly surpassed white U.S. norms on tests involving sustained attention, visual perception, and spatial concepts but fell below norms on verbal and arithmetic tests.

More recent factor-analytic and other studies of ability patterns among different cultures underscore just how widespread these variations are. Irvine (1969) summarizes the data on studies of more than ten different cultures and subcultures from Africa and other continents. Among different groups, general practical, figural, or inductive reasoning; perceptual speed; spatial visualization, and other factors emerge in different strengths and combinations. Vernon (1969) conducted very extensive cross-cultural studies of Canadian Indian and Eskimo, Ugandan, and Jamaican schoolchildren, using an extended test battery of verbal and performance tests, ranging from

Binet vocabulary, English, arithmetic, and information tests, to Kohs blocks, cognitive-style matrices, Draw-a-Man, and an extended subbattery of Piagetian measures. Mean differences between groups ranged, for example, from 13 points below Western norms for Ugandan children to 5 points above Western norms for Eskimos on tests of classificatory sorting, using concrete objects local to the respective cultures. The scores of other groups were scattered in between these extremes. Similar patterns, occasionally more extreme, appeared on other tests.

Vernon traces some differences between groups to cultural experience, as in the relatively high scores of Canadian Indians and Eskimos on design reproduction and form-board test, which he relates to experience in tracking through woods or snow, against the relatively lower scores of Jamaican children, whose experience in nature was more restricted. Although all groups generally fell considerably below the norms of educated groups in industrial societies on nearly all tests, and differences within cultural groups varied in the usual manner with amount and quality of schooling and urban versus rural residence, pattern differences between cultures were marked.

The importance of familiarity with materials, language barriers, and values and concepts about performing abstract, nonfunctional tasks at all, especially for individual merit, is by now widely documented (Glick 1975). What does it mean, for example, to Mexican or American Indian children to be asked to strive for and demonstrate individual competence, when their cultures stress cooperative and familial values above all (Anastasi 1958; Klineberg 1935; Pepitone 1980)? These basic barriers to measuring abilities may reflect fundamental aspects and types of differences in ability that are integral to differences in culture and ecology.

Cultural Competencies and Ecological Adaptation

Many ability differences between cultures are traceable to the different experiences of cultures in adapting to their different environments. Relations between culture competencies and environment are not always direct and contemporaneous. Culture persists with many residual aspects no longer functional, and it changes too, spinning off competencies that bear little relation to conditions of life, in both cases in noncritical areas, that is, involving competencies not essential to survival or ecological adaptation. The legendary ability of Quranic students (students of the Koran) to commit vast religious passages to memory by rote is a prime example (Wagner and Lofti 1980a). Although such highly focused skills are culturally functional for Islamic religious life, they are neither ecologically adaptive nor do they apparently generalize to other memory tasks (Wagner 1978). Plenty of examples exist, however, of quite functional competencies or at least of mental processes that derive directly from living conditions.

In a wide-ranging review and investigation of the influence of environment and culture on visual perception, Segall et al. (1966) report that people from folk cultures that offer little experience with "carpentered" environments were much less subject to certain geometric illusions (such as the Muller-Lyer, Sander parallelogram) than people from industrial societies. Experience with right-angular buildings and other constructions apparently conditions dwellers in an industrialized world to perceive obtuse and acute angles in drawings as if they represented three-dimensional, right-angle structures; for us such perceptual constructions are highly functional. Dwellers in jungles or deserts instead perceive the sides of the Sander parallelogram as approximately equal, failing to compensate by perceptually constructing the left line longer than the right in order to interpret the drawing as a rectangular box.

Cultural experience also affects how people vary in using, naming, and organizing the color spectrum, though not apparently in basic ability to discriminate the actual wide range of color differences (around 7.5 million) (Brown 1965; Heider 1972; Segall et al. 1966). Various cultures divide the color spectrum (actually a continuum) lexically in different ways and to different degrees, ranging for example from the standard English six-color set (purple, blue, green, yellow, orange, and red) to two categories of the Bassa of Liberia who cluster everything into blue-green and yellow-red (Brown 1965). The names cultures employ appear to originate in the names of objects common and important to the people's experience, as in blue-green (aqua, agua) as the name for sea and our use of the color orange as the label for the fruit, orange (Brown 1965). Among Eskimo groups in the Arctic, many of the languages contain a great diversity of terms for designating shades of white, in connection with the many subtle differences they recognize in types of snow, while terms for red and green were formerly unknown (Luria 1976). Thus "color terms are initially metaphorical extensions of what are originally object names, or else of pigment and dye names" (Segall et al. 1966:40). Tribal women in Uzbekistan, whose life centered on weaving rugs of many colors before their integration into Soviet industrial life in the 1920s, reacted with great sensitivity to many subtle differences in the color of the skeins of wool Luria (1976) presented to them experimentally. They applied names of familiar objects, such as peach and calf's dung. The men, in contrast, who had no experience with weaving, tended to label every color blue, and neither men nor women sorted or accepted as legitimate the idea of clustering colors by European categories. Color features frequently in the local natural classification systems of many cultures (Sturtevant 1964). The Hanunóo in the Philippines, for example, classify color on two axes as we do, but in place of brightness and color intensity, they employ light-dark and fresh-dry distinctions akin to the fresh-cut versus dry bamboo distinction important to their culture (Conklin 1955; cited in Lévi-Strauss 1966 and Segall et al. 1966).

   Variations in classification and conservation skills from culture to culture illustrate vividly the role of cultural adaption to the conditions of life. Members of folk cultures generally classify functionally with great skill the fauna and flora of the habitat but are usually less skilled than members of industrial societies in classifying abstractly according to form, color, and the like when faced with the sorting demands of arbitrary tasks (Cole and Bruner 1972; Lévi-Strauss 1966; Luria 1976). Abstract classification and to some degree even conservation of matter, skills built into the problem of ranging across alternatives in complex technological societies, find less place in the simple technologies and relatively fixed and stable environments of folk societies. Since conditions vary from locale to locale, different folk cultures display different approaches to classifying and conserving. Among the Kpelle of Liberia, for instance, Cole and his associates (1971) found that illiterate adults greatly surpassed American adults in both speed and skill in sorting leaves of local trees and vines but did not equal them in working with abstract materials (geometric blocks, designs on cards). Lévi-Strauss (1966) reviews a wide range of ethnographic evidence on folk societies, documenting how systems of classification are universal to human society. Unlike modern scientific systems, however, systems of classification in folk societies are derived directly from practical experience with the natural phenomena specific to the habitat. Folk classifications of the natural world relate to social organization, totemistic and other rituals and practices, and cosmological belief systems the different cultures have evolved. At the same time, though they are not universally applicable without modification to natural life everywhere, Lévi-Strauss points out: "Native classifications are not only methodical and based on carefully built up theoretical knowledge. They are also at times comparable from a formal point of view, to those still in use in zoology and botany" (p. 43). Thus the Hanunóo of the Philippines have developed a hierarchy of eight levels and "classify their local plant world, at the lowest (terminal) level of contrast, into more than 1800 mutually exclusive folk (taxa), while botanists divide the same flora—in terms of species—into less than 1300 scientific taxa" (Conklin 1955:129, cited in Lévi-Strauss 1966:153). Lévi-Strauss describes how these classifications are developed through direct experience in observation and using plants and animals for food, medicine, and other purposes, and that decisions about nuances of classification are arrived at through extensive debate in tribal councils. Earlier travelers could have avoided many errors in scientific classification had they relied on local folk taxonomies instead of working out new ones through trial and error, according to Lévi-Strauss.

   Children in most folk cultures have been found to acquire conservation skills on the various Piagetian tasks of substance, quantity, and the like but frequently at a slower rate than children in developed societies (Dasen 1972). Among Australian aborigines and others, even adolescents and adults seem to fail to develop certain forms of conservation at all. Combinatorial reasoning, Piaget's highest stage of cognitive development, is even more generally absent. Levels of development attained appeared to correlate highly with the amount of Western-type schooling or at least with the degree of exposure to the ideas of industrial societies.

Conservation and similar skills frequently develop according to the ecological problems of adaptation faced by the culture. Dasen (1975) found that Australian aborigines and Eskimos, both of whom followed nomadic, hunting patterns of adaptation, developed conservation of space and other spatial concepts relatively rapidly, whereas Ébrie Africans, who followed an agricultural life, developed conservation of quantity, weight, and volume more rapidly. Adaptation for the first two groups involved problems of navigating across spatial distance, while for agricultural Ébrie manipulating quantities of grain in containers was primary. Cole, Gay, and Glick (1968) in a related study report that illiterate Kpelle farmers were much more skilled at estimating quantities of rice than Yale University students, the difference increasing with the amount of rice to be estimated. They were also better at estimating the number of stones in a pile (though not at estimating distance, length, or other dimensions), presumably because they used stones as counters in their ordinary counting activities. In the same vein Feldman et al. (1974) found that Eskimo children and youth performed substantially better on Piagetian tests of cognitive development using pictures of wild animals and habitats specific to the Arctic culture than tests using abstract geometric materials (colored blocks), though they still did not fully attain Piaget's most advanced stage of formal operational reasoning. The importance of familiarity of materials, testing procedures, language, and cultural values and concepts about performing abstract, nonfunctional tasks should never be underestimated (Glick 1975).

Further evidence of the role of ecological adaptation, this time on occupational differences within an agricultural culture, appear in two studies of Price-Williams, Gordon, and Ramirez (1969). Sons of pottery makers in two Mexican villages performed significantly better on conservation-of-substance tasks, in which clay was the test medium, than sons of families following other occupations and generally better than the latter on other forms of conservation (number, liquid, weight, and volume)—significantly so in one of the villages.

Differences in mnemonic skills also appear to be influenced by factors of cultural adaptation, sometimes related to ecological adaptation and sometimes not. In his seminal studies on memory Bartlett (1932) observed the exceptional memories characteristic of the Swazi people in southern Africa. Herdsmen were able to recall for as long as a year details of a long list of transactions on cattle purchases, recalling colors, types, seller, and amounts with no errors. The Swazi culture centers on the care and herding of cattle. On ordinary tasks of recall on other matters, even over only short periods of no more than a few minutes, Bartlett found that Swazis performed no better than educated Englishmen.

The functional specificity of memory in folk cultures is even more evident in the case of Quranic students, but in this instance culture and ecology are far apart. In his study of memory skills in Moroccan children, Wagner (1978) found no differences between unschooled and Quranically schooled children on most tasks. The legendary superior memory skills of Quranically schooled children appeared to be confined to their ability to ingest large masses of poorly understood religious tracts in a rote manner through cued techniques of "chanting, rocking and toned variation in the verbal production" (Wagner and Lotfi 1980a:248). Wagner (1978) also reports an instance of occupationally based memory skills, in which unschooled Moroccan rug merchants recognized black-and-white photographs of rugs better than did urban secondary school students.

Even simple folk societies may evolve skill differences relatively free of environmental ties. Nadel (1937a,b) found that 16- to 18-year-old Yoruba school children reproduced stories from recall that were more logically organized than the stories reproduced by a similar group of children from another Nigerian folk culture (the Nupe), whose reproductions concentrated on detail. These patterns were linked by Nadel to the high rational coherence of the Yoruba in their religion, against the Nupe, who were more given to magic and detail. Although not tightly linked ecologically, apparently, the cultural patterning of memory skills is nevertheless clear. They appear to form part of wide differences in thought systems that may be traced to the more complex, empire-type social organization and trade relations of the Yoruba in precolonial times (Ehrensaft 1977) before they were conquered in midnineteenth century (Perani 1978-80), compared to the craft-stratified organization of the Nupe.

Showing again the more direct origins of skills in ecological adaptation and a wide generalization of their skills, Eskimo children were found to be much more skilled than children from industrial social settings in drawing reproductions of complex geometrical designs from memory (Kleinfeld 1973). Their excellent visual memory skills are believed to develop from the careful observation necessary for hunting on the relatively featureless snow-scapes. The functional relation between the skills Canadian Indians and Eskimos displayed on form-board and design tasks and their hunting experience (Vernon 1969) is parallel. Similar as well are the refined skills Hopi Indians showed in drawing horses, which grew directly out of their familiarity with horses and of Australian Aborigines in tracking tasks related to their known tracking skills in hunting.

It would be difficult to claim that most skills in every culture are closely tied to patterns of environmental adaption. As cultures develop more elaborate belief systems and more complex technologies, varied occupations, and a written language, many of their skills bear little or no direct relation to the physical ecology, as in the case of Yoruban storytelling and Quranic memorization. Yet at the level of the simple technology of the tribal folk society, skill patterns and environmental adaptation frequently appear to be intimately allied.

The Ecological Basis for Cognitive Socialization

Given the prevalence of linkages between ecology and cultural patterns of competence, it should come as no surprise that child-rearing practices and related developmental experiences of children in different cultures are often closely related to the types of competencies that predominate. These practices and experiences are not always planned, nor are all practices and attendant skills acquired ecologically efficient or even clearly tied to demands of adaptation to the ecology. Enough instances of such linkages can be cited in the case of small, historically stable folk communities, however, to suggest that the modes of childhood experience often grew out of cultural responses to demands of the local ecology and became woven into the culture of childhood.

The practice of swaddling infants (and a similar practice of using cradle boards), for example, has been widespread among folk cultures around the world (Greenacre 1944; Lipton, Steinschneider, and Richmond 1965). It was widely practiced among all classes in Western Europe before the industrial period, where its roots and rationale are traceable at least in part to the ancient Greek physician Galen (Demaitre 1977; Lipton, Steinschneider, and Richmond 1965). Probably drawing from his own folk tradition, Galen argued that swaddling was important to protect the infant from cold and exposure and to toughen the skin. Various cultures have had various rationales for swaddling, including pacification, protection from cold, protection from self-injury, preventing general stimulation, preventing masturbation, aiding the infant to control the emotions, comforting the child, and helping the bones to grow straight. Motor restraint and pacification aided in child care and socialization for conformity in agricultural societies. The practice is associated with climate, more common in cold climes (Demaitre 1977) and less frequently reported in desert and tropical climates (Leiderman, Tulkin, and Rosenfeld 1977). Swaddling and a similar practice, cradling, during the early months appear to have few effects on motor development (Dennis and Dennis 1940), but when swaddling persists through the first year, as it used to in Albania, crawling, walking, mobility, and even fine-motor manipulation and coordination appear to be at least temporarily retarded (Danziger and Frankl 1934). Although immobilizing infants through swaddling or cradling on boards may not permanently retard development, infants cradled even a few months have not been found to be precocious in motor skills (Dennis and Dennis 1940). A related practice, carrying the infant on the back, which is extremely widespread in Africa and elsewhere, appears to furnish infants with extended visual experience and postural motor control in the early months but to impede development later on (Goldberg 1972).

Motor skills are stressed in socialization in low-technology societies, not surprisingly, given the central importance of physical tasks in their life. Early sitting and walking is widely encouraged in folk cultures throughout Africa and elsewhere (Super 1976, 1981). Almost from birth infants are propped up in a sitting position and held vertically for walking, beginning with bouncing in the lap to exercise the neonatal stepping reflex, which tends not to disappear in African babies as it does in the United States. Much of the activity amounts to providing opportunities for practice rather than tutelage. The infant's opportunities to observe the active peer culture of the extended family in a close-knit community provide much of the impetus for early development.

Such skill development is nevertheless selective, crawling in particular being generally discouraged among folk groups because of the obvious hazard to the unknowing infant of crawling into the open fire (Dasen 1974; Super 1976, 1981). While these practices are not consistent with respect to fostering the development of gross-motor competence, and restricting crawling may even slow motor development (Dasen 1974), the too early promotion of motor skill in infancy may conflict with the goal of social conformity and cooperation predominant in agricultural societies (Barry, Child, and Bacon 1959). Although Dennis and Dennis (1940) found no strong specific delay from cradling, walking was generally later among the Hopi, an agricultural society, and Fowler observed among the Bassari, a remote agricultural group in Senegal, that sensorimotor activity was generally dampened during infancy through frequent pacification and protection (Fowler and Fowler 1978). Following infancy, free-ranging motor activity was prominent, including imitation of older peers in adult-type tasks and climbing trees by the age of 4.

An emphasis upon motor competence is thus apparently rarely long delayed and may even extend to the selective acceleration of relatively complex, specialized gross-motor skills. Among the Plains Indians of the United States in times past, boys learned to ride horses well by the time they were 5 or 6 (Ewers 1955; Wallace and Hoebel 1952), while among the Manus of New Guinea infants began to swim as soon as they could walk and mastered the native, very tippy canoes not long after (Mead 1975). The Plains Indian boy was placed on a horse frequently well before age 3 and with little or no direct instruction. As soon as he could stay on a walking and trotting horse without falling, he was given his own pony, on which he then perfected his budding skills through constant practice essentially on his own. He continued to learn as well through observing and interacting with male peers as well as adult males. The horse was a relatively late addition to the culture of various Plains Indian cultures, coming to North America from Europe during the eighteenth century, but it became the ecological mainstay of the Plains Indians' way of life for hunting buffalo and other wild game.

Among the Manus, whose houses are set over water on stilts in tidal lagoons along the shore, movement across the water is the primary mode of transport. During the first year infants observe from the safe vantage point of a veranda the activities of older peers and adults swimming and boating in the lagoon around the house. Close to the time he or she is beginning to talk or as soon as the infant can hold on tightly to the mother around the neck, the infant accompanies her in her daily washing and other activities in the water. Soon the infant is placed in waist-deep water at low tide to play under the watchful eye of the mother, to observe, and gradually to imitate the swimming of able peers only a year or so older. As with the Plains Indians, almost no instruction is given; the child learns to swim through observation, experimentation, and endless practice in the context of intimate interaction with an extended age peer group. Once swimming is fairly well mastered, often before the age of 3, the child is given his or her own miniature canoe in which to experiment in a similar manner, again in playful interaction with peers. As Mead describes the learning process, "in the company of children a year or so older, the young initiates play all day in shallow water, paddling, punting, racing, making tandems of their small craft, upsetting their canoes, bailing them out again, shrieking with delight and high spirits" (p. 28). A great deal of practice is also obtained through frequent opportunities adults offer to the young child to ferry adults in their canoes from place to place on errands. Little attention is paid to errors and clumsiness, and signs of success are met with approval.

Both of these cases illustrate how easy and effective informal cognitive socialization can be for acquiring even quite complex competencies when they are tightly bound to the ecological necessities of daily life in small folk communities. There is no formal institutionalization of education, depending on an organized system, staff, curriculum, and schedules for transmitting a body of skills and knowledge. Deliberate and planned efforts to instruct the infant and young child are also at a minimum. The smallness of the community, the localization of the activities, the simplicity of the technology and skills required all make the process of modeling work well. Daily observation and informal interaction with family and community furnish ample incentive and experience to learn all the culturally needed skills. Formalization of instruction comes only with the appearance of complex technologies and large-scale societies.

Barry, Child, and Bacon's (1959) investigation of 104 folk cultures, few of which were literate, indicates the extent to which patterns of child rearing are shaped to fit the adult culture's forms of adaptation to the ecology.

Agricultural and herding people stressed responsibility, obedience, and nurturance in rearing children, in conformity with the stable, slow rituals and cooperative patterns upon which farming life is constructed. In contrast, self-reliance, independence, and individual achievement were the goals of child rearing in both hunting and fishing societies, to meet the demands for cognitive and personal autonomy in exploring, trailing, and navigating through forest, desert, or ocean wilderness in search of game, fish, and other food. Differences between the patterns of the two societal groupings were generally significant. But again, such patterns were not the product of deliberate instruction. Rather, they were built into the modes of handling children from infancy, the behavior of older peers as well as adults serving as a model until the child formally engages in work tasks.

Similar differences appear in studies by Berry (1966), comparing the Temne peoples of Sierra Leone, who follow an agricultural way of life, with the Eskimos of Baffin Island, whose economy is based on hunting and fishing. The Temne were found to concentrate on conformity and strictness in their modes of handling children, while the Eskimos were more permissive, encouraging children to reach out and explore the environment. The Temne culture's need for close cooperation in farming contrasts with the individual decision making, ingenuity, and courage needed for life alone on the hunt in the Arctic. Measures of (Witkin) cognitive style disclosed differences in the same direction, namely that Eskimos were more field independent, better at perceiving figures against ground, in keeping with their experience in detecting small differences against unrelieved snowscapes. The Temne were more field dependent, in keeping with their experience in a given articulated environment of farms and fields, in which their slow and static mode of existence places few demands for detecting novelty. The consistency with which Vernon (1969), Porteus (1931, 1973), Dasen (1975), and others (Kearins 1981) have found that perceptual design and spatial skills were highly developed in different hunting societies, such as Canadian Indians, Eskimos, and Australian Aborigines, points up the type of influence that socialization in hunting societies has had upon competence development. Similarly the superior quantitative skills of the unschooled Kpelle farmers (Cole et al. 1971) underscores the influence on other competencies of socialization in measuring rice and other farm products. Folk modes of socialization emerge principally from ways of life tied to ecological relations with the environment.

Competence patterns are well socialized in folk cultures, probably in proportion to the adaptiveness of their work patterns to the environment as well as the productiveness of the environment itself. The slash-and-burn practices of Neolithic cultures and of folk cultures in more recent times led in time to soil erosion and exhaustion, unless followed by other practices, such as crop rotation or letting alternating fields lie fallow (Childe 1957;

Harris 1977). Because such practices evolved slowly in the course of millenia, the solution over long periods of prehistory was simply to move on to other forested areas, facing a folk with demands to repeat the slash-and-burn process, but perhaps under different climate or topography requiring novel skill development. The great deserts of the Sahara and the vast arid territories of the Middle East have been ascribed to the intensive overgrazing of domesticated sheep and goats, which crop grasses very closely, coupled with climatic changes following the last ice age (Childe 1957; Kroeber 1948; McNeill 1963). Radical alterations of the physical environment confronted cultures in times past with stringent demands for changes in their ecological patterns of adaptation. Grazing and herding cultures had to become increasingly nomadic, following long desert treks, domesticating camels, and sheltering from sand storms, as Bedouin societies have adapted since those times. Entirely unknown skills like storing and channeling flood water to irrigate crops occurred with those who moved to settle in the fertile river deltas of the Nile and Tigris-Euphrates villages thousands of years ago.

In general, however, though changes in adaptive demands have occurred periodically throughout the history of human culture, the forms of cultural adaptation to the ecology in folk societies have generally been more stable than transient. Except for the occasional catastrophe, such as drought, tidal wave, hurricane, and war, stability in farming or in the historically earlier forms of hunting and food gathering (Harris 1977; Konner 1977), have enabled socialization practices to remain unchanging and nicely woven into the tribal patterns of adaptation to the environment over a period of generations. It takes many years for soil to exhaust itself, for wood to be used up as fuel or building material, or for game and wild fruit, nuts, and grain to become scarce over a stretch of terrain a small folk community could comfortably farm or hunters and food gatherers successfully range. According to archeological reconstruction, our Neolithic forebears in many parts of the world dined quite well on game and crops, wild or domesticated, which were relatively abundant for the sparsely distributed populations (Harris 1977). Adaptation has also worked at some functional level until the last several hundred years in many regions of the world quite remote from the centers of civilization. Only recently have they been altered or crowded out in large numbers by the encroachments of technological society. Lean years have always punctuated periods of plenty. Nonetheless, the ecological arrangements developed by various folk cultures, if sometimes strained, only occasionally had to be restructured. Patterns of competence and modes of socialization through example and practice, rather than instruction and planned guidance, have been comparatively constant. Stability was sufficient to permit a diversity of locally well-developed folk forms, each of which approached pure types or at least could be represented by ideal types of adaptation to local conditions.

Societal Transition, Breakdown, and
Dysfunctional Socialization

Few pure forms of folk culture can be found anywhere in the world today. The encroachment of technology and the political, economic, and social reach of the technologically powerful industrial societies are too pervasive. We live in an age of transition, which some see as eventual decline (Lukacs 1970) and others see merely as necessary transformations that must occur before a better coordinated system of economic organization and cultural life can develop (Harrington 1976). Whatever the future, problems of socialization, child development, and education during this period of transition center on how to bridge the gap between traditional folk forms, which are no longer applicable, and the demand for new forms needed to socialize children in the abstractions, logical thinking, and highly specialized technical competencies of the spreading industrialized world.

Note

1. Competence and skill suggest proficiency in performing certain types of tasks, the former focusing more on overall performance and effectiveness in completing tasks, the latter on the quality of perfomance. Abilities and intelligence connote broader or more abstract qualities of performance or capabilities, abilities for specific areas, types of activity, or domains, intelligence encompassing a broad range of abilities across multiple domains and often implying predominance of biological factors. In this book, the terms *competence, skills,* and *ability* will be employed interchangeably, using the concept of intelligence only as defined.

Socialization in Folk and Hierarchical Societies

The industrial evolution of society has brought about profound transformations in the cognitive socialization of children that impinge on the child's development in every facet of life. At root are changes in the form and complexity of tools we use that alter the nature of our social institutions and our relations with the environment. Technological and social change are continuing at an ever-accelerating pace, though social change lags behind new invention, which is often its source (Ogburn 1922). Social change emerges in such patterns as the revolution in sexual mores resulting from freedom from adult scrutiny the automobile gave youth and later the freedom from the consequences of sexual intercourse the contraceptive pill provided. The realm of child rearing has not escaped the influence of equally unanticipated social consequences, many of them far reaching and of long standing in their evolution from folkways. Perhaps the most recent and still to be assimilated changes are the effects of universally unregulated television upon family life—the recentering of the focus of social activities to the home, but in a different passive, noninteractive form; the shift from primarily printed media to visual media; the emergence of a truly mass programming of uniform popular taste; the penetration of the home with socially sophisticated but stereotyped models for children down to their earliest years; and, not least in importance, the constant availability of cheap, canned child care.

Despite these many unexpected outcomes, large-scale hierarchical societies are fueled by certain systems and modes of functioning that tend to temper and channel the impact of technical change on social development. These are the modes of science, the rational and bureaucratic (in the Weberian (1947) sense of the logical consideration of means to ends), that have developed rational inquiry into the nature of the social world as well as the natural world but also have fundamentally restructured our modes of thought toward the rational in all spheres of life. Science and the rational in fact exercise enormous influence on all our social institutions in general and on the ways in which we rear our children in particular. Despite the persistence of different folkways in many corners of modern family and social life in this possibly transitional period of history, the methods and goals originating in the scientific and the professional influence us in many ways more than we realize.

Inevitably the spread of the rational is uneven and fraught with conflict and incomplete acceptance. If the application of science is to be socially productive and effectively applied on the widest basis, and the folk and the scientific more harmoniously reconciled, we shall need to become more aware of just what implications the forms of complex, technological societies hold for how children are socialized.

Contrasting Social Systems

The first step in the process is to define the characteristics of these modes in order to become conscious of how they work and influence present social patterns and the development of social change. The contrasting structures of folk and industrial systems and the modes of cognitive socialization to which they lead are outlined in summary form in table 2-1.[1] These ideal types vary in practice, of course, in many important ways and overlap to varying degrees, especially as a result of social change. Folk societies may be built on hunting and gathering or on agriculture or some mix of the two and the extended family monogamous, polygynous, or polyandrous. Similarly, industrial systems may be integrated into quite feudal or tribal systems, as in Japan (Lockwood 1954) and Saudi Arabia (Cooper and Alexander 1972), be strongly capitalist, as in the United States, or socialist. Some societies build their life around water transport, others around land. All societies socialize their children in self-care and basic perceptual, motor, cognitive, and linguistic skills. But these variations do not contravene the major distinctions defining the two forms of society, nor do the similarities contravene the basic differences in the practices and forms of organization.

Contrasting Relations to the Environment

Turning to the distinctions themselves, we see that in relations with the environment, folk societies characteristically make use of simple, hand-tool technologies that require close-knit ecological adaptation to the local environment (Barry, Child, and Bacon 1959; Bohannon 1963; Kroeber 1948; Redfield 1947). They kill game with knives, spears, and bows and arrows, or cultivate crops with sticks, crude hoes, and knives, and generally transport and store materials and prepare food in hand-crafted baskets or pots. They are necessarily confined to a marginal subsistence economy and direct bartering relations with others.

The power of a machine-tool technology in contrast permits large-scale production of an endless variety of specialized technical and consumer goods, bearing little relation to the local ecology, and necessitates intricate socioeconomic systems to regulate the organization of production, trade, and credit. The two modes of existence thus diverge widely in the degree and form of their contact with the natural environment. In folk society, because the tasks of daily life are closely tied to the local ecology, their form is shaped by the state of the weather, game supply, soil, and similar factors. In hierarchical society, particularly in its late industrial forms, the development of complex production technologies creates a world of alternatives and artifacts that place the members at some distance from environmental circumstances. They can plan, store, and generate alternatives that enable them to transcend the vagaries of environmental conditions and shifts. People inhabit an environment of highly contrived artifacts and experiences.

Contrasts in Social Structure

These fundamental differences lead to vast changes in the social structure as well, as shown in table 2-1. In the first place the advances in technology make possible enormous changes in the scale of things. Millions can now be supported by the intricate technological productions systems where only hundreds could survive with the meager output of hand-tool agriculture, husbandry, and weaponry in a subsistence economy. Increases in societal size lead to the development of large, hierarchically organized management systems and an endless division of labor to coordinate the many facets of production. Occupational specialization becomes the rule to perform the variety of highly complex, specialized tasks that can no longer be accomplished by means of a set of common skills. Principles of efficiency in which individuals earn specialized roles in terms of merit replace the tight cooperative relations of the folk community in which, except for certain divisions by sex and age, most members perform the same limited set of concrete tasks. Division of labor by sex, roughly into hunting or agricultural tasks for men, and household, child-rearing, and supplemental agricultural and food- and fuel-gathering tasks for women, and role and status graded by age alone work well (if not always fairly) for the few practical tasks performed directly in a local ecology. They no longer suffice for the multiplicity of complex tasks in an industrial world. The direct and informal regulation of economic activity and social life through the interpersonal hierarchy of the extended family must also give way to centrally regulated government and agency control by law and contract to manage the vast enterprises of industrial society. Friendship networks and work associations replace the cooperative kinship systems of control and association for work and social activity, leaving a truncated nuclear family to perform only a few of the functions (child and home care, procreation, recreation) and associations (companionship) formerly performed by the communitywide activities of the extended family.

Table 2-1
Salient Structural Characteristics and Forms of Socialization in Folk and Industrial Societies

	Folk	Industrial
Environmental relations		
Ecology	Direct adaptation—local	Transcendent—indirect
Economy	Subsistence—barter	Mass production systems—formal
Technology	Hand tool—uniform	Machine tool—variable
Social structure		
Size	Local group (hundreds)	Large-scale society (millions)
Form	Communal—kinship	Agency-regulated hierarchical systems
Division of labor	Gender and age	Multioccupational; merit, age, sex
Family	Extended	Nuclear
Status and roles	Ascribed—uniform for all members by sex and age; intuitively and practically defined by cultural prescription	Achieved—widely varied by occupation and task; objectively defined by merit and scientifically regulated practice; career development
Social control	Local—interpersonal: family structure; family heads, chiefs	Centrally regulated—law and government
Associations	Kinship-based associations	Work- and interest-based associations and friendship networks
Social change	Slow and stable over generations except for occasional, sudden ecological events and intrusions from other peoples	Rapid and uneven from spiraling effect of rapid, never-ending worldwide technological change
Socialization Agents		
Family	Extended	Nuclear
Peer culture	Extended-age peer group	Age-graded hierarchy
Formal systems	Communally operated age grading—initiation rites	Professionally operated and ability or age sequenced day care, schools, on-the-job training, and remediation (therapy)
Background	Multiple extended families	Neighborhood; urban-suburban-rural milieu

Curriculum		
Source	Cultural prescription: oral history, traditional practices, myth	Scientific inquiry and rationally accumulated, recorded knowledge; Cultural prescription
How defined	Practical science (observation and experience) Intuitively, traditionally defined practices	Practical science (observation and experience) Objectively defined and hierarchically sequenced goals, roles, methods, and norms
How disseminated	Modeling and oral statements	Professional instruction and mass media (oral, visual, written); delayed exposure to job skills Changing technology and conditions of community life
Content	Self-care and social behavior Fine- and gross-motor skills Uniform work skills (by sex and age) Oral language, myth and literature; limited counting and measurement Concrete, local knowledge and classification Practical reasoning and observation Sports, arts and crafts, dance, integral to production, religious expression, and ceremony	Same plus socioemotional adjustment Same Multiple, alternative work skills Oral and written language and literature; abstract, numerical measurement systems Formal, general knowledge and classification Abstract logical reasoning and inquiry Sports, games, hobbies, and arts
Methods	Primary: modeling (observation and imitation) Own activity and experimentation (play at work tasks, crafts) Peer interaction; graduated involvement in concrete work tasks Occasional instruction, demonstration, and guidance Ritual storytelling of myths and legends Direct controls, sanctions, and incentives	Secondary: modeling (observation and imitation) Own activity and experimentation (play, hobbies, and assigned chores) Peer interaction in sociodramatic, manipulative and construction play (representational, abstract) Primary: extensive planned, hierarchically sequenced programs of formal instruction Texts (books) and mass media Direct controls, sanctions, and incentives

Differences in the Forms of Socialization

Agents. Changes in complexity, size, and scale and changes to impersonal hierarchical forms have produced profound consequences for how children are socialized. The number of socializing agents in industrial society have expanded and changed in character. The personalized care and attention centered in the close daily activities of the extended family and peer culture are expanded to encompass day care, schools, and similar agency-run institutions. While relations may be personalized to varying degrees, depending on size, methods, and other factors, these systems operate by rational, bureaucratic principles of organization and control. The agents are now formally trained and paid professional day-care workers and teachers, working in an organized system of scheduled activities in clearly defined but temporary roles.

The character of the family and the peer culture too are altered, the former by paring the family to its most functional components of mates, parents, and children and the latter by dividing peers into narrow, age-graded segments of one to three years. Functional units are removed from the wider community context. The family becomes a different sort of production unit, modeled on the wider bureaucratic industrial system. Children are now socialized into peer relations through the give and take of relations in tightly age-sequenced hierarchical segments (more or less patterned after the tight age grading of formal school systems), which replace the extended age hierarchy that embraces all children in the extended family living and work units of the folk community (Leiderman, Tulkin, and Rosenfeld 1977; Murdock 1949). The size, diversity, and sprawl of activities in industrial metropolises appear to preclude the continuation of extended family cooperative and community-operated socializing systems.

For the same reasons the background activities of adults in the wider society undergo drastic changes in form. From the daily opportunities to observe concrete work tasks readily visible in the family compound and nearby fields or forest, children in industrial life witness principally only the domestic activities of the home and those of selected service operations (postman, bus driver, street construction worker, retail store clerk) in the neighborhood and wider areas in their commuting and excursions. The multiplicity of complicated and often abstract tasks in the mines, mills, utility plants, offices, and laboratories of modern life are seen only rarely or through second-hand sources of books and television.

Curriculum. In contrast to the cultural prescriptions of folk life handed down through word of mouth and ritual example, the child in an industrial setting is bathed in experiences heavily infused with information and methods originating in scientific inquiry and the written knowledge the society has accumulated. In folk society, because oral history and myth are severely curtailed by the limits of human memory, only a limited range of detail can be provided, usually in repetitive storytelling rituals and sayings that serve to dramatize and focus the message and morality at stake (Bartlett 1932; Langar 1980). For the rest, and perhaps the more important aspects of folk community life, the goals and methods of daily work tasks, the curriculum sources are everywhere at hand in the daily life of the community. A cultural lore of practical activities is the core curriculum for ecological adaptation (Lévi-Strauss 1966; Malinowski 1954). It is only in areas of social form and tribal and human origin that recourse is made to religious myth and the supernatural or in matters beyond the control of practical science, such as control of the weather and disease, that myth and magical techniques come into play.

The use of the written word and the development and institutionalization of science in industrial society not only vastly expand the variety and quantity of knowledge and techniques that can be transmitted to the oncoming generations. Accuracy and detail are increased as well. Writing relieves the burden of memory and makes for precise and unlimited description. But this very expansion shrinks the role of myth and the supernatural as legitimate sources of information. Children are reared more and more according to formally articulated principles in place of myth and intuitively defined, traditional practices, with the aim of optimizing children's development in all possible ways, socially, emotionally, physically, and mentally. Thus the introduction of the printed word and scientific processes fundamentally alter the processes of change and socialization as well. Just as scientific experimentation and written recordkeeeping build rapid change into the realm of production technology, they also build constant change into the processes of socialization. The socialization of children is thus fueled by two novel systems, both of which tend to replace the slow, stable, and concrete practices of the slow-moving folk culture. Socialization practices are constantly influenced by the ongoing experimentations of the social and medical sciences, but the changes in the tools, conditions of living, travel, and communication that technology brings also constantly alter the conditions under which community and family life are organized and thus the conditions under which children are reared.

The advent of the telephone, radio, the movies, and later television introduced a new dimension into the conditions of home life. No longer an island unto itself of earlier eras the middle-class nuclear family in urban industrial society receives through radio and TV daily prepackaged models of social life to influence the child directly and, through their effects on parents, indirectly. The telephone and new forms of transportation—stage coach, train, steamship, and the automobile, bus, and last, the airplane— meant more frequent social contact across geographically wider social networks and increased exposure to different ways of life. A certain worldwide social homogenization of cultures (the global village) has set in, at the same time alternatives are multiplying for the way things are done and for the way children are reared. The automobile expanded the world of local commuting, took parents and children on expeditions to the local shopping mall, moved family life to station wagons and campers, and introduced infant car seats and a host of other items and practices that altered family relations toward peripatetic, consumer-related forms of socialization.

Electric light opened the hours of night, extending the day and permitting longer access to the printed word. Electricity created the world of home appliances as well, of course, at once multiplying the power of the nuclear family housewife, threatened in the middle class at least by gradually emerging industrial opportunities for the poorer, servant classes. Hot and cold running water, washing machines, dryers, pushbutton stoves, and automatic furnaces were probably especially beneficial to the broader population, strata who for the first time were freed from the onerous grind of daily home chores, with a consequent easing of the tensions of family and child relations. These components of the rising standard of living may have contributed to the gradual shift toward greater permissiveness noted by Bronfenbrenner (1958) in American life in the decades after World War II. Related to these are the technological revolutions in food processing—canning, freezing, and packaging—which have changed the pace and form of family eating, communication, and child rearing and, through fast food chains, shifted more of the locus to the car.

The steady growth of technological changes that alter family life are matched by the expanding influences of research and professional activity on our ideas and techniques for rearing children. These influences work both directly on parents, through the various forms of guidance and advice offered, and indirectly through the examples provided by mass media, examples that are themselves influenced by contemporary scientific thought on child development. Professional guidance through pediatricians, well-baby clinics, visiting nurses, parent educators, child-welfare agencies, therapists, teachers, school psychologists and guidance personnel, and similar sources has long been embedded in the fabric of contemporary life. Popular manuals, newspaper columns and articles, radio and television programs addressed to family problems are now so widespread as to be almost as much a source of confusion as a source of clear guidance for parents (Clarke-Stewart 1978). Governments themselves regularly disseminate research-derived information on child care, which of course then change from generation to generation as new studies and concepts supplant the old (Wolfenstein 1953). The influence of countless intervention research projects in the home, day care, and schools also add up to a major source of change (Belsky 1978; Rubenstein and Howes 1979; Zigler and Valentine

1979), directly through the impact on children, parents and teachers in programs and indirectly through the findings published in both professional and popular media.

It is no accident that formal guidance and multiple sources of information on child rearing bombard the nuclear family. Cast off from the working context and support of the extended family and folk community to make its way in the uncharted, ever-changing seas of the metropolises of industrial society, the nuclear family needs something to replace the lost familiar fare of myth, example and interpersonal cooperation. Formal knowledge, formal guidance, and formal agencies, however incomplete, become the maps to hold the family and the socialization of children on course.

In some ways the curricular content of socialization in industrial society has changed very little from that of folk societies the world around, and in some ways it has changed enormously. Children everywhere in all societies must acquire some form of competence in performing routines of personal care in eating, dressing, washing, toileting, and the like. The routines differ in form, and the methods through which they are acquired vary, but they are always social rituals that must be acquired over certain periods and performed in socially prescribed fashion. Forms of address, greeting, and parting, and modes of cooperating and competing are similarly laid out in some socially defined manner in every society. Provisions for acquiring motor skills, both of the small appendages and for the whole body, are obviously always included, and particular forms of movement, skill, and control are often channeled into traditional social forms, though in fundamentally different ways, as in the emphasis on writing in industrial life versus using small hand tools in folk societies. Language and literature, work skills, bodies of knowledge, reasoning are all part of the repertoire of skill acquisition in both folk and industrial worlds. Yet these apparent commonalities in fact mask important differences, as the list of items in table 2-1 indicates.

Much of the difference appears in the wide variety of skills in industrial life, the many occupational branches, the infinite variation in ways of doing things, compared with the limited set of agricultural or hunter-gatherer type tasks that characterize the subsistence economic life in a folk community (Bohannon 1963; Cole et al 1971; Redfield 1947). But the difference is not simply one of increased variety, great as skill proliferation is in the modern world. At the root of the process is a complex and constantly changing technology that calls for novel skills. The skills are generally more intricate and complex, more abstract and generalized than the skills of the past, the total number of skills in which individuals are socialized is greatly expanded, and the repertoire is often changing. Learning to move through the labyrinth of the urban metropolis, to shop, and to negotiate and choose among the myriad of options constantly available for any decision in the realms of eating, clothing, housing, tools, friendship networks, and entertainment are alone formidably intricate and complex skills to acquire. Add the scheduling, juggling, and maneuvering through the hierarchy of school and job rules and tasks, each of which is composed of many component skills, and socialization of the modern child is a wondrous accomplishment. Contrast, for example, the daily migration to the nearby field and the repetitive motions there with a single hand tool experienced by the average folk-culture member with the host of checking, collating, typing, filing, reading, writing, calculating, and varied telephone communication and interpersonal skills demanded in the daily routines of a secretary. Many of the modern skills are in large part constructed with abstract graphic codes and mental manipulations that do not exist in the ancient folk society.

It is the invention of written language and numerical systems, which accompanied the early advances toward complex technology and bureaucratic systems (Havelock 1976; Menninger 1969), that above all shapes the course of socialization so differently from the pattern of socialization in traditional folk life. The life of the secretary, almost all of the school curriculum, and indeed more and more of the postindustrial occupational world and the daily routines of living pivot around written words and calculations. The enhanced scope in tracking, comparing, recalling, planning, and manipulating complex material generated by written codes, recordkeeping, computers and mathematical calculations makes possible a range of activities to solve the most intricate and abstract of problems impossible to solve through oral language systems and mental manipulations alone.

These inventions have also been responsible for recording and thus expanding knowledge. The individual may well acquire and retain large bodies of diversified information through repeated exposure, as merchants do the items of their inventory, physicians the parts and processes of anatomy and physiology, historians the dates and events of their periods and scientists the concepts and procedures of their field. But the information always forms part of elaborately organized, abstractly conceptualized and constantly evolving modes of thought, designed for extended purposes, and is not simply facts anchored tightly in unvarying procedures and rituals. The individual in industrial life is never bound in quite the same way to the single set of work skills of folk life, never wedded to the unchanging, sacred myths and legends that characterize the oral recording of folk history, nor confined to the observations of local fauna and flora that circumscribe practical folk science.

Thus a switch has occurred from local, task-oriented information, recalled in concrete, ritual form, to changing bodies of local and general information, incidental to varying purposes and larger schemes of things, and from particularized skills to general strategies for retrieving and processing information in abstract, constantly changing form. Fewer and fewer of the tasks and occupational skills of our increasingly computer-based society involve repetitive tasks with concrete skills. Individuals increasingly learn abstract codes, general cognitive strategies for problem solving, and basic structures of knowledge that fit them for careers in broad fields. The gradual specialization required for competence in branches of activity is founded on these generalized, abstract skills for acquiring and using knowledge. The industrial or postindustrial person is both an abstract generalist and an abstract specialist, contrasting sharply with the concrete generalizing and the concrete specializing of the person in folk life, as the lag in general levels and the unevenness in development of Piagetian skills in different folk societies suggests (Dasen 1972).

Even sports, crafts, and aesthetics take quite different forms in modern life, all organized and operated with the aid of abstract principles, deliberate planning, and conscious selection among alternative means and ends. Sports were not always highly developed in tribal communities and when they were, employed rules evolved over generations and passed down by tradition, orally and through example, as in the case of lacrosse and other games among American Indian tribes (Sutton-Smith 1976). Competition among clans, though perhaps formal, was always settled by recourse to tradition. Informal games and sports among children and neighborhood adult groups are still widespread in industrial society, presumably part of this legacy, but the bulk of sports and games in modern life are formally organized club, school, and professional teams following highly organized strategies and schedules. Scientific analysis of play, rules, skills, and physical status employs every technique of advanced technology and formal codes—print, video replay, computer, medical diagnosis, and mathematical and symbolic analysis. Competition is between groups or individuals, according to the sport, but also always focused on the further development of the maximum powers of the athlete over the course of his or her sports career. Although not always paid by money, individual achievement and status undergird sports activities in all contexts, and financial perquisites abound in putatively nonprofessional contexts, scholarships of all kinds for college sports, and the lucrative rewards of equipment samples, money, and status from advertising name endorsement for Olympic heroes.

Crafts are perhaps not as widespread as sports in contemporary industrial societies, generally having been replaced by mass production technology, except in countries and regions where traditional folk crafts have persisted. Yet interest in handicrafts for making jewelry, furniture, pottery, and other artifacts revives from time to time. These revivals are actually departures, for they violate cardinal rules that define craft activities in folk societies. In folk life crafts such as rug weaving or basket making follow a standard set of forms and patterns handed down by example in culturally prescribed ways and typically embedded with symbolic significance in tribal myth and ritual (Langar 1980; Lévi-Strauss 1968). Cultural symbolism may have faded where traditional crafts continue in modern contexts, but the repetition of pattern and method persist. Craft revivals on the other hand are relatively open-ended with respect to the choice of both design and method. They may be intuitively constructed by individual artisans, but their guide is design principles respecting aesthetic arrangements of color, form, and current fashion. Their inspiration is individual creativity and the rapidly changing tastes of professional and popular opinion, not the sacred ways of cultural tradition. While folk crafts are based on design principles, there is little interest in experimentation with design and method (including sophisticated machine tools) that governs recreated craft activity in industrial society. Changes in the restricted set of forms available in a given folk tradition occur only slowly over the generations.

Art too in contemporary life follows these same principles of experimentation and the changing opinion of secular professional and popular values, rather than the stable forms of cultural tradition. Actually art as a deliberate attempt to embellish our environment and to reflect on the significance of human existence, values, conflict, and culture is commonly thought to be distinctly a characteristic of large societies. There is no division between the crafts and arts in folk society; they are one, serving the same combined functions of aesthetic decoration, myth recording, and ritual (Langar 1980), Art, like religion, is quite separate from the multiple occupational and recreational activities of our life, however, celebrated only in certain places (books, painting, theaters, concert halls, monuments, art galleries, and some radio and TV programs) and practiced largely by specialists (artists, actors, architects, musicians, fiction writers, poets). As in all other realms, art is deliberately programmed and organized according to scientifically derived, cognitive principles, serving the needs and status of individual creators and consumers, who follow divergent schools in rapidly changing value structures and tastes, that reflect the complexity, diversity, and ever-changing ways of our industrial system.

Methods of Socialization. It is in how children acquire the curriculum of their society that we observe one of the most dramatic yet not widely appreciated alterations industrial forms have produced in the social life of the traditional folk community. As in the curriculum and other matters, old forms persist in many ways; overlap occurs, but novel modes have emerged that are fundamentally at variance with the receding folk modes. The extent of change is perhaps best realized by noting (table 2-1) that modeling is only one of multiple forms of learning skills and knowledge in the contemporary world, yet it is the primary mode for learning skills in the folk community. The children's own activity in imitating and experimenting with the skills they observe practiced among the adults and older peers on daily routines, and their interactions with peers in experimentation are of course also major methods by which they learn. But these personal experimentations and peer interactions are all essentially one integrated social learning process in which the visible daily example of skilled adults at their chores and crafts is the core that engages and binds children in close social harmony in a way of life. There is little need for formal demonstration or verbal guidance because the unvarying activities of tiny communities unitized in the extended family marshals the oncoming generations along a well-trodden course that offers and needs no alternatives. Except in times of crisis—drought, famine, forest fire, flood, exhaustion of land or game, epidemic, or invasion that leads to famine, forced migration, war, and other temporary and sometimes permanent adaptations—these apparently informal social dynamics of modeling-observation-imitation-experimentation-interaction effectively and smoothly socialize all members in stable patterns to maintain the stable ecological balance the folk community itself maintains over substantial time periods. Recall the highly complex motor skills of swimming and canoeing acquired so proficiently by all Manus children by the age of three (Mead 1975). The webs of social and working life are so interwoven that there is no need to teach what no child can fail to learn.

Although the social dynamics of modeling play the central role in folk socialization, other methods are found to varying degrees, usually closely linked to the primary mode. Thus verbal instruction appears less in the form of deliberate instruction in do's and don'ts than in the social lessons buried in the frequent storytelling the child hears. In West Africa the adventures of the hare and the spider indigenous to savannah and forest there tell of the value of cleverness and the pitfalls of egocentrism (Colardelle-Diarrassouba 1975). African hare stories have descended to modern times in the United States through the Uncle Remus stories, originally brought with the culture of African slaves, which tell of the clever rabbit who outwits his adversaries through intelligence and cunning (Harris 1905). Storytelling typically follows a form of group ritual around the campfire or compound, sometimes with various members contributing narrative, as in the traditional Hawaiian folk story (Watson-Gegeo 1981). Cultural history as well is passed along in this way, through the telling of myths and legends about the people. One reason folk history, legend, and storytelling tend to follow a stereotypic, rote form is that, having no means of making a permanent written record, oral, rote forms are essential to preserve some degree of fidelity to the original events and concepts. Thus certain general knowledge and general rules with respect to behavior are transmitted through verbal means in oral form, though more descriptively than analytically, extending the learning of work and craft skills that are learned largely by example and practice.

Physical restraints, verbal directives, and other controls, including sometimes severe punishment and deprivation, are employed to varying degrees (Mead 1928; Witkin 1974), but always secondary to the primary modes of modeling and imitation. Direct controls stressing obedience, cooperation, and conformity appear more in agricultural than in hunter-gatherer societies. They are also more concentrated in infancy than in later periods, given the obvious dependency, and in certain situations, such as in nursing and carrying the infant or preventing the child from crawling near the communal fire (Super 1981). Rewards appear typically in physical form, such as the early bestowal of bows and arrows or the miniature canoe to the Manus child (Mead 1975) or pony to the Plains Indian child (Ewers 1955). Social symbolic rewards and incentives of age-status graduation rites and ceremonies are important experiences in the development of children in every folk culture as well. These controls and rewards appear to work uniformly and smoothly because they are woven into the fabric of an intimate social life where the choices and courses to follow are so clearly defined.

Despite the proliferation of socialization methods evident in contemporary urban life, one modality is primary—formal or deliberate instruction, originating in the methodology of science and the rational systems of bureaucracy. When technology becomes complex and constantly undergoes change, when knowledge becomes abstract, coded in written form and ever changing, and when social organizations become large and hierarchical, it is no longer feasible to guide learning principally through example. Formal planning, organizing, and monitoring progress become indispensable to ensure that the necessary concepts and skills are acquired.

Deliberate instruction takes many forms in industrial society but can be reduced to certain basic processes, which take place in varying combinations according to the context and the goals and media available. These elements, so well known to all of us, consist of demonstration, verbal instruction, guidance of the learner's performance (through verbal comment or pointing to errors or solutions), and arranged experience. No matter what combination is employed nor whether formal or informal, didactic or interactive in approach, the feature that distinguishes planned instruction from the modeling processes that characterize much of the socialization in folk cultures is conscious intentionality. Learning and socialization in industrial society tend to be conscious, deliberate, and planned. There is an awareness of a need to impart systematically information about and skills for how to do things that are too difficult to master without guidance of some kind. Strategies and formal systems develop to meet this need, awareness of which becomes not only widely institutionalized but also embedded in the modes of communication and practice of even our informal modes of activity. For all the reasons of the concreteness, simplicity, and stability of folk life, consciousness of need for instruction and thus strategies for teaching fail to develop. The examples and informal practice of everyday activity work very well. There is no multiplicity and endless hierarchy of skills and knowledge to acquire, only a small body of limited skills that everyone can uniformly acquire quite adequately, some perhaps a bit better than others, but almost no one below minimum levels of competence needed to perform and cooperate as well to maintain the existence of both the person and the group.

How instruction is formalized systematically in the schools, apprenticeship training programs, day care, extracurricular and community sport, game, hobby, and art (music, drawing, sculpture) needs little further elaboration. The role of instruction is easy to document even in the most informal of atmospheres. Even the youngest of infants in day care are talked to, involved in feeding and other tasks, and shown elements of what to do, with at least an intuitive eye to teaching the baby the beginning processes of his or her own self-care, however irregularly and inconsistently in some centers. Honig, Caldwell, and Tannenbaum (1970) have shown that over 90 percent of the information in a day-care setting for children under 4 involves communications from adult to child, largely built around furnishing verbal information and guidance. Moving young children from activity to activity, from indoors to outdoors, getting them dressed, involving them in play, singing, story reading, and similar activities, even when planned learning sessions are ostensibly not practiced in a center, all demand passing information to children and showing them where to move and what to do and not to do. The circumscribed and unfamiliar arrangements of any group setting for children in an urban world depend on guidance and formal control to supervise and socialize children, greatly in contrast to the minimum of guidance required in the open and highly familiar setting of the extended family compound in a folk community (Fowler and Fowler 1978).

Sports, games, hobbies, and art activities as well, however informal the setting, all involve verbally transmitting information and guiding learners about social rules of the club or school, as well as about the rules of the game or task. The most laissez faire of art teachers at least offers suggestions about materials, arranges models, and selected topics, and the class itself is an arranged environment of objects, tools, a teacher who gives examples, and students who interact. Music is of course a highly structured and sequenced domain of formal instruction and practice. To be sure, guidance in rules of the game and ceremonial tasks feature in folk life, particularly in the special ceremonies of unfamiliar puberty rites that occur only occasionally (Thompson and Joseph 1947). But because most work, craft, and game activities in folk communities are limited and unvarying, the degree and scope of attention to guidance and instruction are minimal.

Nearly all the multiple modes of socialization that occur in modern life are accompanied by verbal communication that encompasses intention to teach and inform. The role of teacher may be implicit as in neighborhood peers teaching one another rules for a new card-party game, but deliberate instruction typically continues even after the rules have been verbally explained, as for instance when a would-be teacher suggests, "Just watch and you'll catch on.'' The informal teacher in effect uses the method of the classroom, *instructing* the novice to learn, leaving nothing to the chance of undirected imitation. Board games like Monopoly, moreover, are typically accompanied by written instructions. The realms of media—visual and auditory—are all anchored in the intent to inform and instruct as well. Much of the material may be stories and dramas designed to entertain, please the aesthetic senses, and inspire moral insight, burying the message in art form. But a large portion of the material in all media are deliberately designed to instruct, including children's television programs such as Sesame Street and the Electric Company. Newspapers, television, and radio news programs and whole magazines concentrate on informing the public about current events. It may be argued that news stories are designed to inform, not necessarily to teach. Yet it would appear to be a distinction without a difference, since the method is one of instructing the audience, through planned presentations about the "facts," and in the more sophisticated reporting and news commentaries, explanation of how things occurred is intrinsic to the process of reporting. Needless to add, the various editorial columns, topical guidance articles and commentaries, documentaries, and the vast amount of nonfictional literature for adults and children are directly cast in the form of deliberate instruction, however biased the presentation.

Modeling, peer interaction, experimentation, and practice are still very much a continuing part of socialization in industrial society, but they seldom occur in pure form, without infusions of verbal and other forms of intentional instruction. During childhood they also seldom occur directly in relation to the occupational roles and skills in which the society ultimately expects the child to be socialized. Proficient members of a group are often singled out as examples to follow and their particular skills dissected for the benefit of the learners, through play analysis in athletics, discussion of paintings in art classes, or workshop performances by skilled musicians. Modeling is frequently a more consciously arranged phenomenon than is characteristic in folk life.

Modeling in the home by the parents and older siblings shares much of this same intentionality. The successful parent or sibling is held up for others to emulate, often with quite explicit remarks about skill dimensions and the merits of striving. But the modeling that transpires in the home, except for the task models parents provide as child rearers and housekeepers, is chiefly in the form of general personality and problem-solving models for coping with everyday life. Everywhere the child is exposed to modeling, the home, neighborhood, school, and wider urban community on errands and excursions, the models perform a limited range of tasks. Parents, day-care providers, school teachers, janitors, retail clerks, vehicle operators, and similar service workers are about the extent of the child's direct exposure to the extensive array of occupational roles and skills of the industrial world.

Fortunately exposure comes in many other ways, though it is not as vivid as the exposure a child of folk life is privileged to obtain. The urban child is exposed to the example of role and work models through the examples shown indirectly in visual media and text, often of course in dramatic or narrative form. But just as the exploits of legendary heroes in folk life are more than life size (Radin 1972), so the examples on television are characteristically conventional stereotypes that fail to probe below the surface characteristics of social relations and too seldom depict actual work scenes, let alone the actual skills required in the jobs. Modeling is thus not a primary or at least the most effective mode of socialization in modern life. The modern child learns less about the specific skills of an occupation and more about abstract processes and general knowledge, which is why deliberate, often highly planned instruction, is the foundation method of socialization in industrial life. Abstract use of language, general problem-solving and coping skills, reading, writing, and arithmetic, and a broad and complex hierarchy of pyramiding skills and general knowledge are a fare that is not easy to transmit without mediated learning, the deliberate and often organized verbal instruction, demonstrations, and guidance of skilled adults and older children.

One of the most compelling examples of this shift from concrete modeling to intentional, abstract instruction is to be found in the core curriculum of early childhood education programs of the nursery school and day care. The structure of this curriculum—toys and environmental arrangements—reflects the profound evolution that has occurred from folkways to the modern industrial world in an important method of socialization, namely, the child's own activity or play. How do children play in the two worlds? The core curriculum in our world is made up chiefly of fabricated materials designed specifically for the purpose of play and learning (Fowler 1980b, c; Read 1976). Those for the young child are called toys and play-learning materials. Those for the school aged child are a mixture of toy artifacts, games, science-based learning kits and materials, collections of natural and artificial materials, books, and other media. The entire curriculum of the folk child at all ages are natural and human-made objects designed only for purposes of real work or decoration. Few toys or specialized learning materials are to be found, except for the miniature doll and animal figures that serve as religious fetishes as much as toys (Feitelson 1977; Fowler and Fowler 1978).

Play is widely celebrated as the royal road to learning, particularly for the early years, yet play as practiced in our world is a scarcely developed phenomenon in the activities of folk children (Feitelson 1977). The early childhood activities in the nursery school consist of elaborate manipulations of specialized materials in means-and-end problem solving, creative, construction, and sociodramatic play (Fowler 1980b). Much of the activity is highly imaginative. One basis for stimulating this imaginative, elaborate manipulative and role-playing activity is rooted in the characteristics of the materials themselves, which are essentially abstract in design. There are several categories of materials, none of which faithfully copies real-life objects. One major category is geometric forms that reflect the carpentered world of industrial life (Segall, Campbell, and Herskovits 1966). Variations of these forms find a hundred uses in the early curriculum, including shape sorting and matching in form boards, puzzles, and insertion boxes; size grading; and a variety of modular creative construction activities. A second major category is miniature replicas of vehicles, people, animals, scenes, and similar real-life objects, all of which are manipulated in sociodramatic play, often in combination with specialized manipulative and construction materials. A third category is free-form materials, such as clay, sand, crayons, and paper, which are used for creative activities. A fourth category is the props often added to stimulate social role play, such as hats, service jackets, cans, and boxes with labels, and an occasional tool or piece of machinery.

The principal characteristics that define such materials and activities and even the environment itself in a day-care center or nursery school are selectivity and abstraction. Certain features are selected in the design of materials to represent real-life objects and simulate real-life environments in abstract terms. Other features are deliberately excluded. The selected features are generally the critical features representing a generalized concept of the object or phenomenon in question. Cubes have six equal square sides and only right angles, unlike even most boxes and building materials, to say nothing of other common objects. Miniature vehicles follow the general contours of cars, for example, and include key, well-recognized features, like windows, wheels, steering wheel, a facsimile of the externals of the motor, but usually omit door handles, trim, tail lights, and other secondary features. Irregularities of line and color that characterize objects in real life are also excluded. Thus the various examples of concepts represented in children's play materials are generalized exemplars of concepts, though not exact copies of real-life objects. Not all of the generalized exemplars are alike of course. They vary in size, shape, color and in which principal features are selected for representation, for example, whether car doors open or headlights are included. Such toys are consistently abstractions, however.

Free-form and construction-play materials by the very nature of their amorphous or modular construction are designed to be used for abstract purposes, that is to create or construct summary representations of people, animals, and other phenomena, or to shape and construct abstract forms and designs. The various added props, the benches, cans with labels, and tools, brought in to stimulate occupational role play are also selected items used to suggest—not duplicate—scenes and settings. In other words the basic curriculum for socializing children through play in urban industrial society from the beginning build on processes of abstracting and generalizing.

Very different is the form of experimentation in play followed by the folk child (Feitelson 1977; Fowler and Fowler 1978; Mead 1975; Wilbert 1976a). Living in a highly familiar, well-defined environment of real-life objects, the child who experiments is confined to means-end manipulations of natural and human-made tools and related social objects. The infant is limited to manipulations of body parts, her own or the caregivers' (often the breast itself as a manipulative toy), body adornments, pebbles, sticks, bits of earth, feeding ware, and similar items. These concrete manipulations do serve the advancement of concept learning, as illustrated by the way in which children among the Oksapmin in Papua, New Guinea acquire limited counting skills through the use of twenty-seven body parts (fingers of right hand through arms, face down opposite arm to opposite fingers), which are used in adult life as a notational system (Saxe 1981). Concrete marking systems using body parts are found in many folk societies, which only gradually develop into abstract notational systems as the society evolves in scale and technology or (in recent history) establishes contact with industrial society (Saxe 1982).

As the child becomes mobile and begins to move outside the family and the community compounds, the number and variety of objects explored is extended, though not very much by comparison with the toy repertoire and social artifacts of the urban child's world. The greatest extension is in exposure to the variegated fauna and flora of the region and in the use of tools in the tasks of the adult world. It is a world of functional activity in which the child rarely plays at artificially contrived tasks of the imagination, to represent complicated, distant, and vaguely understood skills, tasks, and social roles, as in industrial life. The play is in fact that of direct and indirect experimentation with the workaday world of the adults and older peers. Skill progression is socialized through following and experimenting in these tasks, a graduated process, embedded in interactions with peers and adults in real-life activities. As skills and motivations develop, the children gradually spend longer periods at the different tasks, engaging themselves more realistically until they are assigned definite task responsibilities on the first stage of the age-hierarchical ladder. Before this formal step the play has always pivoted around simple trial and error in direct means end accomplishment. The net outcomes of these concrete manipulations are quite logically high proficiency in the concrete tasks prevalent in the culture. Logical classification and notational systems do emerge but are largely limited to the local environment and used functionally rather than in terms of universal abstract systems transformable in generalized ways.

Each of the models of cognitive socialization suits its own scene, planned instruction in abstract codes and manipulations for the complex tools, artifacts, and abstract symbols of industrial society, and informal modeling and imitation in the concrete skill manipulations and local abstractions for the socially and ecologically intimate world of the folk community. It is only when individuals socialized in the methods and skills of a folk world, often through the persistence of folkways in a new environment, find themselves encountering the demands of an industrial world, that their adaptation becomes dysfunctional.

Note

1. The terms *industrial* and *large-scale, hierarchical* as applied to society are used more or less interchangeably throughout the chapter and book, although the emphasis is more often on technologically advanced forms of industrial (and postindustrial) society. More distinctions between modern industrial forms and earlier large hierarchical and bureaucratic systems will be made in reviewing the history of formal instruction and early education in the next chapter. Variations from these ideal types, chiefly through the influences power and wealth exercise upon social structure and the various components of production and socialization, probably do not affect fundamentally the polarities between basic modes of the two systems. Much of the conceptual framework for comparing social systems is drawn from Redfield (1947), Tönnies (1940), and Weber (1947).

3

The Social Origins and Development of Early Instruction

The Founding of Educational Concepts and Schools

Socialization, once an informal affair of the family in small communities, has become an elaborate affair of formal institutions in hierarchical societies. Once largely a matter of everyone acquiring language and a few concrete skills differing mainly by sex, it is increasingly a matter of learning abstract, generalized skills and specialized complex skills differing by occupation. The acquisition of skills, which once could easily be left to a few years of direct experimentation and interaction among the young imitating the examples and tales of familiar adults now takes years of planned effort by formally trained child-care and educational specialists designing programs of abstract play and planned instruction. How has this radical shift from socialization to education come about?

The Technological Basis for New Social Forms

The beginnings of this shift in the modes of rearing children are to be found in the traces of change in technology and social forms that produced the first civilization thousands of years ago. The emergence of hierarchical societies occurred not once but several times more or less independently in the river valleys of Mesopotamia, Egypt, the Indus Valley, and the Yellow River regions of China several thousands of years before our era (McNeill 1963; Hawkes 1973; Harris 1977; Toynbee 1947; Wells 1920). Later probably independent beginnings have been identified in Central and South America among the Incas of Peru and the Indians of Central and Southern Mexico. Various hypotheses have been advanced as to why large-scale societal forms should emerge first in such valleys as the Tigris-Euphrates and Nile delta. Many have proposed that favorable conditions for growing crops in these regions led to yearly crop surpluses, which meant leisure time for craft specialization to develop (Hawkes 1973; McNeill 1963; Wells 1920). The year-round hot and sunny climate coupled with the annual flooding of the rivers made large-scale agriculture a highly viable way of life. The rich topsoil deposited along many miles of riverbanks, where grains grew naturally with little effort during the periods of flooding, could furnish a comparatively plentiful existence for large numbers of inhabitants.

Problems confronted the pioneer settlers of these alluvial plains that could not readily be solved by the small-scale systems of folk societies, however. Earlier prehistoric populations had settled in the upper hill regions of the Tigris-Euphrates valley, hundreds of miles above the delta plains, or in the grasslands of Arabia and the areas west of the Nile, which had not then dried up from overgrazing and the change of climate that followed the receding of the last ice age glacier (Childe 1957; Saggs 1965; Williams and Hugues 1980). Intensive cultivation of these fertile areas evolved in Neolithic villages, through domesticating animals and learning to sow the wild grains discovered with simple hand tools. The combination of pressure of population, estimated to have multiplied by a factor of 16 between 8000 and 4000 B.C. (Deevey 1960), and changing climate apparently led members of these relatively rich and successful agricultural communities to move into the flooding, variously swampy, sometimes jungle, and often scorched regions of the lower river valleys (Hawkes 1973; McNeill 1963; Toynbee 1946). Gradual game depletion over thousands of years and the availability of wild grains had much to do with the original shift from hunter-gatherer modes of folk life of earlier eras to the settled folk life of Neolithic villages. In these growing agricultural villages, small and intimate kinship networks working in personalized cooperation still served admirably for an adaptive small-scale communal way of life. Food supplies were not so plentiful, however, even before poulation pressures and changes in climate occurred, nor leisure time adequate to foster the growth of craft specialization, limited as it was to the restricted period between harvest and sowing each year (McNeill 1963).

Chief among the problems of delta cultivation was the unregulated flow of the flood water over vast areas that made permanent settlement difficult, hazardous, and even impossible during seasons when the entire river changed its course by many miles. Unless a supply of water could somehow be maintained in the surrounding plains once the flood receded for the long balance of the year, moreover, crops would wither and die in the parching heat of continuous sunshine. There was very little annual precipitation in these lower valley regions of the Nile and Tigris-Euphrates rivers. Because of the recurring exigencies occasioned each year by the annual cycle of flooding and swamp drying and drought, the latter to the areas farther removed from the rivers, the evolution of irrigation control is likely to have been a rapidly evolving process. Only communities situated in the most favorable areas of alternately mild flooding and parching could have survived, and these sites could not be counted on, given the magnitude of flood variation from year to year. The incentive to flood regulation must have been great even in a series of good years, given the uncertainty and extremes of wetness and dryness of the process at best.

Irrigation and dams, probably originating in quite limited ways in small tributaries (Hawkes 1973), became natural solutions to housing and crop protection from uncontrolled flooding. Once these devices were discovered, perhaps through the accident of natural channeling and bank and settling pond formation from the flow and ebb of flood waters, they would be gradually incorporated into the routines of village practice. As soon as the concept of controlling the direction and timing of water flow was grasped, it was probably a simple extension to the notion of building a network of canals, dams, and reservoirs of varying size to water on demand all the fields in the area. The natural slopes of the land toward the sea and in relation to other contours of the land made the process a comparatively simple though laborious one of working with the course of gravity. Unlike tilling and sowing small plots with a digging stick or even with oxen and plough, which apparently predate the evolution of large-scale social systems and which could be accomplished with the cooperation of the working members of an extended family, constructing irrigation canals and dams are intrinsically large-scale tasks demanding the coordinated efforts of hundreds and preferably thousands of people (McNeill 1963).

Changes in Social Structure

While comparatively simple, the necessity for cooperation among large numbers of workers and the advantage of planning carefully the course, timing, and size of water flow appears to have called forth the development of new social arrangements and more complex technical skills. Coordinating the work of large numbers of workers developed management and administrative skills. Assembling a cast of thousands meant people traveling from distant villages up and down the river for days and weeks at a time, thus destroying the intimacy of the folk community that had made modeling alone quite adequate as the primary method for socializing the young. Planning and monitoring the course of large projects led to the development of new technical skills in measurement and recordkeeping. The simple counting devices of body parts and tally sticks employed everywhere by folk communities at various stages of sophistication (Menninger 1969; Saxe 1981) no longer sufficed for the complexities and precision demanded for predicting time, rate, distance, and volume of water flow and earth removal, land slopes, and ownership, and eventually calendrical calculation to predict the timing of flooding, which in Egypt occurred with comparative regularity each year (Hawkes 1973). Geometry, simple astronomy, and calculating skills emerged to handle the precise land area and other spatial measurements and transactions required. As village size and relations among villages and regions grew, trade expanded in quantity and complexity, involving large and multisided transactions and placing more demands for recordkeeping, measuring, and calculating.

At some early stage of the process, probably long before regional organizations developed (McNeill 1963), transactions became too numerous and complicated to handle through oral report and mental operation. The need to perform and retain transactions in some more convenient, precise, and permanent form led to the invention of written language and number systems. The process began crudely, with pictorial and sign systems for objects, events, and ideas, which when developed in Egypt became the hieroglyphic system and in Babylonia the cuneiform system of writing. Gradually the systems became more condensed and abstract over thousands of years, incorporating phonetic signs and classifiers to clarify meaning, and eventually leading to syllabic and and alphabetic codes (Gardiner 1961; Hawkes 1973; Sarton 1952). Numbers were written down, along with fractions, calculations, and other measurement conventions.

The process of social development went through many stages: first villages were clustered to combine work forces to tame more extensive river areas for crop management, then clusters were organized into regional governments. Society became increasingly differentiated and stratified. At least four socioeconomic classes each with subdivisions have been distinguished: (1) slaves (family servants, serfs, and many craftsmen); (2) artisans, farm owners, merchants, and professional groups; (3) the priesthood and nobility (Hawkes 1973; Saggs 1965). In the fourth class peasants, fishermen, herdsmen, and boatsmen all flourished, fitting the ecological niches available in the network of streams and canals linked closely to the sea and extending over hundreds of miles. Specialized crafts and trades in tool and weapon fabrication, engineering and architecture, business procedure and management, writing, accounting, and recordkeeping; estate management, and religious ritual, court procedure, education, library procedure, food preparation and other fields all proliferated, diversifying and removing further and further the skill practices from the seat of the child's traditional folk forms of socialization.

But while skills grew in complexity, number, and abstraction, they did not grow evenly among the various fields nor especially in the manner in which they were distributed among the population (McNeill 1963). The early societies of Sumeria and Babylonia, Egypt, the Indus Valley, and China were all slave societies built on the unskilled, backbreaking labor of thousands of peasants and fellahs or coolies. Technological progress and skill advances occurred primarily among the specialities in trade, business, engineering, architecture, and similar technical fields that developed into elaborate bureaucratic elites planning and administering the affairs of society and the slave labor of the vast unskilled populace. Aside from a limited number of devices like wheeled carts; the sickle, scythe, and the seed-sowing plow; and the lever, roller, pulley, and sled for moving huge mounds of earth and granite blocks (all developed prior to the formation of centralized state systems in 3000 B.C. (Howells 1954; McNeill 1963; Sarton 1952)), few real labor-saving inventions appeared on the scene in any of these early civilizations. Incentives for change in hand labor were apparently small. The extensive irrigation systems and enormous and precisely constructed pyramids were all accomplished with the combined labor of tens of thousands of unskilled workers, who employed these relatively simple aids and were directed by skilled crews of technocrats (Gardiner 1961). Thus the direction of technological development built on the skills of an elite, who, formally educated in schools established early in dynastic histories (Hawkes 1973; Saggs 1965), were motivated and skilled to perfect further the technical and abstract skills in writing, mathematics, engineering and the like, but not the hand tools of the peasant and laborer. The unskilled, deprived of decision-making roles, were in no position to contribute much to technical advancement.

Once established in large bureaucratic societies, the nature of the social systems apparently limited much further advance in technology (McNeill 1963). Built as they were on the backs of the unskilled, highly hierarchical and operating what has been called a smooth-running "hydraulic society" (Harris 1977) that reliably provided adequate food resources, through elaborate flood control and irrigation systems over thousands of years, both the incentives and the opportunities for continued advancement at any level appeared to freeze. Many of the same types of ploughs, sail boats, bricks, and even technical tools for the elite lasted for thousands of years, some of them remaining little modified in those regions until recent times. Writing systems progressed, especially in Egypt, yet even here evolved only over many centuries from pictograhic (hieroglyphic) to a modified pictorial code (hieratic) using phonetic elements and meaning classifiers, and finally to more of a shorthand script (demotic). Moreover, advances remained at the syllabary level, not reaching the definite alphabetic system the Greeks appear to have been the first to establish (Havelock 1976). Systems for recording numbers and other mathematical symbols made similar advances from pictorial to more abstract modular codes, as in cuneiform writing among the Babylonians, who in fact developed a theoretical interest in mathematics, devising equations more advanced than the Greeks did later (Hawkes 1973; Saggs 1965). Chinese writing, however, hardly changed at all after its first big jump from a pictographic to an ideographic code in the first few centuries. It has remained over more than two thousand years the same cumbersome character system accessible only to a tiny elite for technical and literary purposes (Needham 1969) until recent revolutionary educational reforms have made it accessible to all despite its complexity (Kessen 1975).

Thus the first transformation from folk to formal modes of socialization took forms that severely limited the number of members of society who could be served. Hierarchical control of an efficient food-producing system tended to jell in ways that did little to encourage further innovation, either in technology or in the methods of transmission themselves, that is in the educational process. Schools and libraries were established and elaborate abstract codes and methods of measuring, recording, and calculating communicated and maintained among the privileged. But once technical systems attained certain levels of sophistication, the society continued to operate smoothly with little alteration in form or interruption for centuries. Breakdowns did occur, sometimes for a century or more, in all these civilizations. They were characteristically occasioned by invasion by neighboring tribes and states usually operating at less advanced levels of development (McNeill 1963; Hawkes 1973; Needham 1969; Wells 1920). Interregnums were periods of chaos, hardship, conflict among warring states, and general breakdown in the economy and social system (Gardiner 1961; Hawkes 1973; Needham 1969). Eventually centralized control would be reestablished, but the new dynasties were typically the conquerors from outside the empire who became acculturated to the modes, social structure, and technology of the more advanced hydraulic societies, adding little themselves. The members of the established priesthood bureaucracies apparently perpetuated themselves through their abstract skills, professional organization, and elitism. The growth of a warrior elite with special skills to protect the empire further reinforced the perpetuation of societal continuity in hierarchical form. The preceding Neolithic village societies had been remarkably peaceable and free from conflict (McNeill 1963). Although yielding few food surpluses and low rates of technological advancement, their life was ecologically well adapted. With the advent of large-scale technology and the vested interest of a controlling educated bureaucracy, however, national defense and warfare became intrinsic to the way of life, particularly in Mesopotamia, more vulnerable to invasion from surrounding regions than Egypt, which was comparatively well protected by sea and desert.

Effects of Societal Change on Cognitive Socialization

How much did these early slave bureaucracies transform the folkways of prehistory and just how did these early hierarchical societies differ from the industrial societies of our day in matters that affect socialization and education? The various changes that led to large-scale societies had profound consequences in the ways of socializing children—but not in equal ways upon all members.

The first change of note to alter socialization practices was the ordering of society by occupation and place of work, which gradually paralleled and often supplanted kinship in defining social and work roles, status and duties (Braun and Edwards 1972; Hawkes 1973). Much of the scene of adult activity was removed from the home, severely restricting opportunities for children to observe and imitate adult work skills. While women's work remained largely in the domestic scene, most of the skilled crafts of carpentry, pottery making, wine and beer making, weaving, metal working, and the like were conducted in central locations in temple or royal shops, factories or studios, and centralized bazaars (Hawkes 1973; Saggs 1965). Only residual elements of certain crafts, such as baking and weaving, continued to be conducted around the home for family consumption. Business and most of the skilled professions, such as scribe, architecture, engineering, and accounting, were conducted in centrally operated institutions outside the home—to say nothing of mining, lumbering, and shipping, which were highly organized enterprises demanding movement across great distances.

On the land, local farmers, (estate owners and managers) often resided close to their fields, but actually worked through serfs (Hawkes 1973). The entire agricultural process, as we have seen, consisted of vast centrally run enterprises directed by temple and government authorities, moving about to exploit the centrally operated labor of serfs to till the fields, transport the grain to centralized granaries, and participate in the demanding maintenance of irrigation projects. Although Egypt remained somewhat more a civilization of small towns and villages than the humming and buzzing urban industrial scene of Mesopotamia, it was nonetheless cosmopolitan and hierarchically and bureaucratically regulated. At all levels of society from the domestic and urban laboring slaves and field serfs to the most privileged professionals, occupational life was predominantly out of the home and family control.

This transfer of the site of occupational activity away from the family thus meant that the bulk of the work skills must henceforth be acquired outside the home. Socialization necessarily became more formalized as youth must now travel each day to a centralized place to learn an activity whose sole purpose was the production of specialized products. Since these newly specialized crafts of leather making, carpentry, goldsmithing, and the like all gradually developed quite intricate, highly specialized techniques, the youth, whether freeman or slave (as was often the case), had to spend several years acquiring skill in the craft. While in the past all members of the community learned all the relatively simple skills at least moderately well, except for the skill partitioning by sex, now each youth had to choose in advance from a wide number of highly refined skills to be able to master one of them well. This proliferation of specialties and displacement from the home affected boys far more than girls, since with few exceptions (beer and wine making and textile work) most of the trades were open only to men, further dividing the life of the sexes and paving the way for the development of patriarchal systems built on domination of men over women (Hawkes 1973). Except for the class-linked divisions of concubine, wife, and, occasionally, priestess, the socialization of women was almost entirely confined to the home. Even those few trades in which women participated were chiefly acquired and practiced in the milieu of the home.

The socialization process was complicated by the institution of slavery, but generally speaking, craft skill development apparently followed folk practice in at least two respects. Youths were channeled into the crafts of their fathers and a good deal of the learning continued to be by example (Hawkes 1973; Saggs 1965). In this way the guilds that formed tended to be controlled by certain families and traditional clan networks and skills were acquired through apprenticing in large ateliers or shops dominated by a family or leading family member. Because crafts, though complex and specialized nevertheless involved highly concrete and visible procedures, materials and products, apprentices could learn much through observation, imitation, and practice. But because crafts, though visible were intricate, formal demonstration, guidance, and verbal explanation undoubtedly crept more and more into the socialization process. Thus crafts in the new societies began to develop the modes of deliberate instruction to combine with folk practices.

These important shifts in the form and place of socialization among the skilled trades were matched by even greater changes brought about by the formation of professional classes to plan and direct the operations of the technology and bureaucracy. The development of complex occupational specializations and bureaucratic organizations fostered the development of written codes and complex measurement that led to the establishment of schools. Of all societal changes, schools produced perhaps the most profound transformation in the modes of socialization. Learning for the newly founded professions among the elite now proceeded chiefly through deliberate instruction instead of chiefly by example. The well-preserved records of cuneiform clay tablets tell us much about the earliest schools, which may be traced back to nearly 3000 B.C. in ancient Sumeria (Saggs 1965). First apparently tied closely to temple activities, over the centuries many different schools emerged that were essentially secular in nature, operated by private operators through the contributions of parents.

Needless to say, enrollment was almost entirely confined to the children of the priesthood-governing classes, especially the professional groups, the scribes of all kinds who enjoyed great prestige as the linchpins of the functioning bureaucracy of these first technical societies. Even after their refinement into shorthand signs, these early writing systems were cumbersome and tedious to learn (Saggs 1965; Sarton 1952). Schooling was thus not only necessarily limited to the wealthy professional, business, and priestly noble classes, but many of the nobles, generals, and other high functionaries themselves did not become literate, being assigned scribes of all kinds to serve their technical needs. Because of this intricacy of the written codes schooling occupied much of the daily life of the professionals' children for many years. School continued each day from dawn to dusk, with a break for lunch, under the direction of a master and his assistants, aided by older students who helped to enforce discipline. Corporal punishment in the form of beatings was routine, but was certainly tempered by the power of the wealthy parents who paid the salaries (Hawkes 1973). There were only three free days per month.

Again partly because of the intricacies of the technique, methods were based on rote learning, much of the daily activity year after year consisting of copying word lists on clay tablets (schools were called "tablet houses") until skill in rendering the wedge forms attained a high degree of practical and aesthetic perfection. Skill in writing Egyptian hieroglyphics and Chinese characters (calligraphy) followed a similar long course (Needham 1969; Sarton 1952). Schools in Mesopotamia were organized into at least three levels, beginning around age 8 or probably earlier (Saggs 1965). The curriculum was otherwise composed mainly of learning computational and measurement skills. Very little attention was paid to subject content, except for the semiscientific way in which words were endlessly classified into types of items, such as plants, animals, tools, and other social artifacts. The methods for acquiring this information, which included a vast body of legal, accounting, and other technical terms as well, rested heavily on memorization and oral drill, along with the copying (Saggs 1965). Well-organized grammatical and mathematical texts were composed, literature was also studied, and mathematics and later astronomy became developed as semitheoretical specialties in their own right, divorced from religious conceptions and functions, particularly in later Babylonian times (Hawkes 1973; Sarton 1952). Medicine reached higher levels in Egypt, apparently because of the concern with mummification (Hawkes 1973).

The picture of socialization in the formal school that emerges is thus one of a definite shift to deliberate, planned instruction but with certain defined limits on the prevalent methods and modes of cognitive functioning and on the parties participating. The curriculum was highly organized and sequenced but not conceptualized well in terms of systems of knowledge and inquiry. The relative concreteness, unwieldiness and impreciseness of the various ideographic languages may have played a role in hampering the development of flexible, abstract forms of logical thinking (Havelock 1976), and certainly in extending literacy to the populace (Hawkes 1973; McNeill 1963; Needham 1969). Models and demonstration predominated, though oral instruction was common, even making use of high visiting functionaries to teach in Egypt (Hawkes 1973). Although abstract processes evolved further in later eras, comparative analysis and scientific objectivity never developed much until the invention of the alphabet that came with the founding of Greek society (Havelock 1976; Sarton 1952). Much of the substance of learning remained rooted in drill on techniques and procedures and in ideas embedded in myth and ritual. The emphasis on copying and memorizing through oral drill could be seen to reflect the persistence of imitation and other oral modes carried over from folk society, as well as the intricacies of the languages. Social control and educational instruction were heavily authority centered and based on severe physical punishment, quite in keeping with the brutal methods of maiming and killing by law widely practiced in the extended society.

Outside the schools in the skilled crafts, socialization apparently followed partially traditional folk modes through the apprentice ship system in which youths gradually acquired skill by observing and imitating the methods and modes of their skilled masters. The complexity of the new craft technical skills, however, suggests that verbal explanation and formal guidance may have come more frequently into use. Most important, socialization in the child's early years remained entirely the province of the home, and girls of all classes as well as all children of the population at large rarely were allowed to attend school or follow trades and professions at all (Hawkes 1973).

Educational Evolution—From the Ancient
Societies through the Middle Ages

The history of early education has been amply outlined many times (for example in Braun and Edwards 1972, and Raymont 1937). The focus here is on noting the significant steps in the history of early education on the road from unconscious socialization to systematic education. Of necessity we will continue to extend our analysis to many matters beyond the period of early childhood because issues and techiques in the history of socialization and education often transcend age. The path has not been a straight line, of course, but one marked by diverse turnings and even long regressions. The most extensive of these was the prolonged decimation and deterioration of organized education during the Middle Ages following the collapse of the Roman Empire and the return to many features of folk life, even for the elite (Aries 1962).

The Beginnings of Educational Theory

The presence of vast networks of schools, the development of systematic methods, curricula, texts, and other educational materials tell us that the ancient civilizations of Egypt and Sumeria must have had theorists and educational innovators, but whether their theorists synthesized wide-ranging views on educational matters or evolved no more than pragmatic solutions to practical problems, perhaps couched in religious myths, we do not know. The first great educational visionaries, whose ideas have come down to us in some detail were Plato, Aristotle, and Confucious. Curiously, all three formulated their ideas about the same period in history, around the 6th to 5th centuries B.C. What is not always realized is that these were not isolated writers but simply leading thinkers among a network of philosophers of their times, who tended to cluster together in schools embodying the teachings of leading scholars (McNeill 1963; Winspear 1956). Other prominent schools were the Pythagoreans in Greece and the Buddhists in India, again interestingly both developing in the same historical period (5th century B.C.). While these and other early philosophers developed theoretical world views and ideas of recommended conduct, only the first three seemed to have concerned themselves more directly with educational questions, with varying degrees of influence on subsequent social systems.

The emergence of philosophy, formal theory, and scientific inquiry in ancient Greece has been attributed to the pivotal geographical position of the Greek city states at the confluence of trade on the islands and peninsulas of the eastern Mediterranean. Unlike the monolithic bureaucracies of the hydraulic economies of earlier civilizations, the endless comparison, negotiation and litigation of prices, goods, and arrangements in trade demanded increased abstraction, mental manipulation, and above all flexibility of thought and a comparative point of view (Bernal 1954; Winspear 1956). The origins of parallel but apparently independent developments in philosophy and science in the ancient feudal states of China at about the same period are more obscure. It is noteworthy, however, that Chinese thought may not have been as multifaceted and materialistic as Greek philosophy was. There appear to have been fewer fundamentally different schools of thought, Chinese systems concentrating on matters of social form rather than on a variety of social and material concepts as in the West (Needham 1969).

The Greeks

Plato (431-345 B.C.) was the first to conceptualize the process of socialization systematically in formal educational terms and to link it tightly to the nature of society and the social ideals to be strived for. Though admirable, his dream of communal sharing and cooperative harmony was confined to a landed gentry who were to be educated to rule more effectively over the artisans and slaves (Braun and Edwards 1972; Plato 1980; Winspear 1956).

Plato's views, like those of the Pythagoreans who preceded and influenced him, were developed as a reaction of the oligarchic world of the landed conservatives to the problems and disruptions of the time, the rising mercantile groups, peasant rebellions, rivalries among competing city-states, and the press of population. The comparative successes of the highly repressive Cretan and Spartan regimes in containing the merchant classes in Crete and suppressing them in Sparta, together with the comprehensiveness and integration of their educational systems directly influenced his conception of education and social life. The defeat of Athens by Sparta during Plato's youth and the resultant social and intellectual decay, confusion, and recrimination, including condemnation to death of Socrates, its leading intellectual and Plato's teacher, contributed much to Plato's search for a conservative and utopian solution in *The Republic*, modeled heavily on Sparta.

Plato's theory of education was an idealized system for totalitarian social control of the landed oligarchy over all life and learning of its citizens. Plato formalized and extended what was already roughly general practice, particularly in Sparta. The division of social classes was to be reinforced by providing for a thorough, comprehensive, and lifelong system of education for the chosen elite, who were to rule over the lower, supposedly inferior classes of artisans, peasants, and slaves as enlightened and gentle but firm despots for the good of all. The ruling elite to be educated would be selected according to their apparent fitness, regardless of class of origin, but Plato generally assumed that the bulk of candidates would emerge from the classes of "silver and gold," rather than the classes of "bronze and iron." While formal education was reserved for this elite, artisans and peasants were to be educated in their trades and crafts through apprenticeships (which of course they were already), and slaves simply through performing the required tasks themselves. The unfit would be placed on the mountains to die in infancy. Girls were to be educated jointly with boys, according to their capacities and strength, which Plato considered generally inferior to boys'. The family and private ownership would be abolished, men, women, and children of the guardian class learning, living, and working in a communal existence without knowledge of family ties or personal property. Obviously revolutionary, even for our times, these concepts were particularly so in ancient Greece, where only boys attended school, girls being socialized for domestic duties in the home. Even more, although channeling the education of the lower classes into vocational training, Plato's program for children of the lower orders is worth citing, because it reveals the awareness and probable prevalence of play among the ancients, as well as Plato's own advanced insights about the value of play for cognitive development, albeit in limited ways:

He who is to be good at anything as a man must practice that thing from early childhood, in play as well as in earnest, with all the attendant circumstances of the action. Thus, if a boy is to be a good farmer, or again, a good builder, he should play, in the one case at building toy houses, in the other at farming, and both should be provided by their tutors with miniature tools on the pattern of real ones. In particular, all necessary preliminary instruction should be acquired in this way. Thus, the carpenter should be taught by his play to use the rule and plumb line, and the soldier to sit a horse, and the like. We should seek to use games as a means of directing children's tastes and inclinations toward the station they are themselves to fill when adult. So we may say, in fact, the sum and substance of education is the right training which effectually leads the soul of the child at play on to the love of the calling in which he will have to be perfect, after its kind, when he is a man. (The Laws, Book I, p. 1243).

Plato left large gaps in detailing the curriculum and methods to be employed, yet he stated for the first time in history as far as historical records reveal, theoretical solutions for many of the major educational problems that continue to concern us even in our time. Moreover, he addressed himself to questions of socializing children in early development far beyond what anyone else said even through Roman times. He defined education comprehensively as a cradle-to-grave process of developmental socialization embracing all aspects of learning and community activity. Individuals would follow a step-by-step series of tasks (curriculum sequencing) but would live in groups sharing all activities in common, leading ultimately to the role of philosopher-kings to rule society supposedly in total harmony.

Plato defined the institution, setting, and agents of socialization even in infancy. Infants were to be removed from the home to be reared in professionally run communal group settings by trained nurses. Mothers would be called in only to breast feed infants, supplemented by wet nurses from the general population, without knowledge of whose child they suckled. There was to be a total curriculum ranging from physical exercises and military skills (males and females participating together naked in the square—the custom already for males), through music and all the academic subjects of science, geometry, calculation, and literature, to the social skills and virtues that would be acquired through communal learning and living. Plato also stressed the importance of combining theoretical learning with direct experience and action in the ordinary affairs of the common people.

He took up the question of content selection, advocating rigorous selection of oral tales and other literature for young children, banning horror tales and immoral stories that might frighten them or corrupt their innocence, issues with a familiar ring even today. He was thus one of the first to develop a rationale for censorship and control over media.

Except for compulsory participation in gymnastic and military training exercises, Plato's methods were open and inquiry-oriented; he observed that one could train a body but a mind trained by compulsion did not develop. As we know from his dialogues, Plato employed Socratic methods of dialectical interchange—acquiring knowledge through issue-oriented argument. He even spoke to motivation, arguing that the superior genetic stock from which the elite would be drawn would by definition be innately motivated. Yet he also recognized individual differences, noting that though "inferior in general" the range of individual skill potential among women was as great as among men.

Plato was an innovative and comprehensive founder for all time, whose ideas set much of the course for the concerns, dimensions, and scope of education that occupy us today (Cremin 1965). He articulated the nature and dimensions of the shift from the informal modes of the folk community to the formal modes of the bureaucratic society, searching for the bridges between the personal and communal on the one hand and the systematic and abstract on the other. Although opportunities for planned socialization and formal instruction were to be confined to a ruling elite, genetically biased and genocidal, his solutions nevertheless find live parallels in recent history. The communal rearing of infants in groups by professional nurses outside the home and family is represented to varying degrees in day care, the Israeli kibbutzim (where mothers come on schedule to nurse and play with their infants), the family communes of the 1960s in the United States, and certain boarding care centers in the socialist countries—though in no case is the parent-child identity so completely erased, and planned education or deliberate instruction for the young is obviously most uneven in its spread around the world (H.B. Robinson and N.M. Robinson 1972; N.M. Robinson and H.B. Robinson 1972). Total curricular are common in many places in our time, though unselfconscious nudity and glorification of the human body, dialetical methods, and even equal treatment for women are often nonexistent, rare, or marked by serious breaches. Developmental sequencing is typically hampered by tradition and poor logic and marked by the breaks between institutions, classrooms, age grades, and subjects, while its complement, individual differences, often disappears in the maze of class, subject, and ability grouping and teaching of all kinds. Clearly there are few questions about education for which Plato did not sketch solutions in some form to problems still widely unsolved.

Although Aristotle (384-322 B.C.), a student of Plato, appears generally more liberal in his outlook toward education, less oriented toward a tight systematic approach to educating the citizenry and more concerned with freedom for the individual, his general elitest framework and many of his principles were substantially the same as Plato's. He limited the citizenry eligible for formal schooling to the same oligarchic classes and recognized the total social and lifelong character of education and thus, like Plato, advocated, for example, control over the stories, language, and social experience young children are exposed to, and even advocated infanticide for deformed children. On the other hand children were to remain in home care during their first seven years, and both study and physical labor were to be avoided during the first five "lest . . . growth be impeded" (Aristotle 1941:1303). Aristotle restored the role of the (then) traditional family, including women's place in the home, and abandoned Plato's notions of communal living, child rearing, and property holding. He placed more emphasis on education for the ultimate intelligent use of leisure time as the highest goal, though there was the same serious concern for the inculcation of moral and social responsibility in educating the future ruling elite, and is thus the founder of traditional liberal education for young gentlemen.

In general, while he offered various suggestions on marriage, the family, child development, and education not apparent in Plato, few were developed in detail. Among other things, he touched on such matters as the age and health of spouses as those factors might affect their children, the health of the mother during pregnancy, the importance of abortion for excess children "before sense and life have begun" (p. 1302), and hardiness training for infants. He also explicitly discussed the concept of developmental stages or periods of human development, during which conditions and experiences are likely to vary. This recognition of stages—infancy, early childhood, two ages of education (from age 7 to puberty and from puberty to 21 years)—though only sketchily developed appears to be one of his most notable contributions. Especially interesting was his awareness of how stages are to some extent rooted in biology, yet that development is modifiable by experience: "we should observe the divisions [stages] actually made by nature; for the deficiencies of nature are what art and education seek to fill up" (p. 1305). His moderation and liberal outlook appears again in his criticism of excessive regimens of physical training, particularly in training for Olympic events as leading to unhealthy one-sidedness, and his idealization of the goals of education as habit and reason. His ideas on curriculum were less elaborate than Plato's. Aristotle's major contribution remains more in the realm of philosophy, the general nature of matter and knowledge, and the beginnings of science, of which he was one of the world's great founders, than in advancing educational theory and concepts of socialization.

Confucious and Chinese Society

The theories of Confucious (551-479 B.C.) are important because of the evidence they provide on China, one of the early large-scale bureaucratic slave societies like ancient Egypt and Sumeria. They are also noteworthy because of a certain stress on the democratization of education. Like the thought of Plato and Aristotle, Confucian thought reflected a widespread response among the conservative educated classes of the time wishing to preserve the state feudal control of the past (McNeill 1963). It is important to note that few if any of the writings of Confucious have come down to us in pure form, most having been edited and supplemented by unidentified disciples and later scholars. Nevertheless the general outlook and precepts of Confucianism have exercised an enormous influence on the Chinese social system up to the most recent revolutionary period, effectively serving as the major model and source for the mandarinate (the bureaucratic civil service hierarchy) control of education and social life for more than two thousand years (Galt 1961; McNeill 1963; Needham 1969).

The historical importance of Confucian thought in this context lies in advancing the concept that nobility and virtue were not inborn but were traits open to members of all classes through education, which should be available to all (McNeill 1963; Needham 1969). In this he departed from the aristocratic views of the past espousing an extraordinary doctrine for his time. His views laid the basis for the system (adopted first by individual feudal states and later by the Han dynasty about 200 B.C.) that, while very much elitist and rigidly class bound in practice, recognized and permitted a few individuals among the poor sectors to rise through open examination and education. Confucian ideas are also important, because, unlike ancient Egypt and Sumeria, in China there was no organized priesthood to guide education of the Mandarinate nobility in professional and governing skills; religious training (ancestory worship) was only a minor component. Virtue was not justified through religion, but judged on its own merits, more so even than among the Greeks and Romans. The general ideals of the educational system were those of social virtues of gentlemanliness, decorum, lack of violence, and cooperation, governing through diplomacy rather than confrontation, purportedly for the welfare and social harmony of society as a whole.

Stabilization and Reversion: Schools and
Techniques from Rome to the Renaissance

Confucious had little to say about early development, however, and in fact, even in the Western world, apart from the beginning made by Plato, Aristotle, and a few other Greek and Roman scholars, little systematic attention to the early years appears to have been paid until the Renaissance. Reading, arithmetic, and related skills were regularly taught in Greek and Roman times to children of the wealthy, as they had been in the ancient societies preceding them, and scholars occasionally discussed reading and other teaching methods, individual differences, and the merits of what age schooling should start. Most scholars advocated deferring school until the age period still widely in current use, between 5 and 7, for fear of forcing the child, but a few scholars, such as Xenophon, Chrysippus, and later the renowned Roman educator, Quintilian, observed that children could learn much as soon as they learned to speak or could absorb moral training (Davies 1973). With the development of alphabetic writing by the Greeks (Davies 1973; Havelock 1976), the alphabetic system of learning to read and write appeared, supplanting the various ideographic and syllabic systems in use up to that time (and still used in China). The advent of this simplified system made literacy potentially more accessible to all people, but money and restricted opportunity limited literacy to the well-off.

Reading continued to be taught in part by syllables, however, the child first learning the alphabet by rote, forward and backward and in different combinations, in syllables, then in whole words and sentences, practicing endless exercises by rote (Davies 1973). Writing was generally acquired in company with reading, a stylus on wax tablets being used. Letter sounds are nowhere mentioned. Quintilian later stressed learning the letter shapes and advocated use of letter-grooved boards to guide the child's practice more firmly. Otherwise he generally followed the Greeks. This ancient alphabetic, syllabic, and spelling approach remained little changed all through Europe until modern times. Phonics, or learning letters, syllables, and words by means of letter-sound associations was not widely introduced until early in the sixteenth century in Germany. The idea of a controlled vocabulary, however, was proposed as early as St. Jerome, who also introduced the use of Biblical names, combining reading instruction with religious lore, the former practice eventually developing into the mainstay in our times, though religious themes have widely disappeared in this century. The use of illustrations for reading texts can be traced to their use in early vocabularies or dictionaries as early as the fifteenth century, even before the advent of printing, which were then adapted for children's ABC books and primers. Illustrating letters and word concepts then led quite naturally to the whole-word method of reading, first developed by Comenius in detail.

The position of women and girls was marked by certain advances in ancient Rome (Carcopino 1941). Roman matrons enjoyed a certain respect, based on legal rights, partial equality in marriage, attending school with boys, and frequent participation in politics, athletics, civic activities, and the arts and letters. Many Roman children were taught letters and numbers and some elements of reading at home by their mothers (or educated Greek slaves) in the preschool years, before they were sent off to school (Carcopino 1941). Until the fall of Rome certain Christian leaders too involved themselves in questions of early learning though for different purposes. St. Jerome, in a letter to a Roman matron, suggests that she teach her daughter her letters (in cutout shapes) through play, along with moral precepts, as preparation for religious training in the troubled times of declining Roman power (Braun and Edwards 1972). The practice appears to have continued to some degree among religious groups and the wealthy throughout the medieval era until modern times (Davies 1973). However, interest in education and the very existence of schools in any form were greatly diminished in Europe until the Renaissance.

Outside Europe schools for the governing bureaucracy and the elite were maintained much as before in China (Galt 1951; Needham 1969) and established in similar ways, though more embedded in religious ideology, in the rising Islamic world (McNeill 1963; Peters 1962; Wagner and Lofti 1980a, b; Ulich 1954). Although schools were in some places perhaps more widespread than in medieval Europe, no noteworthy innovations in formal education and child socialization are widely reported. Rote procedures, oral recitation, and confinement to male elites have predominated everywhere, aside from the various brief partial exceptions practiced in ancient Greece and Rome, until the most recent period (Kessen 1975; Wagner and Lofti 1980a, b).

In Europe schools in some form with numbers of children, and these once more largely for boys, did not again become widespread until the sixteenth and seventeenth centuries (Aries 1962; Braun and Edwards 1972; Davies 1973; Huizinga 1954). The ideal for the knight of feudal times was hunting, war, and chivalry, skills for which apprenticeships and modeling, not schooling, were required. Outside the church hierarchy only occasional feudal lords and rulers, such as Charlemagne, acquired any learning or showed any respect for formal learning and the arts.

Even the church hierarchy was very uneven in its concern for literacy and learning (Davies 1973). Methods were again by rote and ritual, of course, typically following group oral practices of chanting and song derived from folk culture (Aries 1962; Davies 1973). Learning was mainly devoted to memorizing the prayers, passages, rituals, chants, and psalms required for the ritual performance of duties in the monastery, cloister, or parish. Reading often became more a means of verifying memory rather than of acquiring new information. Only in special cathedral schools and a few private schools in Italy, Ireland, and England did learning in a somewhat broader form survive through the Middle Ages until the Renaissance. The decline of the Roman empire, the attendant decay of urban life, where schools and intellectual life had been centered, the development of feudal domains around the medieval village, castle, and agricultural life, shrank formal education largely to a process of church ritual and the oral tradition, much like the Quranic schools of the Islamic world (Aries 1962; Wagner and Lofti 1980a, b). Few became genuinely literate and thoughtful, a condition pepetuated by the labor and expense of hand methods employed for writing and reproducing books.

Discipline and attitudes toward children in schools and in the home were frequently harsh and abusive from the earliest societies up to our era (Carcopino 1941; Davies 1973; Raymont 1937). Beatings, deprivation, and other forms of physical and psychological abuse were the common means of commanding attention, demanding learning, and enforcing control. Quintilian, Plutarch, St. Jerome, and other educators in Rome wrote of the need for more enlightened, humanist practices and even the use of play in teaching children. Children should be encouraged and praised and reason employed rather than beatings and other harsh forms of treatment. Yet even Plutarch saw public rebuke as a necessary educational tool and was against "spoiling," writing as he was to sophisticated and often corrupt elites (Braun and Edwards 1972). A certain leavening of treatment occurred from the first century on in Rome, even occasioning concern by contemporary critics that schooling involved too much play in the children's learning (Davies 1973). The Middle Ages brought extension of schooling in principle to the slave as well as the freed men under a decree issued during the rule of Charlemagne in 789, but the methods were generally harsher under Christian precepts of original sin, following the decline of the Roman Empire, even through the nineteenth century. Severe beatings and other forms of punishment have continued in some schools in Europe, America, and elsewhere to our day.

During the Middle Ages the apprenticeship system became once more the mainstay of socialization for people in all classes, professions, and trades alike. Moreover age became irrelevant in determining admission to a trade. One might enter at any age, only conditional upon ability and opportunity to handle in some way the tools of the trade. In practice this meant many children began their trades between 8 and 12 or so, often becoming full-scale workers, even officers in the navy as early as age 12 (Aries 1962).

Changes in Socialization from Folk Society
to the Renaissance: Overview

Many concepts on planning children's socialization as formal education had been advanced and various conscious educational practices established or experimented with in ancient societies up to the fall of the Roman Empire. Some of these concerned the development of young children. Certain concepts and practices were lost or greatly diminished in force, clarity, and scope of application during the prolonged period of agriculturally based feudal life and church dominance that marked social life in Western Europe during the Middle Ages. While formal education in forms similar to those described for the earlier Egyptian, Sumerian, and Chinese slave- and serf-based bureaucratic civilizations continued elsewhere, little change occurred and few novel socialization or educational concepts appeared. Small islands of rational inquiry in certain urban centers in the broad sweep of culture remained or emerged here and there, such as in Constantinople, or in other places in the Middle East and North Africa witnessing the flowering of Islamic culture. But these exceptions exercised few widespread or permanent effects on how children were reared or educated (Bernal 1954; Issouri 1950; McNeill 1963; Needham 1969; Peters 1962) well attested by the still widespread practices of rote and ritual in Quranic schools (Wagner and Lofti 1980a, b).

Certainly the most profound transformation from folk modes of socialization was the idea of teaching and education as conscious acts and their institutionalization in planned systems of instruction, however well or poorly conceptualized and organized in practice. Once developed and practiced, formal education, at least for children of the elites, became an integral necessity to the bureaucratic governing systems that more or less permanently succeeded the tribal communities in Asia and Europe. Literacy, calculation, systematic recordkeeping and administrative and professional skills demanded some conscious and planned instruction for groups of children in schools. These were invariably placed outside the home and relatively separated from the context of daily community activity, thus reinforcing the abstract and generalized nature of the language skills and other concepts and skills to be learned.

Schools may have declined greatly in number and generally in quality during the European feudal era, but this decline and the extensive return to folk ritual and oral transmission regulated by church need was by no means uniform. The collapse of Rome's vast bureaucracy deflated the need for schools for educated leaders and removed the underpinning of an educated urban elite and leisure class with time to devote to learning and the arts. But the process did not occur all at once and the beginnings of church bureaucracy began well before the toppling of the Roman power center in 476 A.D. (Braun and Edwards 1972; Davies 1973).

In a curious way, though quantity and quality declined, educational variety proliferated during the Middle Ages. Although nominally directed from the Church's seat in Rome, church schools, as they gradually extended themselves in the thousand years between Rome's fall and the beginnings of the modern era, took many forms. They were shaped locally in many ways, influenced directly and indirectly by the fragmentation of the seats of feudal power throughout Europe. And the multiplicity of feudal authorities themselves (through growth and conquest evolving gradually into nation states, beginning with Charlemagne and Alfred the Great) as well as leaders in the various urban centers of trade that survived and grew, were influential in maintaining and establishing semisecular private schools of various kinds (Davies 1973). It will also be recalled that the methods of instruction of ancient Greece and Rome, as well as those of the other large-scale slave societies, were themselves still very much the creatures of rote learning, ritual, and oral transmission, as well as of harsh discipline. Thus the declines were uneven and the beginnings of a diversity of new forms ultimately became possible. The major advances toward more rational-analytic methods, enlightened treatment of children, and democratization, however, awaited the Renaissance and the reforms of the industrial era.

The practice of Roman matrons teaching their preschool children letters and counting and beginning reading marked the first conscious use of cognitive socialization in early development. The involvement of learning through play illustrated by the letter of St. Jerome underscores the recognition of developmental stages, earlier advanced by Aristotle, and of play, earlier discussed by Plato as the characteristic form of activity for the young child. Thus by the time of Rome, early socialization had been transformed from folk practice in several ways. Parents thought consciously about stimulating their young children, did so widely among the educated classes and they did it in the realm of graphic symbol learning, one of the more abstract bases of thought. Play itself in its abstracted social forms had also become basic to the modes of cognitively socializing children, however little understood as such. Although girls as much as boys were generally exposed to these practices, except in the occasional writings of scholars like Plato, early education remained an institution entirely embedded in the traditional framework of the family. Though we have few records to go on, and the topic is much neglected even among the elites of the feudal world of medieval society, teaching methods apparently brought together in different combinations folk and formal practices, and didactic and play-centered interaction approaches that have come to be common child-stimulation patterns of middle-class life in Europe and America down to our own times. There was, however, little educational or developmental theory nor much resembling a systematic technology of early education or even of general education.

The next thousand years until the Renaissance brought not only a drastic decline in schooling and the informal abstract teaching in the educated home—which persisted only in cultural islands here and there. Sociodramatic play and the idea of childhood itself, if not quite as lost as Aries (1962) originally proposed (deMause 1974; Forsyth 1976), were diminished or functionally transformed in the agricultural community of the Middle Ages (Aries 1962). The family was again frequently close to its place of work in tilling the land, plying a craft, or practicing knighthood in local tournaments or nearby sieges and battles, obviating the need for elaborate fantasy in abstract social play. Observing the visible, concrete activities of daily life—even the priesthood was constantly about—the children became familiar with adult practices almost as soon as they could move about. Indeed childhood was for the medieval period a barely recognized phase of infancy, before the child could handle a tool or contribute to the daily household and farming chores of the way of life. Even in the later paintings of the Middle Ages we not infrequently see infants and young children depicted as something like miniature adults, who need grow only in size to reach maturity.

For the medieval world the infant was something of a toy or a plaything and a burden of chores because of its dependency before it could pull its weight in the hard struggle for survival (Aries 1962). The diminution of childhood and the world of play in some ways resembles development in folk society, which was, of course, one of the major roots of the Middle Ages, in the tribal societies that overran Rome. There were differences, however, namely the continuation of written material, schooling, and formal apprenticeships for craftsmen, knights, and priests in medieval society, which went along with the craft and professional division of labor, however retrenched from the occupational complexities and hierarchies of the Roman Empire. It must also be recalled that, unlike life in earlier and even recent folk societies, the life of the peasant and craftsman, similar to life in the ancient empires, was burdened by a network of heavy obligations, restrictions, and often great abuse by the elaborate social structure of feudal hierarchies.

Even for the greatly reduced elite, there was little place or function in this world for extended periods of childhood divided into infancy, early childhood for play, and different stages of schooling, as in Greek and Roman times. The child moved from infancy to small duties, then boys quickly to apprenticeship in a craft, soldiering, or knighthood, or studies for the religious professions. Girls were once more pushed back in the scheme of things. Reinforced by church doctrine of the guilt of Eve, along with folk practices, women were generally returned to the domicile of cottage or castle, moving from infancy to domestic chores and agricultural tasks as their primary mode of development and existence. The important exception of the religious orders provided a few women with the best education of the time at the cost of regimentation and isolation in the convent.

Much of the learning for children followed the ancient folk practices of observing and imitating older children and adults in the routines of daily work and the rituals of religion and knighthood. The intimate family circle, the village community, and the stable patterns and simple technology of agricultural life were quite in harmony with such practices. The few children (mostly boys) who went to school, and these were typically religious schools, started at the same variable ages of 7 to 9 or more, typically after contributing to the family workload for some years (Aries 1962; Davies 1973). Life in feudal times was a strange mix of the folk, the mystical, and the bureaucratic that left the early years of life undefined, a period of apparent nondevelopment.

The Founding of Modern Systems of Early Education

Industrial Technology and the Enlightenment

The development of education as a formal but rational and humanist system of instruction and the founding of early education itself as a field are products of the Industrial Revolution, the Protestant Reformation, and the Renaissance. Changes in technology and the growth of trade beginning even before the thirteenth century and expanding rapidly by the seventeenth century led to the establishment of industry and expanding awareness of the culture and ideas of the ancient world (McNeill 1963; Peters 1962). These in turn called for new methods of work and different sorts of skill and training to supplant the prevalent static patterns of village serf, feudal lord, priest, and skilled artisan. Aggressive entrepreneurs who could found enterprises and initiate projects, manage groups of people, the large numbers of skilled and unskilled workers working together in an industry soon blossomed into a new hierarchy of socioeconomic classes. The dynamically changing new production and training systems, interacting with the revival of interest in the rational thought of earlier Greece and Rome, evoked new models of theology and secular thought, to reconcile and guide the demands of the emerging way of life free from the stifling forms and controls of the old feudal and Catholic hierarchies (Peters 1962; Tawney 1926).

The new theology, embodied in the doctrines of Protestantism, propounded the rights of the individual for direct intercourse with the deity, bypassing the traditional sanctions of the church hierarchy (Braun and Edwards 1972; Davies 1973; McNeill 1963; Peters 1962; Tawney 1926). The Bible was translated from Latin into the vernacular languages of the different regions and new demands were placed on the individual to find his or her own way to salvation. Popular education, at least for the growing skilled and professional middle classes and business leaders, became necessary to meet the parallel demands of the new technology and the new theology of individual skill and achievement. Martin Luther (1483-1546), the chief founder of Protestantism in Germany, wrote and spoke widely on the importance of education for the development of the individual (Braun and Edwards 1972). He advocated founding schools for everyone, girls and boys alike, so that all could read to seek their own Christian path. He discussed broad-based curricula, religion, ancient and modern languages, the arts and sciences, professions, music, and physical and emotional development, and vigorously supported the development of libraries of similar liberality everywhere. His educational efforts were enormously successful, leading to the founding of popular elementary education and widespread literacy in the German states centuries ahead of the rest of Europe.

Central to these developments was a focus on rational inquiry that accompanied the humanist concern for the development of the individual, which extended itself to all citizens regardless of social background, as evident in Luther's interest in popular education. The constantly changing technology, the onus on the individual to learn, achieve, and not only to adapt but to innovate, and the responsibility placed on the individual to read and interpret scripture for himself or herself shifted the emphasis in philosophy and thought from what was given to what might be. Doubt, inquiry, reasoning, and the methods of scientific objectivity came into being and rose to the forefront (though not without constant conflict with existing institutions of the time), stimulated by such leaders of the Enlightenment as Erasmus, Francis Bacon, Montaigne, Descartes, and Voltaire. The simple agricultural technology, static institutions, and hierarchy of the Middle Ages could easily accommodate the informal, personalized, and rote modes of socialization and education of the Middle Ages. The new era demanded not conformity with tradition, hierarchy, and religious doctrine, but rational and objective understanding of how things worked and could be improved, which meant a constant inquiry into alternatives. The way was now paved for the eventual establishment of a systematic science and technology of education, combining rational theory and tested practices.

Persistence of Old Forms

The old ways did not die easily, however. The harsh discipline that had grown up with feudal life and oppression and were sanctified in the framework of original sin and the guilt of humankind found firm position in the various Protestant doctrines of the Reformation. Because they were essentially reform movements originating in Christian theology, concern for religious indoctrination remained paramount, and they sometimes saw the corruption of the traditional Catholic church as also lax in attention to the strict moral training of the child (Braun and Edwards 1972; Raymont 1937). Literal interpretation of the Bible and moral rules predominated. Luther, Calvin, and the Puritans all espoused fear of God and the need to root out sin in child training. Susanna Wesley, the mother of the religious leader, John Wesley, herself applied the severest measures in rearing her seventeen children. Writing in 1732, she commented:

> When turned a year old, and some of them before, they were taught to fear the rod and cry softly. In order to form the minds of the children, the first thing is to conquer their will and to bring them into an obedient temper. (cited in Raymont 1937:17)

A very popular children's book of the time, "Divine and Moral Songs," by Isaac Watts (1720) rails throughout against the dangers of amusement, frilly dress, lying, and other forms of sin, depicting an all-watching, all-powerful God, "whom it is dangerous to provoke," because "one stroke of his almighty rod shall send young sinners quick to hell" (cited in Raymont 1937:19).

The primers and hornbooks and much of the content of the lessons in schools that gradually extended themselves in Western Europe and America were, until the late nineteenth century, heavily focused on religious catechism, often of the narrowest and most severe moral precepts (Birchenough 1920; Davies 1973; Earle 1974; Raymont 1937; Smith 1931).[1] Schools did not become established automatically everywhere and the new ideas of humanism, democracy, and rational reform of methods made slow headway. Severe and arbitrary discipline, rote learning, and the most simplistic and frightening religious content continued to dominate the scene of child rearing and education.

The new ideas and ways were often framed as social concerns, frequently stimulating the development of and being stimulated by reform movements that gradually made significant inroads in the scope, theory, and practice of education (Raymont 1937). Many of the ideas and reforms directly concerned the welfare and education of the young child. Among the figures whose contributions to child development and education, and especially early education, stand out historically in the new age are Comenius and John Locke.

The Lost Founder of Early Education: Comenius

Were it not for the fact that much of the monumental work of Comenius (1592-1670), the Moravian educator, exercised remarkably little influence on subsequent educational theory and practice, for either younger or older children, Comenius could easily be considered the modern founder of educational theory and the technology of developmentally oriented education, from infancy to adulthood (Braun and Edwards 1972; Raymont 1937; Rusk 1953). He was to our era what Plato was to the ancients, developing a general plan of education from infancy to adulthood, formulating educational principles, and relating education to societal concerns in the comprehensive manner of Plato, though without the political and sociological scope of the latter. While Plato and other ancients established many of these concepts for the first time, including notions of a general curriculum, developmental stages, the role of play, sequencing, and equal participation for both sexes, Comenius synthesized them with a new humanist and scientific outlook for the total population of all classes. Both his principles and methods were also far more elaborate than those of earlier ages. He had more to build on with the emerging technology and empirically based rationalism of the new age. Unfortunately his chief works were lost to sight until the nineteenth century because of the devastating religious and civil wars of the time such as the Thirty Years War, which led him into exile, moving from place to place, into Poland, England, and The Netherlands, and because of certain theological bents that alienated his writings from wide acceptance at the time (Raymont 1937).

In his comprehensive treatise "The Great Didactic," Comenius defines the types of schools that should be freely available in terms of developmental periods, starting with The Mother's Knee for infancy (the first six years), The Vernacular School for childhood, The Latin School or *Gymnasium* for later childhood and The University and travel for youth (Raymont 1937; Rusk 1951). The first two levels would be open to all, but the successive levels would be designed for those desiring increasingly advanced education, and each level would be based on the simpler learnings of the preceding stage.

Unlike Plato he saw the home as the best educator for the earlier years, anticipating conflicts over the home versus day care that plague our day. But he also developed specific and systematic programs of parent education for mothers, in line with his recognition of the lifelong, cumulative nature of the learning process. He thought mothers would provide greater care and attention, adding—and here he demonstrates awareness of the teacher-child-ratio issue—that young children require more individual attention than teachers can give to children in groups. Yet he also drew attention to the limited time and competence of many parents for instructing their children in the complex curriculum required for older ages and also highly valued schools for the opportunity they provided in advancing social learning through peer interaction, again breaking new ground. As might be expected of an advanced innovator of the emerging humanist era, he placed more weight on care and tenderness over discipline and control and in general advanced notions that school and learning should be pleasurable in their own right, ideas that later form the basis for progressive education, informal schooling, and latter-day concepts of intrinsic motivation. He accordingly placed much stress on play and imitation for young children, describing in detail the kinds of manipulative materials, natural objects, and miniature tools needed for the sorts of experimentation and construction activities that would start children toward learning real-life adult work skills.

What is most remarkable in Comenius is not only his sophisticated recognition of early experience as the foundation for later development, of which the ancients too were well aware, but the insightful beginnings he made in defining in detail children's capacities and the nature of the science concepts of time, space, movement, and causality that young children could absorb (Raymont 1937; Rusk 1951), anticipating mental testing and Piagetian concepts by three centuries. He described infant programs of language and concept learning, similar to the object lessons later developed in greater detail by Pestalozzi and others and the language-labeling activities characteristic of contemporary approaches to infant-language stimulation. His definitions of learning were comprehensive, embracing the importance, not only of knowledge and language ("knowing and saying"), but of activity ("doing") as well (hence the stress on play). In this way he also foresaw the progressive education movement of Rousseau, Pestalozzi, Froebel, Montessori, and Dewey, as well as the action-based theory of cognitive development of Piaget, yet retained a more balanced or multifaceted point of view.

Comenius conceived of the young child as very much open to nurture, using analogies of wax tablets, which when fresh are soft and responsive to impression (Rusk 1951). In this way he was a forerunner of Locke's concept of the child as a blank slate (tabula rasa). Comenius inhabited a world of growing interest in the nature of the material world and an emerging empirical science that was fired by the budding changes in technology. His conception of mental development was thus based directly on the experience of sense impressions as the source of concepts that shaped the mind. Comenius similarly formulated concepts of learning skills through acquiring habits, as Locke did, so that development must be guided by training and control (though very different from the prevalent repressive discipline of the time). He was thus at variance with the subsequent pure biological unfolding concepts of development of Rousseau and later Gesell. Perhaps because of these experientially oriented concepts, very advanced for his time, he displayed considerable insight into problems of learning and what we now term socioeconomic or educational disadvantage, pointing up the importance of establishing a complex concept foundation in early childhood in the home in order to progress well later in school. He recognized organic bases for mental retardation as well, but even here his modernity comes forth in his claim that mental development can be advanced even in retarded children through heightened stimulation, more careful attention, and improved methods. Clearly Comenius is the unrecognized Renaissance mind of educational theory, systematic education, and the founder of planned early instruction.

The Founder of the Concept of Experience:
John Locke

The importance of John Locke (1632-1704) for early education and child development lies less in the originality of his concepts, which were preceded in various ways by Comenius, Elizabethan scholars like Thomas More and

Francis Bacon (who influenced Comenius during his stay in England), and educational scholars of the time of Oliver Cromwell, than by the detail, broadness and eloquence with which he wrote (Braun and Edwards 1972). The syntheses Locke advanced and promoted centering on habit and the experiential basis for development through the role of the senses in shaping the mind, made him an important founder in the history of psychological and educational thought (Boring 1951; Peters 1962). He is credited with introducing empiricism into epistomology in his landmark *Essay on Human Understanding* published in 1690 (Hunt 1979) and may be considered the first theorist to conceptualize the place of experience and stimulation in development. His emphasis on repetition and practice in learning, along with utility and positive attitudes and praise, lie at the root of later formulations of the law of effect, reinforcement, and behavioral theory. His orientation also relates to modern modeling and social learning theory. While stressing nurture and experience, however, he remained fairly eclectic, stressing reason, understanding, and a kind of commonsense balance in his approach to learning and human relations. Curiously, while comparatively insightful and systematic with regard to psychological and educational processes, he remained in some ways a figure of the waning feudal life in his advocacy of the home over the school and of education limited to young gentlemen to which he narrowed his concerns (Braun and Edwards 1972).

Summing up the effects of these early theorists, despite the general failure of Comenius's grand treatises directly to influence events (though one of them did—his works on teaching children first in their native language instead of Latin), the theory and practice of planfully instructing young children followed a continuing if irregular course of development in the succeeding centuries (Braun and Edwards 1972; Raymont 1937; Rusk 1951). History might have moved faster had the synthesis Comenius put together so thoroughly in such detail become more widely known at the time, but change and reform were in any case in the air, pushed by the revived intellectual outlook and the press of the industrial revolution. The Elizabethan scholars, John Locke, and countless other thinkers all contributed to the flow and gradual formation of changing concepts and techniques. The many battles and setbacks that ensued, moreover, indicate that progress could not have followed a straight and rapid course, in part because of social inertia and in part because progress in one concept often meant reversals in a related one: Concepts were bound together with institutions and historical change in complex ways that defied simple solutions.

Incentives for Change: Social Conditions

Social conditions among the unschooled populace, which until the late nineteenth century effectively embraced up to 90 percent or more of the population of even the most technologically advanced countries, were appalling and in many ways worsening as the industrial revolution began (Braudel 1973; Kessen 1965; Morton 1948; Raymont 1937; Sée 1931, 1942; Taylor 1958). Poverty, always widespread during the periodic famines, protracted feudal conflicts and religious wars, and grinding obligations of feudal times, took on particularly severe and inhuman forms with the spreading encroachment of technology and accompanying changes in employment, land control, and living conditions. Increasing centralization of land control in large estates, displacement of small landholders, the beginnings of mass factory work, the movement to cities and tenement conditions, the growth of unregulated child labor, the increasing neglect of the poor child through the movement of women to the factories, all combined to darken the plight of the working population.

To worsen matters, outworn monarchies and vast layers of idle and profligate nobilities, long having lost any useful social function, formed a heavy burden of taxes to support their elegant idleness and chronic wars (McNeill 1963; Morton 1948; Sée 1931, 1942). Revolution and reform more and more occupied the thoughts of the leading intellectuals of the time, moving from the general humanism of the Renaissance and Reformation period to focus on definite ideas and programs to improve the lot of the common people and active consideration of structural changes in society. In France, where the social structure had evolved less than in England to make room for the rising middle classes, the intellectual ferment and stifling oppression culminated in the French Revolution, though the monarchy was soon temporarily reestablished. Efforts at revolutionary change were common against the crusty feudal monarchies of Europe during the nineteenth century, especially in 1830 and 1848, and broad-scale reform movements recurred wavelike in England throughout the century.

Integral to the concepts and plans that governed the direction of these repeated efforts at social change was a deep concern for extending popular education and transforming the atmosphere and methods of mindless ritual, slavish rote practices, and stifling authoritarian control systems (Braun and Edwards 1972; Raymont 1937). Much of the concern encompassed ideals of the rights of all people to general enlightenment, to gain knowledge of science, history, and culture that education was presumed to bring. Enlightenment was part of the spirit of the dawning concepts of democracy and egalitariansm of the emerging era. Flowing quite naturally from this ideal was a concern for educating citizens and giving them access to reading and writing so they could keep informed and participate more fully in the complicated political processes of the social system. Education would be a means of securing and maintaining the rights of citizens. On a less idealistic plane, education for working people was more and more demanded to provide skills to suit the changing character of work. A substantial body of educated professional, clerical, technical workers, and teachers was needed to staff the new industries, administrative offices, and educational institutions themselves—an educated middle class.

The establishment of schools and child-care agencies for children of working people later in the Industrial Revolution was also inspired by the neglect and exploitation of children whose mothers were working in textile mills and mines in large numbers (Kessen 1965; Raymont 1937). Over the course of the eighteenth and nineteenth centuries, mothers and often very young children were increasingly drawn into factory work under horrifying conditions. Young children who were not working were often crowded into the tiny and dismal quarters of some poor and totally uneducated older poor women or man of the community (Raymont 1937). In these infamous so-called dame schools hoards of children sat on the floor, confined from dawn to dusk and controlled by the switch, with little or no occupation of any kind. Children were growing up stunted, deformed, malnourished, ignorant, and poorly socialized. Even toddlers were found in these makeshift child-care arrangements, while babies in England and on the Continent were abandoned in large numbers to overworked and overcrowded baby farms and charitable orphan asylums, where many died (Langar 1974). The desperate state of development of poor children excited more and more clamor inflamed by the scathing satires of writers like Charles Dickens, which led to the beginnings of serious social welfare, child-care, and educational reforms (Braun and Edwards 1972; Raymont 1937).

The Feudal Legacy in Child Rearing

Among the waning nobility and even the multiplying middle class, the formality, foppery, and rigidly stratified hierarchy of lingering feudal structures, propped up by outmoded church doctrines, left a legacy of stultifying practices in the socialization of children (Earle 1974). Well into the nineteenth century, the feudal legacy left an approach to child care and training among the educated classes that was centrally focused on manners, ritual, and status. The dress of the youngest children was elaborate and frilly, girls in broad gowns and long lace panties, boys in fancy suits, matching in miniature the clothes of adults. Clothes were totally unsuited for any play except the prissy formalities of intricate social protocol empty of meanings except those adapted to the long-dead age of chivalry and knighthood (Huizinga 1954). Children were reared precociously, both socially and intellectually (Earle 1974).

The revival of intellectual life that came with the Renaissance generated widespread interest in learning that accelerated in the seventeenth century but continued in some ways into the twentieth. The effect on child rearing was to restore certain earlier practices of the affluent home in ancient Rome. Children as young as 3 or 4 were deliberately taught letters, numbers, and often to read. There were important differences in spirit and method, however. The aim now became a combination of an early start on classical scholarship imposed on the child, reaching the extent of teaching the child to read Latin and occasionally Greek (as in the case of John Stuart Mill) almost as early as his or her native language, combined with a stringent regimen of religious doctrine. Hornbooks and primers well laced with religious precepts, and even the Bible itself, typically served as the first primer material (Davies 1973; Raymont 1937). Whether religious or classical, material was highly abstract, completely unrelated to concrete realities of the everyday world, thus shedding little light to the child on the nature of things.

This forcing-house system of education, as it was called (Earle 1974), produced a rather sterile and artificial culture of manners and forms. The child was reared for display, often asked to perform to company for show, as part of the residue of decaying feudal manners, described so well by Goethe (1963) in his novel *Elective Infinities*, on the elaborate, static, and meaningless charades of country nobility. When scholarship was emphasized, display of learned languages, literature, poetry, and ideas were too often valued more than artistic creativity or scientific inquiry—though both of the latter of course grew with the times in spite of this adulation of the past. The religious aspect developed in children a hive of arbitrary, abstract rules and concepts about morality that masked the complicated social forms and subterfuges of everyday behavior. The severity of discipline accompanying this authoritarian legacy, combined with the religious notions (including original sin) and preoccupation with social forms, infused child-rearing attitudes and practices with callousness, righteousness, and rigidity that was widely cloaked with the grossest sentimentality and superficiality. Rote methods and ritual further colored the practices with a sterile mechanical quality. Catechism, stereotyped questions and answers about doctrine, and recitation of letters, syllables, numbers, times tables, and endless religious, classical, and sentimental verses and passages were routine.

The lost idea of childhood and the persistence of oral cultural practices from folk life were of course also important contributors to this feudal legacy. Oral practice, ritual and recitation permeated society. Age and developmental status were often overlooked in teaching children letters, numbers, and reading, just as they were in apprenticing for a trade. The neglect was characteristic, not only in the early dame schools (where the rudiments of learning were sometimes attempted), but even later in the infant school programs that were started around the 1820s in England. Hundreds of children of all ages and sizes from toddlers to 10-year-olds were typically crowded together in the same large hall with their hornbooks, all following oral drills in unison in the same curriculum at the same pace, regardless of skill or comprehension (Birchenough 1920; Raymont 1937; Smith 1931).

It is true that classical culture, fundamentalist religious doctrine, feudal forms, and oral folk cultural ways were frequently at variance with one another as well as with the new empirical modes emerging with the growth of technology, science, and knowledge. Yet despite these contradictions and despite the newer trends, old forms persisted, strongly influencing the form early education was to take in the mass education system established during the nineteenth century. Taken together, the overall effects on child socialization seemed to unite the worst practices of conscious and planned instruction begun by the ancients with the least efficient aspects of the informal socialization practices of traditional folkways. Children were stimulated to become intellectually and socially precocious without regard to developmental characteristics or the play and other needs of childhood. The forms of oral culture became recitational display without genuine intellectual or social purpose, and the rigidities and literalness of Calvinist doctrine and the concern for form produced mechanistic and rote methods. The stereotype of the child these practices produced, which fortunately were tempered in many children through various doses of tenderness and commonsense attention to reality and the nature of children, was that of a stuffy and righteous priggishness and a pretentious and empty brilliance, given to show without purpose. Although the possibilities of planned instruction and symbolic thinking during early childhood discovered by the ancients was reaffirmed, a long distance remained to be traversed before a complex and humane approach to early education would become widespread.

The Beginning of Developmental Theory: Rousseau

The development of contemporary early education practices, which got their first big impetus from Rousseau and the intellectual ferment and social upheavals of the French Revolution and the Napoleonic era, was marked by the uneven introduction of novel concepts and innovations. The advances in one sphere were characteristically accompanied by lags in another. Over the course of the eighteenth century but especially during the nineteenth, several major theorists formulated ground-breaking ideas on child development and early education. Movements were launched and institutions started that evolved into contemporary practices. No theorist or institution singly provided all the answers nor even determined the shape of the new forms that were gradually emerging. There was a tangle of too many issues and problems, for which each innovation could only contribute in some way, raising awareness of other problems that required further work and still other variations.

The merit of Rousseau was his concern for the rights of children as children, with all the implications this entailed for respect and attention to the characteristics and developmental processes that make them at once different from adults and capable of development as socialized beings (Braun and Edwards 1972; Raymont 1937; Rusk 1951). But in resurrecting the lost concept of childhood and greatly elaborating it in more complex form, Rousseau was bound up in the biology of the times. He confounded the natural with the personal and psychological, failing to see how attention to the concreteness and personal modes of the young child was not simply a natural process necessarily at odds with the psychosocial forms of society. This unfortunate tendency to reduce psychological processes to natural (biological) processes and to place psychological development in opposition to sociological structures continues to exercise considerable influence in developmental thinking. The outlook maintains itself in the tendency to conceptualize maturation as a biologically governed process quite separate from experience or at least to downplay experience, particularly planned instruction, in the equation of development as a process of cumulative interaction between organism and environment. Notwithstanding these limitations, Rousseau blew a blast of much-needed fresh air into the anachronistic outlook on childhood and child rearing that dominated the decaying feudal structures of eighteenth-century Europe. Because he criticized so eloquently the corrupt and artificial patterns of the feudal legacy and illuminated current thought with the characteristics and needs of children, his influence on the development of early education and child study was enormous and long lasting.

Rousseau's influence came almost entirely in the form of novels and treatises. (*The Origin of Inequality, Emile, Julie,* and the *Social Contract*), which resulted in his eventual banishment from France, but he himself established no schools or programs and even abandoned his own children to a foundling hospital (Braun and Edwards 1972; Hunt 1979). In insisting on basing child rearing and education on the natural capacities of children, he cut through layers of outworn feudal images and effectively laid the foundation for direct observation as the basis for child care and education. The empirical basis for a science of psychology and child development also became possible. Gone were the notions of basic depravity that must be rooted out through stern measures, church doctrine, and protocol. The child was a creature of biology who must be taken as is and cultivated as a plant in a garden. The approach was to be based on providing direct experience, concrete and practical, which meant dispensing with fairy tales and telling the child the "naked truth." Unlike Plato, however, Rousseau was concerned with presentations of realistic or phenomenological truths more than he was with presenting selected myths about glories of the elite. He was above all democratic, the implications of natural child rearing and natural man (persons) opening completely an egalitarian outlook of individual development and education for everyone. In stressing direct experience through the senses, he launched the modern outlook, but by casting aside the role of books and accumulated social knowledge, he also paved the way for minimizing the role of mediated learning, verbal concepts, and cognitive and social learning, which strongly influenced the progressive, humanistic trends in early education that developed during the nineteenth century and continue in the nursery school movement and elsewhere in our day. He also established the basis of child-centered education and permissiveness that are integral to the approach and remain foci of conflict as well. Implicit in his definitions are concern for the whole child and a constructionist discovery point of view that sees the child as a major shaper of his own personality and destiny—again shades of the modern day care and nursery school, as well as of current developmental theories, notably those of Piaget.

The Dynamics of Educational Development: Innovators versus Education for the Populace

From the time of Rousseau, there were really two distinguishable trends in the development of early education, one oriented toward reform with respect to how the child was viewed and cared for as an individual, and the other busy with the problem of educating masses of poor children in the symbolic and social basics required for coping in a technological world. Although they overlapped in both theory and methods and even in establishing schools, one stem was inspired by the child-development outlook set forth by Rousseau, the other by the accumulated traditions of formal educational thought and practices traceable to the most ancient large-scale societies.

The Developmental Trend

The Early Infant-Developmental Schools. Integral to the first trend was the founding of numerous experimental infant schools (as they were generally called) in England and on the Continent from the mideighteenth century on. The first such school was begun in France in 1769 by Johannes Oberlin, who built on the preliminary efforts of Pastor Stouber starting in 1750, in a poor and barren rural parish in northeast France (Braun and Edwards 1972; Raymont 1937; Rusk 1951). Oberlin was followed by a long string of founders of innovative schools and care centers for infants and young children all directly or indirectly influenced by the ideals and ideas of Rousseau. Among the best-known founders were Princess Pauline, who established a school (still running today) for children of poor working mothers in Germany; Robert Owen in Scotland, who set up an infant school primarily to serve mothers working in his textile factories; Pestalozzi in Switzerland, who established a kind of school farm for poor children; Froebel, who started kindergartens in Germany; and Montessori, who established the *Case dei Bambini* (Children's Houses) sponsored by tenement owners in Rome as a means of controlling vandalism.

The chief characteristics of all these programs was their point of departure for activity in child-centered care and free play indoors and out (Braun and Edwards 1972; Raymont 1937; Rusk 1951). All of them in theory at least shunned corporal punishment and generally favored positively reinforcing methods of care over the traditional stress on control and strict discipline, though all of them believed in regulating the child's behavior in some way. These schools were the forerunners of the nursery school, which, following the example of the McMillan sisters in the London slums in 1911, gradually spread in some numbers throughout England and across North America in various university, welfare, and private school settings. But these early preschools were also the beginnings of the modern kindergartens, junior kindergartens, and infant schools (in Britain) that eventually became integral to the total public system of education.

The Early Innovators. The curriculum of the early developmentally oriented preschools typically embraced various handicrafts and practical work tasks, such as gardening, carpentry, weaving and sewing, along with simple moral lessons and songs (Raymont 1937). Pestalozzi, Froebel, and Montessori developed more explicit and systematic theories and methods that widely influenced the forms of education generally as well as those of early care and education (Braun and Edwards 1972; Raymont 1937; Rusk 1951). These innovators had much in common. All of them attempted to center activity on the whole child and concrete experience with real-life objects through play, but at the same time all of them designed programs based on sequencing learning from the simple to the complex. They were concerned with the development of the individual in all aspects, including intellectual, physical, and emotional, stressed spontaneity, creativity, and freedom for the individual, though not a freedom from all restraints but a freedom to develop self-control, cooperate, create constructively, and act morally and wisely. Thus all three incorporated routine work tasks for young children, such as domestic chores (setting the table, dressing) or working the garden, which were taken quite seriously and set up as guided responsibilities for the individual to learn for self-development and for the benefit of the group. All three also minimized verbal concepts and explanations on the part of teachers, centering attention on the child learning through the realities of social experience and the physical environment. The message of Rousseau was clear in much of what they did and wrote.

Their similar approaches led to similar problems, and there were naturally differences among them. For various reasons their program sequences tended to be rigid and, particularly in the hands of their followers, became mechanical and sterile rituals slavishly adhered to and tending to assume the status of cults (Raymont 1937).

The First Theoretically Based School. Pestalozzi's difficulty appeared to be rooted in his exaggerated attempts to reduce matters to their concrete elements, shying away from abstract symbols (Braun and Edwards 1972; Raymont 1937; Rusk 1951). But when applied to reading (for older children) he is found to have followed a very abstracted process of learning letters and syllabic combinations in prolonged mechanical sequences that had been typical of the beginning reading process in most circles since ancient times. Pestalozzi was unable to escape from the general problem that plagued the development of rational teaching of abstract and symbolic material through planned instruction. In the attempt to render symbols and signs in their most concrete form, they were reduced to basic elements abstracted from context, making their function and meaning difficult to grasp. Because he was also weak in theory and in articulating his methods, and because he was above all a charismatic figure who loved children and believed in traditional, informal education in the family matrix, when his practices were translated into group settings with other teachers, the dry ritual and mechanistic procedures tended to come to the fore.

Pestalozzi was thus in some ways relating to the folkways and rural life of the past instead of preparing a system geared to the expanding needs for educating large populations of children in groups that the future demanded. He related to the larger world through ideals of Christian brotherhood and cooperation, challenging the traditional social hierarchy but understanding no need for new institutions. Yet he was a ground breaker in his humanity and tenderness to children, his infinite concern for individual needs and differences, his developmental approach, and his combined work and play orientation. He also spelled out for the first time in practice in his object lessons the specifics of teaching young children concepts in concrete terms, defining for example the kind of object labeling and cognitive exploration of common objects through learning their names and their characteristics that has been very much the core of early learning programs in recent years.

The Play Innovator. Froebel, though more theoretical and precise in defining concepts about stages of development than Pestalozzi, with whom he had worked extensively, designed a somewhat logically organized series of limited infant-child developmental learning tasks (beginning with his gifts for infants and working into his occupations for older preschoolers), which chained teachers to a narrow range of activities with children (Braun and

Edwards 1972; Raymont 1937; Wiggin and Smith 1900). The first gift, for example, consisted of only six differently colored balls of wool (for 2- to 3-month-olds) and the second of only a wooden ball, a cube and a cylinder, (for 6- to 8-month-olds). While these did provide beginning stimulus contrasts and manipulable objects to promote sensorimotor concept learning, they were obviously extremely limited in variety and stressed geometric abstractions. Educational exercises confined to these objects became quite stultifying in Froebelian schools and the early kindergartens.

Froebel's chief contribution was his formulations of concepts of play and their relation to stages of development. He pointed out the importance of experimentation in play for the child's creative development and distinguished the process-oriented play of early childhood from the more goal-directed play and games of later childhood. He worked out elaborate programs of fanciful movement play for young children based on their opportunities to observe everyday situations, such as the movements of animals, which would combine exercise with the development of fantasy. Despite the restricted range of materials and activities in his programmed gifts and occupations, his added focus on play, self-activity, and manual experimentation, and the materials and form of many of the activities themselves (such as drawing, block building, clay work) contained the root of the sensorimotor manipulation, creative and constructive activities that became the basis for learning through play with later nursery schools and kindergartens. His awareness that school should relate to real life brought in the stress on socioemotional relations that parallels most contemporary approaches. Nature study and science-concept activities may also be traced in an important way to Froebel.

Despite his tremendous contribution to child-centered schools for young children, and the actual spread of kindergartens under his influence, Froebel too based his thinking on the family, and in fact was quite mystical about his notions of motherhood and his beliefs about nature. Influenced by the biological thinking of Rousseau and the times, he saw development largely as a process originating and controlled from within, an outlook that exercised a continuing influence on child development, the nursery-school movement, and early education for many years (Braun and Edwards, 1972; Raymont 1937).

The First Cognitively Sequenced Sensorimotor Curriculum. Montessori developed a far more elaborate set of sequences and materials, which she built on the earlier work of Séguin with the mentally retarded. These were designed for learning a broad variety of concepts through programmed sensorimotor play (Braun and Edwards 1972; Evans 1975; Montessori 1912, 1967; Raymont 1937), such as size, shape, color, length, weight, number, and even early reading (beginning between 2 and 4 years of age). It is presumably because it is much more cognitively comprehensive and operationally articulated that her program is still widely used often essentially unchanged in our time. Nonetheless, her approach, which has tended to stress defined ways of handling each sequence of materials, has been widely criticized as centering on ritual at the expense of flexible and creative cognitive development.

One of the special strengths of Montessori's theory and program is her stress on spontaneity through self-regulation, which she was able to operationalize practically through the precise form and sequence of her materials. This so-called self-regulation is in fact based in part on initial modeling conducted by the teacher, the child being discouraged or even prevented from exploring nontask uses and ways of handling materials. The strength of the Montessori method is thus also its weakness: there is little place in its scheme of things for open-ended construction and creative play, nor for sociodramatic play. Verbal interaction in spontaneous discourse for language development is also limited, language being largely restricted to the communicative aspects of the formally defined work and sensorimotor tasks.

Education for the Masses: The Application
of Old Forms to the Populace

Although developmentally oriented educational concepts were evolving and experiments with schools and methods being conducted here and there throughout Europe during the nineteenth century, the developmental, progressive education trend made few inroads until our century (Raymont 1937). The major evolution in the nineteenth century was simply in the exponential increase in the number of children of all ages attending school and in the elaboration of the ancient rote methods applied to handling children in mass (Birchenough 1920; Raymont 1937; Smith 1931). This second trend, the development of popular schools, was marked by a number of almost bizarre developments that did not pass from the public education scene until the 1900s. Among them was that young children, and not infrequently infants as young as 2, were mingled with and taught alongside older children in hordes on the same curriculum and in the same classroom, without discrimination as to age, developmental characteristics, and often even ability and achievement. Education truly became a mass phenomenon.

The Mass Model: The Monitorial System. With increasing public and professional recognition of the plight of children and growing societal needs for genuine literacy and numeracy, the mindless custodial centers, the dame schools, of the early phases of industrial life began to be seriously supplanted by the efforts of professionals, entrepreneurs, and religious leaders (Birchenough 1920; Raymont 1937; Smith 1931). Until the latter part of the century much of the educational activity, particularly in Britain, was in the hands of religious societies and similar private welfare organizations. While avowedly educational, the new forms were seldom unquestionable improvements, however.

Around the 1800s two figures with little educational background, Bell and Lancaster, the first a clergyman and the second of poor background, each independently formulated principles and established schools based on an ingenious but horrendous mass method of school organization, the monitorial system (Birchenough 1920; Raymont 1937; Smith 1931). Under their system, which was widely adopted in England for decades, several hundred or more children were assembled in a large hall or gymnasium-type structure for long hours of daily lessons. Presiding over this assembly were one or two adults who directed the program of the three R's and biblical catechism through the agency of older children, usually poorly versed and hardly trained themselves. These older children, monitors, each guided the lessons of about 10 little children aged 2 to 9 or more, grouped around huge pillars (supporting the roof) that were used for posting the lessons. In the interests of economy and efficiency, large crowds of children quietly waited for their turn at a post, sitting with arms folded on the floor or on benches nearby, under the strict eye of a monitor or the school principal. The methods of instruction were the most mechanistic versions of programmed rote and ritual, then still widely employed for acquiring the curriculum. Because of the continuing dominance of hierarchical traditions, the impossibly crowded conditions and the limited skill and knowledge of the child monitors, progress was uneven at best and the iron rule of the rod was the characteristic method of reinforcement.

Pseudo-Reform: Wilderspin. Reform was more or less permanently in the air, however, a chronic by-product of the expanding excesses of the Industrial Revolution and the persisting feudal legacy. The influence of Rousseauian notions directly, and indirectly through the example of Pestalozzi, Robert Owen, and others, directed some of the efforts of this mass educational trend toward reforms in method. As the infant schools grew in number, a modest clerk by the name of Samuel Wilderspin founded a school, which through his practical success with somewhat more enlightened methods and his extensive writing and lecturing, was soon adopted elsewhere (Raymont 1937; Wilderspin 1840). The new schools then being founded by the religious societies in Britain gradually supplanted the original monitorial system with Wilderspin's educational model for children under six, who were then gradually instructed separately from primary school children. Reforms in method and quality of schooling were not drastic, however. Playgrounds and play were made integral to infant schools, but indoor play was limited, and although Pestalozzian object lessons and a more rounded curriculum were adopted, the old rote system predominated. Indeed although supposedly eliminating the monitorial system, Wilderspin hit upon a device that actually prolonged its use in modified form. This was the gallery, in which little ones waited their turn as before, sitting in rows ranging upward in age on tiered benches, to take their turn at posts for their lessons. Child monitors were no longer employed, but the methods and skill levels of the few teachers for hundreds of children, made the new approach a slim improvement. The object lessons, moreover, became a travesty, as children were expected to learn without understanding long strings of obscure words and arcane definitions abstracted from context. Rote learning and mechanical sequencing of the traditional forms, accompanied by harsh discipline, remained the rule.

Even as late as the beginning of the twentieth century, when reform began to make more headway, influenced by the belated hiring of female inspectors (Raymont 1937) and the progressive reforms inspired by Froebel, Montessori, Dewey, and the founding of the nursery-school movement, drill, discipline and mass conformity remained widespread in the English infant schools. Little concession was made to the status of early development. The aims of early education remained dominated by the goals and standards, rigidly applied, of realizing literacy and vocational skills, such as sewing, knitting, or weaving. An infant-school leader in 1893 likened the schools to prisons, in which preschool children were chained to their seats by drills in letters and syllables and even thimble drill (learning to sew) for an hour at a time, making the movements in sequence and in unison by the numbers, like military drill (Raymont 1937). Although publicly supported education gradually supplanted religious sponsored education and was extended to much of the entire population, reform still had far to go. Education had become conscious, planned, and systematic with a vengeance but neither cognitive nor developmental, with few exceptions.

*The Establishment of Developmental Child
Care and Education*

The eventual transformation to a more play-oriented developmental, cognitive, and humanist approach to early education in particular and to all education in general only really got going during this century, fed by the rising expectations, educational levels, and standards of living of the growing middle class. The old ways of doing things in tightly run patriarchical family firms were slowly replaced by large corporations whose operations increasingly depended on large educated staffs that could participate actively and intelligently in organizational decision making (Bowles and Gintis 1976; Riesman, Glazer, and Denney 1950; Whyte 1956). It was no longer possible for a few persons at the head of a family-run business to assume all responsibility and direct the day-to-day activities of a limited number of employees. Delegation of responsibility meant greater autonomy and intellectual participation that called for a new type of individual. The revolution in transportation and communication that also accelerated with the twentieth century served to reinforce these demands by broadening outlooks, inducing greater independence and multiple demands for intelligent, adaptive coping by the individual.

The changes that came, though fast compared with prior centuries, did not come all at once and worked unevenly in different realms of early education and child socialization. In Britain the well-established infant schools changed only slowly (Raymont 1937), saving their most momentous transformation to the new outlook with the trend to informal or open education in the post-World War II period (Braun and Edward 1972; Weber 1971). Public infant schools had never been established in America, making it less difficult in some ways for the kindergartens that were gradually added on here and there, beginning in the last half of the nineteenth century (the first one for English-speaking children was founded by Elisabeth Peabody in Boston in 1860), to adopt more flexible, Froebelian approaches.

The Developmental Educator. Even so, it was not until the influence of Montessori and John Dewey and the University of Chicago Laboratory School at the turn of the century that new forms were adopted in earnest. Building on the concepts of Froebel and others, Dewey centered on play and the development of the individual child through activity, "learning by doing." Dewey wrote about reaching the child through his or her interests, self-expression, relating activities to real-life occupations and flexible programming that would attempt to integrate education in terms of the child and society (Dewey 1971). As he saw it education is a gradual process that must work with two poles in mind, the self-directed, evolving activity of the child interacting with the forces of accumulated social knowledge set out in a curriculum that shapes this development. Dewey was a central figure in founding the interactionist notion of development. In addition to the several university and private progressive education schools and kindergartens that were established, inspired by this developmental outlook, public school education itself gradually changed profoundly in this direction. Social promotion, developmental reading, and similar developmentally oriented methods, and in general a more enlightened psychological approach to curriculum and to the teaching and handling of children can be traced to Dewey and the influences of this period (Braun and Edward 1972; Cremin 1961).

Early Education for the Elite and the Populace: Nursery Schools, Day Care, and Head Start. The nursery-school movement, when it began in Britain under the efforts of Rachel and Margaret McMillan, was totally organized around developmental precepts and practices. Everything pivoted around play and the growth and development of the whole child, physically, socioemotionally, and intellectually. The child study and child development movement, beginning in 1923 under the leadership of Lawrence Frank through grants to universities by the Rockefeller fund (Braun and Edwards 1972; Frank 1962; Senn 1975), utilized and elaborated a framework of these principles that dominated approaches to early education and child care until well after World War II. While serving mainly selected educated and poor populations, they steadily grew in number, following essentially the same developmental philosophy and informal play methods, to reach a total of 1,700 in the United States by 1933. Then under the national crisis of the great depression, money from the Federal Works Progress Administration led to their multiplication as a means of both creating teaching jobs and furnishing child care and education. The rapid expansion of nursery schools and the beginnings of day care that came in World War II with the Lanham Act, patriotically inspired by recognition of the need of working mothers and the desire to ensure success of the war effort, resulted in the further extension of these educational forms to other places (N.M. Robinson and H.B. Robinson 1972).

There were exceptions, of course, principally in the Montessori movement and schools that continued to grow, though more in Europe than in America, and in certain parochial and private schools (Evans 1975; Rambusch 1962). Among the latter different combinations of traditional focus on strict discipline and tight programming, sometimes combined with early attention to the three R's, continued to hold sway. Here and there a few dissident research efforts, such as those at the University of Iowa, also followed a different perspective, exploring the effects of stimulation on intellectual development in the nursery school and other settings (Anastasi 1958; Updegraff et al. 1938).

It was not until the War on Poverty and the resurrection of the day-care movement (which had waned with the peacetime prosperity and stress on family life that succeeded the crisis atmosphere of World War II) in the 1960s that serious consideration of cognitive learning came again to the fore. A combination of sociopolitical forces taking the form of the civil rights movement and the women's liberation movement, together with the impact of several strands of research on early experience, led to a widespread push for day care, The National Head Start Program, and massive programs of early intervention research for children from socioeconomically disadvantaged backgrounds (Hunt 1975; Zigler and Valentine 1979). Social definition and research findings had changed once more. New concerns for cognitive learning and development, inspired by Piaget and the several strands of research on the effects of poverty, institutional experience, and other forms of early deprivation, began to challenge seriously the by then traditional laissez-faire, developmental philosophy as the dominant point of view and open-ended play as almost the sole practice.

The Contributions of Developmentalism
to Early Education

The child-development approach to instruction crystallized by Rousseau has contributed much to rationalizing and humanizing the planned socialization of children that began with the ancient bureaucracies. As technology extends demands for rational learning to more children at younger ages, and as family life is altered and the extension of early child care in group settings grows apace worldwide, the contributions should be recognized at the same time they are placed in perspective.

Central among the contributions is of course growth in awareness of the fact of development itself. On the other hand continuing stress on internal governance, development through biological maturation, which long dominated explanations for how children acquire skills and knowledge, has cost something historically in terms of attention to the influence of learning and experience. That children are different from adults, do not learn in the same way, cannot learn the same things, and require years to acquire the skills and cognitions of adults does not mean learning plays a negligible role in the development of mind and personality. Enchantment with the nature of childhood and development, coupled with the subtleties, complexities, and slowness with which children make major cognitive advances, long dimmed awareness of how the cumulative effect of experience interacting with biological forces, shape mental development. The result was something approaching wholesale abandonment of curriculum programming and planned, adult-mediated concept stimulation in the mainstream of nursery school and day care for more than one-half century.

This direction was perhaps understandable as a reaction to the harshness and narrowness of the authoritarian systems of the past and the battles still to be won in schools at the elementary level, from which the nursery schools were quite separate and looked down upon. The central concern was for wholesome relations, leading to preoccupation with social and emotional relations and the spontaneous expression of interest in play, to the comparative neglect of intellectual skills and abilities. The important thing was to lighten the deadening effect of authority, to let the children themselves relate to one another and to work things out and develop skills on their own. In a society increasingly concerned with social interaction and democratization, and exploring the parameters of social relations, play, and development for the first time historically, it was only logical that theories stressing biological factors and the flowering of mind and personality through natural forces would enjoy large appeal (Hunt 1961). The impact of nineteenth-century Darwinian theory, applied enthusiastically in somewhat over-literal forms by G. Stanley Hall to notions of the ontogenetic development of the individual, filled a theoretical gap of how development comes about that freed the early education theorists and practitioners to center their attention on the world of play and social relations (Braun and Edwards 1972). Intelligence and its development were regarded as underlying, uncontrollable factors of heredity, best left to IQ mental testers like Terman. Developmentalists would study the course of development itself, influenced as well by the rising dominance of behaviorism and psychology's rejection of the study of mental processes (Boring 1951). In this manner Gesell and his collaborators (Gesell and Ilg 1949; Gesell et al. 1974), gathered reams of normative developmental data on multiple aspects of the child's functioning through careful observation, charting patterns of development from birth to adulthood for the first time in history. That the data were almost entirely descriptive, without organizing theory on the nature of relations among phenomena or on how the child progressed from one step or level to the next, other than through biological maturation, and that the data were confined mainly to selected middle-class circles, mattered to few. Gesell was the leading light, and the child was allowed to play and grow unhampered. Parents too were free from guilt over role failure, since the child was biologically programmed to proceed from one age to the next. The child would grow out of any difficulties that arose: the problems of the 2-year-old would simply be succeeded by the tranquility of the 3-year-old, and language delay would be followed by late-blooming development in language skill.

That matters did not work out quite so simply and perfectly was both obscured and compensated for by the amount of attention addressed to the individual child and his or her social relations and development. This individualization of care and degree of focus on the social in an essentially sheltered and cognitively stimulating middle-class world *did* solve many if not all problems. And, if there was no explicitly planned program of care and cognitive stimulation, the ambiance was nonetheless embued with the implicit intellectual goals, patterns, and models of middle-class life. Methods were employed, skills established, and limits set, simply more flexibly and more humanely. That certain behavioral problems did not get solved, and that the full potentials for cognitive development were widely unrealized, as this book will attempt to show, may be counted as one of the costs of the historical establishment of developmentally oriented early-education systems.

One of the additional great by-products of the child-study and child-development movement launched by Frank in the universities and incorporated in the leading nursery schools was the extent of efforts to involve parents in the child's life at school (Braun and Edwards 1972; Senn 1975). Indeed many of the early nursery schools, such as the first nursery school at the University of Chicago, were founded as parent-teacher cooperatives. The general trend, though originally heavily restricted to the world of the upper middle class, and largely to a segment that inhabited selected university and similar intellectual communities at that, may be seen as integral to the general effort to restore early education and child rearing to the community, akin to the folkways of the past. Folk communities have largely disappeared and the impersonal urban life of large-scale, hierarchically structured societies increasingly prevail. Yet the developmental philosophy, the humanist and whole-child concern, the stress on flexible, child-directed play relating to models in the adult world, however personally difficult to bridge, and the focus on acquiring skills through concrete experience, experimentation, and peer interaction, together with interrelating the home and the group institution of planned care, is easily seen as an attempt to draw on many of the better elements of that world, if not recreate it. Indeed the original statement of Rousseau on the virtues of the natural child and closeness to nature seems to have been just that.

The contemporary world of developmental psychology, child care, and early education is nevertheless a rational world, governed by analysis, inquiry, and the methods and findings of science. The nursery-school movement itself was founded in close alliance with the university world of child study and research (Braun and Edwards 1972; Peters 1981). This world has also moved recently with Piaget and early intervention into new realms and new understandings of cognitive development and cognitive stimulation. Thus it would seem now that the informal, developmental systems are well launched if not completed nor everywhere established, that the next step might be how to integrate complex and systematic strategies of cognitive stimulation into the socialization of young children without sacrificing the gains of developmental philosophy that have been won.

Note

1. The hornbook was a learning device in the shape of a hard, short wooden paddle, with letters, syllables, phrases, and religious homilies variously inscribed on one side and sometimes a writing slate on the other. It was conveniently also employed as an instrument of punishment (Birchenough 1920; Davies 1973; Smith 1931).

Historical Paradigms in Research on Early Cognitive-Development Stimulation

Historical Background

The development of child study as an empirical enterprise over the past two hundred years has been shaped by many historical trends. Converging in different combinations at various times, the result has been the establishment of several identifiable approaches to the study of how children develop. Most of these persist in some form in contemporary research and all of them have had significant effects on issues affecting research strategies and the accumulation of knowledge on the effects of early experience and early cognitive stimulation on development.

In this chapter, we shall review some of these important historical influences, including the ones already mentioned, and trace how different approaches to research have drawn from them. The knowledge obtained about experience and development is heavily dependent upon the conceptions of development held and the methodology employed. Systematic reviews of the literature follow.

The major historical forces that have shaped the direction of child psychology and development since the Renaissance fall into two sets. One set is linked to the legacy of thought and way of life that was the feudal world (Huizinga 1954) and the other integral to the birth of new ways and new outlooks integral to the Renaissance and the creation of the industrial world and the development of the objective methods of science (McNeill 1963; Peters 1962; Sarton 1952; Tawney 1926). Though clustering together in this way, various components were not always in harmony with the direction of the respective overall movements. For example, thought and explanation in the feudal world were characteristically pursued on the speculative plane of religion and mysticism, yet the Protestant Reformation revitalized the theological, dogmatic qualities of religion at the same time it democratized religion for the common man in opposition to the fixed hierarchy of the feudal past. Religious reform was thus paradoxically an obstacle to objective understanding yet part of the basic fabric of the enlightenment and new humanism that clothed the spirit of the new technology moving toward rational understanding and scientific inquiry (Tawney 1926).

In the feudal legacy what stands out is the static world view rooted in mysticism and a relatively unchanging status hierarchy (Bernal 1954; Huizinga 1954; Peters 1962). Observation and scholarship were not lacking in

89

feudal times, but they were tied to theological doctrine. Inquiry and scholasticism began and ended for the most part with discourse and treatises on small points on the totally abstract plane of religious myth. A limited, comparatively small-scale technology that hardly changed from century to century was quite supportive of the static institutional hierarchies and intricate social protocol that marked feudal society and made few intrusions into its ethereal world of supernatural explanation. Objective inquiry and the accumulation of new knowledge and techniques were stifled by the oppressive social forms of feudal life and the rigid adherence to myth and doctrine. Oral culture and ritual thrived in the reviving folk practices of the early post-Roman societies (Lot 1971). Though actually also a part of the inheritances of the ancient civilizations themselves (Davies 1973; Hawkes 1973; Saggs 1965), they were particularly well adapted to a world that revered form, ritual, unquestioned obedience, and religious dogma and ritual above knowledge and inquiry.

Given such a static and mystical world view it is not surprising that the ancient belief in preformationism would suffer few challenges in the medieval era. The comparatively frozen social structures, religious doctrine, and technology of the Middle Ages were quite compatible with the idea of all life as preformed at conception, that the essential form of the adult was present in microcosm from the beginning.

It has apparently always been easier to perceive the obvious changes in size that plants and animals undergo in their progression from infancy to adulthood. The small and subtle changes in body proportions, such as head/body size ratios, and the delayed appearance of secondary sex characteristics, for example, could escape casual observation or be written off as insignificant with regard to maintenance of basic structure (including maleness and femaleness) present at birth and even before. The concept of morphological change through development would appear to depend on awareness of fundamental change or transformation as characteristic of all matter, something that is less apparent in the history and prehistory of human societies. Until the acceleration of change characteristic of our technological age, most such changes, such as large-scale, geological alterations of the earth's surface, changes in the distribution of fauna and flora, and changes in technology or cultural forms, occur only occasionally and slowly, in comparison with the span of human lifetime. The problem is compounded by the perceptual disappearance of the original structure, making the links between cheese and milk, for example, difficult to follow. It is easier to believe some magic is involved or to believe that the novel material is somehow contained in the original form, released through some external agent, a god or spirit of some kind (Malinowski 1954).

The problem of grasping change is especially complicated in the case of mind and personality, which are invisible and linked to personal identity and thus are widely seen as innate characteristics of the person present from birth. Even the ancient Greeks, who transformed the technological skills of the earlier river-irrigation civilizations of the Middle East into a central interest in abstract inquiry and general principles (Bernal 1954), failed to penetrate deeply into this question. Only Aristotle formulated a crude notion of epigenesis, apparently from observations of the development of the chicken embryo, and his concepts on this matter were largely ignored until the seventeenth century (Hunt 1961). Aristotle had not only formulated the notion of stages of human development but had recognized both the biological underpinnings and the influence of experience in modifying development.

The keystone of the feudal world view that reinforced the static quality of life and impeded recognition of the idea of epigenetic development was religion (Bernal 1954). The Christian concepts of creation and original sin explained both the creation of the world and the creation of the individual as single acts of a supernatural creator, the first carried out in seven days and the latter originating in the Garden of Eden. The medieval mind was inclined to view children as miniature adults. Except for the brief concession to infancy, children were dressed much like adults, were expected to perform adult tasks, according to their strength, started their craft and professional apprenticeships almost from early childhood about as soon as they could manage, and as lessons and schools became established, often attended them beginning in toddlerhood. Well into the Renaissance paintings frequently depicted children, even infants, as creatures with clearly reflective, adultlike expressions (Aries 1962). The downplaying of childhood, with its absence of provisions for play and for developmental differences in modes of thought and ways of doing things, was highly consonant with if not a direct product of the notion of preformation in human development. It was only with the rise of new technology and the attendant emergence of entrepreneurial and technical classes, along with the revival of secular scholarship, the enlightenment, the development of science, and more particularly the gradual development of more precise instruments such as the microscope (Hunt 1961) that the preformationist concept became untenable. Detailed structural changes in the formation of embryos in their early periods revealed through a series of experiments by the Russian scientist Wolff in 1768 demonstrated beyond any doubt that the movement from egg to embryo was a process of transformations through successive differentiations (Hunt 1961).

The rising world of science and secular thought in a changing social and technological environment had thus mounted its first notable challenge to the fixed notions of the old world about the nature of organisms. Although first demonstrated only in embryology, the way was open to its extension in biology and human social development, which was not long delayed.

Developmental explanations had begun to receive their first scientific boosts, but this did not mean that experience and learning were assigned an important role. As often happens in the history of ideas, an originally insufficient explanation, the notion of people preformed at conception, when challenged led to another improved but still inadequate explanation, predeterminism, the concept that the course of development of organisms is laid out in advance by biology. Wolff himself conceptualized the first crude notion of predeterminism, defining development as a process produced by its own internal force (Hunt 1961).

It was Rousseau, however, who laid out in eloquent detail a grand application of the idea to human social and mental development in 1762 (Ausubel, Sullivan, and Ives, 1980) even before Wolff's definitive experiments and tentative formulation of theory. Obviously the general direction of thought was already questioning on all sides the rigid preconceptions about human life. The spread of technology that accompanied the acceleration of the industrial revolution generated ever widening, if still small, demands for a more empirical, a more pragmatic outlook that could deal with the facts of phenomena as they were, to deal with the needs of the multiplying entrepreneurial system (Boring 1950; Peters 1962; Tawney 1926).

The seventeenth century saw the burgeoning of the new empiricism and rational outlook in the intellectual thought and institutions of the time: Pascal's mathematics and scathing satires on the circumlocutions of religious thought; the laying down of the rational and materialist basis for a mechanistic, objective psychology by Descartes; Leibnitz starting the roots of German psychology; Newton formulating a mechanical view of the physical world in Britain; and the century culminating in Locke's famous *Essay on Human Understanding,* in which he strongly argued against preformationism and predeterminism (Boring 1950; Peters 1962). It was less difficult to propose a general orientation to developmental change, once the concept of the newborn mind as a blank slate had been proposed by Locke. Rousseau's concept of child development as a process controlled from within and proceeding through a series of predesigned stages, though in some ways simply displacing in time the conception of human beings as preformed, was an effective and important antidote to the rigid impositions of the past. By casting off the individual from a decrepid social framework and declaring that development was simply a natural biological process he freed observers to look at children realistically and humanly in terms of their actual needs as they developed. Like most theorists, moreover, Rousseau was not entirely consistent. His writings (*Emile, Julie*) are laced with descriptions of what to do and how to treat children from earliest infancy, implying that preprogrammed biology is not the only force in development.

Predetermined conceptions of development were first established in more scientific terms by Darwin (Hunt 1961), who undergirded Rousseauian educational conceptions of development in his idea of natural selection of inherited characteristics. Although Darwin concentrated on physical characteristics, his ideas were gradually widely applied to mental development, leading to the concepts of inherited or fixed intelligence, as well as the detailed programmatic conceptions of unfolding development through maturation worked out by G. Stanley Hall and Gesell (Hunt 1961; Murphy and Kovach 1972; Watson 1968). Once it is assumed that development is predetermined, abilities and intelligence must necessarily be among the characteristics fixed from birth. Preformationism, predeterminism, and inherited abilities are thus all part of the legacy of ancient conceptions, sharing in common the core concept of denial of experience as a causal agent. That such ideas have historically been interpreted with various degrees of literalness does not dilute this central idea.

The final major trend to be noted before reviewing the paradigmatic history of research on early stimulation originated in the efforts of the new scientific empiricism to combat the abstract mentalism of religious and classical scholasticism. Like the revolt of Rousseau in rejecting experience entirely because of its embeddedness in corrupt social forms, the students of animals and humans who began to form a science of psychology in the late nineteenth century became concerned about the practice of applying anthropomorphic explanations to animals and in general reading into human actions more than was there. Mental characteristics cannot of course be observed directly and the empirical base of science, applied so successfully in physical matters, was transferred rather literally to psychology (Brunswik 1952). Behaviorism and the general tendency to reduce explanation to the simplest tenable basis grew into being.

The rejection of mentalism did not occur with a single swipe of course. Experimental psychology formally began in the laboratory of Wundt in 1879 and was taken up by Titchener and others in the United States (Boring 1950; Murphy and Kovach 1972; Watson 1968). Both Wundt and Titchener incorporated mental processes into their interpretations, Wundt concerned with apperception and higher mental processes through experimentation and scientific explanation, Titchener with sensory and imaginal process, and both freely employed introspective methods. William James, the giant of psychology in the late nineteenth century, maintained a rounded perspective on mental development, discoursing at length on the stream of consciousness in rich terms very readable today. The static quality of faculty psychology and the failure of the introspective methods to integrate a systematic picture of human functioning from the mountains of objective data that were accumulating in the multiplying laboratories, however, gradually led to a shift in emphasis from subjective interpretation to objective description as the main task. Following James there was a brief period of mental functionalism during the 1890s and 1900s, led by John Dewey, Angell and the Chicago School in opposition to the structuralism of mental elements of Titchener, in which they advocated mental processes or mental functions as the basis for psychology (Boring 1950; Murphy and Kovach 1972). But when John B. Watson completed his thesis, "Animal Education: The Psychical Development of the White Rat," in 1903, he found no use for the tradition of inferring mental processes from his thorough descriptions of behavior. Animal behaviorism was inherently functional, but mental processes engaged an extra, speculative step, with which Watson dispensed. Beginning in 1913 through his vigorous and successful promotional efforts he formally defined psychology as objective; this objective psychology became behaviorism (Boring 1950). From that time until the recent past, and the gradual ascendence of Piaget and cognitive psychology on the scene, little theory and few studies could make much headway in bringing mental processes into the mainstream of objective psychology rooted in behaviorism.

Approaches to Studying Early Experience

In the history of the scientific study of children and child development, progress in investigating the effects of early stimulation has not been wholly governed by the influence of theory and historical world views. Once the empirical method began to be accepted into the domain of human activity during the early phases of the Renaissance and later the industrial revolution, the socioeconomic demands of the evolving technology and the new managerial leaders would stimulate opportunities to practice it. Philosophers like Francis Bacon and John Locke would define its parameters and experimenters like Galileo and Newton would come forth to make use of the method to further understanding of how things work. Science as a system to inquire into the nature of things through observation and experiment, established first in physics in the seventeenth century, spread to other fields, including ultimately psychology, education and development (Boring 1950; Brunswik 1952; Murphy and Kovach 1972; Peters 1962). The efforts of scholars and experimenters working in concert took on a life of their own, leading to the discovery and invention of novel techniques and ideas that in many cases led to approaches and even conclusions contrary to the mainstream thought of the time. Historical accident also sometimes played an important role, as in the case of the seminal work of Itard (Malson 1972). Theory and world view were nonetheless always major influences on research.

Classical Beginnings of Child-Development Research

The beginnings of a systematic approach to studying children are generally dated (Dennis 1949) from the contributions of Preyer's (1888-1889) detailed biographical account of his own child's early development in *Die Seele des Kindes* (*Mind of the Child*) and G. Stanley Hall's (1883) extensive investigation of concepts in school children published as *The Contents of Children's Minds*. The work of both scholars illustrates the contending influences of current theory and empirical development in its own right. Both approaches had been used before their time, baby biographies as early as 1601 by the court physician of Louis XIII, Héroard (1868), who kept a lengthy journal of the life of the court that included many observations on the Dauphin's behavior from birth. Preyer made extensive comparisons with observations from the previous biographies, and Hall's study was an elaborate repetition of an earlier study in Berlin (Dennis 1949).

The advances of both consisted of undertaking a more thorough and comprehensive approach and a decided advance in method. Preyer not only made a detailed account of the first three years of his son's development, but he organized the material by topics (sensation, motor activity, expression or emotion, and intelligence), drawing from embryology and the incipient German psychology of the time, an arrangement that has remained a model up to our time (Kessen 1965). His observations were careful, compared with those of earlier biographers, and he provided many valuable insights and interpretations, including those on stranger anxiety and the role of the child's own discovery in cognitive development, which he interpreted as self-regulation in a manner anticipating Piaget.

Hall, with characteristic thoroughness, just about exhausted all possibilities by compiling a list of 134 topics for questioning Boston kindergarten children on the status of their concepts. Hall's chief contribution, however, was to train four kindergarten teachers in uniform procedures of questioning, in place of merely circulating written instructions to regular classroom teachers without further guidance, as was done in the Berlin study that preceded it. The results of both studies indicated much ignorance of common concepts of many natural and social phenomena. Hall went on to carry out many other studies and to become a major figure in training graduate students, many of whom, like Gesell, Dewey, and Terman, became founders of developmental psychology themselves.

The theoretical framework for human development that prevailed well into the twentieth century, predeterminism, appears to have been a major factor in these and other studies in limiting progress for many years in understanding the nature of early experience in development. Certain obvious limitations are inherent in the case study method for getting at objective explanation but none that would have precluded gathering productive insights of a different kind. Preyer's observations were so laced with his views on development as an unfolding process, originating from within, that it is often difficult to disentangle what behavior actually occurred (Kessen 1965). Strongly influenced by the Darwinian conception of evolution, which Darwin himself was inclined to apply as a model of ontogeny in the biography of his own son (Darwin 1877), and following the inspiration of Rousseau, Preyer was attempting to watch his son's development unfold, deliberately withholding efforts to train the child. At every point Preyer was looking for the evidence of heredity at work. There is very little information on the exogenous factors influencing the infant's behavior and development. The strength of the data, aside from organization and thoroughness, is to be found in the insights noted with regard to the emerging internal regulation of activity, the role of endogenous sources of stimulation. But even here the information is truncated, because of Preyer's concern with general forces of heredity, rather than with specific features of the child's cognitive development, and because conceptions of mental processes were extremely limited at the time, being confined to static, underlying general notions of mental faculties (will, vanity, power, ambition) rooted in phrenology, which used head contours to indicate faculties of the brain (Boring 1950). Still Preyer in many ways was anticipating the kind of descriptive norm gathering undertaken so thoroughly later by Gesell. He also provided a great deal of information on development, even though he concentrated on his son's manipulations in his encounters with the environment (tearing paper, opening and closing boxes), which Preyer interpreted as the child discovering and developing himself as a causative agent. In his frequent systematic comparisons with the developmental milestones recorded in other biographies and in his discussion of different performance criteria (such as conditions of smiling employed by different biographers), he compiled the first systematic if crude record of the general course of early development.

Hall's questionnaire was focused on children's concepts at kindergarten age, furnishing no information at all on earlier periods of development, though variations of the questionnaire method have since been widely applied to assess the concepts of younger children. The chief limitation of Hall's study from the point of view of shedding light on experience is that the study was entirely focused on children's concepts without regard to their origin (or development). It was essentially an inventory of children's understanding of the world in schools of one community, with no study of developmental processes at all. Like Preyer, Hall's outlook was completely shaped by the predeterministic Darwinian views of the times; he went so far as to conduct a number of studies in which he attempted (often ridiculously) to demonstrate how individual development in its ontogeny recapitulated phylogeny, the history of all life (Strickland and Burgess 1965). Hall applied freely to the development of culture and to the postnatal development of the individual the original concept of recapitulation that Haeckel has formulated with respect to embryological development in rough morphological terms (Ausubel, Sullivan, and Ives 1980). The flavor of his thinking, including his inspiration from Darwin, is shown in the following excerpts from a study (Hall 1896) he conducted on human fears:

> Cases [cites a string of case numbers] almost suggest atavistic relapse toward the early forms of sessile life. . . . the propensity of children to run away . . . suggests the migratory instincts of birds, fishes, animals, nomadic races. (pp. 162-163)

> The simplest of all hypotheses, and therefore the view that may fairly claim that the burden of proof should rest with any other. . . . passion . . . for children to see, feel, paddle in, play with or sail on water. . . . strongly suggest the earlier and far longer life in the sea. Later. . . . Those best adapted to land were at greatest disadvantage in water, and thus fear of it became chronic. (p. 170)

> the hypothesis of ancestral transmission. . . . the fears of the cat, dog and cow class . . . [not] older than domestication . . . [implies] snake fears runs back to the tertiary age of reptiles . . . wise to keep this larger solution, to which Darwin was so strongly attached. (p. 210)

Elsewhere he formulated more definite notions of stages of human development (infancy, childhood, youth, adolescence) (Hall 1907; Partridge 1912). His conceptualizing and his descriptions remained loose and sweeping, however, loaded with untestable hypotheses based on historical-evolutionary analogies in place of explanations based on specific experiences and developmental processes (Partridge 1912):

> Infancy . . . the shape of the body, movements such as grasping and climbing, the shape of proportions of internal organs, all indicate that the characteristics belonging to the simian period of racial existence are now most dominant. . . . During all this period, and on through childhood, there will be many occurrences that can be explained only by evolutionary principles. The feeding habits of the child, his play, modes of self-defence, curiosity, social instincts, all require study with reference to the stages of life in the race centering about the simian age. (p. 74)

> That the passing traits of the child resemble the characteristics of the savage in many particulars cannot be denied. (p. 76)

The continuity of this developmental-evolutionary thinking from Rousseau is also evident in the following passage:

> Rousseau would leave the prepubescent years to nature and to these primal hereditary impulses and allow the fundamental traits of savagery their fling

till twelve. Biological psychology finds many and cogent reasons to confirm
this view if only a proper environment could be provided. The child revels
in savagery, and if its tribal, predatory, hunting, fishing, fighting, roving
idle, playing proclivities could be indulged. . . . (Hall 1904:xi)

Given this historical developmental framework, Hall displayed little interest in how experience facilitates development, concentrating in his first
study on what children's concepts are at a certain point in development,
rather than on how experience may have contributed to their formation.
Nevertheless, as a starting point for systematic data gathering, his first
study was a landmark. It introduced a certain objectivity in standardizing
procedures and the questionnaire method served as a model easily adapted
later to interviewing parents, observing home conditions, and relating the
two to measures of children's concepts and patterns of behavior.

Taken together, the Preyer and Hall studies reflected both the constraints of contemporary theory and the emergence of important methods
readily adapted to many purposes, and despite their common theoretical
bias, each furnished a certain amount of developmental data. Although
neither study added much to knowledge about early experience, not even
defining a role for external stimulation, methods were established that
could lend themselves to the study of such questions, and in Preyer's case,
internal sources of early experience were first explored.

Historical Forerunners of Research on Early Experience: Experimental Case Studies of Extremes in Experience (Early Deprivation and Acceleration)

In order for case studies to reveal how external experience affects development, there must be changes in the child that are closely associated with
changes in the environment. The larger and more persistent the changes and
correspondence, other things being equal, the more confidence we can take
in the association. In the ordinary course of development, most events are
inconsequential and transient or form a pattern of slow and lasting quality
with few contrasts, making it difficult to separate development from its
context. While average cases may encounter important environmental
variations, it is the extreme cases that usually furnish the most dramatic
evidence of how experience affects development. Two primary extremes are
those of development under conditions of extreme deprivation (or privation) and development in response to exceptionally enriched stimulation,
the former associated with retardation, the latter with precocity. While it is
rarely possible to rule out the influence of organic factors (and often heredity)
in the first extreme and certainly of heredity in the second, several useful

comparisons can be made with experimental case studies of this sort. Among these are comparisons with norms for the age group and baseline comparisons, or the changes that occur with development when conditions are altered. Extreme cases usually contain valuable information about developmental processes as well. Because they are so out of the way of things that we take for granted about normal life, we are led to insights about mechanisms for change of which we are generally unaware.

So it is that the case studies of "wild children," children somehow lost or abandoned in the wilds for their early years and then rediscovered, and case studies of exceptionally well stimulated young children seem to have featured in the evolution of our thinking about the processes of early experience earlier and in some ways more significantly than mainstream efforts in the history of education and child development—though not always through the expected channels. There are countless instances of wild children recorded historically, going back for centuries in many countries (Malson 1972), and similarly frequent instances of precocious children reported in the early literature (Dolbear 1912; Earle 1974). While many of these cases exercised some influence upon education, two outstanding cases, described in the *Wild Boy of Aveyron* by Itard (Lane 1976; Malson 1972; Shattuck 1980), and the *Education of Karl Witte* (Witte 1914), are perhaps the earliest well-documented cases with scientific involvement, in which the influence on later educational thought and research is in some way traceable.

Like most studies of wild children, Itard's work with Victor, the wild boy of Aveyron, came about by historical accident. Pastor Witte's educational experiment with his son, on the other hand, was the result of a deliberate plan. Victor was discovered and captured by French peasants in some woods in southern France just before 1800. He escaped, then was befriended by others and soon brought to the attention of the authorities, who accepted Itard's plan to attempt to educate or "civilize" the boy. A village clergyman, Witte undertook systematically to educate his son from birth in 1800, believing that he could make him into a brilliant scholar. Despite these differences, both Itard and Witte were motivated by similar ideals stemming from the Enlightenment and the empirical approach of John Locke. They were inspired by the ideal of human beings as social animals who required cultivation through education to become fully civilized, and they believed in limitless possibilities for mental development through education. Itard's ideas and methods were modeled directly on those of the French philosopher, Condillac, who saw knowledge and mental development entirely as products of the cumulative effects of experience formed directly from sensations, thus abandoning the role Locke attributed to reflection in integrating sensory experience (Boring 1950). Itard was also influenced and supported directly by Pinel, his teacher and a reforming physician, who followed Condillac's empirical and analytic methods, believing in education and the functional basis of the wild boy's problem. This approach was against the prevalent, conservative view that diagnosed and dismissed Victor as an organic idiot, in keeping with the general hereditarian outlook, the feudal legacy, which conceived of children as miniature adults, socialization and education playing only minor roles in the development of intellect.

The source of Witte's ideas is less clear, but he appears to have been inspired by Helvétius, a French philosopher and empiricist, who argued in opposition to Rousseau that education could do anything, that all intellect is potentially equal (Peters 1962). Witte was clearly a forerunner of the concept of early experience as central to development. He advocated intensive formal education during early childhood, considering that the mind is particularly plastic and open to formation during early development, very much in opposition to the hereditarian and predeterministic views of the time.

Both Witte and Itard were clearly shaped by the period of revolutionary ferment and activity that swept over Europe from France, taking an optimistic view of human nature and believing passionately in the possibilities for change and development. Indeed both men lived and conducted their experiments near the peak of the period, beginning in 1800, Itard actually in France, clearly benefiting from the support of a sympathetic government (Lane 1976).

The experiments themselves were both systematic, long-term programs of intensive cognitive stimulation, Witte's spanning all of his son's childhood from birth and Itard's a remediation program embracing a period of five years from around age 12 to 17. Their methods ran generally parallel, both employing analytic methods and starting with concrete sensorimotor activities, and object exploration and labeling. The material world was the point of departure: they moved from the simple, concrete, and known to the complex, abstract, and unknown, in a regular progression but always focusing first on the child's interests and knowledge, pacing according to his progress. As a physician and scholar following the conceptualizations of Condillac on sensory training as worked out by Sicard in an institute for deaf mutes, Itard used methods far more detailed and systematic. Yet Witte, though a layman, studied Pestalozzi and visited his school. He was a very careful and thoughtful teacher of his son, and a thorough and analytic concern for concept particulars and the child's interests was evident in his writing. From different sources they may be said to have been working with new humanist principles of education, centering on the child's characteristics and development espoused by Rousseau, as opposed to the prevalent educational focus on the body of information to be transmitted regardless of pupil characteristics, as practiced by example in the rigid curricula of the newly founded infant schools. Yet they also explicitly rejected Rousseau's predeterministic natural child concepts in favor of Lockean empirical concepts of development through education, following an approach of rigorous, systematic programming and concept training, however flexibly adapted through interaction, games, and play. Their idealism also framed their work and attitudes into a powerful moral outlook, which was built into their relations with their respective pupils in notions of fair play and discipline as justice to be internalized in the child. Both teachers even tested out their social training, Itard in deliberately falsely punishing Victor, finding moral satisfaction in Victor's strong rebellion against the obvious injustice, and Witte in demonstrating at a friend's house how his son Karl had been morally socialized since the latter would not voluntarily remove his self-inflicted punishment over breaking a rule (spilling milk at the table), despite the urging of the hosts, even with the parents not present.

At first glance the direct relevance of Witte's work to modern understanding of early experience is easier to show. Closer consideration, however, reveals how each experiment and others like them made certain contributions and suffered from special limitations, mainly methodological in form. In his early years Karl Witte acquired a rich store of concepts over a range of areas, could discuss and analyze with adults freely, could read fluently by the time he was 4, was clearly well developed in social behavior, and was to all accounts emotionally well balanced, enjoying play and learning equally well. In his later development, building on this extensive and complex symbolic and cognitive inquiry foundation, the boy Karl went on to learn many languages (again through his father's efforts), obtain his Ph.D. in his teens and become a famous scholar of Italian literature, revolutionizing the field of study of the poet Dante.

As an untutored wild creature Victor had many skills for coping and surviving in the forests (running on all fours, climbing trees nimbly, finding food, cracking nuts with his teeth) but almost no social skills, general information, symbolic skills, cognitive inquiry strategies, or even language. Starting about age 12, he became over a period of five years a boy who knew and followed most of the expected social rules, could cope in a protected household environment, could apply himself diligently to school learning tasks, had acquired a large body of socially defined, common concepts about the social and physical world (colors, shapes, common objects), and could even read and write—though he could say only a few sounds and words. Mainly because he failed in teaching Victor to talk, Itard then terminated the experiment as something of a failure. Victor was left in the care of a woman in her home, subsidized by the government for the rest of his life; he died there at age 40.

The advanced mental accomplishments of Karl Witte during early development are evident, indicating the possibilities of accelerating cognitive development and complex symbolic learning (reading) in a well-balanced way that facilitates both cognitively complex and constructive social development. The results with Victor, though perphaps less immediately evident, are equally significant. No matter which diagnosis of Victor is accepted, long-time acclimated wild child or recently abandoned idiot (or autistic child), Itard's work demonstrates in some way the potentials and limitations for altering the effects of early experience. If he was organically limited, autistic, or otherwise grossly disturbed emotionally, the alterations of the forms of his early development are all the more remarkable. Actually the magnitude of Victor's later recovery makes it unlikely that any organic basis for the retardation was more than minor. It also points up the magnitude of skill retardation and deviance that may be produced through prolonged early privation and deviant experience. At the same time it suggests just how far development can be altered subsequently through later highly intensive cognitive stimulation, including the probability of limits to reversability. (Prolonged privation in the wild was presumably combined with at least some early cognitive socialization prior to abandonment, in order to enable him to adapt and survive through trial and error. But it seems unlikely that it could have continued much past infancy, given his virtually total ignorance of language and social skills.)

Consider his later social and moral adaptation, his general skills and wide knowledge, and his abilities to read and write, in an individual who at the age of 12 commanded few if any of the most ordinary social concepts or symbolic skills, even language, only sensorimotor, and forest survival skills. The extent of reversability of such apparently basic developmental privation is remarkable. The failure to acquire *spoken* language has historically often been misinterpreted obscuring Victor's tremendous attainments, including the fact of acquiring language (evidenced by receptive language and reading and writing skills), in the face of the failure with speech. Whether the latter indicates the effects of a critical period for speech, the failure of technique (Itard failed to provide Victor much opportunity for spontaneous verbal social communication, particularly with his peers), or both is not possible to decide, a difficulty common to case studies.

In single cases, no matter how well planned and systematically implemented, there obviously is no means of separating out special factors peculiar to the individuals and the teaching methods employed, whether positive or negative in influence. Karl and Victor may both have enjoyed superior heredity, for example, and their teachers may both have been exceptionally skilled—as indeed they were. In Witte's study as in most later cases of stimulated precocity (Dolbear 1912; Fowler 1981b), there is no separation of early from later experience, thus confounding the later effects of early experience with the effects of later experience. Early stimulation has many dimensions, which cannot all be explored in a single case study (though some could be explored in limited ways in a series of such studies), such dimensions as age or starting, duration, intensity, and type of stimulation, and a myriad of variations of method, motivational techniques, and other processes.

But while we can only draw certain definite inferences with regard to these children and these teachers and techniques, the results in comparison with norms for any population and any period in history, and the illumination they provide on techniques and the details of early stimulation, and of developmental learning processes themselves in the one case and remedial learning in the other are enormously impressive. Not only as models to be tried out under more controlled conditions with more subjects, but in the variety of techniques and insights they offer, these early experimental case studies have hardly been surpassed. It is probably in part for these reasons that they have exerted considerable influence over the history of research and programming in early education, Itard's work probably much more than Witte's.

Despite the fact that Witte's originally weighty and overlong book enjoyed limited circulation at the time, it apparently inspired many parents to follow Witte's example with their young children, and thus was an early influence on parent education, though to what extent is unknown. Witte did, however, correspond directly with Pestalozzi, who admired his experiment and the outcome, which suggests that Witte may have influenced Pestalozzi's work, as for example in his stress on early reading, a practice continued by one of his later followers in early education, Montessori, who developed the techniques further. The translation into English (Witte 1914) in a shortened more readable form is known to have extended its influence on parent education of the early 1900s among educated parents and a few scholars like Adolphe Berle, Norbert Wiener, and Boris Sidis (Dolbear 1912). Techniques were not always employed as flexibly as Witte himself had applied them (Wiener 1953), but in general the results, measured by the precocity of the childrens' development, were as impressive as the original long-term individual successes of Witte, though no controlled studies were undertaken. Recently interest in Witte has been revived by Fowler (1962a) and others.

The reach of Itard is so great that it is difficult to overestimate. Itard surfaced during a period of optimism with respect to the value of nurture and thus benefited from the body of scholarship on theory and techniques flourishing at that time. He himself was a painstaking scholar and innovator, inventing a large variety of techniques and learning materials (matching to sample devices, forming labels with cutout letters, the beginnings of form boards, discrimination learning devices, fading techniques), later developed in more elaborate form by his major pupil Séguin. In addition to his pervasive influence on the entire field of special education for the educationally and mentally retarded (Ellis 1963; Lane 1976), Itard also directly shaped the field of early education. Montessori took time out from her busy administration of early education programs to study Itard and Séguin in depth, then developed the comprehensive and systematic set of sensory motor learning devices still in use today (Malson 1972; Lane 1976). While the broader field of the nursery school and early education later rejected the stress placed on symbolic learning and systematic programming by Itard, Séguin, and Montessori, many of their concepts and materials were adopted in some form (Braun and Edwards 1972). The Montessori approach received renewed emphasis in the early-intervention programs of the 1960s (Day and Parker 1977; Hunt 1975). It is evident that developmental psychology and early education, particularly with respect to issues bearing on the effects of early experience, trace their experimental forebears to these first efforts of Itard and Witte, which took place much earlier than those of Preyer and Hall discussed by Dennis (1949).

However preliminary their methodology and techniques, the first formal test of the idea of systematically stimulating development (from the earliest years in the case of Witte), and especially the test of the idea of the cumulative effects of stimulation on development, evidenced by the prolonged and painstaking years of effort in both cases that were associated with often day-by-day, recorded incremental changes, can be placed at the door of these early educational experimenters. Not the least of their contribution is their experimental case-study test of the possibilities of *planned experience* cognitively to socialize or resocialize the child, a consequence of their strong belief in the importance of nurture. There were limitations, of course, especially those relating to their limited conception of cognitive learning and developmental processes and thus their limited awareness of learning mechanisms and programming concepts, not surprising since even today there is still widespread disagreement on both theory and method. All the more remarkable that they both could combine considerable tightness, specificity, and system in their methods with concern for motivation and understanding (cognition), avoiding the mindless and slavish rote and ritual carried over from the feudal legacy that continued to plague education through the nineteenth century. Cognitive inquiry, dialogue, and discussion were especially marked from an early age in Witte's approach and were evident in various ways in Itard's efforts, despite the constraints the absence of oral language placed on communication.

Given the persistence of strong authority-centered structures in the society of the era, both Itard and Witte stressed a certain formality in interpersonal relations, more than easy and flexible interaction, though both used games in their teaching. Formal programming and formal instruction as such were strongly emphasized, but they nonetheless worked from a focus on the child, and Witte broadened his son's experience through nature study and visits to museums and other cultural centers, much as advocated by today's early educators. On the other hand both Witte and Itard appeared to limit the scope of the boys' peer experiences, again a product of tradition. In Victor's case broader experience might have facilitated both language and ultimately more advanced concept development.

Twin Studies

The singular potential the common heredity of identical twins offers for distinguishing between the effects of heredity and experience, when experience between them is varied, has long made them attractive to investigators for research. Studies of twins have usually followed paradigms characteristic of their period, yet this singular built-in feature of experimental control has sometimes pointed up dramatically the design and concept limitations of the paradigms better than the common run of studies following the same paradigm. For these reasons we shall review a variety of twin studies representative of historically important strategies for studying maturation versus learning and other issues related to early experience, reviewing additional studies not employing twins where necessary to complete the picture. Sir Francis Galton (1907, 1925) conducted the first formal twin investigation, studying two sets of twins retrospectively through written questionnaries sent directly to adult twins or relatives of same-sex twins. The first set embraced thirty-five pairs reported to have been highly similar during childhood and the second set, twenty pairs who had been highly dissimilar during childhood. His method of analysis, after selecting the two samples from a total of some eighty cases on the basis of descriptive information from the respondents, consisted of clustering the cases empirically in different combinations according to various characteristics and event patterns of similarity and dissimilarity that emerged. Each twin pair had been reared in the same family since childhood.

Galton's report of the findings and the conclusions he draws reveal both the limitations of his strategy for analyzing the role of experience and the extreme bias of his thinking toward heredity and predetermined development. He had totally absorbed the Darwinian explanatory framework that dominated much of developmental psychology during the late nineteenth and early twentieth century, perhaps not too surprising for a cousin of Charles Darwin (Boring 1950; Murphy and Kovach 1972; Watson 1968). No matter what the outcome in adulthood, Galton managed to find nature at work. Among the originally similar twin pairs, a body of cases (number uncertain, because Galton discusses them in different clusters of similar physical and mental traits), remained highly similar to adulthood, which led him to rule out nurture as the prime influence on human development. In the balance of the originally similar cases, the twins were found to have re-

mained basically similar or *would have remained similar* (Galton's interpretation) except for some illness or accident, or some difference in original
endowment that he believed only became manifest with maturation, again
leading him to rule out nurture. He reported that the accumulation of
countless small influences accounted for differences in no more than a very
few cases and then only partly, while the "free will" of a twin counted in
none. Thus Galton attributed almost everything to inheritance. The twenty
cases of originally dissimilar twins remained without exception dissimilar up
to adulthood, proving to him once more that original inherited differences
between twins can no more be altered by experience than endowed similarities in other twins.

Galton's unwavering predeterministic bias has not often been matched,
although a later study of extremely brilliant identical twin girls (both IQs
fluctuating around 180) by Gesell (1922) is a close parallel. Gesell similarly
attributed the closely similar profiles he found with a battery of objective
mental and behavioral measures in these 7- to 9-year-old girls almost exclusively to heredity. He dismissed as unimportant the lifelong daily intensive pattern of cognitive stimulation the highly educated mother provided in
concept learning, foreign languages, and early reading to *both* twins
together from early infancy. The twins would both have become brilliant
anyway, Gesell observed, the training merely serving to allow what was inherited to flower.

Galton's design and methods were intrinsically flawed, calling into
question any conclusions that might have been made. The biggest problem
is that Galton studied twins reared together, confounding the effects of
nature and nurture throughout their development. It is difficult to understand how he could have expected to determine the effects of either factor,
particularly—and this is the second problem—since few quantitative
methods were used. Beyond grouping pairs on the basis of subjective
judgments from descriptive data, and these in different combinations, he
apparently employed no objective rating system or organized system of
classification of the data, let alone using statistics. There is thus not even a
beginning for sorting out similarity and dissimilarity of experiences according to functionally relevant or proximal factors, such as the quality and type
of parental care and stimulation and favoritism, as against the kind of distal
factors of social rank and general exposure to persons (parents, teachers,
peers) that concerned Galton. Galton also reports no basis, other than sex
sameness, for determining identicity of twinness, making it not unlikely that
some fraternal pairs may have been included even in the similar set, and
possibly a few identicals in the dissimilar set of twins. Although Galton was
apparently aware of the distinction, precise measures for determining identicity (fingerprints, dentition, blood typing) were not then employed and the
distinction between twin types was probably not widely understood at the

time among the general population (Newman, Freeman, and Holzinger 1937). Aside from these general limitations, no analysis was made by age and duration of experience, the focus resting on lifelong development, nor by any other factors of relevance for studying any details of the processes of learning and development.

Except for the use of objective phychological measures and a battery of physical measures to determine identity (including blood typing, bone measures from Xrays and palm and sole prints), Gesell's (1922) study of the bright twin girls suffers from similar defects of method and interpretation. Nevertheless, like the long historical chain of studies on precocious development whose systematic documentation began with Witte (1914), Gesell's twins do furnish valuable heuristic information with regard to the evident function of intensive early cognitive stimulation in fostering precocity, in this case in identical twins, without addressing the question of heredity.

Throughout his interpretations, Galton appeared to find everywhere what he was looking for, constants where he expected similarities and continued disparities where he expected dissimilarities, bending his syntheses to fit his hypotheses, even to the point of finding that correspondences due to nature would still be the case even though "it does not follow the same expression should be the prevalent one in both cases" (Galton 1925:161). The thing behind the thing (nature) is always what counted for Galton. As with all empirical work, however, the facts sometimes pull the investigator of necessity, even given the limited methods and measures used by the early investigators. Like Rousseau, Preyer, and others, in a later study of historically eminent great minds Galton (1907) generally attributed the basics to heredity. Yet the developmental patterns he found in his observations led even Galton to note that early experience plays a role, observations that have since been confirmed many times (Cox 1926; Fowler 1981b): "It is, I believe, owing to the favourable conditions of their early training, that an unusually large proportion of the sons of the most gifted men of science become distinguished in the same career" (Galton 1907:189-190).

Identical Twins Reared Apart

The first well-designed study employing the now well-established strategy of studying identical twins reared apart was carried out by Newman, Freeman, and Holzinger (1937). They studied relations between nineteen twin pairs' differences in environmental background and differences in mental ability, educational achievement, personality and physical characteristics, using objective ratings on the twins' background and a battery of objective tests and other assessments to measure the twins' characteristics. They determined the twins' identity by assessing correspondence between twins on many

minute physical characteristics (physiognomy, dentition, and fingerprints).
The three investigators consisted of an investigative team, a psychologist, a
biologist, and a statistician, who were interested in collaborating to find out
the relative contributions of nature and nurture to human development.
While bringing their biases, the psychologist believing more in the potency
of the postnatal environment and the biologist (as a specialist in the biology
of twins) of the prenatal insofar as nurture is concerned, they appeared to
stress the by then well-established cannons of the empirical tradition—to
search for what the facts were on this question. They were apparently more
interactionist than predeterminist compared to many of their colleagues in
the field of child development of the period (Hunt 1961).

As part of the same nature-nurture twin investigation, Newman and
his group also studied differences in twin pair correlations between fifty
pairs each of identical and fraternal twins reared together in the same
families, using many of the same measures. Intraclass correlations for the
fifty identical and fifty fraternal twin pairs were, respectively, .910 and
.640 for Binet IQ and .955 and .883 for educational age (Stanford
Achievement Test), differences that were and are typically interpreted to
reflect the effects of different degrees of closeness in genetic background
on ability. The closer correspondence between identicals and fraternals in
educational achievement is considered to indicate the greater weight that
grade placement, which is close for both types of twins, has upon school-
related achievement skills. While studies using objective ability measures,
precise identicity measures, statistical correlation, and comparisons between two genetically different types of twins are a definite improvement
over the earlier work of Galton and others, the failure of Newman and his
associates to employ precise measures of experience does not bring us
much beyond these gross indices. As the investigators themselves note, we
cannot assume that all of the greater similarity between identicals can be
laid at the door of heredity; identical twins are also generally treated more
alike, further suggested by the lower ability and achievement correlations
between the nineteen pairs of identical twins reared separately (.670 and
.507, respectively).

The great advantage in employing identical twins to investigate the effects of experience on development is to be found in designs where the types
of experience are substantially different for each twin (Gesell and Thompson 1929; Munn 1954), either by plan or by social circumstance. The
former, the method of co-twin control first used by Gesell will be discussed
presently. The latter, studying twins who for social reasons have been
brought up in totally different families, was employed by Newman et al.
(1937) for their other nineteen pairs. They found correlations of .791 between the twin members' educational background differences and their IQ
differences and .908 between their educational background differences

and their educational achievement differences. A smaller though still significant correlation of .507 was found between their IQ differences and social background differences. The remaining correlations were well below significance or do not concern us here (for health, personality).

As the authors conclude, environment appears to have been a significant factor in producing these twin differences in mental ability and educational achievement, despite the presence of several factors (not all recognized by the investigators) that diluted possibilities for observing in greater magnitude the effects of experience. The first one is that, although highly reliable environmental ratings were made by five judges (interrater reliability for each variable above .90) on three distinct environmental variables (education, social, physical) and the ratings correlated poorly with one another, the ratings were essentially global, subjectively scaled ratings on descriptive case records that were apparently not coded in any way. Few of the brief paragraphs describe details on the quality of intellectual interests or discourse, attention to books and hobbies, peer stimulation, grades in school, and the like. The social index reflects broad factors of social status and occupational and rural-urban differences. In other words, except for school grades completed, the focus is not on the qualities of cognitive experience that would be expected to influence mental ability nor on any other specific features of the twins' life experience, but rather on broad distal factors, only partially embracing and indirectly indexing cognitive socialization. In this light the magnitude of the correlations is impressive, particularly considering how other factors, such as the global-ability measures employed and the absence of large educational differences in twelve (63 percent) of the nineteen pairs, worked to diminish them.

The problem with both general IQ scores and general educational achievement scores, which directly assess school skills, is that they furnish no information on the quality of various specific abilities in which individuals are known to differ widely. A pair of twins with similar IQ and achievement scores may well have differed considerably in geography, math, reading, or other skills, and, in fact, markedly different skill profiles of this kind were common between twins who were otherwise close in IQ and general achievement scores. But because the Newman group only correlated global IQ and achievement differences with environmental differences, and because environmental processes that may have shaped these profile differences were not tapped, understanding of how experience may have differentially influenced the twins' cognitive development is greatly diminished.

Newman's group actually found that only four cases (22 percent) accounted for most of the correlations between educational background differences and ability-educational differences between the separated twins. The contribution of these four cases with the relatively greater amount of educational and social differences is dramatically apparent in the reductions of the variance accounted for when they are removed from the calculations. When they are included in the total nineteen cases, 72 percent of the IQ variance is accounted for; when they are removed, only 19 percent is accounted for. Background differences between pair members even in these four cases are not as great as they should be to test seriously the effects of environmental influences. As Kamin (1974) points out, many separated twins are really the products of socialization in socially and educationally quite similar environments. Rarely have background differences between separated twins approached the order-of-magnitude of differences found between the extremes of rearing in cognitively deprived and rearing in cognitively accelerated environments. Only one or two of the Newman group's cases approach this standard. It will require studies involving something not far from this magnitude of differences in experience to determine just how much experience can influence levels of cognitive ability or range or reaction for genotypically identical members of a population (in this case twins). Needless to say, a long series of such studies becomes visible with this perspective, to test the variability potentials for a complex hierarchy of skills. Such a series of investigations will need other strategies than twin controls, however, given changes in ethical values that would discourage extensive experimental manipulation of differences between twin experiences, including separation for adoption (Rheingold 1981), and that in any case placement of separated twins has always gravitated toward placement in equivalent social status and cultural environments (Anastasi 1958; Kamin 1974).

The two cases of Newman et al. (1937) with the largest background differences not only fell far short of such differences in scale but differences were not consistently contrastive in the same direction. In case 8 the advantaged twin was reportedly reared in an intellectually stimulating home environment, associated with a University of Chicago graduate frequently, was exposed to many books, read constantly, and played the violin, while the less-advantaged twin grew up in a home with few books and other intellectual activities, with a foster mother who had only a grade school education. On the other hand the two attended schools of similar quality, and though the first twin was a half grade ahead of her sister, no mention is made of marks, and the supposedly less-advantaged twin did take some music lessons. The description of the advantaged twin's social environment, moreover, suggests constant, lighthearted peer group play rather than intellectually oriented activities, while the less-advantaged twin spent most of her time in solitary play as an only child, a condition often associated with more concentrated cognitive activity (Anastasi 1958; Fowler 1975). The pattern of achievement-score differences as well is not consistently in favor of the advantaged twin (who is lower in spelling; both are about the same in arithmetic), and their overall averages differ by only thirteen months. Genetic limitations notwithstanding, it is difficult to believe the so-called advantaged twin was really stimulated much in view of her below average Binet IQ of 92, her twin sister scoring only 77. All in all, while there were differences, neither the environmental nor the outcome differences were either consistent or very wide.

Environmental differences are both larger and more consistent in the second wide difference case, case 11, though they are neither as extreme nor as consistent as the criterion we have defined. The advantaged twin obtained a bachelor of arts degree in a small college and became a teacher, while her sister attended school for no more than three years, because of frequent family moves. On the other hand both girls grew up in similar modest homes of equivalent status, without evident intellectual or cultural activities. Their home experiences are described as rather similar except that the mother of the less educationally advantaged twin did not believe in education for women. Thus while the contrasting IQ difference of 24 points (116 to 92) and the highly consistent differences in achievement scores, averaging five years nine months, are suggestive of the differences schooling can make in cognitive abilities and skill development, even in identical twins, considering this is the case with the widest extremes, more cases with even wider and more consistent extremes are needed to test better any hypotheses on the range of ability variation experience can induce in identical twins.

Given the vagueness of the ratings on environmental background, this twin investigation, which is characteristic of studies of separated twins, makes very little contribution to our knowledge of the effects of early experience, especially since early experience is incorporated into the entire developmental experience. Nearly all cases were separated in infancy, by the age of 18 months, but almost no data covering their preseparation experiences or even their preschool years are presented at all.

Co-Twin Control

The method of co-twin control, introduced principally by Gesell (Gesell and Thompson 1929; Munn 1954), provides a more experimental, prospective type of controlled strategy for studying the effects of experience, especially early experience, in genetically identical (twin) populations. As it happens, the several experiments of Gesell and his students both speak directly to questions about early experience and serve as excellent examples of basic limitations that have characterized a large body of otherwise well-controlled experimental training studies on this problem. This was the famous series of studies on maturation versus learning in which the aim of the major investigators of the era was to demonstrate that the main characteristics of development were predetermined, unfolding in a natural succession of stages automatically that experience could deflect or alter in only minor ways. As many as four of these classical experimental studies were conducted on *the same pair* of identical twin girls, twin T (the experimental twin) and twin C (the control). Their patterns of development were also studied continuously from birth to adolescence as part of a longitudinal study (Gesell and Thompson 1941), the interventions being limited to the early years. The twins' identicity was reliably established through a running series of anthropometric measures, including fingerprint and dentition patterns.

As may be noted in table 4-1, four comparatively short-term educational intervention studies, ranging in length from five weeks to four months for the twin generally trained first (T), were carried out at intervals between the ages of 46 weeks and 60 months, as well as a continuing series of observations and assessments conducted from infancy to age 14. Twin T's stimulation periods not only occurred first, except in the last study, they were longer in the first two studies, and twin C received no guided stimulation at all in the third study, compared with 4 months of guided play for twin C. The aim of the investigators in three studies was to determine whether learning or maturation were more important for development. This aim was tested in the first two studies through stimulating twin T earlier in development and for longer periods than for twin C. In each case twin C was placed in a nontreatment environment while twin T was being stimulated, after which the experimental conditions were reversed, but for shorter periods, as shown in table 4-1. In the third study designed to test this hypothesis (the fourth study in the series), Hilgard (1933) provided practice with alternative motor and memory tasks to each twin concurrently, then switched the stimulation programs for a second parallel series, each twin thus serving as the maturational control for the other in the first series. The other study, on play by Thompson (1943) was designed to improve the quality of twin T's play, in which she was slightly less persistent than her sister, while also determining the potency of stimulation to change behavior. It should be noted that the various terms, "training," "practice," and "exercise," tended to be employed interchangeably by the investigators of the period, though in fact apparently reflecting differences in the amount of adult mediation involved in stimulating the child. The first indicated direct involvement in guiding the child's learning; the second and third usually indicated mainly arranging materials and tasks, encouraging the child and general supervision of activities, though usually some degree of instruction as well.

In their findings the investigators in the first two studies emphasized the fact that with briefer periods of similar training furnished slightly later in development, the control twin had in each case approximately equaled and

Table 4-1

Sequence of Experimental Intervention Studies in Identical Twins T and C by the Method of Co-Twin Control[a]

Age Span of Treatments	Duration of Treatments T	C	Experimental Training	Investigators
46-52 wks	6 wks		Fine- and gross-motor skills (cube manipulation;	Gesell and Thompson (1929)
53-55 wks		2 wks	stair climbing) [20 min daily]	
84-88 wks	5 wks		Language (object-noun labeling)	Strayer (1930)
89-93 wks		4 wks	[two 1-hr sessions daily, one in Spanish, plus some labeling in other sessions]	
42-46 mos	4 mos	None	Guided vs. free play (C) [two 45-min sessions per week, totaling 25 sessions]	Thompson (1943)
55-60 mos	Two series of parallel 8-wk periods divided by a 4-wk gap		Early and delayed "practice"; fine-motor (cutting); gross-motor (walking board, ring toss); memory (digit and object) [Alternating series, each twin in three 1-hr sessions per week]	Hilgard (1933)

[a]A variety of periodic observations and development assessments were also made from birth through adolescence (age 14) Gesell and Thompson 1941.

in some ways surpassed the skills of the earlier trained twin T. Twin C performed as well as her trained sister in cube behavior, even without training, by the end of T's six-week, daily 20-minute training program, and nearly as well as T in stair climbing after only two weeks of daily training, following the end of T's training. Twin C acquired a vocabulary of thirty words in the later four-week training period it took twin T to acquire twenty-three words. Both twins learned only six words of Spanish, though twin C learned two in a shorter period. The results and conclusions were similar in Hilgard's (1933) study. Each of the twins typically improved more rapidly through the delayed training periods than her twinmate through earlier training in the same tasks, the gains being attributed to maturation. Three and six months following cessation of any training, the twins generally resembled each other in skill levels on the various tasks, much as they had before the experiment began. In the study on modifying play, Thompson found that twin T became more persistent in play in certain ways, but only when alone and even this persistence vanished nine months after the program terminated, again leading Thompson to stress maturation as the basis for skill development.

The predeterministic framework of G. Stanley Hall's famous student, Arnold Gesell, is quite evident in the conclusions emphasizing maturation drawn from the first study:

> There is no conclusive evidence that practice and exercise ever hasten the actual appearance of types of reaction like climbing and tower building. The time of appearance is fundamentally determined by the ripeness of the neural structures. (Gesell and Thompson:114)

It is also evident in the second study by Strayer:

> That training cannot transcend maturational level is obvious . . . in spite of intensive drill and training, neither . . . [twin] was able to attain a vocabulary equal to that of the average child of their chronological age, a result to be expected in view of their consistent degree of retardation rated as sub-average normality. (1930:312)

and again in the conclusion made in the Hilgard study on delayed practice:

> The fact, however, that *both twins "forgot" to the same level in spite of their different attainments with practice does point to the importance of general developmental factors.* [original emphasis] (1933:566)

those made in Thompson's study on play, in which she concluded that the play patterns of twin T were "fundamental and individual characteristics which persist from age to age" (p. 188); and finally, the general conclusions drawn by Gesell and Thompson in their summative developmental monograph on the twins:

> Twin T . . . [was given] hundreds of hours of preferred and specialized training designed to improve her motor coordinations, her neatness, her constructiveness, her span of attention, her vocabulary. . . . There is no evidence that all these systematized experiences added either a cubit to her mental stature or a basic component to her individuality. (1941:118)

Before reviewing the main problems with the study designs, the short-term results themselves, even taken within the investigator's own narrow framework do not unequivocally support their conclusions, particularly in the language study. While the control twin did attain the cube activity skills of the trained twin, with later, much less special training, twin C did not quite gain the mastery that twin T acquired through the longer and earlier training. More important, twin T was superior to twin C in sentence structure and pronunciation, as well as in vocabulary (thirty-five to thirty words), at the end of their respective training periods, differences that had not entirely disappeared three months later. While in the first two studies the later training was briefer, these slightly superior skill levels of twin T were acquired *earlier,* dampening the maturational hypothesis. The earlier trained twin in Hilgard's (1933) study on delayed "practice" *did* show an advantage over her untrained control twin in ten of the eleven trained skills, which was retained in four skills after the delayed training of the control. Twelve weeks following training moreover, the earlier trained twin had declined in only two skills, compared to six skill declines for the later trained twin. In Thompson's (1943) play study, the limited training continued to show some effects, perhaps as long as nine months after training terminated (period not specified precisely). The really important limitations on the findings, however, cannot be shown until we look at the conceptual designs and framework characteristic of these types of experimental interventions, limitations that are not absent even in recent history (as in Brossard and Gouin-Décarie 1971; Hamilton 1977; Koslowski and Bruner 1972).

Studies of this sort abstract the treatment programs from the developmental history, general characteristics, and ecological context of the children. That such considerations are not merely general principles widely stressed in contemporary child research (Bronfenbrenner 1977, 1981) but factors that may have been critical even in these original experiments is suggested, for example, by the report that twin C was consistently more socially responsive than twin T. Obviously, greater responsiveness to tutorial guidance could have been a cogent influence on twin C, motivating her faster rate of learning in both studies. Despite their longitudinal data accumulations on these twins, Gesell and Thompson (1941) failed to synthesize and conceptualize these data and apply them to the context of the experimental treatment programs.

There were a number of reasons for this failure. Despite his developmental orientation, Gesell was caught up in the empirical press and outlook of experimental psychology and behaviorism that eschewed mental functions in favor of description and analysis of specific behaviors without regard to how they might be logically interrelated. The crude state of cognitive theory of the time would have made it difficult in any case to consider logical relations among functions and how they developed. Finally, Gesell was so highly centered on expecting similarities between these twins because they were genetically identical, that differences were not highlighted, were perhaps even overlooked, and because of his maturational outlook as well, he made no attempt to study the processes and mechanisms through which experience and learning interact with a developing organism to bring about development. It is true that these investigators did more or less time the skill training selected for these studies to the readiness of the twins at the time for the development of the respective behaviors. But there was little consideration of the possible impact of study 1 on study 2, the relation of these behaviors to other skills acquired by either twin, or in general to any cumulative and contextual differences affecting learning in the particular studies, such as twin C's greater social responsiveness.

The extent of Gesell's imprisonment in the conceptual framework of predeterminism and inherited traits is underscored by the paradox of his actually tracing the developmental patterns and history of these twins, yet failing to relate them to each other or to the experimental treatments except in the most superficial manner. Unlike most investigators who have not even bothered to gather information on the child's history and developmental status, in this way showing by default their implicit support of predeterminism, Gesell did look but he did not see. The core of the problem lay in his assumption that a child's behavior consists of underlying traits that evolve in terms of programs prescribed from within, enduring regardless of environmental factors and contexts. He was constantly explaining away various factors without investigating them carefully, for example dismissing the possibility that twin T's superior skill as a teenager in the 50-yard dash could be related to her earlier and longer training in stair climbing (Gesell and Thompson 1941:118). He even overlooked the obvious short-term effects the training had upon *both* twins' skill development.

It is interesting to compare the motor skills of Gesell's twins with the performance of children reared under average conditions, without the benefit of specifically focused stimulation. In stair climbing, for example, both twins at close to one year could climb five stairs alone in approximately 10 seconds (T slightly faster than C). According to Gesell's own developmental norms, the average American child does not typically even creep up stairs until 15 months, walks up with assistance only at 18 months, and walks alone only at 2 years (Knobloch and Pasamenick 1974). Even within the short-term experimental framework of these studies, the investigators in their stress upon maturation all but ignored the substantial gains that both twins invariably made as a direct consequence of systematic stimulation. In this way Gesell and his group overlooked many very real specific and cumulative experimental influences that could easily been explored and analyzed in depth in the ongoing developmental study with these twins. Certain ones are worth citing.

Twin C not only was more socially responsive but was reported to be highly favored over twin T by the mother (Gesell and Thompson 1941), a connection that is mentioned only in passing and neither studied nor related to the training studies. Twin C also vocalized more, was more language oriented from early infancy, and later more talkative, perhaps in keeping with her closer relationship to the mother, and certainly holding important implications for her readiness to respond to the language training at a faster rate than twin T. Part of this general pattern appears to be twin C's lifelong social dominance over twin T, taking the lead constantly, showing initiative, responding more to overtures from the investigators, all suggesting more openness to learning. She was early more skilled in fine motor processes, while twin T was more physically active and engaged in a more scattered, object-oriented type of play. None of these patterns were seriously studied nor related to the treatment outcomes, though they certainly have implications for C's slight relative advantage in rate of language learning and cube manipulation and T's slight relative advantage in stair climbing and less focused responsiveness to cognitive stimulation generally.

Several long-term consequences were ignored by Gesell's group. In addition to T's later advantage in the 50-yard dash, twin T remained superior in vocabulary and pronunciation, though not in comprehension as late as age 13, despite less talkativeness, in keeping with her lower social responsiveness. It is true that many of their performances remained closely aligned over the years, but this is only to be expected considering the relative brevity and similarity of their earlier training in relation to the close parallel of their total life experience. There are on the other hand other unanalyzed hints that twin T's general edge in gross-motor skills and later superiority on the 50-yard dash were at least partly developed through the earlier and longer stair-climbing training she experienced. She walked two weeks earlier. Was this a transfer effect from training in stair climbing, which began well before she walked? Gesell describes how she began stair climbing in a crawling posture while twin C (who began when six weeks older, at age 53 weeks) approached stair climbing in a walking posture. Twin T excelled over twin C in several closely related gross-motor skills besides running during adolescence. She walked better and more vigorously and performed generally better on walking boards and tap-dancing, though twin C did better in bike riding, which appears to bring in additional concepts and skills (steering). Unfortunately, design limitations and lack of analysis leave the significance of these patterns unknown.

Perhaps the most interesting unexplored pattern is the developmental course of the Twins' DQ-IQ scores from infancy to age 13 (Gesell and Thompson 1941). Both started and remained at 75 or 80 until age 2, when they began to rise until they reached and remained around 100 IQ at ages 6 through 9. Then they declined slowly until they fell below 90 at age 13. Contrary to the maturational (and premature) conclusions of Strayer, can the gradual upward slope in the early years be attributed to cumulative effects of the series of training programs in which both twins participated, and the later slow declines be considered the result of cumulative effects of living in an unstimulating, poor home environment? The last experimental stimulation study terminated about age 5, and even the frequency of interpersonal contact with investigators for observation fell off markedly. Twin T, moreover, whose accrued time in stimulation considerably exceeded that of twin C, rose and remained 3 to 7 IQ points above the latter between the ages of 6 and 9. Again we see a pattern that appears to anticipate the later findings of the early-intervention studies of the 1960s and 1970s (Bronfenbrenner 1975). Early experience has an impact, even the brief disconnected variety employed here, but the total cumulative pattern of the twins' poor home and milieu was more determining when special stimulation was not maintained at the same levels.

It is of course the design limitations of such early-intervention studies, discussed elsewhere (Fowler 1962a, 1968), that ultimately determine the scope of the findings. The studies were essentially all short-term studies of a few weeks or months whose total time was small compared to the total span of even early development alone. Though described as intensive in the language intervention, the aggregate of diverse stimulation, even for twin T over the four-year span (ages 1 to 5) amounted to less than three months of stimulation, one to two hours per day, plus less than 5 months of hourly (or shorter) sessions two to three times per week. How could enough effects accumulate developmentally to make a difference, particularly when the balance of the life experience during training was spent in the largely common environment of identical twins (Rowe 1981), an environment that also persisted during the much longer periods of no training? Obviously, aside from the brief, matched control period, for the balance of development, maturation was totally confounded with day-to-day, general experience in culturally normative activities that typically promote development in cognitive, language, and sensorimotor skills closely related to the skills in which twin T was being trained.

The limitations of the design are even more evident in the contiguity of the twins' respective training periods, coupled with the brevity of training, severely restricting the amount of maturation that might occur. The fact of comparable training for the control twin, moreover, erased much of the possibility for studying the long-term effects of differentiated early stimulation. And what of diffusion effects between twins sharing a common daily environment and constant intimate relations, effects that forced Gray (Klaus and Gray 1968) to seek a distal control group even for her nontwin intervention study in another community and that this author found particularly strong for identical twins (see chapter 2, volume II)? The problem was compounded in the first two studies by the fact that twin T was placed in a nontreatment environment following her training experience, while twin C was returned to her normal milieu following training. Such an environment was not merely neutral but deliberately depriving, effectively dashing (negatively reinforcing) learning expectations built up during training and the possibility of further learning accumulating through self-initiated activity, what Dennis and Dennis (1941) defined as autogenous (self-generated) learning. Such self-propelled learning has been reported as an essential agent furthering the subsequent development of intensively early stimulated children, but *only* in continuously supportive ecological contexts (Fowler 1981b).

There were other small flaws as well, most of them apparently working against twin T. In every experiment the tutor (who was also the experimenter and tester) tried out the techniques first with the earlier trained twin (always twin T, except in the double control study of Hilgard 1933). But twin C, unlike twin T, would also be quite familiar with the tutor training environment and even the task elements in some cases, from experiencing her nontreatment period with the experimenter in the same setting, which in Strayer's study actually included many of the same games used for her later vocabulary training—only conducted silently!

Given the myriad of limitations, is it any wonder that the total impact of a common, poor home environment, shared over the twins' developmental lifetime, interacting with a common genetic heritage, would not contribute more toward high stability of style and ability similarities than small differences in timing and duration and even smaller differences in type of early stimulation would toward discontinuity and instability of differences?

Maturation in these and other similar studies (such as Hilgard 1932) was confounded with general experience, as the preceding discussion makes clear. Children cannot be placed in cold storage to mature (fortunately), allowing experience to pass them by while the trained twin (or group) experiences special training. Both twins (or experimental and control groups) were encountering a variety of general and specifc experiences, in and out of the training context, more or less related to the concepts under focus in the training program. Gesell's studies did not compare learning with maturation, but the effects of focused stimulation with those of an ongoing, accumulating mix of interacting maturational-experiential processes, intimately woven together.

Some idea of the skill limitations of most training studies from the earlier era is indicated by Mattson's (1933) investigations on how variations in task complexity influences the role of experience in learning. Mattson's tasks consisted of rolling-ball mazes, in which twenty-five average-IQ children of 58 to 72 months were given practice and guidance in manipulating a small ball through trough mazes by means of tipping the corners of the supporting structure to influence the course of the ball through the maze. Experimental children received a total of forty-six days of training and testing, compared to twenty days for controls (included test experience only), who were closely matched in age, sex, IQ, and initial maze scores. There were three levels of maze complexity, one with only around four corners and no blind alleys, one with thirteen corners and three blind alleys, and a third with eighteen corners and six blind alleys. Following training, there were virtually no differences between groups at the simplest levels, but significant mean differences not only appeared at the two advanced levels, the magnitude of the differences increased in proportion to the complexity of the mazes. Mean final differences in terms of both time and error scores for experimental children were about 40 percent lower than control scores on the most complex mazes, compared to only about 25 percent lower on the intermediate mazes. Given the relative simplicity of even the most complex mazes (there is no complex hierarchy of multiconcept-based skills as in language) and the limitations of the training period (about 1.5 months, less than one month more than controls), the study holds important implications for the difference extended training might make in the development of complex systems of competence.

In keeping with the descriptive, poorly conceptualized picture of cognitive processes of the time, in most studies there was little logical basis for the choice of skills stimulated or the organization of the sequence and relations among the various skills. Except for language, most of the tasks were simple fine-motor skills and gross-motor skills with obvious ceiling effects, severely limiting the amount of ability differences that could ultimately be realized. These large nonsymbolic simple skills were taught in isolation from any extended skill context, moreover; even vocabulary was separated from language. Under such circumstances small differences in smoothness of performance and speed (seconds or less) as in the cube-manipulation, stair-climbing, and walking-board tasks were the most that could be expected.

This pattern was true of many experimental training studies until the 1960s with the advances in cognitive theory spurred by Piaget (Fowler 1962a; Hunt 1961; Munn 1954). An early, often-cited experimental study of Gates and Taylor (1925) is characteristic. These investigators compared the learning and retention effects of two groups of preschoolers (ages 4 years to 5 years 8 months) after interspersed periods of practice and no practice in memory for digits, totaling one hundred days of practice for the experimental group and only twenty-two days for the controls. While the experimental children made important gains over the controls after their initial 4½-month training period, the gains faded completely with no practice and no further differences or permanence of gains were found for either group. Here we see not so much the work of brief training periods as the barrenness of an approach that is especially linked to ceiling effects and a total disregard of the meaning and relations of arbitrary rote memorization of random numbers to the developmental history, status, and ecology of the child and to the hierarchy of cognitive skills. The approach is quite in contrast to the recent series of efforts by Case and his associates (as reported in Case and Khanna 1981) to chart the developmental course, experiential origins, and interrelations with other skills of memory span functions in children.

All in all, except for a few hints like those of the developmental shifts in DQ-IQ patterns and the slight edge the more frequently and earlier trained twin T displayed in certain relevant gross-motor skills, and aspects of other skills (such as language), as late as adolescence, about all the information yielded on early stimulation from these and many other studies like them is that planned stimulation does produce effects on the complexity of competence in infants and preschoolers. The effects are definite, immediate, and functionally related to the type of cognitive stimulation offered. Given the design limitations, such as brevity, ceiling effects, poorly controlled conditions, and maturational bias (both in design and conception) and poor conceptualization of mental processes and learning mechanisms, particularly for Gesell's study series, little is added to knowledge about such issues as the effects of varying length of treatment, intensity, developmental matching, sequencing, and pacing of concepts to the child patterns, long-term effects, or transfer. Discounting the limitations, there may, however, be certain effects related to developmental timing (which is a first step toward studying the effects of developmental programming), suggesting the value of timing the type and complexity of stimulation to the state of development of the child in the functions concerned, as Gesell's group attempted to do with cube manipulation, stair climbing, and language, for example. But Gesell thought he was disproving the importance of stimulation and experience of any kind. In fact the aggregate of his intervention studies seems to suggest that timing plays a role, but only within a wider developmental span than he embraced, and that the cumulative effects of early stimulation that continues over a number of years (which he entirely ignored) may be far more significant. We shall take up these issues in more detail in later chapters.

Long-Term Stimulation Twin Comparison Studies:
Deprivation and Acceleration

Not all early investigators confined themselves to short-term training studies abstracted from context or were so strongly predeterministically biased. Two of the most outstanding exceptions were so exceptional in their conception and design—despite the use of fraternal twins—that they contributed highly original information about early deprivation and acceleration. In a sense the two investigations are complementary: both embraced relatively long developmental spans during infancy and the two worked at opposite ends of the spectrum of intensity of stimulation. The first study, by Dennis (Dennis 1941; Dennis and Dennis 1951), explored the effects of rearing infant twins under conditions of selected deprivation; the second, by McGraw (1935, 1939), studied the effects of attempting to accelerate development in one infant twin. Both investigators were strongly identified with the dominant behavioristic outlook of the psychology of the 1930s which followed the empirical stress on learning and experience traceable to John Locke and was rooted in rigorous observation and avoidance of mentalistic interpretations. They attempted to apply this approach to developmental studies, in opposition to the predeterministic framework that governed developmental psychology of the period, one reason there were so few studies of this nature.

Developmental Deprivation. Wayne Dennis and his wife undertook to care for a pair of fraternal twin girls from the age of 36 days to 14 months, rearing them in their home and summer cabin (for three months) confined to a single room they called the nursery, under conditions of severely restricted stimulation. Basic child care of feeding, changing, warmth, and physical comfort was maintained, but there was almost no other care or stimulation of any kind. The environment was equipped with a minimum of furniture (two cribs, bureau, table), but no pictures or toys of any kind, until the twins were close to a year old, when a few toys were provided but without any accompanying stimulation or guidance in using them. The twins spent most of their time in adjacent cribs, between which they were rotated daily and between which a screen was placed to block visual stimulation, until the very end of the experiment. Fresh air and light were ample, but the twins left the nursery only occasionally for trips for anthropometic and pediatric examinations. They were rarely exposed to other persons, except for the daily approximately two-hour presence of the investigators for basic care and extended observations. Dennis and wife attempted to standardize and neutralize their behavior, alternating care between twins, avoiding all rewards and punishment and even acts that might be readily imitated. Occasional tests were made to supplement observations, mostly to assess motor skills, especially reaching and grasping, sitting and standing. Beginning about age 6 months, the regimen was relaxed to accommodate reciprocal smiling (once spontaneous smiling had emerged without apparent modeling), noncontingent fondling and physical play, and speaking to the infants upon approaching them. Around 8 months, the infants were placed on floor pads for a few minutes daily outside their cribs and at 10 months in highchairs for short daily periods.

The results of the study can be summarized briefly. On the vast majority of visual and auditory perceptual motor behavior including vocalization normatively expected during the first 7 months of their development, both twins fell within the age of acquisition ranges of comparable samples of infants the investigators had compiled from forty baby biographies, as well as norms from Shirley (1931-1933). The exceptions embraced the first three items (fixate near object, start at sound, and follow moving object), which Dennis and Dennis attribute to the poor first-month nutrition by the neglecting mother (the father had deserted). Dennis makes no mention of the probable accompanying low level of maternal care and stimulation and he believed that slight delays found on selected items (head up-supine, object to mouth, and visually directed reaching), may have partly reflected sample limitations of the normative group. The twins were, however, seriously delayed on nearly all items for the 8- to 14-months norms, items defining the acquisition of the basic gross-motor skills of creeping, sitting, standing, and more complex aspects of visually directed reaching as well.

Subsequent guidance by the investigators, however, proved sufficient to raise the children's levels to normal standards, except that one of the twins was later found to have a mild left hemiplegia attributed to birth injury, somewhat restricting the use of her left arm and leg. This organic problem may have contributed to the earlier delays of this twin. Her delays were similar to those of her twin sister, however, until the more advanced gross-motor skills concerned with mobility came into play, but also showed up in her later reduced Binet IQ at age 4½ (70 to 107 for twinmate). In this case the weakness of the design through lack of control subjects is tempered through the limited control provided by her twin sister, for whom there was no evidence of organic problems. The Dennises (1951) furnish little other follow-up information on the twins except to note that they both have continued to make a good adjustment, considering that their care has alternated between the care of relatives and assignment to institutions, the mother assuming little responsibility for their upbringing.

This painstaking longitudinal experiment of the development of infant twins was a remarkable enterprise in the care exercised to control experience over time and in the importance of the results obtained. It is in the tradition of the baby biographers like Preyer (Kessen 1965) and comparable to the intensive studies of bilingual language development by Leopold (1939) and others (McLaughlin 1977) and the recent spate of controlled observation and analysis of basic language development. It probably stands alone historically, however, in the deliberate deprivation of culturally usual forms of cognitive stimulation, child care, activity, and social experience— something no longer tolerated since public opinion has pressured social scientists to systematize and enforce ethical standards. It is also not without certain flaws, both conceptually and methodologically.

The most notable finding was the differential effects deprivation of exogenous stimulation produced on two different classes of abilities. Simple motor and manipulative skills like following, grasping, and head turning were delayed relatively much less than more complex skills like sitting, walking, and visually directed reaching. But the investigators also were able to show that ability delay is not difficult to reverse, at least when intervention is not long delayed, thus anticipating W. Dennis's (1973) own later work on orphanage-reared infants in Lebanon and the collected findings on reversibility of early deprivation summarized recently by Clarke and Clarke (1976) and Rutter (1979). In many way as important was their success in demonstrating that maturation or growth alone was rarely if ever responsible for the emergence of skills. In skill after skill, through careful observation of specific expressions of behavior, day after day, which the behaviorist orientation dictated, they were able to show that many skills in these comparatively unstimulated twins originated as successive approximations to competent performance through a process of repeated experimentation on their own. The Dennisses termed this source of learning *autogenous development,* what is commonly referred to now as *endogenous sources of stimulation,* the self-regulated type of exploratory-manipulative activities that are the push for development in Piagetian theory. This type of experience was inadequate, however, without externally guided experimentation to induce the development of competence in the more complex skills.

Certain methodological constraints and conceptual biases of their behavioristic outlook (partly a function of the limited state of cognitive theory) however, made them overlook significant aspects and implications of their results. Aside from the obvious failure to vary experience between twins, using the co-twin control method (even if fraternal), probably the most important of these is the fact that both twins were behind the median in more than half the first 7 months' normative-age items (54 percent) and either or both twins were in the upper range (and only slightly) on no more than three items (12.5 percent), that is, grasping objects, vocalizing syllables, and crying at sounds. What the Dennisses apparently failed to consider are the *cumulative developmental deficit effects* of reduced external stimulation and opportunities to experiment in play through interaction with others and access to common objects and toys. Despite their longitudinal outlook, they, like Gesell, overlooked certain developmental implications of their study. Attaining competence in the lower ranges is seen by them as adequate, when earlier attainment through better stimulation might have served to establish prerequisites to better and earlier mastery of a host of more complex skills, including ones like visually directed reaching and gross-motor competencies at which the twins were found to lag noticeably in the latter half of the study. We must ask what would the abilities (indexed here by the 107 IQ score) of the uninjured twin have been at age 4½ had planned deprivation not been applied, or even better if intensive, high-quality cognitive stimulation been presented over the thirteen-month experimental period. We cannot discount the influence of the apparently less than optimal care the twins subsequently received, as recent intervention studies have shown (Bronfenbrenner 1975). Yet neither the possible cumulative benefits of intensive early stimulation, which have been shown to stabilize at various high levels of ability where the home milieu has remained supportive (Fowler 1981b; McCall, Appelbaum, and Hogart 1973), nor the cumulative deficits of early deprivation (Hall and Kaye 1980) apparently penetrated the thinking of that time. The notion of cumulative influences, positive or negative, does not seem to have touched the Dennisses' thinking at all.

Once again, a root difficulty was the piecemeal consideration of skills as independent behaviors, a product of the descriptive-behavioral framework, which did not conceptualize motor and other skills as a chain of hierarchically linked, cognitively regulated competencies, the learning of which builds up through additions and transformations, one set on the other, cumulatively. The absence of this more Piagetian cognitive and molar framework is also apparent in their analysis of those few behaviors in which relatively little experimentation by the twins was evident prior to their attainment more or less full blown. Actually, in the twins' attempts to turn from supine to prone position, for example, the Dennises overlooked the probable goal the twins had plenty of opportunity to acquire through being daily handled for changing and feeding: vantage points for viewing, once experienced, the twins would want to recreate. The fact that they experimented so seldom until a certain later period in development is easily ascribed to their initial complete failures: further experimentation and success awaited the acquisition of mediating prerequisite skills, in this case better control of head and back, and understandings, such as spatial orientation. Another instance of failure to infer mental processes and linkages between skills appears in the Dennises' oversight of the obvious transfer of one of the twin's earlier skills (pushing head and torso up from prone position with the hands) to later opportunities to practice sitting (in which falling forward with legs astraddle, the twin transfers the earlier pushing against the floor with her hands to push her body to a vertical, sitting position unaided). For the Dennises, learning tended to be synonymous with motorial expression, one behavior (or at best one set of behaviors) at a time, without regard to concepts of means-end relations, space, skill orchestration, and the like.

Thus these relatively advanced investigators were also hampered in grasping just how externally mediated experience facilitates cognitive understanding and in this manner the development and relations among various skills in sequence. In this regard it is interesting that language development is hardly touched on by the Dennises, an area long considered of prime importance in mental development (McCarthy 1954). Both twins tended to develop the early vocalization skills (vocalizing vowels, vocalizing to a person) about on schedule, but fell back toward the end of the year in the only item recorded, duplicating syllables, a progression in babbling that points toward imitation and the beginnings of speech. They report no other indices of language acquisition. The investigators conversed with one another in the presence of the twins from the beginning, but behaved noncontingently and did not talk to the twins until their sixth month and then only briefly upon approaching them, apparently. This was evidently enough to initiate and foster (or at least reinforce) vocalization experimentation on the part of the twins, which is reported as extensive from the fourth month; it was not enough to further progress toward the vital but entirely ignored domain of language in its complex form as speech. The physical barrier erected between the twins' cribs cut off visual-motor communication but not vocal communication. But twins, while stimulating one another freely for the early stages of vocalization, do not serve as good models for advancing comprehension in the complex rules of phonology, morphology, and syntax; language delay has long been known to be typical of twins reared together (Day 1932).

The Dennises seem surprisingly naive about child care as well, perhaps again implicitly reflecting the underlying maturational developmental framework of the period, in their assumption of what constitutes normal care patterns. Two hours per day of undivided attention to the twins by two kindly and highly caring adults, albeit much of it quiet observation and note taking, but later (after age 6 months) including scheduled play and brief conversation, is probably as much or even more time in good-quality care and stimulation than many babies ordinarily experience. It must also be observed that the deprivation cannot really be called long term, compared to the prolonged period of abusive care and neglect an infant from a deprived home may experience, two years during infancy and three more years before entering school. It is not that the experimental conditions were not depriving, compared to the quality of care present in many quite average homes. It is merely that the Dennises may have overestimated the severity of the planned deprivation they provided, fortunately, in view of the (now) questionable ethics of deliberately implementing deprivation in infants.

Specialized Acceleration. The McGraw (1935) study on twins was like the Gesell and other studies of the period, designed to investigate the relative potency of maturation and learning during early development. Unlike almost all other investigators, she attempted to demonstrate that intensive stimulation must be presented earlier and over longer periods, and that it would have more influence on the development of complex skills than on simple skills. Despite certain methodological and conceptual shortcomings, such as the twins' lack of identity and her limited understanding of cognitive factors characteristic of the behavioral orientation of the period, McGraw's study was a prototype in its scope, intensity, and duration of stimulation during infancy and in the detail of information on methods and learning processes, not often duplicated since.

Generally speaking, for these simple functions, McGraw found that the added stimulation with one twin, Johnny, did not materially advance his rates of development beyond those of his fraternal twin or of the group norms of other infants under study. Note that McGraw was comparing a stimulated child with norms for children developing under *average* (not deprived) conditions of stimulation.

McGraw's findings are at variance with the accelerated development with which White and Held's (1966) infants responded to enriched stimulation in visually directed reaching. The discrepancy may be a function of the more defined and complex analysis of experimental conditions of stimulation undertaken by White right from birth, as well as the longer period in which stimulation was apparently conducted on *specific* sensorimotor schemata. It will be recalled that visually directed reaching was one of the skills that Dennis and Dennis (1951) classed as more complex because of its retardation with deprivation. Recent Piagetian analysis of early sensorimotor skills, moreover, has demonstrated their cognitive aspects and a high degree of plasticity with respect to conditions of child rearing and stimulation programs (Paraskevopoulos and Hunt 1971; Hunt et al. 1976).

McGraw's experimental program on complex cognitive-motor learning, which she classed as ontogenetic, meaning more controlled by cumulative experience, produced more dramatic results. The educational program for these complex skills began for Johnny at the age of 7 months, continuing until the twins were approximately 24 months of age. Training for the controlled twin, Jimmy, began only at the age of 22 months and continued for only 2½ months. The list of activities in the program embraced swimming, diving, descending and ascending inclines (slides), jumping and climbing off high stools, skating, tricycling, and grading and manipulating stools and stacking boxes. At the end of the 22-month training period (including the period for simple skills), Johnny was far superior in mastering all skills compared with his unstimulated twin, Jimmy. Differences were marked even following 2½ months of special training Jimmy received from the age of 22 to 24 months.

The effectiveness of the program may be illustrated by the fact that Johnny learned to swim entirely alone, maintaining a horizontal position but remaining submerged six inches below the surface, by the time he was 10 months of age. He could then swim across the tank, a distance of about 7 feet. He had established well-coordinated movements in roller skating on four-wheeled, ball-bearing skates between the ages of 13 and 16 months of age. He could climb up a 61-degree incline at the age of 16 months and a 70-degree incline at the age of 22 months. By the age of 15 months, he dove alone off the edge of the pool with much pleasure. At 17 months he dove similarly from a springboard. His accomplishments were similar in other activities.

This study appears to underscore in a manner almost no other study does, the value of long-term, developmental-stimulation programs starting at the earliest infancy. The remarkable achievements of Johnny by the age of 2 years stand in vivid contrast with the minor achievement differences demonstrated in the short-term learning investigations conducted by Gesell and his followers.

The impact of the early long-term stimulation is further indicated by follow-up measures made on the twins. At the age of 6, Johnny generally maintained an advantage over Jimmy in his overall adaptiveness, coordination, agility, self-confidence, and ability to grasp the requirements of the task (McGraw 1939). He was generally superior in all the earlier trained complex skills, swimming the crawl compared to Jimmy's dog paddle, jumping freely from heights compared to Jimmy's hesitation, arranging stools and stacking boxes to climb for a suspended lure quickly, casually, and without much order or as many steps compared to Jimmy's over-thoroughness and caution; climbing steep slides with a more efficient technique he discovered, using his feet rather than his knees as Jimmy did; and descending from high stools more easily than Jimmy. Johnny was also generally superior in a variety of other ordinary skills, like walking, manner of falling down, and maintaining an erect posture, indicating generalization from the training.

Yet there were skill losses for both twins. Johnny still skated with better integrated movements than Jimmy but with much less skill than before, principally because of alterations in body proportions from infancy that changed his center of gravity upward. Swimming produced some of the same effects, so that Johnny no longer swam without a tire, despite evident adultlike skill. Tasks that had been well mastered and were unaffected by changes in body proportions, such as tricycle riding, showed no loss of skill. In abilities otherwise, there was little difference between the boys. Both boys fell within an average range on standardized ability tests, but Johnny was more imaginative, analytic, and reflective, characteristics that may have generalized from the kind of analytic training received, together with the long enriched guidance relationship with McGraw. At age 22, moreover, a film of their motor skills (unfortunately quite limited in scope) shows Johnny far more skilled and confident in mounting a high ladder, quickly and with ease (McGraw 1976).

Not the least of the findings that emerge from McGraw's prolonged early-training study is the potential of early stimulation that is intensive and long term to generate effective and relatively permanent motivational systems, a sense of efficacy (R. White 1959). At nearly every phase of the training period, there were striking contrasts between the boys in the quality of interest displayed. Johnny consistently demonstrated high self-confidence and enthusiasm as he engaged in the complex motor activities, an attitude that persisted to the later follow-up studies at ages 6 and 22. He tended to throw himself into a task, even a new one, wholeheartedly, with little consideration of the risk. He would also persevere longer than Jimmy in exploring the dimensions of a task in order to work out solutions.

There were, in brief, some sort of generalizing processes at work, a kind of cross-facilitation that not only gained superiority in particular skills for Johnny but led to generally superior muscular coordination and cognitive orientation for learning in the gross-motor sphere. He acquired what may be defined as a general cognitive learning set for gross-motor activities, an orientation to learn and master. Not only his skill level but the manner in which he handled himself in approaching and engaging in a task was quite superior to his twin, Jimmy. The extent of generalization is indicated, for example, when at the age of 16 months he was taken to a lake for the first time. He dove and swam in the water with little hesitation and much delight after having been limited previously to swimming and diving in a miniature pool 7 feet across.

It is evident from this study that motor skills are not simple, mechanical operations. They are also cognitive operations, acquired for analyzing and interrelating task dimensions in a long chain of problem solving. One may conveniently divide these ontogenetic skills into two classes, both of them involving problem solving. In the first there is a heavy proportion of dependence upon the body appendages and torso as instruments for accomplishing certain ends. These skills include diving, swimming, jumping, skating, and the like. The second form of task required complex skill manipulation of physical objects as well as use of the body as an instrument. Johnny had to manipulate, grade, or pile stools and boxes in order to reach an object suspended from the ceiling otherwise out of the child's reach.

In the latter activity McGraw attends more explicitly to the cognitive processes and dimensions required of the tasks. She mentions, for example, that as he approached mastery, Johnny would stand off from the randomly placed set of boxes on stools to reflect. His expression clearly indicated he was analyzing the problem before attempting solution. He also became more sensitive to discriminating the concept of height by the age of 15 months, as a result of his training in manipulating and grading the stools and boxes. By the age of 20 months he was beginning to understand the concept of serial order. At 22 months he had clearly mastered this concept, at least functionally for these tasks, grading as many as five heights in a series.

In this regard it is interesting to compare Johnny's accelerated development of the concept of seriation with norms derived from Piaget's studies (Flavell 1963:314). The youngest children, 4-year-olds, in Piaget's experiments were unable to arrange objects (dolls) in a series according to height, or to insert a missing doll in its correct ordinal position even after the experimenter had arranged the series of dolls in order. Later attempts to train seriation concepts, while successful, go no lower than age 4 (Bingham-Newman and Hooper 1974; Brainerd 1977).

McGraw also conducted an experiment on memory development, training Johnny to locate hidden objects. After several months of training Johnny at 24 months could locate eight unrelated objects, hidden twelve hours earlier in eight different locations, regardless of the order in which asked for. There are no developmental norms for memory functions, but his performance was in fact considerably superior to the unrehearsed trials of adult observers in the project.

Yet there were definite boundaries to the domains of Johnny's competence. The demarcation of competence was highlighted by comparing the boys' performances on a variety of fine, perceptual-motor, problem-solving tasks, given to both children at the age of 24½ months. Most of these tasks required the child to discover that sets of sticks or other means could be combined to obtain a lure otherwise out of the child's reach.

Although similar in a general way to the stool-arranging and box-piling tasks, the fine-motor tasks demanded greater precision and more complex reasoning. On these tasks Johnny was no faster than Jimmy in his rate of learning to solve problems. He was, on the other hand, consistently superior in such general aspects of his cognitive functioning as the amount of searching, exploratory, and analytic operations he employed in solving tasks. He was also superior in his ability to make precise size discriminations involved in one of the tasks. He showed a slight and continuing advantage on the Merrill-Palmer and Minnesota preschool scales over his sibling. Both children, however, scored intellectually somewhat below average norms.

These additional examples of performance discrepancy between gross- and fine-motor spheres of competence would tend to support the notion of cognitive competence as processes partially bounded by or anchored to particular areas and dimensions of activity (Feldman 1980; Fowler 1980a). There was, in brief, a relative lack of transfer across spheres of activity. This point is further illustrated by Johnny's relatively poor language development compared with norms, as well as the fact that he could make good size discriminations on a nonverbal basis but was poor when using language mediation. Although he could skate well at 16 months he had no word for skate, reflecting McGraw's largely nonverbal methods of teaching motor skills. Even at age 6 there was a tendency (on the part of both twins) to lisp.

In view of the unique qualities of this study it is worth summarizing certain principles and methods employed in the training program. In addition to its longitudinal plan for stimulation, one of the most outstanding principles of McGraw's program was the attention she devoted to analysis and grading of the task sequences, programming principles with an ancient history and first developed for infants logically in comprehensive form by Montessori, but not applied extensively in early intervention research programs until the 1960s (Day and Parker 1977). Efforts were made to arrange tasks according to complexity and logical order, following the natural arrangement of skill and cognitive components of a task. In learning to tricycle, for example, attention was first given to the process of learning to pedal, leaving steering until later. Not all the analyses were successful and McGraw was inclined to keep hands off when a bit of guidance was needed, apparently influenced by the laissez-faire developmental philosophy of the period. In the main, however, her attention to task dimensions and guidance were well beyond the practices of the period.

To teach swimming, the first problem was defined as learning to grasp the dimensions of water. During the first month, with careful guidance, Johnny learned to accept submersion and how to spit out swallowed water. Attention was then shifted to learning forearm strokes. Each week the harness around his balance point at the chest was moved a bit farther toward the lower torso, making him increasingly, but only very gradually, dependent upon the movement of his upper appendages to hold himself horizontal, as well as to sustain forward motion. Similar kinds of sequential guidance and well-timed and analyzed intervention were provided throughout all of the activities. The training program was, in sum, long term, carefully graded, and systematic, much like various popular programs for teaching infants swimming and other skills that have become routine in recent decades (Newman 1967; Timmermans 1975).

Motivation was handled principally through establishing a well-defined and systematic framework of routines, in which adult expectations for the child to exercise and be guided clearly produced internalized expectations in Johnny to carry out a daily regimen of activity. But it is equally obvious that forced-feeding and pressure techniques as such were underplayed. Although the experimenter maintained something of a neutral rather than a praise-oriented attitude, it was clearly an accepting attitude and social framework, in which the child came to anticipate with pleasure and confidence the exercises and achievement learning. The semipermissive and interest basis used for generating motivations is suggested, for example, by McGraw's practice of concentrating on activities of Johnny's choice on many days.

The motivational system utilized may be described as primarily intrinsic reinforcement, deriving from satisfaction over achievement and mastery, within a framework of social reinforcement and experimenter approval. The orientation incorporated another principle, namely, the constant analytic, problem-solving orientation of the experimenter in her approach to teaching. She used a light, guiding hand, with little verbal didacticism, often letting the child work out solutions to skill coordination and sequencing. Focus was again and again upon the dimensions and relations involved in a task, perfecting and integrating performances as a consequence of *assessing* and *understanding* task dimensions and sequences.

Finally, the entire program was based upon focused stimulation in specific task learning, nearly all of which concentrated in a single sphere, namely, problem solving in the gross-motor area. The learning of concepts and principles, in other words, was tied to particular contexts and types of perceptual-motor learning. Yet this orientation also resulted in considerable cross-fertilization among the tasks, as witnessed by the development of highly generalized competence, agility, and motor coordination, and the cognitive orientation, self-confidence, and motivation toward the gross-motor sphere in general. The stimulation program and probably especially the close and continuing relationship with McGraw during training may also have been responsible in part for his greater reflectiveness and more highly developed imagination.

In spite of the signal success of this early experiment in long-term stimulation, both methodological problems and conceptual limitations detracted from the value of the outcomes. Aside from the problem of the twins' fraternal status (only discovered after the experiment had begun), McGraw did not conceptualize or control social and general motor experience related to the program as well as she might have. During the three-hour intensive training period each day at the laboratory, Johnny bathed in the undivided attention of McGraw, his tutor, and generally attracted wide notice among the hospital staff with his astonishing developmental acceleration, skating along the hospital corridors and the like. Jimmy—the control—largely alone in his crib, received much less attention and less guided stimulation in all respects, including especially normal gross-motor activities related to mobility, except opportunities for fine-motor play on his own with toys. For the control twin the absence of a program treatment was thus confounded with social isolation and some deprivation (unclear how much) of normal gross-motor activity. On the other hand the mother's awareness of a sensitivity toward Johnny's special treatment led her to favor Jimmy strongly over Johnny with more affection and attention when the twins were at home during the evening, weekends, and during all of the twins' later development. Jimmy was even guided occasionally in some of the skills (such as jumping from heights) that were part of Johnny's program.

It is possible to make some interpretation of these disjunctive arrangements, partly from McGraw's own observations and partly from an extensive report by a psychiatrist who observd the twins frequently during the program and in depth at the time of the main follow-up at age 6. It would appear that Jimmy was deprived in the study to some degree, compared to his twinmate, if not compared to norms, in social support and stimulation, and in gross-motor experience compared to norms as well during the program. This is reflected in Johnny invariably assuming the leadership role between the twins in the laboratory throughout the period of training and the entire follow-up. (The twins came to the laboratory for testing periodically over the entire four-year posttraining period.) He was clearly always more at home and displayed few signs of tension (nail biting, restlessness, withdrawal) that were characteristic of him at home. Jimmy was the opposite, relatively more at ease at home, taking the leadership over Johnny, but shy and more retreating at the laboratory, despite the twins' similar statements that both were well treated by "Dr. McGraw." Despite rather competitive relations and certain tensions (partly a function of pressures in the very large family), the twins were described by the psychiatrist as essentially normal and well adjusted at follow-up. Both twins were enuretic, Johnny apparently more so, but enuresis was a family trait (the psychiatrist stresses), evident in even one of the adult family members.

On the one hand Jimmy's combined social and gross-motor deprivation at the lab may have contributed to his lowered confidence in approaching training at 22 to 24 months, which made him benefit less from training and continue to express uncertainty in all the complex gross-motor tasks. On the other hand the social compensation provided at home, together with his obvious better adjustment and even favored position at home suggests that his anxieties were confined largely to the laboratory situation and to complex gross-motor skills. It is difficult to believe that Johnny's long, intensive, and sensitively guided skill training did not make the principal difference in the specific competencies Johnny acquired. Jimmy brought uncertainty but also some specific skill deprivation to the task and was in the end trained for a shorter period on all tasks. It is in any event important not to lose sight of the significance of Johnny's exceptionally accelerated developmental attainments, not simply to Jimmy alone but in comparison with norms.

McGraw's failure to consider social experience adequately is related in some ways to her failure to consider the longer term developmental perspectives for these twins. In defense, hers was a pioneering effort of exploration that shed valuable information about possibilities, methods, and ages for stimulating complex gross-motor skills, an excuse not enjoyed by the intervention studies begun in the 1960s. She made certain errors in timing stimulation, only natural considering she advanced starting ages for training in all of the complex skills well beyond norms, despite her analytic care in programming and implementation. She did foresee, apparently, how skating would be related to walking and began teaching the child to skate while he was mastering walking, just before he was 1 year old. But tricycle riding proved unexpectedly more complex and difficult than skating. Johnny mastered trike riding at 19 months only after eight long months of trying, also apparently because McGraw furnished too little guidance (for pedaling, steering, and coordinating) on this task, leaving Jonny to work it out too much on his own. He learned to skate well by 16 months, following only three to four months of training. Skating is so close to walking that it was not difficult to help him learn to balance and work out the alternating step movements and their adaptations for rolling on wheels. More important was the evident expectation that Johnny's high competence in gross-motor skills would continue throughout development, a failure to appreciate how changes in body proportions would create new dimensions and relations for Johnny to master, in skating and climbing slides, for example, or to consider how subsequent lack of encouragement or of opportunities at home to practice and perfect skills not originally well mastered and integrated, such as arranging graded stools and stacking graded boxes to obtain lures, would cause competencies to deteriorate.

McGraw herself became aware of these factors in the course of the study and its follow-up, yet she did not quite grasp their theoretical implications for early experience and child development. Part of the oversight may be attributed to the limited state of the cognitive art at the time, especially with respect to its application to gross-motor competencies still not well developed, with some exceptions (Fowler 1976; Fowler and Leithwood 1971). But McGraw's ground-breaking efforts on early stimulation could also find little inspiration anywhere for such notions as hierarchies of skills developed only through the long cumulative experience of continued specialized training. Swimming, tricycling, and roller skating are pretty much culturally normal skills (though for later ages) at the levels McGraw terminated the twins' training. Their serious potential as a foundation or as componential skills for truly complex learning, and long-term cumulative effects of training, can only become evident when the child is led through a long course of skill training in complex gross-motor sports like figure skating, fancy diving, and gymnastics, for which Johnny was given an excellent foundation but no further experience, let alone guidance of any kind. McGraw developed many insights for us. In addition to the many aspects of early stimulation, such as intensity, method, sequencing, earliness, and long-term cumulative effects (in a limited way) she explored, she drew our attention to the special value of concentrating stimulation in specific domains and to how abilities are not merely a function of the academic-type skills reflected in IQ measures. Yet given the era and the mixed reception with which the professional community greeted this work, it was not followed by similar studies until another era, which even then was little used and seldom matched the quality and scope of her monumental efforts.

Variations in Historical Research Trends
Bearing on Early Experience

With few exceptions the many remaining historical strands of research relating to questions on the developmental effects of early stimulation and early experience followed variations of two major directions. One direction was the gradual development of sophisticated experimental manipulation in the laboratory. The second consisted of investigations that took advantage of variations in naturally occurring social and life circumstances to answer questions about development, though not all of them were concerned with how development might be influenced by experience.

Investigations Utilizing Variations in Natural or Social Circumstances

Developmental Norm Collecting. Gesell, a student of G. Stanley Hall, was the founder and chief orchestrator of norm gathering for developmental psychology. The norms of Gesell and his group represented an encyclopedic endeavor to record through careful observation, fitting the behaviorist trends of the time, all that the child did at every successive age level from birth to adulthood (see Ames and Ilg 1950, 1951; Gesell and Amatruda 1947; Gesell et al. 1940; Gesell and Ilg 1946, 1949; Ilg and Ames 1951). They also display a cavalier disregard for how the antecedents of experience influenced their acquisition. These developmental trends in motor skill, language, personal-social, and adaptive development took on something of a sacred status as a universal timetable of development in all cultures, classes, and places. Gesell mistook the trends of selected middle-class groups in New Haven, Connecticut, in the 1930s and 1940s for the patterns of everyone for all time.

Gesell's chief contribution was to chart systematically for the first time in great detail the outlines of development in major areas of functioning, updating the heretofore sometimes careful but less organized work of Preyer and others. In line with the rapid rate of change characteristic of early development, behavioral change was recorded in weeks during infancy, shifting gradually to monthly and even annual units later for adolescent development. But in making us aware of the kind of skills that define different age periods and that development follows a certain orderly progression, Gesell, in keeping with his maturational bias, mixed in some developmental brew the many diverse skills that are the product of cultural and idiosyncratic experience (dressing; toileting practices; complex motor, game, and social skills; reading) that develop to meet the universal requirements of adaptation (basic motor skills, language). In the same manner he tended to confound cultural practice with universal order, as in assigning absolute developmental priority to parallel play over cooperative play (Gesell et al. 1940). Later research, which has extended its scope to embrace experiential antecedents of development and individual differences has observed considerable variation and that cooperative play often begins in simple forms as early as parallel play (Haas and Harms 1963; Howes 1980). In the main, however, the developmental order Gesell found is largely dictated by the logic of necessity (balancing and standing before walking) and task complexity (working puzzles with few pieces before working those with many pieces, single words before sentences), rather than by the internally governed biological unfolding process Gesell conceptualized. Although drawing from the traditions of mental age skill testing founded by Binet (Anastasi 1976), Gesell maintained a useful functional separation of his empirical categories, which were later developed and extended into multiple competence scales of Griffiths (1954, 1970; Thomas 1970) in Britain. The closest Gesell came to cognitive operations, however, was in his adaptive behavior category, which embraced such concepts as means-end relations and organization of perceptual relations, without integrating such concepts into his item descriptions, however.

Gesell norms dominated child development for decades, disposing parents, nursery-school teachers, and other practitioners to wait for children to be ready for tasks before teaching them, believing that even if they were not stimulated or encountered problems and delays, biology would eventually work things out for the best through so-called late blooming. Underlying this outlook was the persistence of hereditarian thinking, in which it was assumed that each child's mental level is ultimately preprogrammed. Early environmental stimulation, far from facilitating development, was frowned on as a definite hazard for the fragile child. It is ironic that such a rich yield of developmental skill patterns should produce so little study on how they develop and how variations in timing and choice of skills occurs. But individual differences were blurred in the maturational mainstream. This predeterministic outlook seriously hampered the field of child development for years in performing genuinely developmental studies on early experience (or experience at any age), except for rare mavericks like McGraw.

Precocity Norm Collecting. A similar emphasis on developmental norm gathering has prevailed for years in the field of high-ability children, who have historically long been known as *gifted*. Usage makes the term difficult to abandon, though it epitomizes the hereditarian bias that has colored the field and particularly the views of its leading founder, Terman, who, it will be recalled, was another student of the great predeterminist, G. Stanley Hall. Much of the effort in the field has consisted of case studies, many of which Terman himself collected (for example, Terman 1919), until he launched one of the most monumental longitudinal investigations ever undertaken. This study started with nearly one thousand California school children of 140 IQ or more and followed the course of the children's development into adulthood and beyond (Burks, Jensen, and Terman 1930; Goleman 1980; Oden 1968; Terman 1925; Terman and Oden 1947, 1959). Most of the data consist of assessments and descriptions of personal characteristics centering on abilities, achievements, and social patterns, usually tabulated in frequencies and percentages without any statistical analyses of antecedent-consequent or any other relations. There are frequent comparisons with developmental and social norms, but the only attention to early experience and stimulation is largely limited to certain cursory questionnaires sent to parents, which included such items as when the child learned to read and how much the child had been stimulated at home.

Unfortunately, for Terman, cognitive stimulation was synonymous with didactic teaching, leading him to summarize the data omitting most of the information on the character and scope of informal interactions between parent and child where the productive forms of cognitive stimulation actually occurred (Fowler 1981b). Evidence of important parental influences on mental development everywhere creep through Terman's case descriptions, despite his repeated dismissal of experience as tertiary to the genetic basis of their so-called genius. His earlier case studies (1919), where more descriptive detail is included, are quite revealing of the uniformity to which exceptional early stimulation was a major factor in promoting the realization of high abilities in bright children. Until recently (Stanley, George, and Solano 1977), moreover, the field of high abilities has been governed by the magic and mystery of the IQ score of the mental-testing movement as the selection criterion (Bakan 1967). The IQ concept, or general intelligence, was in many ways the counterpart of behaviorism, the latter the superficial characteristics subject to manipulation and environmental influence, the former the underlying and immutable biologically programmed governor that really determined the development of competence to perform skills in any area. Even the great promoter of behaviorism, Watson, believed biological development must have its licks before stimulation could take effect (Hunt 1979). This narrow but global conception of development and approach to measurement, which will be discussed in conjunction with the early research on the effects of nursery-school experience, combined with the normative, predeterministic framework, has further masked understanding and retarded research effort on how abilities are richly variegated and shaped by experience from earliest infancy.

Adopted-Child Studies. Like the investigations of twins reared apart, studies of children reared in adoptive homes were another attempt to separate experimentally the effects of heredity from the effects of environmentally induced experience. Unlike studies on separated identical twins, however, this design does not yield the kind of near-maximum control over nature that twin studies do. Since identical twins have virtually identical heredity, by definition, experimental control problems are entirely centered on ensuring maximum differences between the environments in which the twins are socialized, or at the least that differences should be substantial and known in detail with regard to relevant parameters of cognitive stimulation, a condition that has rarely obtained. Foster- or adopted-child studies in contrast are faced with the problem of experimentally controlling both environmental experience and heredity, something difficult if not impossible to do in the light of genetic knowledge of family characteristics, then (1920s and 1930s) or now. The salient advantage of adopted-child designs is the partial control over heredity intrinsic to separating children from their biological parents whose genetic relations are closer than those of unrelated parents and children.

Supposedly the best-controlled investigation of the type during this early period (according to Anastasi 1958), by Leahy (1935), reported correlations between the adoptive children's IQ and some fifteen adoptive parent-home characteristics (including parent IQs, education, and a child-training index of the home) fluctuating around .20, compared to the standard .50 for a closely matched group of control children and their biological parents. There were 194 children in each group, matched in sex, age, and (for the experimental group) foster father's occupational and educational level and mother's educational level. Adopted children had all been placed at no later than age 6 months. These seemingly clear findings favoring the hereditarian hypothesis, which have been more or less replicated several times (see Burks 1928), have nevertheless been frequently questioned because of several flaws intrinsic to their design (Anastasi 1958; Jones 1954). First is the lack of control or even detailed knowledge of the adopted children's early experience, pre- and postnatally, probably quite important in light of the known poor socioeconomic background of many of the adoptive children's original homes affecting such matters as nutrition and quality of attention and stimulation. Second is the more emotionally distant psychological relationship often characteristic of adopted-child-parent relations, coupled with the lowered expectations for development knowledge of adoptive status may have upon both children and parents in foster home relations, knowledge known to 50 percent of Leahy's adopted children and all adoptive parents of course. Third was the greater uniformity characteristic of adoptive homes compared to control homes, which should lead to greater homogeneity of abilities among the adopted children. In fact standard deviations in IQs were 12.5 and 15.4 for the respective adopted and control children, a difference that may have contributed to the reduced foster-parent-child correlation values for the adopted children, compared to control children. Selective placement was also sometimes a problem (though minimal in Leahy's study) resulting in genetic and environmental influences working in the same direction. What has not been discussed historically, finally, is the grossness of measures of home experience and abilities in the Leahy and other studies. As in the twin studies there was less awareness at the time of the nature of cognitive stimulation and developmental processes, most studies focusing on socioemotional relations and stimulation in a general way when they got beyond such distal measures as parental occupation and educational level at all. Abilities were also not broken down into something less crude than IQ measures, making it impossible to isolate the effects of specific types of sitmulation in the home upon the development of specific abilities.

Other studies, notably the investigations by Skodak (1939) and Skeels (Skodak and Skeels 1945, 1949) and by Freeman, Holzinger, and Mitchell (1928) found many more indices of the effects of adoptive-home influence on children. In the last study mean IQ gains after placement were 7.5 points, slightly more for those adopted below the average age of 8; a correlation of .52 between child's IQ and cultural index of foster home for children adopted before age 2; and a correlation of only .25 for sibling pairs reared in different homes, compared to the usual .50 for ordinary siblings reared in the same home and .37 between adopted and biological children in the same adoptive home). The Skeels and Skodak study included a follow-up on one hundred children between 11 and 17 years of age, who had originally been adopted at less than 6 months ($\overline{X}$ = 3 months), and whose IQ levels were determined to be no different than those of earlier children lost through attrition. There were no relations between the child's IQ and either the foster mother's or foster father's education (no data on foster parent IQs), but relations with the biological mother's IQ and education ranged from .30 to above .40 at various testings, including the final testing, when children ranged between 11 and 17 years of age. Although there were no preadoption child-IQ scores, later mean differences between maternal and child IQs were 20 points, 18 points in the case of the groups with the higher scoring mothers (111 versus 129 for mothers and children, respectively) and as much as 41 points for the low-scoring mothers (63 versus 104 for the respective mothers and children.

The design limitations of all such studies, the lack of information and precise measures on selective placement and experience, including earlier preadoptive experience, and the singular quality of adoptive-child-parent relations, coupled with the uncertain status of genetic factors left the knowledge derived from all such studies even more equivocal than the findings from the studies of separated identical twins. Yet there are consistent indications that adoption probably has facilitative effects, the earlier the placement the more powerful the effects. One of the main sources of conflict between findings stems from the differences between relying on correlations and relying on means. Virtually all studies appear to find that parent-child intellective correlations for the biological family dyads are greater than those for the adoptive family dyads, giving weight to genetic factors, though the roles of early preadoption experience and malnutrition, adoptive-parent-child expectations and psychological distance, and relative homogeneity of the adoptive homes cannot be discounted. In contrast, in these studies where they were measured the children's mean cognitive gains after placement or mean advantage over their biological mothers are equally impressive, maternal-child differences reaching as much as 18 to 41 IQ points in the Skodak and Skeels study, suggesting a definite cognitive facilitative effect from the adoptive experience. Even more impressive were the extraordinary outcomes of the very long-term Skeels (1966) study, in which not only did adoption lead to IQ gains, but it also led to almost completely uniform successful occupational and marital adjustment in adulthood, compared to persisting low IQ levels and almost completely uniform occupational and social failure in adulthood for the nonadopted institutionalized children. No doubt some of these changes must be partly discounted for methodological reasons (including selective placement), but the difference in results points up the differences revealed by mean scores (trend of changes or differences) against those revealed by correlation (relative rank and degree of association), the former in this case suggesting the environment produced certain effects, the latter suggesting heredity exercised certain constraints as well.

Early experience is once again not directly addressed in these studies, but the magnitude of the IQ gains Skodak and Skeels found from early adoption (at less than 6 months), compared to the minimal gains Freeman and his group found for later adoption (mean age of 8 years), together with the slightly larger mean gains they found for an earlier adopted subsample, would indicate that the deleterious effects of early malnutrition, neglect, conflict, and poor stimulation frequently reported for these children before adoption are easier to reverse when more facilitative conditions begin early. Unfortunately, again as in so many investigations intending to study nature versus nurture, the combination of variables involved precludes analysis of the effects of stimulation alone, either for the earlier or the later adoptive experience.

Institutional Variations: Orphanages and Nursery Schools. The beginning studies on the effects of early institutional experience upon cognitive development searched out the extremes of institutional variation in deprivation and enrichment but made few attempts to design and control the form and quality of stimulation programs. At one extreme investigators from various disciplines of medicine and social science began after World War I to look at the effects of socialization in orphanages and like child-care institutions. Educators and psychologists began during the same period to study how well young children were developing intellectually in the nursery schools spreading around the United States. The sizable body of studies of both kinds that were collected over the next few decades established that institutionally reared children tended to be delayed intellectually to varying degrees and nursery-school attendees appeared to gain a few IQ points on the average. But on both counts the findings were poorly received by the scientific communities of the era, in part because of the strongly held view of the immutability of biological intelligence that IQ scores supposedly accurately reflected and in part because of the lack of definite conceptions of cognitive processes and stimulation, which limited control over specific variables of stimulation. Just as important, the significance of findings was lost until changing political and social perspectives and the impact of Freud and Piaget following World War II led to the first major interest in the issue of early experience and new syntheses of the accumulating findings (Anastasi 1958; Casler 1961; Fowler 1962a; Hebb 1949; Hunt 1961; Yarrow 1961). Much of the first impetus for this change in theoretical perspectives came in 1949 from Hebb's timely book. Coming as it did with Hebb's outstanding credentials as a behaviorist and experimental psychologist, the new synthesis, summarizing data from both animal and human literature, this presentation of a learning theory framework that could accommodate long-term, experiential developmental phenomena attracted wide interest and helped launch a new age.

Aside from the frequently poor quality of methodological control that marked the first studies on the effects of institutional care often conducted by well-meaning psychoanalysts (Pinneau 1955), the chief problem centered on undefined qualities of institutional care that failed to distinguish what specific characteristics might be hampering development. In particular, separation from the mother and home and the presumed special emotional aspects of maternal care were together assigned the main role, without distinguishing among them or considering much at all the influence of sensory and cognitive stimulation and a variety of specific factors, such as age and duration of institutionalization and number and quality of caregivers (Casler 1961; Yarrow 1961). In these later analyses of the older studies both earliness and duration of institutionalization for example were found to increase retardation, while attempts in certain institutions to improve the quality of individualized care and stimulation tempered the degree of retardation.

The widely cited classic study of the effects of early institutional care by Skeels (1942, 1966; Skeels and Dye 1939) is perhaps the best example of the problems and possibilities for this line of investigation. The gross retardation of infants was linked to conditions of obvious deprivation in a residential orphanage and it is one of the earliest experimentally controlled remedial intervention studies on record, with the longest follow-up as well. The orphanage conditions, which were associated with mean IQs of 64.3 and 86.7 points for the respective experimental and contrast groups, were extremely deprived for infants up to 6 months of age (propped bottle feeding, no toys, and visual barriers around cribs), only a little less so for infants from 6 to 24 months (few toys, a little movement, and limited interaction between infants confined to large cribs, but adult stimulation still limited to hastily executed basic care routines because of the limited staff/child ratios), and highly regimented and monotonous care from 2 to 6 years (adult/child ratio no more than 1:30, with assistance from no more than four 10- to 13-year-olds, the young children sitting in chairs much of each day in a severely overcrowded room 15 feet square).

Discovering by accident the apparent IQ improvement of two infants removed from the orphanage environment to the care of retarded adult women in a related institution, Skeels placed eleven other infants in the same highly enriched, multiple-caregiver environment at the mean age of 19.4 months for a mean period of 18.9 months, the program continuing for each infant until his or her development approached a normal range. Intelligence measures administered during this period of special care showed cumulative mean gains of 27.5 points. Later assessments in adulthood found all of the original thirteen children self-supporting as average citizens, holding jobs or managing homes as housewives, only two in unskilled work, the two who had never been adopted. Mean educational level attained was twelfth grade and eleven had married, nine having a combined total of twenty-eight well-adjusted children ($\bar{X}$ IQ = 104). A comparison group, in contrast, none of whom had ever been adopted (because of lower IQs), showed cumulative mean IQ declines of 26.2 points during early childhood and remained largely incapable of functioning as adults. One had died, four were still institutionalized, and the rest were in unskilled occupations. Median educational level attained was less than third grade and only two were married, one having one child and then divorcing.

There were many problems with this study, recently reevaluated by Longstreth (1981); yet despite its flaws it points up certain features about experience and development and the way they might be studied longitudinally as few studies have. The principal experimental weakness is the fact that the experimental controls were not only not randomly selected, but were a comparison group assembled post hoc from a previous control group, though they were from the same orphanage environment. Much is also made by Longstreth of the fact that maternal-child mean IQs differed significantly by 23.3 points in the contrast group compared to virtually no difference (1.6 points) in the experimental group. Maternal IQs in the latter group were available in only five cases, however, compared to nine in the contrast group (Longstreth counted only eight), mean length of schooling for the experimental and contrast mothers were similar at 7.8 and 7.3 years (N = 11 and 10), and health histories appear to be comparable (contrary to Longstreth's claim).

This study also illustrates well the limitations characteristic of most early educational studies in the types of measures employed and the approach to stimulation used, both of which were undefined general-package devices. Except for the functional observations of competence and social adjustment used years later, the early measures were all IQ tests (Kuhlmann and Stanford-Binet and Iowa Test for Young Children), which furnish little precise information about the nature of the cognitive processes and abilities that are influenced by experience. There was no formative evaluation. When such measures are accompanied by an unanalyzed program that consists merely of large increases in the amount of care and stimulation the infants received (many enthusiastic retarded women playing surrogate mother for each infant, ample toys, peer experience, and excursions for the experimental children, against an overworked orphanage staff handling many infants in a monotonous environment for the contrast children), it was impossible to detect which aspects of care and stimulation were influencing which aspects of development, only that a general program had general intellectual effects as indexed by IQs. Notwithstanding these several limitations, including questions about the contrast group, the fact that the duration of the original treatment before adoption was poorly related to the size of IQ gain and the poor predictive validity of the first infant test scores (Longstreth 1981), the study remains a landmark for several reasons.

In the first place, while all variables of care, stimulation, separation, and so on in the retarded women's institution were wrapped in a single package (as in other early studies of institutional care), the treatment program makes it possible to rule out the influence of separation (both maternal and home) and even continuity of single adult attachment. Since almost every child was "adopted" as the personal charge of one of the retarded women, despite the general pattern of multiple caregiving, a given caregiver for each child was apparently characteristic in the institution, one or two children assigned to each cottage group of retarded women, paralleling home conditions in extended families. The critical change was thus in adult/child caregiving ratios, coupled with a great augmentation of toys and play equipment, which made possible an enormous increase in the quantity, quality, and variety of care and stimulation through play by the mentally retarded women. We are thus at least able to study the effects of a well-described general program of quality care and stimulation, even if such separate variables as language or quality of emotional relations were not isolated. The measured cognitive developmental effects of this program were substantial.

The really significant merits of the study, however, lie in the remarkable magnitude and consistency of both the early and long-term developmental outcomes following such a remedial program of cognitive stimulation and total care in infants given the extent of deprivation and accompanying cognitive deficits described. The mean 27.5-point IQ treatment gains in this study reflect substantial gains for *every* infant, only two gaining as little as 7 IQ points, the other eleven infants gaining from 17 to 58 points. These gains were generally paralleled by staff observations of marked improvement among the children, which together established competence levels enabling eleven of the thirteen children to be eligible for adoption no later than a few months following program termination. All except one of the eleven adopted children made further IQ gains of 2 to 17 IQ points (the exception losing only 5 points) over the first two and one-half years following treatment, which were sustained throughout their entire developmental history in adoptive homes to adulthood, all eleven becoming socially and intellectually competent human beings in their communities. The nonadopted pair lost 9 and 17 IQ points and both ended up as domestic servants as adults. The general IQ declines of the contrast group, leaving their mean IQ still only 66.1 at follow-up, made all contrast children ineligible for adoption, and thus forced to continue their monotonous institutional existence throughout childhood, which led to their low social and intellectual competence as adults. This pattern, coupled with the fact that the later gains of the experimental children were unrelated to the degree of maternal retardation, are further indications of the potentials early positive and negative experiences may have for mental and social development. Another of the significant heuristic aspects of this exceptional study is the separation of early from later experiences, which, combined with placement in a strongly supportive (adoptive) home environment, suggests on the one hand the potency of early experience to exercise profound effects on cognitive development for good or for ill but on the other hand, *only when the later experiences operate in the same positive or negative direction.* It is worth noting that the later intervention studies beginning in the 1960s suffered from just this latter defect: early-stimulated children were invariably returned to the original, preprogram disadvantaged environment, leading to a gradual regression of most cognitive treatment gains (Bronfenbrenner 1975; Palmer and Anderson 1979). Clearly we need more systematic analyses of the scope and magnitude of early versus long-term cumulative effects, by systematically varying the ages and duration of early stimulation in relation to the characteristics of the succeeding later intervening experiences. The fact that in this study initial IQ gains were unrelated to treatment duration may only mean that what there was to learn could be acquired in a comparatively brief period, after which the cognitive level of activity was not sufficiently complex to induce further gains. The program was after all, though excellent for the stimulation-starved levels of deprived infants, a rather diffuse general program, with minimal professional supervision and little planning. Variations in quality among the cottage groups alone may have been responsible for a considerable portion of the variation in outcomes.

Studies at the other end of the continuum, the intellectual enrichment presumed to occur from nursery-school experience, are much the same, both from the point of view of methodology and from the point of view of the use of global measures (mostly IQ tests) and global program definitions (Anastasi 1958; Fowler 1962a). From the 1920s to the 1940s more than fifty studies were carried out, most of them afflicted with certain basic methodological problems, problems of program enrichment relative to the children's background, and problems of global programming and measurement. In Wellman's (1945) compilation of the results of all the numerous investigations of nursery-school experience to that date, she reported that 1,537 children from twenty-two nursery groups gained an overall mean of no more than 5.4 IQ points, compared to 0.5 points for the controls. Such a gain is obviously not impressive, even though significant. Gains tended to be concentrated during the first program year, moreover. Very little additional mean gain appeared with the accumulation of additional years' experience. No consistent differences in various follow-up IQ and achievement measures were reported in several studies that ranged from elementary school through college (Anastasi and Foley 1949). Significant differences in school grades favoring the nursery-school group appeared in one study by third and fourth grade (not before), though not on achievement tests and only with *N*s (10 and 8) for the respective groups greatly diminished through attrition (Kounin 1939, cited in Anastasi and Foley 1949). Methodologically, even these modest gains have been seriously called into question, apparently the result of artifacts, in which the apparent gains were largely the result of a combination of regression and test practice effects (Anastasi 1958). The central methodological problem lay in the selection of subjects who were not randomly assigned to attending and nonattending groups but consisted of self-selecting parents of higher educational and socioeconomic background. In order to match children's groups in initial IQ, children from the higher level nursery school groups were chosen from samples whose scores were systematically underestimated. Their IQ scores tended to rise over time, following the patterns of children from advantaged middle-class homes, perhaps partly a result of regression and partly the result of delayed stimulation effects. Nursery-school children were also found to be exposed more often to routine testing than nonattending controls.

In the case of these enrichment studies the problems of possible effects being masked by the unanalyzed and highly generalized programs and accompanying IQ measures are compounded by the quality of the program relative to both the children's home background and the content of IQ measures. The type and complexity of play with puzzles, construction toys, art materials, gross-motor equipment, and sociodramatic devices in the characteristic nursery school, while perhaps more extensive than in most homes, was essentially similar to the kind of activities encouraged in the typical middle-class home from which these children were drawn. Any gains that occurred would almost necessarily be miniscule, since the children were by and large already quite experienced in these sorts of tasks. But IQ tests also measure verbal and abstract-reasoning skills more than the perceptual motor, spatial, visual perceptual (art), and social skills that pervade the nursery-school fare. In studies that used IQ tests such as the Merrill-Palmer scale, which are composed of a heavy proportion of puzzle and other spatial tasks, the mean gain for seven groups of nursery-school children amounted to as much as 14.5 points, compared to a mean gain of only 6.4 points in four groups of unschooled children (Wellman 1945). Presumably some of this advantage must be discounted because of regression and testing effects, but the results are more in line with what one would expect from the program content.

Skills exercised in nursery-school programs not only vary considerably from the kind of abstract symbolic skills measured by IQ measures, but the programs that elicit them are (or at least were) ordinarily more concerned with the child's enjoyment in play and social development than with cognitive development as such. Nursery schools are thus neither intensive nor systematic in quality of programming, showing less effects even with disadvantaged children, who might be expected to benefit from activities often absent from their homes, than other, more organized programs in the 1960s (Miezitis 1971; Miller and Dyer 1975). Interesting early evidence of this sort of finding appears in a three-year study conducted by Skeels and other members of the Iowa group (Skeels et al. 1938; Wellman and Pegram 1944; Wellman, Skeels, and Skodak 1940). In this well-controlled study comparing the development of residential orphanage children randomly assigned to nursery school and nonnursery school groups, the advantage accruing to the school groups appeared only in maintaining or slightly improving their IQ levels, compared to mean declines of 16.2 IQ points for the controls. Children remaining over 400 days in the program made mean gains of no more than 6.8 points. A similar but especially well-controlled, matched-pair study by Barrett and Koch (1930), however, produced mean IQ gains of 14.9 points for the nursery-school-attending orphanage children (for whom practice effects were also controlled), compared to gains of 5.1 points for the controls, using the more sensorimotor-type Merrill-Palmer scale. When these values are compared with the kind of mean IQ gains of 27.5 points occurring in Skeels's (1966) earlier study in the intensive daily program (though still largely undefined experiences) with mentally retarded but highly motivated and intensively oriented surrogate mothers in a context of many-adult/one-child ratios, the limitations of nursery-school programs for cognitive development are evident. Program analysis and developmentally sequenced measurement awaited the post-World War II advancement in Piagetian inspired cognitive developmental theory and sophisticated input-outcome assessment systems that grew up with the intervention studies accompanying the 1960s' War on Poverty (Gordon 1972; Miller and Dyer 1975; Soar and Soar 1972).

Environment-Child Relations: Correlation Studies. Perhaps the largest body of evidence accumulated on the influence of early experience on development takes the form of correlations between the child's environment, often measured retrospectively, but also currently or even longitudinally over time, and measures of the child's development at some point in time or even over several points in time longitudinally. A great deal of power can be gained in this manner because of the opportunity to forgo the time and expense of experimental efforts yet obtain endless quantities of information on multiple variables simultaneously, unless the children are also followed longitudinally. One reason why so few long-term training studies have been undertaken at any time, past or present, is the time involved, coupled with the fact that the rules of the experimental paradigm severely restrict the number of variables that can be manipulated in any one investigation. There is a well-known price for this apparent power of course. Correlations do not permit the same kind of inferences with regard to the direction of influence of cause and effect as do experimental studies, and there is not the same degree of confidence that third factors, coincidentally correlated with the selected variables, can be ruled out. Many investigations in recent history in fact combine correlational investigation with experimental manipulation.

Galton was among the first to use correlation techniques, which were later developed mathematically by Karl Pearson (Boring 1950). One of the first systematic studies of early environmental influences on cognitive development was conducted by Van Alstyne (1929), who studied environmental factors contributing to children's intelligence. She measured a great many dimensions of environmental-child relations and found a pattern of results not dissimilar to the more conceptually and technically sophisticated recent studies, such as those of Clarke-Stewart (1973) and Carew (1980). Van Alstyne administered IQ and vocabulary tests to seventy-five 3-year-olds and mental tests to the mothers, whom she also interviewed with respect to a variety of hypothesized environmental stimulation factors, such as length of time with child, reading to child, kind of play materials, definite teaching of child, child's activities, and interest of parents in child. While most of the multitude of environmental factors correlated with either the child's vocabulary or IQ between .30 and .60, a composite of the environmental factors correlated .70 and .61 with the respective ability measures. Van Alstyne also correlated the environmental factors with the Kuhlmann subtests, which yielded such correlations as .54 between enumeration of objects in a picture (subtest 1) and the number of constructive toys the child had an opportunity to use. On the whole, relations between factors and subtests were not consistent.

The composition of the sample was so heterogeneous (children's IQs ranged from 79 to 167), that the correlations may have been spuriously high, or in any event left plenty of room for alternative or underlying factors. Environmental factors were all behavioral frequencies, providing little insight into the pattern of cognitive stimulation processes at work, and of course the interview method does not furnish direct observational data. The largely empirical approach is indicated by the use of the hodgepodge of Kuhlmann subtests without any conceptual organization of abilities by type, which, together with the limited behavioral-frequency method of assessing the environment, tended to obscure the pattern of relations between environmental factors and cognitive test items. But if the behavioral-descriptive and general-intelligence (IQ) framework of the period governed Van Alstyne's approach, she did break away from the developmental mainstream of maturational thinking in her exploration of specific environmental influences on the child's mental development, even attempting to study patterns of experience in relation to patterns of cognitive outcomes through use of the Kuhlmann subtests. Unlike recent studies, however, which range over several age periods and also employ a variety of cognitively relevant, complex observational measures set in interaction contexts, Van Alstyne assessed children at a single age, further limiting possibilities for sketching any sequence of developing interactions between child and environment. Although correlational investigations are inherently limited with respect to causality and the isolation and control of variables, latter-day developments with respect to ecological settings, statistical analysis (multiple, stepwise regression, cross-lagged, sequence, and path analysis (Lytton 1980) and, even combining correlation with experimental manipulation, as done in recent large-scale programmatic studies on early education and early intervention (Fowler 1972, 1978a, for example), go far beyond the information yielded in the crude, though historically important, study of Van Alstyne. The Van Alstyne study typified the early correlation work in studying relations between events and developmental outcomes at a single age, or at best several ages, even into recent times (Freeberg and Payne 1967; Walberg and Majoribanks 1976). Classical correlation studies could thus tell us very little about the value of early experience beyond the fact that experience played a role in development as it might at any age, even aside from the fact that correlation does not give us the same control over causality as experimental training studies.

Despite the improved multiple time and interactive developmental assessments that have evolved with the contemporary approaches to correlation, because of the inherent limitations with respect to variable control and the sheer volume of studies, correlation studies are only peripherally considered in these volumes. Unless correlation measures are coordinated with known or planned time-linked patterns of stimulation, in which case some degree of experimental control is also involved, correlation patterns are usually not held to furnish the same firm test of antecedent-consequent relations as does direct manipulative control of stimulation and outcomes across subjects. In some senses the issue is really knowledge, that is, variable articulation and control, versus statistical strategies, that is, degree of difference (correlation) versus group differences (anovar). But since comparisons of differences between groups—or individuals in the manner of the preliminary process stage of case studies—is the principal strategy employed for the kind of planned early stimulation studies with which the book is chiefly concerned, correlation is considered only secondarily, if at all.

Cross-Cultural Studies of Development. Much of the early literature on cross-cultural differences in cognitive development was contained in the review of the cultural and ecological bases for individual differences in ability in chapter 1. It remains only to summarize and point up a few of the special problems that marked the early cross-cultural research on early experience on cognitive development. Very little of it was aimed specifically at early development, its biggest limitation for our purposes.

Comparisons of children reared in different cultures furnish one of the more powerful tools for following the effects of experience at any age upon development, because the totality of experience from all influences derives from apparently distinct sources. Like the studies of identical twins reared apart, however, cross-cultural comparisons have pitfalls. Cultures all face common general problems of adaptation for survival, every culture needing to socialize children in certain basic skills that appear as the universals of cognitive development. Neither separate homes for twins nor separate sources for cultures necessarily mean totally different types of environments. Thus children almost invariably acquire the basics of means-end manipulation, gross-motor movement, social interaction, and language to some minimum degree, though the particular forms in which they are expressed and the degree of refinement in complexity may vary from culture to culture.

Few of the variations between folk cultures probably approached the degree of variation found among members of large-scale, hierarchical societies, where division of labor, occupational specialization, and complex manipulation of written abstract codes and concepts are highly developed and differentiated. Differences in special skills and competencies in abstract manipulations are also bound to be great between all members of folk societies and the educated members and occupational specialists of hierarchical societies, as various studies reviewed in chapter 1 have shown. Differences in competence between folk cultures are probably greatest in the realm of knowledge of fauna and flora in the local environment and mastery of competencies developed over generations to manipulate the local ecology for adaption and survival.

Cross-cultural research faces another caveat as well. Folk cultures are genetically diverse and not infrequently confront nutritional problems that may undermine skill development. While both factors may play a role in determining the complexity of skill levels attained, it appears highly unlikely that such factors play a major role in the dramatic, highly particularized skill differences regularly found to be associated with ecologically relevant socialization practices.

What it comes down to is that differences in ability and cognitive development cross-culturally amount mainly to differences in specific types of knowledge and skills, such differences as variations in the amount of knowledge of different fields and variations in the ability to perform different types of concrete manual skills and abstract manipulations. But even assuming most variations are of this order, we cannot automatically assume that cultural differences make for skill differences. Again, like identical twins reared apart, widely separated cultures may very well share common ecological problems that condition socialization of similar skills to a high level of complexity. The consistency of differences between agricultural and herding folk societies versus hunter-gatherer folk societies in socializing children toward conformity and cooperation versus autonomy and initiative (Barry, Child, and Bacon 1959) is a case in point. More specific illustrations of the relevance of a common ecology to early conditioning of cognitive development appear dramatically, for example, in the earliness and high complexity with which swimming and canoeing skills are socialized among the Manus of New Guinea (Mead 1975), the Motu of Papua New Guinea (Rosenstiel 1976), and the Warao, a lake-dwelling tribal group in South America (Wilbert 1976b), all three of whose basic ecologies have historically been built around fishing and water transport (see chapter 1). On the other hand these patterns are quite at variance with the development of children in most cultures, including that of the Plains Indian children traditionally in the United States, whose pattern of skill development in turn is quite different again from those of boat- and water-reared children and indeed of children in most other cultures.

It is the study of such experiential-ability variation clusters that cross-cultural research would appear to do best and it is a tribute to some of the early investigators, who began in some numbers between the two world wars, that whatever their theoretical and methodological limitations they sometimes made trenchant observations and interpretations on matters of this kind. The earlier investigators appear to have emerged from two separate backgrounds; anthropology and psychology. The former followed an ethnographic, descriptive approach, which in the hands of the earlier imaginative observer and popularizer, Margaret Mead, contributed much to both professional and popular awareness of the effects of cultural variation in experience on development. The second group comprised a small number of socially oriented psychologists, who began to wonder about and measure cultural variations in ability, armed primarily with the general-purpose instrument, the IQ test, which raised as many questions as it answered, for reasons already summarized at length.

Fortunately, psychologists did not limit themselves to the verbal, abstract type of IQ test, but such investigators as Porteus (1931), Dennis (1942) and Havighurst and Hilkevitch (1944) made use of performance measures, including spatial measures, maze tests, and drawing figures that in some cases bore a closer relation to the skills generated in the way of life of various folk groups. Some of them went further, devising special measures modeled after those designed for individuals formally educated in industrial settings but composed of skills indigenous to the particular culture and ecology of a group. Porteus's (1931) foot-tracking maze test for Australian Aborigines and Dubois's (1939) Draw-a-Horse test for Pueblo Indian children were prime examples of this type. Even as early as this period the pattern of results seemed to suggest that folk groups generally lacked the kind of verbal-logical abstractions sampled by IQ measures but that abilities varied widely from culture to culture in terms of the types of skills in which children were socialized, which in turn grew out of their ecological relations with the environment.

Still another line of inquiry by psychologists was directed at assessing less exotic cultural groups residing within the purview of industrial society, such as blacks and isolated mountain people in the American South. Much of the effort of early innovative psychologists like Otto Klineberg (1934, 1935) was devoted to demonstrating how IQ scores among blacks varied with socioeconomic background, place of residence, and educational level. As black populations moved from rural to urban areas in the South, for example, and from South to the more industrialized North and Midwest regions of the United States, their IQs gradually rose, presumably in association with the decreased racial discrimination and expanded opportunities for better schooling and occupational skills. Klineberg also analyzed in detail the cultural basis of IQ measures, pointing out, for example, the inappropriateness of such test items as "_____ [silence] should prevail in churches and libraries," in black folk culture, where church ritual is traditionally physically and verbally expressive (Klineberg 1934). Similarly, Sherman and Key (1932) found that children from isolated mountain folk cultures increased their mean IQ scores by 5 to 35 points, depending on the test used, as they moved to town and attended school. As with studies of Indian children, the isolated mountain children performed better on selected performance measures like the Draw-a-Man test.

There was, however, little conceptual sophistication and no systematic effort then to develop measures to explore cultural differences in ability in relation to experience, nor much communication between disciplines. Cross-fertilization between psychology and anthropology, represented in the growing field of cross-cultural psychology and in general the cognitive diversity and richness of analysis inspired by Piaget, along with the stress on ecological relevance, cultural context, and *emic* (context defined) as opposed to only *etic* (externally originated) measures (Brislin 1980) are all of relatively recent vintage (Ashton 1975; Berry and Dasen 1974; Bruner, Olver, and Greenfield 1966; Cole et al. 1971; Klineberg 1980; LeVine 1970). The effects of early experience were seldom the focus in any of the earlier cross-cultural investigations. Margaret Mead's (1975) informative observations on the Manus, for example, like those of her observations on child rearing in Samoa (1928) were simply part of her general description of socialization practices in the culture. The observations of Danziger and Frankl (1934) and Dennis and Dennis (1940) on the effects of physical restraints such as cradling boards and swaddling on infant's motor development were exceptions.

Probably the most significant contribution of cross-cultural research in the early historical phases was its role in changing the perspectives about the determinants of human development (Klineberg 1980). Founders like Franz Boas (1911), as well as the active recorders of socialization processes in different cultures like Margaret Mead and of intellectual variations with social conditions and instruments like Klineberg and Porteus, above all drew attention to the malleability of human functioning and mental processes. The framework of cultural variation within which they worked opened wide vistas that made the extreme hereditarian and predeterminist views on mental development no longer tenable.

Laboratory Investigations

We have already analyzed in some detail the type of short-term training studies characteristic of the field of learning prior to World War II. Further discussion of the approach, illustrated by a few additional examples, however, should clarify better how the learning-theory framework of the period truncated efforts to devise more meaningful, long-term studies of cognitive learning and development, particularly in certain isolated learning studies that were actually long term in form.

We have seen how the behaviorist, learning-theory framework that dominated psychology until well past World War II, interacted with the predeterminist assumptions of developmental psychology to devise training studies on maturation versus learning, such as those of Gesell, whose methodological and conceptual constraints precluded gathering systematic evidence on the role of experience. The short-term nature of the training, the simplicity of the tasks, the limited knowledge and consideration of cognitive processes and of cognitive relations between the task and the child's developmental status all conspired to blur the nature of developmental learning processes. But even within the ranks of the dedicated learning theorists and learning-oriented experimentalists, little progress was made. Conditioning theory, both the classical paradigm of Pavlov and later the instrumental or operant paradigms developed by Ivanov-Smolensky and Skinner (Munn 1954), were essentially focused on molecular relations between organism and environment for the purpose of generating general principles of how stimulus-response relations worked, rather than on how the organism develops through cognitive learning over time. In working to establish itself as a science, psychology was following what it believed was the lead of physics, to be objective and precise and to deal with the directly observable (Brunswik 1952). The result was a stress on minute, well-defined movements, the immediately visible behaviors of the organism—behaviorism—stripped of the mental meaning, the invisible, mentally regulated intentions and long-range goal-striving, which can only be revealed through observing overarching molar acts. Variable manipulation and experimental control were the order of the day, leading to an emphasis on animal experimentation in the pure state of the laboratory, uncomplicated by the complexities of mental processes and the multiplicity of variations found in real-life contexts. Even among the experimentalists who were interested in learning in children and dealt with issues pragmatically in a less purified state, the absence of a convenient organizing cognitive theory and the stress on control led to a narrow preoccupation with simple behaviors and empirical exploration of intuitively devised tasks. The psychology of learning operated almost exclusively unrelated to the concerns of mental functioning, development, and the ecology of family and community.

Developmental research for the most part was limited to comparing learning capabilities in various tasks of this kind at different ages. It was not developmental at all in the sense of investigating relations between successive stages or processes of the developing child and the mechanisms by which the child progresses from one to the other.

In the strict conditioning framework, aside from questions on the nature of the conditioning processes (types of responses, range of variability of schedules and types of reinforcement, generalization), concern was mainly on how early conditioning could be established in the infant including the possibility of conditioning during the prenatal period (Munn 1954). In spite of the occasional theory put forth on the nature of development, such as Hull's (1934) "habit family hierarchy," postulating the acquisition of sets of increasingly complex responses through association and generalization, there was very little thought or study devoted to how the child develops as a functioning, changing system through the cumulative impact of experience. Tolman's (1932) extensive formulations on purposive learning, even in rats, influenced his own interpretations of how rats operated in maze learning in his own laboratories but did not widely influence the field of human learning and child development as a whole. In a number of investigations of higher mental processes, such as those of Hamilton as early as 1911 (and 1916), subjects at different ages from infancy to adulthood were presented with a multiple-choice (door-opening) problem they were to solve through trial and error. The focus was on how the proportion of inferential responses increased with age, not on the nature of these processes or how changes come about.

Training studies were nevertheless not uncommon among learning-oriented psychologists who experimented with children. But even when the training periods might be said to be prolonged, a matter of a few months at least, there was a curious inflexibility of procedures and perspective that led to setting up arbitrary and often narrow learning tasks without regard to the developmental status of the child. Both the concern for control and the behaviorist framework apparently precluded flexibility and exploration of cognitive learning processes. Consider for example, the interesting study of Ling (1941), who trained infants between 6 and 15 months of age to discriminate geometric shapes under varying conditions over a period of several months. Why geometric shapes and how do they fit into the cognitive potentials and perspectives of the infant's development? A rationale could be developed, but such issues found little place in the empirically directed, laboratory-oriented studies of the period. Or what of the series of studies of Welch (1939 a,b), who through prolonged training was able to induce size discrimination at twelve months and form and area discrimination by fourteen months, using a series of boards graded in width and length to differences as fine as .5 inch. Welch (1940 1946 a,b, 1948; Welch and Davis 1935) did attempt to formulate a conception of concept development in children, involving a gradual extension of abstraction levels, through processes of stepped generalizations up the successive levels of the hierarchy, foreshadowing Gagné's (1968, 1970) later conceptions. But in attempts to test his constructs, he can be seen to have been trapped in the same molecular control framework of the era, as for instance in his extraordinary persistence over five hundred trials with the same narrow task of inducing an infant to associate an arbitrary word, "ate," with a wooden plate (Welch 1939b). Most of the training studies on higher order problem solving, such as those of Richardson (1932, 1934) on teaching infants of different ages to secure a lure by pulling a string or to ring a bell by turning a lever, were restricted to a few days of training. And again the entire design was defined in terms of an empirically selected, predefined task not conceptualized or related to the child's mental development. At most investigators such as Mattson in his 1933 study of 58- to 72-month-old children learning a rolling-ball maze considered such cognitive dimensions as IQ, reflecting the prevalent notion of an underlying general intelligence relatively uninfluenced by experience. Mattson's study did demonstrate quite conclusively, however, that no amount of maturation or unrelated general experience could match the effects of specific training in maze learning with *complex* designs. Only with the very simple designs did untrained older children perform as well at the outset as children trained at younger ages, in the manner of the Gesell, co-twin control series.

Occasionally young children were trained with complex verbal material, but for the most part short-term training and inflexible presentation of poorly conceptualized set tasks remained the rule. Foster (1928), for example, used a series of nine short stories for children between 2 years 7 months and 4 years 9 months to memorize through ten daily repetitions. His only concern for mental development were age and mental age, to which he found learning was proportional in each case. One of the most unusual learning studies of all time broke out of the mold in one important respect, the length of development spanned. In all other respects, H.E. Burtt's (1932, 1937, 1941) extraordinary study of verbal learning and memory in his infant son followed the characteristic course of using a set task, logically unrelated to the child's development and presented in a rigidly standardized manner.

Burtt undertook an investigation of the effects of prolonged but not intensive early training on his son's later development. Between 15 months and 3 years, Burtt read twenty-one 20-line passages of Greek to his infant son, taking less than one minute per day and introducing three new passages every three months. Differences between learning the earlier read material and new material were highly significant at 8.5 years, less so at age 14, and had disappeared entirely by the age of 18. The rigid adherence to the prescriptions of a task totally meaningless to the child and rigid procedures with no regard at all to developmental states or mental processes at any age sets a standard of some kind for all time. Burtt must nevertheless be counted as showing the persistence of the effects of early stimulation over a substantial period of years. If this could be accomplished, given the lack of meaning or close relation of the concepts involved to anything else the child acquired at any point, apparently, and given the lack of further reinforcement until the first follow-up at age 8½, in a similarly arbitrary and short-lived task, the insertion of some meaning, developmental relevance, and follow-through ought to do wonders. Nothing of the kind has been tested since. Most of the research on early stimulation since that period has been devoted to early compensatory education.

As early as the 1920s a controlled experiment was conducted using complex verbal and meaningful concepts; that was Davidson's (1931) then totally exceptional laboratory study on teaching preschool children to read. She selected three groups of four to five children each, all sharing a common mental age (1916 Stanford-Binet) of 4 years, their mean ages being 3, 4, and 5 years, to which their respective IQs of 126, 98, and 77 points were inversely related. Four months of kindergarten activity included 10 to 15 minutes of individualized and small-group daily reading instruction, using a word-sentence method in the context of play-motivating techniques and pretraining in the overall gestalt of word-form silhouettes. All children made some progress in learning to read, but success was directly proportional to IQ level and inversely proportional to age. At the end of the program, two of the high-IQ 3-year-olds were reading fluently, compared to near fluent reading by one of the average IQ 4-year-olds and no more than substantial progress in one low-ability 5-year-old. While there was no nontreatment control group, the application of similar stimulation programs across age and ability conditions is a useful model rarely duplicated in the early-education literature. The fact that progress was related to ability levels, not age alone, resulting in children as young as 3 easily mastering complex perceptual-cognitive operations historically associated in the educational mainstream only with school-age children past ages 5 or 6, strongly suggested the young child's potential for complex learning. The study also found that high IQ ability and success in reading were themselves strongly associated with the quantity of reading to the child previously engaged in by parents. This experiment is also unusual in its concentration on learning in a specific but complex domain of knowledge, not bounded with the sorts of severe skill ceilings marking the usual maturation-versus-learning and other laboratory learning studies of the pre-World War II period. Unfortunately, there was no formal follow-up study, though informal inquiry found at least half the children (those located) to be reading well above average in school. Nevertheless the study remains a classic of its kind, ranking among a handful of landmark studies scattered throughout the literature.

Historical Overview

A broad array of strategies for studying learning and development in children emerges from this historical sampling, but no systematic body of knowledge and nothing like an organized conception or even a core of consistent research activity devoted to exploring the domain of early cognitive developmental stimulation as a field. Investigations of infants' and young childrens' learning were frequently undertaken, but seldom with a more precise aim then merely to explore learning processes in one of the phases of childhood, without relation to development or, as in the conditioning studies, to study general laws or determine how early the infant could make stimulus-response associations. Many studies included early childhood within the age range of investigation without considering that earliness might enjoy special properties of its own or analyzing separately the events and characteristics of the period. Studies of this kind, such as those of twins reared apart or of adopted children, did attempt to locate children who had been separated or adopted as early in life as possible, however, but largely with a view to controlling differences in *total* life experience.

As this selected review has tried to show, most studies that embraced early childhood took two forms, short-term learning studies on rather limited competencies usually facing ceiling effects or developmental descriptions, norm gathering, which under the aegis of Gesell abounded from the 1920s to the 1940s. This may be defined as the period when research in child psychology and child development became established in a regular way, and studies on learning and development in these alternative forms became common paradigms. Longitudinal investigations like the Berkeley Growth Study (MacFarlane 1938) and Terman's continuing study of bright children (Terman and Oden 1947, 1959), were variants of this norm gathering, though a new paradigm, correlation studies of child-environmental relations, like the Van Alstyne (1929) study, which offered tremendous promise for unlimited exploration of the role of experience in any pattern and time combination, began to come more and more into prominence.

Methodological problems are evident in various investigations, usually circling around the question of experimental controls, and of course correlation studies are intrinsically limiting with respect to causality. Since many investigations were concerned with developmental description alone, and even when learning was studied often simply compared how children learned a given problem at different ages, questions of experimental control over experiential variables did not arise. Well-controlled experimental studies were not uncommon, using both matched groups and co-twin control, though random assignment of subjects to groups and blind assessment were rare if practiced at all.

Progress in probing early developmental stimulation was impeded by conceptual and methodological inadequacies of the studies. Conceptions of the nature and origin of human abilities and the nature of the scientific method as applied to psychology, the former coming down from Darwinian and earlier historical conceptions of human nature and the latter marking the struggles of psychology to establish itself as a legitimate science, established a framework that narrowly channeled theory and the kind of investigations undertaken.

Among the most important and pervasive conceptions was the predeterminist idea of development, which in the IQ test and other instruments devised by the mental testing movement, was assumed to reflect in some meaningful way underlying, biologically governed intelligence. Wherever development was studied, the mental age score was assumed to index the maturational state to which the child had progressed at a given age, following the innate level of intelligence (IQ). These biologically governed notions of abilities were widely employed as well in the normative studies of skill development by Gesell and others, as noted previously. Skill development was assumed to reflect predetermined, maturational progress at successive ages. The net effect of the biological predeterminism was to make charting the course of development, rather than studying specific environmental influences on development, a chief activity of the period. Why study what could not seriously be changed? The hereditarian outlook did not stop with the work on mental development but led as well to the expenditure of a great deal of effort to prove or disprove or estimate the proportion of influence heredity had upon intelligence and development. The investigations of twins reared apart and of adopted children and the Gesellian maturation-versus-learning studies represent only part of a large quantity of research on the nature-versus-nurture question in the period between the two world wars—as indicated, for example, by the fact that the Yearbooks of the National Society for the Study of Education for both 1928 and 1940, both two-volume editions, covered the same topic, "Nature and Nurture" (Whipple 1928, 1940).

What is most interesting, moreover, is how the predeterministic outlook seemed to combine with the rigorous scientific stance of classical behaviorism and experimental psychology to discourage investigations of long-term learning of complex abilities. Rigor and precision meant phenomena that were directly observable and specifiable, leading study away from the nebulous world of internal mental processes to the world of behavior. But in practice it meant more than this. Precision and control tended to narrow the problem to small matters of stripped down environments in the immediate situation. Laboratory controlled animal behavior answered the terms best, but when children were studied it was usually on the same terms. Complex cognitive processes and long time spans were more difficult to observe, measure, and control, and in fact did not often enter the research enterprise because by definition they engage internal mental functions and developmental transformations that were scientifically taboo. But by moving toward the molecular and short-term, the learning framework abandoned the very thing it might do best: study the influence of meaningful, cumulative experience. In this manner, the field of explanation for developmental experience was left clear to the predeterminist framework of mental testers and early mainstream developmentalists. Gesell and his group utilitzed these short-term learning experiments with truncated behaviors to demonstrate the irrelevance of experience, and even the more learning-oriented investigators like Welch (1939a, b) and Burtt, (1932, 1937, 1941) were hampered in their endeavors to study concept learning by the mold of experimental rigor and the low state of the art of conceptualizing mental processes that the antimentalist framework prescribed.

The same interaction of rigor, antimentalism, and predeterminism was a major factor in developing mental tests in the global, contentless IQ form that predominated. Rigor meant quantification and reliability at all costs.

But since intelligence was an immutable, general property of the organism, any sample of behaviors that would correlate highly with one another to make reliable predictions about ability would be suitable. Charting the succession of skill samples by age would then yield the course of this underlying maturation through development. No matter that the predictions were not perfect and that most of the information about what actual specific skills might be àt work was lost. Unfortunately, it did and still does matter and decades of research and intervention studies that limited their assessments to the general IQ type measures were unable to trace what was influencing what, notably in the classical studies of nursery-school experience, but also in many of the first post-World War II remedial early-intervention studies as well (see chapters 6-8). Programs were necessarily designed and modified intuitively without benefit of knowledge of why one intervention appeared to increase mean IQs more than another.

Other factors were at work in the case of the multitude of nursery-school studies and indeed in the approach with which young children's learning and development were studied in all circumstances. It will be remembered that nursery schools were first established in the first part of the century, the climax of a historical revolt of the humanist and social reform movement descended from Rousseau. The importance of caring for children lovingly and warmly, appreciating that their characteristics and needs were different in kind from adults', and rejecting the austere and severe traditions of controlling and narrowly training children by rote methods and punishment were at the heart of the new philosophy and methods. As play, social acceptance, love, health, and socioemotional development of the whole child took center stage, everything associated with the earlier harsh methods, including concern for intellectual development and cognitive stimulation themselves were accorded secondary status and even viewed with suspicion. The forced culture of the past was formally decried by many, including Terman and Gesell, giants of the period. Children were too tender and fragile, had rights to their own world of play and relationships, and in any case would follow their own biological schedule of development. Intellectual stimulation, as it was then called, would not in any case change things in any important way and might cause emotional stress, learning problems, and social maladjustment or deprive children of their childhood. Nursery-school programs were designed to reflect these values, making it difficult to measure developmental outcomes with one kind of measure (IQ tests) that were produced with another sort of program (sensorimotor and sociodramatic play).

In this dual atmosphere of orientation toward play, social relations and automatic development, on the one hand, and anti-mentalistic empiricism, narrow experimental control and molecular focus on the other, the wonder is that any systematic studies of early cognitive stimulation of the order of

McGraw's (1935, 1939) intensive training of complex gross-motor skills or Davidson's (1931) study of early reading could arise at all. Even gropings without clear definition, hampered by the period conceptual constraints, like the pioneer efforts of Skeels (1966), the ethically questionable developmental-privation study by Dennis and Dennis (1941, 1951), and the abstracted experimental anomaly of Burtt (1932, 1937, 1941) are to be admired in their own way, as are the extraordinarily advanced developmental learning perspectives and systematic experimentation with stimulation techniques of Itard (Lane, 1976) and Witte (1914) more than a century earlier. They all provide a beginning, a place from which to start searching with more of a plan for how the different facets of early life affect development, in the early period itself and over increasingly longer spans of the developmental cycle.

Concepts and Dimensions of Early Cognitive Stimulation and the Development of Competence

The Rise of Research on Early Learning

Early experience as a concept for research was not really isolated until after World War II although educational theorists like Comenius, Rousseau, and their successors, the early empiricists led by John Locke, as well as Church doctrine all stressed the importance of forming the child's mind through experience from his or her earliest days. Despite practices of early stimulation as early as ancient Rome and down to the Montessori Schools, the field of early education and child development as a whole did not single out early stimulation for special concern until a confluence of theory and investigations from various fields occurred after World War II to establish early experience as a problem of singular importance for study. Until recently the field of early education, represented mainly by the nursery school and its offshoot, day care, was more preoccupied with matters of the whole child's development through play and social relations. Reacting against the stringent methods of child control and stimulation from earlier times, practitioners downplayed intellectual development and were especially suspicious of early cognitive stimulation as pressure. This attitude was reinforced by developmental theory, which stressed the fragility and play orientation of early childhood rather than its potential for understanding and cognitive learning, and the still widely dominant predeterministic view of development. The field of developmental research, under the hegemony of Gesell, was highly influential in this regard, widely propagating these views and backing them up with charts of the natural, universal course of children's development. The taboo on the study of mental functions in favor of behavioral descriptions further hampered research on cognition and stimulation and, coupled with predeterminism, made it difficult even for learning-theory-oriented investigators to mount studies on early cognitive (then termed intellectual) stimulation.

The point of departure for this new direction can probably be dated from Hebb's classic book *The Organization of Behavior* (1949), in which he presented a plausible neurophysiologically based theory on development that gave special prominence to early stimulation in influencing the formation of basic neurological structures. He also brought to bear for the first time evidence from widely separated sources suggesting that early experi-

161

ence might produce long-lasting effects on development. He summarized evidence from diverse human and animal studies, including perhaps the first study of its kind, Hunt's study on "The effects of infant feeding-frustration upon adult hoarding in the albino rat" (1941). He pointed up such findings as the deleterious influence of sensory deprivation in infancy on later perceptual functioning, the potential effects of early deprivation on adult behavior and intelligence, and the differential effects of brain injury occurring early or later in development. The book was widely influential in both animal and child research, and in clinical work, which was already responding to the impact of Freud's stress on the vital importance of early life experience upon personality formation and neurosis (Orlansky 1949), as well as to early studies on the effects of institutional and maternal deprivation. By the 1960s when Hunt lauched his seminal analysis on *Intelligence and Experience* (1961), reviewing a vast array of research in terms of a framework laying bare the historical preformationist and predeterminist biases in psychology and child development, studies on early experience had become a well-established multifaceted enterprise, following several directions, such as early training, sensory deprivation, and institutional deprivation (Hunt 1975, 1979).

Various other reviews of the period served to point up issues. Casler (1961) and Yarrow (1961) sought to disentangle such issues as the effects of maternal care from those of stimulation. Studies suggesting the complexity of cognitive learning even infants were capable of and how early stimulation might increase potential for learning throughout development were reviewed (Fowler 1962a). The deficiencies and biases in the historical research on early learning and development reviewed in the preceding chapter were analyzed. By this time the sociopolitical forces of the civil rights movement were ready to launch Head Start and a decade of early-intervention research to compensate for the claimed mental deficits of the child from impoverished environments (Hunt 1975).

That intervention era has largely vanished as a result of cutbacks in government spending for research and disenchantment over the apparently modest results of the numerous intervention studies. But the field of early stimulation and early experience had its critics from the beginning. As early as 1949 Orlansky demonstrated in a major review of the various psychodynamic theories and studies, including cross-cultural investigations, that the collected studies on early experience had regularly confounded variables, failing to distinguish between psychosexual influences and overall family child-rearing patterns, for example, and between early versus later influences on development. Similarly Pinneau (1955) in a scathing analysis of the accumulating observations by psychoanalysts, pointed out the total lack of experimental controls and the failure to isolate variables. Even reviews of those not unfriendly to the notion of the importance of early experience, such as Casler and Yarrow, drew attention to the abundance of methodological problems in the research on early deprivation to 1960.

More recently, a number of investigators have conducted studies (Kagan et al. 1979, for example) and reviewed bodies of evidence (Brim and Kagan 1980; Clarke and Clarke 1976; Kagan, Kearsley, and Zelazo 1978; Moore and Moore, 1975; Ogbu 1981) suggesting that early life may play no particularly vital role in development. Much of the argument of these critics rests upon the apparent later reversibility of many of the effects of early privation, as found, for example, in the studies of Kagan and his group (1979) in Guatemala and of Dennis (1973; Dennis and Sayegh 1965) on motor retardation of institutionalized infants in Lebanon, along with the general washing out over the course of later development of many of the basic cognitive gains, particularly as reflected in IQ scores, acquired by disadvantaged children through early-intervention programs (Bronfenbrenner 1975; Clarke and Clarke 1976; Miller and Dyer 1975). Kagan and his colleagues have also drawn attention to the generally modest and inconsistent correlations between patterns over long time spans of development, buttressing their view on the essential discontinuity of human development (Brim and Kagan 1980; Kagan, Kearsley, and Zelazo 1978).

Such conclusions may be premature. The analyses that support them play down the rather remarkable persistence of certain cognitive, social, and motivational effects displayed as late as the high-school years by early-stimulated disadvantaged children over their controls (Palmer and Anderson 1979), persistence that might not be expected in the face of the social obstacles in the typical ecology of the impoverished milieu in which these children develop. Their main defect stems from the lack of system and strategy for investigation and analysis in the field of early experience and early stimulation. Research in this field is in a state of disarray. No organized conception exists of early stimulation and experience or of how stimulation variables and cognitive processes may interact in various combinations in the short run or cumulatively over the long term to influence development. The effects on cognitive development are not distinguished regularly from those on socioemotional development and motivation, and there is no systematic strategy for, nor even much current interest in, making definite investigations on early (long-term) learning in relation to development. Many of the numerous studies of early stimulation have been geared to special, disadvantaged populations, combining multiple types of stimulation and often global measures of cognitive development. And now that programs and measures have become more sophisticated, new research on early education has dwindled because of funding cutbacks. What is most needed is a considered synthesis of what we do and do not know about the properties peculiar to developmental earliness, if they exist, and a conceptualization of the dimensional structure of early cognitive stimulation and developmental learning. It is particularly important to distinguish between short-term stimulation that may influence performance on simple tasks and what may be termed developmental stimulation, or stimulation that continues over weeks, months, or years—long enough to produce important changes in the child's cognitive abilities and processes. As in Piaget's work, the focus needs to be on the development of the organism as a cognitive system, but unlike Piaget's work, more weight needs to be placed on exogenous over self-regulatory factors in development.

An effort is made in this book to distinguish a number of dimensions of early developmental stimulation as they relate to the acquisition of cognitive processes both in early development and in relation to the persistence of effects through later development. The dimensions identified will be explored conceptually in terms of a general scheme and tested against selected samples of studies in which the dimension appears to play a prominent role. The best investigations of the type are reviewed.

While we are concerned with the general question of how susceptible to learning the child is at different ages, the criterion is not simply ease of learning comparable material. An advantage accrues with age because the older child has already developed a more complex cognitive structure through experience, as the history of education and Piagetian research have amply documented. The perspective is instead to determine whether earliness increases the potential for mastery over the long term. At the same time the special characteristics of early learning and development are interesting in their own right. We shall survey various conditions and dimensions of early stimulation and learning, such as the intensity, duration, type, and rate of stimulation, with a view to discovering which ones make a difference, their order of importance, and how they interact with one another and with the child's pattern of developing cognitive processes. Such explorations have been relatively common in the realm of animal learning and development for some time (King 1958), but except for some preliminary efforts (Caldwell 1962, 1967; Fowler 1965b, 1967a,b, 1971b; Yarrow 1968), have yet to be undertaken systematically with human learning.

Early experience can influence development in two directions: accelerating it or retarding it. This analysis will concentrate on the first, efforts to facilitate or accelerate early learning. The framework is developmental learning, learning that involves the acquisition of an interrelated body of concepts and skills related to cognitive development and important aspects of competence. Learning of this type usually requires stimulation that continues over time to generate significant and complex effects on development, as opposed to short-term learning, which affects only simple skills or limited components of complex skills and leaves little trace on development. The focus is on the patterns and problems of learning in relation to development, universally in all populations, though taking account of culture, ecological context, and social experience. The large body of literature on early intervention with children from socioeconomically disadvantaged populations will necessarily be covered, because it is the largest single body of experimental literature on early developmental stimulation available, although the focus is general and not on issues of compensatory education for special populations. The review is restricted mainly to experimental training literature because of the limitations inherent in correlations study, discussed in chapter 4. Because it is the second largest single source of experimental early-stimulation literature, short-term experimental studies on early learning will be selectively reviewed. As will become evident, among the many difficulties that appear to obscure understanding of the role of early experience is the confounding of variables and lack of conceptual precision in the bulk of the studies.

One of the most difficult problems is to sort out the differential influences of cognitive learning, motivation, and social and emotional factors on the development of competence. They are all always intrinsic to the general processes of mental functioning and development. Yet they can be distinguished analytically and in fact frequently appear to vary in different proportions, and sometimes even in direction, as for example in the case of relations between cognitive complexity and socioemotional adjustment, as in certain cases of the extremely brilliant (Hollingworth 1926, 1942; Miles 1954). Our chief concern is with cognitive learning and the development of competence, but the development of motivational systems and interest patterns, and the status of socioemotional processes will necessarily enter the picture.

A Profile of Cognitive Competencies

The variability of skill development between and within individuals makes it essential to explore the dimensions of early experience in terms of a variety of abilities. Relying on IQ measures and related concepts of general intelligence that mask the often highly selective effects of individual and cultural experience will no longer do. There is unfortunately no widely agreed upon conception of how different cognitive abilities and processes are organized in mental systems, but there is enough consistency for plausible models to be constructed. Regardless of conception, the important thing to recognize is that mental functioning, though integrated, is not unimodal but is highly differentiated into a variety of component cognitive processes and domains of activity that can be developed to different degrees or levels of complexity.

The scheme to be employed here (developed in Fowler 1971b, 1977, 1980a) is based on a triad of intimately interrelated types of cognitive skills.

In this scheme cognitive processes are conceptualized as operations involving rules defining concepts of phenomena, whether of the external world or of our own mental and physical activities. All human mental processing seems to make use of general concepts, in which for example the single object (a book, say) or the single means-end manipulation (reaching for a glass) are treated as representations of a general type (a concept, distinguished by the selective abstraction of features and operations (pages of print, extending arm and grasping glass) according to defined rules. The single item has no meaning—that is, it cannot be understood—except as an example of some type. The range of concepts and the rules that define them are extensive, however, though they may be grouped into several overall categories as shown in table 5-1. The three main categories or types of cognitive skills indicated, together with motivation (sometimes classified as a cognitive style in prior formulation; see Fowler 1980a), constitute the major sources of variation for the development of cognitive skills. Knowledge consists first of formal concepts about the general forms and processes of matter in any form, the type of operations that Piaget (1952)

Table 5-1
Classification of Cognitive Competencies

Concept Categories	Examples
Knowledge	
Formal (general nature of phenomena)	Means-end, object permanence, causality, conservation, classification, seriation
Information (content)	Natural world; human world; artifacts, activities, idea systems, and social structures and relations
Codes	
Motor	Gross and fine motor skills
Perceptual representation	Visual, auditory, tactile, olfactory, gustatory, and kinesthetic
Sensory channels	
Motor manipulation	
Symbolic	
Verbal	Language
Specialized	Math, music, dance, games (e.g., chess)
Problem-solving strategies and styles	
Focus (structural orientation to problems)	Analyzing - interrelating
Tempo	Fast – slow
Memory	Short- – long-term; scope
Reflectiveness	Reflective – impulsive
Adaptiveness	Standards oriented – flexible
Achievement orientation	Productive, creative
Motivation	Intensity, scope (areas of interest) Attentiveness, inquisitiveness, concentrativeness, persistence

has so brilliantly assembled in relation to a sequence of cognitive development, such concepts as the permanence of objects, the relation of means to end, causality, conservation of matter, and the classification of objects according to type. But knowledge also varies according to the domain or area of the world involved, embracing everything from natural categories (plants, animals, earth structure) to human artifacts and activities (dishes, clothes, housing, theater), idea systems such as religion, and social practices such as manners and, styles of personal dress. Each of the formal processes can be applied to all domains of information.

Codes are the concept systems through which we represent and summarize knowledge to simplify and make possible the manipulation of vast bodies of material. At the simpler, more concrete levels, we have the alternative grammars of rules that are built up through the various perceptual motor channels of looking, hearing, touching, tasting, smelling, and moving. Chief among these for the normal individual is the visual mode, which works typically in coordination with the fine-motor, tactile manipulative processes. Gross-motor processes develop primarily out of kinesthetic processing but are also closely intertwined with visual and often fine-motor activities. In more abstract form, symbolic codes like language and such specialized codes as mathematics, music, and symbolic logic open unlimited vistas for processing knowledge of all types in highly flexible, abstract and generalized yet precise forms. Symbolic codes are limited only in losing directness of relation to phenomena, in the way perceptual-motor codes function.

Strategies or styles are concepts governing modes employed for solving problems of any kind, whether in a domain of knowledge, in learning or using a code, or in perfecting a strategy itself. We figure things out, take action, produce and create at different rates (tempo) and with different degrees of reflectiveness, attention to standards, and concern for detail (analyzing) or relations between things (integrating). We also have different degrees and types of mnemonic skill (short versus long term). Motivation may or may not be considered a style variation, but in any case has to do with the intensity with which energy is developed, marshaled, and invested in the type of task concerned, both immediately and in the long-term pursuit of a domain of activity (interests).

The development of intelligence is thus a matter of acquiring skill in these diverse concepts and defining rules, making human variation as much a matter of variation in skill type as of variation in ability levels. Because development typically occurs in different skill combinations, there is a tremendous variety of individual differences from skill to skill and quite often a considerable range of differences in competence from skill to skill in the same individual. There is almost an infinite variety of skill combinations and individual profiles, each with its own hierarchy of cognitive complexity, derived from the great diversity of human experience from individual to individual and culture to culture. Farming life and urban life, for example, each generate many combinations of quite different skills and interests and, although occurring in patterns affecting clusters of individuals, the number of combinations is practically limitless.

Each of the three major categories of concept systems is necessarily represented for every individual in some combination of subtypes at some combination of levels of complexity. Knowledge (both formal and informational), codes (at least minimal language and perceptual motor processing), and problem-solving strategies (at some speed, with some degree of focus, memory, and motivation) must all be engaged in some manner for mental processing and action to occur at all. The only question is at what level of skill complexity (skill in drawing, for example, or judgment of painting, from scribbling to Picasso) and what subtype combinations get developed (olfactory and gustatory rules for gourmet cooking, say, versus visual form and color taste for fashion design). This engagement of subtypes is chiefly responsible for the great range of possible combinations of competencies. Human tasks and activities do not draw neatly on this or that perceptual motor mode, domain of knowledge, and style of solving problems. Playing a musical instrument for example, depends on knowledge of a musical code, but it may vary from the limited scale of a simple folk flute, using only the autitory mode, to the classical Western scale of the violin, using complex musical notation as well. The demands of simple flutes, violins, and other instruments for other subskills, such as breath control and finger dexterity, each with its own rules to be mastered, also vary enormously. Operating lathes, acting in plays, performing office work, and running the mile similarly encompass many different combinations of skill subtypes.

Variations in skill combinations are multiplied further because there are alternative routes to competence in the same domain or even task. No two tennis players or golfers employ quite the same stroke patterns or playing strategies; the former sometimes using hard straight strokes and sometimes using subtle curve-ball techniques, the latter varying from high to low in their putting to fairway control ratio. Writers vary markedly in their reliance on composing drafts mentally, Ernest Hemingway reputedly having written as many as seventy drafts for a single chapter whereas Katherine Mansfield recorded her stories essentially in a single draft, writing it down only after composing it all in her head.

Development is viewed as the broad, large-scale changes that result from many small acquisitions of concepts that accumulate in the day-to-day tasks of learning and problem solving. Learning and problem solving both concern the mental manipulation of rules about concepts experimenting with alternative means to attain goals. They differ only in that learning involves coming to terms with novel rules. Cognitive development is a process of acquiring hierarchies of concepts and rules in various combinations of skill types and domains through daily experience. Experience comes in spurts and combinations, different periods of the daily and even yearly cycle being devoted to different tasks. There is, however, a certain consistency of repetition and commonality among members of the same culture and family in folk societies, or the same family, subculture, class, occupation, and school in industrial societies. The years of early life are usually characterized for everyone in all cultures by repeated daily exposure to stimulation in basic skills, the sensorimotor and language codes, the formal Piagetian knowledge concepts, and the elementary content categories of the community (body parts and functions, clothes, household arrangements) and the basics of problem solving and coping in daily tasks. This commonality transcending culture leads to a certain universal minimal level in basic skill acquisition, though problems of poverty, neglect, child abuse, and the like in large-scale societies appear to depress skill levels at the lower range much below the levels found in the traditional, well-regulated folk community (Fowler and Fowler 1978). At the other end of the scale, exceptionally facilitative early cognitive stimulation in selected middle-class and occasional working-class families appears to inflate mastery levels in various areas much above these universal minimal levels (Fowler 1981b).

Although skills are acquired in many combinations, generalization and transfer occur across skill categories, leading to a certain degree of hierarchical organization of skills across common domains and types. Transfer occurs more or less in proportion to the similarity of skills to one another. Ball handling is a skill common to many sports, for example. There are many basic skills of this type, such as language, arithmetic calculation, measurement, reading, and the basic formal concepts like casuality, conservation, classification, and seriation, that serve as modules laying the groundwork for facilitating skill acquisition in numerous complex competencies and tasks. The elemental rules for employing the body are the indispensable modular foundations for acquiring an infinite variety of competence hierarchies.

Learning and development follow a certain sequence, as Piaget's extensively confirmed observations on the stages of acquiring basic formal concepts have made researchers and educators acutely aware. But the order is not limited to formal concepts nor characterized solely by cognitive transformations in stages. Many component acquisitions lead to each of the broad transformations in Piaget's developmental scheme, from preoperational to concrete operational status, for example (Furby 1972), and probably throughout the entire developmental cycle (Case 1981; Case and Khanna 1981). The process may not occur in broad stages or in stages of any kind (Brainerd 1977; Siegel and Brainerd 1978), or else stages may be limited to developmental transitions within particular concept domains (Feldman 1980;

Fowler 1981b). The cross-cultural research on Piagetian concepts itself points to how component skills may vary in alternative concept hierarchies (Dasen 1972). Learning may be defined as a process of becoming familiar with many small elements of a task or concept, which leads to a generalization, or the apprehension of a concept, of which the elements are exemplars. These elements are, for example, the critical defining rules or features of pants (two leg holes, trunk hole, top and bottom), which, along with those of other items of clothing, become the critical rule features defining clothes, building up a hierarchy of knowledge that becomes interwoven with even larger and more complex hierarchies of weather, fashion, class, culture, and history. Learning combines and alternates between both incremental learning of elements and transformations, in which elements are interrelated to be grasped as concepts, and, at more complex levels, integrated into hierarchies and concept systems. These are the broad transformations we identify as cognitive development, in which several skill subsets are synthesized to form novel hierarchies, such as reading fluently, mastering multiplication, mastering dressing skills or table manners, and in the Piagetian realm, classifying, seriating, and conserving at a concrete-operational level.

The process does not necessarily follow a single course from elements to concept, but interweaves within and among concepts and elements, working down as well as up the hierarchies. For example, the child over the same time period may concurrently be differentiating items of clothing as both exemplars of clothes and types of clothes, with their own exemplars and feature distinctions, feature rules being gradually sorted out in both directions. Learning takes place concurrently in multiple domains and skill processes, leading to broad syntheses across various categories, as when the inferences that have been progressing in clothes, dishes, furniture, food, and family activities come together to form the social hierarchy of family and home. Again, in the Piagetian realm, the constancies observed in how superficial changes occur in form and position of objects finally leads to the cognitive integration of conservation regardless of object, shape, or arrangement.

As rules and skills become thoroughly mastered through familiarity and repeated use, they take on a life of their own, becoming habitual. Once they have what Allport (1937) termed functional autonomy, the new concepts and skills can be drawn on without serious effort or thought. Much of the permanence of skills must be attributed to their continued, selective use as modular components of the many tasks encountered in occupations and other activities of daily life. These are the basic sensorimotor and language codes, the common cultural repertoire of knowledge, and the well-honed strategies of analyzing and interrelating problem elements in familiar domains of daily life. Once this stage of automaticity is attained, as it is characteristically for many tasks of daily living, the active or conscious cognitive grappling with problems diminishes in intensity and scope. Cognitive awareness recedes to the periphery as we carry out the familiar activity of driving a car, dressing, or drawing on our common vocabulary and grammar to converse or compose a routine letter. Only in the face of a novel demand, a gap in the individual's skill repertoire, is cognition brought into play at higher levels to search for a substitute, a less-familiar concept, or an alternative arrangement of the problem elements.

Analysis of the Effects of Early Stimulation on Development

Tables 5-2 and 5-3 present a model for the analysis of relations between variables of early cognitive stimulation and varieties of developmental effects,

Table 5-2
Hypothetical Dimensions of Early Cognitive Stimulation

Dimensions of Stimulation	Knowledge		Codes			Strategies /Styles (see table 5-1)
	Formal	Content	Perceptual	Motor	Symbolic	
Primary variables[a]						
Earliness (age)						
Duration (including long term)						
Intensity/frequency						
Secondary variables						
Cognitive breadth (molar-molecular)[a]						
Sequencing/matching[a]						
Interaction[b]						
Diagnosis/monitoring[a,b]						
Cumulative review[a]						
Ecological framework (milieu)[a] (consonant-dissonant; short and long term)						
Socioeconomic						
Intellectual (value) ambiance-interests						
Emotional climate/conflict						
Motivating techniques (social relations and dramatic play)[b]						
Inquiry/problem oriented (versus rote/fact accumulation)[b]						
Special handicaps-advantages (genetic/injury)						
Child						
Teacher						

[a]Developmental considerations (strategies).

[b]Situational factors (tactics).

Table 5-3

Illustrative Measures of the Effects of Different Types of Early Stimulation on Cognitive Competence over Early and Later Periods of Development

	Early Development		Later Development	
	Short Term	Early Childhood	Childhood	Adulthood
Knowledge[a]				
Complexity				
Quantity				
Variety				
Depth				
Originality				
Code use[a]				
Complexity				
Breadth				
Frequency/proportion				
Flexibility				
Strategy/style use[a]				
Efficiency				
Intensity				
Breadth				
Frequency/proportion				
Autonomy (self-propelled)				
Creativity				

[a]See table 5-1 for the types of knowledge, codes, and strategies to which the different developmental effects can be applied.

from the most immediate to those traceable as far as adult life. Potential stimulation variables are presented down the leftmost column of table 5-2 and various cognitive abilities or competencies across the top row, since dimensions will be explored (as the evidence permits) in terms of the areas or types of stimulation employed. Some of the developmental effects that might be considered significant for cognitive development, from various types of early stimulation, are listed in the leftmost column of table 5-3. These could be assessed in terms of their impact on development at four (or even more) periods of development, as indicated in the column headings, namely, the most immediate or short-term effects, lasting not more than a few weeks; those prolonged or delayed effects that continue to be found throughout early childhood, perhaps to school age; the developmental effects that persist throughout childhood into adolescence, producing continuing influences on development; and, finally, any characteristics or attainments in adult life that are empirically traceable to early experience, as distinguished from later, intervening experiences.

Many of the dimensions tend to be confounded in most studies, and various subtypes of competence, even one of the three major categories, in particular, studies attempting to facilitate the development of cognitive strategies, are poorly represented in the literature. For this reason most of the discussion here concentrates on the three designated primary variables of stimulation, with much the greater portion devoted to the effects of earliness (the next two chaps) paying some attention to age, distinguishing between immediate and long-term effects, and making an attempt in chapter 7 to group studies in terms of different types of competence, as outlined in tables 5-1 and 5-2. Chapter 8 extends the discussion to the other two primary variables (duration and intensity) and selected secondary variables, in the same manner but in greatly condensed form. The dearth of studies specifically addressed to any stimulation variables beyond earliness (and rarely age specifically) will largely restrict the effort to probing existing early-learning literature for signs of potential importance of other variables. All variables will be analyzed within the framework of how they interact with early stimulation. Since few investigations are likely to label or conceptualize developmental effects in the same form as presented in table 5-3, the terms employed will generally follow each investigator's usage.

Certain questions should be borne in mind. Among the most important is whether earliness itself is critical or at least advantageous for the generation of competence, especially with regard to the persistence of effects during later development. The question of earliness can be cast in a strong or a weak form. A positive answer to the weaker or more general form would indicate that on the whole advantages accrue from stimulating children earlier rather than later in development, but no exact age is associated with this advantage or critical period beyond which stimulation produces qualitatively less potent effects, as long as the process occurs sometime during the first years of development. In the strong form the potency of earliness would be identified with a definite early age range, a critical, or at the least a sensitive period during which the neurophysiological properties associated with growth would be peculiarly responsive to stimulation, and after which stimulation would be substantially less efficacious in generating learning. Alternatively, the strong form could imply the earlier the beginning, the more powerful the potency of early stimulation.

This issue has been framed historically in terms of whether early development may be a critical period for skill development, beyond which mastery cannot be attained at the same levels, whether it may be merely an optimal period, or whether competencies of the same magnitude can be attained regardless of the developmental period in which relevant stimulation occurs (Caldwell 1962; Dennenberg and Bell 1960; Hebb 1949; King 1958; Orlansky 1949; Scott 1968; Thompson 1955). In the first case biological programming and developmental readiness are necessarily primary, unless the nature of learning itself is somehow so complex that an early start is essential to allow for prolonged duration needed to attain competence. The latter concept fits more closely with the notion of optimal period, however, since variations of even four or five years at either end of the formative developmental cycle alone (which lasts twenty to twenty-five years, more or less) amount to no more than 15 to 25 percent, not likely to make a critical difference and easily made up by a slight prolongation past the normative period. Even then, the concept of optimal period comes into question, since duration alone does not encompass the issue of special properties or circumstances of early development having implications for mastery. There is no escaping the need to identify features of learning processes or circumstances surrounding the period of early learning that uniquely facilitate competence development if the concepts of either critical or optimal period are to remain tenable. If the former, then biological bases must be presumed, reflected in the kinds of neurological changes in brain structures that have been associated with stimulation, but not yet conclusively demonstated to be the more potent for early than for later stimulation even in animals (Uphouse 1980; Walsh 1981). If the latter, then characteristics of the first stages of learning itself, or of social conditions singularly favorable to inducing competence when stimulation is supplied early in life, or both must be implicated. Assuming social conditions as the major factor, however, implies that early cognitive stimulation no longer holds singular importance; favorable conditions for later developmental stimulation could be expected to compensate for the failure to experience optimal or quality stimulation early in life—as the reviews of Clarke and Clarke (1976), Brim and Kagan (1980), and others claim to show.

Our dimensional review is expected to indicate that the equation is more complex than the reviews on deprivation and recovery suggest. Thus included as primary variables are the duration and intensity of early stimulation, which, combined with earliness, may demonstrate what earlier analyses and isolated studies, focusing mainly on age period alone, occasionally linked with duration, have failed to reveal. This combination of dimensions that have been earlier conceptualized mainly for the field of animal development (King 1958; Thompson 1955) should enable us to explore a second important question about early experience, a question that is really a matter of focusing in depth on the question of earliness.

Is there a critical or optimal amount of early cognitive stimulation needed to form a critical ability mass, a special foundation, a specially efficient or more highly motivated cognitive system for learning and problem solving that greatly facilitates competence development at later periods of development? The kind of self-propelled, intensely motivated learning behavior, cognitive autonomy, and creative project activity emerging very early in highly competent children, which has historically been attributed almost exclusively to genetic giftedness, may to an essential degree be a function of unusual early stimulation as well, as certain extensive case-study analyses have suggested (Fowler 1981b; Feldman 1980). Perhaps it is the implantation of high motivations and intense interest patterns alone that are the outcomes of advantageous early stimulation, varying with the types of competence stimulated. Such a distinction would become evident if studies are found that show, for example, persistence of effects only in cases where high motivation accompanies complexity, or in the less likely instances of early high motivation, without notable early skill complexity, that leads to later high competence.

Scott (1968) on the other hand has formulated the question in more general terms as inherent in the very nature of the development of behavioral systems. Earliness is primary because the first behavioral systems are established that determine the direction in which later learning will follow. Learning does not occur at random but becomes organized into systems, rooted in physiological processes, that establish a commitment of the organism to proceed in the same direction. Integral to this concept of organizing systems is a self-limiting process, since once organized they become increasingly difficult to replace or alter. Although resembling Piaget's progression through assimilation and accommodation except for the behavioral in place of the cognitive locus of organization, Scott's concepts are more open ended in terms of the directions development can take than Piaget's biologically based sequence of developmental stages. It thus makes more of a difference *which* behavioral systems get organized early in life. This is essentially a foundation theory of development, in which earliness becomes the primary dimension. In any case exploring developmental effects in terms of the efficiency, creativity, and motivation in cognitive processing, and the extent of self-directed cognitive activity, should furnish evidence bearing on this question of the nature of the concept systems generated by early stimulation.

The distinction between primary and secondary variables of stimulation (table 5-2) is fairly arbitrary, resting simply on the notion of trying to isolate major factors that may emerge from the sparse literature available. It is quite likely that various other, secondary factors may well prove significant in inducing complex competence early in development and especially an efficient, self-directed learning system. There is evidence that such variables as maintaining a cognitive-inquiry orientation and interacting with the child rather than directing him may contribute to the development of cognitive complexity, creativity, and independent knowledge seeking (Fowler 1981b; Sigel 1982). Unfortunately, we have hardly reached the stage where research has begun to sort out the developmental effects of variation among the primary variables, let alone meet the intricate control demands for answering questions on the myriad of secondary dimensions. This discussion on the latter is likely to be quite preliminary, exploring a few of the incipient trends that will probably reflect combinations of stimulus dimensions.

The question of cumulative effects of learning on development, which is linked closely to duration, is more complex. What may matter most is not an early start but simply the opportunity, time, and effort available to accumulate concepts and skills in order to acquire depth and scope in any complex field of knowledge. In this case earliness, duration, efficiency of stimulation and other factors all play no more than marginal or secondary roles in a complex equation of developmental learning processes. The nature of the current and subsequent intervening ecological framework and emotional and stimulating support systems bear importantly on this question of cumulative effects. We need studies varying earliness alone, keeping other facilitative factors of stimulation and ecology equal, in order to sort out the differential effects of earliness and cumulative learning. Some of these distinctions appear to group themselves between developmental and situational factors, as noted in table 5-2. (A further discussion of these problems will be found in the first chapter of volume II.)

Many other questions guide or are likely to emerge from the multidimensional nature of this review, questions like the age-old issue of whether intensive early cognitive stimulation is hurtful or helpful to the child's emotional development and social competence, and of course many questions concerning the effects of employing different strategies and methods. Given the limited literature deliberately addressed to them, our evidence is for the most part more likely to raise questions for future research to probe than it is to furnish answers. The comprehensiveness of the structural analysis of dimensions, the varieties of competence, and the variations in developmental effects should permit us to test the usefulness of the analytic framework, however, and perhaps yield selected substantive information as well as disclose the limitations and problems of research to date.

The Effects of Earliness and Age: General Cognitive-Stimulation Programs

Much research on earliness was begun in response to a social need or to evaluate an educational system. The pre-World War II studies on whether nursery-school attendance advances intellectual development were clearly designed to answer both questions. So too were the early-intervention studies on disadvantaged children in the 1960s, which were concerned with redressing a social problem, the school-learning failures of millions of poor children, but were also designed to evaluate a general strategy of compensatory education, providing a head start to children early in life, an improved cognitive foundation with which to perform better in later school learning. They have also compared the value of group (center-based) programs and home programs. Regardless of their purpose, we may ask whether any of these studies furnish information on the value of early stimulation to development. It would not be the first time research designed for one set of purposes yields information serendipitously on another set of questions.

Studies of Nursery-School Attendance

It is clear from the review of nursery-school studies in chapter 4 that little can be said about the advantages of earliness of stimulation as practiced in the nursery school, stated in either its strong or its weak form. Even overlooking the supposed methodological flaws of the various studies, mean IQ gains for middle-class samples were minimal (averaging around 5 IQ points across many studies), except on the Merrill-Palmer scale (whose sensorimotor tasks resembled the nursery-school curriculum more closely) where mean gains across seven groups averaged 14.5 IQ points, compared to 6.7 points for controls (Wellman 1945). Even the best-controlled nursery-school studies, with disadvantaged, institutionalized orphans, produced no gains for experimental children, while controls, who remained institutionalized, declined by 16.2 mean points (Skeels et al. 1938; Wellman and Pegram 1944; Wellman, Skeels, and Skodak 1940), or again, mean gains of 14.9 points, compared to 5.1 points for controls, on the sensorimotor-oriented Merrill-Palmer scales (Barrett and Koch 1930).

On the criterion of complexity of attainment then (compared to norms), the nursery-school programs did not improve even the short-term functioning of middle-class children much if at all beyond the norms of their own advantaged population group, whose experiences in the home were already similar in the quality of cognitive stimulation experienced, except on sensorimotor types of tasks. Studies of orphanage children from less-stimulating institutional backgrounds, however, did indicate that nursery-school programs would at least prevent further IQ score declines and might even produce gains over population norms on performance tasks.

Among the few investigations of long-term developmental effects only a single study (Kounin 1939) on middle-class children suggested some persistence of effects, this in the form of significantly higher school grades than nonnursery-school-attending controls in third and fourth grade but only with very small samples ($N = 10$ and $N = 8$, respectively). No follow-up studies on deprived children are reported, leaving untouched the vital question of what effects enriched early cognitive stimulation may have on the later competencies of children who are returned to an institutional ecology that fosters quite different competencies.

Underlying the limited results with such studies has been the diffuse nature of nursery-school programs, whose content appears to have been more directed toward socioemotional development, play, and sensorimotor skills than the type of verbal-logical, abstract skills characteristic of most general IQ measures, the measures overwhelmingly employed to assess outcomes. Thus IQ gains have generally appeared primarily where sensorimotor performance measures were employed, or mainly with children from institutionalized backgrounds, who are deprived relative to controls, given the close parallel between nursery-school and home experiences for middle-class children. Neither programs nor measures have been either well defined or focused on specific competencies. Aside from the broad assessments in terms of general and performance IQ tests, the only other criteria of developmental competence explored in a few studies have been socioemotional adjustment or competence and motor skills, in neither of which have nursery-school attendees been found to be consistently superior to non-attending children (Swift 1964). Since nursery-school studies have been almost entirely confined to children between 3 and 5 years of age, the findings are at best concerned with the effects of stimulation introduced after a few years of culturally normative middle-class stimulation or culturally deviant forms in an institutional environment.

Effects of Day Care

Investigators of the effects of day care on cognitive development are a comparatively recent enterprise. Although the care of young children outside the home has a long history, most of the care in group settings has been designed for educational purposes or has involved the placement of children under the care of neighbors, relatives, or untrained commercial operators (Low and Spindler 1968). Day care in group settings began in the United States as early as 1854 in New York, for poor children. While it was extended temporarily during the Civil War as a means of aiding war widows, and again after the Great Depression through the government programs, its first big boost came during World War II, spurred by patriotism and the need for women workers in the factories (Braun and Edwards 1972; Lazar and Rosenberg 1970; Rudermen 1968). Group day care did not die out in the ensuing years, but it waned tremendously under the postwar shift of opinion that discouraged mothers of young children from working, and very little research on what was formerly called the "day nursery" was carried out (Swift 1964), until the recent revival of day care in the 1960s with the growth of the women's liberation movement (Etaugh 1980; Fein and Clarke-Stewart 1973) and the return of women to the workplace.

There is no difference in principle between the curriculum of day care and that of the traditional nursery school (Swift 1964), despite the fact that the former became established under the aegis of the child-welfare movement and the latter in the course of the establishment of the fields of child development and education. Welfare concerns were very much involved in the founding of the first nursery schools in Britain, shortly after the turn of the century (Raymont 1937; Braun and Edward 1972). Regardless of the origin of sponsorship, the same general developmental philosophy and concepts traceable to Rousseau of internally governed development of the child as a whole in wholesome socioemotional relations and extensive opportunities for sensorimotor and sociodramatic play have guided the structure and techniques of both the nursery school and day care. Since development has been viewed largely as emanating from within, the child's own experimentations with materials and initiatives in informal interactions with adults and peers have been assigned first place at the expense of planned programs to stimulate language and other features of cognitive stimulation from exogenous sources.

A certain amount of research has nevertheless grown up with the spread of group and family-day-care systems in the 1960s, aided by government subsidy from the municipal to the national levels. A great deal of this research has taken the form of the evaluation of effects on development of special programs devised by research investigators (Belsky and Steinberg 1978; Etaugh 1980). In line with the newly founded emphasis on cognitive processes and early stimulation of the time (Hunt 1961; Fowler 1962a), these programs have varied from the developmental, laissez-faire emphasis of the traditional practice in child care and early education, adopting the framework of planned, externally regulated cognitive stimulation of the Head Start and early-intervention movement with the disadvantaged, of which indeed the specialized research centers have formed an integral part

(Belsky and Steinberg 1978; Etaugh 1980). This literature will be reviewed in detail and the limitations of the type of research with respect to furnishing understanding of the potentials of early experience on development will be discussed in the sections to follow. Since the programs and evaluation techniques are much the same, whether the programs are traveling under the label of day care or early education, no further general distinction between them will be made.

A few projects have been designed to evaluate the effects on infant and child development in day-care centers, both group or center-based and family-operated in the home, some community operated and municipally regulated (Belsky and Steinberg 1978; Etaugh 1980). The curricula of these programs more nearly resemble that of traditional nursery and day-care practice, geared to providing care and a good play environment above all. While undoubtedly influenced by the cognitive stimulation concerns of the period, including what were believed to be the implications of early intellectual experience for later development, for the most part, traditional practice and simply maintaining a going concern of child care on practical grounds have been the chief guides to practice. This day-to-day practical need, away from the distilled intellectual focus of the university and the research community, combined with the child-care, socioemotional, and play orientation, is probably why the developmental outcomes found in these programs are if anything smaller than those reported so often in the research on educational attendance in the 1920s to 1940s (Belsky and Steinberg 1978; Etaugh 1980). Nearly all of the earlier research was conducted in university-run nursery schools, a great deal of it on middle-class and upper middle-class populations (Anastasi and Foley 1949; Swift 1964), with occasionally special projects for lower class or poor children from what were then called underprivileged backgrounds or institutional environments. Most of the day-care research has been focused on the development of infants who have been brought into group and family-day-care systems in numbers as the number of mothers working outside the home has increased (Golden et al. 1978). Thus the possibly small cognitive (IQ) gains observed with middle-class children and the somewhat larger gains with children from less-advantaged backgrounds, compared with no change and sometimes mean declines for largely lower class and poor infants in the contemporary, community-operated centers (Belsky and Steinberg 1978; Etaugh 1980), must be seen in the context of these program and population differences.

In the most extensive recent investigation on infant day care, Golden and his associates (1978), studied the development of several hundred infants in eleven group and twenty family programs in New York City between the ages of 6, 12, 18, and 36 months of age. The study included both cross-sectional and longitudinal components. Approximately 90 percent of the families were black or Hispanic and 90 percent were from the two lowest classes on Hollingshead's indices of socioeconomic status, including 16 percent welfare families. Using the Bayley Mental Scales and later the Stanford-Binet and Peabody Picture Vocabulary Test at the oldest age, there were no mean score differences between the longitudinal groups through 18 months, but mean differences significantly favoring the group-care children appeared on the Stanford-Binet by 36 months. What the study seems to show is that group-care programs, which have somewhat more professional, planned input than family-day-care programs, prevented the usual marked intellectual decline of poor children (Wachs, Uzgiris, and Hunt 1971) in terms of the type of verbal-logical skills measured by IQ tests but did not stimulate cognitive development of this type above the norms for the general population. Children from both samples had fared reasonably well until 18 months, though the family-day-care sample had declined more than the group-care sample. As may be seen in table 6-1, children in both groups actually declined from their initial mean levels (between 2 and 21 months of age on entering programs) over the course of the entire experience, those in family day care than the group-care sample, the latter remaining just about the general population mean, while the former fell considerably below. Mean scores on the Peabody, which is particularly focused on receptive language, are even lower for both groups at 36 months (81.1 and 75.7, respectively). No follow-up study on this or any other similar study is available.

It seems evident from this and other studies that ordinary day care, whether group or home based, as presently constituted at best prevents the cognitive decline in abstract skills typically found in children from the poor folk communities of different minorities. It does not, however, transcend their backgrounds enough to generate cognitive skill development in these academically oriented directions above the general norms. Like the nursery programs of the past, the type of care and stimulation offered appears to be doing many healthy things for children's socioemotional development, but in the cognitive sphere the goals of the program are neither closely allied with the nature of the measures employed nor particularly stimulating for

Table 6-1
Mean Mental Test Scores of Group-Care and Family-day-care Infants at Three Age Periods[a]

| | Bayley Mental Scales | | Stanford-Binet |
Type of Day Care	Initial Scores	18 Months	36 Months
Group care	108.5	100.4	91.1
Family day care	112.5	98.0	92.0

[a]Ns range from 68 to 133 in the two groups at different ages.

the development of verbal-logical skills. Little information is added on the potentials of early stimulation to influence development.

Compensatory and Preventive Education: Early Intervention Among Impoverished Folk Groups

Considering the volume of research on early intervention since the first wave of programmatic studies centering on nursery-school education died out with World War II, it is surprising how little we know about the significance of early experience to development. Certainly the chief source of difficulty is that research addressed to a social need, now as then, has a way of skirting many of the main questions. The vast bulk of research has been conducted on special populations, various constituencies of young children from the poorest and least-educated strata of society, white, black, Spanish-speaking, Native American, and other minorities. Stimulation programs almost without exception have been compensatory or preventive care and education programs of one sort or another. They have been concerned with providing stimulation believed lacking in the homes and communities of the target population, either because of a general cognitive developmental deprivation (deficit rationale) or because cultural and community lifestyles emphasize different competencies (difference rationale) (Horowitz and Paden 1973). Either way, the aims are to facilitate competencies needed for later successful school learning and social adaptation to the mainstream verbal and abstract cultural modes of industrial society. Only secondarily have projects been concerned with analyzing patterns of early cognitive stimulation in relation to development from a theoretical point of view.

Had more been known about the nature of early cognitive stimulation and development the 1960s intervention studies might have been designed somewhat differently. Their programs and measures took off where the strategies employed for the nursery-school attendance studies of prior generations had left off, and both were highly generalized (Hunt 1975; Zimiles 1970). Programs first followed traditional nursery-school practices, particularly in the first Head Start programs, and measures consisted primarily of IQ tests. While the experimental research programs soon began to experiment with a variety of different concept-learning, problem-solving, and language-oriented activities, and to supplement IQ measurement with various concept inventories, language measures like the Illinois Test of Psycholinguistic Abilities, and other specially devised research measures, the stress continued to be placed on IQ measures because of their norm-referenced properties, which were widely accepted as assuring promise for success in academic learning. Unfortunately this direction also obscured analysis of just what aspects of stimulation were producing what effects on the individual child's learning and development. Programs tended to remain addressed to a broad spectrum of concept and language skills that generated mean gains in IQ scores for the group, and insufficient attention was paid to the cognitive progress in depth of the individual learner.

Probably most important, program designers were ignorant of differences in cultural patterns and ecology, and the role they might play in the children's assimilating and maintaining the competencies stressed in early-stimulation programs (Bronfenbrenner 1975, 1977, 1981; Zigler and Valentine 1979). Much discussion ensued about the need for increased stimulation among children from these disadvantaged backgrounds, though studies began to show that high levels of strident, diffuse forms of stimulation might be more of a hindrance than a help to development (Wachs, Uzgiris, and Hunt 1971). The need seemed rather to be for diminished general sensory stimulation and more directed, specific forms of cognitive stimulation. More than this, the debilitating conditions of poverty and poor job perspectives undermined family and community life, producing widespread malnutrition, family conflict, despair, child neglect, and a developmental orientation toward a street community culture that failed to support and often worked actively against the cognitive patterns, motivations, and value structure of the establishment emphasized in early-intervention programs (Horowitz and Paden 1973; Hunt 1975; Ogpu 1981). Cultural folk traditions further stressed the functional uses of language and concepts in the context of everyday activities, not the abstract comparisons and manipulations demanded of school life and skilled occupations.

Critics of early intervention laid the problem of cognitive disadvantage or difference at the door of institutional constraints and economic class and racial barriers that trapped entire communities and cultural groups in poverty and social discrimination. They asserted that compensatory education falsely placed the blame on the individual, family, and local community and could not work until these institutional arrangements were restructured (Baratz and Baratz 1970; Bowles and Gintis 1976; Gross and Gross 1969; Ryan 1971; Stipeck, Valentine, and Zigler 1979). In an effort to address such problems at least partially various projects incorporated parent guidance to educate parents in child care and stimulation techniques consonant with the cognitive and social goals of the intervention. Follow-up programs of different sorts were introduced, including a national follow-through program to bolster family life and lend continuing support to the children over later periods of development (Hunt 1975; Zigler and Valentine 1979).

However effective or limited these various supplementary efforts might be in certain cases, it is clear that, from the point of view of research on questions of the effects of early experience, the basic design of virtually all early-intervention programs on socioeconomically disadvantaged children really embraced two curricula. There were essentially two different forms of developmental stimulation: (1) the stated cognitive-stimulation goals toward cognitive abstraction of the intervention programs and (2) the traditional folk modes of socialization toward concrete community adaptation of the different cultural minorities and poor whites. The root problem was not simply the question of difference, but, rather, that the two modes of stimulation were at variance with each other and that the folk modes themselves operate at a high social cost, undermined by institutional barriers, poverty, and the attendant problems of malnutrition, conflict, and hopelessness that make socialization among the poor a difficult enterprise of adaptation at best.

In reviewing the investigations on early intervention, then, we must keep in mind this basic conflict between curricula and the sharp variance between formal program modes and the ecological context of poverty and the folk community. Stimulation programs that begin typically at ages 3-5, working with strategies of planned instruction directed at cognitive abstractions in a general way, *against* the intuitive curricula of the poor folk community, make poor tests of the role of early stimulation. They were dissonant with what transpired in the home and community before, during, and after the year or two of formal stimulation and can only be considered as a test of an extremely strong version of the earliness hypothesis.

Short-term Effects

General Programs. The questions remain how much of an impact a comparatively evanescent experience makes on development and how long it will endure. The answers to both these questions are by now well documented. Nothwithstanding the apparent odds against impact, the average cognitive short-term or immediate change from the better controlled, research-engineered early-intervention programs, measured by IQ tests (mostly Stanford-Binet), has been typically on the order of 5 to 20 points, surprisingly (Bronfenbrenner 1975; Ryan 1974). Three-year-olds in at least one program (Bereiter-Engelmann) gained as much as 30 IQ points (Hunt 1975; Weikart 1969; White et al. 1973). As research efforts multiplied, a wide variety of additional measures were employed that indicated children from these special populations responded favorably to stimulation in ways that any population of children might respond, though at reduced levels, effects varying to some degree according to the type of abilities and processes emphasized in the programs (Beller 1973; Miezitis 1971; Miller and Dyer 1975; Ryan 1974; White et al. 1973).

Looking at developmental effects in terms of the pattern outlined in table 5-3, including both IQ and other types of measures, children in these programs attained complexity levels generally approaching population norms, but seldom above. Thus mean IQ changes generally moved from around 80-90 IQ up to 90-100 IQ, but only occasionally to 110 IQ or more (Bronfenbrenner 1975; Hunt 1975; Ryan 1974; White et al. 1973). In other domains children generally made equivalent gains in a variety of language and other school-related concept skills, the greatest gains in IQ and other measures appearing in the programs that stressed verbal-abstract skills the most (Bronfenbrenner 1975; Hunt 1975; Meizitis 1971; Miller and Dyer 1975; White et al. 1973), as indicated for example by the outstanding 30-point IQ gains to a mean IQ of 121 in a Bereiter-Engelmann program.

Stimulation programs that defined more specialized emphases generally produced comparatively stronger developmental effects on competencies in the stressed areas (Hunt 1975; Miezitis 1971; Miller and Dyer 1975; White et al. 1973). In this way Piaget-type programs such as one by Honig and Brill (1970; Starr 1971), advanced infant development in Piagetian skills over controls, and significantly only in skills most emphasized in the program, namely means-end relations and object permanence. Programs focusing on motivations for concept learning, such as the Darcee program, produced their strongest effects on motivations and attitudes toward learning (Miller and Dyer 1975). Traditional nursery-school and Montessori programs, both of which encourage open-ended, exploratory activity, were found to develop children scoring relatively higher on curiosity (Miller and Dyer 1975), though results were not always consistent. Both Montessori and the relatively structured teacher-directed Darcee program produced higher levels of inventiveness than either the more open-ended traditional or the structured Bereiter-Engelmann programs. On the other hand, traditional, open-ended nursery-school play practices, which Montessori programs lack, have proved to generate more creative behavior in children than Montessori in other comparisons (Beller 1973).

Despite such differences the character of recent early-intervention programs has been broad-gaged and oriented toward a mix of academic verbal-numerical concept skills. Children in almost all programs gain *generally*, to different degrees, despite some of their special emphases (Miller and Dyer 1975). Thus Ramey and Haskins (1981), for example, reported cognitive gains in all of the McCarthy subscales (verbal, perceptual performance, quantitative, memory—verbal and numerical) from their generalized program except motor skills.

In line with the problem of the dual curriculum, for the most part, neither the general IQ and related cognitive gains nor the gains in specialized competencies reported from time to time have reached even the average levels of the U.S. population at large. Competence development is ordinarily reported in terms of comparisons with experimental controls from the same disadvantaged populations who are functioning at below-average levels, rather than with reference to general norms. Although mean posttest levels, which usually range between 90 and 100 IQ, characteristically encompass cases of 100 to 110 IQ and sometimes higher, this distribution does not begin to match the pattern frequently attained by socioeconomically and educationally advantaged children whose mean levels often reach 120 IQ or more and typically embrace cases ranging from 130 to 140 IQ and higher. Taken in this context, therefore, we much conclude that, overall, the short-term effects of planned early developmental stimulation are heavily diluted by competing or contradictory forms of cognitive stimulation, thus failing to produce competencies above population norms in any of the verbal-abstract domains under scrutiny. What the gains might be in stimulation programs centering on skills consonant with the milieu of the special populations is a matter for speculation. No programs of this nature have been located and are unlikely to enjoy wide currency because of their functional dissonance with the ecology of the mainstream culture.

Specific Age Effects. The question whether certain early-stimulation strategies on special disadvantaged populations, such as studies varying the age of intervention and the scope and intensity of stimulation, may have produced more favorable effects is difficult to answer. The difficulty is that age of intervention is often confounded with other variables, such as type, intensity, and scope of program, as well as duration of treatment. The few programs that have varied age of intervention alone have usually reported small and inconsistent differences in IQ levels and related language and cognitive measures (Beller 1979; White et al. 1973). Gordon's group (Gordon, Guinagh, and Jester 1977; Guinagh, Olmstead, and Gordon 1975) found mean differences between infants stimulated through parent home training from 3 to 12 months and 12 to 24 months ranging from 0 to 11 mean IQ points (Bayley-Binet scales) annually between 2 and 6 years. Although differences generally favored the first-year group, they were seldom significant, and reversals occurred (Gordon 1973). The more equivalent comparison, measuring the first-year group at 12 months and the second-year group at age 24 months (though 9-months versus 12-months duration for the two groups) employed different mental scales (Griffiths at 12 months), but in any case the mean difference compared with controls was only 4 GQ points (IQ equivalent), against a 2-point mean difference over controls on the Bayley for the second-year group (Gordon 1969; Starr 1971).

Levenstein (1970, 1977; Bronfenbrenner 1975) found 10- to 20-point mean IQ gains for different samples of 2- and 3-year olds in her parent home tutoring projects. Gains varied more or less inversely with differences between initial IQ levels and all groups ended the first program year at close to the same level, around 100 to 105 IQ. Moreover, mean differences were not significant at the end of the respective third- and fourth-year testings. Similarly, Caldwell (1970; Beller 1979) reports a small difference in mean gains of 14 and 18 IQ points respectively, for children enrolling in her specialized, cognitively oriented day-care program between 12 and 24 months ($N = 86$) and children enrolling after age 3 years ($N = 22$). Measures were administered after 2 and 1½ years in the program for the respective age groups, but there was no relationship between intervention age and IQ gains.

In the same replication of the Bereiter-Engelmann program that resulted in 30-point IQ gains on the Binet for 3-year-olds over the course of a year, children starting at age 4 gained only 20 points. Both age groups started at 80 IQ (Hunt 1975; Weikart 1969). On the other hand Weikart's (1967) first two experimental groups, one starting at age 4, the second at age 3, gained about the same amount over one year (13 and 12 points, respectively), but the third group, starting at age 3, gained 20 points. Klaus and Gray (1968) found that children entering their program at age 3 gained 14 IQ points during the first year, compared to gains of only 3 points for children entering at age 4. Significance values for either of these comparisons are not reported, however, and Klaus and Gray's younger group started the program 7 points below the older group (88 to 95), probably in part because of the effects of repeated testing of the older group in their earlier role as controls for the younger group between the ages of 3 and 4. Mean gains for the latter group might thus be more difficult to attain, as suggested by the small mean IQ difference of only 4 points separating the groups at the end of the respective years (102 against 98). Mean differences over successive years ranged between 0 and 5 points and were never significant (Gray and Klaus 1970). Palmer (1972) found that children starting his eight-month-long program (all boys) at age 3 outperformed those starting at age 2, but the mean difference on the posttest Stanford-Binet was inconsequential (99.29 versus 96.43).

Taking the findings more generally in terms of comparing intervention during infancy and intervention during early childhood (ages 3-5), again there are no consistent differences in mean cognitive changes. Mean IQ changes range over the same magnitude for both age levels, from 0 to 20 or so IQ points (Beller 1973, 1979; Bronfenbrenner 1975; White et al. 1973). Levels varied slightly, infants usually ranging up to 20 points or so higher than the preschool groups, since, as widely reported (Bayley 1970; Starr 1971), IQ scores of disadvantaged populations tend to decline only after the first year. Mean differences over controls were of about the same order as well, though sometimes the mean advantage was the result of mean declines in control group IQ scores (Schaeffer 1972; Bronfenbrenner 1975) rather than of gains in the experimental group (Beller 1979). Extreme mean IQ changes are not found at the infant level to quite match the 30-point IQ gain for 3-year-olds, however, at least within a one-year time span. This difference may be in part because scores for disadvantaged children do not decline substantially below general population norms until past infancy, making IQ gains more difficult to realize during infancy.

There were mean differences in cognitive gains between programs at different ages, but short-term gains do not appear to be associated with specific ages of intervention, and program differences would make such age differences difficult to interpret, unless they were found to cut consistently across programs. The best that can probably be said from these collected findings on age variations is that there are indications of a slight advantage accruing from starting at earlier ages that require more rigorous tests, using larger samples, better controls, and more powerful programs. The watershed age, if there is one, appears to fall between ages 3 and 4. No program for children past age 3 has resulted in cognitive gains on levels of the same magnitude (30 points or 120 IQ) as some programs have produced for the 0-3 age range.

The problem with this pattern of findings, however, is the same general problem of ecology and the dual curriculum discussed earlier. Interventions that start at different ages, leaving children following a totally different course of cognitive socialization before or after the age period for which abstract cognitive stimulation is undertaken, are truncating the lives of the children in certain ways, washing out age or any other fine-grained effects. Even during the supposedly beneficial period of participation in a program of special stimulation, the abstract verbal and cognitive aims of the program are in conflict with the informal patterns and concrete coping modes of the folk life of urban blacks and other target poor populations in the programs.

The broad nature of verbal concept learning in the programs and the global character of the main (IQ) measures employed have probably contributed to the problem of tracing specific age or other program effects on development as well. But even when selected features have been emphasized and corresponding measures devised that show appropriately patterned outcomes, these have occurred in a context of general concept-learning of an abstract nature. Neither specific nor general cognitive changes have often reached levels above general population norms, and usually levels have remained at or below such norms (despite significant advances over controls), regardless of the age of intervention or the type of program undertaken.

Thus the main problem does not appear to rest in the diffuseness and generality of program and measurement. The problem lies, rather, in the dichotomy between the abstract and formal achievement values inherent in experimental programs and the informal and concrete ecology of the folk community, compounded by the pervasive problems of poverty that undermine efforts not devoted to immediate coping and survival. This pattern of findings and lack of clear age effects tells us less about the complexity, quality, and efficiency that early stimulation can produce in development than it tells us that conflicting forms of stimulation produce contradictory effects. Yet in another sense it also tells us about the remarkable potency of proportionally small amounts and periods of early stimulation to produce consistent effects in the face of a pervasive socialization of the folk community pushing in an opposite direction. But equally, it suggests the need for alternatives with populations in poverty.

Home- and Parent-Oriented Programs. Quite early in the early-intervention movement, a number of investigators, aware of the basic conflict between program and community, began to stress the importance of alternative approaches designed to function in relation to community ecology (Bronfenbrenner 1975; Gordon 1969, 1973). Unless programs took responsibility for building support for the family and community in which programs are undertaken, how could abstract skills learned for a brief period in the life of the infant or young child and for only one segment of her or his milieu be expected to transform the child into a model of the successful verbal abstractor idealized in middle-class life?

The most natural beginning for this type of effort was to work directly in the home, guiding poor and little-educated parents to modes of child rearing that would incorporate the desired verbal-abstract modes of concept stimulation in some planned fashion. It was assumed that the new curriculum would thus be integrated into the family and community way of life, removing the conflict between program and community, and developing new forms of parenting that would socialize poor children toward effective school learning. The question of what would happen to traditional modes of the folk community, however, was seldom confronted.

Home-Stimulation versus Center-Based Programs. Parent tutoring or guidance has produced about the same effects as center-based programs stimulating the child alone. Cognitive gains, as indexed by IQ score changes and similar measures, have varied between 0 and 20 points, precisely the same mean range, bringing disadvantaged children to the same below-average to average levels characteristic in center-based programs (Beller 1979; Bronfenbrenner 1975; Hunt 1975; Starr 1971). We have already noted the change pattern and levels of infants in the programs of Gordon (Gordon, et al. 1977; Guinagh et al. 1975) and Levenstein (1970, 1977; Bronfenbrenner 1975), both of which employed elaborate kits and schedules of cognitive-play interaction sequences to guide the parents in the home. The mean first-year IQ gains for Levenstein's 2- and 3-year-olds amounted to 10 to 20 points, bringing them all to slightly above 100 IQ. Gordon's infant groups, whose parents were guided in different combinations during the infants' first, second, and third years, gained between 5 and 15 points (not always clear because different scales were used in different years), almost invariably remaining in the 90s or below at program termination. Gordon's lesser gains have been attributed to using paraprofessionals (Hunt 1975), while Levenstein used social workers but is reported to have later realized slightly less effective results with low-income, high-school-educated aides (Beller 1979; Madden, Levenstein, and Levenstein 1976). Individuals from the same folk background may have the best rapport with parents but might not be the best educators to deliver a cognitive curriculum in which they themselves are not strong. On the other hand in Weikart's (Lambie, Bond, and Weikart 1974) infant program, in which trained schoolteachers were employed, there were only slight differences between experimental and comparison groups, few of them significant. Final, end-of-program mean scores on the Bayley scales ranged close to 100 IQ or slightly above for both groups. Other studies have shown similar variations in mean gains, all falling within the same range as the center-based gains, even when the child has been the chief focus of stimulation in the home (Beller 1979; Hunt 1975; Painter 1968; Schaeffer 1972; Starr 1971). The general pattern is consistent across almost all parent-home studies, regardless of intervention age, except for the usual tendency of mean scores to be higher in early infancy, more often rising above 100 IQ in keeping with the norms for poor folk populations, which do not begin to decline until the second year.

There is little mystery to why special efforts in the home with parents produced no better results on the whole than working with the child alone, in or out of the home. The typical program consisted of one hour per week of interaction, guidance, and toy demonstration with parents, almost always the mother, with a little counseling on family problems sometimes included. The programs were not really geared toward helping parents cope with the massive personal and socioeconomic problems occasioned by poverty (Gordon 1969, 1973), or for compensating for an educational background that was poorly equipped to meet the kinds of abstract cognitive goals intrinsic to programs. A superior potential for parent-oriented programs might be there, since one hour per week could apparently produce as many gains as many hours per week could produce with a child in a center-based program. Yet something more was clearly needed, something more ecologically complete and comprehensive, or perhaps more intensive, of longer duration, or even more selectively persistent in a given type of concepts, to produce more significant short-term developmental effects and demonstrate the power of early stimulation in poor folk populations. Before presenting the long-term developmental effects of specialized early stimulation with disadvantaged children, we shall review the short-term effects of certain exceptional programs having greater scope and selectivity.

Selected Comprehensive Programs for Disadvantged Children. Two investigations using special programs have produced effects considerably beyond those found in typical early-intervention programs. Both appear to demonstrate the value of beginning cognitive stimulation in earliest infancy, but earliness alone does not appear to be sufficient to account for the findings. One is a comprehensive program for disadvantaged infants in Milwaukee, Wisconsin, by Heber and his associates (1972),[1] which combined parent guidance with center-based stimulation, extending from 3 months to 6 years. The families were drawn from the most disadvantaged sectors of the black population, whose mothers had a Wechsler IQ of less than 80. The other investigation consists of related programs of Hunt and his colleagues (1976), one conducted in a residential-care institution for foundlings and orphans in Tehran (well before the revolution), the other program conducted by Badger (1971) with markedly disadvantaged infants in Mt. Carmel, Illinois, beginning during their first 6 months. The latter, like Heber's program, combined a tutoring program for mothers with a specialized day-care program in which some of the mothers were teachers.

Heber's program embraced a very intensive pattern of cognitive stimulation of language, perceptual and motor processes, general-concept learning, and social functioning. Infants from age 6 months attended a special day-care center of highly structured and individually sequenced and reinforced (in small steps) activities all day, 5 days per week, 12 months per year until age 18-20 months, when the children were shifted gradually to a similarly structured, all-day preschool program. Teacher/child ratios were 1:1 in the infant program, with one teacher assigned responsibility for the same infant continuously, using trained paraprofessionals under close professional supervision, and apparently around 1:3 in the preschool program, in which children moved among area teachers in small groups of two, three, and four. Math and reading processes were introduced into the preschool program. The mothers underwent an extensive program of basic skills in reading and arithmetic, job training for such fields as dietary aide and nursing assistant working with an experienced employee, and home-making and child-rearing skills. The latter two aspects were apparently not as extensive as the vocational training. Peer interaction among the mothers was also a major feature of the program. Fathers were encouraged, but only a few participated. There was a total subject pool of forty infants, twenty assigned randomly to an experimental and twenty to a control group. A wide variety of measures were employed to measure the children's developmental outcomes, including general IQ (Gesell, Catell, Binet, and Weschler series), language, concept learning and problem solving, but few formal measures of maternal outcomes. No data seem to have been reported on the reading and math learning.

The cognitive development of Heber's infants has surpassed the mean gains and levels attained by disadvantaged infants and preschool children in almost any other U.S. intervention program. Experimental and control groups were roughly comparable and slightly above test norms on all four component Gesell scales (motor, adaptive, language, and personal-social) until age 14 months, when they increasingly diverged on all subscales, reaching a mean difference of over 5 months in mental age on a composite for the scales by 22 months, the controls falling slightly below test norms. From age 18 months to age 6 years on the Gesell-Catell-Binet series the experimental group averaged above 120 IQ over all testings given at three-month intervals (at six-month intervals after age 4), while the controls consistently declined, sinking to around 95 IQ or below from age 2 on and ranging between 25 and 30 points below the experimental group's mean scores at successive testings. At program termination, mean IQ scores on tests administered blind by an independent testing agency for the respective groups were 120.7 and 87.2, a difference of more than 30 points (Heber 1976; Trotter 1976). The distributions, moreover, are virtually nonoverlapping. Few of the controls have scored above 100 IQ (most remain around 90 or below), while hardly any experimental children have scored below 100 IQ.

Among the other measures, language assessments showed the same pattern of acceleration, both over controls and in relation to norms. On the Illinois Test of Psycholinguistic Abilities at age 6, the mean PLQ (IQ equivalent) for the experimentals was 108.3, against 86.3 for the controls, a difference of 22 points. Again there was almost no overlap between distributions. Language differences emerged by age 18 months on the Gesell language scale, reaching 4 months over norms and 6 months in advance of controls by age 22 months. Similar results are reported for analysis of children's free speech and various other measures of grammar comprehension, imitation, and production, experimental children scoring generally one to two years in advance of controls. On free speech measures, experimental children were generally one year in advance of controls in cumulative vocabulary and MLU (mean length of utterance), scoring at levels generally comparable to middle-class samples (Miller and Chapman 1981; Wells 1979). Speech patterns follow traditional black dialect patterns of the community in both groups.

On the several measures of learning and problem solving, experimental children performed substantially better than controls on all tasks, including color-form preferencing, probability matching, and oddity discrimination, between the ages of 2 1/2 and 6 years. Experimental children were also more category oriented and field independent on measures of cognitive style. Particularly significant is the fact that the experimental children developed an active hypothesis-testing strategy for problem solving and responded effectively to feedback from error-success patterns. The controls, in contrast, followed stereotyped patterns, often demonstrating no strategy and remaining passive and uninterested in the tasks. The extent of the experimental children's abstract, concept-oriented approach to problem solving is indicated as well by differences between experimental and control dyads in the classic Hess and Shipman (1965) maternal-teaching task. The source of the difference in favor of the experimental dyads emerged in the greater initiative in engineering problem solving on part of the children, not the mother, the children guiding the task, using verbal direction and questioning to teach the mother, who followed some of the child's examples.

The Heber study is exceptional for several reasons. Young children from the most impoverished and educationally undeveloped sectors of a black community were stimulated to attain cognitive levels not only as high as but often higher than controls in nearly all other investigations. They scored much higher than general population norms, reaching levels characteristic of highly advantaged middle-class populations, and they did so on a broad variety of measures of ability, language, concept learning, and problem solving, encompassing many of the knowledge, coding, and strategy dimensions outlined in tables 5-1 and 5-3, though not conceptualized in the same way. Their active approach and abstract, verbal, and concept-oriented strategy toward solving tasks, moreover, matches the dominant verbal-abstract modes demanded for successful school learning and coping in contemporary industrial society. How well such levels with these modes have persisted will be reported in reviewing all studies in terms of long-term developmental effects.

Apparently a combination of dimensions distinguishes this investigation from most if not all other early intervention studies on disadvantaged children. Few if any studies have started as early as 3 months, and even fewer have extended specialized cognitive stimulation over the first 6 years of development; moreover, no other studies located have carried out so intensive and extensive a program of stimulation. The 1:1 teacher/child ratios during infancy and the low ratios thereafter, combined with the highly individualized and sequenced program, made possible the extremely intensive and comprehensive program. It is interesting that, while the mothers were involved in a comprehensive vocational-training and family-guidance program, most of the effects appear to be attributable to the child stimulation component of the program. Heber (1976) reports generally improved and stable job patterns for the mothers but little improvement in maternal social patterns, and as the child-mother interaction analyses indicated, most of the experimental advantage over controls came from the children's contribution. Parental involvement coupled with the extraordinary daily, dawn-to-dusk, 12 months' program with the children over the entire span of early development, must nonetheless be counted as essentially countering a great portion of the dual curriculum that has generally impeded efforts on early intervention projects with the poor.

The Hunt investigations contained several comparisons, with N's ranging from 6 to 20 infants per comparison. One studied the developmental effects of rearing infants under a variety of experimental program conditions in the Tehran orphanage in successive waves, each program beginning during the first few weeks of life. A second was the Badger program in Mt. Carmel, Illinois, and a third was a study of developmental effects of predominantly middle-class infants in Worcester, Massachusetts, under culturally normal rearing conditions. The latter was employed by Hunt as a normative yardstick of the effects of relatively optimal developmental stimulation. The Piagetian sensorimotor cognitive scales of infant development developed by Uzgiris and Hunt (1975) were employed to assess development. Although providing the advantage of differential scaling, Piagetian sensorimotor scales have been found to correlate highly with global IQ measures like the Bayley scales (1974).

Both the Mt. Carmel and the Tehran program drew extensively on Piagetian concepts as conceptualized by Hunt (1961, 1969), and modified in different ways for the various experiments, particularly with respect to the emphasis on language, which is not stressed by Piaget. The Badger program consisted of an elaborate series of carefully sequenced sensorimotor activities, continuously matched to each infant's developing rate of understanding, mediated principally through the mothers in training but with little emphasis on language stimulation. The successive waves in the Tehran orphanage consisted first of a control group (basic minimal institutional care, very little attention and 1:10 caregiver/child ratios). Wave 2 brought into use experimental audiovisual devices, consisting of automatically operating tape-recorded music and mother talk, together with infant-operated mobiles, but the program was never carried out, so it was adopted for wave 4, with a few manipulative toys added. Waves 3 and 5 consisted of supplementary human enrichment, wave 3 mainly through improving care ratios to 1:3 and wave 5 through both improving ratios and training caregivers in the Badger program plus language stimulation techniques (vocal play followed by word, interaction learning play).

The pattern of results from the Hunt investigations is important in two respects. The development of infants from the institutionally deprived backgrounds in the most stimulating programs was accelerated more rapidly than the cognitive develpment of infants from advantaged, middle-class backgrounds. Second, these and other differences in infants among the different programs followed the patterns of stimulation experienced in the programs. Thus the infants in the multiple-enrichment orphanage program (wave 5) attained the top levels on five of the seven Uzgiris-Hunt scales (object permanence, means-end relations, vocal and gestural imitation, and causality) from 1 to 29 mean weeks in advance of the Worcester middle-class sample and lagged them by only 3 to 4 weeks on spatial relations and variety of schemes, respectively. In the Mt. Carmel program, the infants who benefited from multiple forms of intensive sensorimotor stimulation but little language, attained top-scale levels in object permanence and means-end relations at means of 73 and 79 weeks respectively, 25 and 21 weeks ahead of the Worcester sample. Hunt has worked out their object-permanence level in terms of IQ ratios, which amounted to 150 IQ. On the other hand, in vocal imitation (the only other cognitive sequence validly measured in the study), the Mt. Carmel infants trailed the Worcester infants by 20 weeks, failing to develop vocal language skills until a mean of 114 weeks (that is, after age 2 years).

None of the rates of development in the other waves in the orphanage approached the rate of development of the foregoing groups, all of them lagging by 10 to 40 or more weeks behind the Worcester middle-class sample. But there were differences between them that shed light on the effects of different conditions and specific forms of stimulation. Waves 1 and 2 were consistently the lowest, often approaching age 3 before reaching scale ceilings, in keeping with the unmodified, extremely unstimulating institutional environment. Waves 3 and 4 were generally each 20 to 30 weeks in advance of waves 1 and 2 on all scales and more or less closely matched. Wave 3 revealed some special effects of improving caregiving ratios, beyond the improved attention and language that produced the multiple effects across all scales, namely much earlier ages in sitting and standing, at means of 27 and 41 weeks, respectively, quite comparable to standard motor-scale norms for general populations. This is attributed by Hunt to the ameliorated routines caregivers introduced of holding and carrying infants about and placing them in walkers, which the improved ratios made possible. The intensity of adult/child care ratios (of 1:3 or better) has proved to be a widely demonstrable dimension, influencing the intensity of cognitive stimulation parents and child-care workers employ with infants to generate a broad range of improved cognitive outcomes (Fowler 1975).

The findings for wave 4 are also significant in that the results point to the effects that mechanical devices and manipulation of the physical environment can have on the developmental learning of infants over a period of two years or more. These findings are in line with the significant correlations found by Yarrow and his colleagues (1972; Yarrow, Rubenstein, and Pedersen 1975), ranging from around .30 to .50, between dimensions of the physical environment (variety, responsiveness, and complexity of toys and other objects) and infant functioning in terms of Bayley IQ and a host of other measures of language and cognitive functioning (goal-directness, problem solving, object permanence, exploratory behavior) through home observations at 5 months in a sample of low-education black families. This effect extended to a more rapid increase in language development, including spontaneous use of words, from hearing tape-recorded language over roughly the first two years of development, an effect that matched the rate of language development that came with improved ratios for wave 3.

The Hunt investigations differ from most other studies on children from poor folk communities on much the same set of dimensions that Heber's study does and probably the original experimental program with orphanage infants as well (Skeels and Dye 1939; Skeels 1966), though program details for the latter are not recorded. Stimulation started in the first few months of life and continued over a period of two to three years. In the two most successful programs (wave 5 in the orphanage and the Mt. Carmel study) it was also clearly quite intensive, highly individualized, paced to each child's development, and comprehensive (with the exception of the sparseness of language in the Mt. Carmel study), as indicated by the general cognitive gains across most scales. But Hunt's investigations also point up the advantage of designing stimulation and assessing development in terms of cognitively differentiated approaches. Using this matched input-outcome strategy, Hunt was able to show just what was and what was not being stimulated and to obtain sensitive measures of just what concepts each infant was acquiring and at what level in a precise sequence. There were almost no step reversals reported in any of these investigations, and he was able to demonstrate how widely cognitive development can be varied as the result of the cumulative effects of stimulation concentrated in different areas.

Taken together these two sets of investigations strongly suggest that planned programs of early cognitive developmental stimulation can have extended short-term effects for poor and deprived institutional children of roughly the same magnitude regularly induced by socialization in abstract verbal and cognitive concepts in the normal milieu of the advantaged middle-class family, despite the competing basic curriculum disadvantaged children experience in their everyday folk community. But these investigations also underscore that it takes more than the limited stimulation of typical programs of a few hours per week continued over a limited period of a few months of a year or so, even if started early in infancy. Highly intense and variously sequenced individualized stimulation of extended duration, sufficient to allow effects to accumulate and to temper the effects of poverty and the dual curriculum: this combination of conditions is apparently needed to produce effects of this scale. Now we must see whether or to what degree the short-term effects produced in these and other programs have any lasting effects on children's development, once programs are terminated.

Persistence of Effects

Broad Early Effects. The measures for follow-up studies are somewhat different from those employed by investigators for assessing the short-term outcomes of the original early interventions. As follow-up investigations were conducted over an increasing number of years, investigators found a gradual decline in mean IQ scores occurring quite consistently across all experimental groups of disadvantaged children. As children were enrolled in school, however, they were naturally compared on their performance in school, on formal achievement tests, school grades, and a number of broader measures indicative of academic coping, such as retention in grade and enrollment in special classes. On these measures fairly consistent advantages for experimental children over their controls were generally maintained well into the teen years. As in the foregoing discussions, we shall use the investigator's own categories, commenting on them occasionally in relation to the overall patterns outlined in tables 5-1 to 5-3. The categories break down into general and specific abilities and a variety of indices of coping in school, all of them useful in their different ways, but incomplete for providing a clear picture of the pattern of competencies developed. Basic abilities are as usual indexed mainly by IQ tests in the follow-up studies, typically the Wechsler series, in particular the Wechsler Intelligence Scale for Children (WISC) by agreement among members of a research consortium of some eleven major investigators of the early interventionists of the 1960s organized to pool data and coordinate efforts on the better controlled investigations (Lazer et al. 1977; Lazar and Darlington 1978, 1982). But the WISC, like other IQ measures, is an empirically derived measure without a clear logical framework. The verbal scale, for example, is composed of an aggregate of general and social information, vocabulary, arithmetic, verbal classification and other skills, without any inclusion of grammar and syntax at all. The performance scale similarly combines different skills, such as pictorial coding and spatial organization. The various achievement test skills reported come closer to measuring specific abilities (Schweinhart and Weihart 1981), such as math and reading, but the other measures of grade retention and special classes give some assurance of success in school without shedding light on just what aspects of competence, motivation, behavioral conformity, grades, or some combination of these and other factors are involved.

Looking at the long-term effects in detail, the pattern of findings is nonetheless remarkable, given the original problem of the dual curriculum. Although mean differences between experimental and controls in IQ scores on both the verbal and performance scales, as well as on the full WISC scale, gradually diminished over the years from their earlier range of around 5 to 15 points or so immediately following intervention, to become no longer significant, differences remained significant until about ages 9 to 12 in several investigations, mostly on the Stanford-Binet (Beller 1973; Brown 1978; Carter and Capobianco 1976; Delaporte 1976; Guinagh and Gordon 1978; Palmer and Anderson 1979). And although no longer significant, mean score differences continued to favor experimentals by 1 to 4 points in a few studies as late as ages 12 to 16 (Lazar and Darlington 1978). Differences in favor of the experimental children (all boys) in the Palmer study remained significant and as much as 6 points on the performance scale to age 12, the latest assessment point, a long-term impact from an original intervention that had only amounted to 2 hours per week for a year at ages 2 and 3 (Lazar and Darlington 1978). Mean differences in the Levenstein investigation (Lazar and Darlington 1978), which it will be recalled consisted of a home-tutoring program for parents of children from less than age 2 to age 3, were significant as late as age 9 years 9 months (9-9) on the WISC total and verbal scales. Levenstein's study, moreover, appears to be the only investigation among the main body of studies in which children's IQ levels were maintained at the level of general norms, that is, at 102, 98, and 105 for the respective full, verbal, and performance scale, though Palmer's mean scores are not much below norms to age 12. Considering that the original posttest means in both projects were obtained on the Binet, whose norms run consistently higher than WISC norms (Buros 1975), the later declines may in part reflect Binet versus WISC test standardization differences as much as they do real declines.

Thus in the main body of intervention studies, the original early mean gains of 5 to 20 points (from an 80-90 IQ level to 90-100 and occasionally more) have slowly declined to near the original low levels and sometimes below (where the original interventions may not have been as uniformly well implemented in replication, Miller and Dyer 1975). They have, however, usually remained a few points above pretest levels and follow-up control scores, though seldom significantly so (Lazar and Darlington 1978, 1982).

Among the more intensive and comprehensive selective programs Hunt et al. (1976) conducted no follow-up studies, but they note that the high cognitive levels attained in the successful combined language and problem-solving Piagetian program with wave 5 made it possible for nearly all of the infants to be placed for adoption. They speculate that the probable long-term outcome would as a result be similar to the developmental outcomes in the classical study by Skeels (1966). Adopted into generally socioeconomically advantaged or at least well-functioning homes, the children were expected to build on this early competence base to continue to develop at least as well, and probably better, than norms for the population on most social and formal indices of functioning. The projected effects of early cognitive stimulation in the Hunt (and Skeels) design are thus traceable in part to the benefits of experiencing a continuing framework of social support and stimulation the early gains made possible, not as a source independent of this supportive ecology, as in most studies of disadvantaged children.

Despite their originally tremendous IQ and other cognitive gains, the children in Heber's group are showing a similar trend decline during their school years. The level to which they have declined, however, ($\overline{X} = 105$ on WISC on the latest testing at age 10) are still slightly above general population norms and substantially (20 points) and significantly above the low IQ level ($\overline{X} = 85$) common among children from severely disadvantaged backgrounds and to which the controls have regressed (Heber 1976; Garber and Heber 1981). A telling comparison is represented in the differences between experimentals and controls in the number of children whose IQ scores fall below 85. Since program termination at age 6, fewer than 10 percent of the experimental children have fallen below 85 IQ at any testing, and none at ages 9 and 10. The percentage for controls in contrast has increased steadily from none during infancy to the 60 to 80 percent range between ages 6 and 10. Half the controls have scored below 80 IQ at 10. Seventy-five percent of the original sample was assessed at age 10.

Although impressive, testing has not proceeded as far in age or as long since program termination in Heber's groups, compared to other investigations. It remains to be seen whether the scope and intensity of the Heber program can sustain these relatively higher levels in the face of counterpressures from the community and poverty these children, like most disadvantaged children, face once a special early program is terminated. In point of fact, mean scores in Heber's group at age 10 were only 3 IQ points higher than mean scores for Levenstein's children at age 9-9 (105 versus 102) on the WISC measure), hardly a difference worth noting in respective samples of 20 (Heber) and 51, considering the magnitude of difference in the duration and intensity of early stimulation between the two projects. It would seem that intervening competing pressures from the poverty folk culture take their toll whatever the scale of the early effort, without continuing support from an ecology that matches the cognitive forms of the original research program.

Two widely reported measures of school achievement in many followup investigations, reading and mathematics, are the best indices available of the children's cognitive abilities in specific domains (Lazar et al. 1981; Lazar and Darlington 1978, 1982; Palmer and Anderson 1979). Since children attended many different schools, a wide variety of different standardized achievement tests were employed, including the California Achievement Test (CAT), Metropolitan Achievement Test (MAT), and Stanford Achievement Test (SAT), and administered at different grades according to school policy. Because these tests are norm referenced, the results can be compared with general population levels as well as in terms of controlgroup comparisons. The findings were positive but uneven in general, different projects showing mean experimental group competence significantly greater than controls in both reading and achievement scores at different elementary grade levels, but trends consistently favored experimental children in nearly all comparisons. A generalized comparison made by the research consortium found significant differences favoring experimental groups for the pooled data, on math achievement through fifth grade and on reading achievement through fourth grade (Lazar and Darlington 1982).

Among the most impressive findings in particular investigations are the highly consistent and significant differences favoring experimentals over controls to age 14 (eighth grade) on a wide variety of achievement ability and other measures in the Perry Preschool Project (Schweinhart and Weikart 1980, 1981). Mean differences were highly significant in language, as well as in reading and arithmetic on the CAT, and moderately significant on all eight cognitive, motivational, and social factors derived from a Pupil Behavior Inventory and an Ypsilanti Rating Scale (academic motivation, academic potential, verbal skill, social development, emotional adjustment, classroom conduct, socioemotional status, and personal behavior).

The latest age to which any long-term effects of early stimulation have been reported is around 19.2 years (median), in the Institute for Developmental Studies (IDS) investigations (Jordan et al. n.d.). Of 1,200 poor black children who originally participated in the special program set in the Harlem public schools, 158 18- to 22-year-olds (clustering heavily around the median) have been located, approximately two-thirds from the experimental group and one-third from the controls (originally randomly assigned subjects to groups). The persisting experimental group effects are entirely restricted to males, however. Higher percentages of experimental groups males are attending college than comparison group males (32 versus 20 percent) and are employed full-time or part-time (57 versus 44 percent), while no differences appeared between female follow-up experimental and comparison groups (*Science* 81 1981). In a separate analysis certain factors discriminated strongly between experimental and comparison-group males—in descending order, educational attainment levels, vocabulary, sense of control of academic outcomes, and academic self-concept—all dimensions that were associated with the goals of the early education program (Jordan et al. u.d.). (Only vocabulary discriminated in favor of controls, as a result of certain artifacts, according to Jordan et al.) The lack of long-term advantages for experimental females is believed to be the result of greater ecological pressures for girls to pursue traditional home and child-care roles. These potentially important findings are unfortunately diluted by the serious problems of sample attrition encountered. The total percentage of subjects recovered was small (13 percent) and experimental-control samples were not representative of the original samples in terms of the end-of-program Binet IQs at age 5. Experimental follow-up scores were biased upward and controls were biased downward, thus favoring experimentals and making the design quasi-experimental (Lazar and Darlington 1978). The period since intervention (14 years, from age 5 to 19) is also diminished (to 11 years) because a special enrichment program continued in the elementary grades through grade 3.

The latest Beller (1980) follow-up study covered a similarly long interval following early intervention (14 years, age 4 1/2 to grade 12), but the twelfth grade level presumably extended to a mean age of 18 and included few youths as old as the IDS follow-up. Beller (1974) found experimental subjects, especially girls, consistently ahead of controls on all school subjects except science through the fourth grade, though differences did not reach significance for boys at fourth grade. Mean differences favored experimental children significantly as well through the fourth grade on a Maturity of Moral Judgment Test and on Kagan's Matching Familiar Figures test of cognitive style (the experimental children being generally more reflective than impulsive) and through the twelfth grade for certain dimensions of the Pier-Harris Self-concept scale (intellectual and school status, physical appearance and attributes, and popularity). The composite self-concept score differences were close to significant ($p < .10$) (Beller 1980). Experimental boys were also significantly less impulsive than control boys in cognitive style through twelfth grade.

In the Palmer investigation, in which only boys had been stimulated, mean differences in reading were significantly greater for experimentals over controls, through grade 7 for reading and through grade 5 for arithmetic (last grade assessed) (Palmer, Semlear, and Fischer 1981).

The additional set of data derived from long-term follow-up assessments of coping in an academic environment show experimental children consistently superior to controls on all measurs. Data compiled by the research consortium on seven of eleven long-term follow-ups from the third to the twelfth grades found only 13.8 percent of experimental subjects versus 28.6 percent of controls placed in special education classes; only 25.4 percent of experimentals versus 30.5 percent of controls retained in grade, and only 25.4 percent of the subjects versus 44.1 percent of the controls underachieving (placed in special education classes, or retained in grade, or dropped out of school; Lazar et al. 1981). The figures are median percentages for six projects for special education class placement and seven projects for the other two comparisons. Significance values ranged from .01 to as high as .0001. Percentages for grade retention are probably conservative figures because of social promotion (diminishing experimental percentage more than controls) and the fact that the larger percentage of controls assigned to special-education classes reduced the percentage coded as retained in grade (Lazar and Darlington 1978). The consortium conducted more detailed analyses as well, controlling for differences in sex, ethnicity, initial and posttest IQs, family size, family structure (father absent or present), and mother's level of education (Lazar and Darlington 1978, 1982). All effects remained positive on the various analyses, including, additionally, comparisons of eleven individual programs (project subgroups) at five sites as the unit of analysis. The effects for posttest IQ and individual programs were significant for special education class assignment only. The analysis controlling for posttest IQ gives a measure of the power of the early-intervention programs to assess long-term effects on broad aspects of competence development.

The consortium looked further into the long-term effects on non-cognitive aspects of development, finding some but neither strong nor widespread effects (Lazar and Darlington 1978, 1982). Somewhat greater achievement orientation for children having experienced specialized early stimulation over their controls was found across projects on children feeling proud of themselves for achievement-related reasons (school or job achievements, straightening oneself out, helping out at home). Overall mean differences were highly significant ($p = .003$). Experimental girls were more likely to give school-related reasons for being proud of themselves (or said they had no reason to be proud of themselves), control girls for having babies. Otherwise, groups did not differ on their educational expectations, though experimental subjects by the teen years tended to have lower vocational aspirations, which the investigators interpret to be more realistic aspirations. In the same vein mothers of the experimental subjects had higher vocational aspirations for their children than did control mothers, and higher vocational aspirations than their children did, further indicating the trend of realism among the children. The high maternal aspirations suggest the influence early-intervention programs had upon family ecology in supporting the long-term cognitive gains of the children. Control mothers varied widely on how they corresponded with their children's aspirations. Gray (Gray, Klaus, and Ramsey 1981; Gray, Ramsey, and Klaus 1982) in one of the most interesting achievement-related outcomes, found that teenage girls who had been subjects did not become pregnant less often than control girls, but when they did, they significantly more often attempted to finish school.

Few other attitudinal, relational, and motivational mean differences were either significant or substantial. In self-evaluation, older experimental children (the later follow-up studies) rated their own academic performance significantly higher than controls did, but there were essentially no differences between groups in getting along at home, in school, or in spare time activities, or in the percentage reporting participation in organized community activities.

Specific Long-Term Age Differences. Are there any age effects more precise than these rather remarkable long-term general effects of broad-gaged programs of early stimulation? The long-term effects of varying ages of entry into programs are generally negative or inconclusive for the same reason differences in starting ages resulted in inconsistent differences in short-term effects. Age variations built into the design of investigations using the same program at different ages were typically confounded with program duration and sometimes differences in ability starting levels (Bronfenbrenner 1975; Klaus and Gray 1968; Levenstein 1970, 1977). Comparisons of starting ages across programs is risky for the obvious reason of program differences (intensity, methods, concepts emphasized). Palmer and Anderson (1979), in their detailed analysis of the effects of entry age in the main body of intervention studies compared by the research consortium, concluded that stimulation programs beginning at 2 and 3 tended to produce stronger long-term effects on both IQ and achievement than did programs beginning at age 4. But they also drew attention to the inconclusiveness of the pattern because of the problem of confounded variables and the inconsistency of the results. Gray (Gray and Klaus 1970; Gray 1974), for example, found no IQ differences between starting at 3 or 4, in successive follow-up tests, nor did differences appear later in achievement scores. Weikart (1967) found similar short-term results, and though the Bereiter-Engelmann replication conducted by Weikart (1969; White et al. 1973) showed greater immediate gains for 3-year-olds, neither of the latter two investigations have apparently been followed up.

Essentially the other within-program variations reported for short-term effects were repeated for long-term effects, variable confounding making the results difficult to interpret. The earlier Beller's (1973; Palmer and Anderson 1981) experimental children entered his school program (nursery school, versus kindergarten, versus first grade), the greater the IQ gains (Binet and Peabody). Group IQ differences were significantly maintained through grade 6, as were significant differences in school achievement (reading, spelling, science, social studies, and arithmetic, the last approaching significance). But the groups varied in length of schooling as well. Guinagh and Gordon (1978) found mean specific ability differences consistently favored early-versus late-entering children in Gordon's home-stimulation programs up to six years after program termination, as measured by reading and math achievement tests, percentages of children performing above grade and assignment to special education classes. Mean differences over controls were generally significant for the former but not the latter group.

But, again, earliness is confounded with duration. The children entering at 3 or 12 months (early group) followed the program for two to three years, while children entering at 24 months (later group) participated only one year. In the case of Palmer's (1972; Palmer, Semlear, and Fischer 1981) comparison of the long-term effects of intervention at ages 2 and 3, small IQ differences that had favored those starting at 3 over those starting at 2 gradually disappeared. No differences were found between groups (70 percent of original sample retained) in IQ scores, arithmetic and reading achievement, or in grade retention through grade 6. That early stimulation can yield persisting developmental effects when started as late as age 6 is indicated by a study of Carter and Capobianco (1976). An intensive 12-week, 1-hour-per-day language intervention program in first grade resulted in 11-point mean IQ gains for thirty-two disadvantaged children compared to only 3 points for their thirty-two controls (matched pairs on Binet IQ and mental age, Illinois Test of Psycholinguistic Abilities, language age, chronological age, and social class). The IQ levels and experimental-control differences, while not of the same magnitude as in some of the projects involving earlier stimulated children, are significant and persisted through seventh grade (89 versus 82 for the respective groups). Following first grade, mean differences in reading achievement gradually appeared and increased, reaching 1.5 years by seventh grade.

Despite the uncertain and conflicting pattern of findings, there are certain significant long-term effects that suggest earliness, beginning as early as infancy, may produce more powerful effects. In only two projects have mean IQ differences remained at or above general population norms as late as age 10, Heber's (Garber and Heber 1981) and Levenstein's (Lazar and Darlington 1978), the former 105 IQ at age 10 and the latter 102 IQ at nearly age 10 (9-9) (both on the WISC). Intervention in both projects started during infancy, Heber's during the first 6 months and Levenstein's at age 2 (for three of five experimental groups who are pooled for follow-ups) and age 3. Palmer's experimental children, moreover, remained above 90 IQ ($\overline{X} = 92$), as late as age 12, compared with all other projects in which children typically regressed to the 80 to 90 IQ range (Lazar and Darlington 1978; Palmer et al. 1981). Half of Palmer's group entered his program at age 2, the rest at age 3. Earliness does not guarantee results, of course. Gordon's (Lazar and Darlington 1978, 1982) subjects regressed to the low 80's ($\overline{X} = 83$), but Gordon indicated retrospectively that his methods were not as articulated as they could have been (noted in Palmer and Anderson 1979: 451), and within his groups, children starting in infancy did consistently better than children starting at age 2, though earliness is confounded with duration (Guinagh and Gordon 1978). It is true that differences among programs might have produced continuing effects of this magnitude. Some of Levenstein's children also started at somewhat higher IQ levels than children in other projects did, though not higher than in others, and Palmer's groups started at the 80 IQ level. Heber's investigation is in a class by itself, combining earliness, duration, intensity, and comprehensiveness and a scale of socioeconomically disadvantage in a way almost no other project did. The trend on age is provocative and should be followed up by more systematic studies.

*Conclusions on Earliness from Compensatory and
Preventive Education and Care Studies*

If it is difficult to pinpoint precisely at what age or how early cognitive stimulation may make a difference, it is nonetheless clear that stimulation at any early age can produce high-magnitude short-term cognitive and other effects and remarkably enduring if small long-term cognitive and related competence effects. In the context of the dual curriculum, that is, the essential discrepancy between the goals and cognitive culture of intervention programs and the folk patterns of the poor black and similarly disadvantaged communities, such effects are almost hard to believe. Yet when Head Start and the research programs on early intervention began, they were widely heralded as a panacea to the cycle of poverty, low competence, school failure, unemployment, and delinquency. The transformation of the children's competence was deemed to be a forgone conclusion (Helmuth 1970; Hunt 1975; Zigler and Valentine 1979). But as the investigations progressed and follow-up studies began to disclose the regression of IQ scores toward the norms of poor blacks and similar folk populations everywhere, the faulted Westinghouse (1969) study appeared to bury Head Start; and the premature pronouncements of Jensen (1969) and others claimed that early education could make no substantial difference, that blacks were inherently inferior mentally—in retrospect of the ensuing pessimism, the later actual long-term results seem quite unexpected.

These results tend to suggest that the wide-ranging early-stimulation programs appeared to have broad cognitive, social, and motivational effects, quite in keeping with the broad nature of the original early-intervention programs, in which stimulation was seldom specific or aligned closely to outcome measures. A variety of dimensions listed in table 5-3 (complexity, quantity, variety, intensity) and numerous others that could be proposed to assess developmental outcomes for all three types of cognitive domains (knowledge, codes, and strategies) and their subtypes outlined in table 5-1 appear to be involved to some degree.

There is some evidence in the Weikart and other studies that differences expanded with age, indicating cumulative effects developmentally. That they were not of great magnitude, however, is suggested by the failure of IQ gains (which reflect the more abstract form of verbal and other general concept skills) to hold up as development progressed, and the tendency for children in all studies consistently to lag behind general population norms. Thus Weikart reports (Schweinhart and Weikart 1981) that experimentals were advanced in achievement over controls by 1.2 grades at grade 8, but still lagged general norms by 3 years, performing at only a grade 5 level. Only in the Heber group's follow-up study have cognitive gains of the children from low educational, impoverished environments been maintained at least slightly above the general population level for several years (to age 10), following termination of the early-stimulation program. Mean score declines appear to have been less in the Heber group (around 5 IQ points), compared to the declines of 5 to 10 points or more characteristic in most investigations. Mean scores declined from 110 to 105 on the WPPSI-WISC series from program termination (age 6) to follow-up at age 10. (Mean Binet scores were around 120 IQ at program termination, reflecting the higher norm pattern characteristic of the Binet, Buros 1975). Levenstein's and Palmer's follow-up patterns have also varied from those in the main body of studies in that the IQ levels of both groups have remained at (Levenstein) or close to (Palmer) general norms, as well as remained significantly greater than control levels longer than in other studies (Lazar and Darlington 1978). Unfortunately, Heber's group has so far reported no follow-up data on other cognitive abilities, achievement test patterns or other indices of long-term developmental effects.

Nevertheless the general pattern is impressive, considering the countless ecological obstacles the children and their families confront: pervasive poverty; minimal education; chronic unemployment that has averaged for blacks double the percentage for whites since World War II (Kenniston 1977), embracing the period in which early intervention occurred and the children progressed through school; the devastating quality of inner city schools (Gross and Gross 1969; Frost and Hawkes 1966; Silberman 1970); and widespread social and racial discrimination (90 percent of the children in the eleven research consortium studies are black, and Heber's group is all black), which often blamed the poor families and their children for their own misfortune (Ryan 1971), rather than the ecological snare of poverty and the nature of the social structure.

How the second curriculum—the ecological curriculum of poverty and the different styles of the poor folk community—systematically precludes the possibility of large cognitive gains from early stimulation, except in sweeping efforts like those of Heber's group, and erodes the modest effects from all programs, once the stimulation program is terminated, is illustrated by many findings in the follow-up investigations. Beller (1980), for example, found that the special preschool experience in his program failed to yield any long-term effects for children from broken homes or homes where neither parent was employed when the child entered school. Shipman reports (1976:52) that children's competencies among the impoverished black families were directly affected by economic factors: "even small differences in material possessions and household density were associated with children's higher achievement" that Head Start programs did not erase. The research consortium analysis of eleven different follow-up studies found that a number of background variables in the home (low maternal educational level, broken home, and number of siblings), all of which are integral to patterns of the poor community, tended to reduce children's IQ scores significantly by age 6, following the period of preschool intervention, though preschool intervention tempered some of the reduction (Lazar and Darlington 1978).

In one sense the long-term cognitive successes of the early-intervention programs might be viewed as passing something of a strong test on the impact of early stimulation, given the persistence of influence in the face of countervailing forces from the folk community over the years. In another sense, given the smallness of the continuing impact, its gradual diminution with time, and the greater persistence where family circumstances lent greater support, the evidence would suggest that it is obviously not the early stimulating experiences alone that determine cognitive development over long time spans. Rather, it is the effects of early stimulation combined with the succeeding experiences accumulating in harmony with the original experience that determine long-term outcomes. In this context it might be worthwhile to consider what the impact of special early-stimulation programs, designed to intensify the skills intrinsic to the folk community, might be on poor black children. The problem with this strategy, however, is not that such verbal narrative, interpersonal, streetwise, and similar coping skills (Ogbu 1981) would not be reinforced by the social ecology in both early and continuing periods of development. It is that poverty and the attendant circumstances of anomie and oppression in ghetto life undermine family and community folk life and muddy the waters of experience to make such programs questionable in the context of the overarching demands of a modern technological society.

The extent to which the ecology of poverty undermines the effects of the verbal-logical types of early stimulation offered in the intervention programs appears strongly in the National Follow-Through study as well. This was a program designed in the latter part of the 1960s to remedy the erosion of developmental gains by the poverty ecology, through following up the Head Start program with enriched educational support services during the first several grades of elementary school. Unfortunately the program was relatively ineffective in that "differences in effectiveness between sites with each model were greater than overall differences in effectiveness between models. None of the seventeen models in the evaluation demonstrated that it could compensate consistently for the academic consequences of poverty" (Anderson et al. 1978:162). In a more detailed, precise, and comprehensive research evaluation of outcomes conducted by Miller and Dyer (1975) in selected sites and programs, Binet IQ scores underwent the same pattern of mean score declines reported for follow-up investigations, as where no follow-through support was provided. Mean score declines ranged from approximately 4 to 12 points from the Head Start posttesting to grade 2, and there were hardly any other later mean differences between experimentals and controls on any cognitive ability, motivational, or noncognitive measures. Even mean achievement scores in reading and mathematics were not consistently above controls and all mean ability and achievement scores remained generally well below general norms. Similarly, only inconsistent results are reported in the Seitz (Seitz, Apfel and Rosenbaum 1981) follow-through study. Follow-through boys but not girls were generally superior to their same-sexed non-follow-through counterparts in cohort 1, but the opposite was true in cohort 2. Mean differences favored the respective sex groups in Peabody IQ, mathematics, and general information (the last two significantly) as late as ninth grade, but there were no differences in reading achievement.

Not all programs were equally ineffective, but the pervasiveness of the trend tells the story best regarding the role of the dual curriculum among impoverished folk groups in society generally. Wang, Leinhardt, and Boston (1980), for example, observed a rising score trend across school sites in their highly systematic, academically oriented program that began at the preschool level and continued through several elementary grades. Grade-equivalent scores in reading and math of disadvantaged children rose progressively from kindergarten through third grade. Even in this relatively favored program outcome, however, the rate of gain dropped during third grade, especially in math, leveling off at or falling below general population norms.

It is interesting to speculate on the mechanisms through which gains in cognitive processes derived from early stimulation persisted across such long spans of development, well into the high-school years and beyond in some projects, in a broad range of cognitive and coping indices, but seldom in IQ measures. Studies on middle-class populations have shown how IQs wax and wane during development with the vicissitudes of family life and other problems (Honzik, MacFarlane, and Allen 1948; McCall, Appelbaum, and Hogarty 1973; Richards 1951), so the IQ regressions under the appalling conditions poor blacks face is hardly surprising. But given the ecological obstacles, how did any school related skills persist at all? Although earlier analyses (Bronfenbrenner 1975) reported that projects that directly involved the family produced more persisting cognitive (IQ) effects than those that did not, later analysis of longer follow-ups have not borne this out (Palmer and Anderson 1979; Lazar and Darlington 1978). Children in projects with minimal family involvement (Palmer) have done as well as those with family involvement the primary focus (Gordon, Levenstein). Although it is reasonable to believe that educating parents in the target modes of stimulating and caring for their children would provide a mechanism for ensuring continuing progress in the children's school-related abilities, reason exists to believe that it is changes in the child's self, coupled with changes in family attitudes and methods, and some minimal base of family support that make the difference, but not necessarily parent stimulation itself. In Heber's study it was *children*, not the mothers, who had become developed enough to guide the mothers in a complex learning and problem-solving task, not the reverse, an interesting indication of the advancement in self-propelled learning or autonomy in learning that can be developed early in life even in children from impoverished environments. Heber's group (Heber 1976; Garber and Heber 1981) believes that this development has become characteristic of many of the experimental group and will serve to support their ability to cope academically and otherwise, despite their difficult ecology. At the same time ample evidence underscores the difference family support and economic conditions made to maintenance of early gains over the course of later development, including the changes in maternal aspirations for their children's school and life goals.

But why is maintenance reflected in a variety of specific cognitive and noncognitive functions and coping processes but not general ability (IQ)? General IQ measures appear to reflect the most abstract and generalized form of verbal-logical skills of the mainstream middle-class culture. In the past they have been largely standardized on white, middle-class populations, drawing their content as noted in chapter 1 from the interests and activities of middle-class life. The problem progresses with age. Reading and mathematics achievement, motivation, cognitive style, and similar measures of ability, while abstract, draw their content much more closely and consistently from the activities to which the child and youth in school are daily exposed. Thus IQ measures draw as much from the home and community of the middle class, which penalizes the poor black child who inhabits a home and community with quite different interests and patterns. Had the IQ measures employed drawn more from the culture and ecology of the poor black community, perhaps the more abstract differences characteristic of IQ measures might have persisted to a higher degree as well, even if not quite at the original levels at the point of terminating early intervention, given the erosion from the way of life.

Studies on Average and Advantaged Populations

The modest to potent short-range effects and the few modest long-range effects from early cognitive stimulation that studies on poor black and similar folk children have shown must be considered remarkable, given the ecological conflicts, social barriers, and artifacts with which their developmental course is strewn. This pattern suggests an underlying potential for early stimulation still very poorly explored. If effects of such magnitude can be so consistently produced with such essentially limited periods of specialized early stimulation in disadvantaged children, what may be the potential for early learning with children from socioeconomically and educationally average or above-average backgrounds who do not have to contend with such barriers and cultural dissonances?

Only three experimental early-education investigations of advantaged children appear in the recent literature and none of them are well controlled (for example, no pretests). (The inconclusive findings from the earlier nursery-school attendance studies will not be repeated here.) One of the three studies (Metzl 1980) suffers from the same global program-outcome asynchrony encountered in many studies on disadvantaged populations. The other two, however, while either restricted to a very small N (4) with no controls (Drash and Stolberg 1977, 1979) or conducted on mixed advantaged-disadvantaged populations (Ulrich, Louisell, and Wolfe 1971), both make use of a better match between stimulation and outcome measures that despite design limitations yields highly interesting results.

Metzl developed an essentially language-based program of stimulation to be presented by parents interactively in six different life situations, ranging from quiet talk to excursions outside the home, between 6 weeks and 6 months of age. Two experimental groups of twenty firstborn infants, each from a normal, middle-class home (seventeen white and three black) were stimulated through instructing parents in two experimental groups (the mother only in one group and both parents in the second) for 1½ hours at each of three ages (6, 12, and 18 weeks) (with random assignment of subjects to group). Mean experimental group gains were significantly greater than controls on the Bayley Mental Scales and on the quality of home environment, as measured by the Caldwell HOME inventory, and means for each experimental group were significantly greater than controls at post-testing on both scales but significantly different from each other only on the Bayley Mental Scales (favoring the two-parent instructed infant group). There were no significant group differences on the Bayley Motor Scale at 6 months.

Metzl's program is strikingly thorough and precise. The modest IQ levels attained by her experimental groups at posttesting (109 and 112 for the respective one- and two-parent instructed experimentals, against 104 for the controls), however, are far from uncommon among the middle-class groups with whom she worked. The relative brevity of her program, the infrequency of delivery to parents, and the global nature of her single mental-development-outcome measure, probably all contribute to these apparently limited results. Motor skills were apparently not stimulated, and not enough time elapsed for cognitive developmental effects to accumulate, especially in light of the lack of specific language measures to detect changes that might have been occurring from a heavily language-focused program. But it is also questionable how faithfully parents would carry out a program so sparsely introduced and monitored, compared to the weekly guidance and monitoring typical of home-based intervention programs with disadvantaged children.

The investigation of Drash and Stolberg on the other hand was better articulated with respect to delivery and to the match between stimulation and measurement, and though about equal in length and age (seven months for three 6-month-old infants and five months for one 3-month-olds), was much more intense (one three-hour session per week, tapering off to one session per month near program termination). The familial socioeconomic and educational background is not described but may be assumed to be around average or at least functionally quite adequate, inasmuch as they were intact families and the type of parent training included weekly staff lectures on infant development, an approach usually considered inappropriate for families from low educational backgrounds. Infants were Caucasian firstborns. Parent training consisted also of modeling and discussion of behavior-modification stimulation techniques and review of infant progress each week. The early-stimulation program covered cognitive, linguistic, and social development.

Infant development was assessed by program-matched measures, the Catell and Binet to measure cognitive development, the Peabody Picture Vocabulary Test and a research-devised measure to assess language, and the Vineland Social Maturity Scale and the Behar Preschool Behavior Questionnaire to assess self-help and interpersonal skills respectively. At post-testing (age 12 months) the infants' mean IQ was 136, rising to 145 at first follow-up (23 months), and 157 at the second (43 months, $N = 3$). On the other measures (administered at follow-ups only) mean language quotients were 149 and 133 ($N = 3$) for the first and second follow-ups. Social skills were similarly advanced: Vineland quotients were 169 and 207 and Behar percentile ranks were 55 and 35.5 (on total disturbance indices) at the respective follow-ups.

The small N and absence of controls dictates a cautious interpretation, particularly since no replication or further follow-up has been carried out (Drash 1982). Certain parallels with results to be reported in later chapters lend additional weight to certain implications the Drash and Stolberg study holds for early stimulation in cognitive development. Further long-term follow-up studies are essential, but even if the evolving home milieu were not to prove supportive of these early exceptional cognitive levels established, the infant-ability levels themselves hint at possibilities for stimulating cognitive complexity that need serious research study. The combination of earliness and intensity, as in the Heber group's investigation, appears to be central to the high-level outcomes, although with important modifications. The program was much less intense (though more intense than the one to two hours per week typical of home guidance programs with most disadvantaged infants), but the focus was on thorough parent education in infant care, training in highly specific stimulation techniques, fairly tightly articulated to measured cognitive goals, and, at least as important, involved educationally advantaged families whose milieu was consonant with the program goals. There was thus no dual curriculum, in which the home curriculum often works in a different direction than the verbal abstraction goals of the program.

Studies with longer term follow-up would prove interesting to determine the degree to which the middle-class ecology is indeed capable of assimilating and maintaining the special stimulation practices, or at least supporting the child's own advanced cognitive system. Here, as in many early-intervention studies, there are only hints as to the nature of this cognitive system in terms of the criteria outlined in table 5-3. It is clearly ad-advanced and complex in the verbal-abstract realms, indicated by no Binet IQ falling below 135 at ages 2 and 3½ and the advanced linguistic skills, prob-ably indicating considerable fluidity and autonomy in these realms. We are given few details, however, about quality, reasoning skills, originality, effi-ciency, and the like, beyond mention of rapidly expending vocabularies and production of long sentences, together with the advanced self-help skills in-dicated by the Vineland (lowest quotient, 128) and the low frequency of hostile, anxious, and hyperactive behavior on the Behar, which are sug-gestive. The substantial mean advances in IQs and social development be-tween posttesting and follow-ups over 2½ years also signal that parents had thoroughly absorbed and continued to practice the program's stimulation techniques. But the accelerating social development may also indicate that the skills developed by the children had included considerable cognitive autonomy that might have contributed to the furtherance of their own in-tellectual advance through experimentation and initiative in utilizing parents as concept resource systems, much as described by White, Kahan, and Attanucci (1979) for highly competent children. The fact that Heber's infants tended to decline later (Garber and Heber 1981), despite their observed executive skills at program termination, however, lends weight to the first hypothesis, at least with regard to the supportive value and con-sonance of the milieu for the child's high verbal-abstract skill system.

A similar comprehensive behavior-modification type program was de-veloped by Ulrich et al. (1971) at Western Michigan University in a center known as the Learning Village. The program was scheduled to furnish con-tinuous academically oriented multiskill stimulation from early infancy through the elementary grades, divided into three phases, an infant nursery (2-30 months), preschool nursery (2½-5 years), and elementary school beginning at age 5. The infant program was designed to teach motor, perceptual, conceptual, language, and personal and social skills. The nursery program combined instruction in language, reading, arithmetic, social studies, science (including "manipulation and analysis of the environ-ment" p. 34) and based most instruction on the tightly programmed Engelmann Distar programs. From kindergarten on, instruction followed the same emphases but more intensively. The child-care and teaching staff in-cluded both trained professionals and paraprofessionals, including college and high-school students, staffed with teacher/child ratios of 1:3 in infancy and 1:5 in the nursery program. While methods were essentially closely con-trolled and programmed behavior-modification techniques, certain skills were taught semiformally, and constructive peer interaction in play was encouraged throughout the Learning Village programs.

The results reported in the literature to date cover preliminary findings on children attending the nursery-school and kindergarten program for one to two years, before the infant program was in operation. Children were from both middle-class ($N = 11$) and lower class, disadvantaged (on welfare) ($N = 7$) backgrounds. Preliminary results on IQ changes with ten children (six advantaged, four disadvantaged), showed mean IQ levels of 114.7 and 124.1 following one year in the nursery program and a second year in kindergarten, respectively, compared to mean IQs of 107.2 and 114 for comparison groups in a one-year traditional nursery program and a two-year traditional nursery-public-school-kindergarten program. (Pretest scores are not reported.) Experimental children gained over both program years (details incomplete and not evaluated statistically), but advantaged children gained slightly more (10 points) than the disadvantaged (8.5 points), the postkindergarten means reaching 130.7 and 114.3, respectively.

On measures of school achievement, which included the total N of 18, all except one child scored at greater than the 90th percentile on reading in the Wide-Range Achievement Test at the end of kindergarten, including all seven disadvantaged children. In arithmetic achievement and spelling the means were better than the 70th percentile. Children attending public-school kindergarten scored at a mean of approximately the 45th and 50th percentiles for the respective achievement areas. Mean grade levels were 3.02 and 1.78 for reading and arithmetic for the Learning Village group, and low first grade (ranging from 1.22 to 1.37) for both categories for both comparison groups, including those who had attended the experimental nursery program, then shifted to public school.

These highly tentative findings, which, though needing confirmation, expansion, and follow-up, and are from a prematurely phased out project (Ulrich 1982), nevertheless provide some support for the promising findings of the Drash and Stolberg (1977, 1979) pilot study. The gains with the small disadvantaged sample are slightly less than those reported with other highly intensive programs, except for the inclusion of an intensive, apparently successful follow-through reading and arithmetic program, in which children attained levels a year in advance of the normal age and grade (age 6, first grade) reported in few other projects (see chapter 7). It is interesting to note, however, the possible operation of age effects. The highly intensive Heber program began in early infancy, as did the Drash and Stolberg program, while the Learning Village program (for this sample), though highly intensive and of one to two year's duration (compared to around twelve to eighteen months for the Heber children to reach their IQ maximum and about seven months for the Drash and Stolberg infants plus many months of probable continuing stimulation from trained parents), did not begin until the ages of 3 to 4 years. Are these age differences related to the 10- to 25-point higher IQ levels attained in the different programs, around 125 (Heber) and 157 (Drash and Stolberg) compared to 115 and 130 for the respective advantaged and disadvantaged groups in the Learning Village program? Observe as well the consistency with which the levels of the advantaged children remain 15 to 30 IQ points above those of the disadvantaged, whether starting in infancy or in the preschool years. Once again the effects of the contending dual curricula appear to be involved.

It would appear that children from all backgrounds can improve their levels of abstract and academic types of cognitive functioning as a consequence of planned stimulation during the early years. Almost any period during the first six years of development will produce cognitive gains above the norms for the population group, though persistent evidence indicates that greater levels in the short term at least are easier to come by when stimulation is applied in infancy, both with poor children from different folk backgrounds and with advantaged, middle-class children from the societal mainstream. Studies on advantaged children are extremely limited, in number, sample sizes, experimental control, and stages of implementation, comparisons among techniques and conditions, and follow-up evaluation. With this caveat in mind, note the consistent trend suggesting that planned-intervention programs conducted with advantaged children may generate cognitive levels up to a standard deviation higher than levels realized with even the earliest, longest, and most intensive and comprehensive programs with disadvantged children. It remains to be tested whether these research-engendered high levels will persist or gradually fade in the manner characteristic of poor children over the years, once such specialized program efforts are terminated. The large-follow-up mean IQ gains (21 points) attained by the Drash and Stolberg infants supports the hypothesis that the verbal and abstract-reasoning competencies stressed in these programs and assessed in IQ tests are much more consonant with life in the middle-class world than they are for children from poor folk communities. Once specially guided, parents may sustain their child's development even beyond the brief one-year follow-up period assessed, perhaps even over an indefinite period. Studies on precocious children to be reported in a later chapter suggest that they will, though the child's own early-generated skills appear to play a strong role as well.

Evidence has cropped up here and there that there is a definite association between the forms of stimulation introduced and the types of outcomes developed. The evidence so far presented, however, is entirely on programs embracing broad, abstract cognitive skills, and for the most part designed as preventive or remedial programs for disadvantaged children from dissonant backgrounds. Similar outcroppings have strongly indicated that earliness alone is not responsible for the cognitive gains regularly attained.

Obviously the nature of the program itself, the type and quality of methods used, must contribute importantly to outcomes, but we have also already found instances (Heber, Hunt) where at least two other primary factors, intensity and duration of stimulation may greatly magnify the cognitive effects of early stimulation. The various so-called secondary dimensions outlined in table 5-2, such as the form of adult-child interaction and the degree of program sequencing, would seem to serve important functions as well. In the next few chapters the effects of using different forms of stimulation, are analyzed as well as the effects of the additional dimensions; more studies of average and advantaged populations are included.

Note

1. The basis for some of the Heber group's findings has been questioned, in particular the equivalence and hence the random assignment of the experimental and control groups (Beller 1979; Page 1975). Because the issue has not been resolved, data have continued to emerge from the project, and above all, even if controls are treated as a quasi-experimental design-comparison group, the developmental outcomes of the experimental subjects are sufficiently impressive to warrant discussion.

7

The Effects of Earliness and Age: Specialized Stimulation

Competence and cognitive processes do not develop all of a piece as the classical views of general intelligence would have us believe. While the broad programs reviewed in the last chapter indicate how malleable the young child's development is to general cognitive stimulation and how persistent the developmental effects can be, in some ways these programs are not as all encompassing as they seem. They pivot around verbal-logical skills of an abstract sort that define academic-type competencies, ignoring such major domains as motor skills, music, and the arts. Yet even in their comparative breadth, they embrace a number of specific competencies, from formal concepts to perceptual skill. In the light of the wide range of variation between competencies regularly found in the same individual (chapter 1), a range of developmental effects from early stimulation concentrated in particular domains might be expected. Taking a good sampling of the major and minor domains, including both those like music, which are bypassed by the corpus of early-intervention studies, and those buried in the generalized early-intervention context, like perceptual and language codes, what can be said about domain-directed stimulation?

Following the pattern outlined in table 5-1, the review of the literature and issues on the differential effects of early stimulation by specific types of concepts will be divided into the three major domains: general knowledge, codes, and strategies and styles of cognitive processing. Under knowledge, we shall first explore how formal concepts or general dimensions about the material world (concepts of form, magnitude, seriation, conservation) have been stimulated, centering largely on work inspired by Piaget. We shall then touch on the neglected domain of information concepts, which has been little researched at any period. The effect of early stimulation in particular areas of coding, such as sensorimotor action, visual perceptual, and language codes, will comprise much of the remainder of the chapter because research on strategies has also attracted little organized interest with respect to early learning. The discussion of learning coding concepts will encompass derivatives of verbal language, reading, and writing, as well as more specialized symbolic domains of mathematics and musical learning. The fact that a review embracing so many domains and subdomains can be confined to a single chapter says something about how few investigations have been conducted on early developmental learning. Except for the area of early reading, only scattered studies among the several domains have seriously addressed the problem of the impact of how early stimulation influences the development of mental functions and competence in a field, as opposed to isolated skills.

Knowledge

Training in (Piagetian) Formal Concepts

The review of classical research on early development in chapter 4 revealed a number of historical constraints that operated to impede study of the potentials for complex early learning. Scattered investigations of learning in several concept areas were undertaken, including formal concepts of magnitude, shape, color, and the like (Munn 1954; Thompson 1952). But the strong behaviorist empirical framework working in opposition to mentalism, combined with the persistence of predeterminist assumptions about development and the absence of meaningful cognitive theory, cast the bulk of the research in one of two forms. On the one hand were dozens of conditioning and other short-term learning studies, often devoted to determining what children could learn at different ages, along with the similar, truncated maturation-versus-learning studies inspired by Gesell. Characteristic is Hicks and Stewart's (1930) investigation of how learning capability progressed with age in 2- to 5-year olds in learning the concept of middle-sized through presentation of a toy under the middle one of successive sets of boxes varying in relative size. On the other hand was an accumulating body of material, a good portion produced by Gesell and the Yale school, that simply recorded what children could do at different ages. The result was massive charts of developmental progressions assumed to be universals for all children in every culture. In the domain of formal concepts, the series of observations by Gesell's student Ames (1946), on the development of the sense of time from infancy, is typical.

Only a few investigators, such as Ling (1941), Long (1940), and Welch (1939a-c, 1940) attempted to pursue formal-concept learning through longer term training studies, Ling with infants in geometric forms and Welch and his collaborators in a variety of studies on size, length, roundness, number, and even abstract concepts of classification and reasoning ability. Despite Welch's efforts to conceptualize formal-concept development in cognitive terms and the relative success of Ling and of Welch's group in demonstrating infants' and young childrens' capabilities to grasp concepts of form, size, and other concepts across conditions, the narrow empirical framework with which they persisted with stimulation over longer than the usual time spans (several months in Ling's case), resulted in an overfocused mechanistic approach that appeared to inhibit learning to some degree (Welch 1939c). Welch's effort to study learning potentials through a complex hierarchical sequence, linking one set of concepts to another, was not picked up at the time. Ling's success in demonstrating that infants could acquire stable, generalized or abstract concepts of many geometric forms (circle, square, triangle, cross, ellipse) considerably younger than 15 months was perhaps the most impressive example of early potentials for complex learning of formal concepts. Infants do not begin to match normatively even the simplest form, a circle, until 13.6 months, and a square only at 19.3 months, on the Bayley Mental Scale, and this only in a simple perceptual match. The findings were not linked to developmental processes or perspectives in any way, however. They were not followed up with successively more complex tasks to determine the extent of what infants could learn, nor related to other competencies, nor were follow-up assessments made to discover the implications of such early advancement for later development. Indeed no follow-up studies of any kind in this domain have been uncovered from earlier eras. The significance of learning for development was hardly touched on in the empirical, yet preterminist mold of the time. This sort of perspective for developmental learning of complex systems could not emerge until the advent of Piaget and cognitive-development theory, though, as we shall see, the availability of a theory does not mean that it will necessarily be applied in a certain way.

Since the assimilation of Piagetian theory in the United States, beginning effectively in the 1960s, much of the research on formal concept learning has been conducted in the Piagetian framework. The long tradition of norm gathering in developmental psychology has continued in the domain of concept development, but the work of recent decades is more complex. One of the fruits of cross-age comparison is the discovery of how early infants appear capable of classifying objects in rudimentary ways—as early as 12 to 24 months (Nelson 1973)—manifested through selective ordering and handling (Ricciuti 1965; Starkey 1981) or measured by habituation and novelty paradigms (Ross 1980). Several Soviet investigators have shown evidence of infants as early as 1 year responding to stimulation involving concept labeling and classification of familiar single objects and pictures, using a conditioning paradigm and children's blocks in play (Koltsova cited in Brackbill 1960, 1962; Mallitskaya 1960). In the course of repeated conditioning trials over several weeks, infants were able to group selected balls and blocks, for example in response to the verbal cue "toy," following the kind of functional basis for grouping Nelson (1973) found in her pilot study and which she believes is characteristic of early preferences. Children at a slightly older age (2 to 3 years) were successfully stimulated by Denney and Acito (1974) to group geometric forms by shape and size through modeling techniques alone in only two demonstration sessions. Thirteen of seventeen experimental subjects formed complete concrete-similarity groupings in a posttest, compared to only three of seventeen controls (who had only played with the materials). Eleven of the thirteen experimental subjects met the criterion on a transfer task with different materials (pattern substituted for shape), compared to two of the three successful posttest controls. Such brief forms of training draw heavily on immediate cognitive-development potentials, rather than generating development, however. Nonetheless this more recently accumulating normative data and the responsiveness of even infants to the beginnings of classification training make one wonder why no real long-term developmental training studies of this kind have been undertaken, even in the Piagetian framework, to which we now turn.

Virtually all of the still-burgeoning Piagetian training studies have centered on training children in specific concepts integral to various stages of Piaget's general scheme of cognitive development. History tending to repeat itself, short-term training has remained the paradigm. The only exceptions have been a number of long-term educational programs, including ones for infants and preschoolers (Day and Parker 1977; Lawton and Hooper 1978), that have been based on or at least have incorporated Piagetian theory on self-regulatory learning and other Piagetian concepts. Since the programs have been included in the foregoing review on compensatory education, they will not be discussed further in detail.

The bulk of Piagetian training studies have concentrated on inducing concepts forming part of the cognitive structures of the concrete-operational stage (defined as the second major stage of development if the preoperational stage, following the sensorimotor stage of infancy, is excluded). Most of them have worked with conservation of number, length, quantity, mass, area, or volume, with a sprinkling dealing with seriation and classification (Brainerd 1977, 1978). One series was concerned with facilitating the development of object concepts in infants (Siegel and Brainerd 1978).

As might be expected, much of the later Piagetian research has been devoted to children at or close to the age when children have typically been found in industrial societies to acquire the concepts from experience normal to daily life in the culture, that is, during infancy for the studies on object permanence and related concept learning and during the first elementary-school years (ages 6-9) for stimulating conservation and other concepts related to the hypothesized concrete-operational period (Flavell 1963; Siegel and Brainerd 1978). Some training studies have succeeded in inducing concept learning in these areas in children well ahead of the prevalent norms.

The collected studies, impressive with respect to the immediate effects of complex early cognitive stimulation, are extremely limited in their designs in precluding the generation of much information on the potency of early-versus-later experience, particularly with respect to long-range effects. The studies do show that infants under 1 year can be regularly and reliably accelerated in object permanence, means-end relations, and similar sensorimotor concepts, and that 3-5 year olds can be tutored to acquire conservation and similar concrete-operational concepts, and in both cases by a variety of instructional methods (passive versus active observation, guidance and feedback, peer modeling).

Simoneau and Décarie (1979), for example, found that 3- to 5-month-old infants advanced more than controls in concepts of object permanence through perceptual training (repeated viewing of a moving object) and through cognitive schema training (coordinating stimulation with objects through touch, sight, and sucking), over one month. Infants trained through the multiple-sensory-modes strategy learned significantly more rapidly than both control infants and perceptually trained infants. Other studies (Nelson 1974, for one) have shown similar short-term effects.

In a series of studies on advancing conservation, Rosenthal and Zimmerman (1972) first trained middle-class 5- and 6-year-olds on six types of conservation (spatial, substance, weight, number, and continuous-discontinuous quantity) through modeling, then later in the series of experiments trained a similar group of 4-year-olds in the same tasks, modifying training by interspersing modeling procedures with assessment tasks to reinforce the lower attention spans of the younger children. Of children who had failed all six conservation tasks at pretesting, approximately two-thirds of the older children passed six tasks at posttesting. They passed over half the tests for types of conservation on which they were not trained. Younger children passed more than one-third of the types of tests and about 30 percent of the transfer tasks. Two later studies included 4-year-old children from culturally very different backgrounds, Papago Indians from Arizona (Henderson, Swanson, and Zimmerman 1975) and children from lower class neighborhoods (Anglo-Mexican and black American) in Tucson, Arizona. A variety of other training studies employing different strategies have induced substantial numbers of 4- to 5-year-old children to conserve on various dimensions or develop classification or other aspects of concrete-operational modes (Brainerd 1977, 1978; Lasry and Laurendeau 1969; Lefebvre and Pinard 1974; Rothenberg and Orost 1969; Vadhan 1976).

What these studies show regarding the value of early experience is that cognitive complexity can be accelerated in infancy and early childhood, in the case of concrete-operational concepts, several years in advance of norms. The findings also show that cognitive development can be advanced considerably in one concept area while remaining behind or essentially at norms in others. Thus children stimulated in two areas (seriation and classification) may advance in one (seriation) but not the other (Bingham-Newman and Hooper 1974). In fact, one or more of the various types of conservation is characteristically singled out (often conservation of number or length) for stimulation, following which a much higher performance is obtained (either higher percentage of children or higher mean scores) for the stimulated areas than for other areas. While transfer effects are common, they do not produce mean scores as high as scores in the trained areas, nor do they generalize equally in all directions. For example, Brainerd's (1974) 4-year-olds (who had failed all conservation-of-length and -weight pretests), trained in conservation of length, passed 50 percent of the length items but only 34 percent of the weight items (untrained) at posttest one week following training. Other studies have shown transfer percentages ranging from 30 percent to 60 percent on different tasks (Brainerd 1977).

Perhaps the most telling aspect relevant to the role of early stimulation is the advancement of trained children over control children and norms by several *years* in cognitive level for the areas trained. The studies also show that it is mediated stimulation, that is, tutoring or guidance by adults (including modeling and feedback and film viewing), that produces the changes, not simply the child's own experimentation, the discovery or self-regulation strategy advocated by Piagetian theorists. Although studies using discovery techniques have not been made on preschoolers, preschoolers trained through guidance advanced about as much as or more (Brainerd 1978) than elementary-school children stimulated through discovery techniques alone in a series of studies conducted by the Genevan school (Inhelder, Sinclair, and Bovert 1974), despite the fact that the former often failed all pretests, whereas the latter had often made partial progress at pretesting. The proportion of Genevan elementary children who made perfect posttest scores ranged from 20 to 40 percent, while in one study Zimmerman and Lanaro (1974) report that 50 percent of the 4-year-olds gave correct judgments on conservation of length at posttesting and 63 percent on a delayed test (nine days later).

What these accrued studies on training Piagetian concepts fail to reveal is how the child's cognitive processing system is affected in other ways, particularly with relevance to how acquiring competence in this or that area of conservation may affect the child's cognitive development, in either the short-term or the long-term. Nothing at all is reported on the status of children at later periods with regard to how early acquisition may have influenced later competencies. At best, follow-up or delayed posttests are administered a few weeks (usually less than two), occasionally a few months (Lefebvre and Pinard 1974; Rothenberg and Orost 1969), following training (Brainerd 1977, 1978).

But even in the short term, we are given no insights on how acquiring a selected concept may influence the child's competence in daily activity of any kind, such as in his or her efficiency of cognitive processing, self-propelled motivation, creativity, competence in schoolwork, or social competence (as listed in table 5-3 and 5-1) or even to perform and produce in tasks of any sort that might be related to the Piagetian concepts in which the child is successfully trained. The pattern of educational experimentation is almost entirely related to proving or disproving issues relative to Piagetian or developmental theory in the narrowest and most abstract terms. It leaves out the functional significance of such acquisitions for child development, especially with regard to the larger perspective of the cumulative, broad-gauge, and long-range functions of stimulation relative to the development of competence.

It is reasonable to believe that acquiring basic formal object concepts earlier in infancy and similar concrete-operational concepts of conservation and classification in the preschool years, well ahead of norms, could establish a more effective foundation to facilitate later cognitive learning and development. But, like the maturation-versus-learning and other short-term learning experiments conducted by Gesell and others in the 1930s, the experimental strategies applied have not tested this concept. We do know that development can be considerably advanced beyond norms in most of the concept areas stimulated, but the evidence runs against the notion that a broad cognitive foundation is being established by such selective concept-training approaches. Indeed transfer is selective and development apparently remains uneven, although again the effects of such selective advancement on extending cognitive development more broadly remains unassessed. Further evidence against such effects appears in a report on several case studies of child prodigies by Feldman (1980). Young elementary-school children skilled tremendously beyond any conceivable norms in chess and music, for example, were only slightly above norms on Piagetian tests of concrete-operational development. Even more significant with respect to the limitations of the generality of Piagetian concepts is Lovell's (1968) finding that a group of twenty-nine precocious 8.5- to 11.7-year-old children (IQs 140-155 +), though more flexible in their thinking, performed no better than average on Piagetian measures of concrete and formal operations.

The design of these Piagetian training studies is nevertheless a considerable improvement over the 1930s' vintage selective training studies. The stimulation programs are highly articulated logically with respect to both the cognitive processes and developmental phases, and the developmental measures are intimately matched to the concepts in which the children are stimulated. Because of this logical articulation, the issue of ceiling effects (effects of training truncated by the simplicity of the task) does not come into play, since training is defined in terms of finite goals. Unfortunately, because we do not learn about the later comparative developmental fates of experimental and control children, the developmental meaning of highly accelerated but selective advances remains obscure with respect to the issue of nature versus nurture and, relative to our problem, of the role of early experience. Only long-term follow-ups and long-term maturation-versus-learning studies, following through on longer complexity sequences of Piagetian and related concept hierarchies, including school learning, can furnish the answers.

Something of this order is illustrated by a science-training study with 3-year-olds of mixed racial and socioeconomic background, the only study located to present a relatively long-term (eight months) program of articulated formal concept training with average populations (Zeitler 1972). The program was carefully designed, implemented, and measured to teach children ($N = 30$) elements of a broad range of formal scientific concepts (odor, color, temperature, phase, hardness, size, and so on)—but no experimental control group was used. Because of the detail and clarity with which the program was conducted, however, a precise profile of the children's preprogram-to-postprogram progress is disclosed on exactly what concepts children did and did not improve. The percentage of both boys and girls identifying properties increased in nearly all categories, mean pre-posttest gains overall reaching significance ($p < .001$) for both groups. Differences in changes between dimensions varied widely, however. For example, the largest increases were found in certain aspects of color, temperature, and hardness (at least 50 percent change each), while no change at all occurred in certain features of odor and direction. The study resembles Palmer's (1972) concept-directed program for poor black children, but is less broad, more concerned with exploring the possibilities of developing observational skills and scientific concepts in preschool children, and lacked any long-term follow-up. The study is important in breaking away from global measures like the IQ test as the central arbiter of cognitive development.

More such programs, in which hierarchies of different concepts are explored, are needed to determine how variations in the depth and breadth of early concept-learning influences children's cognitive development, particularly with regard to the long-term development of cognitive strategies and readiness to progress to complex levels in science and math. The body of developmental information that is mounting under Piagetian influence could readily be used to design and test quite sophisticated and selective long-term developmental stimulation programs. These would progress from the very roots of grouping to high-level, multihierarchical classification in well-ordered, perhaps greatly accelerated sequences that might also be generalized to function usefully in many daily activities.

Stimulation of Information Concepts

Early concept learning, not about the formal, general nature of things, but about their specialized features and functions, has seldom been investigated with the idea in mind of children's potentials for complex development. Like the developmental sequences for time, number, motor, and other skills and concepts charted so untiringly by Gesell's group, children's common knowledge about the world, their concepts of birth, sex, death, and life, political views, family, industry, transportation, offices, and even the common social artifacts and natural phenomena of everyday life have been widely collected since the beginnings of developmental psychology (see Bibace and Walsh 1981). The first formal investigation in developmental psychology, G. Stanley Hall's (1883) exhaustive assessment of *The Contents of Children's Minds*, summarized in chapter 4, was in fact a survey of all the information concepts of first graders Hall could think of to ask, ranging from concepts of ponds and sunsets to those of cubes and business.

Curiously, few efforts have been made to investigate children's potentials for learning such concepts, despite the recent work on formal concepts, which reveals that even infants under 2 can begin to classify common objects like miniature cars, animals, and other toys functionally as well as formally. Limited reports available of Russian investigators (Brackbill 1960, 1962) using a conditioning paradigm do suggest that functional classificatory skills may be accelerated in early infancy, but almost no other studies of information-concept learning can be found. The studies that have been undertaken have been buried in other contexts, usually learning formal concepts, from Welch to Piaget. Children, engaged to learn an abstraction, are necessarily working with content of some kind, using dolls, furniture, marbles, clay, pennies, sticks, or whatever types of objects an investigator happens to choose. Since the entire focus is on learning the formal abstraction, not on learning about dolls and furniture in depth, such studies are no measure at all of children's potentials for content learning. At best a few exemplars are exposed, but these are usually selected because the child is already familiar with them.

A second introduction to information-concept learning appears in educational contexts, but rarely before school age. Studies of learning in schools are restricted to children past the preschool period by definition, and preschool programs, even the few for advantaged children, include information concepts only incidental to the main formal-concept program. One of the earlier programs, a study by Dawe (1942), did include a definite program of information-concept learning in a specialized language-stimulation program for orphanage children between 43 and 82 months. Children were taught information and formal concepts through planned discussion of some 845 pictures taken largely from magazines and depicting clearly a representative variety of common objects and activities such as food and eating, number concepts, and clothing. They were also taught through six excursions to places of interest to the children and through information contained in stories and other activities of the language program. At the end of the program the experimental subjects were found to have progressed significantly more than controls on a broad variety of common categories of information assessed through home living and general science tests.

This promising learning project does not seem to have been replicated or pursued elsewhere. Programs for the disadvantaged have incorporated content into the typical language-stimulation and generalized cognitive-stimulation curriculum, simply using common objects and knowledge to serve the language-labeling processes and the time, size, space, causality, and similar formal-concept learning that constitute the substance of early-intervention programs. Even when separate concept inventories are devised to measure development (Caldwell 1970a; Englemann 1967; Victor and Coller 1970), the bulk of the material is composed of formal concepts, not common information concepts. In any case, outstanding concept complexity has not been the mark of developmental attainment in children whose efforts are divided between folkways and verbal abstraction. Follow-up measures, moreover, have been limited to broad indices of achievement and coping in school, rather than the quantity and complexity of concepts in the repertoire.

The omission of information-concept learning for special study in early development may be more unfortunate than at first it might seem. It is conceivable that stimulating young children early with a useful body of general knowledge or even in some cases with knowledge in depth in selected content areas could be a useful avenue to facilitate children's apprehension of formal concepts and an important vehicle for advancing cognitive development. High familiarity with a wide range of content, for example, may enable children to detach themselves from content more readily in order to grasp abstractions, provided the content is not stimulated in an overly concrete manner or offered in disconnected rote fashion. Development of knowledge in depth in specific areas, ranging from history to cars to postage stamps, may also prove to be a productive means of laying an early basis for later competence, as will be discussed further on in conjunction with the discussion of the development of precocity.

Codes

The codes employed for mental processing, or the medium in which an activity occurs, it will be recalled (see table 5-1), range from the most direct and concrete sensorimotor level of action to the most abstract and symbolic forms, including such coding systems as ordinary language, mathematical systems of various kinds, and symbolic logic. Given our focus on early development, it is fitting to begin at the most concrete level with motor skills, because they are among the first to develop and obviously take up much of the child's life during the early years. It is no doubt for this reason that, historically, a large portion of the research on young children's learning (Munn 1954) and developmental norm collecting (Gesell et al. 1940; Gesell and Amatruda 1947) has been concentrated in this area. The great focus on motor development as such, however, was probably at least equally a function of the behavioral outlook, which mired investigation in sterile description, motor actions being among the most likely candidates for attention.

As the scheme described in chapter 5 indicated and as various authors have conceptualized in different ways (Piaget 1952; Bruner 1973; Fowler 1976), basic motor competence consists of complex schemas, sequences, and hierarchies of routines and subroutines, which are mastered only through extensive periods of developmental experience during the first few years. Motor skills are not neatly compartmentalized separately from concept learning in other areas, however. Tasks are typically composed of a number of different subsets of skills, most often combining motor with perceptual operations, usually visually, and quite often language as well, as in showing someone how to make a cake while using words to explain the procedures demonstrated. We must expect then that studies of motor competencies that involve complex skills like gymnastics, ballet, skiing, and musical instrumental performance would necessarily demand cognitive mastery of highly intricate pyramids and chains of complex motorial concepts, quite apart from the involvement of various combinations of musical, aesthetic, and other concepts. We shall review visual-motor activities together, combining in the same discussion studies of both fine- and gross-motor skills because so few studies of either kind meet our criteria.

Stimulation of Motor Skills

Studies on stimulating motor competence are afflicted by the same problem that plagues research on concept learning in other areas. The vast majority of motor-learning studies of all periods are short-term training studies, which are inherently limited in their potential for illuminating the role of early experience in development. For the most part they made use of simple, isolated tasks without regard to ceiling effects and possibilities of building competence in a complex hierarchy of skills. The tasks embraced skills like cube manipulation, stair climbing, cutting with scissors, walking boards, tossing rings and other similar simple skills. In the maturation-versus-learning studies with twins as subjects, for example, maturation and general experience enabled the control twin (later, in shorter periods of training) to attain much the same levels as the trained twin had achieved (in some cases more practice than guidance was given, as in a study by Hicks 1930). The investigators failed to note that in each case children attained levels much ahead of developmental norms for the skills in question and that ceiling effects effectively limited any further gains to asymptotic increments. For example, in stair climbing both the earlier and later trained twin were able to climb five stairs in ten seconds (T slightly faster than C) at close to 1 year, compared to age 2 for walking upstairs alone for the average child (Gesell and Thompson 1929). Later motor gains for either twin were measured by Gesell in fractions of a second (Gesell and Thompson 1941), not much of a change in competence.

In the few instances where relatively complex skills were involved, maturation or general experience did not equal the effects of the earlier training (Mattson 1933; see chapter 4). Even within the limits of the comparatively restricted range of skills (manipulating a ball in a maze, with no concept hierarchy involved) and time for training (six weeks) in one of the few investigations studying the problem, the effects of specific training increased enormously and proportionally to the complexity of the skills in the task. Short-term training investigations also tended to show that older children learned motor skills at faster rates than younger children, (Gesell and Thompson 1929; Hilgard 1933), but again this interpretation overlooks the developmental perspectives of the advantage that earlier acquisition may offer for complex skills that are built on cumulatively over extended periods of development. Children of different ages also appear to learn at much the same rate for material at their own level (Munn 1954).

Gesell and others also overlooked indications of cumulative effects of early stimulation. In Gesell's twins (Gesell and Thompson 1941), both twins maintained scores of 90 to 100 IQ, above their own base level ($<$90 IQ prior to the training study series) for several years (to age 9), before falling back to earlier levels. The earlier stimulated twin T also maintained a *generally* greater competence in all gross-motor activities and some aspects of language, suggesting a cumulative advantage from the combined effects, in motor training of a generally earlier start and more training experience, and in language training of an earlier start in the infant language-training study and the continuing greater language stimulation accompanying the greater total amount of training received in all studies. Another investigator (Mirenva 1935) found the usual short-term advantages accruing from specific motor-skill training (jumping and throwing and rolling balls at targets) in four identical twins over their untrained twinmates. But she also reports the trained twins gained much over the untrained twins in general motor dexterity, similar to those evident but minimized by Gesell in twin T, and the advantages observed by McGraw (1935, 1939) in her long-term motor-stimulated infant twin. Like Gesell's twins, moreover, Mirenva's twins gained substantially in IQ (10 points) from the four and one-half months of training in the skill series, compared to no gain at all for the untrained twins.

As observed in the cross-cultural studies reviewed in chapter 1, gross-motor competence is a valued domain of socialization among tribal societies. Early sitting and walking are encouraged in advance of norms characteristic in industrial societies (Super 1976, 1981), and in several societies selected complex skills, including swimming, canoeing, and bareback horseback riding are socialized from earliest infancy to high competence levels between ages 2 to 5 on the different complex skills (Ewers 1955; Mead 1975; Rosenstiel 1976; Wallace and Hoebel 1952; Wilbert 1976b). In folk society few aspects of any skills are formally taught. Rather, children begin acquiring the skills that are ecologically necessary in the context of daily informal interactions with the extended-age peer-hierarchy and adults in the small, close-knit communities. Such cross-cultural data furnishes evidence for the high potential of infants and young children to learn complex motor competencies without stress, but since skills in folk communities are in every case defined and reinforced throughout the life cycle to meet the adaptation requirements of the culture, there is no possibility of assessing the effects of early stimulation alone. Instead these obviously superior competencies maintained throughout development and over the course of adult life give weight to the cumulative effects of stimulation over the span and the importance of continuing ecological support and reinforcement for skill maintenance and refinement.

A related study by Williams and Scott (1953) on black infants from contrasting low and high socioeconomic backgrounds in the United States, shows similar effects of differences in socialization practices on the development of motor skills. Lower class infants were significantly advanced over infants from largely upper-middle-class families in gross-motor competencies on the Gesell Developmental Scales (crawling, sitting, walking, jumping, throwing, and so on), and consistently accelerated by about 7 DQ points over controls from 10 to 15 months, the lower class group mean reaching 119 DQ at a mean of 15 months. Differences between the two groups were associated with child-rearing practices, in particular, absence of mechanical restrictions, permissiveness in discipline and in permitting child-initiated reaching, and flexibility of schedules, on all of which lower class families were rated significantly higher ($p = .01-.03$) than middle-class families. Again, the data indicate the effects of variations in class-based, culturally stimulated practices but say nothing of long-term outcomes.

In his studies of infants reared in several different residential orphanages in Tehran, Dennis (1960s) found gross differences in gross-motor competence between infants reared in public and private residential institutions, which varied enormously in the quality of care and opportunities for motor learning. Only 2 percent of infants between 1 and 2 could walk in the public institution (none of fifty could walk alone), only 14 percent could creep or scoot, and only 42 percent could even sit, compared with respective percentages of 60, 75, and 90 in the private institution ($N = 20$). These compare with U.S. norms for sitting and creeping of around 6 to 9 months and walking between 12 and 14 months (Bayley 1969). Older children in the same or a similar public institution remained similarly retarded in motor skills to age 4, only 15 percent of children between 3 and 4 having learned to walk unaided and 63 percent walking supported, compared to 94 percent of the children between 2 and 3 ($N = 31$) walking alone in the private facility. Children in the public institutions were almost totally confined to small cribs from the time they were admitted as foundlings, usually less than a month after birth. Except for alternate-day bathing and periodic changing, they were rarely handled, even for feeding, being fed with propped bottles and left alone in their cribs supine without toys nearly all the time. Children in the private institutions, on the other hand, were handled frequently, held in laps, held for feeding, placed frequently in playpens with toys, and the trained staff emphasized behavioral development. Untrained staff and supervisors and staff/child ratios of 1:8, compared to 1:3 or 1:4 in the private setting, were behind the dramatic differences in care. The quality of ratios has proved to be an extremely important setting variable influencing the quality of care and stimulation and the corresponding developmental outcomes (Fowler 1975). Dennis was able to show that nutrition was not a factor, given the vigor with which infants scooted, a mode of self-taught, hitching movements, which requires more energy than walking. This mode was adopted by 75 percent of the infants, instead of creeping, without progressing to walking for some years, as a result of the confining conditions and absence of stimulation. Confinement was reinforced by soft mattresses that greatly inhibited sitting and mobility from the constant supine position.

It is tempting to compare this monkeylike mode of locomotion with the kind of animallike movements observed in the many so-called wild children when they are first discovered (Lane 1976; Malson 1972). In this cruder, less-efficient method of movement what is likely to result in the absence of adult guidance? In any case Dennis draws attention to the characteristic skipping of the creeping mode, a supposed inevitable, biologically programmed stage of motor development enshrined by Gesell and the other early-developmentalists, as evidence of developmental variability with respect to order and form, even in this supposedly sacred maturational sequence. In the private institution, employing open, stimulating methods of care, all infants at the prewalking stage ($N = 15$) progressed by creeping rather than scooting.

Dennis himself considered the extreme effects of the prolonged motor deprivation on skill development, in contrast to the relatively minor delays observed in the twins he and his wife reared under restricted conditions (Dennis 1941; Dennis and Dennis 1951), as indicating the profound effects early experience can have upon maturation, in opposition to the classical developmental view. Those twins, it will be recalled, were handled minimally until 9 months, then gradually handled more and talked with during their second year. Few and small delays were registered in the simpler, early skills (hand and object play), but skill delays became more noticeable with the later skills of creeping and mobility. Skills were not nearly so delayed, however, because the twins were handled more from the start, were typically placed in a prone position (on a firm mattress) in a manner that facilitated motor experimentation (head up, rolling over, pulling to sit), and deprivation was less prolonged, in fact including compensatory guidance in sitting and standing soon after delay became evident. In the same way the absence of gross-motor retardation among cradle-bound Hopi Indian infants appeared to be the result of frequent holding and handling and opportunities to experiment from a prone position during many waking hours (Dennis and Dennis 1940). However, cradling could be said to be associated with slower rates of development than those observed in many cultures in Africa and elsewhere (Hindley et al. 1966; Super 1976, 1981; Williams and Scott 1953).

With respect to the effects of this early deprivation on later development, Dennis observed older children in the same institution, children over 3 (age 6-15) attending school, playing games, doing chores, and learning to weave Persian rugs. Because they were from the same institution, he assumes they too experienced motor deprivation during early development, though he furnishes no information on whether deprivation had in fact occurred to the same degree in these individuals. Institutional crowding and care deterioration may have been a recent phenomenon, however, as a function of the then recent rapid growth of Tehran and the accompanying social disorganization he reports, as peasants moved to the cities in accelerating numbers. He gives no details on the skills observed, mentioning in passing walking, running, and weaving, the latter a fine motor skill, about which no deprivation was reported. Nor does he describe the competence levels attained, which might well have been lower than norms for Iranians socialized in other settings. At best all we can infer is that considerable recovery from early deprivation may have occurred (assuming it did occur in the older children Dennis observed). Such recovery has by now been widely documented for many settings (Clarke and Clarke 1976) and indeed is one of the hallmark achievements of the compensatory education movement (Zigler and Valentine 1979). But again, as in all studies with all deprived or culturally different populations, there is reason to doubt whether the (assumed) later recovery generated competence levels as great as those realized through development in which skill stimulation for a specified domain has never been deprived, hampered, or diminished at all.

There have been comparatively few early-motor-stimulation studies since World War II. The focus has generally shifted from the learning studies and descriptive norm gathering of the prewar practices to the cognitively guided tracking of sensorimotor-based Piagetian sequences of the object concept. Studies on object-concept-learning, which center on motor action, are invariably short-term. Certain limited training investigations following a less Piagetian conception can also be found, such as one by Kaye and Marcus (1981), in which infants were stimulated in a variety of simple fine-motor actions (touching ear, shaking toy, mouthing) once a month between the ages of 6 and 12 months. The results demonstrated that infants learned the gestures modeled through imitation, and in a certain order, but while such studies are valuable for exploring learning mechanisms and sequences, like the Piagetian studies, they hardly begin to probe early potentials for motor learning in relation to the development of competence in depth.

One of the few exceptions to this trend is the extended series of investigations carried out by White and his associates (White, Castle, and Held 1964; White and Held 1966) on the potentials for stimulating infants almost from birth in a sequence of interrelated visual motor skills. The approach is something of a model for charting and stimulating motor competencies from a developmental perspective. Earlier brief training studies had demonstrated that an infant could be induced to grasp a rattle through less than a week of training between 4 and 5 months of age (Curti 1930). With similarly limited training an infant could even grasp and hold its own bottle to suck liquids, becoming quite proficient at manipulating the bottle, inserting and removing the nipple at will during the next few weeks (Sherritt 1922). I have produced similar results on self-feeding in a later unpublished study of my three daughters. But, while bottle feeding is a complex, cognitively mediated, fine-motor manipulative task for the age (independent grasping begins modally around 5 months on the Bayley (1969) and other infant scales), such studies do not systematically explore conditions facilitating the learning of interrelated skills over substantial spans of development.

More recently, White and his group studied the etiology of these kinds of visually directed movements through experimentally controlled observations. Working with institutionalized infants, they traced and classified a normative sequence of development over the first 6 months of life in terms of eight stages of development, culminating in visually directed reaching just prior to the age of 5 months.

Of significance in the present context is the success of the investigators in manipulating the crib conditions of the institutionalized children in a way that experimental groups achieve top level reaching in approximately 60 percent of the time required by control groups, or at less than age 3 months. The various combinations of experimental stimulation include greater opportunities for self-initiated movement, exposure to a great variety of color-form stabiles in the crib, and extra handling by adults.

Certain focused forms of stimulation, particularly placing decorated pacifiers at the point of normal infant visual accommodation (8-10 inches), accelerated further the development of visually directed reaching. On the other hand, there was a tendency of specially stimulated infants to be slightly delayed in hand regard and swiping responses. This unevenness of development might be avoidable if all aspects of a series of learning tasks are subjected to careful analysis to ensure the coordination of sequencing operations. In this manner components of each sensorimotor cognitive structure could become integrated into effective schema.

One problem with these studies is the lack of follow-up with complex motor skills, to discover how accelerated development for visually directed reaching might be built on to foster greater proficiency with more complex skills. Visually directed reaching is an important component of the thousands of fine visual motor manipulations of everyday life—handling minute objects, tying shoelaces, working puzzles, sewing, writing, drawing, playing a musical instrument. Nor is any follow-up reported to determine how longlasting these early advances might be. Since White's studies, like the series by Hunt and his associates (1976) in Tehran, used institutionalized infants who encounter the same difficult ecology that works against development in its optimal form, the methods also need to be tested with average and advantaged populations. Would a more facilitative ecology produce more dramatic outcomes or would the results of specialized stimulation for such simple skills be buried in the already stimulating context much like the parallel between school and home provided in the classical nursery-school studies?

In the White series, stimulation sequences are more behaviorally articulated with the developmental outcome measures than in the Hunt studies, as well as more precisely focused on motor competence in particular forms. The latter investigation utilized more generalized, cognitively oriented, means-end activities and cognitive-developmental assessments. Unfortunately, without continuation and expansion of these lines of inquiry on stimulation, and comparisons between the effects of narrower or broader and more cognitively conceptualized stimulation and competence development, there is little to show of the potentials for early perceptual motor stimulation.

We are left then largely with the single study of McGraw (1935, 1939—except for studies by the authors of this book, to be reviewed later) that seriously explores the potentials of early developmental stimulation over time in the motor area. The many classical short-term early-training studies repeatedly verified that children's fine- and gross-motor competencies could be accelerated during early development in a variety of specific ways, though given the narrowness and simplicity of most skills, much of the specific gains largely disappeared after a few weeks or months. Repeated training of Gesell's identical twins, much of it on interrelated motor skills, gave hints Gesell overlooked or played down, that broader, more extended, more complex, and more purposive types of training might generate more important, cumulative effects on development. The Mirenva (1935) studies suggested that multiple early experiences in related skills tend to generalize in the motor area, while Mattson's (1933) study indicated that the dependance of perceptual motor competence on directed stimulation would show up only on skills sufficiently complex for something besides a few test trials and the ordinary culturally programmed experiences of daily life to make a difference. Cross-cultural observations and deprivation studies suggested that both basic and complex gross-motor competencies could vary widely as a result of gross differences in the character of early gross-motor experiences, experiences that appeared to establish a strong or weak foundation for later skill development. But only McGraw directly experimented with augmented motor stimulation extended in time, although popular early-swimming (Newman 1967; Timmermans 1975) and other motor stimulation programs (such as Suzuki music training), which would make fertile areas for long-term study, have since become quite successful and widespread.

In McGraw's lengthy, intensive, and systematic programs of stimulation on a variety of relatively complex skills—skating, tricycle riding, swimming, and diving—the trained twin became highly skilled in these activities by 22 months of age, long before the usual norms for acquisition. After two months training, his fraternal twin by age 2 years was much less successful in acquiring these skills, and at age 6 very substantial differences remained between the twins in skills in which changes in body proportions through growth were not involved (tricycle riding, climbing down, swimming, stacking). But above all, the quality of coordination, agility, and confidence with which the early-trained twin continued to tackle these and other gross-motor tasks of any kind, like walking, running, and falling down, were far superior at all times. Even as late as age 22 in a film of their performance in climbing a high ladder, the trained twin, Johnny, remained far more agile and at ease in ascending the ladder, mounting quickly to the top (roof high) in alternating steps, compared to his twin brother Jimmy, who displayed considerable hesitation and uncertainty (McGraw, 1976). Jimmy mounted the ladder slowly, placing the same foot foward each time, then dragging the other onto the same step before advancing the first foot again. Johnny climbed and descended with equal ease and alacrity, whereas for Jimmy the descent was as painfully slow as his ascent.

The fact that the control twin was fraternal does not detract from the significance of early-stimulation development for the complex skills. Nor should we be deceived by the apparent simplicity of ladder climbing into writing off Johnny's later advantage to motivation and emotional factors alone, or to continued practice. No doubt emotional factors are important, and quite possibly lifelong differences in skill reinforcement through practice were involved. Yet coordination and sequencing of complex movements, in which Johnny's training led him to excell over his untrained twin in all skills by age 2, as well as later at ages 6 and 22, make up the complex cognitive core of concepts and operations that Jimmy never mastered very well in any task in the gross-motor sphere. The behavioristic framework of the era that constrained McGraw's grasp of the cognitive dimensions of motor tasks need not lead us into the same error.

Together with the hints of developmental complexity, generalization, and permanence in the Mattson, Mirenva, and Gesell twin studies, the McGraw findings suggest that early motor stimulation may lay down certain cognitive and motivational dispositions to competence across a domain that may to a degree become self-perpetuating, even when not particularly reinforced in later periods. But when they are reinforced throughout later development, as in certain folk cultures or as in certain sports and musical activities, these early-induced motor dispositions and competencies may be beneficial if not essential to outstanding mastery in the field. We shall have more to say on this point when we discuss precocity and the influence of other dimensions of stimulation on development.

Visual Perceptual Skills: Ikonic Codes and the Visual Arts

Visual perception is in many ways closely linked to fine-motor competence because of the manner in which motor activities are engaged in learning about the nature of visual spatial phenomena, as Piaget's highly original observations on sensorimotor development suggest (Piaget 1952). Piaget himself, however, tends to conceptualize perception as a process proceeding in a separate channel from the development of cognitive processes beginning with perceptual-motor activities (Flavell 1963; Gruber and Voneche 1977). Let us treat visual perceptual processes as concept-learning activities taking off from perceptual-motor processes and to some degree intertwined with or at least depending on them for their expression. Their development is one of building up a visual spatial conception of the world, one step removed from sensorimotor action codes, which become coded in visual imagery, symbols, and three-dimensional depiction (Bruner, Olver and Greenfield 1966). Visual perceptual codes are thus the basis for producing and interpreting pictures and the entire aesthetic world of the visual arts—drawing, painting, sculpture, and the like—each with slight variations in the rules for how the visual world is represented. Contrary to Piaget, visual spatial perception of the world would seem to be related to concepts about the environment, and indeed the perception of phenomena is highly dependent on the meanings we attach to them, which in turn emerge from the concepts of the world built up through many years of experience.

There is nevertheless an apparent distinction between concepts and perception, which probably proceeds in part from the way in which concepts are typically defined in verbal form. Concepts rely on generalizations about classes of phenomena, abstractions that summarize ideal types, defined by certain critical rule features, deliberately ignoring or excluding variations in perceptual detail. Yet visual perception usually also embraces general forms and patterns, representations of ideal types, that transcend the irrelevant details that appear in actual examples. For this reason we might have included here Ling's (1941) geometric-form simulation study, but the emphasis was on learning a generalized concept of form, abstracting across conditions (despite Ling's employment of a discrimination learning-theory framework) and thus an important basis for formal-concept learning. While the focus for spatial perceptual processes lies in the business of representing visual reality in detail, the problem is to integrate into depictive detail general types. The concern is upon both generalities and how they are represented. In language coding the latter is not directly implicated. It is concepts and rules of perceiving and representing concepts of the world in visual form that are involved in ikonic coding.

At the simplest levels studies have shown that the hierarchy of perceptual preference for faces, other perceptual patterns and color can be altered through conditioning in normal infants between 3 and 7 months of age and even in retardates between 3 and 9 months (Lu 1967). No long-term training studies have followed up this work, however, to determine the developmental consequences of altering perceptual hierarchies.

At more complex levels skill in perceptual coding appears to be tied to a certain extent to knowledge of the concepts being encoded and decoded (regarding knowledge of letter and number forms see Gibson and Levin 1975). But while school-readiness tests like the Metropolitan have been found to correlate from .575 to .674 with various subtests of the Stanford Achievement Tests, such tests actually embrace additional cognitive operations (vocabulary, arithmetic) found on IQ tests, with which they also correlate highly (.76), along with the multiplicity of perceptual skills closely allied with letter and numerical forms (Anastasi 1976). Research on such perceptual skills has thus been largely directed toward improving readiness for reading, writing, and arithmetic, rather than competence in perceptual coding as such.

A good illustration is provided by a program undertaken with preschool disadvantaged children. In one of the most comprehensive programs of the type a highly systematic and sequenced perceptual-skill program, beginning at age 4, extending through grade 2, and leading directly into teaching reading and arithmetic in the Primary Education Project (PEP), was organized and conducted at the Learning Research and Development Center at the University of Pittsburgh (Rosner 1972). Both visual and auditory perceptual skills were carefully sequenced in a behavioral objectives program that included copying and analysis of geometric patterns and gradually letters (including grapheme-phoneme relations) and numerals. Cumulative mastery expanded from grade to grade. But individual differences remained wide at every grade, and correlations with reading and arithmetic achievement for visual and auditory perceptual motor tests designed specifically for the program ranged only between .40 and .55. (The effects of the program on reading and arithmetic achievement will be summarized later.) While these and other similar programs seldom as tightly sequenced indicate the possibilities for accelerating early perceptual-skill learning, the narrow academic task and area focus of the skills in question does not seem to add much to our understanding of how children can be induced to grasp and represent visual spatial reality in the broad sense.

Much of our knowledge about the development of the child's understanding of visual reality is derived from children's drawings. Measures of how children draw figures, especially people, are widely used as measures of intelligence (Harris 1963) and almost every mental scale from the original Gesell scales (Gesell and Amatruda 1947) to the Bayley scale (1969) and Binet scales (Terman and Merrill 1972) include items marking the development of infant and child skills in depicting objects visually through drawing. Children progress through a number of stages to arrive at the ability to make use of elaborate rules for coding objects in two-dimensional representations, such as the rules for perspective, shading, relative size, and composition (Gesell and Ames 1946; Harris 1963). Harris (1963) has summarized the various conceptions investigators have devised to describe the course of development. In general, children progress from a scribbling phase when they learn the functions of the drawing instrument, through a series of steps in which they first gain control over the direction and form of movements, then begin to label the apparently meaningless markings, and gradually become able to make and plan crude representations. These evolve from designs and star-shaped figures or mandalas radiating from a center (Kellog 1969; Kellog and O'Dell 1967) to tadpole forms and finally increasingly complete human and other figures.

Most of the attention in developmental psychology and mental testing has been devoted to how the child develops skills in literal or assumed naturalistic representation, according to Western concepts of drawing and painting that were slowly developed historically (Gombrich 1961). In keeping with the predeterministic outlook that has governed these fields for much of this century until quite recently, the evolution of the concepts and skills employed have been assumed to be sequential universals. The mandala, for example, is believed to appear everywhere and in all cultures in a definite form during a particular phase of the supposed developmental order (Kellog 1969; Kellog and O'Dell 1967). This outlook has led apparent developmental progression in drawing skill to be taken as an index of general intelligence and mental age (Harris 1963). It has taken time for the gradually accumulating evidence from cross-cultural studies and other lines of thought and inquiry to make inroads, to recognize, for example, that the crude stick figures Dennis (1960b) observed in the drawings of Bedouins were a matter of cultural proscription against iconoclastic representation, not a matter of inferior underlying general ability.

Ives and Gardner (1980) have discussed a number of ways in which cultures define perceptual experience for children that channel visual coding concepts of drawing, painting, sculpturing, and other art media. The availability of materials affects children's development in different media: for example, plenty of clay but a dearth of two-dimensional devices will stimulate three-dimensional development. A lack of pencils but plenty of sand in rural Honduras made unschooled children more skilled in copying geometric figures in sand than with a pencil on paper. The availability of culturally valued referents influences children's perception as well, as in the tendency of children from industrial societies, surrounded by letter forms, to form and label letters very early, in contrast to the orientation toward fauna and flora in nonliterate societies. The early emphasis on visual realism and linear and spatial perspective in industrial life, compared with the early appearance of stylism in Bali and the lack of concern for spatial perspective in Nepalese children's map drawing are similarly rooted in the ecological perspectives and cultural practices of the different cultures.

In a somewhat broader framework, Barry (1957) rated ten works of graphic art from each of thirty nonliterate societies, on which Whiting and Child had presented socialization data, in terms of eleven variables defining complexity of art style. The variable complexity of design (which correlated highest with the overall measure) correlated .71 ($p < .01$), higher than any other art variable, with the Whiting and Child measure of severity of socialization among the thirty societies. Unfortunately this relatively isolated earlier work does not seem to have had much impact on the unfolding developmental orientation that has governed work in art education. One does not need to subscribe to the psychoanalytic framework underlying this study on socialization and art complexity, which may have been partly responsible for the study's failure to influence the necessarily cognitive thrust of education, to appreciate that severity of socialization might be associated with training the child in perceptual cognitive particularities.

Cross-cultural studies on perceptual and aesthetic skill development are a rich source of concepts for designing studies on art stimulation that are only just beginning. Given the predeterministic framework, however, it can hardly be unexpected that little research has been conducted on how experience might influence the development of perceptual coding processes and representation. The problem is especially magnified in this domain because the visual arts are widely identified as a special category of experience. They are not only considered subject to the laws of preordained developmental universals, but ability is thought to take the form of special talents, which one either does or does not possess, that can emerge only when allowed to grow and flower with complete spontaneity (Eisner n.d., 1972; Gardner 1980; Grossman 1970). Any attempt to exercise direct influence upon the child's skill development is felt to be likely to stifle the full richness of the imagination and to lead to the narrow production of stereotypic forms using such conventions as a bird as two connecting arches or a sun as a smiling circle with spokes radiating outward. Few experimental training investigations of any kind at any age can be found that attempt to study the conditions of stimulation that influence the development of competence in art.

There are, nonetheless, a few advocates of planning children's art education who have attempted to explore the parameters of stimulation through which children acquire perceptual and artistic skills. While generally adhering to a universal developmental theoretical framework, Gardner (1973, 1980) has shown how cultural and personal experience, including the influence of sophisticated models in the family, may enrich and advance the development of artistic skills. Ives and Gardner (1980) have explored the dimensions of art experience cross culturally, as just noted, and Fucigna, Ives, and Ives (1982) have conceptualized a developmentally based art curriculum beginning in early childhood, which would furnish extended personal experience in motor skills, psychological autonomy, social relations, and symbolic communication, closely related to opportunities for the child to master visual art techniques. Eisner (1972) has advocated the need for more systematically designed training programs. Grossman (1970) has stressed the importance of cognitive and sensory exploration and is one of a handful of investigators to conduct studies in which preschool children have been stimulated with different techniques to foster the development of visual and art skills, particularly in drawing and painting. He conducted two 12-week training studies with kindergarten children centering on both cognitive analysis and sensory processes to develop visual-perceptual, aesthetic, and creative skills in drawing. Experimental groups improved significantly more than control groups in all areas (significantly so in the second study), generally improving more in the use of detail and in the employment of such design skills as composition, line, and the use of color as judged by a group of eight artists.

Two studies from the USSR report that teaching drawing skills improved technique and representational skills. Ignat'ev (1951), using a direct guidance approach to drawing by dividing up drawing areas into sections, not only found that the children's spontaneity was not impaired but that their perceptions were sharpened and their overall conception of representation was improved. Sakulina (1947) had children read and discuss stories, which they then represented in drawings. Themes rather than drawing skill was emphasized. This approach was found to improve drawing technique and analytic ability, as well as interest in drawing and appreciation of literature.

Several additional studies have been conducted in the United States, involving brief to moderately long periods of exposure to different understandings of representation, as well as technique. Douglas and Schwartz (1967) instructed 4-year-olds in several basic art ideas, namely, art as nonverbal communication, art as an artist's idea, using what he or she sees, thinks, and feels, and the great variety of materials available for artistic representation. Ideas were illustrated through pointing to features in professional ceramic pieces, encouraging the children to verbalize the concepts themselves. At the conclusion of the program, children were found to utilize and interpret these ideas in their own clay-modeling work.

One of the best-controlled studies included some of the youngest children (2-0 to 4-8) in one of the longest training programs (six months). Dubin (1946) verbally guided twenty-six nursery-school children in easel painting techniques, matching children with a control group in pairs by age, sex, and interest in drawing. Guidance, provided at the completion of each drawing, was adapted to each drawing and the stage of representational drawing ability of the child, as classified by Monroe (1929) (scribble-unnamed, scribble-named, diagram, design, and representation). Mean experimental-group improvements in representational drawing skill and interest in drawing significantly exceeded the gains of the control group, who had followed a program of unguided, free drawing activity. In an interesting well-controlled study by Smilansky and Boaz (1976), Israeli disadvantaged 4½- to 7½-year-olds ($N = 120$) were randomly assigned to two experimental groups and one control group for a five-month-long educational program in clay modeling. The first experimental group was provided concept-oriented group discussion on clay modeling followed by clay-modeling activities with technical guidance, while the second experimental group combined similar group discussion followed by clay modeling without technical guidance. Controls experienced only unguided, free clay-modeling classes. The first group generally advanced in both clay-modeling skills (including skills in working on novel tasks) and verbal-cognitive skills over the second group, which in turn advanced more than controls. In a brief experiment, Mott (1945) found that specific motor movements made in the context of group activities, in which the children were asked to verbalize the movement (this is my head; I nod it), increased the probability that the moved part of the body would be included in a drawing of a human figure made immediately following the exercises and would be executed with more attention to detail.

It is evident from these several studies that young children's perceptual coding skills can be substantially advanced over norms represented by control subjects in both two- and three-dimensional media. Even a few sessions, as in the case of Mott's (1945) surprisingly simple cognitive-focusing movement activities, have an influence, though the more extensive and the longer the program, apparently, the greater the magnitude and scope of the advances. The greater changes of the combined verbally and technically trained group over the verbally trained group in the Smilansky and Boaz (1976) study are especially indicative.

Unfortunately, as in so many other areas, short-term stimulation studies of this type, even those of moderate duration (months), tell us little about the significance of the effects for long-term development. The substantial cognitive gains in competence complexity, the gains in motivation and even in creativity that appear regularly with such stimulation can at best be taken as encouragement for the possibilties for early stimulation and as evidence against the popular educational myth (Eisner n.d.; Grossmar 1970) that artistic development will automatically flower without the benefit of planned stimulation of some kind. It is not unimportant that specific stimulation pursued over a few months or so can greatly improve the visual perceptual and artistic skills of young children, but the effect of such early stimulation upon the child's competence and perceptual and aesthetic skills in drawing, painting, and other art areas in the long run is unknown. Do the skills persist more than a few weeks or months? Is the heightened motivation only temporary, or does it lead, fed perhaps by the sharpened skills, to more permanent interests in the art field, which in turn result in seeking further art education and definite talent in the field? At least two of the studies (Grossman 1970; Smilansky and Boaz 1976) indicate that the stimulation generates more than highly limited, task-bound skills, but instead skills generalize across a wide area. How wide and how permanent is the transfer? These and related questions require follow-up studies and preferably a sequence of studies in which the timing, duration, and other dimensions of timing are systematically varied on the parameters of early stimulation.

Especially desirable are studies on coding and representation in the other sensory modes. How much of the world can be constructed in the auditory, olfactory or other modes? Fraiberg's work (Jastrzembska 1976) with blind infants would suggest that the auditory mode fails to compensate for the loss of the visual mode, but what if systematic early stimulation in auditory-spatial relations were undertaken? Can the superlative but highly auditory skills of musicians and bird-watchers or the legendary olfactory-gustatory skills of wine tasters be generalized across domains, in the manner drawing and painting skills seem to do? And can such skills be advanced beginning early in life through stimulation, as the few preliminary studies on visual art stimulation suggest?

Language Stimulation

Language is so central to mental development that many theorists, among them Vygotsky (1962), Luria (1961), and Bruner (1973) consider it to be the chief vehicle of thought. It is in any case such a primary tool and the common denominator of so much school learning that it has characteristically featured strongly in early-education programs from the most ancient times, though not necessarily in a conscious, systematic way (Braun and Edwards 1972; Davies 1973; Raymont 1937). Curiously, learning the letters and early reading often received more of a conscious focus than language itself from the ancient times to the mass infant schools of the nineteenth century. Nursery rhymes, stories, conversation, and verbal instruction have been the common fare in rearing children from the earliest periods nonetheless, at least in the advantaged classes, and educators of infants beginning at least with Pestalozzi's object lessons have long accorded language-labeling activities a central place in the curriculum, as Witte (1914) did in the education of his son.

Yet research on early language learning did not fare any better in the burgeoning research activities of the early part of this century than it did with learning in any other concept domain. Short-term learning studies and developmental norm collecting were the mainstay of most investigations on language in young children (McCarthy 1954) until the advent of the Chomskyian (1957) revolution in linguistics and the early intervention studies of the 1960s got into full swing (Hunt 1975). Until then, early educational programs that grew with the child-development movement in research (Senn 1975; Peters 1981), principally the nursery school, stressed sociodramatic and sensorimotor play and the development of the whole child. Language and cognitive development were accorded complex treatment by some earlier educational theorists (such as Isaacs (1930), but much of the stress was on socioemotional relations and the informal use of language and concept learning through discovery in self-directed play. Following this pattern, research on the influence of nursery-school experience on cognitive development illuminated little in the way of language development, mostly because language outcomes were buried in the principal measuring device, IQ tests (mainly the Binet), along with other cognitive processes, but also because the curriculum itself placed relatively little stress on language.

Early-intervention research equipped itself with a new environmentalist philosophy, which grew out of the sociopolitical demands to remedy the plight of the poor ethnic minorities: tackle the problems early in development before the intellectual patterns of poverty and the folk cultures become entrenched in the child (Hunt 1975; Zigler and Valentine 1979). The momentum of the civil rights movement demanded change and the volume of research expanded enormously, spreading the doctrine of early stimulation and making inroads into the prevalent developmental philosophy of predetermined sequences, which had dominated early education for so long.

The emergence of structural linguistic theory at about the same period, however, led to contradictory perspectives in the mainstream of developmental research on language. Noam Chomsky's (1957, 1965) generative theory of grammar, in identifying a hierarchy of complex rules that must be grasped cognitively to be used, appeared to demolish purely behavioral explanations for language functioning, but because of its manifest complexity, the learning basis for language development as well. Adult speech was too complex for infants to learn, it was argued, and therefore it must be biologically programmed. There followed years of preoccupation with the nature and course of development of these rules, which children were presumed to acquire through the aid of a biologically blueprinted language acquisition device (LAD). The effort in some ways resembled the norm collecting of the early developmentalists, except for its concern with mechanisms, mental operations, and logical sequences, compared to the behavioral descriptions of the traditional developmentalists (McNeill 1970). Only gradually did challenges emerge to the strong hereditarian stance, which began to reestablish a role for learning and experience, through demonstrating how adults adapted their speech patterns to the evolving comprehension of children (Snow and Ferguson 1977). The protracted period of preoccupation with basic questions of linguistic theory and the predominance of the biological outlook, however, seriously delayed interest in experimental research on early language stimulation in relation to development, except for research embedded in the early-intervention framework. The concepts of predetermined development and inherited intelligence have left their stamp in every corner.

Compensatory education programs for young children, beginning in the 1930s with the ground-breaking project of Skeels (1942, 1966; Skeels and Dye 1939) to farm out infant orphans to the care of retarded women in institutional cottages, have rarely centered attention on language learning and development alone. Skeels's own program was obviously a highly generalized program of care and stimulation with no analysis of the concepts encompassed. The few additional pioneering investigations on compensatory education (though they were not then called that) for poor and institutionalized children that were carried out by Skeels's group (Skeels et al. 1938) and other investigators (Anastasi and Foley 1949) during the same period simply enrolled children in a nursery-school program. The uncertain inclusion of language in these programs seemed to prevent cognitive declines in verbally oriented IQ tests but generated cognitive gains only in sensorimotor-oriented IQ tests (the Merrill-Palmer scales).

Perhaps the first early-intervention study to define language as a central component of the program was conducted in 1942 by Dawe, whose assessments of information-concept learning were recorded above. As a result of the fifty hours of weekend stimulation spread over a period of three months, the 43- to 82-month-old deprived orphanage children gained significantly over their matched pair controls in mean sentence length, the Smith-Williams vocabulary test and other language measures, as well as making a significant mean gain of 14.2 points in Binet IQ (to 94.8 IQ), compared to a control loss of 2 points. Like most later studies on disadvantaged children, those studied by Dawe did not exceed or even reach the population mean and there was no follow-up, making the study's chief significance historical in its stress on language and deliberate early compensatory education, demonstrating the responsiveness of children to early stimulation despite the countercurriculum of a barren institutional environment.

The fact that the study did not focus on language alone makes it uncertain how much each of the component types of stimulation were separately contributing to development in the respective domains, though some idea would be evident had the language and information measures been comparably scaled. One of the problems with focusing on language is that it is a code and among the most abstract of codes at that. It is virtually impossible to stimulate language without incorporating knowledge concepts for the language to code, though it is possible to place a considerable portion of the attention on the grammatical and other structural rules of language, giving second place to other cognitive content.

Dawe's stress on information concepts was unusual. Nearly all early-intervention projects since that time have included a broad spectrum of cognitive learning activities, ranging from sensorimotor and spatial concepts to quantitative concepts and language. In all of these studies, including the highly intensive and comprehensive studies of Heber et al. (1972) and Hunt et al. (1976), where particularized assessments of language outcomes were made, children have displayed gains in language development generally proportional to the gains in IQ and other cognitive areas. Because of the unassessed, multidimensional nature of program content, however, we are unable to determine how much separate components of stimulation contributed to individual outcomes. Nevertheless, the consistency of language gains across programs and the increase in language (and other) gains with the intensity of the program as in the Hunt and Heber programs, underscore the responsiveness to early stimulation of language processes, as much as other domains. We also know from the Hunt orphanage studies where language was omitted or less stressed in the program, language skills did not develop as well.

Not all the main body of studies, including the Heber and Hunt investigations, report separate assessments of language competencies in follow-up studies of later development. Hunt did not conduct a follow-up study and the Heber group reports only general IQ scores (Garber and Heber 1981). Of those that do, the status of later language development reveals a mixed picture. Schweinhart and Weikart (1980) found significant mean experimental-control differences as late as age 14 in language usage and structure, spelling, and language capitalization and punctuation, attributable to the original intervention program at ages 3 to 4. Other groups, however, found no differences in various language achievement tests scores at age 19 (Gray, Ramsey, and Klaus 1982), or even at age 10 (Guinagh and Gordon 1978). Further complications appear when IQ measures (the WISC) are broken into the verbal and performance components (Lazar and Darlington 1978), in light of the fact that the verbal scale is a broad measure of verbally, mathematically, and pictorially coded cognitive skills rather than of language processes alone. As mentioned previously, few experimental-control group differences on basic ability measures remained after about age 9 or 10 from any of the original early-intervention, general cognitive stimulation programs (Lazar and Darlington 1978, 1982; Palmer and Anderson 1979, 1981). Mean differences between experimental and control groups remained significant on both the verbal and performance scales, to age 10 in Levenstein's follow-up, but only on the performance scale in Palmer's group, at age 12 (Lazar and Darlington 1978, 1982).

There have been a few studies on young children from socioeconomically disadvantaged backgrounds, however, in which programs were highly concentrated on intensive language stimulation, although other cognitive content (knowledge concepts) was of necessity incorporated to some degree. The more recent work has tended to zero in on language delay and linguistic deficits but still mainly concern socioeconomically disadvantaged populations. Spangler, Smith, and Rosen (1976) conducted an intensive program using individual operant conditioning combined with a classroom approach and parent counseling, with forty-eight preschoolers, children with marked linguistic deficits. Mean IQ gains from the program leveled off over a two- to three-year period following termination, but receptive and productive skills in language continued to progress. In another recent investigation, a remedial language-intervention program in the classroom was set up four days per week, three hours per day over a period of seven months, with a group of twenty-five 36- to 60-month-old children diagnosed as 1.5 standard deviations below the mean on the Reynell Developmental Language Scales and 1 standard deviation below the mean on the Leiter International Performance Scale (Van der Spuy et al. 1980). Children were matched in age, sex, socioeconomic status, nonverbal IQ, and language comprehension scores with twenty-four children from the same diagnostic set who were assigned to a delayed treatment control group. Both groups made significant mean gains on language comprehension and expression, but the experimental group made significantly greater gains than the control group in comprehension.

A somewhat earlier study is notable for the later age of intervention and the length of its follow-up (Carter 1966; Carter and Capobianco 1976). In this investigation a systematic remedial language program (twelve weeks, one hour per day) with socioeconomically disadvantaged, low-IQ first-graders resulted in significant mean gains in IQ (74.2-84.3) and Language Age for the thirty-two 6-year-old experimental children, compared to their controls, matched in pairs by age, social class, Binet IQ and MA, Illinois Test of Psycholinguistic Abilities, and Language Age. Groups were balanced for sex. (Mean control IQ scores move from 74.2 to 77.1). By seventh grade, six years later, the mean IQ gap between experimental and controls ($N = 17$ pairs remaining) was still 7 points (82-89.2). Experimental children scored significantly higher than contols on language IQ and total IQ of the California Test of Mental Maturity, the comprehension, vocabulary, and total score of the California Reading Test, and on math fundamentals and math reasoning of the California Arithmetic Test. Grade-point averages were also significantly higher in language arts, social studies, and physical education but not in math or science. There was also no difference between groups in nonlanguage IQ on the California. Thus a certain selectivity occurred in the facilitative and transfer effects of the original language program toward language-coded domains, compared to the numerically coded domains of mathematics and science and the perceptual-spatial coding involved in the nonlanguage IQ, though not entirely consistently. The advantage in physical education might well have been a motivational spinoff, but the advances in certain math-achievement tests may have resulted from the contribution improved linguistic skill would make to understanding the problem descriptions.

Although it is not clear from the follow-up report that the diminished samples were comparable to the original total groups, the study is interesting in the lateness (age 6) with which remedial stimulation can alter folk-socialized poverty patterns with a high degree of permanence (to age 13), alterations that encompassed abstract, general IQ scores—which was not true of the study by Spangler et al. The closest any other study has come to producing such relative permanence is age 12 (Lazar and Darlington 1978; Palmer, Semlear, and Fischer 1981). The Palmer program ran over the children's third and fourth years, however, making it eight to nine years since program termination, compared to six to seven years for the Carter and Capobianco children. The differentially facilitative effects of language stimulation contrasts with the Palmer study, where mean IQ differences over controls remained in performance but not the verbal (nor the total) IQ.

In the Levenstein study, where significant mean differences remained to nearly age 10 thus also six to seven years since program termination (Lazar and Darlington 1978, 1982), differences included the total and verbal WISC scales but not the performance scales. The latter program was defined as a verbal interaction program (Levenstein 1977), emphasizing language (though not exclusively as in the Carter and Capobianco program), while the original Palmer program was apparently less language oriented (Palmer and Siegel 1977).

The power of early language stimulation to exercise large and highly persistent effects over a wide period of early development among socio-economically and linguistically disadvantaged populations seems quite clear, in the same manner general cognitive-stimulation programs produced rather general cognitive effects, against the ecological tide of the counter-vailing curriculum of poverty folk culture. The wide range of ages within which substantial and persistent, if not equally strong effects can be produced from early language stimulation is evidence against the concept of earliness tied to any specific age. Although the Carter and Capobianco study at age 6 produced gains at the lower end of the range found in disadvantaged programs with younger children, 10 IQ points versus 15 to 20 or more in a number of programs, including Dawe's (1942) similarly brief three-month program limited to weekends, most programs were of longer duration and more comprehensive, as was Dawe's program, and Dawe herself embraced a few 6-year-olds in her 3½- to 6-year sample. However, no program for disadvantaged children older than age 3 has produced gains of the same magnitude as those for children age 3 and younger, as noted earlier. Like the general-program effects, however, it must be kept in mind that the *levels* to which these children are brought in language codes and related skills with all except the highly intensive Heber-type program remain typically at or below general norms, and thus considerably below the above-normative levels characteristically produced in the verbal-logically oriented ecology of middle-class milieux.

The bulk of these programs cast little light on relations between language and thought, given the admixture of general cognitive stimulation covering a broad base of concepts with almost all language programs. The apparent exception, the Carter and Capobianco program, though occurring in slightly older children, suggests an important role for language in generalizing competence to the abstract-oriented concepts characteristic of academic abilities and achievement, but more precise control over concept content would be useful, as discussed earlier.

It is disappointing to find few programs exploring the potency of early language stimulation with advantaged children. One of the programs described earlier for middle-class, advantaged children did define language as the chief aspect of the program (Metzl 1980), but unfortunately no separate measure of language was employed. Metzl used only the Bayley Mental and Motor Scales to assess outcomes. The selected effects of language stimulation from 6 weeks to 6 months are suggested by the significant experimental group changes in the Bayley Mental Scales, compared to the lack of change in Bayley Motor Scale scores. But the comparatively small mean difference between experimental and control groups (maximum, 8 points) and modest final level of the most stimulated experimental group (IQ = 112), considering the infants' middle-class background, may well reflect the limited contribution of language to the Mental Scale (which also has age gaps in the language components, Kohn-Raz 1967), as much as the comparative brevity and low intensity of the program.

The other program for advantaged infants, although multidimensional, was highly intensive and did measure separately each skill area stimulated (Drash and Stolberg, 1977, 1979). The enormous cognitive gains in this pilot study in all areas, including language, are impressive. The mean language quotients of 149 and 133 (N = 3) at the ages 2 and 3½ follow-ups, underscored by the multiword sentences and highly expanded vocabulary of 500 to 700 words for three of the four infants at the age-2 follow-up, well beyond norms, offers a great deal of promise with respect to the potential of language to be accelerated. The study is unusual in the gains achieved and the accumulation of further gains following program termination, saying as well something about the potential of the ecology of the middle-class world to respond to planned intervention, as noted in chapter 6. It does not tell us whether language can be advanced independently of development in other areas or whether such precocity will be maintained over later development, however.

The balance of the studies on stimulating language in early life are relatively more focused studies, designed to compare different approaches or analyze in greater detail relations between language stimulation and the structures and functions of language competence developed. Although most of them were conducted on special, disadvantaged populations, their value lies in their experimentation with stimulation techniques and demonstration of the range of possibilities for planned control over stimulation of language development. The studies vary greatly in duration of treatment, from a few weeks to as long as eighteen months.

Two unusual, fairly long-term training studies concentrated on phonemic development. In his classic study, Irwin (1960) guided working-class (blue-collar) mothers to label, talk about, and tell stories from infant picture books for fifteen minutes daily to a group of infants (N = 24) from the age 13 months to age 30 months. By age 18 months infants began to exceed control infants (N = 10) in the frequency of phonemes employed in spontaneous vocalizations. In something of a similar study, Shvarchkin in the USSR (cited by Ervin and Miller 1963:111) presented Russian words varying one phoneme at a time to infants between the ages of 11 and 22 months. Following a planned sequence beginning with vowels, the infants gradually learned to discriminate all phonemes in the Russian language.

Two other specialized comparatively extended language-stimulation studies utilized a broader set of measures. Luria and Yudovich (1959) worked with one of two severely language-deprived, 5-year-old identical twin boys in a carefully constructed eleven-month program (punctuated by a two-month break after three months), embracing object labeling, repeated phrases, guided question answering, and picture description. Following ten months separation, during which the control twin (whose speech had been less deprived) participated in routine kindergarten activity only, both twins shifted from what the investigators defined as highly concrete and limited private (autonomous) speech (low and specialized vocabulary and crude syntax) to a high proportion of planned and narrative speech production, embracing an extended vocabulary and largely grammatically complete sentences. The specially stimulated twin produced a greater proportion of abstract speech and extended sentences than his control.

In a shorter, three-month program, Cazden (1965, 1972) found that a modeling technique (using well-formed sentences) was superior to an expansion technique (expanding on the child's last utterance), and both were superior to no-treatment controls in advancing disadvantaged children's rate of language development (ability to repeat sentences, mean length of utterance, and noun phrase, verb complexity, copula and sentence-type indices). Three matched groups of black 28- to 38-month-old children participated in the program.

Various other brief experimental training studies are sprinkled throughout the literature, demonstrating the modifiability and advancement of different aspects of language development through stimulation. There was first the classic study of Gesell's student Strayer (1930) with identical twins (chapter 4). Though designed to prove quite the opposite (maturation), Strayer in fact furnished quite a nice demonstration of the effectiveness of vocabulary-training techniques, what are now often termed labeling strategies, in accelerating vocabulary development. Following a behaviorist framework, Rheingold (1956) some time later found that two months of individualized experimental care in 6-month-old institutionalized infants improved their social responsiveness (but not IQ or other indices of development), which included increased vocalization, over their institutionally cared for controls. Mean differences remained significant one year later (age 19 months), after the infants had been adopted in homes at 9 months, on the number of infants who vocalized, but not on other features of the social tests nor on IQ, though trends on IQ and vocabulary (17.9-13.7 words for controls) favored the experimental subjects (Rheingold and Bayley 1959). Following this multistimulation-care experiment, in which language stimulation and outcomes were embedded in the general-care context, Rheingold, Gewirtz, and Ross (1959) showed how frequency of vocalization in 3-month-old infants could be brought under control of social reinforcement (smiles, sounds, and caresses) in a matter of days. They pointed out, however, that nonsocial reinforcement might be equally effective. Later Weisberg (1963) demonstrated that vocalizations of 3-month-olds would increase through social reinforcement (over an 8-day period), but not through nonsocial reinforcement. In the USSR, Mallitskaya (1960) devised a set of highly successful, cube picture-labeling techniques (in play) to stimulate vocabulary development in 9- to 17-month-old infants, enabling infants by 11 months to learn words at a rate of two to three repetitions each, mastering as many as nine words. Over a five-week period, (Hamilton 1977) trained 9- to 15-month-old infants ($N = 20$) in three conditions of vocal modeling and operant conditioning, plus a control (four infants per group). Infants improved significantly in some measures of vowel, consonant, and word utterances in the modeling conditions over the control condition but not in the operant condition.

While the effectiveness of a variety of approaches to advancing linguistic competence in a number of ways is evident from these studies, spanning almost the entire period of early development, more extensive and systematic studies are needed with less disadvantaged populations to explore the full range of competencies that might be advanced. It would also be important to study in greater detail the extent to which language stimulation influences cognitive development in related domains (other symbolic codes, such as math) and less-related domains (visual perceptual codes). The centrality of language to thought in the eyes of many theorists makes investigations of the relations between language and cognition of particular importance. Much evidence points to the role of language in mental processes characteristic of school learning and verbally loaded IQ tests and of its boundaries reflected in the poor transfer from language stimulation to nonverbal measures, but few studies have addressed themselves systematically to this problem. If language codes exercise some sort of generalizing function, it might be through their potency in representing concepts, or perhaps through the mediation of (or possibly in conjunction with) strategy enhancement. Early language stimulation may facilitate memory, for example, or the kind of cognitive autonomy in motivation for intellective activity that is characteristic of precocious children with high verbal abilities (Fowler 1981b). Studies that explore a variety of interactions of this kind (as outlined in tables 5-1 to 5-3), such as the breadth of effects and interactions with knowledge development, are needed.

One limited study addressed to this general question found no differences in 3- to 5-year-old black children from an urban ghetto in the effects of verbal versus gestural (modeling) training on ability to sort objects by color or form (Moskovitz 1972). Differences were found in favor of verbal training on ability to sort by function, which contrary to Nelson (1973)

Moskovitz believes to be more abstract than formal concepts. But since even infants have been found to be responsive to rudimentary sorting by both form (Ricciuti 1965; Starkey 1981) and function (Koltsova cited in Brackbill 1960, 1962; Mallitskaya 1960; Nelson 1973; Ross 1980) and the training consisted of no more than two sessions on a special folk population of children, the training may have involved teaching unfamiliar verbal labels more than teaching classificatory skills. Despite these limitations, as Moskovitz suggests, processing functional concepts, for which verbal concepts are the basis, constitutes a great deal of the cognitive realm.

There are no follow-up studies reported on these special language-training programs, so the best we can say with respect to development is that language complexity is easily accelerated in a variety of ways during almost any period of early childhood, but we know little about the long-term effect from such focused techniques. The fact of clear follow-up effects over periods of two to ten years or so in a number of programs on disadvantaged children that stressed language to varying degrees is encouraging, however. It is also quite clear that an important source of young children's acquisition of language is experience itself and that planning and regulating the nature of the language stimulation will systematically affect the character of the language the child acquires, at least for short-range development. The notions advanced by the Chomskyian linguists (N. Chomsky 1957, 1965; McNeill 1970) that infants are equipped with a basic language acquisition device that controls language development biologically does not fit the pattern of these data. Supporting this trend is the accumulating evidence on how parents generally adapt speech to facilitate language learning for their infants (Snow and Ferguson 1977) and on the fact that when this does not occur, language deprivation results (Clarke and Clarke 1976; Leonard 1979; Luria and Yudovich 1959; Malson 1972). One of the additionally interesting features apparent from these studies is the diversity of aspects of language that can be influenced, directly and indirectly, by early language stimulation. Virtually all aspects have been shown to respond to stimulation—phonology, syntax, and semantics, the effects on semantics ranging from vocabulary (Strayer 1930) to such broad features as the ability to narrate meaningful text (Luria and Yudovich 1959). The results can be direct, as in the close matching of stimulation to outcomes in the phonemic stimulation study of Shvarchkin (Ervin and Miller 1963:111), or indirect, as in the effect on phonemic development of a general language program in Irwin's (1960) study.

Early Reading

Historical Basis. Reading is the cornerstone and one of the earliest specialized skills in the ediface of planned education that grew up with the first establishment of hierarchical societies. Learning to read in schools or through tutoring by scribes dates back to ancient Sumeria, Egypt, China, and wherever the demands of the new large-scale socioeconomic systems for abstract verbal skills and recordkeeping came into being (Davies 1973; Hawkes 1973; McNeill 1963; Saggs 1965; Smith 1955). The evidence suggests that instruction typically began at about 5-7 as it still does, although the age was not as fixed as modern bureaucracies have made it.

Aristotle (1941) advocated not starting reading instruction prior to age 5, but Chryssipus and others advocated beginning at age 3 (Davies 1973), as if the social rules were not yet clear on this point. Reading instruction was not uncommonly conducted in the home, often beginning in infancy or at least before entering school. Ancient Jewish (Baron 1942; Zborowski and Herzog 1952), Indian (Keay 1938), and other scholars tutored their own children from an early age, to lead them as apprentices in the expected path toward their own profession (Smethurst 1970, 1975). The tradition of early home instruction, usually through informal methods incidental to play of some kind, has continued since the Roman era in many societies, including Medieval Europe, wherever urban centers of culture and hierarchical social systems persisted at all. The practice of beginning reading at 2-5 was long ago extended as well to school practices in certain societies and cultures, such as the Jewish *shtetl* of Middle Europe, with its strong tradition of verbal intellectual scholarship in religious practice, and the first mass infant schools established by Wilderspin (1840) and others (Davies 1973; Raymont 1937) in Britain during the nineteenth century.

The methods employed—rote learning, rigid and mechanical alphabetic-syllabic sequencing, severe discipline, and religious catechism—were differentially effective. Failure was apparently widespread and it is not clear at all what proportion of the preschool learners made any real progress, though it is clear that numerous preschoolers actually became fluent readers, probably more so in the homes of the educated and well off than in the mass settings of the infant schools (Davies 1973; Earle 1974; Forest 1927; Raymont 1937; Reisner 1930; Rusk 1933; Wilderspin 1840). It is well documented that many of the historically eminent learned to read well before school age (Cox 1926; Davidson 1931; Earle 1974; Fowler 1962a). Thus it would seem that on the basis of the historical evidence alone, early childhood is a period quite receptive to accelerating the development of complex reading skills to younger ages (2-5) not normally attained in contemporary societies until age 6. It is not clear from this evidence what the relationship of early reading attainment is to other abilities, such as language or verbal concept development, nor how easily and thus how early and with what frequency, competencies as complex as reading can be established in young children, though it is evident that the younger the age, the fewer the early readers. Nor is it clear what effect early competence in reading has upon later development in reading and other competencies. Some insight into this question was provided by Davidson (1931), using data on the historically eminent from Cox (1926). She inferred that abilities as measured in terms of estimated IQ-type ratings must be reflected in a mental age of at least 4, even if like Macaulay (IQ 180) the child learns at age 3, and that reading early may confer certain lifelong advantages for learning. (For more on precocity and reading see chapter 9.)

School Practices and Research on Age. Research on early reading, like research in other areas, is essentially a development of this century and the institutionalization of science. Yet it is already widely established that almost any program that attempts to teach children of age 5, and sometimes earlier, to read meets with considerable success (Fowler 1971a). A carefully graded sequence of manipulative procedures is built into the Montessori system of early education, often leading children to begin reading by the age of 4 or 5, and to letter recognition even earlier, but not much formal data has been compiled on problems and success rates. Reading instruction beginning at age 5 has been standard practice in much of the British school system for many years (Chall 1967; Dunlop 1942; Raymont 1937). Kindergarten programs that incorporate reading instruction using many different methods, or beginning reading activities (sound and letter recognition, along with learning isolated words and a few sentences, as a basis for breaking the code) have been common in recent years (Artley 1966; Blanton 1972; Fowler 1971a; McKee, Brzeinski and Harrison 1966; Stevenson 1964), a number of them experimental programs with varying degrees of sophistication in controlled evaluation.

Appleton (1964) found, for example, that in a free-choice situation, twenty-three of twenty-six kindergarten children (aged 4.6-6.6) elected to participate in a reading program. All of them made progress in learning to read, some reading as many as nine beginning books. In another program, the mean reading grade level of a group of 208 children, selected for their cognitive readiness ($\overline{X}$ IQ = 116) for beginning reading during kindergarten, reached 1.9 years after three months of first grade in word-recognition skills (Dominion Achievement Test, a Canadian Test), compared to 1.6 for their controls, who had not been instructed in kindergarten (Stevenson 1964). Many other programs report similar results. It thus seems comparatively easy to advance skill complexity in reading for children around 4-6 years of age, even in fairly standard conditions of the public schools. schools.

Generally speaking, success rates are directly proportional to age and few school programs or even studies have undertaken to teach children to read younger than age 4 (Fowler 1968, 1971a). In an interesting exception, which nevertheless confirms the success-with-age rule, Findley (1968) found that, while forty-nine (82 percent) of the 5-year-olds in his program could read and understand one preprimer with a twenty-five-word recognition vocabulary by the end of the first year, only twenty-four (40 percent) of the 4-year-olds and six (10 percent) of the 3-year-olds had progressed that far. The problem is complicated by the children's abilities in other areas, however. The children were all at the 100-105 IQ level, and it will be recalled that Davidson's (1931) success rates were *inversely* proportional to age, more 3-year-olds nearing fluent reading than 4-year-olds, who in turn made more headway than 5-year-olds, apparently as a function of higher IQs and reading to the children in the home being associated with the younger age levels.

There are many other reports of children acquiring reading skills by 3 and sometimes even 2 years of age, but few formal investigations with published data. In one of the most elaborate programs, Moore (1967) designed a multistage sequence for teaching and writing to 3- to 5-year-olds, in what he defined as a responsive environment, following Montessori concepts in part and using manipulative materials and a talking typewriter. The program functioned in a private school for upper-middle-class children, many from a university community, and thus presumably children of high verbal-abstract skills and IQ. Moore (1967) reports that by the end of first grade the average child who had been in the program at least two years read at the sixth-grade level on the Metropolitan Achievement Test. No other details have been reported, unfortunately; thus we do not know whether any of the children learned as early as age 3, except for two children, one daughter each of Moore and myself, both of whom learned fluently at home before entering Moore's group program.

Developmental Components and Prerequisites. One of the complications is that reading is often loosely defined by investigators to include beginning stages of letter and individual word recognition (Cohen 1961; Dunn 1970; Lado 1977; Perlish 1968; Smethurst 1970, 1975), rather than reading and comprehending sentences and text. The former consists essentially of foundation skills for reading, that is, limited lower order, unit-identification processes commonly developed in at least many middle-class children out of their normative experiences of socialization during the first 2 to 3 years (Ilg and Ames 1950). The fact that 3- to 5-year-old, Down's Syndrome children ($N = 13$, mean IQ 83), were able to learn word-recognition skills (at least thirty words each after four program quarters) but did not read sentences or text is perhaps indicative (Hayden and Dmitriev 1975). Nevertheless, there are enough well-documented reports available of children reading sentences and text as early as age 3 and even 2 years (Brown 1924; Davidson 1931; Durkin 1966; Fowler 1962a; Terman 1918) (including investigations to be discussed further on—Fowler 1962b, 1965a, 1971a) to indicate that specialized stimulation of rules for reading can generate higher order reading competence well in advance of norms in many children, who may or may not be intellectually advanced in other areas.

It seems reasonable to expect that there might be lower age limits to teaching children to read, since reading processes are obviously composed of a variety of skills closely linked to and apparently dependent on language and concept development. The concept of word and the task of applying it to extracting meaning from written words and strings of written words is clearly contingent on the development of the object concept and necessarily associated with language. Yet the fact that reading competence is so regularly correlated with MA-IQ scores (usually ranging between .40 and .60, Chall 1967) may mean only that IQ tests are heavily loaded verbally. On the face of it, reading printed material would seem to confront the learner with a number of demands beyond those already required to master language, such as attending to visual material, which requires deliberate focusing, in contrast to hearing speech, which pervades the child's aural world. Reading also requires mastering several dimensions reflected in the fact that written codes are language codes written down on the basis of several visual-auditory correspondences (letter-sound and word-word representation, word spacing, punctuation, capitalization, left-to-right and vertical-line progression). Written material also lacks the interpretive cues of intonation and stress. Reading is in many senses no more abstract a code than oral language, however, both making use of the production and interpretation of strings of arbitrary modules that are coded to represent classes of phenomena; yet the strings themselves are presented in a concrete perceptual form, unlike abstract concepts like conservation, for example.

Although certain theorists (Elkind 1977; Furth 1978) have argued that reading is contingent on the development of Piagetian stages (concrete operations), in fact various studies do not seem to bear this out. Several studies have found correlations between Piagetian concepts and reading skills (Lunzer, Dolan, and Wilkinson 1976; Walter 1977). But even when significant, correlations are still modest (.30 to .56, Colter 1965), and sometimes minimal (<.20, Waller 1977), leaving plenty of room for advancement in the domain of reading comparatively independent of formal Piagetian concepts, just as reading varies across a wide range of IQ levels, correlating between .40 and .60 with IQ (Chall 1967) as already noted. It may be noted that Durkin's (1966) early readers (see below) ranged in IQ from 82 to 170, correlations with reading skills ranging from around .40 to .80 at different ages. Thus studies in which significant differences between reading and nonreading 5-year-olds appear on a Piagetian operativity factor (Briggs and Elkind 1973), and between early reading and nonearly reading prekindergarten children on conservation, two measures of the Illinois Test of Psycholinguistic Abilities and Creativity (Briggs and Elkind 1977), can also be interpreted, at least in part, as cognitive facilitation and transfer as a *result* of advanced reading instruction, instead of as causal of early reading potential. Broad abilities no doubt facilitate reading acquisition, even as IQ correlations suggest. But again the limited proportion of the variance (< 36 percent) accounted for by concrete-operational concepts, and the wide range of abilities evident in early readers makes general abilities only a modest part of the story. As Waller (1977) points out, little advantage is to be gained in identifying yet another factor or set of factors to the 62 tasks out of 103 tasks that Doehring (1968) found distinguished good from poor readers in his classic monograph, unless some theoretical (*causal*) basis is established. In view of the relative ease and selectivity with which concrete-operational concepts of all kinds can be induced in preschool children through brief training programs, the evidence for the role of a generalized Piagetian cognitive factor as a prerequisite for reading is quite limited.

Perhaps the most compelling evidence that reading codes may not be quite as generalized in their cognitive dependence on other concept areas and even on language skill appears in several studies that demonstrate the capability of individual children to learn to read in parallel or in association with their beginning progress in learning language (Steinberg and Steinberg 1975; Söderbergh 1971; Terman 1918). The Steinbergs and Söderbergh were linguists who taught their respective children to read, the Steinbergs beginning at the prelinguistic age of 6 months with their son and Soderbergh with her daughter at 28 months, after speech production was well established, though still in the early stages. Both researchers employed systematic, sequenced methods, beginning with letters (but not sound values), then words and sentences, but in neither case did the child crack the code and read text independently until the age of 3½ years. The developmental achievement is nonetheless important because of the high level of autonomy in fluent reading used as the criterion, in which highly skilled competence in reading was realized at roughly the same pace and levels as language development. Most reports on the reading achievements of 3-year-olds define reading as reading a few sentences or one or two primers, usually with aid, not success in reading alone a cumulative series of books.

In an impressive and seminal study reported by Terman (1918), a father accomplished the same developmental levels of fluent reading and language with his daughter, Martha, by 26 months of age. From 14 months, when word learning had just started, Martha began with capital letters, her third and fourth words being "pretty" and "pretty B" (treated as a unit). Much of the stimulation consisted of object word-learning activities over the next five months, presented in sensorimotor play, which included letters and gradually homemade sentence charts on cardboard. At 19 months the child suddenly mastered all capitals, then small letters within a month. The concept of word representation appeared at 21 months, 10 days (recognition vocabulary, 35 words), and she began to read with enjoyment at 23 months, at *less than 2 years of age*, having acquired a reading vocabulary of 150 words (speech vocabulary is not reported). Just past age 2 (26.5 months), Martha had completed four and one-half primers, was reading fluently, with comprehension, and was using a reading vocabulary of 700 words. Since a Binet IQ test administered at age 3 years, 11 months registered a score of 140 IQ, the mental age extrapolated to age 2, when she began to read fluently, works out to be only 3-0, or a year younger than the mental-age floor that has been found to be characteristic in the early-reading literature (Davidson 1931; Fowler 1971a). It is evident that integrated reading is a set of cognitive competencies highly responsive to stimulation during early development, even given wide variation in methods employed and the lack of systematic investigations on substantial samples of children, making reading a field of fertile potential for study. But if short-term potentials are great, what then of the long-range developmental effects?

Early Reading in the Home. The most extensive investigation of the long-term effects of early reading in the home was conducted by Durkin (1966), who measured the reading progress of forty-nine early-reading children in the California school system over the first five years of school ($N = 25$ through six grades) in one study, and the progress of another 156 readers in the New York schools over their first three years in a second study, in which she gave more intensive study to a selected sample of thirty experimental-control matched pairs. The early readers, who were selected through elaborate screening and testing procedures, ranged between 1.5 and 4.5 in grade level achievement in the first study and between 1.4 and 5.2 in the second study, two weeks prior to first grade and the beginning of school instruction in reading in both studies. They constituted slightly less than 1 percent of the population tested in the first study and only 3.5 percent in the second study. All children had been taught to read at home between the ages of 3 and 5 by parents, siblings, or neighbors. The methods typically included a rich store of school resource materials in the home, frequent reading to the child, and responding to the child's curiosity about letters, words, and text in a variety of contexts. Spelling and writing were often part of the process, and while methods were characteristically informal, usually conducted through play, at least eleven children were deliberately taught through planning the instruction.

A number of methodogical problems mar these studies, in particular subject attrition and the lack of a prearranged control group in the first study, in which the children's performance was compared with achievement norms for school populations. In the second study the 156 early readers were also compared with school populations, and, in the more intensive component study of thirty matched pairs, the match for sex and classroom teacher could not be maintained in the face of problems in readjusting IQs to reduce differences when shifting from group tests to individual IQ tests.

The findings are nonetheless provocative, particularly in the light of supportive data from other studies to be summarized below. In both studies Durkin found that early readers consistently maintained superior achievement in reading over grade norms and over the various comparison groups, in the first study through grade 6 and in the second study into grade 3. The mean reading grade level attained by the total group in the first study was 7.6 through fifth grade, and for the diminished group (N = 34, the balance had been double promoted out of elementary school) 9.0 through sixth grade, or three grades above norms, despite the exclusion of double-promoted children. On selected comparisons of available subsamples with local school populations, mean differences in favor of the early readers were significant through grade 3 on the Stanford Reading Test (N = 12 versus 241 for controls), and substantial, though not significant, on the same test (N = 25 versus 631 for controls) through grade 6, probably because children who had been advanced in grade (N = 12) were not available for the sixth-grade comparison. The median reading grade level of the 156 early readers in the second study was 6.1 as far as grade 3, and the mean difference significantly in favor of the experimental subsample of thirty children over their matched pair controls was .9 years (p = .025). There were no sex differences in the second study, both boys and girls reading at the 6.1 level. Mean sex differences fluctuated back and forth between .1 and .6 of a grade through grade 5 for the total sample in the first study, but girls were superior to boys in the reduced sample in grade 6 (9.6 versus 7.9).

Especially interesting is the comparison of age effects in the first study. Children (N = 13) who had been taught to read beginning at the age of 3 (3.0-3.9) read on the average at the ninth-grade level (median 9.2) in grade 5, compared to the seventh-grade level (median = 7.6) for children (N = 14) who had been taught to read beginning at age 5 (5.0-5.9). That general-IQ ability differences did not play any role in this comparison is indicated by the closeness of IQ scores for the two groups (medians of 128 and 127 for the respective groups).

In the second study Durkin also analyzed the effects of early reading on other skills, such as memory, visual motor skills (Bender Gestalt), and creativity, at the end of first grade, but found generally small and insignificant mean differences between all experimental-control comparisons. The largest differences were in teacher ratings on intelligence, memory, and self-reliance, which appeared to favor early readers.

Durkin makes no analysis of the effects of early reading upon IQ, focusing instead on so-called general intelligence as a contributor to success in early reading and school achievement and thus as a control variable, as for example in her selected comparisons, where she matched early readers and nonreaders for IQ. Yet the consistently high correlations between reading achievement and IQ (.40-.80 in the first study between the first and sixth grades) and the markedly above-norm IQ levels Durkin found for her early readers in both studies (medians of 121 and 133, respectively), could easily have been partly the *result* of advances in cognitive skills generated by early reading (and related) stimulation, in the manner Davidson (1931) interpreted her findings. Reading is after all basically a derivative of language, and language skills are the strongest component of IQ measures, particularly the heavily verbally loaded Binet used in the study by Durkin. The entire question of the scope and boundaries of influence of early reading (and other) stimulation on cognitive development needs careful experimentation. Unfortunately Durkin's data does not lend itself to much analysis of this kind. Information on what other kinds of stimulation may have been conducted in the home is sparse, the study was partially retrospective, and Durkin made no assessments of school achievement in mathematics or other areas.

Both earlier and later investigations have generally supported Durkin's findings, though few of the studies have been as comprehensive or as carefully implemented. One of the earlier, large studies, by Almy (1949) on 106 first-grade children, found a significant correlation (.26, p = .01) between success in reading in first grade and the quality of home reading experiences the previous year. The best readers in the group were children who had been stimulated in relation to the reading process in some way. Unfortunately Almy's definitions were so broad as to encompass parents who had done little more than simply read to their children, the first-grade reading test used as criterion did not discriminate well, and the data were not quantified very systematically. A later study by Moon and Wells (1979), however, found that knowledge of literacy by the child at age 5 correlated .79 with reading accuracy at age 7. Parent provision for the child's literacy between 5 and 7 correlated .72 with the child's knowledge of literacy at age 5. McCracken (1966) identified eight early readers of a total first-grade population of 360 children. While these children tended to lack the scope of knowledge usually expected of advanced children, mean reading achievement on the Stanford Achievement Test was 3.3 and 4.5 during the respective first and second grades, or more than two grades above grade-level norms. No child scored less than one grade above norms. Their mean IQ was 132, which again may have been a consequence of, as much as a factor contributing to, success in early reading (and later school learning). A similar, but larger study by Clark (1976) in Britain on 32 children with a wide range of IQs (98-146, $\overline{X}$ = 123), who were fluent readers on entering school (around age 5 and sometimes younger), found children, when tested between just under age 5 and 6½ years, were reading from 2 to 6 grades ahead of their age norm. Unfortunately, there is very little additional quantified information, despite the extensive descriptive data. Reading stimulation began with the majority prior to age 4. Subsequent school achievement in reading, spelling, and written work remained "impressive" (p. 102) through several grades.

The school achievements of Terman's (1918) case of Martha, who was taught to read before age 2, were all much above average in all areas (Davidson 1931). At age 7-5, she was in the third grade and scored at an educational age of 11-1 on the Stanford Achievement Test. Her grade levels were low sixth, high fourth, and low fifth in reading, arithmetic, and spelling, respectively. By age 11-10, she was in the high eighth grade (about 2 years ahead of grade), was skilled in all subjects, but especially literature, and planned to become a writer, having already written two short books for children.

Early School Programs. An early study by Keister (1941) will be given more attention than its methodology deserves because it has been widely cited and is one of the few raising questions about the value of early reading. Keister interpreted his results on children's reading at age 5 in the school to indicate that, while children learned well, gains were less permanent than with older children because they forgot more over the summer vacation following the first year and failed to make up the loss in successive grades, through grade 4. Because there was no kindergarten in Nebraska schools, but state law required school attendance beginning at age 5, all first grades included a high proportion of 5-year-olds. There were no controls used in the study, however, not even baseline comparisons with norms of a school population, only statistically unevaluated comparisons with a subsample ($N = 17$) at the end of the first year, whose mental age was at least 6-0 and who regressed in reading less than those whose MA was less than 6-0. Since we are also not told what portion of the higher MA children were less than age 6 (chronologically) and by how much, nor is there any breakdown of reading achievement by age or MA for the later grades, the study is really little more than a descriptive analysis of trends, suggesting the influence of general verbal-abstract skills on progress in reading.

Actually, progress through the later grades was not consistent among the three early-taught cohorts. The first cohort, the only group followed as far as grade 4, maintained average levels throughout; the third cohort, followed only as far as grade 2, attained slightly above average levels; and the second cohort, followed through grade 3, fell 0.7 of a grade below average by grade 3. In the absence of background information on socioeconomic status and family support of academic learning and reading skills, as well as of details on the flexibility of the school program, coupled with the inconsistencies, the lack of controlled comparisons, the simplest conclusion is that the findings represent a picture of normal progress and variation in reading achievement in a school in which neither the school population nor the school reading program was outstanding. Certainly, little evidence is presented contraindicating the value of early reading, but even a slender bit of evidence that children regularly beginning reading in school at age 5 can keep up with national norms standardized for children who characteristically begin reading instruction around age 6.

A later investigation by Durkin (1974) on the later developmental effects of early reading experience in the school tends to corroborate the findings of her two earlier investigations, but the contamination of the control group early experiences and rigid later programming illustrates well problems of research in the schools. Using a fairly open-ended and flexible language-arts approach to reading, Durkin set up a two-year experimental preschool program for 4-year-olds in a public-school setting. On entry to the elementary grades (in the same school), the experimental subjects were consistently advanced over their controls in the same classrooms through grade 4, but significantly so only through grade 2 when IQ differences were controlled. Experimental children continued to exceed controls in their mean reading test scores (Stanford Reading Achievement and Gates-MacGinitie) and reading grade level (6.14 to 5.26 for controls) through grade 4, even controlling for IQ, though not significantly. This relative convergence of the two groups seems far from unexpected, in hindsight. The potential for continuing, long-term effects was seriously undermined for at least three major reasons. School authorities attempted to match the early-reading experience of the experimental children by providing letter- and number-naming experiences and a small reading vocabulary in the kindergarten (the second year of the early-reading program) for the control children, apparently as a result of parent pressure. Upon entering first grade, experimental subjects and controls shared the same classrooms, in which all children rigidly followed, by and large, the same lockstep basal reader program, with little or no extra reading offered *or permitted* in school to advanced readers, even as late as the fourth grade. The large bulk (more than 90 percent) of the families of both groups were upper lower class and lower middle class, milieux not noted for strong support of academically oriented skills like reading in the home. In the face of these factors working toward convergence, the persistence of even trend differences for several years gives more weight to the hypothetical potency of the effects of early reading.

One of the more interesting long-term investigations of the effects of beginning reading during kindergarten used a carefully graded and systematic program of instruction and the design offered special features that permitted separation of early from later effects (McKee, Brzeinski, and Harrison 1966). The experimental program focused on prerequisite language-skill activities, letter-sound associations, and a high-frequency word vocabulary during the earlier phases of working up to basal preprimers in the latter phases, but in a four group design. Children started either in kindergarten or grade 1, and different groups followed alternatively flexible or standard lockstep programs throughout the early school grades. Four different groups, each with very large samples, followed different program combinations. Two groups ($N = 750$ each) followed regular kindergarten and reading readiness activities, group I then continuing on through the grades in a standard reading program, group II starting the experimental beginning-reading program in grade 1 and following an adjusted reading program thereafter. Two other groups ($N = 1,250$ each) received the special experimental reading program in kindergarten, one group (group III) then continuing through the grades in an ordinary reading program, while group IV followed the programmed reading sequence from first grade on.

By the end of first grade, mean reading-achievement-test score differences (Gates Primary Reading Tests) among groups were significant ($p < .001$), the groups achieving in reverse numerical order, group IV achieving the highest. By the end of grade 5, the order had changed. Group IV (which had followed the experimental program beginning in kindergarten) was still significantly more advanced in reading (Stanford Diagnostic Reading Test) than the basic controls, group I, which had not begun until grade 1 and had followed the regular program throughout. But group III, which had followed reading instruction in the kindergarten with a regular reading program, though advanced over the basic control (group I), was no longer significantly so, and group II, which had begun the experimental program in first grade, was significantly advanced over the basic controls and ahead of group III, though not group IV. On the Stanford Achievement Test in reading, group IV was significantly advanced over all groups ($p < .001$) on all two group comparisons in grades 2-5, while the short-term experimental kindergarten group (III) was only barely advanced over controls (grades 3 and 4), and never significantly so. On the other hand the delayed experimental group (II) was significantly advanced over both the basic control group (I) and the experimental kindergarten group (III) at all grades 2-5, though not by as much as group IV. Other tests (Gates Speed of Reading, number of books read) produced parallel gains.

The importance of the McKee et al. (1966) study lies in demonstrating that early stimulation is likely to have permanent effects only when followed up with stimulating experiences that reinforce and cumulatively build on the successful early experiences, as the authors themselves conclude. The short-term experimental group (III), whose nicely sequenced kindergarten reading program was succeeded by a return to a more rigid basal reader program that was poorly articulated with the special kindergarten reading experience, failed to maintain its advantage over the later beginning groups past grade 1. The advantage group IV continued to maintain over the later-starting group II, which followed the same flexible experimental reading program as group IV (but a year later), indicates that it was *age of starting*, and not program quality that gave group IV the special advantage. It is nonetheless interesting that the short-term experimental group held up as well as it did, considering that the experimental reading program in kindergarten was only moderately intensive and was only one year in advance of the basic beginning reading program. This age was not nearly as early as the three- to five-year age range of learning to read moderately to fluently reported in the Clark (1976) and Durkin (1966) studies, where children read one and one-half to six years in advance of grade level on entering school. The return to the rigid basic program, too, may have occasioned some fall in motivation.

The results overall are particularly impressive because of the generalization of effects and the findings on positive social adjustment (both of which will be reported below), but especially because they involved randomly assigned classroom to program groups, analysis of covariance, controlling for IQ and sex, and such large samples, embracing the entire Denver elementary school population. At grade 5 there remained 225, 496, 707, and 759 pupils in the respective groups.

Other studies of children reading in kindergarten versus first grade have produced similar results (Beck 1973; King and Frieson 1972). One small, well-controlled study (including IQ) also found significant experimental advantages over controls in reading achievement through grade 5 (Beck 1973).

The highly promising program on early reading by Findley (1968) described previously was unfortunately altered in midprogram to eliminate or minimize the reading and arithmetic components in favor of a linguistically oriented curriculum (Findley 1982). Notwithstanding this shift, at entry to first grade, the experimental group, which had had three years of preschool experience, including an unknown amount of early reading), surpassed the comparison group, which had had no preschool experience, on nearly all of a wide range of reading and arithmetic achievement measures, as well as on Binet IQ (115-107) (Huberty and Swan 1974). Mean group differences were not evaluated statistically, however, and the follow-up sample composition may not have been entirely representative (the follow-up experimental group was lower in SES).

Two additional investigations of the effects of early reading in a school setting tend to document both similar and different patterns of decline, with one showing a remarkable persistence for girls and to some extent boys through many years of schooling. In a ten-year longitudinal study in Germany, children were taught to read in school between 4½ and 6. Experimental group ($N = 118$) advantages over controls ($N = 48$) in reading and language skills declined gradually during the first two grades, presumably in part as a result of lack of provisions for capitalizing on the early acceleration, either through the school program or parent involvement (Rudiger 1971). No generalization to other skills was clearly demonstrated.

Results were quite different in a long-term investigation comparing reading and other forms of school achievement through age 14 of Scottish ($N = 124$) and British ($N = 68$) children in two towns with similar social profiles (Vernon, O'Gorman, and McLelland 1955). (Scottish children are introduced to reading and other aspects of academic learning earlier than British children.) The results showed that Scottish girls generally maintained an overall advantage in all subjects (including all aspects of reading) over British girls through age 14, while boys remained advanced through age 8 in all subjects, but only in spelling and arithmetic by age 14. Considering that IQ scores for Scottish children (both sexes) were slightly (1-2 points) below those of the British children, the results are impressive. Actually the continuing advantage appears to be due as much to the greater concentration of formal learning and adherence to rules throughout the grades in Scottish schools than the earlier start, which at best appears to be only a matter of months. Both groups start learning around age 5, but academic programming begins more slowly in the British schools (Chall 1967; Dunlop 1942; Vernon et al. 1955).

Early Reading with the Disadvantaged. Special reading stimulation in the home has been long believed to be a phenomenon associated with well-educated, middle-class families (Durkin 1966). But Durkin herself found that the predominant group represented in her first study came from blue-collar backgrounds (47 percent were black or from other minorities), and over half the matched sample of thirty children came from lower-middle-class families or below, largely because other groups were poorly represented in the population from which the sample was drawn. She also found evidence that lower echelon families were less responsive to the popular professional dicta that long widely condemned parental efforts to teach reading or otherwise engage in early stimulation (Boney 1949; Durkin 1966; Fowler 1968; Morphett and Washburne 1931).

Morrison, Harrison, and Auerbach (1971) were able to identify fifty-eight early-reading children out of a disadvantaged population of 1,378 children (nearly all black) entering first grade in New York City schools. Despite the restricted definition of early reading ("Identify words in print, no matter how few," p. 4) and certain methodological flaws, the trends reported on later reading achievement are suggestive. Measures (Stanford and Metropolitan) favored the early readers over their preschool nonreading peers through third grade, and six of the seven score differences remained significant in third grade ($p = .01$ level). The total sample of nonearly readers unfortunately included the early readers, but the percentage the latter represents of the former is so small (4 percent) as not to materially affect the comparisons. While sex and SES were apparently not controlled and no IQ measures were administered, selected groups of early readers matched on the Murphy-Durrell Learning Rate Subtest with nonearly readers ranged from .4 to 1.1 grades in advance of the latter on the Metropolitan Achievement Test in grade 3. Nonearly readers were reading at grade level (the entire project was directed at comparing special methods of teaching reading), while the mean test score grade level for early readers was 3.75.

Not many investigators have incorporated reading instruction into early intervention programs with disadvantaged children, beyond occasional attention to familiarity with letters (and numbers) (Day and Parker 1977; White et al. 1973). Most of the exceptions have reported little success beyond children learning to recognize a few individual letters and words as isolated units (Bereiter and Englemann 1968; Strodtbeck 1964). The later follow-up advantage of disadvantaged children in reading achievement skills must therefore probably be attributed in most projects primarily to the oral language, reading readiness, and other cognitive components of the early stimulation programs (Palmer and Anderson 1979; Lazar and Darlington 1978, 1982).

At least two investigations on mixed populations of children are noteworthy, however, one of which was described in detail in the last chapter along with general programs on advantaged children, who constituted the main body of children in the investigation (Ulrich et al. 1971). In that study, all except one child, but including all seven disadvantaged children, who had attended the graded, multiskill, behavior-modification program (included perceptual-motor, language, reading, and other skills) from one to two years beginning at age 4, were all reading at higher than the 90th percentile on the Wide Range Achievement Test by the end of kindergarten. The mean reading grade level for the Learning Village children was low grade 3, compared to only low grade 1 for children who had either the Learning Village Nursery Program plus public school kindergarten or ordinary nursery school plus public school kindergarten.

The other investigation consisted of a similar (but not behavior-modification), multiskill, carefully individualized and sequenced program in reading, mathematics, and general-concept learning, the Primary Education Project (PEP), beginning for many children in the preschool at age 3 and continuing through the early elementary grades (Resnick, Wang, and Rosner 1977; Wang, Leinhardt, and Boston 1980). The children were from mixed social classes, but predominantly poor children in both urban and rural settings at seven different sites from a diversity of folk backgrounds, such as inner city black, Southern Appalachian white, and Native American. The emphasis in the program has been on school-related skills, mainly reading and arithmetic, and although significant mean Binet IQ gains of around 5 points have been reported in the kindergarten for early samples, later reports have dropped the IQ measures. For this reason the investigation is not reported along with the general learning programs of the previous chapter. In this program experimental subjects in all cultural groups progressed in all schools from about grade-level reading achievement at the end of the kindergarten year to half a grade or more ahead of grade by the end of third grade, thus progressing cumulatively faster than norms for the general population, as well as advancing significantly over controls, who generally read below grade, at all grade levels. Although some groups advanced more than others, even sites with a high representation of poor inner city blacks and Native Americans (from a reservation) advanced at faster rates than the national norms.

The results in these two programs are impressive, pointing up the possibilities for early preventive stimulation to enable children from diverse folk and impoverished backgrounds to achieve well in school in reading and other academic skills. Like the studies by McKee et al. (1966) and Vernon et al. (1955), however, much of the success of the programs appeared to depend as strongly on the continuing, individualized cumulative learning programs as it did on the earliness of starting. Because neither program separated duration of stimulation from age of starting, or early from later effects, as the McKee study attempted to do, it is not possible to assign weights to the factors. The fact that reading achievement is not reported until kindergarten, however, suggests that much of the prekindergarten experience in reading was limited to the kind of unit-learning activities (letters, sounds, words) employed in other programs attempting to teach reading to disadvantaged children. Drawing an inference from the McKee study, it would appear to be the *combined* effects of the early start and the cumulative, graded stimulation in the program that produced high achievement in children against the stream of their folk background in their dual curriculum.

Influence on Other Skills and Socioemotional Development. The collected studies on long-term effects are not clear on the degree to which early skills in reading transfer to other domains, as we have noted, though there is evidence of parallel competence developing in related verbal areas and early readers appear to perform generally above average in most school subjects. The process has not been systematically studied, however, and no effort has been made to determine whether and to what degree other forms of cognitive stimulation accompanied the instruction in early reading, especially those learning at home. Although early reading through the family yields clouded if any information, one study on reading in the kindergarten, the large-scale, well-designed investigation of McKee et al. (1966) yielded more systematic data. Group IV, with a combined early reading and specially sequenced program through the grades, surpassed all other groups in fifth grade in all domains involving extensive use of verbal skills and reading. The same group performed significantly better in the less-related concept domains of science and math, but less consistently so, especially in arithmetic computation. Group II, the group not beginning reading until first grade but following a special program through the grades, performed at the next best level. But differences among the other groups were less consistent, suggesting that at least some of the generalization of effects was a function of a motivational halo effect from prolonged participation in special programs (which both groups I and III missed) as the authors themselves conclude.

Also poorly studied but on which a certain amount of evidence exists is the question of how early readers have fared in their later socioemotional functioning. This issue historically draws its importance from a pervasive concern in the field of education and child development that preschool stimulation in general and early reading instruction in particular may have dire consequences for the child's learning and overall development. The concern is integral to the developmental philosophy that evolved from Rousseau. The general outlook, which is by no means moribund (Elkind 1981; Hymes 1965; Roderick 1979), stems from the predeterminist framework that development will unfold more or less according to a biological timetable, each child following his or her own natural course. In the field of reading, the developmental sequence for the acquisition of reading skills, as originally outlined by Ilg and Ames (1950), epitomizes this framework. Attempts to foster development systematically in the early years, particularly to teach preschoolers to read, is seen as unwholesome acceleration, likely to distort development or at best bypass the natural experiences of play and fantasy of childhood. Recent expressions of concern, embracing educational leaders from many countries, indicate that underlying the concern is the problem of how to teach reading to young children in the institutionalized setting of schools in a developmentally broad and appropriate manner (Roderick 1979).

But what is a technical problem of mass education should not be confused with individual readiness and cognitive potential. Many children have learned in the early years and the studies reviewed report little but generally positive short- and long-term effects on the early readers' social and emotional development. Davidson's children and Martha, taught to read at age 2, all appear to have benefited from the advantage higher skills gave them in school learning, at least in verbal subject areas, and from the enhanced status these skills gave them with teachers (Davidson 1931). The early fluent readers in the British study by Clark "appeared well adjusted to school and to be seen as generally acceptable to their classmates" (1976:102) through the first several grades of school (to ages 7-8).

More systematic investigations of social and personality outcomes by Durkin (1966) and others yielded parallel findings or reported no difference between the patterns of early and nonearly readers. Rudiger (1971) found no adverse emotional effects accruing in experimental early reading children during his 10-year longitudinal investigation. The only differences Durkin reports (in her second study) are essentially more interest in private play and in concentrated or quiet types of activities, and less interest in school during first grade (but not in achievement), probably at least in part a function of boredom from facing the rigidly lockstep curriculum that did not challenge their advanced skills sufficiently. Otherwise children were similar as judged by both teacher and parent ratings, except for a slight edge for early readers, in a gamut of largely positive characteristics, including friendliness, happiness, self-reliance, persistence, competitiveness, sensitivity, tendency to worry, and dominance in social relationships.

In a more focused study, but with a small N (six pairs) and limited to bright children (again perhaps a partial consequence of early reading, and probably other cognitive stimulation) Scott and Bryant (1978) found early-reading kindergartners enjoyed several advantages over their matched controls who had not learned to read prior to attending school, though they found no difference in social skills. Early readers interacted with adults more, cited adult-defined social rules more, were more independent, more purposive and task oriented but socially they manifested no more negative behavior and interacted with peers as much as nonearly readers.

In the McKee et al. (1966) investigation, which admittedly is not a very early start, kindergarten-starting children (groups III and IV) were not significantly different from first-grade-starting groups through grade 5 in percentage of eye defects, hearing loss, or manifestation of socioemotional adjustment problems, the last assessed through observation and formal clinical evaluations. No group had as much as 3 percent of its children maladjusted. Special diagnostic tests administered (the Stanford Diagnostic Test) found fewer disabilities in all experimental groups (group IV, the combined early-starting, special-sequenced program group the least) than in the control group (I).

It is difficult to conclude from the literature that early reading instruction itself is a source of emotional difficulties, social maladjustment, or even visual problems, though few studies have investigated the question in detail. The long-range advantages early reading appears to bestow on cognitive development in reading itself and very probably in relation to related verbal areas of school learning and academic functioning generally, in themselves reflect an important measure of adequacy in an important socially valued domain. If learning to read at an early age does not necessarily promote social development—and the coincidence of continuing good social adjustment generally appearing among early readers suggests that it may—at least there is little evidence so far that it undermines social development and it does promote academic coping and competence.

Conclusions. Overall, a sizable volume of material now indicates that many children enjoying a wide range of IQ and other abilities encounter little difficulty in acquiring skill in reading between the ages of 3 to 5, one to three years ahead of prevailing developmental norms. They go beyond unit recognition of letters, a few words, and several pat phrases, to read simple preprimers and quite often acquire skill enough to read fluently and with understanding advanced readers and popular children's books by the time they enroll in school. Once having learned to master text in this way—which in school-based early programs may require flexible, sequenced instruction continuing over a period of years, as is the McKee et al. (1966) study—few studies fail to find that early readers maintain an advantage over nonearly readers in reading achievement on many indices through one to as many as six grades in school. There is also evidence that early skill in reading may confer long-time advantages in any subject area where reading is a prime component, such as social studies. There are further indications, moreover, that, holding IQ ability constant, learning to read at 3 may be additionally beneficial over learning to read at 5 insofar as maintenance of advantages in later reading achievement is concerned (Durkin 1966), one of the few specific age effects (the degree of earliness of stimulation) that has appeared for a specific domain.

One of the problems repeatedly encountered in early reading (and elsewhere), however, is the difficulty of separating the effects of earliness from those of the duration of stimulation. The problem is particularly acute in the reading sphere because reading is the primary activity throughout the school years, constantly reinforced and consequently making it difficult to sort out early from later effects. We are distinguishing here duration of the original early stimulation from duration of total time engaged in this sort of reinforced experience over the years subsequent to the early-stimulation experience. Children learning to read one or more years in advance of their peers necessarily have been reading one or more years longer than their schoolmates at any later age tested.

In studies where data presentation makes any breakdown possible, such as in Durkin (1966), children are found to be reading in advance of their nonearly-reading peers by an amount approaching the difference in age. In a more pointed analysis, Durkin found that children beginning reading instruction at age 3 read 1.6 grades in advance of those beginning at age 5, but in fact the gap had been steadily widening over the years, beginning with a mean difference of only .9 at the beginning of grade 1. There is almost no other precise information comparing age and duration effects. Clark (1976) describes the early-reading children she studied as far more advanced than their schoolmates in later reading and most other school subjects, but they were also high in IQ and the information is not compiled systematically. The McKee et al. (1966) kindergarten-instructed children apparently increasingly widened the gap in reading competence over normal first-grade starters (both groups following the continuing sequenced-instruction programs) between first and fifth grade in the same way Durkin's early readers did. The groups did not change in the relative numbers of books reported read during the second semester of each year between second and fifth grade, but this measure takes no account of skill and the quality and difficulty of books read. Thus, in all of these cases, as the ratio of the difference between groups to the duration of total years in reading experience diminished with the years, earliness remained a constant that meant an increasingly wide advantage for the earlier starters.

This small bit of evidence is encouraging, but the problem needs extensive investigation, comparing skills according to time since beginning instruction or acquisition of fluency. The problem is complex since one of the advantages of earliness might just be the greater number of years available for reading experience, though the criterion is a weak one. By the time children graduate from secondary school, around age 18, the percentage of total years spent in reading constituted by differences of one to three years in starting age seems miniscule, only 8 percent for beginning at age 3 versus beginning at the normal age 6. The more significant criterion is or ought to be how well reading ultimately gets mastered by children at different starting ages. The latter may be partly a social learning phenomenon. Starting before school or at the very beginning of school (in kindergarten) may establish a direction for activity that ensures higher competence and an enduring interest, likely to survive vis-à-vis tempting alternatives like sports or TV watching.

Most of the early readers, or at least those learning at ages 3 and 4 before kindergarten, learn through stimulation at home, incidental to or planned for the routines of reading to and play with the child by the parents. The PEP (Wang et al. 1980) programs taught in a school setting suggest that children, even the disadvantaged, can benefit from beginning early reading as early as age 3 or 4 and that the advantages over their school comparison group classmates may persist for several years—if they continue to attend an individualized learning program in reading. The McKee et al. (1966) study (and to some extent the Vernon et al. 1955 study on Scottish children) indicates that the benefits of early reading can be available even when the reading begins only a year earlier, in kindergarten, in a school setting, compared to the 3-5 range typical of home-taught early readers. The

McKee program was also well designed and followed through with a commensurate well-paced reading program whose absence apparently failed to produce equivalent long-term advantages in the Keister (1941) study, in both the Durkin (1974) and the Rudiger (1971) early school (age 4) reading programs, or in the McKee study itself (one group), when after the early reading programs, the children were in all cases dumped back into the ordinary, lockstep school programs. Davidson (1931) made no formal follow-up study. It is worth reiterating that the most successful early readers in her schoollike program were 3-year-olds whose parents had stressed reading in the home more than the parents of the 4- and 5-year-olds—again making it difficult to separate earliness from probable continuing support in the home ecology. About half the successful early readers who were contacted informally in later grades all were reading ahead of their school peers, some avidly. Studies directly comparing home- and school-stimulation efforts would be useful, along with studies coordinating stimulation at school with parent involvement. One of the little-discussed but at least partially documented advantages early home readers seem to have over their early school-taught counterparts, beyond the informality, interaction, and motivational framework the home often provides (Durkin 1966; Fowler 1981b) is the continuing high support in the home for reading activities.

On the whole, children instructed in reading early at home have fared better, longer, compared to normal rates of progression, than children instructed in school settings. Only when school programs have followed through with individually graded or at least intensive programs through the early elementary grades (McKee et al. 1966; Ulrich et al. 1971; Vernon et al. 1955; Wang et al. 1980), have children maintained their advantage over their normal peers. What these individualized, continuous school programs suggest is that early beginnings help but only when cumulative mastery at more and more complex levels is fostered as a continuous developmental process.

At first it might seem as if children learning at home maintain their advantage over many grades without the aid of special follow-up programs. But while the generally earlier start and the somewhat higher levels of mastery they attain by school age, compared to children instructed ahead of the usual age in school programs, may be factors as well, it is reasonable to infer that parents who start early at home are not a random group (and the case-study information supports the inference—Durkin 1966; Fowler 1981b). They are among parents most likely to maintain continued support of their children in reading and related school learning to refine and build cumulatively on what they have learned to ensure expanding mastery of what the parents valued enough in the first place to become involved in teaching ahead of the usual developmental schedule. Reading is usually integral to the total ecology of the home in such families. It may well be that, while early experience alone in reading (and other areas) *can* produce certain effects that persist for years, as in the case of the general functional coping and competence advantages of disadvantaged children, more significant as a winning combination from the broadest development perspective is the joint effects of earliness and later ecological maintenance and utility. Learning a skill early is not likely to be of much value unless it leads to mastery and continued use, enabling the learner to build cumulatively on the early start.

Among other key problems is the question of how dependent reading skills are on concept development in basic formal concepts and other areas. Certainly, we would expect language to be all important, but it turns out that reading can apparently be taught almost concurrently with the acquisition of language. The role of Piagetian concrete-operational concepts is also uncertain. Davidson's (1931) original index of mental age 4 as the benchmark, general (IQ) ability level necessary for beginning reading seems to hold up in a general sort of way. Most early readers are found to have high IQ abilities, so that 130 IQ at age 3 is about age 4 MA. But there are enough exceptions of early readers with no more than average abilities apparently floating around (and thus with MAs of 3, when only age 3 or younger), as in Terman's (1918) case and Durkin's (1966), Findley's (1968), the Ulrich (Ulrich et al. 1971), and the PEP (Wang et al. 1980) samples, including disadvantaged children from a variety of folk cultures, to warrant precise study. Once again the global verbal-logical-abstraction processes that IQ tests represent tell us painfully little about just what specific cognitive processes in the various branches of knowledge, codes, and strategies learning to read may be constructed of or contingent on.

Early Writing Competence

Writing is an ambiguous concept, referring to both visual motor skill in *recording* the graphic language code and *composing* stories and other original material. But no matter which definition is employed, there is very little research at all on stimulating young children to write and determining its significance for development.

There is the usual gathering of developmental norms common to many fields. Earlier efforts followed the lead of Gesell, whereas later work has been more concerned with conceptualizing the nature of writing in relation to the phonology of language and the role of writing in the process of learning to read. Thus even the later work is primarily centered on the mechanics of structure and recording processes rather than composition and meaning.

In the early research Ames and Ilg (1951) recorded the prewriting and writing patterns of groups of infants and children from 36 weeks through age 10. Children move from crude preoccupations with the process of manipulating objects (crayons and pencils) as paper-marking instruments to the problems of marking paper in various stages of single and multiple scribbles in different directions, to making recognizable forms (vertical and horizontal lines, circles, squares), eventually to forming capital and small letter forms of increasing clarity, and finally words and phrases. Ames and Ilg present a separate defined sequence for the development of manipulative and postural control of writing with paper and pencil. IQ tests have long included many specific items of these sequences. Bayley (1969) and Griffiths (1954), for example, list the first adaptive attempts to hold a crayon or pencil at just under 1 year, controlled scribbling at before age 2, followed soon after by vertical and horizontal marking. The first capital letters appear at age 4, words at 5-5½, according to Ames and Ilg, though Griffiths (1970) does not include the first letters until age 5 and the first words until 6. The difference appears to be a function of the populations from which the samples were drawn. Ilg and Ames observed a middle- to upper-middle-class sample, in which a great deal of attention is normally paid by parents to literacy quite early; Griffiths standardized on a general population sample. Because the beginnings of writing can be so readily traced to the early years, it is odd so little early-stimulation research had been conducted even on the mechanics of early writing. The discrepancy between Ames and Ilg and Griffiths in the norms reported alone suggests that writing competence is very early quite open to variations in the quality of stimulation.

Recent developmental work on children's writing has focused on the apparent ability of children, beginning as early as age 3, to devise crude spelling systems of their own, based on a literal utilization of the names of letters for their sound values (Bissex 1980; C. Chomsky 1971a,b; Read 1971). Many of the standard consonants are employed, though certain ones may be omitted (nasals are merged with succeeding consonants, as in AD for and). Vowels may also be omitted, because of their phonological incorporation in a consonant (the A within the R, as in STRT), or another vowel whose name sounds more like the vowel as pronounced in a word may be substituted (using E for I, as in BEG for big, because the letter name of I is the long sound). The first efforts tend to run words together, recognizing no concept of word units. Gradually, over a long period of years, well into the early school years, children move in stages toward more conventional forms of spelling, making use of the standard phonological and other arbitrary rules that determine how English words are spelled. But the rate at which the process evolves toward conventional forms apparently depends very much on how much guidance in standard usage the child receives. This line of inquiry adds a dimension to how the young child's first understandings of written forms are tied to language, but the hands-off developmental approach, like the earlier charting of the child's development of visual-motor control, appears to sidestep the problem of how writing skills can be facilitated.

The advantage of keeping hands off, even in the early school grades, is seen as increasing the child's opportunity to work creatively in expressing his or her own thoughts, to concentrate on meaning and composition (C. Chomsky 1976; Gerritz 1974). There are alternatives, however, which may make it possible to foster creative compositional skills while concurrently advancing the young child's mastery of the visual, perceptual-motor, and phonological rules for writing, to enable the child to utilize earlier the production and communicate advantages offered by conventional writing systems. For example, Terman (Terman and Fenton 1921; Burks, Jensen, and Terman 1930) cites a case of a child, Betty, who composed extensive stories and poems by the age of 4, beginning at the age of 2 with the aid and stimulation of parents who recorded her oral compositions, thus keeping the composing process separated from the mechanics of learning letter forms. She was also taught to read fluently before she was 4, the parents employing indirect techniques of stimulation that will be discussed more in chapter 9, on precocious mental development. By age 6 Betty was composing material on the typewriter, and writing prolifically; she completed her first novel by age 18. The method of writing down the child's crude narrative statements from the earliest years is occasionally found in preschool programs, is not uncommon among families who have stimulated early reading in their child (Fowler 1981b), and in any case is an intrinsic aspect of a language-arts experiential approach to teaching reading in the elementary grades (Durkin 1972).

The frequency with which early reading is allied with early writing (many of Durkin's (1966) early readers were "early scribblers") makes it something of a puzzle as to why stimulating early reading has been the subject of a substantial body of research but not early writing. Durkin and others often mention the efforts of parents to help their child form letters and words, as they help in the process of reading, but almost nowhere have the effects of stimulating the writing process been measured, either in the short term or the long term. Writing was integral to the curriculum of the early infant schools in nineteenth-century Britain and elsewhere (Adamson 1905; Rusk 1933) and indeed was an accompaniment of the tedious alphabetic-syllabic exercises used everywhere in teaching reading from the most ancient times (Davies 1973). The results of these efforts, when undertaken in early childhood are even more obscure than the results of teaching reading, however. At least we know that a good number of young children learned to read in the early infant schools, but reports on writing skills are sparse. Montessori (1912; Kent 1974) built writing into her sequenced sensorimotor, symbolic curriculum as a primary basis for learning to read. Children begin at age 4 to trace raised, sandpaper geometric figures with their fingers, following soon after with finger-tracing exercises with sandpaper-covered letters and eventually simply with cutout letter forms with no special surface. When a certain number of consonants and vowels are mastered, the teacher guides the child in composing words with letters the child knows, until the child can compose words independently. Montessori herself observed that the transfer from letter manipulation as the basis for composing words and sentences to chalkboard and paper writing, came quite easily without stress. It usually also occurred quite suddenly as an exciting discovery, independent of any adult verbalization, leading to an inspired release of the child's efforts to write.

The process is easier in Italian because of the phonological consistency of the spelling rules, though the methods have been introduced into English-speaking Montessori schools (Durkin 1968; Evans 1975). But while there is a body of research on the effects of learning in Montessori schools embracing a wide range of abilities, much of it is on disadvantaged children (Beller 1973; Miezitis 1971; Miller and Dyer 1975), there seems to be very little research addressed to the development of competence in writing (or reading) in terms of either mechanics or composition. Hardly any studies on stimulating early writing have been located in the enormous corpus of work on early intervention with disadvantaged children. An exception is the systematic perceptual-skill training program in the University of Pittsburgh Learning Research and Development Center, which led into training in writing skills as well as reading and arithmetic in the PEP program (Rosner 1972). Children advanced at varying rates from age 4 on through grade 2, generally accelerated in advance of norms. Although few details are reported on writing, the investigation appears to demonstrate that many children, including the disadvantaged, can be accelerated in learning the mechanics of writing by beginning before kindergarten, as they can be in other school subjects. Unfortunately, the long-term effects on writing skills and the effects on creative writing are not reported.

The chief example of research on early writing, Moore's (1967) program, has never reported detailed findings on either reading or writing competence, unfortunately. Moore combined the process of stimulating reading with writing, children working on a talking typewriter, which would voice the letters and words the child punched on the keys. One-to-one guidance by adults was given, the child eventually composing words and stories independently, similar to the manner of Montessori, but using the typewriter rather than letter forms and paper or chalkboard as the primary beginning media. Moore reproduces several one or two sentence statements that different nursery-school children had composed for their class newspaper but does not specify numbers nor the conditions under which they were composed. This highly promising field of early experience is thus greatly in need of systematic investigations, particularly with regard to the long-term effects on creative compositional skills, but even the problem of mechanics has scarcely been touched.

Mathematical Abilities

Mathematics concepts of counting and measurement and the derivative symbolic codes and accompanying cognitive operations are perhaps inherently more complex than the basic concepts that constitute the structure and operations of ordinary language and the printed word. Language is composed of several levels (phonology, syntax, and semantics), each with multiple units and complicated rules for patterning and processing in sequence, which must be woven together as an intricate system for representing and organizing information about the world in abstract ways (N. Chomsky 1959, 1965; McNeill 1970). The apparent pure and abstract simplicity of math concepts, codes, and operations, in contrast, may in fact be a source of difficulty for mastering it. Everything about math is a universal abstraction: concepts and coding units (such as the number 7) represent all phenomena in all times and all places, regardless of particular features, until qualified by verbal modifiers (seven red cherries). There are no perceptual cues for the young child to grasp in learning the elements of this abstraction system, and the cognitive edifice the child must construct on these elemental abstractions adds multiplicity and intricacy in the levels and varieties of codes and operations the child must master, in abstraction upon abstraction (arithmetic operations, fractions and decimals, algebra, geometry, the calculus).

It may be argued that abstraction and complexity in language dominate from the beginning, in infancy. The many phonemes to be acquired and how they must be sequenced, altered with context, and related to both grammar and meaning in complex ways, seems to be an extraordinarily difficult, abstract task, a task which, as Noam Chomsky (1965) originally hypothesized, seems to require some prearranged biological programming, a language acquisition device (LAD) to succeed at all. True enough. The maze of rules the typical child wades through during the first three or four years to become a certified member of his or her speech community may make the few rules required for basic understanding of primary math structures (one-to-one correspondence, cardinality and ordinality, numerosity, the numeral code, seriation, and conservation of number, length, and other dimensions) and even arithmetic operations of adding and substracting and the like, seem simple by comparison.

Yet however complex from the earliest stages, language is characteristically anchored in perceptual events and most often related to limited classes of phenomena that can be identified by specific features to serve recognition and memory. Sounds and sound sequences are modeled for the infant to imitate (recognizing that the child must learn to master a class of sounds in each case, a range of sounds to represent phonemes in different contexts). More important, sound sets (words, morphemes, phrases), unlike math concepts, are related through modeling and guidance to objects and actions of definable, specific types (birds, trees, run, blue). Math codes and concepts in contrast, invariably represent *all* classes of phenomena under *all* circumstances. Modeling and guidance can and are used in instructing the young child, but the number 4, for example, must be learned as applicable to all things, not just four birds, concretizations, which for language, serve as memory aids. In fact, tying the concept to limited sets, such as birds or pillows, violates the principle of universal abstraction the child must grasp to master the concept of 4 and the general concept of number.

Whatever the truth about the relative difficulty of mastering the domains of language and math, the incidence of language in ordinary usage in common cultural contexts gives it a certain advantage in ease of mastery. The infant, moreover, does not confront the complexity of grammatical structure in the pure technical form Chomsky visualized—fortunately. Adults and older children routinely modify the speech they employ in caring for and communicating with infants and young children (Snow and Ferguson 1977). And it is language, not counting and measurement concepts, they utilize as the primary coding tool for much of their daily activity with children.

Language is integrated into social life far more than counting and measuring activities. Math concepts *are* modeled for children and children *are* to different degrees guided in their meaning and use from the earliest period, in the course of core routines of matching and manipulating clothes, food, containers, and other objects by size, number, and other dimensions. Counting and measurement in some form has been a staple of all cultures, apparently, even in the most ancient folk cultures (Menninger 1969). Children have long learned to count pebbles and sticks in daily life, or more commonly fingers and toes and other body parts (Saxe 1981), as noted in chapter 1. But the procedures through which infants and young children have traditionally learned, observation and imitation in the daily rituals of a close-knit folk community, may not construct the sound basis necessary for competent development of the complex mathematical codes and thinking demanded in our technologically dominated world. In any case the separation of home from occupation and many other adult activities effectively deprives the child of extended opportunities to observe and interact in their use. Systematic research on cognitive socialization of mathematical concepts would seem to demand first priority, to ascertain the parameters of just how early, in what form, and to what degree the basis for mathematical thinking can be established, and in relation to its effects on later development.

Yet there has been very little research on the developmental experiential origins of number and other mathematical concepts, perhaps in part because of the apparently greater inherent abstractness of math concepts and in part because of its less prominently functional qualities in everyday traditional life, particularly for young children. One of the few studies to consider early child-rearing influences found that freedom to explore and experiment was the most important antecedent of nonverbal competence (Bing 1963). But this study on the development of abilities (verbal and nonverbal—space and number) was retrospective, starting from age 10, and the investigation of nonverbal skills was limited to contemporaneous observations of parent-child interactions on spatial tasks (puzzles) and interviews on availability of toys, tools, gadgets, and opportunities to play and experiment during early development. There was nothing on the specifics of adult-child interaction influences during early childhood.

Mathematical development has been the subject of norm collecting beginning systematically with Gesell in the same way norms have been collected on the child's development of language, reading, writing, and other skills. Ilg and Ames (1951), following earlier efforts of Descoeudres (1921), Giltay (1936), Long and Welch (1941), Piaget (1961), and others on the development of concepts of number, charted the benchmarks for the child's development of arithmetic skills from the first year through age 9. Providing more detailed descriptions of normative behavioral repertoires then conceptualizations of cognitive dynamics, they noted the infant's first skill in manipulating objects in succession at age 1, through the gradual discrimination of one versus many, of sets of less than five, then more, to the gradual acquisition of numeral labels and terms of comparison (more, big, equal, same), rote counting, one-to-one correspondence, familiarity with money, addition, and abstraction and other operations. Norm collecting has continued more or less unabated through the present day, though latter-day emphasis has been on studying the mental operations and the sequence with which different concepts and skills are grasped, rather than the precise age at which they may be acquired (D'Mello and Willemsen 1969; Gelman 1972; Gelman and Gallistel 1978; Schwartz and Scholnick 1970; Wang, Resnick, and Boozer 1971; Wohlwill 1960).

Research on early learning of mathematics skills has, however, been confined to certain restricted channels. One channel has been the focused training studies on dimensional concepts of size, number, length, and the like, which because of their basis in the formal, general nature of phenomena were reviewed extensively under formal concept learning. Dimensional concepts are, however, equally the conceptual foundation for mathematical abilities, the concepts that lead to the acquisition of complex mathematical codes and operations of arithmetic, geometry, algebra, and other math systems. Without exception these studies have been short-term investigations of the child's present knowledge or briefly delayed training in specific dimensions, beginning with the first groping experimentations of Welch and his associates (Long 1940; Long and Welch 1941; Welch 1939a-c) on size, form, number, and similar concepts and encompassing the more recent extended investigations on Piagetian concepts of conservation, seriation, and classification (Brainerd 1977, 1978; Gelman and Gallistel 1978). The results of these collected investigations appear to demonstrate quite clearly that children at least as young as age 4 can often readily be induced to master selectively various basic concrete-operational concepts of seriation and conservation and be advanced through planned stimulation in their grasp of size, number, length, and related concepts even earlier. (See earlier discussion on formal concept learning.) While there is some degree of transfer across dimensions, for example from number to length when the child is trained in number, the findings are inconsistent and there are not enough studies yet undertaken to map the boundaries of the transfer terrain.

Because virtually all the later research of this type is inspired by Piaget, there appear to have been no focused investigations on early stimulation of a host of other mathematics concepts and skills, such as counting, numerals, one-to-one correspondence, ordinality and cardinality, and various arithmetic operations. Most prominent of the shortcomings in these isolated dimensional studies in a short-term mould is the failure to orchestrate the child's learning and development of an interrelated hierarchy of mathematical skills that might establish a significant foundation in the domain. Gelman (1972; Gelman and Gallistel 1978) speaks to this problem in a selected review of early, short-term training studies and of her own detailed studies and analysis of overlooked mathematical potentials of preschool children but reports no research investigations framed with longer and broader perspectives. It would seem useful to launch a comprehensive early training investigation of this kind and follow through a complex sequence of skills to determine the cumulative effects that might make a difference for the child's long-term development of mathematical abilities.

Probably the closest in conception are the early-intervention studies on children from disadvantaged backgrounds. A number of these programs have included number concept and numeral-learning activities, including counting and simple addition and subtraction (Bereiter and Engelmann 1966; Gray et al. 1965; Miller and Dyer 1975; Weikart 1967; White et al. 1973), and all of them have embraced some type of formal concept learning of basic dimensions of size, length, number, and the like (White et al. 1973).

Since all of the investigators designed comprehensive programs for the purpose of developing the abilities of disadvantaged children in all cognitive domains, the program components directed at math abilities necessarily interacted with the concept stimulation programmed in other areas (beyond that normal to the child's milieu). Both the short- and long-term developmental effects must necessarily be evaluated with this interaction in mind, as in the case of the evaluation of language stimulation. The problem is magnified by the fact that the skills taught in most programs were simple counting and measurement concepts preceding arithmetic operations, and the measures employed were typically standard readiness and achievement tests, in which there was not a precise match between the specific math skills taught in a program and the set of concepts and skills assessed in the math component of the test.

Within this framework the general findings of the early intervention studies indicate that children frequently gained in mathematical abilities often significantly greater than controls, for both the short-term and the long-term, sometimes attaining or even exceeding the norms characteristic of the general population. Since many of the projects relied on broad ability measures such as IQ tests and the Illinois Test of Psycholinguistic abilities, they furnish no assessment of changes in math skills during the period of the program itself. By kindergarten and the successive school grades, however, investigators increasingly incorporated standardized readiness and achievement tests. The Wechsler scales were also introduced in some projects at this time, giving a measure of math skills in the subtest of arithmetic. The pattern of initial changes has been extensively summarized by White et al. (1973) in a comprehensive report on early education prepared for the U.S. Department of Health, Education, and Welfare. Both White's survey and the reports of myriad of individual investigations demonstrate that the children who were experimental subjects frequently made substantial advancements in a variety of mathematics concepts and skills, often significantly greater than controls, rising in some cases above general norms, as measured by the various tests administered in kindergarten and later grades.

In one of the better programs beginning for some children at age 3, for example, termed the Primary Education Projects (PEP), which encompassed a comprehensive program of math, reading, and other cognitive skills extending through the primary grades, children were found to have attained once the program was well established at least average grade levels in math and reading from the end of kindergarten through third grade, significantly above control levels, which tended to fall below grade levels (Resnick, Wang, and Rosner 1977; Wang, Leinhardt, and Boston 1980). The PEP program was not restricted to the early years but provided continuing, well-sequenced stimulation, area by area. It furnishes a good example of the importance of effective continuing stimulation for disadvantaged children in the area of academic skills to compete with the differently oriented curriculum of the poor folk community. Children participating in the carefully sequenced, and individualized PEP Follow Through program, not only maintained at least grade-level competence in math (and reading), compared to the non-Follow Through controls; they tended to advance progressively from grade to grade (Wang, Leinhardt, and Boston 1980). They generally moved in all school sites from about grade level in their kindergarten year to half a grade or more ahead in grade 3, when rates began to lag, even tending to fall below norms, particularly in math, illustrating once more the potency of the competing folk curriculum of the poor.

Examples of the effects of early stimulation of one to three years, with little or no follow-through stimulation are also available (White et al. 1973). One is provided by the Learning to Learn program, in which different experimental groups surpassed controls on math (and other) subtests of the Primary Mental Abilities, Metropolitan, and the Stanford Achievement tests at different times from kindergarten through grade 2, sometimes above grade level (Sprigle 1974; Van De Riet, Van De Riet, and Resnick 1970). Another is furnished by the program of Karnes, who reported 4-year-olds advanced substantially and significantly in math and other academic skills over controls and slightly above grade level on the California Achievement Test through grade 1 (Karnes, Hodgins, and Teska 1969), apparently regressing in math (though less in reading) gradually to average levels or below by grade 3 (Karnes, Zehrbach, and Teska 1974). Possibly the most outstanding levels were registered by the initial Bereiter and Engelmann project, where children reached the beginning second grade level at the end of the preschool program, still achieving at a grade equivalent of 2.6 by the end of kindergarten (Bereiter and Engelmann 1968) but regressing to average and below thereafter (Karnes et al. 1969). In the realm of early, highly intensive programs, the Heber group (1972) also fail to report immediate math learning effects and have not reported any math or other achievement data to date (Garber and Heber 1981).

By no means all of the programs reported gains in math skills, even though such concepts were integral to the program. Disadvantaged experimental groups in the Deutsch (Deutsch et al. 1971), Durham Education Improvement (Spaulding, n.d.), and Howard University Preschool (Herzog, Newcomb, and Cisin 1971; Kraft, Fuschillo, and Herzog 1968) projects found little or no improvement in various math skills, and children in the Perry Preschool Projects (Weikart et al. 1970; Schweinhart and Weikart 1980, 1981) were not significantly advanced over controls until first grade or after (White et al. 1973). It is thus evident that children improved in various programs, sometimes enormously, but that problems of program delivery, lack of program-articulated measures, and later intervening environmental problems in the early grades characteristically encountered with and by disadvantaged children, often diluted or undermined the effects of the early math stimulation. It is also not clear why effects should be delayed in some instances, as in the Weikart investigation.

Two investigations already summarized under early reading have reported on the development of math skills in middle-class children as a result of early stimulation. A study by Stevenson (1964) shows that it is not difficult under modified, standard school conditions to accelerate the development of math skills of selected high verbal-logical skills children (mean IQ = 116) by beginning instruction in kindergarten, a year in advance of norms. The mean grade level attained on the Metropolitan Achievement Test in arithmetic concepts and skills by the end of grade 1 was at least 2.9. In the program of Ulrich et al. (1971), the mean percentile for arithmetic achievement in first grade exceeded the 70th percentile and a mean third grade level, compared with less than the 50th percentile and a first-grade level for children, who were either attending only the special preschool program followed by the standard public school program or attending neither program. The Ulrich study included seven disadvantaged children, whose results are not reported separately except that they did as well as the others.

Taken together, the investigations underscore the potential for advancing math learning ahead of norms in advantaged children, and for the Ulrich study, like the PEP program, in disadvantaged children in continuous learning programs. The point seems well established, though in neither study is it possible to separate early from later effects, or to ascertain the effects of interaction with other forms of stimulation (reading, general concepts).

Do any of these specialized cognitive effects persist beyond a few years? Analysis contained in the consortium investigations of math achievement of early stimulated disadvantaged children reported by Lazar and Darlington (1982) furnishes data on six studies combined. On the basis of pooled data ($N = 325$) mean experimental advantages over controls remained significant through grade 5 ($p = .040$). Different standardized achievement tests were employed by the various projects, including the Iowa Test of Basic Skills, the Metropolitan Achievement Test, the Wide Range Achievement Test, the California Test of Basic Skills, and the California Achievement Test. The investigators also asked whether the significant difference was actually a substantive difference (Lazar and Darlington 1978). Taking one of the projects (Beller) at the median and controlling for age, sex, and pretest IQ, the experimental-control difference was .52 grade equivalents, or about one-half year's difference in grade achievement in mathematics. Separately, Palmer, Semlear, and Fischer (1981) in the same project have reported a mean grade equivalent advantage of experimentals ($N = 136$) over controls ($N = 45$) in grade 5 in math on the Stanford Achievent Test of 8.3 months (5.35 to 4.52, $p < .001$) given by the New York City schools (and thus independently). Palmer's children experienced one year of stimulation, either at age 2 or 3. Since these are all projects measuring effects some four to eight years after children experienced no more than a year or two of stimulation some time between 6 months and 6 years of age without intervening specialized stimulation, the magnitude of the persisting effect is both highly practical and developmentally significant with respect to the potency of early math stimulation.

Not all individual project investigators report the same degree of long-lasting effects, though all the major ones report some persistence of experimental advantage through at least grade 2 (Lazar and Darlington 1978; Palmer and Anderson 1979, 1981). Gray, Ramsey, and Klaus (1982) report mean differences between experimental and control groups remained as far as grade 4 but were no longer significant. The most long-lasting effects reported so far appear in the Perry Preschool Project, in which an experimental advantage in math (and other forms) of skills over controls did not really emerge until after grade 1 and have grown with the years (Schweinhart and Weikart 1980; Lazar and Darlington 1982). On the California Achievement Test mean differences favored the experimental group ($N = 110$) through age 14 in grade 8 on all mathematics subtests, including concepts, problems, and computational skills. It is important to note, however, that the characteristic math ability levels on the disadvantaged experimental children in these follow-up investigations remain with some exceptions (PEP, Berieter-Engelmann), consistently below grade-level achievement norms, usually lagging by a few months to a year (Begab, Haywood, and Garber 1981; Gray, Ramsey, and Klaus 1982), as in the 5.35 level for the end of fifth grade noted above in Palmer's project. There are no follow-up studies reporting mean achievement levels above grade level norms beyond grade 3.

All in all, mathematics concepts and skills represent another domain in which early focused stimulation, intensified beyond cultural norms, proves to generate corresponding math competence above general norms for the age period in the short run, and above the disadvantaged norms for selected (disadvantaged) populations over many years. Children from various advantaged, average, and some disadvantaged populations seem to be able to be advanced in dimensional concepts (magnitude) in infancy and to acquire many of the Piagetian concepts of conservation and seriation, which are among the important foundations of mathematical thinking, between 4 and 6 years of age, well in advance of the usual 6-9 age period reported for developing these and other aspects of concrete operations (Flavell 1963). But all of this type of focused stimulation study is of the classical short-term variety with all its problems. There is no developmental perspective looking at possible interactions between the child's history and current pattern of cognitive abilities and cumulative effects building up over extended time spans, nor any follow-up to study whether any of the accelerated complexity in these basic math skills persists more than a few weeks.

For some reason, except for large-scale studies on the disadvantaged, studies devoted to stimulating a broader array of math skills, such as counting, number names, and arithmetic operations are almost nonexistent, either in the past or in the current Piagetian paradigm. The large-scale studies with the disadvantaged, however, are highly encouraging in this regard. Some of the math programs utilized in the children's early years were quite comprehensive, extending across a range of beginning math skills and concepts for as much as a year or two. The effects, as we have seen, have been sometimes enormous and in many cases moderately long lasting, up to eight years. Given the debilitating ecology of poverty and the countervailing press of the folk community, persistence of effects of this kind, even if diluted from original levels and not even at societal norms, let alone the high level often found among advantaged children, furnishes a kind of measure of the potency of early experience (chapter 5). Selective, domain-focused early stimulation in the abstractions of math can apparently be sufficiently potent to persist in the face of little obvious further positive reinforcement and much negative reinforcement from the community of poverty, folk life, and ghetto schools (Silberman 1970).

Cognitive gains in the domain of math, as in the domain of reading, tend to persist at higher levels, however, where well-designed programs are continued past the preschool period into the elementary grades, underscoring further the importance of the role of later conditions for development. It would appear that no continuing, above norm or even at-norm levels for math and other abstract formal skills can be expected in poor children without the aid of specially planned, intensive stimulation programs that continue through the grades (unless the school system and poverty itself were to be thoroughly restructured). Even then, gains in these highly articulated follow-through programs seem to fall off by the end of grade 3, unfortunately about the latest grade to which any successful follow-through programs have apparently been designed and assessed.

On the other hand it would be interesting to know about persistence of effects in some of the more intensive early programs with an exceptionally strong focus on math concepts (without follow-through), such as the original Bereiter-Engelmann program where initial gains were so high, reaching several years above age norms. Regrettably, only weaker replications of these strong programs appear to have been followed up and achievement gains in no other areas appear to have been maintained more than in other projects (Lazar and Darlington 1978, 1982; Miller and Dyer 1975). No follow-up achievement data have so far been reported for the Heber investigation (Garber and Heber 1981). The consortium (Lazar and Darlington 1982) did find that the long-term effects were more persistent on math skills (grade 5) than on reading achievement (grade 4), however.

Because early-intervention studies combine early math stimulation with a host of many other verbal-abstract, perceptual-motor, and social skills, we do not obtain a precise test of domain stimulation articulated with developmental outcomes, though an evident trend of greater concentration on specific mathematics concepts than actual reading skills in the programs is consonant with the later advantage in math over reading. Because these investigations are designed primarily as compensatory education to raise depressed cognitive levels or induce different learnings not widely prevalent in the impoverished folk community (depending on whether the deficit or difference model is employed), consideration of the effects of differentiated stimulation as such in relation to basic questions of experience and development are secondary to the social concerns of the investigative context. Alternative, systematic investigations, concentrating on varying parameters of math stimulation across several ages and in relation to overall experiences and development over extended time spans must be conducted before we can learn much about the deep potentials of early math experience.

Musical Learning

Something as common in its popular appeal as music might be expected to be the subject of widespread investigation in early childhood. Yet, for some reason, there are not only few early experimental training studies in the realm of music but there has been virtually no systematic norm collecting in the field. The visual arts were similarly short on training studies, but at least the Gesellian developmentalists charted the course of development in drawing skills (Gesell and Ames 1946), one of the basic branches of competence for the field. Observations on musical skills have been scattered. Jersild and Bienstock (1934) assessed the ability of 407 children between 2 and 10 years of age to sing a range of tones and half-tones of the C-major scale, comparing their performance with that of 65 adults. They found the usual steady progression with age, in this case in pitch competence, but wide individual differences at all ages, many of the children as young as age 4 being able to sing a range as great as that of the average adult.

The small number of studies on early musical learning all date back to an earlier era. Even the massive outpouring of effort with the disadvantaged beginning in the 1960s generated no programs studying the effects of musical stimulation, probably because music and art are often viewed as peripheral to the academic competence the programs were designed to ameliorate. Curious, in many ways, because music is widely assumed to be one of the areas of strength in the Afro-American culture from which most of the disadvantaged were recruited. A focus on music might have been a strong basis on which to build competence in other areas, as well as heightening competence in music itself and enhancing cultural self esteem. Here and there music is alluded to in the various intervention programs (Parker 1972; Day and Parker 1977), but typically almost in passing as a minor feature and only occasionally as a basis for building language

(Bereiter and Engelmann 1966). The slim weight assigned to musical education is reflected in the failure to measure any developmental outcomes in the realm of music itself.

Yet there are many reasons that music should prove to be a fertile area for early education as well as a useful domain to test out the impact of early experience on development. Leventhal and Lipsitt (1964) report, for example, that neonates have no difficulty in localizing sound and discriminate differences in pitch. Because infants have no difficulty in mastering the intricacies of language rules during the first few years, why should they not be similarly adept at mastering musical language, which is certainly no more difficult than verbal language and enjoys the added intrinsic dimensions of tone, rhythm, and melody, combined in ways that charm and capture the sensual and aesthetic senses in a singularly powerful manner?

The few experimental training studies on young children, most of them centering on singing, show quite promising results. Jersild and Bienstock (1931, 1934) conducted two studies on singing, the first a controlled study in which one of two groups of nineteen children 31-48 months old, matched according to singing score and age, was trained to sing eight songs in twice-weekly ten-minute lessons over a period of six months. The songs were selected to contain tones and intervals beyond the children's normal range. Children rotated among small groups of two and three, and the groups were balanced to include strong and weak singers. A variety of added motivational devices, such as sociodramatic role actions, and songs with simple (mainly monosyllabic) words were employed. Repeated testing (which were counted as training sessions) was utilized with experimental children to monitor progress and pace learning of new tones and intervals.

Children in the experimental group improved significantly over controls during the course of training in the range of tones and intervals they could reproduce, more than doubling the mean length of their ranges, despite the fact that controls improved by about 50 percent on both dimensions during the same period. Four months later, experimental subjects ($N = 15$) were still significantly higher than controls on both dimensions, despite slight increases of both groups. Experimentals still performed 60 percent above controls in tonal range and almost double in interval range.

In a later uncontrolled study with twenty-three children between 3 and 8½ years, training was organized into slightly larger groups in sessions that combined group singing with individual guidance and the same number of sessions collapsed into a sixty-day span. Mean gains ranged between 30 and 40 percent for the different age levels, suggesting that the extended training during the first experiment allowed skills to be better assimilated. Children were able to learn semitones as well as whole tones, however, and to sing with wider intervals (perfect fourths and fifths, major and minor sixths, sevenths and octaves) and to move to different keys better than before training. The study is noteworthy not only because of its replicative value but because of follow-up. Two years following termination of training, experimental children ($N = 12$) were found to have maintained a calculated musical achievement quotient of 123 compared to respective pretest-posttest quotients of 105 and 168.

Updegraff, Heiliger, and Learned (1938) and Hissen (1933) report highly similar results, the former with 3-, 4-, and 5-year olds progressing significantly more than control children, in singing tones and phrases, the latter with 21- to 54-month olds improving in tone discrimination and reproduction. In the former study, children progressed so well that the post-test scores of 3-year-olds matched the pretest scores of the 4-year-olds. The training also greatly extended the musical interests of the children, which generalized to a variety of nonexperimental preschool musical activities.

In an interesting small study by Fullard (1967), the sole recent musical training study located, 42- to 59-month-old experimental and control children were randomly assigned to two training groups ($N = 5$ each) to evaluate the effects of aural discrimination training on recognizing musical selections played with six different musical instruments. Each group was trained to recognize the six instruments in sets of three, presented in alternating order to the two groups to assess transfer effects, over a brief series of nine trials (to criterion of 7 of 9 identifications correct). Pre-post test gains over all six instruments were significant, as were transfer effects from the first to the second set of instruments. The study's potential and its limitations are indicated by the progress made in such a brief training study, in which the only guidance was corrective feedback through rewards of candy (M&M's).

Two additional early studies report essentially negative results, one on teaching 3½- to 4½-year-olds to play a tin fife (Colby 1935), the other a short training study in which rhythmic training was attempted with pre-school children (Jersild and Bienstock 1931). Both studies suffer from the obvious limitations of the short-term training framework that precludes development of skill complexity through attention to a broad set of inter-related hierarchy of skills in relation to a developmental perspective.

It might be thought, as Colby concluded, that instrumental skills are too complex for preschoolers to learn. Singing and recognizing a few bars played by different instruments are after all probably more closely related to children's common musical experiences. Learning new tones, intervals, and phrases and the phrases in the singing studies occurred functionally in the context of singing, not as isolated operations in complex movement-sound patterns on an instrument too big for the children's small hands, as exposure to instrumental playing was in Colby's experiment. Yet just as infants regularly accomplish in swimming what not long ago might have seemed extraordinary (at least in Western culture, though not New Guinea—see chapter 1), so, too, do young children routinely accomplish developmentally by the thousands in Japan and all over the contemporary Western world in extensive learning programs with the Suzuki method of playing the violin (Cook 1970; Holland 1982; Suzuki 1969).

Often beginning in early infancy, the Suzuki program is conceptualized as an interrelated set of musical listening and performing experiences, in which the child acquires familiarity, interest, and ultimately mastery of violin playing through a carefully graded series of activities that are usually embedded in the context of family life. The child acquires concepts of musical language functionally in a graduated, extended contextual manner, the dimensions of pitch, rhythm, tempo, interval, phrasing, order, key, and the like, just as the infant becomes familiar with the ordinary dimensions of language—phonemes, morphemes, order, grouping, parts of speech, and meaning, through daily experiences over many years. The chief difference is the carefully planned, systematic programming of the musical learning experience, usually essential in all except a few already musical families, where music is bread to the daily life, like ordinary language (Bloom and Sosniak 1981). Unlike Colby's tin fifes, but like the tradition of training musicians (Fowler 1962a), which Colby did not seem to consider, violins in the Suzuki programs are all scaled down to child size, even one-tenth size for the very small 2-year-olds. In like manner, rhythm is not acquired through a relatively limited series of sessions in a single activity, clapping and beating feet to piano accompaniment as in Jersild and Bienstock's (1935) unsuccessful rhythmic training study, but through an interrelated set of activities involving music, in which rhythmic learning is embedded in the tasks. The child is only engaged in precise rhythmic controls through analysis as he or she grasps a broader, multidimensional understanding of musical events in context.

Numerous children following Suzuki's total developmental-learning program are reported to have become skilled performers in the musical world (Cook 1970; Holland 1982; Suzuki 1969), yet no systematic research seems to have been inspired by this highly promising system of developmental education. Because the Suzuki programs are lifelong, ecologically grounded developmental experiences, they preclude the possibility of easily separating the effects of early from later stimulation among the early starters. They do, however, offer ample opportunity to measure the effects of starting at different ages, since despite Suzuki's ideal type model, children in fact start at a wide range of ages, beginning skill in playing Bach, for example, emerging in children ranging from age 10 or 11 all the way down to age 3 or 4.

Music appears to be an area in which the promise from research and the example from practice (in the Suzuki program) have greatly surpassed the effort in research on early experience. If even six weeks of selected training in singing can produce effects that last as long as two years, and current practice regularly generates complex instrumental performance between the ages of 3 and 5 that continues to develop over many years, we have barely skimmed the surface of musical learning possibilities. There are certain parallels with the field of athletics, though with less-defined ceiling effects; superior skills seem to be regularly produced among swimmers (Newman 1969; Timmermans 1975) beginning in infancy in practical programs unaided and apparently uninformed by the scientific psychological research community.

Styles and Strategies:
Stimulating Memory Development

The realm of styles and strategies is a prickly one, full of multiple component domains that are difficult to define. It is a realm in which the volume of research on early developmental stimulation is miniscule compared to the substantial amount of literature on cognitive styles (Kagan and Kogan 1970), including a growing body on early development (Kagan 1976), and endless material on what we are here considering as closely related functions like motivation and memory (table 5-1), both of which have a long and respected research history in psychology and education. Yet styles and strategies are one of the three main pillars of mental systems, as conceptualized in chapter 5, as indeed they are in other major conceptual schemes of cognitive structures, such as Guilford's (1967) model for the structure of intelligence, in which he defines strategies as operations and to which he also subsumes memory. Clearly, how the individual goes about solving problems and processing information is as vital to competence and coping as the body of knowledge acquired and the skill in using codes to represent concepts. Curious, then, that so little research on stimulating strategies has been done, compared to the enormous body of training literature of work on knowledge (IQ, formal concepts) and codes (language, reading). Part of the difficulty, as we shall see, is the way in which styles are buried in other contexts such as IQ and tied to knowledge.

Most of the work on styles has been addressed to the manipulation of variables to answer questions about the general nature of human functioning and behavior, rather than the influence of experience on development. As developmental psychology became established between the two world wars, norm collecting on processes of memory development and problem solving drew an increasing amount of attention (Munn 1954). A certain amount of attention was also directed toward questions of learning but once again, almost invariably short-term in design. The early work of Hamilton (1911, 1916) on children's methods of problem solving in a door-opening problem, cited briefly in chapter 4, is characteristic of the earlier research on strategies. In this and many other studies children were found to move gradually from trial-and-error approaches to increasingly logical and rational approaches, in which hypotheses and inferences were evident. Evidence of children employing a principle to solve such problems were reported by Roberts (1932) in children as young as age 2, however, and Richardson (1932, 1934) broke down problems of pulling strings or turning crank levers to obtain lures in gradients of difficulty that indicated degrees of "perceptive attitude" or insight in infants between 28 and 52 weeks of age. But the work was essentially normative in orientation. No follow-through training studies were undertaken to determine how well or to what extent strategies could be generated in young children. The descriptive, behaviorist framework of the earlier era left analyses rather limited in form.

It was not until after World War II that the advent of cognitive orientations in psychology seriously introduced questions about mentally governed strategies and styles. Starting especially with the investigations on thinking by Bruner and his associates (Bruner, Goodnow, and Austin 1956), as well as the work on cognitive style or controls originating in psychoanalytic thought by Rappaport (1967), Gardner (Gardner, Jackson, and Messick, 1960), Klein (1958) and others, concepts of various types of cognitive style were applied to developmental studies, as in the work on descriptive-analytic styles by Kagan (Kagan, Moss, and Sigel 1963) and Sigel (Sigel, Jarman, and Hanesian 1967). By the 1970s a large body of literature on many different styles had grown up (Kagan and Kogan 1970; Wallach and Kogan 1965) but without a common framework and rarely if ever addressed to questions of whether or how styles originate in early experience. The focus was principally on establishing the validity and reliability of style measures, conceptualizing their role in mental functioning (often without interrelating them), gathering normative data, and exploring how they operated under different conditions and in different populations, including between the sexes and cross-culturally. (For an expanded discussion of styles and strategies, see Fowler 1977, 1980a).

Despite the multiplying number of formulations on development of style processes and expanded interest in cognitive shifts in modes of thinking, learning, and problem solving, involving essentially developmental shifts from positional and chance and trial-and-error approaches of early childhood to the mediational, logical, and functional win-stay strategies of later childhood (Kendler and Kendler 1962; Levinson and Reese 1967; White 1965), very little work has been done on how learning over time might influence development of the different cognitive modes and strategies. One of the typical series of short-term training studies was concerned with variables contributing to the young child's characteristic lower level of cognitive mediation, as in studies focused on reversal-nonreversal shift discrimination (the tendency to shift or not shift, respectively, to the opposite pole or a new dimension). In a study of size and brightness discrimination, for example, Wolff (1969) found that verbalization facilitated brightness-discrimination learning in a nonreversal-shift problem among preschoolers, though it had no effect on size.

More promising in terms of its implications for facilitating broader, cognitive aspects of strategy development is a study by Fagen (1977). Following the work of Harlow (1949) on learning set with monkeys, Fagen, over a series of eight sessions on a series of two-choice, object-discrimination problems, found that 10-month-old infants improved their performance to 76.5 percent correct, adopting elements of a win-stay, lose-shift strategy more characteristic of older children. Had the study ventured to go beyond the short-term mold, one wonders if the infants could have overcome the positional preference tendency that continued to plague them. Also promising, but again confined to the self-limiting short-term practice of brief sessions, is the experiment of Richards and Siegler (1981) with 3-year-olds. Children guided in employing an analytic style in solving balance-scale problems with weights improved in their use of relatively systematic rule strategies in predicting the effect of weight shifts on the balance scale.

The big exception to the measurement and short-term focus trend came with the early-intervention studies on disadvantaged poor children in the 1960s, but like so many other dimensions, strategies and styles, when studied at the time generally were buried in the matrix of general cognitive-stimulation programs and measures. Taken with this constraint in mind, the findings were in many cases positive, both for the short term and the long term, although not invariably, the emphasis being on cognitive measures like IQ tests and language. The various little logical-abstract puzzles, of which IQ tests are composed, embrace a variety of common concepts, language and numerical skills, and some perceptual-spatial skills, but they also assess a number of strategy processes such as convergent and divergent thinking and memory, which Guilford (1967) has identified. Yet because they are contained in a single package, strategy development, like development in other categories, is not specifically identifiable. Few of the developmental training studies have even availed themselves of analytic devices like Meeker's (1969) templates (based on Guilford), which in any case leave age gaps in the subordinate skills.

To the extent they were separately measured, however, achievement motivation, curiosity and similar processes were found to be increased in experimental subjects compared to the controls (Beller 1973; Miller and Dyer 1975; White et al. 1973), and in many cases differences persisted well into the early grades. Thus Miller and Dyer (1975) reported experimental subjects superior to controls in all four programs studied, following the preschool experience, and differences persisted in inventiveness through grade 4, though differences between programs were not consistent with program emphases upon curiosity and inventiveness. (Both Montessori and the supposedly more structurally programmed and teacher directed Darcee program resulted in higher scoring children). Schweinhart and Weikart (1980) found mean differences in motivation for school favoring experimental children (N = 95) over controls on the Perry Preschool Project, as measured by teacher ratings through third grade, and an increased commitment of experimentals to schooling and educational aspiration for college and related academic concerns through grade 8 (age 15, N = 99) as measured by self-ratings. On the other hand Klaus and Gray (1968) reported no motivational differences between stimulated and unstimulated groups even in the early grades. Moreover, the consortium group found no consistent differences across projects during the secondary school period, except for the significant tendency of experimental children to feel proud of themselves in relation to school matters, compared to controls, to have more realistic vocational aspirations and (for three investigations) to evaluate their school performance higher (Lazar and Darlington 1978, 1982). (Motivational technique as a separate dimension will be discussed in the next chapter.)

Mean differences in cognitive style have also appeared in the literature on early intervention for the disadvantaged, both immediately and persisting for a number of years (Beller 1973; White et al. 1973). Children in experiments by Heber et al. (1972) were superior to controls in field independence, as we have noted, which is generally associated in Witkin's studies (Witkin 1964, 1974; Witkin et al. 1962) with a more analytic and abstract mode of cognitive functioning. The superior executive and analytic strategies in problem solving manifested by Heber's experimental subjects when guiding their mothers in a learning task have also been discussed. Beller cited significant differences in reflectiveness favoring early-stimulated experimental children over their later-starting (kindergarten and first grade) comparison groups through the last year of high school, but only under favorable home conditions (parent(s) employed, father present). The importance of a favorable ecology to maintain the effects of the early experience appears to operate with styles as well. Reflectiveness is associated with a more analytic and cognitively oriented strategy than impulsiveness in Kagan's scheme and is generally associated with better academic performance (Kagan et al. 1964). The fact that Beller specifically stressed reflective styles in his original program adds more weight to the relations found between early stimulation and later development, suggesting connections between the form of stimulation and the type of outcome.

The problem of designing training programs to measure the impact of strategy training is similar to the problem of assessing the effect of early language and other forms of coding stimulation. The modes of problem solving must be guided with content of some kind, concepts in one or another area of knowledge, either formal or informational. Yet the problem can also be resolved in the same way, necessarily teaching analytic-synthesizing strategies, for example, by focusing on the process of pulling problems apart and searching for meaningful connections among key elements, rather than on learning the particular knowledge concepts. Strategies can also be applied to the context of learning coding skills of sensorimotor action, mathematics, and language. In this context codes become the content, even though the coding concepts to which the analyzing may be applied will still utilize samples of knowledge of some kind (verbal representations of agents, actions, and objects that are samples of phenomena).

Whether stimulating strategies across a variety of domains of knowledge might facilitate a broader competence in strategies is an important question. Much of the evidence reviewed in chapter 1 and the style literature generally (Kagan and Kogan 1970), however, indicates that competence tends to be concentrated in specific domains or related areas of knowledge, and mastery of strategies may in fact be sharpened by expanding knowledge in depth in a complex hierarchy of related concepts, which in turn may well facilitate skill in handling the knowledge of the domain. Motivation too is likely to be attached to patterns of attention, concentration, and persistence in particular kinds of knowledge, patterns that we call interests that would seem to arise through accumulating a substantial body of concepts of a particular kind and enjoying the growing status of expert and a sense of efficacy (White 1959) in manipulating the material well. Thus even the improved and partially persisting motivations of the early-stimulated disadvantaged children were improved and persisted in the domains in which they had been or were closely related to those stimulated, all in the general realm of school learning. It was for example, specifically pride in relation to school, not sports or community activities in which the consortium found the experimental children differentially favored.

Memory is apparently also tied to competence in particular areas. Thus Dempster (1981), in an extended review of the literature on memory span, found that of a wide range of dimensions (rehearsal, grouping, chunking, retrieval strategies, capacity), the speed with which items can be identified is by far the most important factor determining both individual and developmental differences. Although Dempster is inclined to attribute this variability to underlying, mainly biological differences in processing efficiency, familiarity with items appears to play an important role. Thus Case (1978), for example, found that even when sequence familiarity was controlled, the class of concepts (words, digits) from which the items were drawn affected memory span. Familiarity or knowledge of the domain appears to be paramount.

Memory processes of all kinds have attracted increasing attention in developmental psychology in recent years (Brown 1975; Dempster 1981; Hagen, Jongeward, and Kail 1975; Meacham 1972; Reese 1976; Perlmutter 1980; Werner and Perlmutter 1979). Yet the focus remains on age differences, general mechanisms, and cognitive dynamics, with comparatively little attention to investigations of how experience influences development longitudinally, especially in terms of experimental training. Memory processes do not seem to have featured at all in the early-intervention research on disadvantaged children, except as contained within the various IQ and other ability and achievement measures. Nor is memory studied as such in the body of Piagetian-inspired investigations of formal concept training, despite the explicit formulations of Piaget on memory as functionally related to stages of cognitive development (Gruber and Vonèche 1977; Piaget and Inhelder 1973).

Memory was of cardinal interest in the learning studies of former eras, despite the typical procrustean time frame that cut off understanding of the influence of developmental experience and the absence of the more recent breakdown in terms of cognitive and dimensional factors, such as short-term versus long-term, semantic versus episodic, chunking, storage and retrieval (Brown 1975). The favorable influence of the effects of distributed over mass practice were the order of the day (Munn 1954; Woodworth 1938). For many decades, until Thorndike and his contemporaries undertook to reveal their fallacy (Thorndike 1963; Woodworth 1938), memory was thought to be one of the general faculties of mind that could be generally improved through training in specifically so-called rigorous disciplines like Latin and mathematics. It was noted in chapter 1 how memory in different cultural contexts is a function of specific ecologies and domains of competence, as in Bartlett's (1932) demonstration that the legendary memories of Swazis in South Africa was confined to the facts and transactions surrounding the life of cattle herding.

We have seen how the short-term learning framework restricted the earlier developmental findings (chapter 4). One of the prime examples discussed was Gates and Taylor's (1925) widely cited study on memory training (totaling 100 days) for digits, out of context and unrelated to the meaningful development of competencies, which produced substantial gains following training, followed by later forgetting after a few months. Hilgard's (1933) study of eight weeks each of early and delayed practice (involving much training) separated by only four weeks, in Gesell's identical twins, produced similar results from the similar, arbitrary form of short-term training for digits and objects. Important gains for both the early and delayed periods were followed by substantial forgetting and approaching equivalence between twins after twelve weeks, though there was evidence the early-trained twin had retained a slight advantage in memory for objects (but not digits) over the later-trained twin.

The importance of meaning and context are also illustrated by a number of recent studies involving memory. Memory has been shown to serve a crucial function in abstract cognitive processing even among preschoolers, for example. Children unable to perform Piaget's transitive inference task, given memory training to criterion on the inequalities, were then able to produce the correct inferences (Bryant and Trabasso 1971; Riley and Trabasso 1974). Where memory served a definite function, the gains from memory training were essential. Children at all ages have been found to improve their memory performance when free-recall lists contain items that belong to culturally common categories (Hagen, Jongeward, and Kail 1975). In a task for remembering pictures, even 2-year-olds (26 of 30) clustered the items in the task above chance levels, apparently as an aid to memory, and clustering increased with age across the 2-5 age range of the children. Yet short-term training studies of very recent vintage continue to adopt arbitrary procedures with effectively abstract material. Kurland's (1981) efforts, for instance, to train 6-year-olds in hundreds of trials daily on counting speed for digits and similar printed, patterned figures over a period of three months produced little improvement.

The possibilities of stimulating memory abilities have been shown in infant recognition memory as early as 5 to 7 months (Cornell 1979; Fagan 1978). Recent reviews and observational studies of infant memory indicate quite clearly that infants early begin to acquire large bodies of information (knowledge or semantic memory) in the form of anticipating, recognizing or engaging in routines, language, people, and objects of all kinds (Nelson and Ross 1980), and to recognize and recall specific events (episodic memory) that involve a variety of different concepts (perceptual and functional attributes of objects and people, locations, and social interactions) (Ashmead and Perlmutter 1980). Yet these indices of possibilities for early stimulation and the manifest influence of daily experiences on memory development have not been matched with developmental training studies that might significantly improve the quality of early memory and mnemonic processes and have great implications for prolonged developmental effects on memory and cognitive development.

Only two long-term experimental stimulation studies with young children have been found, by Burtt and by Smith, both limited to rote learning and verbal memory. Mention may also be made again here of McGraw's (1935) successful stimulation of object memory in the experimental twin

Johnny because of the relatively extended training period and the obvious acceleration of competence in the short-term, despite the odd failure of McGraw to conduct any follow-up assessment of this skill at age 6. Over several months of finding hidden objects in play, Johnny by 24 months could find as many as eight miscellaneous objects, hidden twelve hours earlier in eight different locations, in any order asked for. McGraw's interesting success in this training, in which Johnny's object-location recall far exceeded the skill of untrained adults on the project, can be attributed to her developmentally appropriate play model of stimulation, furnishing meaningful experience to the child, as much as to the relatively extended period of training, which was actually similar in length to that of certain other studies (Gates and Taylor 1925). Johnny was also younger than the children in most other studies of memory training, however.

Burtt's (1932, 1937, 1941) extraordinarily extended but narrowly conceived developmental training study with his infant son (15 months to 3 years), reading passages daily to him in Greek drama (in Greek, which was meaningless to the child) resulted in differences in the child's ability to learn novel compared with the earlier exposed passages as far as age 14, eleven years after termination of the highly particularized early stimulation. All detectable differences faded by age 18. The study is a model for its synthesis of precision and developmental scope with mechanistic procedures and use of meaningless abstractions, nevertheless providing in its way exceptional evidence for the potentials and limits of a strong test of the function of early stimulation.

The second study, by Madorah Smith (1935, 1951, 1963), is truly vast in its developmental scope, extending over sixty years, and much more meaningful in its substance as well. Although not a study on early stimulation within the preschool age period of our concern, it is worth citing because of its developmental implications and because a similar form of memory stimulation has been employed in short-term training that would indicate potential application during early development. In the latter study Foster (1928) found that providing 10 daily repetitions of 9 stories in sequence to 31 children (2-7 to 4-9) resulted in 22 children learning 8 of the 9 stories, the 9 others learning 3 to 4, even the youngest children mastering substantial portions.

In her original experiment, Smith trained one child (unclear whether her child or herself) through methods of systematic distributive practice to learn without error the 107 answers to the Westminster Shorter Catechism between the ages of 8 and 13. Answers were recited at a single sitting. During the next ten years, there was considerable incidental practice to the first but not the later portions of the Catechism. In later memory tests at ages 23, 49, and 59 years of age, the learner recalled about the same number of answers for each of the first two follow-ups (54 and 53 answers, respectively, without prompting, and 44 and 39 with one prompt), and not much less (41 and 32) as long as 50 to 60 years after the original memory training. Fourteen of the 22 answers in the first fifth of the total were recalled perfectly, a period of approximately 50 years since the end of incidental practice, and 5 of the last 22, in which she has had no practice of any kind since the original experiment, were recalled, 2 without prompting and 3 with a single prompt. In general, the less difficult or shorter answers were recalled better than the longer ones.

Such studies leave a tantalizing but pitifully small legacy of the potential for early developmental memory (and other strategy) training, all concentrated on memory of a comparatively limited set of tasks. More in order are long-term, experimental early training studies that would engage a variety of control processes, or the memory strategies (rehearsal, clustering, chunking, coding, retrieval devices) that increasingly appear to be open to development through experience (Brown, 1975; Hagen, Jongeward, and Kail 1975), though the hypothetically less modifiable structural processes (fixed sensory and short-term memory capacities, forgetting rates) need systematic attention with developmental stimulation as well (Brown 1975; Hagen et al. 1975).

Even the early studies on transfer of learning, rote memory included, showed that techniques acquired in the course of training would transfer to new material (Munn 1954). Much of the learning of daily experience is based to an important degree of memory, semantic and episodic memory, as we have noted, and memory was heavily involved in the myriad of short-term training and transfer of learning studies of the past, visual motor or verbal memory in the various motor or language learning tasks in the Gesell's co-twin studies, for example, and in the problem-solving tasks of Richardson (1932, 1934) and others. Without retention, no improvement in later performance can be expected. Much of early learning is culturally reinforced from the modal daily experiences that abound, and learning and memory are in fact closely tied to the ecology and modes of thinking in an environment and culture (Wagner 1978).

Yet the improvement of certain types of cognitive strategies and other cognitive skills reported in the long-term follow-up of early-intervention studies with disadvantaged children from impoverished folk settings suggest that planned training can to some degree transcend culture and ecology, or at least partially transform individuals at an early age to cope and find reinforcement in other cultural realms of the larger society. Given the focal value of memory and other strategies in making productive use of knowledge and codes, and the superordinate demands for abstracting and processing information in the maze of modern technology, strategy training that is *not* necessarily regularly reinforced in the specific content of knowledge and coding concepts of the culture might be a useful task for strategy training studies in early childhood.

Conclusions

It is evident that early learning can be differentially influenced according to the areas of competence stimulated. It is equally evident, however, that the state of the art with respect to developmental stimulation over substantial time spans remains relatively untilled. The most definitive evidence on both the immediate and long-range effects of early stimulation are in the area of early reading, a derivative of language but distinct in its development. The number of studies on early reading is by now substantial, many with large sample sizes and considerable experimental control, in which both early and later effects are measured separately from the development of other skills. The collected studies seem to show that early reading can easily be accelerated in the preschool years, both in the home and at school in special programs. The main problems with these studies is the frequent failure to assess how much other forms of cognitive stimulation may have been operating or to assess how development has been influenced in other areas. At least in studies in the home, there is evidence that more generalized academic stimulation has been a frequent accompaniment of early reading instruction, which may be a factor in producing some of the transfer effects observed that were largely concentrated on language-based areas of competence. Early reading instruction appears to produce an advantage that persists through the early grades of school (as far as fifth or sixth grade) but probably only when the early fluency is followed up by some degree of continued support and stimulation, particularly in the school. There is also evidence that children learning as early as age 3 gain an even greater advantage than children learning around age 5.

The issue of the effect of degree of mastery over the original material, the extent to which a critical mass or effective cognitive processing system is attained through the original early stimulation, versus the role of the later ecology in producing permanent effects still needs a clear test, for other areas as well as for reading. Early reading studies in the school setting have neither been as early nor have they generated the same degree of mastery as reading instruction at home, while studies in the home have furnished little information on how much reinforcement and guidance continued in the later home ecology.

Except for a handful of variously controlled musical training studies, almost all the early stimulation studies in other domains have been short-term, variable-oriented studies or long-term experimental-training case studies. Systematic instruction of 3-year-olds in singing has resulted in tremendous gains in competence approaching adult competencies, gains found in one study to persist for two years. Short-term training in a variety of areas, from motor skills to formal concepts, have invariably resulted in skill levels much in advance of developmental norms, but the motor and memory skills have usually been narrowly conceived or task defined, and rarely have long-term effects been investigated. In the few instances where they have (Gesell and Thompson 1941), contrary to the investigators' conclusions, there are indications that long-term effects may have ensued despite the restricted character of the early stimulation. A certain body of information in the areas of mathematics, language, and reading achievement and cognitive styles comes out of the early-intervention research (both with the advantaged and the disadvantaged), which suggests a certain correspondence between selective stimulation and later developmental outcomes (early as well for language). But the early stimulation of math and reading competencies have generally been limited to the preliminaries, in which few short-term measures were made, and the generalized, loosely and broadly defined stimulation context makes it difficult to sort out interaction effects. Despite the obvious methodological limitations, the experimental-training case studies are not to be underrated. In their way, despite these limitations and lack of cognitive framework, the studies of Burtt and Smith on verbal memory training and of McGraw on motor training are models and monuments of the kind of research that needs to be done systematically on a larger scale to explore the potentials of early developmental learning. All of these case studies are products of another era, whose promise remains to be studied.

Research on Dimensions of Early Developmental Stimulation

Given earliness, what other dimensions count? Is there a combination of dimensions that operate in certain ways to optimize development? Is there more than one combination to bring about similar results, particularly among the different concept domains? Do certain dimensions override others in the magnitude of their effects? Obviously a tangle of such questions is concerned in trying to understand the range of possibilities for early developmental stimulation. We can do no more than touch on a few of them, principally because systematic investigation of developmental learning has barely begun, let alone been recognized as a field of research. For example, the question of earliness ought properly to be expanded to compare the developmental outcomes of systematic stimulation started at widely separated periods of development, even infancy versus adolescence, using equivalent forms and dimensional combinations. It ought to test whether the application of selected dimensions in great strength at later periods would produce effects as great or even greater than systematic early programs utilizing milder applications of the selected dimensions. Intensity and duration of stimulation would seem to be promising candidates for such tests, especially for determining whether such dimensions might be crucial factors enabling late starters to attain equivalent cognitive heights in adulthood.

Few of such issues can be reviewed simply because there are no investigations comparing the effects of stimulation begun at widely different ages, to say nothing of manipulating component dimensions. Except for age and duration, and these almost exclusively on specialized populations from poor, folk communities, investigations in which selected dimensions of stimulation are explicitly varied are rare. The common approach has been to make use of a package of dimensions, different investigators clustering different combinations organized in general cognitive-stimulation programs aimed at compensating for culturally based skill deficiencies (the deficit view) or generating novel skills (the difference view), in either case to prepare the child in abstract, school-oriented skills not stressed in the various folk cultures among the poor. At best one can compare different programs analytically on these clusters, as Miller and Dyer (1975) have done, looking for differential effects from different combinations and possibly even cases where the virtual omission or the inclusion of key dimensions has resulted in marked differences in outcomes. Such analysis would apply if stimulation were entirely didactic, without child initiative,

301

experimentation (rehearsal) or any adult-child interaction, or if all activity were intrinsically motivated without external rewards, or if every concept and exemplar were carefully graded in difficulty in one case and nothing ordered in another. A similar strategy of analysis would apply if important or specialized domains, such as language, sensorimotor, mathematical or musical codes were to be exceptionally stressed or be all but excluded, as was attempted in the domain review in chapter 7.

The same neatness of separation does not occur in the literature of dimensions other than domains. Early intervention with the disadvantaged has, as the term implies, been above all concerned with total programs designed to solve a social problem. Most investigators have been well aware of the gamut of dimensions, from sequencing and programming to external rewards, emotional climate, and self-esteem, but they have generally employed a common set of values for the several dimensions (positive versus negative reinforcement, for example), displaying a practical (and humane) sense, whatever their theoretical bias. Variations among stimulation dimensions in early-intervention programs are matters of relatively small degree, for the most part, much as we have already found to be true of their multiskill emphasis directed at academic competence (language, formal concepts, abstract logical reasoning, mathematical concepts, prereading skills, social competence) and thus wide in cognitive breadth. Investigators of average populations have almost entirely ignored questions about program dimensions, following their own philosophy and intuitions, which in the end appear also to incorporate in a quite practical and humane manner selected values among the important dimensions with unimportant variations. The underlying problem, once again, is the paucity of anything but brief training studies in any domain.

Given sparseness of the experimental early-stimulation literature on the remaining dimensions, the balance of the dimensional review will necessarily be less systematic. The effort will be placed more in identifying issues and problems, drawing largely on selected studies from the general literature already reviewed, where they appear to suggest or illustrate the matters in question. The dimensions will be treated in broad terms, more on clustering small variations and indicating how they may interact at different points. The general framework at all times is on the significance of dimensions for early developmental stimulation.

Duration

It is only reasonable to believe that the advantages of applying stimulation early can only be realized when it is continued long enough to produce a significant effect. How long is long enough? There is no doubt a complex interaction between the type of stimulation, the intensity and sensitivity with which it occurs, and its duration. Yet if stimulation is to have an effect, it must last a certain period, holding other things constant. Changing the intensity with which it occurs, for example, might shorten the period needed for substantial learning and development of concepts to occur, but some time is still necessary for the child to master a body of material, to accumulate the many concepts typically involved. In the case of the infant and young child, the process is an extended span needed to build a foundation of knowledge of the physical and social world, master the elements of language and sensorimotor codes, and acquire some basic general strategies for coping and problem solving. Depending on which aspects and what domains are emphasized, time is obviously an indispensable ingredient of all learning. Because a few early intervention studies bear on the question of duration of stimulation, we shall review briefly the historical material on nursery-school studies and the recent intervention studies.

Nursery-School Attendance

Even casting aside the methodological weaknesses found in the body of studies on nursery-school attendance, investigations designed specifically to test the effects of length of attendance at nursery school yielded generally negative effects. Jones and Jorgensen (1940) found no significant differences between children who had and had not attended nursery school at any follow-up age between 5 and 9. They also found attendance at nursery school correlating .34 with IQ changes on the California Preschool Scale ($N = 66$); but when the number of tests was held constant, the correlation was reduced to .05. Attendance had varied from 50 to 499 days. Two other groups ($N = 68$ and $N = 87$) in the California growth study showed similar reduced correlation values of $-.06$ and .03 when testing effects were controlled.

Wellman's (1940) extended analysis of the records of 228 children from a larger subject pool of 652 children who attended school for at least two years, 67 of whom attended for at least three years, revealed similar results. While there were continuing mean autumn-to-spring gains in successive years for each of the two- and three-year groups, 7.0 and 3.8 IQ points for the first and second years for the two-year group, and 7.7, 4.3, and 1.7 years for the three successive years for the three-year group, it is obvious that the second- and third-year gains were trivial. There was also no significant relationship between length of attendance during a school year (thirty-seven to one hundred forty-eight days) and IQ changes. As in the studies generally, the overall mean gains themselves were marginal (6.6 IQ points).

For the reasons discussed at length in preceding chapters, nursery-school experiences add little to the life of the middle-class child who is already leading an intellectual life comparatively rich in abstract verbal concepts more stressed on IQ measures than in the nursery school. Lengthening attendance only added more of the same redundant and irrelevant curriculum, however salutary it may be for the general social and personal development of the child.

Early Intervention with Impoverished Groups

Analysis of studies by variation in the length of the early-stimulation experience brings the same inconclusive results reported in chapter 6 for the analysis of variation by the exact age of intervention. There are few programs deliberately varying program length, those that did generally confounded treatment length with age of entry into the program or initial IQ, and other comparisons run afoul of the effects of differences between programs. Since most programs lasted about one year, there is little possibility of comparing program clusters in terms of length of program.

With respect to immediate posttest effects, both the 3- and 4-year-old entering experimental groups of Weikart (1967) tended to decline slightly (2 points each) on the Stanford-Binet (and other measures) in the second year of the special stimulation program, as did Beller's (1973) 4-, 5-, and 6-year-old-entering groups in the second and third years (except for continuing slight to moderate rises on a measure of language), but his programs may have been less intensive after the first year. Mean Binet differences in IQ between Gray's (Klaus and Gray, 1968) 2- and 3-year groups were miniscule (3 points favoring the three-year group, controlling for initial score differences) and Caldwell (1970) found no relationship between IQ gains and length of time in program on her children ranging from infancy through the preschool years, though Levenstein's (1970, 1971, 1977) experimental group who participated a second year gained an additional 8 IQ points, following a first year mean rise of 11 points between ages 2 and 3. (Note that Levenstein used the Catell for earlier tests and the Binet later, perhaps affecting the results.) Gordon's (1969; Guinagh, Olmstead, and Gordon 1975) results are more complex, but essentially no consistent difference emerged from length of treatment. There were no differences between experimental and control groups after one year of training (age 3 to 12 months), and subsequently, from age 2 on the three experimental groups with one-, two-, or three-program years tended to fluctuate on the Binet between 85 and 100 IQ over the successive years. No group showed a consistent advantage and few mean differences were significant. Heber's investigation (Garber and Heber 1981; Heber 1976; Heber et al. 1972), the program of longest duration (six years) also confounds duration with starting age, in fact starting earlier in age (< 6 months) and being more intensive than programs in almost any other project. The experimental group mean scores ranged narrowly up and down between 120 and 135 IQ on the Stanford-Binet between 2 and 6 years and between 110 and 115 IQ on the Wechsler Preschool and Primary Scale of Intelligence (WPPSI) between 4 and 6 years (51 to 69 months). The biggest change recorded, a gain of about 10 IQ points on the Catell scales that brought experimental children to their continuing high program levels, occurred around 12 to 16 months.

The findings in which age is controlled through comparing the progress of the same experimental group over successive program years, appear to reflect the usual differences between subgroups, tests, and programs more than they do the effects of program duration. The general trend with respect to short-term duration effects seems apparent. Most of the cognitive gains of disadvantaged children from early stimulation, as reflected by changes in IQ scores and other measures (which generally follow the same pattern), tend to occur during the first year of a program, scores usually leveling off or perhaps declining slightly during the successive program years. Even Heber's big gain between 12 and 16 months reflects this pattern, since his program started between 3 and 6 months, assuming the difficulty with measures for children less than 12 months of age (global infant tests may be measuring different skills at this early age, Hunt 1975) can be discounted.

The pattern is similar in some ways to the results obtained with nursery-school programs in the earlier era, though mean gains in nursery schools were smaller and less consistent, given the parallels between nursery school and home for the middle-class clientele. Both the earlier nursery school and later compensatory-education programs could apparently offer proportionately much less after their initial contribution, in the former because of the strong parallels between home and nursery school and the inappropriateness of IQ measures, in the latter because basic levels had been reached that were difficult to surpass in the face of the competing folk and poverty curriculum of the children, and because of the global nature of the programs as well perhaps. The fact that Heber's program raised the children's mean scores levels so much above norms during early infancy suggests that his program was more powerful than other programs, but not with respect to duration except in its role of maintaining the early gains. Rather, it appears that it is earliness combined with intensity of stimulation, including its unusual comprehensiveness for both school and home that were the main agents. Although certain programs starting in early infancy (like Gordon's) did not produce continuing effects of the same magnitude, they were known to be less intensive or less well articulated, and the programs that combined gains of relatively greater magnitude and permanence (Heber; Levenstein; Palmer) all included a high proportion of infants (children under 3).

The research on long-term effects of varying program duration are even less certain. With the inevitable subject attrition, reduced sample size often made it impossible to make comparisons among the various subgroups varying in duration. For follow-up comparisons, moreover, baseline comparisons for the same group is no longer possible, because the effects of the longer duration necessarily enter all subsequent assessments. Thus in Beller's (1973, 1974) investigations, program duration is confounded with age of entry. Thus the significant experimental control differences reported in IQ, moral maturity, and school achievement through fourth grade (the last mainly for girls) and self-concept and cognitive style (boys) through twelfth grade, are based on comparisons of a group starting school at age 4 in a three-year program with groups starting at age 5 and 6 for two- and one-year programs, respectively. Similarly, Gray's (1974; Gray and Klaus 1970; Gray, Ramsey, and Klaus 1982) two- and three-year program groups started at the respective ages of 4 and 3, but in any case there were no significant differences between subsequent IQ and achievement test scores at any age. Gordon (Guinagh and Gordon 1976, 1978) did find significant mean differences between experimentals and controls in reading and arithmetic achievement in grade 3 for experimental children experiencing 2 or 3 years of early intervention, compared to no experimental-control differences with those given one year of intervention, but the latter group started at age 24 months, while the former started at 3 or 12 months.

Since all studies entangle duration with starting age, one way or another, and mean IQ differences between experimental subgroups typically vanish very early with age over successive testings, our best evidence is in the short-term effects where the bulk of the studies indicate that the first program year appears to be decisive. We can only conclude very tentatively that as far as compensatory early education with socioeconomically disadvantaged populations is concerned, cognitive stimulation past the first program year is probably more important for its maintenance role in countering the countervailing ecology of family and community patterns, but again systematic research effort has hardly begun.

Studies on Average and Advantaged Populations

Because there are apparently no investigations on early stimulation in which duration was a variable, we can do little but compare contrasting investigations for trends. If we ask the question, do the longer term studies appear to produce the greater effects, regardless of area or other dimensions, there is a bit of evidence supporting the influence of longer periods of stimulation, but almost as many contradictory findings. McGraw's (1935) banner success in the twin, Johnny's gross-motor achievements, learning to swim, dive, roller skate, ride a tricycle, and stack boxes and stools in serial order before he was 2 occurred over the course of two years. The program of complex skill training did not begin until 7 months, however, and skill mastery was attained on different skills over varying periods. He could swim alone (though under water) by 10 months, for example, dive by 15 months, skate reasonably well after less than four months, and climb a 61-degree incline by 16 months but mastered tricycle riding only at 19 months after eight months training. Problems McGraw herself encountered in guiding the infant's learning, almost inevitable in a first trial-and-error experiment of this kind, and the relative difficulty of different skills served to vary the duration of training periods. For the most part, training on specific skills was a matter of less than six months, the balance of the training period up to age 2 being devoted to honing the child's mastery of the various skills.

The few studies on early musical stimulation lasted no more than six months, as did Dubin's (1946) art stimulation as well as the training in the classical short-term learning studies in memory and motor skills, and usually far less, yet substantial amounts of learning were almost invariably produced. In the sphere of math concepts and related formal concepts of conservation, classification, and seriation, training amounted in most cases to a few sessions, extending at most over a period of a few weeks, usually less than two. The earlier work of Welch (1939a-c) and Ling (1941) on magnitude and form-concept training are exceptions, but even then training was again a question of a few weeks or months in the investigations of Welch and his colleagues, though lasting as long as nine months for Ling's infants.

There are additional exceptions besides Ling. While the global, pilot programs for middle-class children of Drash and Stolberg (1977) and Metzl (1980) lasted only about six months, in the more extensive general stimulation program of Ulrich et al. (1971), major IQ and reading- and math-achievement gains were made during the course of both the first and second program years. In the studies of Burtt (1932, 1937, 1941) and Smith (1935, 1951, 1963) on verbal memory, which produced such amazing long-term residues, the former embraced daily, brief stimulation over a period of twenty-one months (age 15 months to 3 years) and the latter continued over a period of five years (between the ages of 8 and 13), though only on Sundays. The persistence of advantages during later development lasted only into two or three years of elementary school for early readers taught in prekindergarten kindergarten school programs, however, as we have seen in the Durkin (1974-1975), McKee et al. (1966) and similar investigations—unless followed by school reading programs that built systematically on the early program, as McKee did with one group. Otherwise the ordinary school programs created conflicts similar to the school-versus-home dissonance experienced by disadvantaged children.

It is with children instructed at home, beginning at 3 to 5 years of age, that at first we appear to obtain the best sense of the value of enduring stimulation. Children starting at age 3, who retained stronger long-term advantages than those beginning at age 5, had been stimulated at home for two years against one year for those starting home instruction at age 5. Unfortunately, as in so many cases, it is not possible to separate earliness from duration. Those stimulated two years longer, even before starting school, had started two years earlier. The difference between duration effects become relatively minimal by fifth grade (8 to 6 years), moreover, compared to the two-year difference in starting ages, which remained constant.

Thus longer periods of early stimulation sometimes appear to produce greater, and (where measured) longer term effects. But if we ask the question in stronger form, are there any cases where short periods produce substantial learning effects, the answer also seems to be in the affirmative. A few months, weeks, or even only a few sessions of early stimulation also can produce significant changes, both immediately and in the long term, as in McGraw's motor program, the singing program (one, only two months' duration), and Piagetian concepts (brief training only). The problem with this interpretation is that it takes no account of variations in complexity among the different abilities stimulated and it overlooks interactions with other variables, such as earliness, intensity, and the organization and quality of stimulation. Much of the weight of the findings on the magnitude of the success of brief training in formal-concept studies rests on the aura of Piagetian theory, which holds that acquiring conservation in different dimensions, for example, is intrinsic to the major long-term cognitive-developmental transformations of the life cycle, in this case mainly the stage of concrete operations. But the findings themselves challenge this perspective, both in the apparent ease with which they can be effected several years in advance of norms and the comparative dimensional focus with which stimulation appears to operate. Since there are no really long-term developmental assessments, we might write off the significance of these findings on the effects of brief training for complex development for the moment, but what of the substantial advances in complex skills from no more than a few months' training in a number of investigations, such as in singing and gross-motor skills, competencies that endured in some form for at least two years in the former and to early adulthood in the latter?

In the case of singing or the Drash and Stolberg multistimulation program, the length of the follow-ups of four months to two-and-a-half years do not match the extended developmental follow-ups of motor skills (McGraw) and verbal memory (Burtt; Smith), or the four- to six-year follow-ups of early reading. Other studies, such as Dubin's on drawing, report no follow-up. The follow-ups on general stimulation programs with disadvantaged children, which in all cases lasted at least a year, are also far longer. Thus while the advantages in singing skill (or drawing or formal concepts) may well also last many years, we have no evidence that they do. And given the failure of the benefits from the relatively short-term, school-run reading programs at age 4 to 5 to last beyond two or three-years (recognizing they are at age 4 to 5, compared to ages 2 to 5 for children in the less than six-month-long training studies) these advantages may well also evanesce, assuming no further reinforcement. It seems this leaves only the McGraw study as a model of how no more than a few months of training can produce long-lasting effects. But are we even left with this one? Is it not misleading to abstract the training on separate skills, each enduring from about three to eight months, from the general context of motor stimulation extending from birth to 22 months of age? The skills in fact constitute a set of closely interrelated gross-motor skills, whose stimulation was not only well coordinated but built on an earlier program of simple motor-skill stimulation (reaching), the advanced gross-motor stimulation in some form continued from ages of 7 to 22 months (15 months), and the skills all made use of an overlapping set of basic gross-motor concept-movement modules with the body appendages. The few months' periods needed for the twin Johnny to learn the different motor skills reasonably well, moreover, were in all cases supplemented by continued guidance and experimentation for several additional months, during which competencies were greatly refined to the point of high mastery. In this light we perhaps must redefine the concept of duration.

The investigations in which the early stimulation appears to register significant effects and effects that may last are generally marked by programs that develop the competence(ies) in question to some threshold of mastery. The experimental twin Johnny was highly proficient in all skills stimulated in McGraw's study. It was in fact just such proficiency, which extended broadly across the gross-motor sphere, that appeared to make the permanent advantage. Although the evidence is less clear, because of differences of earliness and degrees of continuing stimulation or support in the home among the different groups, it was just this fluency in reading text that appeared to characterize the home- versus school-instructed early readers. Yet in a larger sense, the same relative mastery is apparent in some of the shorter studies, including the school-instructed early readers, the young singers, drawers, and the like. Mattson (1933) found, in one of the typical relatively short-term studies in complex maze training, that gains and losses in skill, following interim periods of no practice, were related to the degree of proficiency established. Some of the significance of Ling's study may lie in the fact that her training stimulated infants to grasp the concept of geometric form in a variety of types and across several perceptual conditions, thus establishing a firm general mastery of geometric form concepts. Great mastery of the material similarly marked Smith's catechism experiment, and high familiarity with the particular Greek passages (three months each), but especially of the phonology of Greek generally, characterized Burtt's study. Thus in most cases, it is not length as such that determines outcomes (or contributes toward learning, to speak more accurately) but, rather, the process of pursuing stimulation with concepts long and well enough to attain substantial mastery of the concepts involved.

In the Gesell series of co-twin control investigations (Gesell and Thompson 1929, 1941; Hilgard 1933), like most of the other historical short-term training studies on specific, often simple skills, competencies tended to disappear over a period of weeks or months of nonuse (we shall get to ecology later). But, unlike the other investigators, Gesell both measured and found (though he overlooked and minimized) certain more general, long-term developmental effects. The (almost) always earlier trained twin T was slightly superior in gross-motor competencies and some aspects of language generally, and both twins, who had in the end fairly sizable amounts of specialized stimulation over the course of their preschool years (the control twin C usually after twin T), demonstrated IQ gains that might well be attributable to the cumulative effects of continuing early-concept stimulation that come in the course of the general language and cognitive operations entailed with the specific skill training. The gains in cognitive levels that continued to accrue over successive years in the Ulrich et al. (1971) and Wang et al. (1980) programs, unlike the single-year gains characteristic of most early-intervention programs, appear to be a function of the continuing careful building of skills systematically in reading, arithmetic, and formal concepts—in much the same fashion as reading in McKee's follow-through reading programs for kindergartners—competencies in which there are few limits on complexity. True, some of the children came from advantaged backgrounds, but disadvantaged children progressed proportionally well, and early reading and extended math concepts were rarely taught in other early intervention programs. This inclusion enabled children to continue to progress through several grades in advance of norms and may have contributed toward the continuing improvement in IQ scores (in the Ulrich study) as well.

It would appear then that the duration of stimulation is more of a *condition* that makes it possible for a body of concepts to be learned than an aspect of the stimulation process itself. Although time must elapse for stimulation to be applied, duration is only the passage of time, saying nothing with respect to what is applied, how complex it is, how well concepts are learned, and how far the child progresses in relation to how complex the material. Duration would appear to play some role then in how many and how well things are learned, but its effects must be assessed in terms of the actual relations between the child and the process of stimulation, the cognitive developmental learning processes cumulatively as they actually occur, and the influence of other dimensions. Presumably the more complex the concepts or extensive the body of concepts, the longer the period of stimulation required, other things being equal. But other things, as we all know, are rarely equal. The intensity of stimulation, for example, is likely to make some difference, as in the case of five years of no more than a *single day per week* for Smith's stimulation, against *daily* stimulation over twenty-one months for Burtt's program, as we will now consider in detail.

Intensity of Stimulation

The concept of intensity is perhaps ambiguous, carrying within it implications of several subordinate dimensions, such as the frequency with which stimulation is conducted over a given period, the length of the training sessions, the pace at which stimulation is conducted within a session, and the ratio of the volume of concepts exposed to the time expended. It is essentially in the last sense that intensity is employed here, although something of all aspects necessarily enters into the problem. The issue is closely related to the classical problem of how distributed and massed practice affect rates and success in learning, practice that is spread out (distributed) over longer time spans, allowing more intervals without stimulation, having proved over a long series of studies during the first half of this century to be more conducive to learning (Woodworth 1938). Intensity of program would in general concentrate the learning into less widely separate periods of stimulation and thus be closer to massed practice, yet even fairly intensive programs can allow considerable latitude for spacing the length and number of intervals between actual periods of stimulation. In a given day, for example, it is possible to schedule all stimulation in one intensive hour or spread it out into a half dozen or more brief sessions of a few minutes each. Similarly, each week might encompass two full days in succession with several hours of stimulation, or at the other extreme, spread out numerous five- to ten-minute sessions, scheduling a few well-spaced sessions each day, three to five days per week, thus allowing ample room for both breaks between sessions each day and breaks between days. How has program intensity as we define it actually fared in influencing children's development?

Because investigators have not deliberately varied the volume of stimulation in relation to time span, we can do no more than scan the scattered literature, searching for signs of trends and perhaps making tighter comparisons between selected studies. Starting with the examples of Burtt and Smith is intriguing but does not take us far because of the great difference in ages of stimulation (infancy versus middle childhood) and the nature of the learning task (later memorization of passages of Greek drama—there were no early childhood measures—versus recalling verbatim earlier memorized answers to questions). Still, both are verbal, rotelike tasks, and both programs made use of well-distributed practice sessions.

In fact, Smith intentionally scheduled the learning weekly over five years in the interest of distributing practice. To the extent one can discount the effect of age, duration, and task and concept differences—admittedly a large order, the sharp differences in persistence of effects (eleven years versus fifty to sixty years) could be attributed to the greater intensity of stimulation, apparent in the concentrated one-hour sessions in the Smith program, that effectively transcended the distributed spacing. Burtt simply read three different passages of Greek for two minutes, daily, substituting a new one every three months, in contrast to Smith having the child learn (and understand) the material (answers to questions) to criterion of rote mastery, which included cumulative reviewing. Although there is no measure of follow-up effects, Foster's (1928) high success with 2½- to 4½-year-olds learning large portions (in some cases all) of nine stories in sequence through ten daily repetitions (still fairly well spaced) may also indicate the value of intensity of stimulation even as it also hints at the value of meaningfulness in learning, as did Smith's study compared with Burtt's.

If we compare selected sets of early intervention studies on poor children, however, the results at first glance are not so clear. Investigations by Heber et al. (1972; Garber and Heber 1981) and Hunt et al. (1976) clearly fall on the side of high-intensity stimulation, many interactions per day every day in center-based or institutional programs, which produced outstanding cognitive changes in these differently disadvantaged infants. In the Heber study, IQ levels were raised to well above average (125 IQ) and far above the 80 to 90 IQ levels characteristic of the population, levels that remained higher (105 IQ) than those of any other study through age 10. Yet the Levenstein (1977) and Palmer (1972) programs, much less intensive on the surface at least, produced comparable, if not quite as large effects that have lasted at least as long (at last reports). Appearances may be misleading, however, since only the Levenstein program effects are comparable. The children she studied maintained about an average IQ (105 on the performance scale) through nearly age 10 (9-9) despite starting at lower levels than Palmer's (84 versus 94), though her later control group means were higher than Palmer's (94 versus 89) (Lazar and Darlington 1978, 1982). Palmer's later experimental group IQ effects, while significantly greater than controls on one scale (performance), are actually only just above 90 on all scales (92-93). In fact Levenstein's program contained an intensity multiplier factor, in the form of parent instruction, which through the twice-weekly sessions presumably mediated extensive stimulating parent-child interactions throughout the course of the week. In Palmer's program, in contrast, stimulation may have extended little further than what the child could grasp from the twice-weekly, hourly sessions to contribute to home interactions, because they were center-based, directly with the child alone without educational involvement of parents. Since the

Levenstein and Palmer programs were similar in duration (eight versus seven months) and age (around ages 2 to 3), intensity of stimulation may have given the Levenstein children a slight edge.

Intensity of stimulation, like other factors, will not guarantee comparable outcomes of course. A variety of early-intervention programs of more or less equally high intensity produced less high and persistent cognitive effects, presumably as a result of variations from other factors (age, program type, and quality), while certain even brief, fairly low-intensity programs produced rather substantial changes (Palmer and Anderson 1979). The earlier language- and information-concept program of Dawe (1942), for instance, generated mean 14-point IQ and similar language and concept gains following a three months' program limited to a few hours each weekend. The novelty of the weekend jaunts for orphanage children, combined with the highly personalized style and richly motivating approach (stories, pictures, books) seems to have had much to do with her relative success, though it must be added that the final short-term IQ level (95) remained below the level of the most successful, relatively high-intensity projects (Bereiter and Engelmann cited in Weikert 1969 and White al. 1973 for preschoolers, Heber et al. 1972 and Levenstein 1977 for infants), and no follow-up results were reported.

Among the pilot programs for middle-class infants, the greater intensity of the Drash and Stolberg (1977) stimulation program (one three-hour session per week of thorough parent tutoring and instruction during the bulk of the approximately six months' span) compared to the Metzl (1980) program (a total of three training visits spread over the course of the program), given the similar duration and ages, may have contributed to the signally greater cognitive outcomes (mean IQs of 136 versus 112 for Metzl (1980) at program termination). The Ulrich et al. (1971) program, which combined advantaged and disadvantaged older children (4 + -year-olds) and produced IQ levels 10 points above norms for both groups, combined a very intensive program with extended duration (two years).

On the other hand, how can we account for the numerous investigations of Piagetian formal concepts of seriation classification and conservation, which demonstrate that minimal training will acelerate the grasp of selected concrete-operational concepts in 4-year-olds, with some transfer across dimensions (from quantity to length, for example), three or four years in advance of norms (Brainerd 1977, 1978)? This contrasts with the earlier highly intensive, individualized approach to stimulation utilized by Welch (1939a-c) to induce form, area, and size concepts, and by Ling (1941) to generate broadly generalized concepts of geometric form. In both cases successful outcomes with infants came only through months of painstaking efforts with multiply reinforced training-testing trials, daily or several times per week.

Any number of explanations may be offered, but the advancement in understanding of cognitive processes and corresponding developments in techniques for arranging stimulus conditions to dovetail with concept-learning problems from a cognitive against a behavioral perspective may be at the root of the difference. A few closely spaced sessions (thus fairly intensive), are sufficient to induce certain concept transformations, apparently as result of the close articulation of critical features (such as reciprocal relation between length and density in conservation of numbers of units) illuminated through precise arranging and modeling, usually accompanied by explanations. Compare this with the Welch's repetitive presentation of paired stimuli varying slightly along gradients of form or size, in which differences are to be learned through reinforced trial and error alone. Even our assessments of infant capabilities of classification concepts (the precursors) are greatly advanced in the past few years in company with the growth of sophistication of techniques articulated with cognitive theory (Denney and Acito 1974; Nelson 1973; Ricciuti 1965; Ross 1980). Learning two or three concepts (such as aspects of conservation, seriation) is also perhaps not the complex, generalized cognitive-developmental affair Piagetian theory has been wont to believe, compared to, say, the body of abstract and other concepts represented in 10-point or so gains in an IQ test.

Reading provides a sharp contrast with math and formal-concept learning, as we discussed at length in the review of domain-specific forms of stimulation (chapter 7), where the relatively few, if abstract, concepts to be mastered compares with the myriad of anchored perceptual-motor concepts needed to become fluent in reading. As a result of the endless body of specific letter-sound associations and other dimensions of reading to be learned (words, sentences, spacing, lines, capitalization, punctuation), attempts to teach preschoolers to read are almost invariably affairs of daily stimulation. Sessions may not be long, as in the case of Davidson's (1931) and the author's (1971a, volume II) fifteen-minute sessions, but they are typically scheduled daily, to minimize forgetting and maintain continuous progress with the many details of the process. Details are not entirely clear on the processes of home reading instruction, but the general picture (Clark 1976; Durkin 1966; Fowler 1981b) is one of daily encounters between child and parent, older sibling, or other mentor(s) who interact informally and frequently in the context of a variety of activities in the home, in particular, reading children's picture-story books, looking at magazines, ads, and in fact any other printed material (including children's letter blocks and other letter sets, and, in the contemporary world, following such programs as Sesame Street (Dunn 1970; Perlish 1968). Kindergarten programs and the occasional preschool institutional program, including Montessori and special research programs, all similarly follow a daily course of activities that include a steady diet of reading stimulation, when reading is a program goal (Bereiter and Engelmann 1966, 1968; Durkin 1968, 1974-1975; Keister 1941; McKee et al. 1966; Ulrich et al. 1971). Thus while there are undoubtedly variations in the amount of daily focus on reading processes from program to program and child to child, a certain degree of intensity is instrinsic to success in teaching children to read.

An interesting contrast furnishing information on the effects of varying intensity appears in music, in which Jersild and Bienstock (1931, 1934), sought to improve the singing skills of young children in two similar programs, varying markedly in intensity. Similar programs of singing simple songs making use of sociodramatic techniques were presented to two groups of children, in the first program twice weekly in ten-minute sessions over a period of six months, in the second the same number of sessions collapsed into a two-month period. Since mean gains amounted to more than 50 percent during the first study, compared to 30 to 40 percent (varying with age and practice, which were confounded) in the second, the more-extended program appeared to allow more time and development for the concepts and skills to be assimilated, a process of consolidation well known in the literature historically (Woodworth 1938). Duration appears to have enjoyed greater weight than intensity in this instance. The children ranged slightly older in the second study, however, 3½ to 8 years against 2½ to 4 years) and methods involved less small group work. Since age may have worked slightly against the younger subjects in the first study, however, given the possibly lesser rate of gain for younger versus older children in the second study the contrast is perhaps even sharper.

Because duration is so greatly truncated in the second study, and differences in the amount of learning were not marked (apparently none in the complexity of concepts mastered), there is perhaps a balance between intensity and duration, in this case somewhere between the two and six months with respect to duration and somewhat less intensive than the second program but more than the first. Or would a more strung-out program have been even more effective? We are also not informed as to whether the longer spans and intervals between lessons in the first study may simply have allowed more time and a greater amount of reinforced practice in singing at home, not unlikely where children are taking a subject commonly valued and engaged in contemporary culture.

This pattern of findings on limited data, in which variables are generally confounded and comparisons uncertain at best, nonetheless suggests that the amount of stimulation that occurs over the course of a given time span is a dimension to be considered and investigated with precision. The large majority of studies suggest that weekly attention and perhaps daily or alternate-day stimulation is more conducive to learning progress than less-intensive patterns of stimulation. But it also depends on the number and intricacy of concepts in the domain being stimulated, as in the obvious contrast between the highly focused, limited number of concepts in the specialized math and other related formal-concept training studies, compared with the multiple-concept early-reading and general cognitive-stimulation programs. As on the question of duration, it is evidently not intensity as such that makes the difference. It is rather that concept learning needs to be scheduled and maintained with sufficient frequency for the child to attain competence on the succession of concepts with which the domain or aspect of the domain is constructed. Concepts must come frequently enough and be repeated often enough within a given time span for progress to be sustained, yet not so frequently the concepts and skills are not well mastered.

Once more the McGraw's approach with the infant twin Johnny furnishes a good example. Johnny was guided and encouraged to practice each skill daily until first moderate competence then gradually smooth mastery was attained. Johnny spent each day from 9 to 5 o'clock in McGraw's laboratory, as if he were in an intensive, center-based program, alternating periods of play, practice, and guidance with the different skills. Yet because of the wide and often unknown amounts of variations in intensity in different programs, often within the same domain, research on what balances need to be struck for each body of material is very much needed. Could McGraw have made faster and more assured progress, at least in certain skills like tricycle riding, (which required eight months, including a long period of initially futile guidance, compared to only three months for skating), had she diminished the intensity? So many untested variables are at work in such trial-and-error efforts, not excluding the technology of instruction, as in reading (Resnick and Weaver 1979), especially in the realm of stimulating infants developmentally, that the main problem remains one of making substantial advances of any kind in a body of complex concepts. The ground is hardly broken.

Secondary Dimensions

The potential for variation among dimensions of developmental stimulation is logically very great, particularly when the possibility of endless refinements and cluster combinations among dimensions are taken into account. Cognitive-inquiry strategies for example may be either pure discovery, involving setting and material preparation with adult mediation confined to responding to the infant or young child, or more Socratic, in which the teacher prepares a sequence of problems and takes the initiative in guiding the child to inquire into phenomena. Dimensions inevitably appear in a variety of forms that combine in many different ways.

The remaining dimensions are even more prey to the problems of confounding and lack of defined experimental control than those of earliness or age, duration, and intensity. Their secondary status is more a reflection of this state of affairs, however, than of their known proportion of contribution to the matrix of stimulation generating cognitive development. For example, there is a great deal of discussion in the early-intervention and early-education literature, as well as in education generally, on the issues of structure and programming—witness the controversy over progressive education and informal schooling versus traditionally structured methods over many decades (Cremin 1961; Weber 1971). But in fact the concept of structure in early education is widely applied to different mixes of dimensions, such as the degree of sequencing of concepts presented, the structure of materials or the physical setting, the structure of the teacher-child interactions, and the degree of structuring in the modes of exploring concepts or materials (see Fowler 1970 for a discussion of program structure). Attempts have been made to investigate the effects of structure, but most of them are essentially post-hoc analyses, or at best comparisons of packaged programs that combine a multiplicity of factors according to program designer propensities (Miezitis 1971; Miller and Dyer 1975).

Much of the discussion of the so-called secondary dimensions, as a result, will be addressed to problems of clarifying definitions, sorting out concepts, and exploring how they may interrelate with one another. Selected studies will be drawn on to illuminate points as available and warranted. The dimensions to be discussed will follow the set outlined in table 5-2.

Sequencing or Matching

The term *sequencing* is employed to avoid some of the problems associated with the widespread, loose use of the term *structure*, though the latter term will be discussed at various points to clarify issues. Sequencing is most often applied to the practice of ordering the presentation of stimulation according to levels of difficulty or complexity in some way. Criteria for sequencing can vary all the way from the precise and invariant ordering of each example or item in a series to the use of a broad set of concepts defined as belonging to a general cognitive level of development, much as Piagetian stages of cognitive development are claimed to do. For sequencing to be developmentally meaningful, that is, to facilitate cognitive development, it must involve more than ordered steps. The steps or levels must be ordered in terms of a logical order of complexity, whether in terms of a sequence for a specific dimension (such as ordering length in series), a domain (like furniture or language), or a broad level of Piagetian concepts (say, concrete operations). Hunt (1961, 1969) has written extensively about the importance of the concept of the "match," or coordinating curriculum sequences with the child's cognitive complexity of development, and has devised logically sequenced

Piagetian measures of infant development (Uzgiris and Hunt 1975), in which developmental progress follows a highly reliable, invariant sequence, though the programs he has employed do not appear to be as tightly sequenced as the measures (Hunt et al. 1976). The problem of sequencing is complicated by the fact that difficulty is determined by additional factors, such as domain and task familiarity and cross-fertilization across domains, as will become evident in discussing the early intervention studies.

Controlling the order of complexity in which concepts are introduced has an obvious appeal. It should make it easier for a child to learn by isolating two points on a scale (bipolar, as in wet or dry versus three or more degrees of wetness) before three, for example, or two levels of classification prior to three, or single causes prior to multiple causality and chains. How much and in what way have early-stimulation programs actually stressed the order of presentation of items? Is there any evidence that sequencing helps or hinders learning?

The answer to the last question is not so simple as it would seem. The commonsense logic that presenting easy items before difficult ones would facilitate if not be essential for learning finds no easy set of answers in the literature. It is true that among the early-intervention programs, the more structured programs have generally resulted in the larger cognitive gains (Miller and Dyer 1975; White et al. 1973), as we noted, for example, in the high gains for the Bereiter-Engelmann programs against the traditional unstructured nursery-school program. Yet the structuring of programs typically combines structuring of the teacher-child relations as much as the organization of the curriculum, above all in the Bereiter-Engelmann program (Bereiter and Engelmann 1966; Evans 1975; Miller and Dyer 1975). Curriculum *is* highly structured, but it is the economy and precision with which the concepts are illuminated in behavioral rules that are the paramount qualities. Sequences here and in all structured programs are for the most part sequenced by *levels* of difficulty rather than exact order of logical complexity. Palmer (1972), for example, developed a program with five levels of difficulty for learning bipolar concepts, ranging from *up* and *down* at level I to *bigger than* and *littler than* at level V. Difficulty levels were determined through the children's responses to concept inventories. A precise order for introducing each concept is often followed in the highly structured programs; that is, the stimulation is *programmed* in steps. But the sequence is not necessarily entirely logical and the levels do not necessarily reflect difficulty levels for any given child.

Although initial gains have been generally higher, gains have not necessarily held up better from structured programs. Evidence exists in fact that they may not have held up as well, though the Bereiter program may not have been delivered as efficiently in the replications where long-term development has been assessed (Miller and Dyer 1975). On the other hand gains have held up as well or better in Montessori programs (where they have been compared with other unstructured programs), which in some ways is one of the most tightly sequenced curricula designed. The Montessori curriculum does allow choice for children among tasks, but each task is highly sequenced, as is the order between tasks of the same type, and the manner in which children are to manipulate materials is closely structured and monitored (Banta 1972; Evans 1975; Montessori 1912, 1967). However, all cognitive gains for all groups (compared with controls) disappeared by grade 4, where such program comparisons have been made. If we look at the long-term comparisons by the research consortium discussed at length in chapter 6, there is no strong evidence that concept sequencing was an important variable (Lazar and Darlington, 1978, 1982). All of the original early-intervention programs were moderately sequenced as far as can be determined (Parker 1972; Day and Parker 1977) and the Levenstein program, which produced the highest final IQ levels (around 100 IQ), was certainly not high, either in structure or sequence, compared to any other, partly because there is necessarily less control over parents than over professional teachers. Both the PEP program (Resnick et al. 1977; Wang et al. 1980) and the Learning Village program (Ulrich et al. 1971), which were both exceptionally highly programmed, the former at least more logically sequenced, both produced outstanding cognitive gains, particularly in the programmed domains (reading, math, perceptual skills). But preschool gains do not seem to have been larger than those in other programs, and later school-achievement gains were clearly a function of the continuing, specialized school-learning programs as much as they were of the early stimulation programs.

The Palmer program, perhaps the most closely sequenced and structured of those in the consortium comparisons, included two sets of children in the follow-up study, only one of which had followed the sequenced curriculum. The other set were members of a discovery group, with whom trained teachers played with materials identical to those used in the sequenced program, but without following the curriculum and only in response to the child's initiatives. The Palmer study may be one of the best available on testing the effects of curriculum sequencing, because of its implementation in a single study, using the same population, tutors, and setting. Other variables are confounded, however, such as form of interaction, and the original curriculum was not necessarily followed at all in the discovery program. For this reason, this becomes a less-than-perfect test, and the disappearance of all advantages to the sequence-trained group that were found at program termination, after two years for those stimulated at age 2 and after only one year for those trained at age 3, is not fatal to the concept of sequencing.

Mean differences at any time had favored the sequence-trained groups only on the Concept Familiarity Index (CFI), an inventory scale synchronized with the concept-training sequences. Both groups (combined) maintained superiority to controls to age 10 on the performance scale of the WISC and on a variety of school achievement and coping measures, as noted in chapter 6. Yet differences in concept training may have been fewer than at first was apparent and it may be questioned how much Palmer's sequences actually defined levels of cognitive complexity. The learning materials were selected to elicit behavior reflecting concepts employed in the curriculum, such as a doll with a zipper moving up and down, and in fact such common concepts are intrinsic to the use of almost any varied set of toys (Fowler 1980b). Since the same instructors were employed for both programs, they were naturally familiar with the relevant program concepts, which they would undoubtedly demonstrate from time to time following the child's initiatives in play. But even assuming less overlap, there are a host of cognitive operations (means and ends, seriation, grouping and a broad array of language terms and concepts) that would certainly arise in the course of the interactive play in at least simple forms, if not in a planned order. The fact that the groups did not differ from each other except on the CFI, yet both groups were superior to controls on various ability measures (Binet, WPPSI, Peabody Picture Vocabulary Test), to different degrees at different points, suggests the extent of the nonprogram concepts (means-end relations, causality, language) that must have been acquired in both groups to produce gains on such multiconcept ability measures.

The sequencing itself may be faulted on two counts. Difficulty levels were established empirically, but not individually, and, at least as important, it may be argued that the range of concepts was logically in fact entirely on the same level, namely that of two-point comparisons of opposites. The empirical differences found among concepts probably reflected differences resulting from cultural socialization more than they did anything more than small differences in actual difficulty. Is there any reason to believe, for example, that *on top of* is logically much more difficult to grasp than *next to*? Yet they were assigned respectively to the lowest and highest levels (1 and 5) in Palmer's program (Palmer, Semlear, and Fischer 1981).

Thus sequencing seems to have proved itself only in the short run within the narrow framework in which Palmer employed it. The underlying difficulty of assessing its impact here and generally from the early-intervention literature is essentially the same as the problem that affects the interventions among the disadvantaged generally: global programs and global measures, on the one hand, and special populations whose ecology runs counter to program learning objectives, on the other. Program aims, here as elsewhere were aimed at generating a broad set of academically oriented skills, not simply the specific bipolar opposites Palmer stressed, which is why he and everyone else found themselves saddled with general ability and language measures as the major developmental criteria for improvement (Bronfenbrenner 1975; Palmer 1972; Zigler and Valentine 1979). The sequencing in

Palmer's curriculum happened to be more apparent than real, but other programs, like Levenstein's relatively successful program, used even less, and the programs of Bereiter and Engelmann (1966; Evans 1975), Hunt et al. (1976), and Heber et al. (1972), although apparently better sequenced *logically* than Palmer's, were in fact seldom tightly sequenced. They were simply ordered in precise steps as much as they were logically sequenced, ordering in fact being frequently violated. The programs encompassed a tremendous range of concepts from many domains (formal, informational, language, beginning reading, arithmetic), domains seldom sorted out logically in terms of complexity, and which in any case resulted in much cross fertilization of concept learning, in some ways parallel to culturally natural forms of early developmental experience. While, except for the Palmer and Hunt measures (with which Hunt's program was only loosely articulated, it will be recalled), global measures that themselves were not logically organized or sequenced became the measure of development. There were also too many variables (age, duration, interaction forms, setting, intensity—Palmer's program was limited to two hours per week, and many others) mingled in these designs to get any real measure, or even sense, of the value of sequencing and developmental matching. It may be that structure and sequencing (or programming) of all kinds serve more important functions in culturally different folk children than they do with children whose ecological background matches better the type of abstract verbal patterns of these intervention programs, as Bereiter and Engelmann (1966) and others have suggested, but the evidence is far from clear. How much has sequencing been employed and what effects has it had on children's rates of learning in other studies?

No other studies among the sparse literature on average populations have apparently deliberately set out to compare the effects of ordering curricula systematically. Comparing effects across investigations, even ignoring the obvious effects of differentiating variables, yields the same uncertain picture, though for different reasons. The pre-World War II, short-term learning literature was often quite well ordered in curriculum programming, but the learning material was typically so limited that complexity levels seldom entered the picture, as in the cube manipulation, stair climbing, digit memorization, story recitation, and similar tasks. The limited cognitive perspectives did not induce much work on sequential complexity. Mattson's (1933) rolling-ball mazes varied in complexity but not enormously or by level, and in any case children were exposed to them repeatedly in a systematically varied order, yet all mazes were learned well. In Foster's (1928) story-learning task, for instance, children learned the better part of nine stories, presented in a certain order, but stories were all on roughly the same level of complexity, and in this as in most all tasks of the time, children generally learned about all there was to accomplish because of the ceiling effects that were typical. Strayer's (1930) language-stimulation study offered more potential, but only simple, concrete nouns were included and the program, as in most investigations, was too short lived to bring about advances in levels.

In studies that projected more complex gradients, there is no evidence that sequencing was ordinarily used to any degree, though some precision in the concepts to be learned may have been involved. Thus Jersild and Bienstock (1931, 1934) aimed at expanding children's pitch and interval ranges but they do not mention any grading of concepts. Different tones and intervals, beyond the preschoolers' beginning range, were simply embedded in the simple songs selected, but without regard to order, apparently. Dawe (1942) clustered the concepts in her language and information-concept program, but again no description of sequencing by complexity is recorded, yet the 14-point IQ and equivalent language and information-concept gains were about as great as those in most of the later early-intervention programs. Dawe's subjects were also institutionally deprived, raising again questions of special programming and sequencing needs, though the program seems to have worked moderately well without them. The findings in other complex, early-language-stimulation programs are contradictory, but the evidence generally does not suggest that logical sequencing or even programming were indispensable variables. Luria and Yudovich (1959) found that planned, intensive stimulation in one twin worked much better in stimulating language and general cognitive development than an essentially open-ended discovery (standard nursery school) setting for his twinmate, but while conceptually analytic and planned, logical order does not seem to have figured prominently in the planning, and remedial stimulation may present different problems than enriched stimulation (both twins were seriously deprived). In Schvarchkin's successful Russian phonemic stimulation program (cited in Ervin and Miller 1963:111), words that varied one phoneme at a time were introduced in a certain order (vowels versus consonants, then sonorants versus articulated obstruants, and so on), apparently logically based, to second-year infants. But Irwin (1960) was able to substantially multiply phoneme frequency in an entirely open-ended program of story reading to third-year infants.

In other areas Dubin (1946) followed the children's self-selection in tailoring her concepts on how to draw to the children's spontaneous drawings—though it can be said that in itself this approach was developmentally matched better than in most programs. There was no order at all in Burtt's (1941) verbal-memory study, insofar as complexity was concerned, only reading a set of passages, Greek, all of more or less equivalent difficulty and equally meaningless to the child. McGraw (1935) seems to have had some general notions of complexity, starting out with simple skills before complex skills, yet she started the complex skills all more or less in parallel, without determining questions of relative complexity or difficulty. Differences only became evident post hoc, and they appear to have been in part related to problems of teaching method (as in learning trike riding versus skating). Since the diverse forms of stimulation all produced gains of the type and magnitude they were designed to produce, we can only note that more sequencing than was tried might have resulted in greater impact, but of course only in the few studies where the skills stimulated were not truncated by ceiling effects.

Studies on early reading used widely different strategies, as in Durkin's (1974-1975) relatively open-ended ordering in her language-experience approach compared with McKee et al.'s (1966) at least partially sequenced approach, in which letter-sound relationships were generally stressed before word learning and sentence reading, and both appear to have been about equally effective, aside from the obvious advantage accrued in McKee's follow-up program through the grades. Methods and order varied enormously among parent-tutored early readers, with no information available on how sequencing may have facilitated or impeded progress.

About the only small-scale studies where something approaching sequencing has been applied with more precision, the studies on formal concept learning, are nevertheless limited in the scope of complexity. They are all pretty much all-or-nothing transformations in the acquisition of conservation or seriation. The only Piagetian training studies where a genuine gradient of complexity was involved were all embedded in general cognitive-learning programs for disadvantaged children.

Sequencing, however appealing, has thus yet to be tested. It is also very evident that young children can learn a great deal even with little or no thought devoted to ordering concepts in terms of complexity. It is true that programs characteristically present concepts within the same projected general-ability range or level of complexity of the child. The Gesell tasks were all selected to suit the expected developmental range of the twins' motor, language, and other skills, as were the singing tasks of Jersild, the stories of Foster, and in fact the curricula of most studies the early-intervention programs for disadvantaged. Palmer's discovery curriculum, for example, was, like Dubin's drawing program, determined by the use the child made of the materials, thus matching (by self-selection) the individual child's range. At most tasks were set at something above the child's current level but not outrageously beyond, so as to stimulate or challenge but not discourage development.

Formal concept learning for 4-year-olds and classification learning for infants (by Welch) might well be considered exceptions, but Welch's early work was very much trial and error, and utilization of the later understanding of how infants demonstrate the rudiments of grouping suggest that it was his cognitive techniques that were further off the mark than his developmental timing. Many of the early experiments on formal-concept learning

failed, until greater understanding of various factors influencing understanding developed through repeated experimentation. Early reading, too,
is a violation of still widely accepted canons, yet many preschoolers are
regularly taught to read successfully by untrained parents, often mingling
letters, words, and phrases with little regard for order, and school programs
like Durkin's have demonstrated more formally that it can be reliably accomplished without harm. McGraw's tasks for Jimmy ranged far beyond
cultural expectations, yet we see that McGraw succeeded through patience
and persistence, and similar tasks (swimming and canoeing) are normal to
the socialization of infants in certain cultures.

It seems clear that we do not always know what is a good developmental
match and that sequencing, at least for early education, is in its infancy.
Certainly, the complex hierarchies of abstract concepts and reasoning processes that coping in the world of industrial societies demand would seem to
require some degree of developmental matching and logical ordering, compared to the largely concrete motor skills and direct language communication demanded in folk societies. But the case remains to be proved and there
may be important advantages to flexibility and the opportunity for the child
to range around concepts, even across levels, in stimulating curiosity, inquiry, comparisons, and initiative in experimentation, and the acquisition
of knowledge. Certain advantages to sequencing or at least a degree of programming may appear in the assurance that material gets covered and
reviewed and knowledge accumulates, as we shall discuss in volume II in
connection with discussing strategies employed in our own research.
Something between tight programming and highly logical sequencing and
completely open-ended discovery strategies may combine the advantages of
logic, order, and flexibility. Tests like the Palmer study projected seem to
define the extremes. What would appear to be useful is an ordered series of
studies that would systematically vary the number and variety of dimensions
and exemplars on which stimulation is both programmed and sequenced,
logically by complexity, even varying the degree of match with the child by
developmental assessments at several stages of the program.

Forms of Interaction

Interaction refers to the modes of relations between child and adult (or
other instructor) in a learning task, which may vary in many ways, as in the
frequency, length, and type of concepts employed, but here specifically concerns the different proportions of initiative assumed by teacher and child.
Variations on this dimension can range all the way from highly directive
teaching, in which the teacher initiates every exchange with all stimuli, to
highly responsive teaching, in which the teacher invariably waits for the

child to initiate action with all stimuli and only responds to the child's actions or overtures, but never initiates. Most stimulation programs obviously fall somewhere between extremes. Even so-called discovery programs usually allow room for the teacher to make initiatves in interactive play once the child initiates the process (Palmer 1972). Contemporary approaches to child development and education, particularly with young children, lay great stress upon learning through interaction, ensuring the child ample opportunity to initiate action and experiment with materials. The twin developmental goals of autonomy and concept assimilation can only be realized, it is believed, through interaction techniques of some kind. A rationale and an extensive body of principles and techniques has been developed in which interactive learning is one of the core concepts (Fowler 1980b,c, 1981a, and chapter 1 of volume II). Indeed virtually all early-education textbooks talk about the importance of interaction to varying degrees.

Problems are inherent in realizing a balance in the number of initiatives exercised by child and adult in a learning situation, however. The basis of the difficulty is located in the fact that learning programs are designed by adults to teach children concepts of one kind or another. Unless children are to be left entirely to their own devices, adults as teachers at the least must serve as guides to steer the directions of the child's efforts to learn. But more than this is involved. Manipulation of materials alone will not serve to teach verbal concepts, which many believe to be the key to cognitive development (Bruner 1973; Drash and Stolberg 1977; Luria 1961; Vygotsky 1962). Adults (or similar developed mediators) must supply the labels in some manner. Nor does the child's play with objects of different sizes guarantee that he or she will make systematic inferences about magnitude. At the very least demonstrations and guidance accompanied by explanation will usually greatly accelerate the process. Yarrow and his associates (Yarrow et al. 1972; Yarrow, Rubenstein, and Pedersen 1975) have shown that the variety and complexity of learning materials in the home environment significantly influence children scores on mental tests, but children were not left without any adult mediation. The frequency and variety of adult-child interaction in play were at least as important.

Dewey, one of the great developmental educators establishing principles of humanistic educational practice for our time, early pointed out in the *Child and the Curriculum* (1971), that the task for education was striking a balance between transmitting the knowledge and values of the culture, historically accumulated, and fostering the development of the child's own self-regulation. Technology and bodies of knowledge have grown enormously since Dewey's day in our postindustrial world, making it increasingly difficult to strike a good balance. The problem of socializing children in abstract intricacies can no longer be left solely to the idyllic model of the folk community, where children acquire, mainly by daily observation and experimentation, the small set of common, concrete skills routinely performed by adults and older children in their presence, gradually taking on more and more of an active role in cooperative interaction with community work groups. Now we must also *contrive* learning situations that deliberately involve the child in active experimentation as well as plan the series of concepts and tasks to be acquired.

Because of this fact about the role of adult mediation in cognitive learning in our modern life, it should come as no surprise to find that there are few early-intervention programs or early-stimulation projects of any kind in which the adult as teacher, whether parent or professional, was not the primary and often the most frequent initiator of interaction in the learning situations. This very much includes the Piagetian early-intervention programs, despite Piaget's stress on the importance of self-regulation, discovery, and mental constructing in cognitive development (Parker 1972; Day and Parker 1977; Evans 1975). The teacher in the Kamii program, for example, not only arranges the environment and materials generally, but she or he does so for specific learning tasks, making demonstrations and interacting with the child verbally, often asking key questions to guide the child's concept acquisitions.

Even the discovery programs, as we have noted, as well as the traditional nursery-school approach and Montessori, define a very definite role for teachers as knowledge mediators. Nursery-school teachers are expected to arrange the environment and materials, move around among children, organizing and guiding planned learning activities, interacting with children individually and in groups in play. They must offer information and brief demonstrations at well-timed moments and in general supervise and interact with children in the routines, social relations, and management problems inherent in running a preschool and a program (Weikart 1972). Ecological assessments through coded observations in one study in a nursery school day-care setting reported that 97 percent of all information processing in children from 1 to 2 years originated with adults, declining no lower than 90 percent at age 3 and 70 percent at age 4 (Honig, Caldwell, and Tannenbaum 1970). The teacher in Montessori is constantly active in moving among the children, guiding them in the rules for sensorimotor play with materials according to explicit Montessori definitions, as well as demonstrating and verbalizing concepts intrinsic to the materials in highly defined ways (Banta 1972; Evans 1975; Miller and Dyer 1975; Montessori 1912). Behavior-modification approaches are of course highly mediated, if contingency, forms of teaching (Thoreson 1973).

It is equally evident that the individual learning experiments of the past and those of the current, Piagetian era all specify very active roles for teachers in transmitting information and guiding children in the learning tasks. Jersild and Bienstock (1931, 1934), Foster (1928), Ling (1941) all formulated programs and directly instructed and guided children in specific ways. The so-called practice activities in learning motor and memory skills (Hilgard 1933) included specific instructions for carrying out tasks during the tests repeatedly administered, as well as guidance to spur the child's experimentation in task learning. Even in her study on teaching representational concepts in drawing, though in response to the child's initiatives in drawing, Dubin (1946) freely offered verbal comments about the children's drawings, giving concepts after each drawing and thus setting the general direction in which successive efforts should go.

Despite this general thrust toward programming and teacher mediation, however, the degree of active initiative and participation allowed for the child varies among the different programs, ranging from the high initiative and constant experimentation in discovery programs, the traditional nursery school, Montessori, and Dubin's drawing study, to the completely passive listening role assigned to his son by Burtt (1932) in reading passages of Greek to him. Most programs have prescribed a leading role for the teacher to introduce and demonstrate the use of concept-relevant materials, typically first allowing the child to explore and play with them briefly, later encouraging the child to imitate and verbalize the concept. Usually there is a cycle of interaction, in which the child and teacher, more or less in play, alternately engage in concept experimentation, the teacher introducing new concepts and examples as the child masters earlier ones. The child's imitation has not been restricted to copying but has typically offered a certain amount of opportunity to experiment with different exemplars of each concept. In certain specific learning studies, however, such as those of Jersild and Bienstock, and Foster, the items, here the songs and stories, were totally prescribed. Given the common basis of teachers stimulating and initiating in definite ways in all studies, has the variation in the form of child participation anywhere made a measurable difference?

What is immediately evident, as with the analysis of the preceding dimension, is that nearly *all* approaches to early stimulation, whether in group programs or small-scale learning studies, have generated substantial amounts of learning, but that confounding variables makes it difficult to determine, when differences appear, whether any particular dimension exercised an important contributory function. Rather than reviewing the litany of negative and blurred findings, which must by now be quite familiar, we may ask at the outset, are there any crucial studies or clusters of studies that hint at the importance of interaction? Again, the Palmer (1972) investigation appears to be the sole study surfacing where relevant methods were deliberately varied in a controlled design in a single context. Unfortunately, as we know, curriculum programming was, on the surface at least, confounded with the type of interaction. Was the short-term advantage accruing to the curriculum-oriented group a function of programming concepts (not logical sequencing as we have defined it) or teacher directiveness? Actually, it seems likely to have been mainly the result of programming. Although the teacher often made the first initiatives and maintained general control over the direction of the program in the nondiscovery approach, the children were quite active in manipulating materials. On the other hand the teacher is described as having actively participated in interactive play in the discovery program. In any case no lasting advantages remained after a year or two.

It would appear that we are looking for the wrong outcomes. The so-called highly structured programs, such as those of Bereiter and Engelmann, Heber, and Palmer are known to have produced the greatest cognitive gains, at least in the short term (Miller and Dyer 1975; White et al. 1973). And though we know structure here meant both tight programming and a high ratio of teacher-to-child initiative and control, we also can say that in at least some programs with high teacher directiveness, both long- and short-term cognitive gains have been as large as those in which less teacher control and more child initiative was encouraged (Levenstein 1971, 1977; Lazar and Darlington 1978). Similar equivalents are evident in the various small-scale learning studies of Burtt, Smith, Jersild, and the Piagetian training studies, where children sometimes learned concrete-operational concepts almost entirely from observational learning alone (films and other modeling, with explanations variously added) (Brainerd 1977, 1978), making the process physically passive and without an initiating role for the child. Perhaps it is only when we scrutinize studies for the developmental effects of varying child activity on process variables related to autonomy, curiosity, and problem-solving strategies that differences may be detected. Few comparisons of this kind have been undertaken, and although Miller and Dyer (1975) compared the multiple effects from four different programs, the results were small and inconsistent. It will be recalled that the Montessori approach resulted in more inventiveness in children through grade 2 than the more teacher-directed Bereiter-Engelmann program. However, inventiveness was also low in the traditional, more open-ended, child-active nursery-school approach, and high in the Darcee approach, where teacher directiveness and social control were both high. Little can be made of these uncertain findings, where differences in concept emphasis and concept programming were also involved.

However great the appeal of interaction and an active role for the child, as in the case of sequencing, little support can be found for the virtues of active child participation from the collected experimental-stimulation literature. Case-study analyses of young children stimulated by parents employing different models of parent-child interaction also fail to yield certain differences in cognitive or stylistic outcomes (Fowler 1981b). Although theory and various correlation studies that yield, for example, values of around .35 or even as high as .67 between measures of infant competence and different measures of maternal contingency behavior (Yarrow, Pedersen, and Rubenstein 1975) or interactiveness (Clarke-Stewart 1973), respectively, may underwrite its importance, much more systematic dimensional manipulations than have so far been undertaken will be necessary to demonstrate experimental training effects.

Motivational Techniques (Play)

No matter what label the different early-intervention programs go by, they all make extensive use of certain fundamental techniques for motivating children that form the essentials of modern theory and practice in child care and early education. To start with, all research staffs working with infants and preschoolers, whether from impoverished backgrounds or relatively affluent settings, stress the importance of building attachments with children and creating a climate of warmth, friendliness, and encouragement. Positive social reinforcement is common to all approaches; only the degree and form of expression varies. Punishment, either physical or psychological, is discouraged and seldom practiced, except for the occasional, (usually) mild lapses of control by harassed or fatigued staffs, and the more widely variable behavior of parents, both of which are probably constants from project to project. Supplementing positive approaches, however, are varying amounts of social control exercised through mild physical restraint and isolation from peers coupled with verbal instruction and guidance that take on overtones of negative reinforcement (disapproval, censure, criticism, frustration). Such negative control behaviors, however, are directed more at regulating children's relations with the group than at eliciting and maintaining children's interest in learning activities—again discounting parental techniques.

In addition to the high level of positive relating, affectional interaction, and often praise that characterizes motivational strategies in all projects, the other assumed basic source of children's motivation is the motivation intrinsic to performing age-appropriate tasks. Much has been written in recent decades on the value of learning and development through the satisfaction the child derives from accomplishing tasks, starting especially with White's (1959) seminal paper on competence motivation. This concept has been greatly extended by Hunt (1961), drawing from Piaget and others, to encompass the manipulative processes themselves, and applied to the field of early cognitive learning and development. Children are viewed as motivated to learn in tasks essentially in the interest of becoming familiar with the novel, resolving discrepancies and understanding how things work. It is the task itself, experimenting with materials and processes, that engages children and makes them persist to master the concepts intrinsic to experimentation with the means and end of tasks. Nearly all investigators have employed this line of reasoning one way or another in designing programs and activities for young children. The latter-day theoretical explanations have provided the conceptual underpinnings to what has been the philosophy of the child-development movement and the nursery school for decades. All programs have taken their point of departure from perceptual-motor manipulation, appropriate to the physical-world-based explorations and manipulations of early development, supplemented by pictorial materials, which make visual representations of the object world for the child to begin to explore abstractions. While language and elements of formal concept and quantitative thinking have been widely incorporated, in the interest of establishing the roots of verbal-abstract processes directed toward school learning and the goals of socialization in an industrial society, interactions have heavily anchored these codes and spheres in sensorimotor activities, to provide the referents and build a stable concept system from the base up.

If all programs have been more alike than different on these two pillars of motivating techniques, a salutary social framework and intrinsic manipulation, we must look for differences in program outcomes from other sources. We might look to the use of play and extrinsic, nonsocial incentives or reinforcers as a source of difference. Play is a very elusive concept, however, and turns out to be pretty much the satisfaction intrinsic to the sensorimotor experimentation process of how things work that is uniformly capitalized on in all projects, which may or may not have the descriptor "play" applied by an investigator (Gordon Guinagh, and Jester 1977; Schaefer and Aaronson 1972; Weikart 1967, 1969, 1972). Even the so-called no-nonsense approach of the original Bereiter and Englemann (1966) program made constant use of concrete materials and incorporated dramatic play into the verbal-interaction learning activities, such as deliberately employing a totally nonclass exemplar (a dog for a piece of furniture) to heighten awareness of the concept and the learning process. Different programs incorporated different degrees of peripheral or nonprogram-centered sociodramatic and other forms of free play, but programs have differed less on sensorimotor play than on the degree of programming and the form of interaction, which are somehow often confused with the experimentation process itself.

Programs have differed in the use of extrinsic reinforcers, however. Behavioral approaches (Ulrich et al. 1971) and pragmatists like Gray (Gray et al. 1965) have built in token or concrete rewards of some kind into their program to varying degrees, in the case of behavior-modification and related learning-theory approaches as a definite theoretically based rationale. It is clear, however, that program differences cannot be traced to the use of such concrete, external incentives or reinforcers, because projects showing the largest cognitive gains include both types of orientations, those exclusively or predominantly intrinsic (Hunt et al. 1976; Heber and Garber 1972; Levenstein 1977) and those utilizing substantial proportions of extrinsic reinforcers (Bereiter and Englemann 1966; Ulrich et al. 1971). Programs resulting in more modest program outcomes have similarly included both orientations, those with (Gray and Klaus 1970) and without (Gordon 1969) extrinsic reinforcement. Admittedly, such comparisons must be interpreted with a great deal of caution, not only because of the general difficulty in comparing programs that vary on so many stimulation variables, but because the particularities and amount of both intrinsic and extrinsic reinforcement vary so greatly. Technically, social reinforcement is an extrinsic device, but the question of extrinsic reinforcement in this context concerns only the realm of material, activity, and symbolic rewards, because positive social relations are stressed in all projects. In short, although variations in extrinsic and other forms of motivational arrangements can be found, special effects attributable to these differences are not very evident. The differing orientations may have a variety of consequences found in experimental studies specifically addressed to such issues (Rotter 1966). They do not appear to have materially influenced the magnitude of cognitive gains in the early-learning studies reviewed, however. On the other hand the designs of the individual investigations on early stimulation do not make it possible to trace the source of other developmental consequences, often considered to be the important effects of the type of reinforcement, such as differences in the amount of internally versus externally governed interest in learning.

What of the various short-term and other small-scale investigations with average populations? In some ways the range of variation between studies, has been greater than the variation found among the many early-intervention studies or even among the earlier, nursery-school attendance studies. The latter investigations, conducted in the heyday of developmental philosophy, invariably constructed programs that placed a high premium on warm social relations and sensorimotor and sociodramatic play. Yet the bulk of the short-term and other small-scale studies addressed to specific learning problems manifestly followed the same philosophy as well. All the various early-reading programs in schools, early reading at home (insofar as information is available), the Gesell-directed series of studies, the set of studies on musical learning by Jersild and Bienstock (1931, 1934) and others, and many of the other short-term learning studies, all appear to have followed principles of positive social reinforcement and sensorimotor or sociodramatic play in stimulating the children. Not all investigators deliberately incorporated play or game techniques as did Davidson (1931), the Gesell group, and Jersild and Bienstock. But in most studies the tasks themselves were, regardless of formal intent, constructed in terms of experimentation and guidance in sensorimotor actions that in fact constitute what is generally regarded as process play in the young child. Flexible procedures, free play with the materials, choice of tasks and the like, which have been common as well, added to the play experimentation involved. The Piagetian object-permanence and concrete-operational training tasks of recent years, of course, have been very much built on sensorimotor manipulation, appropriate to Piagetian theory, and often with playlike procedures (Brainerd 1977, 1978), and sometimes using modeling in films in a dramatically interesting manner—though excluding active manipulation by the child in the latter cases.

In any case motivation was not studied as a variable in any of the studies and outcome differences among studies cannot easily be related to differences in motivational framework, with certain exceptions. The principal problem, other than a wide similarity among motivational techniques and the obvious influence of other variables, such as task complexity and clarity, sequencing, and so on, is that nearly all studies produced substantial learning gains for the defined task, usually as much as was projected by the investigator. Early reading might be the exception, since achievement levels varied widely, but motivational techniques appear to have varied less in reading studies than methods for organizing material (use of phonics).

The learning tasks in certain studies appear to have deviated more substantially from these procedures and motivational or learning problems were evident in a handful of investigations. Ling (1941) treated infants to geometric forms coated with sweeteners, an extrinsic agent, but also relied on the intrinsic properties of perceptual-motor manipulation as well. Some of the verbal memory studies, such as the study on digit memory training of Gates and Taylor (1925) (see chapter 4), not only employed verbal, abstract codes, but appear to have made no provision for a play approach, to compensate for the lack of sensorimotor, trial-and-error play characteristic in the other learning studies on sensorimotor and problem-solving skills. Yet there is no question that very large memory gains were recorded in these and similar studies, most of them short-term gains certainly comparable to any of the gains recorded in motor or language skills (as in Strayer 1930) reported for any studies utilizing play and any other components of a developmentally appropriate sensorimotor experimentation strategy. The verbal memory studies of Burtt (1932, 1937, 1941) and Smith (1935, 1951, 1963), both of which followed a highly verbal, task-oriented approach without play, sensorimotor or otherwise (though Smith's child was somewhat older, 8-13, and was given more meaningful material) produced long-term cognitive gains as great as any reported in the literature. But if sensorimotor experimentation or play proved unnecessary, there is no evidence that positive social reinforcement was not virtually a universal inclusion in all early-learning studies, including those on verbal memory. The Burtt and

Smith studies both apparently involved close and continuing social attachments between parent and child.

When motivational or learning problems have been identified by an investigator, the difficulties appear to be more often attributable either to poor techniques in organizing the exemplars to illuminate the concepts or to presenting concepts and skills whose level of complexity is beyond the immediate range of the child to learn, than to errors in motivational strategy. The source of McGraw's (1935) reported difficulties in teaching twin Johnny to learn to ride a tricycle were found to be insufficient and improperly analyzed guidance for mastering the dimensions of the task, since McGraw used plenty of sensorimotor play and social reinforcement. The frustration and motivational loss Welch's (1939c) infants encountered in learning to classify objects according to genus-species relations appear to be similarly due to poor stimulation techniques. Welch pursued the task in a mechanical, repetitive conditioning framework that may have conditioned boredom instead. Since recent studies (Nelson 1973; Ricciuti 1965; Ross 1980) have demonstrated some capacity of infants to classify, using more open-ended suggestive techniques, and Welch otherwise employed something of a game atmosphere, the poor quality of the cognitive stimulation he employed, not the nature of the motivational technique, again appears to have been an important source of the failure of the infants to learn. The rigidity of Welch's repetitions and the fact that the infants resided in depriving institutional environments and were generally low in IQ, however, must also be considered in this case. The motivations of the 2-year-old Martha, recounted by Terman (1918), receded from time to time despite the father's extensive employment of sensorimotor manipulative devices and games to maintain the child's interest in learning to read. On one occasion (the sole one reported), the father resorted to spanking the child, which he reported worked wonders, in that the child then persisted and made rapid headway in reading vocabulary learning. A single instance in a single case probably tells us very little, however, and it is noteworthy that the pervasive motivational framework appears to have been built on manipulative play and close social attachment.

Little that is conclusive can be taken from the collected literature, given the lack of study and control of motivation. Yet because the value of play and wholesome social relations is universally acclaimed on the basis of a long history widely documented in research contexts and elsewhere in early child care and early education; and because this framework is common to most studies on early learning, it appears to need no justification other than the general welfare of children. Many questions remain unanswered that controlled studies, if not too extreme in varying the quality of social relations, might well begin to probe. A host of variables on play and related motivational techniques could be systematically varied in studies that otherwise followed a common program and methods of stimulation. Among such variables would be degree of task versus play orientation, flexibility in the use of materials and task structure, use of sensorimotor play extraneous to the manipulation of concept exemplars to be mastered, degree of neutrality versus praise in social attitude, and many others.

Inquiry/Problem Orientation

Obviously closely related to the third major domain of cognitive systems, strategies, or styles of functioning, the topic needs little further discussion. Like the concept of motivational techniques, the concept is discussed as a dimension in this context in order to focus more on the properties of cognitive stimulation rather than survey developmental outcomes, the main thrust in the previous chapter.

The basis for an inquiry- or problem-centered approach to stimulation is the assumption of rationality. Activity and learning have as their purpose the solving of problems, becoming familiar with the materials and arrangements of a task or concept area, figuring out how they work and manipulating them for the purposes desired. The process is the same in essence, regardless of the domain (music versus clothing) or its breadth (singing a musical phrase versus understanding or composing a symphony). Underlying the entire process are the primary principles and perspectives of scientific thinking that the material world and all that we do in relation to it operates according to causal principles that can be understood and regulated in predictable though limited ways. Learning and problem solving then are processes of acquiring functional concepts about phenomena to understand how they work and can be utilized. Moreover, each aspect of reality and the tasks we confront in coping are made up of parts and wholes in interrelations and sequence that require analysis and synthesizing of components to identify key elements and how they are or can be functionally interrelated, as in working with the structure of language or a poem, music or a sonata, or geology or a mountain. These are among the primary problem-solving strategies needed for cognitive development.

Inquiry approaches are often pitted against approaches that stress learning knowledge as a body of concepts. The latter is viewed as (sometimes mindless) fact accumulation, rote learning that dulls the senses at best and in any case fails to develop meaningful understanding that can be applied adaptively across a variety of circumstances. This would seem, however, to be something of a pseudoissue, akin to acquiring strategies without a knowledge base, having no information or a body of concepts to which strategies can be applied. Dempster's (1981) review of memory processes indicating that memory span was a function of familiarity is relevant here (see chapter 7).

A body of concepts about a terrain *is* essential to develop competence in an area, whether it is mathematics or rug manufacturing. The expert is highly knowledgeable about the myriad of concepts in a field, as well as in maintaining a rational inquiry approach to anticipating and solving problems as they arise. Although many details must become highly familiar to master a field, learning them need not, indeed should not, be a mindless, rote-learning affair. These details of fact are actually features and processes that are linked functionally as rules belonging to concepts, which are also interrelated into networks, systems, and hierarchies. Rug manufacture will be better mastered if rug sizes are learned as graded series, varying with some regularity in both length and width, rather than as arbitrarily distributed random sets. When applied to young children, learning geometric figures as an arbitrary set is more difficult and less meaningful than learning features that distinguish between triangles, circles, and squares, such as the lack of or type of angularity, straightness of edges (discriminating from nongeometric forms), and the like.

The concept of inquiry is related to the idea of logical sequencing, but since domains have broad areas of concepts interrelated horizontally, an approach that recognizes the importance of analyzing and interrelating features and functions may be more important than establishing a rigorous order of steps in a hierarchy. Inquiry presupposes logical analysis but not a determined order.

Most experimental investigations on early learning took definite account of the principle of inquiry orientation. It is especially clear that the early-intervention programs for the disadvantaged were manifestly working on developing children's understanding, not simply on fact accumulation. If anything, the opposite problem may have occurred, as was apparent in the dearth of programs that engaged children in learning information concepts, though the use of common social materials (clothes, food, selected furniture) in daily activities may have partially made up for this comparative exclusion. All programs were above all vitally concerned with helping poor children from folk communities, in which opportunities to understand the nature of things from the rational perspectives of science was paramount. How and why things worked was the focus. Even the so-called drill type program of Bereiter and Engelmann (1966, 1968) was in fact highly precise in its analysis of the fabric of commonly employed language and other concept domains. Contingency-governed behavior-modification programs, even when relying on extrinsic, material reinforcement, are equally as rational and problem centered as other Piagetian and similar cognitively oriented programs. The reinforcement serves as a signal and as information feedback, as well as a reward that tells the child she or he has the right explanation for how things work, in the same manner that social reinforcement such as praise works. There appears to have been little systematic difference between programs in the goals of facilitating understanding and inquiring into what makes things tick.

On the other hand the issue may pivot around not simply the question of a rational orientation and inducing understanding but of teaching the child to inquire autonomously, closely related to the goals of fostering initiative and experimentation in play. This presumably requires an active investigatory role on the part of the child, which in turn presupposes a curriculum format that opens possibilities for alternative concepts and problem solutions. Unfortunately the existing early-training literature sheds little light on the question. Neither the degree of child initiative encouraged (form of interaction) nor the amount of structural programming seem to have made a substantial difference, as we have seen, and except for Palmer's (1972) related concept-directed versus discovery program, no regular comparisons seem to have been implemented. Again, even if we ignore the confounding of differences in curriculum substance and degree of child initiative with the dimension of inquiry in Palmer's discovery versus programmed approaches, differences appeared only in the short run, only on the particular concept-inventory measures, and were against the impact of inquiry discovery orientation. The long-term differences Beller (1974, 1980) found from reflectiveness style training, it may be pointed out, were differences between groups that varied on a multiplicity of general cognitive-stimulation variables as well. Finally, it might be well to note that many approaches to early intervention and other early-education programs that organize even tightly programmed curricula have not necessarily ruled out inquiry about alternatives. In behavioral-modification programs reinforcement is typically contingent upon child-initiated operants for any one of a variety of exemplars of a *class* of concepts or behaviors (Thoreson 1973), and similar programs with well-defined behavior objectives work with a range of alternative materials to represent the same concepts (Resnick, Wang, and Rosner 1977).

The small-scale studies add little knowledge to our understanding. As in our scrutiny of differences between developmental outcomes for sequencing, whether or not there was room for the child to inquire about the nature of the phenomena seems to have made little difference. There was, however, generally a difference between the organization of these small-scale programs and the organization of the general cognitive-stimulation programs for disadvantaged and advantaged alike. The concept goals of the small stimulation programs were characteristically spelled out in advance. The investigators have almost by definition been trying to test the child's ability to learn specific concepts and skills, such as singing, cube manipulation, memory for digits, maze tracing, form concepts, swimming, conservation, and the like, as opposed to the goal of facilitating verbal and cognitive development in general. The aims have often included comparing learning under different conditions, especially with respect to variations in age, but also across materials, as with the Piagetian studies employing a variety of materials (Brainerd 1977, 1978) and Ling (1971) experimenting with different exemplars of form, Jersild and Bienstock (1931, 1934), Foster (1928), and Burtt (1932) using a series of songs, stories, and Greek passages, respectively, and Ling with position as well. Yet most variations have provided little room for the child to pursue alternative routes. The set of exemlars has in fact usually been tightly programmed, though not logically sequenced. The same songs, stories, Greek passages, digit series, conservation materials and geometric forms were employed for all children and in a constant order.

More room for maneuver was generally evident in the motor and language learning activities. The former often offered opportunities to manipulate the materials in play, as noted above, or to approach the task in the child's own way, and sometimes include variations in the setting, as in Johnny's opportunities to practice in different sections of the hospital (McGraw 1935). Except for the highly programmed phoneme-word learning sequence of Schvarchkin (cited in Ervin and Miller 1963:111), the latter were all rather broad and flexible in scope. Luria and Yudovich's (1959) approach centered on inquiring, though with definite grammatical rules, and Dawe (1942), Strayer (1930), and the others all involved a great deal of open-ended interaction, which in the case of Koltsova (cited in Brackbill 1960, 1962) centered on sensorimotor-language play with picture blocks. Problem-solving tasks also provided ample opportunity for the child to inquire on his or her own, picking various solutions through trial and error in a door-opening task (Roberts 1932) or a lever-pulling task (Richardson 1934), for example. Dubin's (1946) experiment in stimulating drawing skills was perhaps the most open-ended, inasmuch as not only the form of the exemplars, but the concepts the child chose to represent were her or his own, except as influenced by experimenter inquiry and comment. Yet greater structuring does not seem to have hampered investigators from realizing the goals specified, and greater opportunity for inquiry cannot really be said to have made a difference, as much as one can compare across programs and conditions.

The problem here as elsewhere, however, is that the child's inquiry strategies have never been measured in any of these studies, either in the short or the long term. It is also quite conceivable that the more cut-and-dried programs, while developing the skills in question, may have impeded the child's ability to transfer concepts to other areas or tasks. Again, this has not been measured, though the varying amounts of transfer evident in the short-term Piagetian training studies might be shown to be related to variations in the range of exemplars employed. Few small scale studies have made use of more than a very limited set of stimulation materials, however.

Inquiry orientation is really the opposite side of the coin from programming and sequencing. Both may be useful or even sometimes essential for the development of significant skills and concept mastery, but can both be accommodated? Is there a balance that can be struck between the two? One way, of course, is to stress the different aspects in separate learning tasks or programs. Although it should probably be tested, this solution might lead to a certain compartmentalization. Children might fail to apply the acquired inquiry strategies in the domains of knowledge in which they had been strongly programmed without inquiry. In the short run there may well be social tasks to be learned where the value is on the skill alone, such as dressing and table manners. For the most part, however, the logic of inquiry would suggest that broader, more cognitively adaptive modes of mental processing and skills acquired through inquiry modes, are preferable for the vital areas of knowledge, like language, literature, and science.

The root of the matter is that there are common, culturally agreed upon concepts in all realms, from the culturally trivial world of custom and manners to the most abstract and scientific, which must become part of the child's repertoire in order for her or him to become cognitively well socialized. Dimensions of magnitude, conservation, the number system, language, and the graphic code all operate with finite sets and hierarchies of concepts that must be learned. New discoveries and inventions appear from time to time, but children do not contribute to these cultural innovations that, as Bruner (1965) once observed, are the product of the well-prepared mind. Discovery and invention are the realm of the highly skilled scientist, musician, writer, and artist. Yet the fact that certain bodies of knowledge, codes, and strategies must be learned, does not preclude inquiry as a basic dimension of cognitive development. Indeed it is one of the basic strategies in our model for cognitive development (see table 5-1). Stimulating the child to be oriented to rational explanation, to search for problems and solutions, and even to search for alternatives can easily be integral to mastering each of the relevant specific concepts (circularity, hats) and bodies of knowledge (geometry, clothes). All that is required even when programming or logical sequencing is employed, is to ensure, first, that a variety of materials with different exemplars are built into the activities, preferably setting up many different perspectives, situations, and conditions; second, to indicate that these are not the only alternatives; and, third, to ensure that there is plenty of opportunity for the children themselves to manipulate material so as to make inferences on their own. The last is less simple of course, since closely directing the child's learning might at first glance seem to accentuate the process of concept mastery at the expense of experimentation. But interacting with the child in joint inquiry may pay off in the long run, freely allowing for the child to initiate and experiment by generating broad-ranging, creative skills for solving problems and even, perhaps, producing a more elaborate mastery of the programmed concepts in question.

Cognitive Breadth

The inclusion of a rich variety of examples or exemplars and encouraging the child to explore alternative arrangements and routes to the same problem is closely allied with the question of the breadth of knowledge the child develops. The greater the number of examples and the more varied the routes, the broader the cognitive grasp of a field. Multiplying the number of exemplars might be said to widen perspectives, however, while an increase in alternatives, at least within certain limits, may simply involve rearranging the same material to accomplish equivalent goals and thus is a matter of deepening rather than broadening one's grasp of a sector of knowledge. Yet working with alternatives by developing a strategy of analyzing and comparing, should presumably create a disposition toward wider horizons in one's thinking.

The breadth of one's knowledge can extend all the way from familiarity with every domain under the sun to knowledge and skill of nothing except one narrow corner of a single field. The legendary skills of idiot savants in calculation skills that may encompass only the ability to mentally manipulate calendar dates or square roots, but not both, or to vocally imitate any melody but not sing on one's own (Anastasi 1958; Duckett 1976; Fowler 1962a) illustrate the second extreme, while Aristotle and Leonardo da Vinci (the Renaissance person) illustrate something of the scope of the first. Historically, in Western industrial society, the goal of general education has been held up as the ideal, culminating in the liberal arts curriculum in the college or university, in which the cultivated individual should at least be conversant with the ideas of all fields, from science and philosophy to the arts and humanities. This perspective perhaps underlies the concept of general intelligence that cuts across all fields and is rooted historically in the biological concepts of preformationism and, later on, of predetermined intellectual development (Hunt 1961). But it also harks back to the folk world of nonspecialization and slow variation. The age of the specialist is upon us, however, and whatever the role of general ability (g) in cognitive functioning, it is clear that a great deal of the contribution to competence is made up of a variety of specific abilities (s) that develop differentially to an important degree, through experience with the concepts and skills of various domains and tasks. How broad and how specialized should experience be in human development? The general and liberal education ideal, after all, encompassed the concept of a major field, but the specialization of trades and professions that grew up with the first founding of hierarchical societies, seems to have led to an extraordinary concentration of skill development in many occupations and inidividuals. Yet the technological world we inhabit also places increasing demands on our competence from the ever-widening bodies of information with which we are daily bombarded.

There are a number of components to the problem of breadth. Domains themselves vary in breadth, ranging from the broad sweep of world history, geology and transportation systems to knowledge of the history of a place, of a particular mountain, or of a particular boat. Knowledge of codes and strategies may also vary in scope, from competence in cross-cultural linguistics to knowledge of a dialect or even of the verb alone, and from the nature of cognitive strategies to knowledge about stamp collecting strategies. Bruner and his associates (Bruner et al. 1956) and Gardner and his colleagues (Gardner et al. 1959) have conceptualized differences between individuals on the basis of the number of exemplars they encompass within their conceptions of a cognitive class or category, the former group using the term *category width* and the latter group *equivalence range* for the dimension defining the differences in cognitive style. In Gardner's work individuals embracing a narrower band of exemplars tended to employ more detailed and precise standards for inclusion, those embracing a broader spectrum were likely to use looser, less-precise criteria for inclusion. The differences amount to variations in the breadth of one's knowledge horizons.

Breadth of knowledge or competence need not mean superficiality, however, as is sometimes supposed and reflected in the homily about "Jack of all trades, master of none." Nor is the opposite true, that narrowness implies limited complexity, even as the Gardner observations suggest. Both developments can probably be of a surface kind, involving meaningless sweeps (broad sorters) or trivial detail (narrow sorters), or be highly complex in the intricacy of concept networks grasped, though there are perhaps limits to how narrow a focus may be and remain complex. Cross-cultural linguistics obviously involves comparing complex rule structures of many languages and affiliated linguistic communities, but knowledge of a specific dialect leads one into the intricacies of a structure and how it functions under different conditions unlikely to be developed by the cross-cultural linguist. On the other hand great knowledge and competence about a particular boat might involve a great deal of painstaking pedantry in record-keeping about trips, races, passengers, fuel-speed ratios, repairs, and remodeling that may be detailed, but unlikely to match the intricacies of familiarity with differential organization, functions, efficiencies, usages, and history of types of transport. We may nevertheless assume that knowledge, whether great or small in scope, can vary enormously in complexity.

The traditional opposition in which breadth and depth of knowledge is placed may thus be something of a pseudoproblem. In the nature of things, matter and structures are endlessly complex, whether one compares across a vast range of domains or explores in detail the local microsphere. In both cases one is often led as well into different levels of analysis that draw one into acquiring knowledge of other fields.

Since there are undoubtedly limits to human capacities, however, varying from individual to individual, choosing to be complex in many domains is quite likely to mean less-particularized complexity of development in any component hierarchy. Competence across a broad range of mathematical fields is likely to result in integrative or comparative contributions, perhaps equally complex, but quite different from the contributions of the specialist in linear equations. And great artists and great scientists are unlikely to be, and have in fact seldom been equally competent in one another's terrain (Cox 1926; Snow 1964).

The question about cognitive breadth then comes down to two questions, the social value of concentration versus scope and the fact that which path one follows may have implications for later development. Assuming that cognitive complexity is determined to an important degree by the cumulative effects of stimulation, how broad or wide an arc of complexity is developed may be rooted in early experience. Experience in one domain equips one better for pursuing competence in that domain, or, as Scott (1968) puts it, organizes one's system to process further and more easily material in that realm. It is partly a matter of repetition. Continuing experience in a domain such as language exposes the child to repeated use of the basic concepts already familiar, which become better mastered, second nature or integral to automatic operations that free him or her for more advanced learning. It is not repetition alone, however, but building up an ever more complex hierarchy of knowledge and skill in a certain direction, earlier concepts serving as modules to facilitate learning and problem solving with the increasingly more advanced members of an hierarchy. Whatever the mechanisms, we must consider such questions in any decisions we make about the forms of early stimulation in which the child is engaged for substantial periods. How has the literature approached this question?

It is obvious that the history of research on early learning has moved in two opposed directions, reflecting a polarity of goals on breadth versus specialization. On the one hand is the socially governed trend of early-education and early-intervention research with programs and special populations, beginning with studies on the effects of nursery-school attendance in the 1920s and 1930s, followed by the large-scale efforts to educate institutionally deprived and socioeconomically disadvantaged children and more recently the studies of children in day care. Early stimulation in these programs, as we have noted, has been uniformly directed toward generalized types of cognitive stimulation. While in fact varying in certain definite ways—the socioemotional, sensorimotor-play orientation following the developmental philosophy of the nursery school versus the stress on verbal abstraction geared to school learning in the later early intervention research versus the child-care functions stressed in day care—the conception and goals in each case have always been broad and general in scope. The developmental outcomes of such broad cognitive stimulation sweeps on disadvantaged populations, which has the most extensive literature, are correspondingly broad in their scope. The short-term gains have encompassed a variety of academically based language and mathematical skills in logical abstraction and reasoning, which have tended to fade with time in the long run in their more abstract IQ-test form, but have persisted to varying degrees in the functional abilities measured by school achievement and coping.

The outcomes from both nursery programs and day care are less certain. There have been few differences favoring program children over children reared entirely at home, either for the short or long term (they have not been measured in the long term for day care), with the exception of two highly cognitively oriented day-care programs by the author (Fowler 1972, 1978a) and, more generally, of moderate short-term advantages for children in day care from disadvantaged backgrounds or for institutionally reared children (Anastasi 1958; Anastasi and Foley 1949; Belsky and Steinberg 1978; Rubenstein and Howes 1979; Wellman 1945).

While the modest gains or lack of gains in the nursery-school and day-care programs have been largely attributed to the poor match between the broad child-care, child-development goals (socioemotional, sensorimotor, play) of the programs and the verbal-logical abstract functions reflected in IQ tests, some of the problem is perhaps inherent in the broadness of the approach. Programs that attempt to do everything are unlikely to produce concentrated effects in any single area. The problem is similar with the early-intervention research, despite the program shift in emphasis toward the verbal abstraction of IQ tests and the schools. The effect of the disadvantaged folk commmunity pushing development in a different direction from the abstractions of the school curriculum only serves to compound the problem. The broad set of skills acquired in broad programs, generally never outstanding (compared to general norms), are at best only modestly sustained when not actively undermined by the ecology of the community and the weaknesses of the schools poor children characteriscally attend (Gross and Gross 1969; Silberman 1970).

On the other hand the small-scale research on early stimulation, whether short or long in duration, has been uniformly directed at more focused or narrower forms of processes. Much of it is task focused, concentrated on a highly limited set of motor, memory, or problem solving tasks, such as cube manipulation, walking boards, memorizing digits, or pulling a string or opening a door to obtain a lure (Munn 1954). Many of these tasks might well have more generalized consequences for cognitive development, at least across the domain in which the task is embedded (motor), but as we know, most of the studies have been short term and also have not measured skills more broadly. The more recent research on training young children in formal concepts in the Piagetian mold (Brainerd 1977, 1978), while more cognitively based and indicating selective transfer effects (and thus potentially promising), remain short term without follow-up and without consideration of developmental processes outside selected Piagetian concepts of concrete operations. The relative ease with which such concepts have been induced years in advance of age norms with only a handful of training sessions, moreover, raises questions of whether such concepts are as broad and generalized as Piagetian theory would suggest.

But what of the exceptions: those that pursued learning more in depth and time on a set of interrelated skills broadly across a domain, and sometimes measured later developmental effects? Among such studies are Ling's (1941) study of geometric forms, Welch's (1939a-c) on magnitude, Jersild and Bienstock's (1931, 1934) and Updegraff, Heiliger, and Learned's (1938) on singing, Dubin's (1941) on drawing, McGraw's (1935) and Mirenva's (1935) on gross-motor skills, several language-stimulation studies (Luria and Yudovich 1959), and a few others. All of these resulted in impressive effects on the infants' or young children's development, effects directly linked to the training and quite functional and more generalized than the effects typically found in the narrower, short-term studies. Children displayed refined discrimination of magnitude concepts, broad perception of geometric forms, or greatly improved ability to sing, draw, perform multiple gross-motor skills, or better language competencies, according to the thrust of the programs. Some of the studies did not really involve a broad set of skills. For example, Ling embraced only geometric forms, Welch a variety of exemplars of form and area, and Mirenva no more than two interrelated gross-motor skills (throwing and rolling balls at targets), but all produced generalized effects.

But while these studies may indicate considerable potential for advancing developmental norms in skills of some breadth, few of them included precise follow-up assessments to determine what and how generalized the long-term developmental effects might be. Those that did demonstrated, for example, that in music, gains remained after two years (Jersild and Bienstock), and in gross-motor processes certain specific skills remained after four years and a comparatively generalized gross-motor competence remained as late as age 22 (McGraw). Almost none of the highly promising, language-focused early-stimulation studies were followed up, unfortunately. The best is the Carter (1966; Carter and Capobianco 1976) study of children at age 6, in which the original language gains generalized to IQ scores and other aspects of school achievement, mainly in language-involved areas, gains that were generally maintained to almost age fourteen. There is also the substantial body of literature on early reading, which frequently shows high early mastery in advance of norms between ages 2 and 5 and for many studies continued advancement over norms throughout the early years of schooling. These advantages were more characteristic of children taught at home, however, where children appeared to have consolidated their mastery more and probably continued to enjoy the support of an academically oriented ambiance of the home throughout the school years. In many cases, moreover, stimulation was probably, though not always, more generalized than learning to read (often included language, math, writing and general cognitive concepts). The child's developmental ecology has too rarely been traced in early-stimulation studies, however, and in fact the McGraw study is the only investigation in which something about the intervening ecology is reported: there was no definite follow-up support for the twin Johnny's early-induced skills in either the home or the community.

This highly tentative evidence that stimulating interrelated skills across a domain may be more effective than stimulating isolated skills in limited tasks is further supported by the cumulative effects apparently emerging from the series of co-twin control investigations conducted over a period of several years on the same pair of twins by Gesell and his students. There was evidence that twin T, who was almost always trained earlier, developed small gross-motor and other selective advantages over her control twin C through adolescence, and that both twins gained cumulatively from the training series in general cognitive skills assessed by IQ tests for several years following the training (Gesell and Thompson 1941). (See chapter 4 for details.) Several of the co-twin series involved related motor skills, and language and cognitive processing were constant general enrichment aspects of training in all studies, supplementing the vocabulary stimulation of Strayer's (1930) original language-training study.

It might seem at first glance that the long-term results of both the Burtt (1932, 1937, 1941) and Smith (1935, 1951, 1963) studies on verbal memory contradict this general trend in favor of the value of a certain breadth to cognition stimulation. The answer may lie in the very extended period of training, twenty-one months for Burtt's son (age 15-36 months) and five years in Smith's case (age 8-13), in which extensive repetition (and mastery for Smith) of the same material was extraordinary. The Piagetian object-permanence and concrete-operational training studies, though apparently narrower than Piagetian theory assumes, were cognitively more functional than the relatively fleeting, isolated and arbitrary skills stimulated in the earlier short-term studies of the descriptive behaviorist era. This cognitive integration may be the basis of the tendency for learning to generalize to closely related formal-concept skills that find currency in daily life, and apparently fade less than the isolated less-cognitive functional skills of the earlier era. It is too early to tell before the scope of Piagetian skills is better established and extended follow-ups are undertaken.

It is reasonable to suppose that stimulation directed functionally at concept development, rather than at task competence alone, and particularly when embracing skills involving a set of concepts drawn from a common hierarchy, might prove to have greater impact on cognitive development, especially for the long term. The changes should be more relevant and potent for current functioning and therefore contribute to ease in making significant further advances in development in that domain over longer periods, much as Harlow's (1949) original studies on interproblem learning in monkeys showed. Yet, prolonged stimulation, even if narrowly based, isolated, relatively task oriented, and only slightly intense (the Burtt and Smith studies), can apparently produce remarkably persisting effects as well. But certain developmental effects may also persist for many years at the other extreme, when the early stimulation is broadly based, as long as it is cognitively functional and continues over some reasonably extended time span of, say, a year or more, even when moving in opposition to many forces in the child's ecology, as in the multitude of early-intervention studies on socioeconomically disadvantaged children from folk communities. The consistently successful outcomes of the cognitively oriented intervention studies of the post-World War II period contrast sharply with the indeterminate effects realized by the pre-World War II nursery-school attendance studies, in which play and social relations were stressed more than intellectual development, and with the effects of the amorphous day-care programs as well. The broad-based stimulation effects are greater, and possibly longer lasting at higher levels, when stimulation is more intensive and continued over prolonged periods of early development, as in the Heber and Garber study. There is an obvious need for systematic investigations, in which the scope and depth of the hierarchy of concepts is controlled, along with other dimensions like intensity and duration. In this context organizing stimulation in terms of cognitively functional categories that are moderate in breadth and constructed with an interrelated set of concepts from a single domain (language, gross- or fine-motor coding, formal concepts, interrelated body of knowledge like mammals, insects, or transportation) seems a promising avenue of research to pursue.

Ecology and Context

The possiblity that the child's ecology, the pattern of relations and supports that characterize the child's primary milieu of the family, community, and school, may exert profound and pervasive influences on the child's cognitive development has been a recurring theme cropping up at many points throughout the book. Ecology is constructed of several components we shall attempt to explain, to sketch how planned early-learning experiences may interact with background environmental forces over the course of development. Because of the restricted character of the evidence, however, we are confined to the same cautions in drawing conclusions that we have met in analyzing the impact of other dimensions of developmental stimulation.

It is possible to divide the ecology into a number of levels and types of factors that could influence the child's development for good or ill (Bronfenbrenner 1977, 1979) with respect to development in general and to the developmental outcomes of early stimulation programs in particular. One major division in levels is between the macrolevels of the milieu and community, including general socioeconomic factors, and the microlevels of the child's particular relations with family members, teachers, and peers. Within this framework there are such factors as the quality of socioemotional relations, the quality, intensity, and types of cognitive stimulation, financial circumstances and needs, physical circumstances, health and physical development, including handicaps. Few of these factors can be reviewed in detail because the influence of the ecology has seldom been treated at all in experimental studies of early stimulation, let alone separately. Early-intervention studies with the institutionally deprived and with poor children from folk backgrounds are exceptions, but much of the concern is addressed to the respective general conditions of deprivation and life in poor folk communities, rather than specific factors. There are also little data on questions of health, physical development or handicap as they relate to early stimulation.

It is perhaps quite reasonable that general conditions have been the main concern, despite the fact that individual differences in modes of child care, stimulation, and cognitive development probably vary widely in the various poor folk groups in industrial societies (Anastasi 1958; Clarke-Steward 1973; Giovannoni and Billingsley 1971; Riessman 1962), if possibly not quite so much among institutionalized children (Dennis, 1960a, 1973; Flint, 1966; Hunt et al. 1976) or among folk groups in tribal societies (Fowler and Fowler 1978). Whatever the role of specific factors, the general patterns of the ecology appear to exercise pervasive effects on the average levels and forms of skills of the groups. In other words, matrices of socioeconomic conditions and accompanying cognitive and interpersonal patterns interact to produce a general phenomenon of cognitive deprivation or difference with respect to the typical academic goals espoused for the early-intervention programs. Although certain specific factors have been identified, such as caregiver/child ratios in institutions (Hunt et al. 1976) and unemployment among the disadvantaged (Beller 1980), given general stimulation programs at variance with the multifaceted conditions and patterns of both institutional or folk socialization, the importance of the general conditions as a set is likely to outweigh the influence of any component in the set. We shall briefly summarize the general effects reviewed in preceding chapters, singling out the influence of specific factors where they have been identified in the various studies or appear to play a role in studies that include, but do not analyze in detail, background data on ecology.

The evidence with regard to disadvantaged folk children and to some extent with institutionally deprived children is quite clear. Early cognitive stimulation, either preventively from early infancy or remedially beginning with the preschool years, can significantly alter the different cognitive patterns characteristically associated with these groups in the short run, in the direction of abstract verbal reasoning and school skill patterns stressed in the intervention programs. Generally speaking, a year or two of planned early cognitive stimulation, whether occurring at age 3 or 4, in the preschool range, or the 1-3 infant range, moves the general IQ and related cognitive levels from 70 to 90 IQ toward the general population averages (90-110 IQ) for our industrial society. But these gains seldom attain the above average levels (110-130 IQ) typical of children from advantaged middle-class backgrounds in the mainstream of the majority culture. When the specialized cognitive stimulation is particularly intensive, more articulated, and of longer duration, in some combination, levels attained can match the levels normatively attained by children from the more academically oriented upper-middle-class business and professional families, as in the Bereiter and Engelmann (1968; White et al. 1973), Heber and Garber (1972), and Hunt et al. (1976) programs. The first program was highly articulated and intensive, started at age 3 (to produce 30 point IQ gains); the second was from early infancy (before 6 months), intensive, long lasting, and comprehensive; and the third was similar, except that it lasted two years rather than five and one-half. The most reasonable interpretation of this pattern of short-term results is that it reflects the differential impact of early specialized stimulation working at variance with patterns of socialization in residential care institutions and poor folk communities. Let us look in detail at the role of ecology in relation to outcomes in the respective populations.

The Institutional Ecology. In the institutional setting, children have been reared (when and where these studies were executed) under conditions of minimal care from infancy (Dennis 1960a, 1973; Dennis and Najarian 1957; Flint 1966, 1978; Hunt et al. 1976; Skeels 1966). The extremely poor adult/child caregiving ratios and poorly trained staffs, coupled with the priority placed on cleanliness and antisepsis, derived from traditional medically based attitudes regarding health hazards in crowded conditions, resulted in confinement, immobility, and very little perceptual-motor, language, or general cognitive stimulation during the early years. Infants were usually confined to screened cribs, isolated from one another, sometimes on soft mattresses, making turning to a more active-exploratory prone position difficult, and toys were virtually nonexistent—all in the interests of ease in handling and cleaning, and pacification to diminish curiosity, exploration, and demands for attention. Infants were tended only in the course of widely spaced, rigid routines for eating and changing. As infants became mobile, they continued to be marshaled in large groups, furnished with few toys and periods of play, and generally restricted in opportunities for movement and exploration. Patterns of development following socialization under such conditions of privation were generally retarded cognitively (and socioemotionally) in all areas, ranging from lateness in sitting and walking to greatly diminished abilities in language and concept development. Care and development in all residential care institutions have not always been so uniformly bleak (Yarrow 1961), but in studies where preventive or remedial programs have been undertaken the pattern is characteristic.

Given such extreme conditions and depressed patterns of development, improvements in cognitive functioning, in all areas from the most basic sensorimotor (Dennis and Sayegh 1965) to the most abstract verbal and logical cognitive process (Dawe 1942; Dennis 1973; Flint 1966; Skeels 1966) in almost any program were often dramatic and far reaching, the pattern of changes generally following the amount and type of stimulation offered. The greatest gains, however, were in the earliest starting, highly articulated, and relatively long-lasting program initiated by Hunt et al. (1976).

The nature and role of the ecology in all such investiagtions is stark and unambiguous. Under institutional conditions of this sort, cognitive socialization is pervasively understimulating and infants and young children lag markedly in cognitive development. Intervention programs appear then to be a matter of adding stimulation that is commonly available in the ordinary course of development in all cultures. While cultures vary in the types and intensity of stimulation offered in early life (Kagan et al. 1979), few if any cultures appear to be as low on stimulation in any area as institutions are characteristically low in so many. Evidence on conflict between the dynamics and consequences of socialization in the institutional environment and those in planned-intervention programs is not prominent in any of the studies. Rather than conflict, understimulation seems to lead to eager desires to absorb the concepts presented in the special programs, in large part because of the hunger for human attention, personal attachment, and emotional support. But definite interest in the material itself with regard to concept learning is also evident (Dennis 1960a, 1973; Sayegh 1965; Flint 1966; Frumhartz 1970; Hunt et al. 1976). Not all children learn equally well or are equally interested, of course. Privation and rigid handling take their toll in apathy and hyperactive patterns, sometimes in alternation, and, except in Hunt's preventive program, children seldom attain levels usually reached by children reared at home under richly stimulating conditions. The earlier depressed cognitive levels mean problems of acquiring complex concepts on a poorly or sometimes deviantly developed concept base, in which some inefficient patterns and misconceptions must be discarded in favor of new strategies and concept hierarchies (Dennis 1960a; Flint 1966, 1978; Frumharz 1970). The problem, though important, has been too little studied.

Ecology in the Poor Folk Community. The pattern of contrasts between planned stimulation and folk socialization in poor communities in industrial societies is less marked and far more complicated. In the first place the competence patterns have been more varied and less reduced below norms in any skill area in poor folk children than in institutionally reared children. Mean IQ levels, reflecting especially abstract verbal skills, have typically ranged between 80 to 90 before intervention (Bronfenbrenner 1975; White et al. 1973) compared to 50 to 80 in the various studies on institutionally deprived children (Clarke and Clarke 1976; Dawe 1942; Dennis 1973; Skeels 1966). A variety of perceptual-motor competencies, including even acceleration in gross-motor competencies (Williams and Scott 1953), and well-developed language, concept, and social skills that are functionally effective for coping in day-to-day life in the urban ghettoes and similar settings of impoverished folk communities have also been characteristic (Labov 1972; Ogbu 1981; Riesmann 1962, 1964), compared with the grossly generalized retardation often found in institutionally reared children. A rich and varied emotional life similarly contrasts sharply with the chronic depression or apathy developing in the impersonal and often cold and sterile atmosphere of understaffed institutions.

At the same time, the very existence of this alternative set of competencies and coping skills is at once a psychological resource to draw on and an obstacle to acquiring the kind of abstract, generalized competencies that comprise the bulk of the planned early-intervention curricula. The alternative competencies develop in the first place out of the kinds of demands for coping under the harsh circumstances of social and economic life, the cluster of problems and strategies rooted in endemic poverty and racial, social and class discrimination; the chronic unemployment and employment at low-paying, menial jobs that lead nowhere; the stigma of alleged inferiority; the enforced idleness and boredom leading to fantasy, invention, and fierce and violent competition for unevenly distributed short-term rewards wrested from others; the broken and poorly organized but intensely cooperative and personalized family and community living; and the coping, catch as catch can from moment to moment, punctuating endless want, without perspective and hope for career or complex skill development, but with warm personal relations, periodic celebrations, makeshift feasts, drugs, and other forms of transitory relief. Whatever else life in a folk community for poor blacks and other ethnic minorities may be, it is not a life of uniform bleakness, depression, and retardation, but a life of alternating struggle, despair, cooperation, and colorful and tragic drama, always close to the personal and the concrete.

Thus the skills that are socialized are adaptive to the concrete and the immediate and geared toward conceptions and strategies that are flexible and manipulative to deal with the constant uncertainty, few rewards, and extensive buffeting and suffering marking the struggle for survival in a hostile, unyielding environment. Directness, mobility, and invention in movement; perception, verbal narrative, and interchange; and social relations find expression in experiences that fluctuate widely between cooperative networks of the extended family and temporary alliances of the street culture on the one hand, and unrelieved competition between individuals, groups, and levels of the various street hierarchies on the other. But if they are the consequence of socialization and the substance for adaptive survival in a poor folk community, such an armamentarium of flexible and imaginative pragmatism, pivoting around the raw reality of daily living, does not blend or give way easily to the abstract generalities, formalities and long-range planning and problem-solving strategies of planned stimulation designed to meet the roles of school and career in the halls of conventional success in industrial society. Deliberateness, delayed gratification, manipulation of abstract categories for long-range purposes and even for play find little use in and directly clash with the concrete press and practical manipulations of daily folk life. The so-called disadvantaged child is caught between the pull of a community and the often illusory promise of a career, while for institutionally reared children the abstract strategies and skills of an intervention program are embedded in what for them is perhaps the nearest thing to a human community they have ever experienced.

Comparison of Developmental Outcomes. It is not so much in the short run or in the immediate conflict between rational programs and original setting that findings diverge, however. Early stimulation of both institutionally reared and folk-reared poor children seems to produce roughly equivalent results, suggesting the high malleability of children for change during the early phases of development. The abstract cognitive skills of children from both backgrounds typically approach general population levels in most early programs, reaching around 90-100 IQ and the equivalent in all areas included in the program, from language to specialized perceptual-motor skills. In the institutionally deprived, skills stimulated may encompass the ordinary gross-motor skills of walking, running, and jumping, which are brought to full development (Dennis 1960a). In selected, more comprehensive programs, ones usually also starting in earliest infancy, like those of Hunt et al. (1976) for the institutionally deprived and Heber et al. (1972) for the disadvantaged, gains may reach well above population averages, to the levels as high as those of the highly advantaged.

But at this point, once the programs terminate, what happens? It is here that the force of the social ecology is exercised with full force to make the difference. Turned back to cope in the folk life of poverty, discrimination, and second-class ghetto schools, children from all programs gradually regress across the board in all academic abstract skills close to the norms for the disadvantaged population, the more abstract (especially IQ) the more pronounced the regression. Even groups of children registering the highest early cognitive levels (120 IQ), are found to follow a similar course of decline (Garber and Heber 1981), considering the shorter interval since program termination—though it is possible further studies and broader measures later in development will show the eventual decline to have been less severe. That the effects of early stimulation can be tenacious in the face of many ecological obstacles is indicated by the persistence over many years of cognitive school-achievement competencies and coping skills attributable to the original program, compared with the children's nonearly-stimulated controls. But the persistence is modest compared to the decline and above all the unrealized potential. And that it is the ecology of poverty at work is increasingly documented by the negative relations reported in chapter 6 between the persistence of early gains and a variety of social factors such as father absence and unemployment (Beller et al. 1980; Shipman 1976).

In contrast the subsequent development of early-stimulated institutionalized children shows no change at all, or if anything a slight rise or definite consolidation of the generalized cogntive skills at or slightly above the magic level of 100 IQ. The difference of course is apparently the direct result of profound differences in the kind of social ecology the two groups inhabit, once the original planned programs expire. While disadvantaged children return to their poor folk life, originally institutionalized children, where follow-up studies are reported, without exception are placed out for adoption in families carefully chosen for their properties of nurturance and socioeconomic stability, where the children continue to thrive and maintain their newly found skills of early childhood (Clarke and Clarke 1976; Dennis 1973; Flint 1978; Skeels 1966). The families may not be notably stimulating cognitively or intellectually ambitious for their adopted children, but they clearly provide the kind of close-knit familial support, affection, and cognitive base that enables the children to continue their development academically and cope in the wider world of community and job life at the level attained through the original, planned-early-stimulation programs.

The effectiveness with which Skeels's classic group of adopted children coped and functioned in adulthood (chapter 4) is characteristic, making a dramatic comparison with the sad later destiny of the comparison group who, never experiencing specialized early stimulation, were for the most part forced to live out their lives in the privation of permanent institutionalization. It is regrettable that children in the Iranian orphanage studied by

Hunt have not been followed up to ascertain how well the unusual superior gains from the planned early stimulation have held up in the supporting ecology of adoptive homes. It might be that the superior levels would persist at that level only in cases where the adoptive home ecology cognitively stimulates children, as well as nurtures and supports them economically, throughout development in the same modes and in the same intensive manner conducted in the original program.

Ecology in Small-Scale Studies. The picture we can sketch from the small-scale studies on early stimulation is more limited. Most of the short-term studies, whether in the classic behaviorist model or the latter-day Piagetian framework, furnish no information about the child's ecology, beyond bare identification of socioeconomic background or culture. About the best we can do is venture a few inferences from the sketchy information occasionally provided in a few of the long-term investigations. There is seldom any reference to whether any circumstances of family life or in the general milieu interfered with or facilitated the child's learning of any of the projected concepts, even when background information is provided. The poor socioeconomic background of Gesell's famous identical twins is referred to a number of times in the various studies with them, but it is never mentioned in relation to possible learning difficulties or advantages, only as the *genetic* outcome associated with the below-average IQ scores (Gesell and Thompson 1941). In one of the few studies where marked learning problems were encountered, Welch (1939c), in his attempt to teach genus-species concepts to institutionally deprived, low-IQ infants, nevertheless apparently failed to take account of the children's background in designing and implementing the program. It may not have been Welch's repetitive methods alone that were responsible for the difficulties in learning, as suggested earlier. His methods after all involved a certain amount of play and seemed to work quite well on length- and width-discrimination learning tasks (see chapter 7), and might have worked in classificatory learning with children from advantaged backgrounds, as the recent studies on infant classifitory skills suggest (Nelson 1973; Ricciuti 1965; Ross 1980).

Among the long-term investigations, only McGraw (1935, 1939) and some of the follow-ups of early reading in the home furnish a few details on home background, though seldom much on what the ecology was like following the early instruction, once the child had entered school. Ling (1941), like so many of the classical early short-term training studies, though continuing stimulation for nine months, furnished no information on context. It is not difficult to surmise, however, that the children of research investigators like Burtt and Smith would experience a continuing life of language and other cognitive activities closely related to the verbal memory activities employed in their respectrive training, though obviously closer for Smith (or her daughter) than for Burtt's son (who was apparently not exposed to Greek meaningfully at any time); or that Jersild and Bienstock's nursery-school children might find continuing support for their early advanced singing competence that would maintain their advantage over a period of years.

In the case of early readers taught at home, the family probably supports the child's continuing development in reading and other academic areas (compared to the relatively random background of children taught to read early in special school programs). The ecology of the home appeared to be a major source of persistence for the early developed skills. In early reading in the context of the school, gains persisted only when the school itself restructured its own ecology to provide specialized support and stimulation to sustain the early advantage, as in the case of the individualized reading programs developed through the elementary school years in the McKee et al. (1966) and Ulrich et al. (1971) and Wang et al. (1980) studies. The last-named study, it will be recalled, is one of the few where disadvantaged children continued to progress above general population norms in reading and math achievement as far as the third grade. The program was more closely detailed and individualized with respect to school skills than in many follow-through programs (Miller and Dyer 1975; Seitz et al. 1981).

Slightly more information was provided by McGraw (1935, 1939) about the early home relations and follow-up conditions of the twins Johnny and Jimmy. Their essentially, modest lower-middle-class background provided little special stimulation of any kind at home, except with respect to the family's efforts in the course of the special training Johnny underwent to provide the untrained twin, Jimmy, compensatory gross-motor activities during intervals at home. The training was limited, however. There was no consistent program, nor did it cover the range of skills in which Johnny was stimulated at the lab. The parents tended to downgrade Johnny's status and achievements. Another measure of how the planned training was at variance with home practice appears in the lack of opportunity for either twin to practice most skills learned between training and follow-up at age 6, and presumably to age 22. There was, for example, no opportunity to swim, dive, or roller skate, though they did occasionally ride a bike. However, the mode of play in the community around the twins' neighborhood would suggest that opportunities for gross-motor skill activity in a variety of areas were not lacking, though specific information is missing. In this case the highly intensive and prolonged training in a total environment was able to work for skill development in Johnny in some ways similar to the manner general abstract cognitive skills develop in disadvantaged children in planned center-based programs, despite the absence of strong support in the home and community ecology. On the other hand, although the community ecology failed to provide support for the specific skills acquired, the family values and neighborhood life probably furnished more background support for the sort of general motor competence, in which Johnny but not Jimmy had been developed through the specific skill training across a variety of interrelated skills.

The persistence of a slight edge in motor competence and selected functional language skills (vocabulary, pronunciation) for Gesell's twin T as late as adolescence (Gesell and Thompson 1941) might be similarly attributable to the consonance of these skills, particularly the motor skills, with the lower-class patterns of life. On the other hand the general rise in cognitive skills indicated by the IQ's rising to average levels following the repeated experience with cognitive guidance in specific training tasks, would be expected to revert (as they did) to earlier below-average levels (around 90 IQ), over subsequent years in a generally unstimulating, nonacademic home ecology.

Conclusions

It would appear in sum that planned early stimulation can contravene the direction in which the ecology of the home and community has led or is currently leading the child. Stimulation will take the child in different directions according to the type of program followed, either specifically in a relatively narrow focus (geometric form concepts, verbal memory), across a domain (singing, gross motor), or on a broad set of cognitive skills (IQ, language). The earlier (infancy) and hence the more preventive the program, in which planned competencies get founded before the competing competencies of the normal ecology of the home and community or institution become well established, the more pronounced the effects or greater the levels attained in the area or areas stimulated, though later (preschool) markedly intensive efforts may produce very substantial if not totally equivalent effects. The later the adoption, for example, the less effective the recovery from institutional deprivation, yet the original remedial Bereiter and Engelmann (1966, 1968) program, for which there is regrettably no good follow-up produced very high IQ levels (120+ IQ) as late as age 3 (Hunt 1975; Weikart 1969; White et al. 1973).

Such dimensions of early stimulation as the orientation toward inquiry and rational problem solving, flexible interaction, logical sequencing (or at least programming), and provision for arousing and sustaining interest through play, social support and reinforcement, all appear to be common to most programs, but are not universal. When minimized—especially, logical sequencing and open-ended inquiry—the amount if not the quality of concepts and cognitive strategies acquired does not appear to be greatly affected. Intrinsic versus extrinsic reinforcement appears to be a completely optional matter whose impact, like that of most dimensions, has never really been tested in well-controlled long-term developmental learning studies. Program duriation, also yet to be thoroughly tested, needs redefining in terms of a framework of the time and methods necessary to generate learning in a related set of concepts in a hierarchy. It is the process of acquiring competencies to the point of functioning that is important, rather than time of exposure to stimulation alone. Interactions between intensity, type of interaction, and concept complexity, and the role they may play in the child's life situation also need to be studied in detail.

If the direction and amount of learning can be altered quite easily in early life, without the support of or even against the flow of the ecology, through the operation of planned early stimulation, the long-term role of the extended ecology is quite another matter. When the originally accelerated or advanced skills persist in something close to the early advanced form for more than a few weeks or months, the ecology invariably appears to have played a significant role. Wherever fading or some sort of decline sets in, functional disuse or lack of support or even direct conflict (the disadvantaged) with the early achievements appears to be at work. There are no cases of competence continuing at the same level without some degree of continuing functional advantage and support.

9

Cognitive Precocity

Children develop abilities at different rates. Some acquire skills slower than average, others at average rates, and still others more rapidly than average. Variations in ability are not clustered sharply by levels but are continuously distributed across the spectrum of complexity. A high concentration of numbers appears in the middle range, the more extreme the variation from the norm, the fewer the number of cases. The significance of these extremes is not found in the deviations in rates of development alone, however, but in the status of the final outcomes in later life. Between the ages 3 and 6 the abstract abilities measured by IQ tests begin to predict later abilities at age 18 rather substantially (r = .46-.82, Bayley 1949). The later development of children's abilities may vary quite markedly, of course, fluctuating from period to period with the vicissitudes of life they encounter. McCall, Appelbaum, and Hogarty (1973) found, for example, in their longitudinal study of mental development that the average amount of IQ change between 2½ and 17 was 28.5 points, one in three children changing more than 30 points up or down. Planned-stimulation programs beginning early in life can drastically improve the IQ and other abilities of institutionalized, deprived children, bringing them to at least normal levels, and early intervention with poor children from folk communities can substantially alter their functioning in abstract, school-related skills. Early deprivation and recovery and alterations in the form of children's skill profiles through stimulation have been widely demonstrated.

Developmental Stability and
Earliness of Stimulation

Less well known is the trend among highly precocious children to maintain the high IQ abilities acquired early. One of the most systematic pieces of evidence of this stability comes from the large, lifelong developmental investigation of Terman and his associates (Burks, Jensen, and Terman 1930; Terman 1925; Terman and Oden 1947, 1959) of children Terman called geniuses (Genetic Studies of Genius), who would now be called gifted children. The mean IQs of the original sample of well over 1,000 children have remained remarkably stable, declining only slightly more than 10 points from the early Binet IQ mean of 151 ($\overline{X}$ age 9.7, N = 1,070), to 139

357

($\overline{X}$ age 16, $N = 54$), to 140 ($\overline{X}$ age 28, $N = 954$), to 137 ($\overline{X}$ age 40, $N = 1,004$), thirty years later at midlife. (An adult IQ measure, the Concept Mastery Test, whose equivalence with the Binet was independently established, was employed for the measurement at ages 28 and 40. The mean IQ at age 16 (greatly reduced in sample size to $N = 54$ because of test age limits) was believed by Terman to be slightly reduced by ceiling effects. The mean of this diminished sample at 9-11 had been 148 (compared to 151 at 9-7 for the total sample of 1,070).

Historically the concepts of genius and high ability were often associated with mental disturbance, as in Lombroso's famous work on "Genius and Insanity" (1891). The serious investigation of the development of superior abilities, which began in this century with the IQ test, has long since disproved any automatic linkages of this sort. In fact the picture is quite the opposite. Subjects in the Terman series, for example, and indeed in virtually all studies, have been generally much better adjusted socially and emotionally, both as children and adults, as well as more successful in their career development than the generality of the population in industrial society (Miles 1954).

What can be made of this combination of the precocious development of abstract verbal abilities in some children, their relative stability, and accompanying better than average social adaptation? Earlier views obviously looked no further for answers than heredity and predeterminism, believing brightness to be the product of biology just as they believed biology was the primary determinant of ordinary and retarded development. Hollingworth (1926, 1942), Terman (1905, 1915, 1919), and Witty (1930, 1940), among the leading investigators during the first half of the century during the formative period for the investigation of superior abilities, all placed most of the weight on heredity, in the same manner as Gesell and the early developmentalists. Indeed innateness is inherent in the mystery implied by the widely employed term *gifted*. The disproportionately high proportion of precocious children regularly appearing among the highly educated classes did not disturb these investigators (Miles 1954; Gowan 1977). The proportion of children whose father's occupation was professional or semiprofessional was typically around 80 percent or more, for example, 81.4 percent in Terman's famous study, 82.6 percent in Root's (1921) study of fifty-three "supernormal" children, and 78 percent in Freeman's (1979) study of eighty-two children with a mean IQ of 155. They found this pattern, together with the high representation of majority ethnic groups, quite in keeping with their beliefs in the inherent superiority of populations of Anglo-Saxon and other northern European backgrounds (Kamin 1974). They did not trouble to account for certain glaring discrepancies, such as the large number of precocious children from Jewish background appearing in many studies, far beyond their representation in the population (Sheldon 1954;

Terman 1925), as noted in chapter 1. Yet there was a great deal of evidence in the case records that suggested how significant the influence of experience on mental development might be, evidence that all investigators, with certain exceptions (Root 1921), sweepingly ignored. During the early establishment of the field of study of bright children, which was concentrated on high IQs and academic competence, case studies were routinely and painstakingly collected, in the interest of charting the parameters of precocious development, similar to the way Gesell and his followers were charting the course of normal development. Perhaps the most interesting feature of this pioneer research is the revealing detail recorded that points up how stimulation contributes to cognitive development and the regularity with which certain forms of intense parent-child interaction beginning early in life were associated with intellectual precocity. The bias is evident in the manner in which descriptions were recorded and the omission of much information about interaction patterns. Yet there remains a surprising fidelity in the records that suggests something of the nature of the developmental interaction processes. In rereading these old case records, the arrival of interactionist theory, propounded especially by Hunt (1961, 1975), enables us now to give experience its due in the equation of development as the process and product of cumulative interaction between genetic dispositions and cognitive stimulation.

Take as an example a sample of twenty-three cases of precocious development recently compiled (Fowler 1981b) from a set of case studies by Terman (1919) of forty-one children whose IQ equaled or exceeded 130. The selected subsample included all cases with IQs of 139 or more to match the 140 IQ criterion for giftedness established in the field (Terman 1925). (Two cases at 139 IQ were included to enlarge the sample and because of the way in which the data clustered.) It was not until recent years that measures of high ability and talent development broader than IQ scores began to be included (Stanley, George, and Folano 1977). Inspection of case records in these twenty-three cases indicates that in the vast majority of cases (87 percent) the early cognitive stimulation in the home from various family members was intensive from at least the preschool period. Intensive early stimulation is evident in the remaining three cases (13 percent), though descriptive data are less complete; the only issue in the latter cases is whether stimulation proceeded from external as well as internal sources. The problem is something of a pseudoissue; the child's active exploratory and manipulative initiatives are characteristically a central ingredient of the developmental dynamics of precocious intellectual development. In these three cases, though Terman assigns the development of early reading skills entirely to the child's self-instruction, in fact a child can only learn the labels and meanings of symbols from cultural agents already socialized in the cultural repository of language and graphic symbols. Children do not invent what has required millenia for cultures to evolve.

Data gathered in other case study and systematic investigations, in both early and later research periods, provide much the same picture. Of twenty-three cases of 6- to 13-year-old precocious children whose IQ equaled at least 140, taken from Root's (1921) study of fifty-three children with IQ 120 or higher, 87 percent of the children had experienced a highly superior amount of early home education (rated by Root as A or A+) (Fowler 1981b). (The $N = 23$ and 87 percent figures are coincidentally identical with those from the Terman 1919 study.) Data are again sparse in the remaining three cases, in this instance probably in part because they were older children, by which time (at least age 9) parent recall is likely to have dimmed. Root, who was clearly less biased toward heredity than most investigators of the period, reported that home training was a definite factor in the vast majority of his cases. (The scores of most of his other above-120 IQ cases, who were older than age 10, were probably artificially depressed because of ceiling effects that appeared in the 1916 Binet at age 10.) He commented that in many cases the mother had "devoted her time to [the] pre-school education [of her children]" (Root 1921:130).

Information on home background collected by the investigators themselves in Terman's (1925) later and much better known investigation of 1,000 children and in a recent investigation by Freeman (1979) found highly similar patterns of early home stimulation, though as might be expected, Terman downplayed the role of experience, stressing heredity at all times throughout the lifelong series of investigations. On the basis of questionnaires, to which 595 of the 1,000 families responded, Terman reported that between the ages of 2-3 and 6-7 63.9 percent frequently told or read stories to their child, 25.4 percent taught their child to read or write, 24.5 percent frequently engaged in number work with their child, and 16.5 percent stimulated their child through nature study. Freeman found that 64 percent of mothers of the high-IQ group she studied admitted to giving help to the child before the child attended school. These are undoubtedly minimum figures for several reasons, the chief of which was the way these and indeed most investigators were inclined to restrict their definitions of stimulation to didactic instruction and the pejorative tone of the investigators with respect to parents "pressuring" their children's learning, obviously discouraging parents from responding. Both Terman and Freeman also present overlapping percentages (parents could respond to more than one category) which were not broken down, suggesting that in any case the percentage more nearly paralleled the 87 percent of the better documented studies. Freeman mentions specific teaching (49 percent) and is more forthright in describing the early cognitive stimulation by the "parents [who] had been assiduous in teaching their children, from the time they were born; they taught them to count and read before they went to school" (1979:176). Terman, in contrast, after describing in some detail the case of a mother's intensive stimulation of her boy in play from early infancy, comments that "Some would perhaps account for it [IQ 150 at age 17] on the ground of his early instruction, but we doubt the validity of such an explanation" (1919:236).

In other investigations of high ability, children manifest the same pattern of precocious cognitive development concomitant with intensive stimulation from earliest childhood, both in studies from earlier periods (Hildreth, 1958; Hollingworth 1926, 1942; Witty 1930; Yates 1920, 1922) and in the more recent studies (Robinson, Jackson, and Roedell 1978). In most investigations, while the early development of skills in language, reading, number concepts, and other cognitive skills is well documented, and information on the contributions of early experience is strongly suggestive, details on stimulation are sparser and less systematically presented.

A body of literature also exists on the intellectual precocity of the historically brilliant and eminent, a great deal of it assembled shortly after the turn of the century (Dolbear 1912; Fowler 1971c, 1981b). This was a period during which a number of notable academic figures, particularly at Harvard, set out to demonstrate with their own (or other) children that brilliance must be cultivated from infancy and is not simply a matter of inherited talent (Bruce 1911; Dolbear 1912; Stoner 1914; Wiener 1953). For whatever reasons, all of the cases reported at the time succeeded in developing highly precocious children in a variety of academic competencies, a number of whom graduated from Harvard in their teens, and at least one of whom later became an internationally famous scholar—Norbert Weiner (1953), in cybernetics.

One of the most notable achievements of the period was the painstaking collection by Cox (1926) of extensive biographical information on 282 of the best-documented cases of the historically brilliant, distilled from Catell's (1906) original classification of 1,000 great geniuses. Her capsule biographies are replete with instances of unusual attention to the individual's intellectual development beginning early in life and her conclusions emphasize the frequency with which early stimulation, along with special later education and social opportunities, featured in the development of their genius. McCurdy (1957) has given us a more precise and refined analysis of the role early stimulation and other factors have played in a selected sample of twenty cases from Cox. All of McCurdy's sample had IQs of at least 160 (estimated by complex techniques by Cox, which, given the biases, stressed academic achievements at the expense of musical, literary, or artistic brilliance. They were also selected by McCurdy because of the scope of detailed and reliable biographical information available. Again, McCurdy did not quantify his results as one might have wished, but he describes the kind of exceptional stimulation experienced, such as Goethe, who "throughout childhood was carefully and energetically supervised in varied studies by his father" (p. 453) and Bentham, who was given "a rigorous schedule of instruction in everything from dancing and military drill to Greek from a very early age" (p. 454), leading McCurdy to conclude after examining their biographical records closely, that all twenty members of the sample of historical geniuses received in childhood "a high degree of attention from their parents, as well as others" (p. 451), "expressed in intensive educational measures" (p. 461).

Specific Abilities and the Forms of Stimulation

If, as it appears, early brilliance is contingent on early, intensive stimulation, as well as on advantaged heredity, is the pattern evident in all domains or only in verbal-logical types of competence stressed by IQ tests? To the extent it has been studied, the answer to this question is rather straightforward. Intensive stimulation appears to be a major factor in the early lives of most of the able and talented, no matter what the field of endeavor. But if the signs are clear, the problem has not been studied in other fields in the same organized way the precocious abilities of high-IQ children have. Much of the information on how specialized abilities develop is contained in collections of case studies in popular media or as part of larger collections of material subordinate to studies of ability in general. The Cox (1926) collection of studies in particular, one of the best comprehensive sources of reasonably detailed information on the historically brilliant, encompasses musicians like Bach, playwrights like Shakespeare, and physicists like Newton. But the material is not analyzed according to specialities, and the significance of exceptional competence in one domain, sometimes far exceeding skills in other areas, tends to remain buried in the author's concern for general brilliance. Cox's criterion of intelligent behavior manifested during development, defined in terms of mental-test skills, resulted in such anomalies as an estimated IQ for Bach of 125 IQ, compared to 200 IQ for Goethe, the bias against musicians (and the visual arts) being particularly strong. The earlier collections of Galton (1925) and Catell (1906), the interesting brief probes on early experience by Dolbear (1912), and the later systematic investigations of bright children by Hollingworth (1926, 1942), Terman (1919, 1925), Witty (1940), and Yates (1920, 1922) have all been oriented toward the generality of intelligence, later defined as IQ. The predominance of the belief in fixed, general intelligence and predetermined development, enshrined in mental tests, has long made the IQ the standard against which competence has been measured, often eliminating from consideration at all or at least obscuring the study of competence in less academically based fields. Indeed at times the glories of a high IQ have been celebrated more than high competencies and achievement (Hollingworth 1942).

As a consequence of this generalized orientation, both the systematic, IQ-based investigations and the case-study collection of Cox and others all furnish only limited documentation that early brilliance in a field is commonly associated with stimulation related to that domain. The case collections are studded with musicians, writers, poets, mathematicians, and artists whose earliest years were founded on unusual attention in the milieu, usually by family members, attention usually built around concepts related to the domains in which the child became competent. But because the investigators' prime concern was typically with ability in general, details on how closely related the early stimulation is to the later field are usually lacking. Even in McCurdy's (1957) selective set of twenty cases there is little information on how the skills of Leibnitz and Pascal (two mathematicians in his subsample) developed in mathematics, other than mention of the scientific atmosphere in Leibnitz's home and the intention of Pascal's father to provide a comprehensive education that would include mathematics. Yet in both cases intensive stimulation began extremely early, for Leibnitz the father teaching the boy to read and absorb historical and biblical concepts in the preschool years, and for Pascal, having his father devote all of his time to his son's education from the age of 3. Thus the general verbal-concept basis for their later philosophical eminence can be retraced, but the basis for their mathematical eminence is less precise. The omission of any cases of musicians, painters, or sculptors from McCurdy's subsample underscores the generalist bias.

The later case studies and systematic investigations built around the IQ test also yield evidence of early stimulation related to various specific skills. But while the evidence is a bit clearer in the few investigations where background experience is recorded at all, the use of the IQ as a selective index of ability obviously leaves the frequency of competence achievement in different fields uncertain or blurred by the emphasis on general ability. Some idea of the prevalence of specific skill development arising from specialized stimulation appears in the percentages found for stimulation in different areas in Terman's (1925) study of 1,000 children. Thus verbal skills and concepts were clearly predominant (63.9 percent for stories and 25.4 percent for teaching reading or writing), with math taking second position (24.5 percent), followed by nature study (16.5 percent), though Terman does not analyze these figures in relation to the development of children's ability profiles.

More precise information has been dissected in the analysis of the twenty-three high-IQ cases from Terman's (1919) earlier collection of forty-one cases (data not published with the study, Fowler 1981b). In this set of children, early stimulation, beginning between early infancy and age 5, is directly linked to accelerated skill development in the areas stimulated: learning to read (74 percent), learning to write (22 percent), acquiring high interest and competence in arithmetic or math concepts generally (35 percent), developing advanced musical skills (9 percent), acquiring exceptional logical and reasoning skills (30 percent), and developing an exceptional memory (13 percent). Children were often competent in more than one category of course, but the associations between types of stimulation and types of competence were well delineated in the twenty-three case descriptions.

The same pattern of relations between the form of developmental stimulation and the type of outcome is well established in the research on early reading as well, of course, as our review in chapter 7 indicated. Children who learned to read in advance of age norms, whether at home or in special school programs, learned because of the stimulation directed toward the reading process itself. The few studies available on advancing musical skills, form concepts, and motor skills are also examples of this linkage. So too were the cross-cultural profiles on children learning to swim, paddle canoes, or ride horses bareback, years before the age at which such skills are ordinarily learned, if they are learned at all (Ewers 1955; Mead 1975; Wallace and Hoebel 1952; Wilbert 1976b). The popular educational literature on hundreds of young children learning to play the violin in Suzuki type programs (Cook 1970; Holland 1982; Suzuki 1969) and specialized programs on teaching infants to swim, many later becoming fine musicians or swimmers, are further examples of this pattern.

Case studies of great musicians, artists, mathematicians, and other great minds in special fields do exist, but the concept of inherited intelligence and genius has so long been dominant that their focus has been almost exclusively on achievement rather than on how the abilities developed. In any investigations of the development of mathematical talent, when childhood has been considered at all, the account usually starts in middle childhood or youth and marks the onset of intense interest and early accomplishment, to the almost total disregard of the early processes with which the interests and skills got their start. Bell (1927), for example, in his book on *Men of Mathematics*, in addition to his historical account of mathematical geniuses (Pascal, Poincaré, Gauss), inquired of a sample of contemporary mathematicians about the age at which interest in the subject had "seized" them, to which ninety-three replied. Such strong commitments, reported before age 10 for 38 percent (thirty-five) and between 11 and 15 for another 46 percent (forty-three), do not surface suddenly without an extended background of stimulation and activity in the area in the preceding early years. The bare details Bell provides on early history, such as no more than passing reference to a mathematically and mechanically talented uncle associated with Gauss's ability to calculate mentally before he was 2, is simply tantalizing. A recent conference explicitly aimed at the discovery and fostering of the development of mathematical talent again concentrates on intervention only in the middle and later grades (Stanley, Keating, and Fox 1975). About the only data on early development are bare mention of age benchmarks like walking, talking, and the first evidence of interest in math. The discussions are barren of information on early environmental influences. Other investigations of mathematical development (Aiken 1973; Krutetski 1969) have also noted the earliness with which great abilities develop, Krutetski, for example, concluded that there is "a very early manifestation of abilities (3 to 5 years)" (p. 103), reviewing studies of the development of mathematically precocious children in great detail without supplying a shred of information on their environmental experiences. One has to go back to original sources to piece together a less-fragmented picture of the early life of leading intellectual figures than emerges from secondary sources.

One of the most extreme in its exclusion of life history data is Scheinfeld's (1939) rather comprehensive, semipopular survey of musical talent. Music and the arts are particularly vulnerable to the concept of inherited intelligence, which in the arts assumes the form of a concept of specialized talent. Scheinfeld's survey follows this tradition almost to perfection, devoting the study to genetic speculations of musical skills inherited through family lines. While he does mention elements of family background associated with skills in many musicians, the focus is almost entirely on the presence or absence of high musical talent in other family members, in terms of hypothesized gene distributions, regardless of their personal association with the subject. There is hardly any account of the processes leading to the development of the subject's abilities and interests. We do, nonetheless, glean some rather startling bits of information from Scheinfeld's tabular summaries of talent development. Among the most interesting of these are the fact that the average age at which exceptional talent was first expressed for virtuoso instrumental artists ($N = 36$) was 4.75 years, for metropolitan opera singers ($N = 36$) was 5.75 years. Similarly, Mayer (1964) in a popular article observes that every great musical figure (except singers and occasional composers) was a child prodigy. Again we are confronted with a phenomenon of earliness of achievement that could not have occurred without a developmental history, in the case of music one that apparently begins in the earliest years. In fact there is enough material in these two studies, other popular accounts (Maazel 1950) and those from the scientific community such as Cox (1926), to demonstrate that certain exceptional musical atmospheres in the home or similar early opportunities of an unusual nature were the rule that created the possibilities for extraordinary musical talent to develop. Despite their lack of unusual musical ability, for example, the parents of Yehudi Menuhin, the renowned violinist, in their love of music took Yehudi as a baby regularly to symphony concerts and arranged for violin lessons by a skilled musician before he was 3. Jascha Heifetz enjoyed a similar background, and the beginnings of instruction for Mozart at age 2 are legendary. As in all case studies, the realization of exceptional creative ability early in life does not preclude a vital role for biology. Case studies of success stories omit the many failures of early stimulation that may have occurred where potential was absent. Yet the consistency of the evidence suggests that heredity alone is not a sufficient condition for the generation of talent.

That the development of high ability is often precocious in many fields is supported by the lifelong work of Lehman (1949, 1953) on *Age and Achievement*. He gathered information on the productive development of leading performers, historical and current, in a wide variety of fields, ranging from philosophy and science to the arts, music, and athletics. Although the age of creative achievement extended from almost the preschool period to very old age (beyond 80), the most productive periods were modally in the twenties and thirties, some fields (chemistry and poetry) earlier than others (novelists and business leaders). Of special interest is his finding that many of the individuals making the greatest contributions or skill achievements in athletics, music, and other fields began their productive careers well before age 25, often in their teens and sometimes earlier, as in the case of great musicians in particular. While once again there is very little information reported on early life histories, he, like Cox (1926), Galton (1907, 1925), and others before him, noted that greatness is characteristically associated with early oportunities for experience in the domain. Among other skill areas, he comments that unpublished notes "disclose a surprisingly large number of professional golfers who either were born close to a golf course or who served as caddies when quite young" (p. 198).

Similar observations by Pressey (1955) indicated that the flowering of musical achievement historically in German culture was rooted in a community life in which every little town had several bands, orchestras, and choral groups. The greatness of a number of Bachs seems related to the total concentration of the extended Bach family on musical activity over several generations. Thus all members lived and breathed music from their first awakening, making it possible for all talents to reach closer to their maximum potential and for the development of several really great talents like Johann Sebastian and Phillip Emmanuel. Pressey also noted parallel achievements arising from early opportunities for stimulation in athletics, as for example the public community support of tennis in Pasadena, California, which led to the early start and later attainments of several great tennis players, like Bill Tilden. Here we are coming close to the theme of talent development and community- and ecologically-based socialization, so closely intertwined in folk society, as in the case of the many skilled horsemen among the Plains Indians (Ewers 1955) and the skilled canoers and swimmers among the Manus of New Guinea (Mead 1975).

In several graduate seminars taught by myself, students were asked to conduct biographical research on leading historical figures from various fields. Among the (generally) randomly selected samples of playwrights (Durbach 1979), leading scientists (Tetroe 1979), visual artists (Bennett 1967), and Victorian novelists (Este 1979), the later talents were almost invariably founded on exceptional experiences during the first 6 years that were closely related to the field in which the figures later became pre-eminent. In three of the investigations, random samples of 5 each were drawn from a larger pool of eminent figures in the field. In the fourth study, fourteen of thirty major twentieth-century artists were selected on the basis of availability of biographical material from the university library (University of Toronto). At least two and usually a larger number of biographical sources were employed to study the life history of each case in all investigations.

The overriding dimension common to all cases and all categories, without exception, was the home atmosphere throughout development. Each child grew up in a family and usually a wider milieu of intense verbal intellectual or artistic interests that dominated family life from the child's earliest years. In nearly all instances, moreover, parental values were icnoclastic and critical of the status quo or at least decidedly at variance with social patterns common to the larger community and society, except with respect to the specialized intellectual milieux with which the families were often intimately related. Association with adults and adult intellectual values and interests, as opposed to peers, was highly characteristic of the child's development in all categories, and extensive involvement with stories and adult literature and usually early reading was true of all cases in the nonvisual art categories. In at least eleven and probably thirteen of the fifteen nonvisual art cases, children had been taught to read well before age 6, and children rapidly became involved in reading adult literature. Of the other two cases, Einstein was very early more involved in natural science concepts, his father and uncle being engineers, though he later became an avid reader of scientific material. Yeats, the other case, had difficulty learning from his first home instruction, but was taught soon after early childhood by his father and in any case was richly bathed in stories and literature from his earliest years.

A great deal of individual attention was evident in nearly all cases, beginning early in life, typically centered in intellectual activity related to symbolic learning, either in literature, general knowledge, and the arts, or the visual arts and crafts in the case of the visual artists. In nearly all cases there was direct and continuing engagement by a parent or close family friend who served as mentors or skilled models for the children.

While relations between the early experiences and the later career choices were not perfect, there were remarkable correspondences. Without exception, all of the playwrights and novelists were exposed to a broad range of literature of all kinds throughout childhood. All five of the scientists were continually stimulated by scholars, scientists, or engineers whose fields were directly related to the scientists' later fields of work (Einstein and Fermi to engineers; Davy to several chemists; Lister to a physician, and Wiener, a founder in the field of computers, to a mathematician and physicist (his father tutored him from infancy); and in all cases to other scientists as well). The visual artists all either had as models and guides family members who were practicing artists and crafts people, or, as in the case of Frank Lloyd Wright, the architect, for example, created a highly specialized artistic environment for the child. Wright's mother reared the boy from his first months of infancy in a nursery papered with pictures of the great buildings of Europe and elsewhere, constantly showed him pictures and books, talked endlessly about architecture, and was determined that he would become a great architect. At least twelve of the fourteen visual artists were actively engaged with the visual medium during the preschool period, while information for the other two is uncertain. Considered the most creative, versatile, complex, and prolific of modern artists, Picasso began to draw on the tile floors of his Spanish house by the time he was 2, guided by his father, an artist.

A substantial body of heuristic evidence thus shows not only that exceptional cognitive competence gets its start early in life through exceptionally facilitative stimulation that accelerates development, but that some relationship exists between the domain or domains in which stimulation occurs and the field(s) in which the exceptional competencies are ultimately concentrated.

The Developmental Ecology of Precocity

It is equally evident that early stimulation alone is never a sufficient condition to generate superior development of the adult intellect, regardless of the domain involved. The evidence in all the case studies of great creators from the seminars, as well as the investigatory and historical literature cited, including the selected samples from Root (1921) and Terman (1919) cited in Fowler 1981b, strongly indicates that the unusually rich quality and quantity of stimulation does not stop with early development. It may take different forms during different phases of the child's development, but it is a continuing process that shapes the child's development cumulatively in certain directions. And while there are variations in the strategies and techniques parents and others employ and the conditions under which stimulation occurs, there is a certain set of commonalities to the developmental stimulation-learning patterns that cuts across domains and family styles and milieu to an important degree.

The analysis of case studies from Terman (1919) by Fowler (1981b) and a recent investigation at the University of Chicago of a research team directed by Bloom (1982; Bloom and Sosniak 1981; Pines 1982) furnish the rudiments of a model for how the developmental process leading to specialized intellectual precocity and later achievement may occur. They also shed additional light on which aspects of the original set of dimensions of stimulation (see table 5-2) may bear the most weight in the process. The Bloom investigation, for which no more than preliminary data are available, is a retrospective study of developmental experiential processes in one hundred highly talented, world-famous individuals in a variety of fields (concert pianists, tennis players, Olympic swimmers, and mathematicians), who attained international excellence between 17 and 35 years of age. The findings in this study largely mirror the findings reported in the seminar studies above, except for the more prominent role formal (professional) teaching may take at an earlier age. Some of this difference may be a consequence of the different eras in history, as well as of differences in fields involved. Formal teaching was characteristically carried out by family members in times past more than today, before institutional schooling became mandatory and widespread. The modern sports world is also highly organized and highly skilled teachers are widely accessible. The visual arts by their nature appear to have been characterized by a great deal more informal modeling and guidance, compared with musical performance in particular, which both now and in the past has always demanded systematic, highly scheduled instruction and practice from an early age (Schneideman 1939; Mayer 1964). But actually, as we shall see, one-to-one relations with mentors and models, small-group interaction in intimate situations of communication and analysis, and informal, even play-oriented techniques are the rule for early childhood in both Bloom's sample and all of the data cited earlier. Bloom found that home values are the primary ingredient of the entire process. The child is bathed from the earliest years in the examples, intensive interests, and everyday practices of the chosen domain of the family. The home and milieu of Olympic swimmers is above all sports; of musicians it is musical appreciation and concerts. Bloom also found a strong stress on the work ethic, which is also paralleled in the seminar cases and other literature cited. There is intense interest in the family to live the life of the intellect, to strive and create, sometimes expressed in direct demands to learn and achieve, but sometimes simply intrinsic to the processes of everyday involvement in the activities and concerns of the adults' scientific, literary, musical, sports, or artistic life from early childhood on.

The Chicago study reports a series of stages through which stimulated children generally appear to progress, but which vary to some degree with the field. The process begins first with children informally observing, imitating, and interacting, often in play, with the skilled and highly interested adults, most often the parents, who concern themselves with the child's development personally. At some point toward the end of the preschool period, parents seek out a skilled teacher, as the child manifests precocious skill in the area, following the exceptional early experiences. They then gradually seek out a series of increasingly more sophisticated and skilled teachers, and more hours are devoted to learning and practice in the field, culminating in many hours weekly and serious commitment begining in early adolescence. Swimmers may follow a more telescoped schedule because of the demands for Olympic participation by age 15, and mathematicians may delay even the decision to pursue mathematics until college, though the competence is evident earlier, if not always in the concentrated manner of the prodigy.

The case-study analysis of bright children (Fowler 1981b) displays quite similar patterns, though the later adult outcomes were not available and the skill levels may not have been as consistently outstanding. A number of additional insights are available, however, on the nature of the developmental learning process. Distilling information from the twenty-three high-ability cases recorded reveals a pattern of family-child interaction techniques centered on cognitive stimulation that is coded and tabulated in table 9-1.

Table 9-1
Percentage of Types of Home Stimulation in Terman's (1919) High-Ability Children (IQ = 139 or more) (N = 23)

Strategies and Techniques	Infancy (0-2), %	Early Childhood (3-5), %	Middle Childhood[a] (6-13), %
Systematic (intentional) instruction	9	48	27
Incidental stimulation			
Answering child's questions endlessly	35	48	41
Encouraging child extensively	17	48	50
Arranging highly varied experiences	30	78	100
Dramatization			
Reading many stories or poems to the child	4	35	14
Using play techniques extensively	17	30	23
Child's own activity (endogenous stimulation)	43	87	100

Source: Reprinted from W. Fowler. Case studies on cognitive precocity: The role of exogenous and endogenous stimulation in early mental development, *Journal of Applied Developmental Psychology* 2 (1981):319-367.

[a]N = 22 because one child less than age 5 at time of study.

Following the outline of dimensions of stimulation from table 5-2, which has been guiding our review of early stimluation thus far, it is immediately evident that the three primary variables—earliness, duration, and intensity of stimulation—are strongly represented in the percentages listed in table 9-1. The percentages in the table overlap to some degree, both horizontally across age periods and vertically among strategies and techniques. That is, all percentages for infancy comprise cases in which stimulation began in infancy and continued at least through early childhood, and all cases on which the percentages in middle childhood are based started to stimulate their child in some way either in infancy or during the 3-5 age period. Among stimulation categories, various combinations of techniques were employed in different families, resulting in most families being counted in several categories. But although the categories overlap, there are only two cases in which no specific technique is mentioned in the case description other than supplying richly varied experiences or exceptional learning through the child's own activity. In both cases, however, parental expectations for learning are described as high from infancy on and, as we have observed, the failure to describe behaviors the parents (or some skilled mediating agent) must have performed to enable these two children to learn to read (one at 2, the other at 3), especially labeling, does not mean they did not occur. The omission may be traced to belief systems and social concerns to be discussed shortly.

Thus although parents of precocious children used different combinations of techniques, they virtually all employed some specific combination of techniques, or one preferred technique, such as reading to the child constantly. They also all began the stimulation process at least during the 3-5 age period, often earlier, and the process was highly intensive, as indicated by the pointed descriptors taken from the case records ("endlessly," "extensively," "many"), and it continued over a number of years, not just months. The case records were brief summaries, amounting usually to about one printed page, or less each, and were compiled by Terman, whose reaction to one family's extensive involvement with early stimulation was recorded above. The impression from many of the records is that these patterns reflect only limited comments on outstanding practices, that in fact there were probably others parents were shy to mention or did not recall, and that whatever patterns were employed were, as in the seminar studies and in the Bloom investigation on talented individuals, practices that infused family life as an intensively held and lived value structure oriented toward verbal-logical thinking (as might be expected from studies using IQ level as the basis for selecting cases).

The extent to which stimulation tends to be embedded in the ecology of the family is illustrated by the several families in the sample whose child is one of many high-ability siblings. Two cases were each one of four bright children, another two cases, one of five, and in one instance, one of no less than seven brilliant children, for all of whom intellectual stimulation was the common fare from early infancy. Eight cases in the sample were sibling pairs, only one pair being from one of the foregoing multichild families.

Several things stand out among the strategies and techniques used, possibly the most unexpected the fact that in 48 percent of the cases parents deliberately and planfully instructed their children during the early years. The percentage of families involved is slightly diminished by eight cases drawn from four families, three of whom planned their children's stimulation, but even so the percentage of families intentionally instructing their children remains at 42 percent. Again this figure is probably minimal because of the fear families had (and still have) of being perceived as pressuring their child. Thus nearly half and possibly more families deliberately attempted to induce high abilities and skills in their child.

The second thing that stands out is that the other half of the parents achieved much the same end with incidental techniques of stimulation, the various categories of answering their children's questions, providing encouragement, arranging varied experiences, dramatizing through reading or telling stories to the child, and stimulating their children in play. Even more interesting, the distribution of percentages clearly indicates that the vast majority of *all* parents, both those disavowing and those claiming intention to teach, employed such informal or indirect practices in one way or another. It would appear that parents who deliberately instructed their children were nevertheless seldom didactically inclined. At least five of the nine planned cases built all their teaching around play, in which parents set up sensorimotor and dramatic play activities or brought various concepts to be learned into the child's own play. But the matter extends further: deliberate instruction was never the sole technique these parents employed. They all used other incidental and dramatic techniques as well, typically reading many stories and often answering questions, as well as arranging varied experiences (78 percent of all cases). It is evident from the data that using informal techniques was the common mode of early stimulation for *all* families. Something else appears to have divided them on the basis of whether or not they defined what they did as planning the child's stimulation activities.

Turning to how the remaining, "secondary" dimensions are represented in the stimulation patterns of table 9-1, the striking thing is that all except one of the dimensions of stimulation from table 5-2 discussed in the last chapter feature very strongly among the common parental strategies, namely, ordering the concepts presented in a tight logical sequence or step-by-step program. There is only one instance from the Terman (1919) case records in which parents stuck to anything resembling an ordered series of concepts. In one case, the brother of the early reader, Martha studied by

Terman (1918), the father appears to have mapped out a program of reading, arithmetic, and other school activities patterned after the first three grades of school. Root (1921) describes a similar case and more attention to planned order may have been more common among Durkin's (1966) early readers, where reading itself (rather than general abstract verbal abilities) was the primary focus.

The involvement of other dimensions is marked, however. Interaction was a constant, almost invariably including a great deal of child participation, frequently even when reading to the child by actively involving her or him in pointing to pictures and talking about them and the text. More often than not, the child's initiative was cultivated, as reflected (during the preschool period) in the substantial percentages of parents responding to questions (48 percent) and using play techniques (30 percent) and the high proportion of cases in which the child's own activity was stressed (87 percent). The inquiry and rational basis for these parents' approaches is equally evident, as the half who routinely answered their children's curiosity in responding to questions underscores. Throughout the case descriptions, moreover, there is a strong current of emphasis on the rational. Parents maintain a focus on solving problems and a firm belief that young children can comprehend and advance rapidly in knowledge and skills if only they are treated rationally. The stress on the rational and inquiry underlines the kind of domains valued and the cognitive breadth characteristically involved in the cognitive socialization of these high-IQ children. Answering any and all questions and employing flexible, open-ended approaches, coupled with the emphasis on language, books, early reading, and often math, indicates at once the wide scope of their concept horizons and the high value placed on symbolic learning and the verbal-logical perspectiveness. This informal but intensively stimulating approach defines a powerful motivational paradigm of strategies, techniques and intimately reinforcing social attachments that seem conducive to inducing persisting efforts to learn.

What these various combinations of informal but intensive early stimulation strategies devoted to symbolic learning add up to is a specialized, well-constructed ecology that socializes and adapts children well to the demands of academic learning and later professional and intellectual accomplishment and leadership. Only a small fraction of the symbolically oriented families from any of Terman's (1919, 1925) studies, any of the other investigations of high-IQ children, or any studies of great historical figures emanated from nonprofessional milieux. Among those who did not, even including a few skilled working-class families, there was often an unusual ethos in the family, in which the parents maintain a close system of relations directed toward intellectual learning and achievement. Sometimes there was a religious basis, as in the case of a Christian fundamentalist family whose mornings, evenings, and weekends were devoted to learning exercises with their eight children, from infancy onward, using the Bible and an old encyclopedia as a basis for discussion, but using a modern, interactive approach (Barbe 1958). The pattern has historically been particularly strong among poor European Jewish immigrants (Root 1921; Sheldon 1954), among whom intensive stimulation of verbal-logical skills from earliest childhood and high intellectual aspirations have been commonplace among all classes (Zborowski 1949). Where family interests have been directed toward specialized areas of talent, such as athletics, music, or the arts, the ecology has been equally effective and organized in socializing the adapting children to high competence in the valued domains.

The question of whether early stimulation alone produced the different exceptional talents and cognitive abilities hardly needs further discussion. Running through all the investigations is endless evidence that stimulation does not stop when the child reaches school age. Bloom and Sosniak 1981 and Pines 1982 describe the several stages of guidance that carry the child through the formative span of development, really a continuous process of constant family attention and concern for the child's developing mastery of the chosen areas of ability. The seminar cases, McCurdy's (1957) cases, and the other cases from Cox (1926), all (where information is available) chronicle a pattern of continuing cognitive stimulation and motivational support that remains every bit as strong as those found in the early years. The ecology does not suddenly break apart but continues to operate as a matrix inspiring and guiding the child and later youth toward fine mastery of the domain. Not a single case among the scientists and writers failed to experience such an atmosphere during later development, and while a number of visual artists later encountered family opposition to specific artistic career choice, the ecology of the milieu served to stimulate further at least general artistic development well into adolescence (Bennett 1967). Occasional career opposition from parents has also been found in more verbally oriented careers, as in the case of Pascal, whose father forbid him to study mathematics in middle childhood but nevertheless continued to instruct him with the greatest intensity in the natural sciences (and thus certain mathematical concepts) and the humanities throughout his development and in mathematics itself from age 12 on (Cox 1926; McCurdy 1957).

Some idea of the extent of continuing developmental stimulation and support typically found in the milieu of high-IQ children is evident in table 9-1. It may be seen that all families arranged highly varied experiences for their child or children throughout middle childhood, as far as the cases extended. At least half the parents furnished extensive encouragement, and 41 percent continued to answer questions, while as much as one-fourth of the families provided systematic instruction, beyond what the child encountered in school (27 percent) or used play (or games) as a learning activity (23 percent). There is, on the other hand, a marked shift in the nature of the learning activities, the sources of stimulation, and the degree of initiative toward learning provided by the children themselves. The gradual evolution of this development is indicated by the increase in the percentage of cases attributing learning to the child's own activity, from 43 percent in infancy, to 85 percent in early childhood, to 100 percent by school age on.

The nature of this developmental and behavioral progression is synthesized in figures 9-1 and 9-2, the first illustrating the pattern with families who follow incidental stimulation strategies alone, and the second illustrating the pattern with families who plan their children's instruction. As we have noted, *all* families in fact employed informal, even incidental techniques of stimulation, regardless of their claimed or disclaimed intent to stimulate, and this commonlity is reflected in the strong developmental orientation toward cognitive autonomy in learning evident with both strategies beginning no later than stage II (extensive question asking for the incidentally stimulated child versus active cognitive experimentation for the deliberately stimulated child).

What then is the difference between the strategies and the developmental outcomes? There appears to be no important or consistent difference in outcomes detectable in the case records. As summarized in the later stages III and IV, early fluent reading and a broad array of related academic competencies and general knowledge become firmly established and acceleration continues apace in both patterns, more and more fueled by the child's own independent efforts, based on the strategies, knowledge, and coding skills being acquired. Yet this increasingly self-propelled system of cognitive learning does not operate in a vacuum, but is undergirded by parental guidance in coping at school, including monitoring to ensure the child is placed or accelerated in grade commensurate with skill development; by the challenging home environment that is more and more the inquiry, experimentation, and discussion of intellectual equals; and by the social role of child prodigy (or at least competent intellectual that socially reinforces the child's efforts toward autonomy and achievement in preferred areas, in the home, the school, and the community. The social attention the highly skilled child attracts is repeatedly documented in the case records.

It would appear that there are few if any real substantive differences in strategies and techniques among parents who claim or disclaim planful strategies to teach their child from early childhood on, other than certain belief systems that influence what they say and how they perceive and define how they are interacting with their child. There is some evidence that planful parents more often teach or arrange for supplementary teaching even after the child begins school, but this is really no more than an extension of early practices. What *is* different is the way planful parents believe that experience and education are primary factors in the development of ability and talent, and heredity is less important, while the opposite is true of

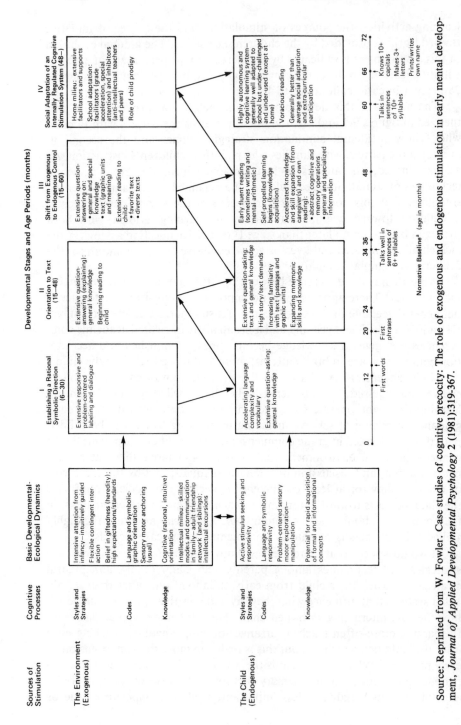

Source: Reprinted from W. Fowler. Case studies of cognitive precocity: The role of exogenous and endogenous stimulation in early mental development, *Journal of Applied Developmental Psychology* 2 (1981):319-367.

[a]From Bayley (1969) and Griffiths (1970) Mental Scales.

Figure 9-1. Stages in the Development of Symbolic Precocity through Incidental Stimulation Strategies

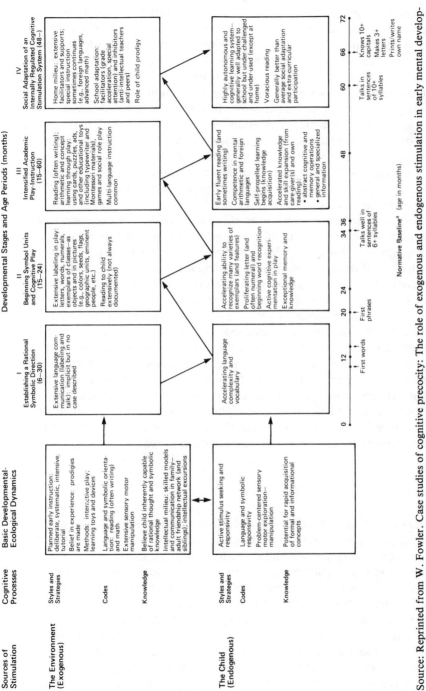

Source: Reprinted from W. Fowler. Case studies of cognitive precocity: The role of exogenous and endogenous stimulation in early mental development, *Journal of Applied Developmental Psychology* 2 (1981):319-367.

[a]From Bayley (1969) and Griffiths (1970) Mental Scales.

Figure 9-2. Stages in the Development of Symbolic Precocity through Planned Stimulation Strategies

parents disclaiming responsibility for any deliberate teaching. Thus where questions of special domains of talent development are involved, as the Bloom (1982) investigations and the several sources of case-study investigations cited here show, even hereditarians do not hesitate to employ the best professional teachers at some stage, or even occasionally to *admit* to the role of teacher themselves in stimulating a common symbolic activity like reading or math to their preschooler. But in all cases hereditarians make sure to say they are merely *responding* to the child's "inborn" irrepressible flow of talent. The techniques are much the same in both strategic camps; in most cases only the attitudes and rationale vary.

Case studies do not permit us to decide on this question of course, and in fact biological disposition probably happily coincides with parental effectiveness in stimulation in these successful instances. What is curious is how parents who attribute most to heredity nonetheless are such marvelous stimulators, using the best developmentally oriented interaction and inquiry techniques to be found anywhere. But again so do the parents who intend. Much of the difficulty at least in the earlier historical periods must be laid at the door of the investigators, who like Terman (1919, 1925) persisted in defining all stimulation as formal, didactic teaching, which conveniently enabled them to minimize the role of exogenous sources of stimulation and attribute everything to the endogenous stimulation of the child rooted in biology. Under such pressures from the professionals, it is almost surprising that any parents at all admitted to engaging in educational practices with their young children. As Durkin (1966) noted (see chapter 7), only blue-collar families, who are more separated from professional educators can fail to be concerned with the social stigma that attaches to early stimulation as pressure. They more often tended to label what they were doing in stimulating early reading as teaching the child to read.

Conclusions

Studies of the academically and verbally highly competent and studies of the highly talented, among both the great minds of history and the high-IQ performers among schoolchildren, yield a valuable source for hypotheses about the role of cognitive stimulation in development. They do not permit us to sort out the relative weights of heredity and environment, nor the relative importance of early as opposed to later stimulation. They do suggest rather strongly, however, that experience from exogenous sources of stimulation in general and during the early phases of development in particular are essential ingredients to the formation of exceptional abilities and talent without ruling out an equally essential role for biology. The regularity with which specific manifestations of ability or talent are associated with milieux in which the corresponding types of competencies are highly valued and fostered may indicate, however, at a minimum, that the inherited components of ability are general rather than specific. Given a high potential, abilities that are stimulated may be malleable in most any direction stimulation is applied, but a great deal of more controlled investigation is necessary to explore these relations, because of course heredity and experience are combined in familial patterns.

The patterns of development of bright and talented children begin very early as a consequence of patterns of interaction in certain kinds of facilitative mileux. Although certain parents consciously set out to induce precocity and superior competencies according to their areas of interest more than others, most parents, regardless of original intentions, make use of remarkably open-ended interactive styles that generate a great deal of autonomous inquiry in the child toward the areas of interest of the family. In other words, while the form of the stimulation is most often one of facilitative interchange and active experimentation and problem solving for the child, which expands with development, the substantive basis for the body of concepts and skills in which the child becomes precociously competent derives from the bodies of material the family values or is competent in themselves.

With regard to the variety of dimensions of stimulation originally proposed (table 5-2), a preferred combination of dimensional values definitely appears to generate competence most successfully. Stimulation begins very early, often in infancy, is extraordinarily intensive and pervasive, permeating much of the child's activities in daily commerce, and it does so over many, many years. Certainly, the cumulative effects of learning the intricacies of skill patterns and large bodies of detailed knowledge associated with superior competence should not be underestimated, though neither should the early, establishing role of getting "founded" or launched in an increasingly successful direction, before competing or less effective skill patterns get a foothold. We do not know that inquiry, free and easy interaction, and play and similar dramatization devices are necessary conditions for the development of high competence, or even that a warm emotional climate, close social attachments, and positively socially reinforcing modes are indispensable agents to the process. But they all occur with such frequency in the case records of the great minds and the intellectually precocious that they deserve to be an important basis for systematic programs of research. Certain instances can be found historically, moreover, such as John Stuart Mill (Packe 1954), Norbert Wiener (1953), William James Sidis (Weiner 1953), and the poet and playwright Yeats (Durbach 1979), in which one or another of these dimensions moved in a contrary direction, particularly in terms of less positively reinforcing techniques, absence of play, and the use of a heavier, more didactic and dictorial hand.

Such cases suggest that too much variation from the ideal may lead to later serious emotional problems, even if the later competencies do not appear to be in any way diminished.

   Possibly the potentially most interesting feature of the developmental process leading to high competence that can be identified is the ecological basis for these forms of cognitive socialization. Unlike the formal, remedial stimulation of poor children from various racial and ethnic-minority folk cultures, which no matter how early it is begun, constitutes only a single prong of a dual curriculum, in channeling a course of conflict between the traditional and street ecology of the home and community and the planned verbal-logical prescriptions of the research program, the ecology of the intellectually precocious child is one of social harmony. The result is not without effort and conflict. Indeed the high expectations, aspirations, and unceasing pressures to learn and achieve may be great and unrelenting. They are also likely to involve certain conflicts with the wider relations among peers, most often in reducing their frequency or at least their scope in the extended society of school and the everyday community (Bennett 1967; Bloom and Sosniak 1981; Durbach 1979; Fowler 1981b, Goertzel and Goertzel 1962; Hollingsworth 1942; Tetroe 1979). Nonetheless the outcomes for all except a few of the most extremely competent (Holingworth 1926, 1942) demonstrate generally better coping in their careers and social adjustment than the norm (Burks, Jensen, and Terman 1930; Miles 1954; Terman 1925; Terman and Oden 1947, 1959). The pattern is often of a piece, the kind of whole that appears so integral to the traditional, informal patterns of socialization that characterize the modes of folk communities from the tribal societies. The parents seldom teach their children didactically, and quite often do not even plan the early instruction the way research-based early-intervention programs do. There is instead an informal mode of communication and experimentation that is steeped in what the family knows and values, which stimulates the infant to observe, imitate, and experiment in the manner folk children do with the skills practiced by the folk family and community. Precocity appears to be an ecological outcome of special subcultures in some ways resembling traditional folk cultures, socializing the child to acquire the competencies the subculture values.

   The manner in which precocious, highly competent and talented individuals appear to be cognitively socialized, regardless of domain, has many implications for education, child rearing, and child development in the population at large in modern society. Among questions raised by the data on precocity are the following: Is there a threshold of abilities, which, if generated early in development, is relatively easy to maintain through minimum social support throughout development? Can more complex abilities and special talents be more widely cultivated among the general population, verbal abstract abilities increasingly demanded by our accelerating high technology world and talents to enrich cultural-aesthetic and intellectual life? And can planning for the early years be widely undertaken without greatly eroding the informal folk quality of family and community life, as certain subcultures among professional elites now appear to accomplish? Some working-class families, including black working-class families (Jenkins 1943), manage the combination on their own, but what of the rest?

References

Abrahams, R.D. *Deep down in the jungle*. Chicago: Aldine. 1970.

Adamson, J.W. *Pioneers of modern education, 1600-1700*. London: Cambridge University Press, 1905.

Aiken, L.R. Ability and creativity in mathematics. *Review of Educational Research* 43 (1973):405-432.

Ainsworth, M. Sensory motor development of Ganda infants. In L.J. Stone and L.B. Murphy, eds., *The competent infant*. New York: Basic Books, 1973.

Ainsworth, M., and Bell, S. Mother-infant interaction and the development of competence. In K. Connolly and J. Bruner, eds., *The growth of competence*. London: Academic Press, 1974.

Al-Issa, I., and Dennis, W. *Cross-cultural studies of behavior*. New York: Holt, Rinehart and Winston, 1970.

Allport, G.W. *Personality*. New York: Henry Holt, 1937.

Almy, M.C. *Children's experience prior to first grade and success in beginning reading*. Teachers College. Contribution to Education no. 954. New York: Teachers College, Columbia University, 1949.

Ames, L.B. The development of the sense of time in the young child. Journal of Genetic Psychology 68 (1946):97-125.

Ames, L.B., and Ilg, F.L. Developmental trends in writing behavior. *Journal of Genetic Psychology* 79 (1951):29-46.

Anastasi, *Differential psychology*, 3rd ed. New York: Macmillan, 1958.

Anastasi, A. *Psychological testing*, 4th ed. New York: Macmillan, 1976.

Anastasi, and Foley, J.P., Jr. *Differential psychology*, rev. ed. New York: Macmillan, 1949.

Anderson, R.B., St. Pierre, R.G., Proper, E.C., and Stebbins, L.B. Pardon us, but what was the question again? A response to the critique of the follow through evaluation. *Harvard Educational Review* 48 (1978): 161-170.

André-Thomas, S., and Dargassies, St. A. *Etude neurologiques sur le nouveau-né et le jeunne nourrison*. Paris: Masson, 1952.

Appleton, E. Kindergarteners pace themselves in reading. *Elementary School Journal* 64 (1964):248-252.

Aries, P. *Centuries of childhood*. R. Baldick, trans. New York: Knopf, 1962.

Aristotle. *Basic works*. R. McKeon, ed. New York: Random House, 1941.

Artley, A.S. Reading in kindergarten. In M.A. Dawson, ed., *Combining research results and good practice*, vol. 2. New York: International Reading Association, 1966.

Ashmead, D.H., and Perlmutter, M. Infant memory in everyday life. In M. Perlmutter, ed., *Children's memory, new directions for child development*, vol. 10. San Francisco: Jossey-Bass, 1980.

Ashton, P.T. Cross-cultural Piagetian research: An experimental perspective. *Harvard Educational Review* 45 (1975):475-506.

Ausubel, D. Viewpoints from related disciplines: Human growth and development. *Teachers College Record* 60 (February 1959):245-254.

Ausubel, D., Sullivan, E., and Ives, S.W. *Theory and problems of child development*, 3rd ed. New York: Grune and Stratton, 1980.

Backman, M.E. Patterns of mental abilities: Ethnic, socioeconomic, and sex differences. *American Educational Research Journal* 9 (1972):1-12.

Badger, E.D. *Teaching guide: Toddler learning program*. Paoli, Pa.: Instructo Corporation, 1971.

Bakan, D. *On method*. San Francisco: Jossey-Bass, 1967.

Banta, T.J. Montessori: Myth or reality? In R.K. Parker, ed., *The preschool in action*, Boston: Allyn and Bacon, 1972.

Baratz, J.C. A bi-dialectal task for determining language proficiency in economically disadvantaged Negro children. *Child Development* 40 (1969):889-901.

Baratz, S.S., and Baratz, J.C. Early childhood intervention: The social science base of institutional racism. *Harvard Educational Review* 40 (1970):29-50.

Barbe, W.B. Case study of a gifted family. *Education* 79 (1958):45-48.

Barch, R. *Achieving perceptual-motor efficiency*, vol. 1. Seattle: Special Child Publications, 1965.

Baron, S. *The Jewish community*, vol. 2. New York: The Jewish Publication Society of America, 1942.

Barrett, H.E. The effect of nursery school training upon the mental test performance of a group of orphanage children. *Journal of Genetic Psychology* 37 (1930):102-121.

Barry, H. Relation between child training and the pictorial arts. *Journal of Abnormal and Social Psychology* 54 (1957):380-383.

Barry, H., Child, I., and Bacon, M. Relation of child training to subsistence economy. *American Anthropologist* 61 (1959):51-63.

Bartlett, F.C. *Remembering*. Cambridge, England: Cambridge University Press, 1932.

Bates, E., Benigni, L., Bretherton, I., Camaioni, L., and Volterra, V. From gesture to first word: On cognitive and social prerequisites. In M. Lewis and L. Rosenblum, eds., *Interaction, conversation and the development of language*. New York: J. Wiley and Sons, 1977.

Bates, E., Benigni, L., Camaioni, L., Bretherton, I., and Volterra, V. *The emergence of symbols*. New York: Academic Press, 1979.

Bates, E., Bretherton, I., Snyder, L., Shore, C., and Volterra, V. Vocal and gestural symbols at 13 months. *Merrill-Palmer Quarterly* 26 (1980): 407-423.

Bayley, N. Consistency and variability in the growth of intelligence from birth to eighteen years. *Journal of Genetic Psychology* 75 (1949): 165-196.

Bayley, N. *Bayley scales of infant development.* New York: The Psychological Corporation, 1969.

Bayley, N. The development of mental abilities. In P.H. Mussen, ed., *Carmichael's manual of child psychology,* vol. 1, 3rd ed. New York: J. Wiley and Sons, 1970.

Bayley, N., and Schaefer, E.S. Correlations of maternal and child behaviors with the development of mental abilities: Data from the Berkeley growth study. *Monographs of the Society for Research in Child Development* 29, Serial no. 97 (1964).

Beck, I.L. A longitudinal study of the reading achievement effects of formal reading instruction in the kindergarten: A summative and formative evaluation. Unpublished Ph.D. dissertation, University of Pittsburgh, 1973.

Beers, H.W. A portrait of the farm family in central New York state. *American Sociological Review* 2 (1937):591-600.

Beilin, H. Constructing cognitive operations linguistically. In H.W. Reese, ed., *Advances in child development and behavior,* vol. 11. New York: Academic Press, 1976.

Bell, E.T. *Men of mathematics.* New York: Simon and Schuster, 1937.

Beller, E.K. Research on organized programs of early education. In R.M.W. Travers, ed., *Second handbook of research on teaching.* Chicago: Rand McNally, 1973.

Beller, E.K. Impact of early education on disadvantaged children. In S. Ryan, ed., *A report on longitudinal evaluations of preschool programs. Vol. 1: Longitudinal evaluations,* DHEW Publication OHD 74-24. Washington, D.C.: U.S. Department of Health, Education and Welfare, 1974. ERIC Document Reproduction Service no. ED 093 500.

Beller, E.K. Early intervention programs. In J.D. Osofsky, ed., *Handbook of infant development.* New York: J. Wiley and Sons, 1979.

Beller, E.K., McNichol, J.E., and Root, M. The impact of preschool on disadvantaged children: A twelve year follow-up study. Paper presented at the International Congress of Early Childhood Education, Tel Aviv, Israel, January 1980.

Belski-Cohen, R., and Melnik, N. *The use of creative movement for promoting the development of concept formation and intellectual ability in young culturally disadvantaged children* (Final report). The National

Council of Jewish Women Research Institute for Innovation in Education, July 1974. ED 164681.

Belsky, J., and Steinberg, L.D. The effects of day care: A critical review. *Child Development* 49 (1978):929-949.

Bennett, B. The childhood environments of famous artists. Unpublished manuscript, Ontario Institute for Studies in Education, Toronto, 1967.

Bereiter, C., and Engelmann, S. *Teaching disadvantaged children in the preschool.* Englewood Cliffs, N.J.: Prentice-Hall, 1966.

Bereiter, C., and Engelmann, S. An academically oriented preschool for disadvantaged children: Results from the initial experimental group. In D.W. Brison and J. Hill, eds., *Psychology and early childhood education.* Monograph Series no. 4. Toronto: The Ontario Institute for Studies in Education, 1968.

Bernal, J.D. *Science in history*, vol. 1. New York: Cameron Associates, 1954.

Bernstein, B. Social class, linguistic codes and grammatical elements. *Language and Speech* 5 (1962):221-240.

Berry, J.W. Temne and Eskimo perceptual skills. *International Journal of Psychology* 1 (1966):207-229.

Berry, J.W., and Dasen, P.R., eds. *Culture and cognition: Readings in cross-cultural psychology.* London: Methuen, 1974.

Bibace, R., and Walsh, M.E., eds. Children's conceptions of health, illness and bodily functions. *New Directions for Child Development*, Serial no. 14 (1981).

Bing, E. Effect of child rearing practices on development of different cognitive abilities. *Child Development* 34 (1963):631-648.

Bingham-Newman, A.M., and Hooper, F.H. Classification and seriation instruction and logical task performance in the preschool. *American Educational Research Journal* 11 (1974):379-393.

Birdenough, C. *History of elementary education in England and Wales.* London: W.B. Clive, 1920.

Bissex, G.L. *GNYS AT WRK: A child learns to write and read.* Cambridge, Mass.: Harvard University Press, 1980.

Blank, M. A methodology for fostering abstract thinking in deprived children. In A.J. Biemiller, ed., *Problems in the teaching of young children.* Monograph Series no. 9. Toronto: The Ontario Institute for Studies in Education, 1970.

Blanton, W.E. *Preschool reading instruction.* Prep report no. 39. DHEW Publication no. (NIE) 73-27625. Washington, D.C.: U.S. Department of Health, Education and Welfare, 1972.

Bloom, B.S. The master teachers. *Phi Delta Kappan* (1982):664-668, 715.

Bloom, B.S., Davis A., and Hess, R.D. *Compensatory education for cultural deprivation.* New York: Holt, Rinehart and Winston, 1965.

Bloom, B.S., and Sosniak, L.A. Talent development. *Educational Leadership* 39 (1981):86-94.

Bloom, L. *One word at a time.* The Hague: Mouton, 1970.

Bloom, L., Hood, L., and Lightbrown, P. Imitation in language development: If, when and why? *Cognitive Psychology* 6 (1974):380-420.

Boas, F. *The mind of primitive man.* New York: Macmillan, 1911.

Bohannan, P. *Social anthropology.* New York: Holt, Rinehart and Winston, 1963.

Boney, C. Shall beginning reading be delayed? *Childhood Education* 26 (1949):168-172.

Boring, E.G. *A history of experimental psyhology*, 2nd ed. New York: Appleton-Century-Crofts, 1950.

Bowerman, M. *Early syntactic development: A cross-linguistic study with special reference to Finnish.* Cambridge, England: Cambridge University Press, 1973.

Bowles, S., and Gintis, H. *Schooling in capitalist America.* New York: Basic Books, 1976.

Brackbill, Y. Experimental research with children in the Soviet Union. *American Psychologist* 15 (1960):226-233.

Brackbill, Y. Research and clinical work with children. In R.A. Bauer, ed., *Some views on Soviet psychology.* Washington, D.C.: American Psychological Association, 1962.

Bradley, R.H., and Caldwell, B. Early home environment and change in mental test performance in children from 6 to 36 months. *Developmental Psychology* 12 (1976):93-97.

Brainerd, C.J. Training and transfer of transitivity, conservation, and class inclusion. *Child Development* 45 (1974):324-334.

Brainerd, C.J. Cognitive development and concept learning: An interpretive review. *Psychological Bulletin* 84 (1977):919-939.

Brainerd, C.J. learning research and Piagetian theory. In L.S. Siegel and C.J. Brainerd, eds., *Alternatives to Piaget.* New York: Academic Press, 1978.

Braudel, F. *Capitalism and material life: 1400-1800.* New York: Harper & Row, 1973.

Braun, S.J., and Edwards, E.P. *History and theory of early childhood education.* Belmont, Calif.: Wadsworth, 1972.

Briggs, C., and Elkind, D. Cognitive development in early readers. *Developmental Psychology* 9 (1973):279-280.

Briggs, C., and Elkind, D. Characteristics of early readers. *Perceptual and Motor Skills* 44 (1977):1231-1237.

Brim, O. Jr., and Kagan, J. eds. *Constancy and change in human development.* Cambridge, Mass.: Harvard University Press, 1980.

Brislin, R.W. Translation and content analysis of oral and written materials. In H.C. Triandis and J.W. Berry, eds., *Handbook of cross-cultural psychology*, vol. 2, *Methodology*. Boston: Allyn and Bacon, 1980.

Broadbeck, A., and Irwin, D. The speech development of children without families. *Child Development* 17 (1946):145-146.

Bronfenbrenner, U. Socialization and social class through time and space. In E.E. Maccoby, T.M. Newcomb, and E.L. Hartley, eds., *Readings in social psychology* 3rd ed. New York: Henry Holt, 1958.

Bronfenbrenner, U. Is early intervention effective? In M. Guttentag and E.L. Struening, eds., *Handbook of evaluation research*, vol. 2. Beverly Hills, Calif.: Sage, 1975.

Bronfenbrenner, U. Toward an experimental ecology of human development. *American Psychologist* 32 (1977):513-531.

Bronfenbrenner, U. *The ecology of human development*. Cambridge, Mass.: Harvard University Press, 1979.

Bronfenbrenner, U., Belsky, J., and Steinberg, L. Day care in context: An ecological perspective on research and public policy. Department of Human Development and Family Studies, Cornell University, December 1976.

Brossard, M., and Gouin-Décarie, T. The effects of three kinds of perceptual-social stimulation on the development of institutionalized infants. *Early Child Development and Care* 1 (1971):111-130.

Brown, A. The development of memory: Knowing, knowing about knowing, and knowing how to know. In H.W. Reese, ed., *Advances in child development and behavior*, vol. 10. New York: Academic Press, 1975.

Brown, B., ed. *Found: Long-term gains from early intervention*. American Association for the Advancement of Science Selected Symposium, no. 8. Boulder, Colo.: Westview, 1978.

Brown, M.W. A study of reading ability in preschool children. Unpublished master's thesis, Stanford University, 1924. Summarized in W. Fowler, Cognitive learning in infancy and early childhood, *Psychological Bulletin* 59 (1962):116-151.

Brown, R. *Social psychology*. New York: Free Press, 1965.

Brown, R. *A first language*. Cambridge, Mass.: Harvard University Press, 1973.

Brown, R. The maintenance of conversation. In D. Olson, ed., *The social foundations of language and thought*. New York: Norton, 1980.

Bruce, A. *New ideas in child training*. American Magazine 72 (1911):286-294.

Bruner, J.S. *The process of education*. Cambridge, Mass.: Harvard University Press, 1965.

Bruner, J.S. Representation in childhood. In J.S. Bruner (J.M. Anglin, ed.), *Beyond the information given.* New York: Norton, 1973. (a)

Bruner, J.S. Skill in infancy. In J.S. Bruner (J.M. Anglin, ed.), *Beyond the information given.* New York: Norton, 1973. (b)

Bruner, J. S. The ontogenesis of speech acts. *Journal of Child Language* 2 (1975a):1-19.

Bruner, J.S. From communication to language: A psychological perspective. *Cognition* 3 (1975b):255-287.

Bruner, J.S. Learning how to do things with words. In J. Bruner and A. Garton, eds., *Human growth and development.* Oxford: Clarendon Press, 1978.

Bruner, J.S., and Anglin, J.M., eds., *Beyond the information given.* New York: Norton, 1973.

Bruner, J.S., Goodnow, J.J., and Austin, G.A. *A study of thinking.* New York: J. Wiley and Sons, 1956.

Bruner, J.S., Olver, R.R., and Greenfield, P.M. *Studies in cognitive growth.* New York: J. Wiley and Sons, 1966.

Brunswik, E. *The conceptual framework of psychology.* Chicago: University of Chicago Press 1952.

Bryant, P.E., and Trabasso, T. Transitive inferences and memory in young children. *Nature* (London) 232 (1971):456-458.

Brzeinski, J.E., and Elledge, G.E. Early reading. In R. Aukerman, ed., *Some persistent questions on beginning reading.* Newark, Del.: International Reading Association, 1972.

Bullowa, M. Introduction. Prelinguistic communication: A field for scientific research. In M. Bullowa, ed., *Before speech: The beginning of interpersonal communication.* Cambridge, England: Cambridge University Press, 1979.

Burks, B.S. The relative influence of nature and nurture upon mental development: A comparative study of foster parent-foster child resemblance and true parent-true child resemblance. *Yearbook of the National Society for the Study of Education* 27, pt. I, 1928.

Burks, B.S., Jensen, D.W., and Terman, L.M. The promise of youth. *Genetic studies of genius*, vol. 3. Stanford, Calif.: Stanford University Press, 1930.

Burnett, A. Assessment of intelligence in a restricted environment. Unpublished Ph.D. dissertation, McGill University, Montreal, 1955.

Burnett, A., Beach, H.D., and Sullivan, A.M. Intelligence in a restricted environment. *Canadian Psychologist* 4a (1963):126-136.

Buros, O.K., ed. *Intelligence tests and reviews.* Highland Park, N.J.: Gryphon, 1975.

Burtt, H.E. An experimental study of early childhood memory. *Journal of Genetic Psychology* 40 (1932):287-295.

Burtt, H.E. A further study of early childhood memory. *Journal of Genetic Psychology* 50 (1937):187-192.

Burtt, H.E. An experimental study of early childhood memory: Final Report. *Journal of Genetic Psychology* 58 (1941):435-439.

Bzoch, K.R., and League, R. *The Bzoch-League receptive-expressive emergent language scale.* Tallahassee, Fla.: Anhinga Press, 1970.

Caldwell, B.M. The usefulness of the critical period hypothesis in the study of filiative behavior. *Merrill-Palmer Quarterly* 8 (1962):229-242.

Caldwell, B.M. What is the optimal learning environment for the young child? *American Journal of Orthopsychiatry* 37 (1967):50-67.

Caldwell, B.M. *Cooperative preschool inventory,* rev. ed. Princeton, N.J.: Educational Testing Service, 1970. (a)

Caldwell, B.M. Impact of interest in early cognitive stimulation. Paper presented at the meeting of the National Association for the Education of Young Children, Boston, 1970. (b)

Caldwell, B.M. Can young children have a quality life in day care? *Young Children* 28 (1973):197-208.

Caldwell, B.M., and Richmond, J.B. *The Children's Center: A microcosmic health, education and welfare unit.* Progress report submitted to the Children's Bureau, U.S. Department of Health, Education and Welfare, 1967.

Capra, F. *The Tao of physics.* Berkeley, Calif.: Shambala, 1975.

Capra, F. *The turning point: Science, society and the rising culture.* New York: Simon and Schuster, 1982.

Carcopino, J. *Daily life in ancient Rome.* Harmondsworth, England: Penguin, 1941.

Carew, J.V. Experience and the development of intelligence in young children at home and in day care. *Monographs of the Society for Research in Child Development* 45, Serial no. 187 (1980).

Carter, J.L. The effect of a language stimulation program upon first grade educationally disadvantaged children. *Education for the Mentally Retarded* 1 (1966):169-174.

Carter, J.L., and Capobianco, R.J. A systematic language stimulation program—revisited. *Education and Training of the Mentally Retarded* 11 (1976):112-116.

Case, R. Intellectual and linguistic development in the preschool years. Unpublished paper, Ontario Institute for Studies in Education, Toronto, 1978.

Case, R. *Intellectual development: A systematic reinterpretation.* New York: Academic Press, 1982.

Case, R., and Khanna, F. The missing links: Stages in children's progression from sensorimotor to logical thought. In W. Fischer, ed., *New directions for child development. Cognitive development*, vol. 12. San Francisco: Jossey-Bass, 1981.

Casler, L. Maternal deprivation: a critical review of the literature. *Monographs of the Society for Research in Child Development* 26, Serial no. 80, 1961.

Catell, J. McK. A statistical study of American men of science: III. *Science* N.S. 24 (1906):732-742.

Cazden, C.B. Environmental assistance to the child's acquistion of grammar. Unpublished Ph.D. dissertation, Harvard University, 1965.

Cazden, C.B. *Child language and education.* New York: Holt, Rinehart and Winston, 1972.

Chall, J.S. *Learning to read: The great debate.* New York: McGraw-Hill, 1967.

Chall, J.S. The great debate: Ten years later, with a modest proposal for reading stages. In L.B. Resnick and P.A. Weaver, eds., *Theory and practice of early reading.* Hillsdale, N.J.: Lawrence Erlbaum Associates, 1979.

Chall, J.S. *Stages of reading development.* New York: McGraw-Hill, 1982.

Chapman, R., and Miller, J. Analyzing language and communication in the child. In R. Schiefelbusch, ed., *Nonspeech language and communication: Analysis and integration.* Baltimore: University Park Press, 1980.

Chazan, S. Development of object permanence as a correlate of dimensions of maternal care. *Developmental Psychology* 17 (1981):79-81.

Chi, M.H. Short term memory limitations in children: Capacity or processing deficits. *Memory and Cognition* 4 (1976):559-572.

Chomsky, C. Invented spelling in the open classroom. *Word* 27 (1971): 1-3. (a)

Chomsky, C. Write first, read later. *Childhood Education* 47 (1971):296-299. (b)

Chomsky, C. Approaching reading through invented spelling. Paper presented at the Conference on Beginning Reading Instruction, University of Pittsburgh, May 1976.

Chomsky, N. *Syntactic structures.* The Hague: Mouton, 1957.

Chomsky, N. Review of "verbal behavior" by B.F. Skinner. *Language* 35 (1959):26-58.

Chomsky, N. *Aspects of the theory of syntax.* Cambridge, Mass.: MIT Press, 1965.

Chomsky, N. *Reflections on language.* New York: Pantheon Books, 1975.

Chomsky, N. Several sections in M. Piatelli-Palmarini, ed., *Language and learning: The debate between Jean Piaget and Noam Chomsky.* Cambridge, Mass.: Harvard University Press, 1980.

Chomsky, N., and Halle, M. *The sound pattern of English*. New York: Harper & Row, 1968.

Clark, M.M. *Young fluent readers*. London: Heineman Educational Books, 1976.

Clarke, A.M., and Clarke, A.D.B. *Early experience: Myth and evidence*. New York: Free Press, 1976.

Clarke-Stewart, K.A. Interactions between mothers and their young children: Characteristics and consequences. *Monographs of the Society for Research in Child Development* 38, Serial no. 153 (1973).

Clarke-Stewart, K.A. Popular primers for parents. *American Psychologist* 33 (1978):359-369.

Clarke-Stewart, K.A., VanderStoep, L., and Killian, G. Analysis and replication of mother-child relations at two years of age. *Child Development* 50 (1979):777-793.

Clébert, J.P. *The gypsies*. Harmondsworth, England: Penguin, 1967.

Cohan, M. Two and a half and reading. *Elementary English* 37 (1961): 506-508.

Colardelle-Diarrassouba, M. *Le lièvre et l'araignée dan les contes de l'Ouest Africain*. Paris: Union Génerale d'Editions, 1975.

Colby, M.G. Instrumental reproduction of melody by preschool children. *Journal of Genetic Psychology* 47 (1935):413-430.

Cole, M., and Bruner, J.S. Preliminaries to a theory of cultural differences. In I.J. Gordon, ed., *Early childhood education. Yearbook of the National Society for the Study of Education* 71, pt. II (1972).

Cole, M., Gay, J., and Glick, J. Some experimental studies of Kpelle quantitative behavior. In J.W. Berry and P.R. Dasen, eds., *Culture and Cognition: Readings in cross-cultural psychology*. London: Methuen, 1974.

Cole, M., Gay, J. Glick, J.A., and Sharp, D.W. *The cultural context of learning and thinking*. New York: Basic Books, 1971.

Cole, M., and Scribner, S. *Culture and thought: A psychological introduction in experimental anthropology*. New York: Basic Books, 1971.

Colter, M.W. Cognitive maturity and the development of early reading skills. Unpublished Ph.D. dissertation, Boston University, 1965.

Conklin, H.C. Hanunóo color categories. *Southwestern Journal of Anthropology* 11 (1955):339-344.

Cook, C.A. *Suzuki education in action: A survey of talent training from Japan*. New York: Exposition Press, 1970.

Cook, T.D., and Campbell, D.T. *Quasi-experimentation: Design and analysis issues for field settings*. Chicago: Rand McNally, 1979.

Cooper, C.A., and Alexander, J.S., eds. *Economic development and population growth in the Middle East*. New York: American Elsevier, 1972.

Corrigan, R. Patterns of individual communication and cognitive development. Unpublished Ph.D. dissertation, University of Denver, 1976. *Dissertation Abstracts International* 5393B (1976):37.

Corrigan, R. Language development as related to stage 6 object permanence development. *Journal of Child Language* 5 (1978):173-189.

Corrigan, R. Cognitive correlates of language: Differential criteria yield differential results. *Child Development* 50 (1979):617-631.

Cornell, E.H. Infants' recognition memory, forgetting, and savings. *Journal of Experimental Child Psychology* 28 (1979):359-374.

Cox, C.M. *The early mental traits of three hundred geniuses. Genetic studies of genius*, vol. 2. Stanford, Calif.: Stanford University Press, 1926.

Cratty, B.J. *Physical expression of intelligence.* Englewood Cliffs, N.J.: Prentice-Hall, 1972.

Cratty, B.J., Ibeda, N., Martin, M.M., Jennet, C., and Morison, M. *Movement activities, motor abilities and the education of young children.* Springfield, Ill.: Thomas, 1970.

Cremin, L.A. *The transformation of the school.* New York: Knopf, 1961.

Cremin, L.A. *The genius of American education.* New York: Random House, Vintage Books, 1965.

Cross, T. Mothers' speech and its association with the rate of language development in young children. In N. Waterson and C. Snow, eds., *The development of communication.* New York: J. Wiley and Sons, 1978.

Cross, T., Parmenter, J., and Johnson. Effects of day care experience on the formal and pragmatic development of young children. Paper presented at the Second International Congress for the Study of Child Language, Vancouver, B.C., September 1981.

Curti, M.W. *Child Psychology.* New York: Longmans, Green, 1930.

Danzinger, L., and Frankl, L. Zum problem der functionsreifung. *Zeitschrift für Kinderforschung* 43 (1934):219-255. Summarized in P. Greenacre, Infant reactions to restraint: Problems in the fate of infantile aggressions, *American Journal of Orthopsychiatry* 14 (1944):204-218.

Darsie, M.L. Mental capacity of American-born Japanese children. *Comparative Psychological Monographs* 15, Serial no. 3 (1926).

Darwin, C. Biographical sketch of an infant. *Mind* 2 (1877):285-294.

Dasen, P.R. Cross-cultural Piagetian research: A summary. *Journal of Cross-Cultural Psychology* 3 (1972):23-39.

Dasen, P.R. Concrete operational development in three cultures. *Journal of Cross-Cultural Psychology* 6 (1975):156-172.

Davidson, H.P. An experimental study of bright, average and dull children at the four-year mental level. *Genetic Psychology Monographs* 9 (1931):119-289.

Davies, W.J. *Teaching reading in early England.* London: Pitman House, 1973.

Dawe, H.C. A study of the effect of an educational program upon language development and related mental functions in young children. *Journal of Experimental Education* 11 (1942):200-209.

Day, E.J. The development of language in twins. I: A comparison of twins and single children. *Child Development* 3 (1932):179-199.

Day, M.C., and Parker, R.K., eds., *The preschool in action*, 2nd ed. Boston: Allyn and Bacon, 1977.

Deevey, E.S., Jr. The human population. *Scientific American* 203 (1960): 195-204.

Delaporte, K.L. The long-term effects of a human development program on the intellectual performance, school achievement, and auditory-verbal learning aptitude of economically disadvantaged children. Unpublished Ph.D. dissertation, University of Oklahoma, 1977. *Dissertation Abstracts International* 37 (1977):5031-5032.

Demaitre, L. The idea of childhood and child care in medical writings of the Middle Ages. *The Journal of Psychohistory* 4 (1977):461-490.

deMause, Lloyd, ed. *The history of childhood.* New York: Harper & Row, 1974.

Dempster, F.N. Memory span: Sources of individual and developmental differences. *Psychological Bulletin* 89 (1981):63-100.

Denenberg, V., ed. *Infant education.* Stamford, Conn.: Sinauer, 1970.

Denenberg, V. Paradigms and paradoxes in the study of behavioral development. In E.B. Thoman, ed., *Origins of the infant's social responsiveness.* Hillsdale, N.J.: Lawrence Erlbaum Associates, 1979.

Denenberg, V., and Bell, R.W. Critical periods for the effects of infantile experience on adult learning. *Science* 131 (1960):227-228.

Denney, N.W., and Acito, M.A. Classification training in two- and three-year old children. *Journal of Experimental Child Psychology* 17 (1974): 37-48.

Dennis, W. Infant development under conditions of restricted practice and minimum social stimulation. *Genetic Psychological Monographs* 23 (1941):143-189.

Dennis, W. The performance of Hopi children on the Goodenough draw-a-man test. *Journal of Comparative Psychology* 34 (1942):341-348.

Dennis, W. Historical beginning of child psychology. *Psychological Bulletin* 46 (1949):224-235.

Dennis, W. Causes of retardation among institutional children. *Journal of Genetic Psychology* 96 (1960):47-59. (a)

Dennis, W. The human figure drawings of Bedouins. *Journal of Social Psychology* 52 (1960):209-219. (b)

Dennis, W. *Children of the Crèche*. New York: Appleton-Century-Crofts, 1973.

Dennis, W., and Dennis, M.G. The effect of cradling practices upon the onset of walking in Hopi children. *Journal of Genetic Psychology* 56 (1940):77-86.

Dennis, W., and Dennis, M.G. Development under controlled environmental conditions. In W. Dennis, ed., *Readings in child psychology*. New York: Prentice-Hall, 1951.

Dennis, W., and Najarian, P. Infant development under environmental handicap. *Psychological Monographs* 71 (1957):1-13.

Dennis, W., and Sayegh, Y. The effect of supplementary experiences upon the behavioral development of infants in institutions. *Child Development* 36 (1965):81-90.

Deregowski, J.B. *Illusions, patterns and pictures*. London: Academic Press, 1980.

Derwing, B. *Transformational grammar as a theory of language acquisition*. Cambridge, England: Cambridge University Press, 1973.

Descoeudres, A. *Le Développement de l'enfant de deux à sept ans* 3rd ed. Neuchatel: Delachaux et Niestlé, 1921.

Deutsch, M., Victor, J., Taleporos, E., Deutsch, C., Faigao, B., Calhoun, E., and Ponder, E. *An evaluation of the effectiveness of an enriched curriculum in overcoming the consequences of environmental deprivation*. Institute for Developmental Studies, New York University. Final report to the U.S. Department of Health, Education and Welfare, Washington, D.C., 1971.

Deutsche, J.M. *The development of children's concepts of causal relations*. Minneapolis: University of Minnesota Press, 1937.

deVilliers, J., and deVilliers, P. *Language acquisition*. Cambridge, Mass.: Harvard University Press, 1978.

Dewey, J. *The child and the curriculum and the school and society*. Chicago: University of Chicago Press, 1971.

D'Mello, S., and Willemsen, E. The development of the number concept: A scalogram anlaysis. *Child Development* 40 (1969):681-688.

Doehring, D.G. *Patterns of impairment in specific reading disability*. Bloomington, Ind.: Indiana University Press, 1968.

Dolbear, K.E. Precocious children. *Pedagogical Seminary* 19 (1912):461-491.

Doll, E.A. *The measurement of social competence: A manual for the Vineland Social Maturity Scale*. Minneapolis: Educational Test Bureau, 1953.

Donaldson, M. *Children's minds*. Glasgow: Fontanal Collins, 1978.

Douglas, N.K., and Schwartz, J.B. Increasing awareness of art ideas of young children through guided experiences with ceramics. *Studies in Art Education* 8 (1967):2-9.

Downing, J., ed. *Comparative reading*. New York: Macmillan, 1973.

Downing, J., *Reading and reasoning*. New York: Springer-Verlag, 1979.

Downing, J., Ayers, D., and Schaefer, B. Conceptual and perceptual factors in learning to read. Unpublished paper, University of Victoria, Victoria, B.C., 1978.

Downing, J., and Thackray, D. *Reading readiness*. London: Hodder and Stoughton, 1975.

Doyle, A-B. Infant development in day care. *Developmental Psychology* 2 (1975):655-656.

Drash, P.W. Personal communication, 1982.

Drash, P.W., and Stolberg, A.L. *Acceleration of cognitive, linguistic and social development in the normal infant*. Tallahassee, Fla.: Florida State Department of Health and Rehabilitation Services, March 1977. ERIC Document Reproduction Service no. ED 145 938.

Drash, P.W., and Stolberg, A.L. Intellectual acceleration in normal and Down's Syndrome children through infant stimulation and language training. Paper presented at the annual conference of the Southeastern Psychological Association, New Orleans, Louisiana, March 1979.

Dubin, E.R. The effect of training on the tempo of development of graphic representation in preschool children. *Journal of Experimental Education* 15 (1946):166-173.

DuBois, P.H. A test standardized on Pueblo Indian children. *Psychological Bulletin* 36 (1939):523.

Duckett, J.M. Idiot savants: Super specialization in mentally retarded persons. Unpublished Ph.D. dissertation, University of Texas, Austin, 1976. *Dissertation Abstracts International* 37 (1977):5032A. University Microfilms no. 77-3894.

Duncan, H.F., Gourlay, N., and Hudson, W. A study of pictorial perception among Bantu and white primary school children in South Africa. Human Sciences Research Council Series, no. 31. Johannesburg: Witwatersrand University Press, 1973.

Dunlop, A.B. Observations on the reading attainment of a group of infant school children in Glascow. Abstract. *British Journal of Educational Psychology* 12 (1942):76-77.

Dunn, B.J.S. The effectiveness of teaching selected reading skills to children two through four years of age by television. Unpublished Ph.D. dissertation, University of California at Los Angeles, 1969. University Microfilms no. 70-14, 274, Ann Arbor, Mich., 1970.

Durbach, E. Untitled manuscript on the development of five eminent playrights. Ontario Institute for Studies in Education, Toronto, 1979.

Durkin, D. A fifth-year report on the achievement of early readers. *Elementary School Journal* 65 (1964):76-80.

Durkin, D. *Children who read early*. New York: Teachers College Press, Columbia University, 1966.

Durkin, D. When should children begin to read? In P.M. Robinson, ed., *Innovation and change in reading instruction. Yearbook of the National Society for the Study of Education* 67, pt. II (1968).

Durkin, D. *Teaching young children to read*. Boston: Allyn and Bacon, 1972.

Durkin, D. A six year study of children who learned to read in school at the age of four. *Reading Research Quarterly* 10 (1974-1975):9-61.

Durkin, D. Facts about pre-first grade reading. In L.O. Ollila, ed., *The kindergarten child and reading*. Newark, Del.: International Reading Association, 1977.

Durkin, D. *Teaching young children to read*, 3rd ed. Boston: Allyn and Bacon, 1980.

Dye, N.W., and Very, P.S. Growth changes in factorial structure by age and sex. *Genetic Psychology Monographs* 78 (1968):55-88.

Earle, A.M. *Child life in colonial days*. Folcroft, Pa.: Folcroft Library Editions, 1974. Originally published, 1899.

Ehrensaft, P. The political economy of informal empire in precolonial Nigeria, 1807-1884. In P.C.W. Guthond and P. Waterman, eds., *African social studies*. New York: Monthly Review Press, 1977.

Ehri, L.C. Beginning reading from a psycholinguistic perspective: Amalgamation of word identities. In F.B. Murray, ed., *The recognition of words*. Newark, Del.: International Reading Association, 1978.

Ehri, L.C. Linguistic insight: threshold of reading acquisition. In T.G. Waller and G.E. MacKinnon, eds., *Reading research: Advances in theory and practice*. Vol. 1. New York: Academic Press, 1979.

Ehri, L.C. Orthography and phonology in printed word learning. Paper presented at the biennial meeting of the Society for Research in Child Development, Boston, Mass., April 1981.

Eisner, E.W. *The Kettering project of Stanford University*. Stanford, Calif.: Stanford University Press, 1972.

Eisner, E.W. The mythology of art education. Paper presented at the School of Art Education, Birmingham Polytechnic, Birmingham, England, n.d.

Elardo, R., Bradley, R., and Caldwell, B. A longitudinal study of the relation of infants' home environments to language development at age three. *Child Development* 48 (1977):595-603.

Elkind, D. Reading, logic and perception. In J.F. Hellmuth, ed., *Educational therapy*, vol. 2. Seattle: Special Child Publications, 1969.

Elkind, D. Perceptual development in children. *American Scientist* 63 (1975):533-541. (a)

Elkind, D. We can teach reading better. *Today's Education* 64 (1975): 34-38. (b)

Elkind, D. Cognitive development and reading. In H. Singer and R. Ruddell, eds., *Theoretical models and processes of reading*, 2nd ed. Newark, Del.: International Reading Association, 1977.

Elkind, D. *The hurried child.* Reading, Mass.: Addison-Wesley, 1981.

Elkonin, D.B. Development of speech. In A.V. Zaporozhets and D.B. Elkonin, eds. *The psychology of preschool children.* Cambridge, Mass.: MIT Press, 1971.

Ellis, N.R., ed. *Handbook of mental deficiency.* New York: McGraw-Hill, 1963.

Ellis, R., and Wells, G. Enabling factors in adult-child discourse. *First Language* 1 (1980):46-62.

Engelmann, S. *The basic concept inventory: Teacher's manual*, Field research ed. Chicago: Follett, 1967.

Englefield, F.R.H. *Language: Its origins and its relation to thought.* London: Pemberton, 1977.

Ervin, S.M., and Miller, W.R. Language development. In H.W. Stevenson, ed., *Child psychology. Yearbook of the National Society for the Study of Education* 62, pt. I (1963).

Este, H. Five Victorian novelists in the making: Their early and middle childhood years. Unpublished paper, Ontario Institute for Studies in Education, Toronto, 1979.

Etaugh, C. Effects of nonmaternal care on children. *American Psychologist* 35 (1980):309-310.

Evans, E.D. *Contemporary influences in early childhood education*, 2nd ed. New York: Holt, Rinehart and Winston, 1975.

Ewers, J.C. *The horse in Blackfoot Indian culture.* Smithsonian Institute Bureau of American Ethnology Bulletin, no. 159. Washington, D.C.: U.S. Government Printing Office, 1955.

Ewing, G. Presyntax: The development of word order in early child speech. Unpublished Ph.D. dissertation, Department of Linguistics, University of Toronto, in preparation.

Fafouti-Milénkovic, M., and Uzgiris, I.C. The mother-infant communication system. In I.C. Uzgiris, ed., *Social interaction and communication during infancy.* San Francisco: Jossey-Bass, 1979.

Fagan, J.F., III. Facilitation of infants' recognition memory. *Child Development* 49 (1978):1066-1075.

Fagen, J.W. Interproblem learning in ten-month-old infants. *Child Development* 48 (1977):786-796.

Farber, S. *Identical twins reared apart: A reanalysis.* New York: Basic Books, 1980.

Farnham-Diggory, S. Symbol and synthesis in experimental "reading." *Child Development* 38 (1967):221-231.

Farnham-Diggory, S. *Cognitive processes in education.* New York: Harper & Row, 1972.

Farnham-Diggory, S. *Learning disabilities: A psychological perspective.* Cambridge, Mass.: Harvard University Press, 1978.

Farnham-Diggory, S., and Bermon, M. Verbal compensation, cognitive synthesis, and conservation. *Merrill-Palmer Quarterly* 14 (1968):215-228.

Farnham-Diggory, S., and Gregg, L.W. Short term memory function in young readers. *Journal of Experimental Child Psychology* 19 (1975): 279-298.

Fein, G., and Clarke-Stewart, A. *Day care in context.* New York: J. Wiley and Sons, 1973.

Feitelson, D. Cross-cultural studies of representational play. In B. Tizard and D. Harvey, eds., *Biology of play.* Philadelphia: Lippincott, 1977.

Feldman, C.F., Lee, B., McLean, J.D., Pillemer, D.B., and Murray, J.R. *The development of adaptive intelligence.* San Francisco: Jossey-Bass, 1974.

Feldman, D.H. *Beyond universals in cognitive development.* Norwood, N.J.: Ablex, 1980.

Ferguson, M. *The Acquarian conspiracy: Personal and social transformation in the 1980s.* Los Angeles: J.P. Tarcher (distributed by Houghton Mifflin, Boston), 1980.

Feuerstein, R. *Instrumental enrichment: An intervention program for cognitive modifiability.* Baltimore: University Park Press, 1980.

Fillmore, C., Kempler, D., and Wang, W., eds. *Individual differences in language ability and language behavior.* New York: Academic Press, 1979.

Filmore, E.A., and Skeels, H.M. Mental development of children from underprivileged homes. *Journal of Genetic Psychology* 50 (1937):427-439.

Findley, W.G. Early education as continuous stimulation. *Journal of Research and Development in Education* 1 (1968):46-50.

Findley, W.G. University of Georgia. Personal communication, 1982.

Firth, I. Components of reading disability. Unpublished Ph.D. dissertation, University of New South Wales, Kensington, New South Wales, Australia, 1972.

Fischer, K. A theory of cognitive development: The control and construction of hierarchies of skills. *Psychological Review* 87 (1980):477-531.

Fisher, M.S. Language patterns of preschool children. *Child Development Monographs* 15 (1934):16-88.

Fisichelli, R. A study of the prelinguistic speech development of institutionalized infants. Unpublished Ph.D. dissertation, Fordham University. Summarized in F. Catalano and D. McCarthy, Infant speech as a possible predictor of later intelligence, *Journal of Psychology* 38 (1954):203-209.

Fiske, D.W., and Maddi, S.R. *The functions of varied experience.* Homewood, Ill.: Dorsey Press, 1961.

Fitts, P.M., and Posner, M.I. *Human performance.* Belmont, Calif.: Brooks Cole, 1967.

Fjellman, J. The myth of primitive mentality. Ph.D. dissertation, Stanford University, 1971. *Dissertation Abstracts International* 32 (1972): 5585B. University Microfilms no. 72-11549.

Flavell, J.H. *The developmental psychology of Jean Piaget.* New York: Van Nostrand, 1963.

Flesch, R. *Why Johnny can't read.* New York: Harper, 1956.

Flint, B.M. *The child and the institution: A study of deprivation and recovery.* Toronto: University of Toronto Press, 1966.

Flint, B.M. *New hope for deprived children.* Toronto: University of Toronto Press, 1978.

Fodor, E.M. The effect of systematic reading of stories on the language development of culturally deprived children. Unpublished Ph.D. dissertation. *Dissertation Abstracts International* 27 (1966):952A.

Fodor, J.A. Several sections in M. Piatelli-Palmarini, ed., *Language and learning: The debate between Jean Piaget and Noam Chomsky.* Cambridge, Mass.: Harvard University Press, 1980.

Forest, I. *Preschool education; a historical and critical study.* New York: Macmillan, 1927.

Forsyth, I. Children in early medieval art: Ninth through twelfth centuries. *Journal of Psychohistory* 4 (1976):31-70.

Foster, J.C. Verbal memory in the preschool child. *Journal of Genetic Psychology* 35 (1928):26-44.

Fowler, W. Cognitive stimulation, IQ changes, and cognitive learning in three-year old identical twins and triplets. Abstract. *American Psychologist* 16 (1961):373.

Fowler, W. Cognitive learning in infancy and early childhood. *Psychological Bulletin* 59 (1962):116-152. (a)

Fowler, W. Teaching a two-year-old to read: An experiment in early childhood learning. *Genetic Psychology Monographs* 66 (1962):181-283. (b)

Fowler, W. Multiple birth and mental health. In A. Deutsch, ed., *Encyclopedia of mental health.* New York: Franklin Watts, 1963, Vol. 4, 1267-1275.

Fowler, W. Structural dimensions of the learning process in early reading. *Child Development* 35 (1964):1093-1104.

Fowler, W. A study of process and method in three-year-old twins and triplets learning to read. *Genetic Psychology Monographs* 72 (1965): 3-89. (a)

Fowler, W. Concept learning in early childhood. *Young Children* 21 (1965): 81-91. (b)

Fowler, W. Design and values in the nursery school. *Inland Architect*, 9 (1965):12-15. (c)

Fowler, W. The design of early developmental learning programs for disadvantaged young children. *Supplement to IRCD Bulletin*, ERIC Information Retrieval Center on the Disadvantaged, 3 (1967):1A. (a)

Fowler, W. The dimensions for environmental control over developmental learning. *Psychologia Wychowawcza* 10 (1967) no. 3, pp. 265-281, and no. 4, pp. 385-397. (b)

Fowler, W. The effect of early stimulation in the emergence of cognitive processes. In R. Hess and R. Bear, eds., *Early education*. Chicago: Aldine, 1968.

Fowler, W. The patterning of developmental learning processes in the nursery school. In A.J. Biemiller, ed., *Problems in the teaching of young children*. Monograph Series no. 9. Toronto: Ontario Institute for Studies in Education, 1970.

Fowler, W. A developmental learning strategy for early reading in a laboratory nursery school. *Interchange* 2 (1971):106-125. (a)

Fowler, W. Cognitive baselines in early childhood: Development learning and differentiation of competence rule systems. In J. Hellmuth, ed., *Cognitive studies: Cognitive deficits*, vol. 2. New York: Brunner/Mazel, 1971. (b)

Fowler, W. Mental prodigies. In *Encyclopedia of Education*. New York: Macmillan, 1971. (c)

Fowler, W. A developmental learning approach to infant care in a group setting. *Merrill-Palmer Quarterly* 18 (1972):145-175.

Fowler, W. Language: Development and stimulation program. Unpublished paper. Toronto: Ontario Institute for Studies in Education, 1974.

Fowler, W. How adult/child ratios influence infant development. *Interchange* 6 (1975):17-31.

Fowler, W. The role of cognitive learning in motor development. In final report, State of the art research review and conference on the psychomotor development in preschool handicapped children for the Bureau of Education for the Handicapped, Office of Education, U.S. Department of Health, Education and Welfare, Contract N. 300-75-0225. Milwaukee, Wis.: Vasquez Associates, 1976.

Fowler, W. Sequence and styles in cognitive development. In I.C. Uzgiris and F. Weizmann, eds., *The structuring of experience*. New York: Plenum, 1977.

Fowler, W. *Day care and its effects on early development: A study of group and home care in multi-ethnic working-class families*. Toronto: Ontario Institute for Studies in Education, 1978. (a)

Fowler, W. *Supplement to day care and its effects on early development: Guides to early care and teaching*. Toronto: Ontario Institute for Studies in Education, 1978. (b)

Fowler, W. Cognitive differentiation and developmental learning. In H.W. Reese, and L.P. Lipsitt, eds., *Advances in child development and behavior*, vol. 15. New York: Academic Press, 1980. (a)

Fowler, W. *Curriculum and assessment guides for infant and child care*. Boston: Allyn and Bacon, 1980. (b)

Fowler, W. *Infant and child care: An approach to education in group settings*. Boston: Allyn and Bacon, 1980. (c)

Fowler, W. A strategy for stimulating infant learning. In R.L. Schiefelbusch, ed., *Early language: Acquisition and intervention*. Baltimore: University Park Press, 1981. (a)

Fowler, W. Case studies of cognitive precocity: The role of exogenous and endogenous stimulation in early mental development. *Journal of Applied Developmental Psychology* 2 (1981):319-367. (b)

Fowler, W., and Burnett, A. Models for learning in an integrated preschool. *Elementary School Journal* 67 (1967):428-441.

Fowler, W., and Fowler, J. Competence development in a tribal society. Unpublished paper, Ontario Institute for Studies in Education, Toronto, 1978.

Fowler, W., and Leithwood, K. Cognition and movement: Theoretical, pedagogical and measurement considerations. *Perceptual and Motor Skills* 32 (1971):523-532.

Fowler, W., and Swenson, A. The influence of early language stimulation on development: Four studies. *Genetic Psychology Monographs* 100 (1979):73-109.

Fox, B., and Routh, D.K. Analyzing spoken language into words, syllables and phonemes: A developmental study. *Journal of Psycholinguistic Research* 4 (1975):331-342.

Fox, B., and Routh, D.K. Phonemic analysis and synthesis as word-attack skills. *Journal of Educational Psychology* 68 (1976):70-74.

Frank, L.K. The beginnings of child development and family life education in the twentieth century. *Merrill-Palmer Quarterly* 8 (1962):207-228.

Frankenberg, W., and Dodds, J. The Denver developmental screening test. *Journal of Pediatrics* 71 (1967): 181-191.

Fraser, C. Discussion of McNeill's paper: The creation of language in children. In J. Lyons and R. Wales, eds., *Psycholinguistics papers: Proceedings of the 1966 Edinburgh conference*. Edinburgh: Edinburgh University Press, 1966.

Freeberg, N.E., and Payne, D.T. Dimensions of parental practice concerned with cognitive development in the preschool child. *Journal of Genetic Psychology* 111 (1967):245-261. (a)

Freeberg, N.E., and Payne, D.T. Parental influence on cognitive development in early childhood: A review. *Child Development* 38 (1967): 65-87 (b)

Freeman, F.N., Holzinger, K.J., and Mitchell, B.C. The influence of environment on the intelligence, school achievement, and conduct of foster children. *Yearbook of the National Society for the Study of Education*, 27 pt. I (1928).

Freeman, J. *Gifted children*. Lancaster, England: MTP Press, 1979.

Frost, J.L., and Hawkes, G.R., eds. *The disadvantaged child*. New York: Houghton Mifflin, 1966.

Frostig, M., and Maslow, P. *Movement education: Theory and practice*. Chicago: Follett, 1970.

Frumhartz, D. The effect of planned social interaction on institutionalized infants. Unpublished Ph.D. dissertation, McGill University, 1970.

Fucigna, C., Ives, K., and Ives, W. Art for toddlers: A developmental approach. *Young Children* 37 (1982):45-51.

Fullard, W.G., Jr. Operant training of aural musical discriminations with preschool children. *Journal of Research in Music Education* 15 (1967): 201-209.

Fuller, R. Breaking down the IQ walls: Severely retarded people can learn to read. *Psychology Today* (October 1974):97-102.

Furby, L. Cumulative learning and cognitive development. *Human Development* 15 (1972):265-286.

Furrow, D., Nelson, K., and Benedict, H. Mother's speech to children and syntactic developments: Some simple relationships. *Journal of Child Language* 6 (1979):423-442.

Furth, H.G. Reading and thinking: A developmental perspective. In F.B. Murray and J. Pikulski, eds., *The acquisition of reading*. Baltimore, Md.: University Park Press, 1978.

Gagné, R.M. Contributions of learning to human development. *Psychological Review* 75 (1968):177-199.

Gagné, R.M. *The conditions of learning*, 2nd ed. New York: Holt, Rinehart and Winston, 1970.

Galt, H.S. *A history of Chinese educational institutions*. London: Probsthain, 1951.

Galton, F. *Inquiries into human faculty and its development*. London: J.M. Dent and Sons, 1907.

Galton, F. *Hereditary genius: An inquiry into its laws and consequences*, 2nd ed. London: Macmillan, 1925.

Garber, H.L., and Heber, R. The efficacy of early intervention with family rehabilitation. In M.J. Begab, H.C. Haywood, and H.L. Garber, eds., *Psychosocial influences in retarded performance. Vol. 2: Strategies for improving competence*. Baltimore: University Park Press, 1981.

Gardiner, A. *Egypt of the Pharoahs*. London: Oxford University Press, 1961.

Gardner, H. *The arts and human development*. New York: J. Wiley and Sons, 1973.

Gardner, H. *Artful scribbles: The significance of children's drawings*. New York: Basic Books, 1980.

Gardner, R.W., Holzman, P.S., Klein, G.S., Linton, H.B., and Spence, D.P. Cognitive controls: A study of individual consistencies in cognitive behavior. *Psychological Issues* 1, no. 4 (1959).

Gardner, R.W., Jackson, D.N., and Messick, S.J. Personality organization in cognitive controls and intellectual abilities. *Psychogical Issues* 2, no. 4 (1960).

Garrett, H.E. Differentiable mental traits. *Psychological Record* 2 (1938): 259-298.

Gates, A.I. *Gates primary reading tests*. New York: Teacher College, Columbia University, 1943.

Gates, A.I., Huber, M.B., and Salisbury, F.S. *The Macmillan readers*. New York: Macmillan, 1951.

Gates, A.I., and Taylor, G.A. An experimental study of the nature of improvement resulting from practice in a mental function. *Journal of Educational Psychology* 16 (1925):583-593.

Geber, M. The psychomotor development of African children in the first year and the influence of maternal behavior. *Journal of Social Psychology* 47 (1958):185-195.

Geber, M., and Dean, R.F.A. Gesell tests on African children. *Pediatrics* 20 (1957):1055-1065.

Gelman, R. The nature and development of early number concepts. In H.W. Reese, ed., *Advances in child development and behavior*, vol. 7. New York: Academic Press, 1972.

Gelman, R., and Gallistel, C.R. *The child's understanding of numbers*. Cambridge, Mass.: Harvard University Press, 1978.

Gerhardt, L.A. *Moving and knowing: The young child orients himself in space*. Engelwood Cliffs, N.J.: Prentice-Hall, 1973.

Gerritz, K.E. First graders' spelling of vowels: An exploratory study. Unpublished Ph.D. dissertation, Harvard University, 1974.

Gesell, A. Mental and physical correspondence in twins. *The Scientific Monthly* 14 (1922):305-331, 415-428.

Gesell, A. *Studies in child development.* New York: Harper & Brothers,1948.

Gesell, A. *Infant development: The embryology of early human behavior.* New York: Harper & Brothers, 1952.

Gesell, A., and Amatruda, C.S. *Developmental diagnosis*, 2nd ed. New York: Hoeber, 1947.

Gesell, A., and Ames, L.B. The development of directionality in drawing. *Journal of Genetic Psychology* 68 (1946):45-61.

Gesell, A., Halverson, H.M., Thompson, H., Ilg, F.L., Castner, B.M., Ames, L.B., and Amatruda, C.S. *The first five years of life: A guide to the study of the preschool child.* New York: Harper, 1940.

Gesell, A., and Ilg, F.L. *The child from five to ten.* New York: Harper & Brothers, 1946.

Gesell, A., and Ilg, F.L. *Child development: An introduction to the study of human growth.* New York: Harper, 1949.

Gesell, A., Ilg, F.L., Ames, L.B., and Rodell, J.L. *Infant and child in the culture of today* rev. ed. New York: Harper & Row, 1974.

Gesell, A., Ilg, F.L., and Bullis, G.E. *Vision: Its development in infant and child.* New York: Hoeber, 1949.

Gesell, A., and Thompson, H. Learning and growth in identical infant twins: An experimental study by the method of co-twin control. *Genetic Psychology Monographs* 6 (1929):1-124.

Gesell, A., and Thompson, H. Twins T and C from infancy to adolescence: A biogenetic study of individual differences by the method of co-twin control. *Genetic Psychology Monographs* 24 (1941):3-121.

Ghiselin, B. *The creative process.* New York: Mentor, 1955.

Ghuman, P. *The cultural context of thinking.* London: Heineman, 1975.

Gibson, E.J. Learning to read. *Science* 148 (1965):1066-1072.

Gibson, E.J. The ontogeny of reading. *American Psychologist* 25 (1970): 136-143.

Gibson, E.J., and Levin, H. *The psychology of reading.* Cambridge, Mass.: MIT Press, 1975.

Gibson, J. *The ecological approach to visual perception.* Boston: Houghton Mifflin, 1979.

Gilmore, J.V. *Gilmore oral reading test (Forms A & B).* Yonkers-on-Hudson, N.Y.: World Book, 1952.

Giltay, M. Sur l'apparition et le développement de la notion du nombre chez l'enfant de deux à sept ans. *Journal de Psychologie Normale et Pathologigue* 33 (1936):673-695.

Ginsberg, H. *The myth of the deprived child.* Englewood Cliffs, N.J.: Prentice-Hall, 1972.

Giovannoni, J.M., and Billingsley, A. Child neglect among the poor: A study of parental adequacy in families of three ethnic groups. In S. Chess and A. Thomas, eds., *Annual progress in child psychiatry and child development*. New York: Brunner/Mazel, 1971.

Glick, J. Cognitive development in cross-cultural perspective. In F.D. Horowitz, ed., *Review of child development research*, vol. 4. Chicago: University of Chicago Press, 1975.

Goertzel, V., and Goertzel, M.G. *Cradles of eminence*. Boston: Little, Brown, 1962.

Goethe, J.W. *Elective infinities*. Chicago: Henery Regnery, 1963.

Goldberg, S. Infant care and growth in urban Zambia. *Human Development* 15 (1972):77-89.

Golden, M., Rosenbluth, L., Grossi, M.T., Policare, H.J., Freeman, H., and Brownlee, E.M. *The New York City infant day care study: A comparative study of licensed group and family infant day care programs and their effects on children and their families*. Medical and Health Research Association of New York City, 1978.

Goldstein, D.M. Cognitive-linguistic functioning and learning to read in preschoolers. *Journal of Educational Psychology* 68 (1976):680-688.

Goleman, D. 1,528 little geniuses and how they grew. *Psychology Today* (February 1980):28-53.

Gombrich, E.H. *Art and illusion*, 2nd ed., rev. Princeton, N.J.: Princeton University Press, 1961.

Goodwin, W.L., and Driscoll, L.A. *Handbook for measurement and evaluation in early childhood education*. San Francisco: Jossey-Bass, 1980.

Gopnik, A. Early locative terms and concepts of space. Lecture at the Linguistics Department, University of Toronto, November 6, 1981.

Gordon, H. *Mental and scholastic tests among retarded children*. Pamphlet no. 44. London: Board of Education, 1923.

Gordon, I.J. *Early child stimulation through parent education*. Final report to the Children's Bureau, Social and Rehabilitation Service, U.S. Department of Health, Education and Welfare. PHS-R-306 (01), June 1969.

Gordon, I.J. An instructional theory approach to the analysis of selected early childhood programs. In I.J. Gordon, ed., *Early childhood education. Yearbook of the National Society for the Study of Education* 71, pt. 2 (1972).

Gordon, I.J. *The Florida parent education early intervention projects: A longitudinal look*. Gainesville, Fla.: Institute for Development of Human Resources, College of Education, University of Florida, 1973.

Gordon, I.J. Intervention in infant education. Paper presented at the Texas Conference on Infancy, Austin, June 1975.

Gordon, I.J., Guinagh, B., and Jester, R.E. The Florida parent education infant and toddler programs. In M.C. Day and R.K. Parker, eds., *The preschool in action*, 2nd ed. Boston: Allyn and Bacon, 1977.

Gottfried, A.W. Interrelationships between nomological networks of psychomotion and Piagetian measures of sensorimotor intelligence. Unpublished Ph.D. dissertation, New School for Social Research, New York, 1974.

Gowan, J.C. Background and history of the gifted-child movement. In J.C. Stanley, W.C. George, and C.H. Solano, eds., *The gifted and the creative: A fifty year perspective*. Baltimore: Johns Hopkins University Press, 1977.

Grassam, E.H. *Beacon teachers' handbook: Old Lob approach*, 2nd ed. London: Ginn, 1952.

Gray, S.W. Children from three to ten: The early training project. In S. Ryan, ed., *A report on longitudinal evaluations of preschool programs: Vol. 1: Longitudinal evaluations*. DHEW Publication no. (OHD) 74-24. Washington, D.C.: U.S. Department of Health, Education and Welfare, 1974.

Gray, S.W., and Klaus, R.A. The early training project: A seventh year report. *Child Development* 41 (1970):909-924.

Gray, S.W., Klaus, R.A., Miller, J.O., and Forrester, B.J. *The early training project: A handbook of aims and activities*. Nashville, Tenn.: George Peabody College for Teachers and Murfreesboro, Tenn., City Schools 1965.

Gray, S.W., Klaus, R.A., and Ramsey, B.K. Participants in the early training project: 1962-1977. In M.J. Begab, H.C. Haywood, and H.L. Garber, eds., *Psychosocial influences in retarded performance. Vol. 2: Strategies for improving competence*. Baltimore: University Park Press, 1981.

Gray, S.W., Ramsey, B.K., and Klaus, R.A. *From 3 to 20: The early training project*. Baltimore: University Press Press, 1982.

Green, D.R., Ford, M.P., and Flamer, G.B., eds. *Measurement and Piaget*. New York: McGraw-Hill, 1971.

Greenacre, P. Infant reactions to restraint: Problems in the fate of infantile aggressions. *Journal of Orthopsychiatry* 14 (1944):204-218.

Gregg, W., and Farnham-Diggory, S. How to study reading: An information processing analysis. In L.B. Resnick and P.A. Weaver, eds., *Theory and practice of early reading*, vol. 3. Hillsdale, N.J.: Lawrence Erlbaum Associates, 1979.

Griffiths, R. *The abilities of babies*. London: University of London Press, 1954.

Griffiths, R. *The abilities of young children*. London: Child Development Research Centre, 1970.

Gross, M. *Learning readiness in two Jewish groups*. New York: Center for Urban Education, 1967.

Gross, R., and Gross, B., eds. *Radical school reform*. New York: Simon and Schuster, 1969.

Grossman, M. Art education for the young. *Review of Educational Research*, University of South Florida, 40 (1970):421-427.

Gruber, H.E., and Vonèche, J.J., eds. *The essential Piaget*. New York: Basic Books, 1977.

Guilford, J.P. *The nature of human intelligence*. New York: McGraw-Hill, 1967.

Guinagh, B.J., and Gordon, I.J. *School performance as a function of early stimulation*. Final report to Office of Child Development, Grant no. NIH-HEW-OCD-09-C-638. Gainesville, Fla.: Institute for Development of Human Resources, University of Florida, 1976.

Guinagh, B.J., and Gordon, I.J. School performance as a function of early stimulation. *Catalog of selected documents in psychology*, American Psychological Association 8 (1978):31-32.

Guinagh, B.J., Olmsted, P.P., and Gordon, I.J. Untitled paper presented at the biennial meeting of the Society for Research in Child Development, Denver, Colo., April 1975. Gainesville, Fla.: Institute for Development of Human Resources, University of Florida, 1975.

Haas, M.B., and Harms, I.E. Social interaction between infants. *Child Development* 34 (1963):79-97.

Hadfield, C. *The canal age*. Newton Abbot, England: David and Charles, 1968.

Hagen, J.W., Jongeward, R.H., Jr., and Kail, R.V., Jr. Cognitive perspectives on the development of memory. In H.W. Reese, ed., *Advances in child development and behavior*, vol. 10. New York: Academic Press, 1975.

Hall, G.S. The contents of children's minds. *Princeton Review* 2 (1883): 249-272.

Hall, G.S. A study of fears. *American Journal of Psychology* 8 (1896): 147-249.

Hall, G.S. *Adolescence*. New York: Appleton, 1904.

Hall, G.S. Aspects of child life and education, T.L. Smith, ed. Boston: Ginn, 1907.

Hall, V.C., and Kaye, D.B. Early patterns of cognitive development. *Monographs of the Society for Research in Child Development* 45, Serial no. 184 (1980).

Hall, V.C., Salvi, R., Seggev, L., and Caldwell, E. Cognitive synthesis conservation, and task analysis. *Development Psychology* 213 (1970): 423-428.

Halliday, M. One child's protolanguage. In M. Bullowa, ed., *Before speech: The beginning of interpersonal communication.* Cambridge, England: Cambridge University Press, 1979.

Hamilton, G.V.N. A study of trial and error reactions in mammals. *Journal of Animal Behavior* 1 (1911):33-66.

Hamilton, G.V.N. A study of perseverance reactions in primates and rodents. *Behavioral Monographs* 3, no. 2 (1916):1-65.

Hamilton, M.L. Social learning and the transition from babbling to words. *Journal of Genetic Psychology* 130 (1977):211-270.

Hanfmann, E., and Kasanin, J. Conceptual thinking in schizophrenia. *Nervous and Mental Disease Monographs* no. 67 (1942).

Hanson, R. Consistency and stability of home environmental measures related to IQ. *Child Development* 46 (1975):470-480.

Harlow, H.F. The formation of learning sets. *Psychological Review* 56 (1949):51-65.

Harrington, M. *The twilight of capitalism.* New York: Simon and Schuster, 1976.

Harris, D.B. *Children's drawings as measures of intellectual maturity.* New York: Harcourt, Brace and World, 1963.

Harris, J.C. *Told by Uncle Remus.* New York: McClure, Philips, 1905.

Harris, M. *Cannibals and kings: The origins of cultures.* New York: Random House, 1977.

Harty, K.F. A comparative analysis of children who enter kindergarten reading and children of the same age who require additional readiness for reading. Unpublished Ph.D. dissertation, University of Wisconsin, 1975.

Havelock, E.A. *Origins of Western literacy.* Monograph no. 4. Toronto: Ontario Institute for Studies in Education, 1976.

Havighurst, R.J. *Developmental tasks and education,* 2nd ed. New York: Longmans, Green, 1952.

Havighurst, R.J., Gunther, M.K., and Pratt, I.E. Environment and the draw-a-man test: The performance of Indian children. *Journal of Abnormal and Social Psychology* 41 (1946):50-63.

Havighurst, R.J., and Hilkevitch, R.R. The intelligence of Indian children as measured by a performance scale. *Journal of Abnormal and Social Psychology* 39 (1944):419-433.

Hawkes, J. *The first great civilizations.* New York: Knopf, 1973.

Hawkridge, D., Chalupsky, A., and Roberts. A. *A study of selected exemplary programs for the education of disadvantaged children.* American Institute for Research in the Behavioral Science, Palo Alto, Calif., 1968.

Hay, J., and Wingo, C.E. *Reading with phonics,* rev. ed. Chicago: Lippincott, 1960.

Hayden, A.H., and Dmitriev, V. The multidisciplinary preschool program for Down's syndrome children at the University of Washington model preschool center. In B.Z. Friedlander, G.M. Sterritt, and G.E. Kirk, eds., *Exceptional infant. Vol. 3: Assessment and intervention*, New York: Brunner/Mazel, 1975.

Hebb, D.O. *The organization of behavior*. New York: John Wiley, 1949.

Heber, F.R. Sociocultural mental retardation: A longitudinal study. Paper presented at the Second Annual Vermont Conference on the Primary Prevention of Psychopathology, Burlington, Vt., 1976.

Heber, R., and Garber, H. Progress report II: An experiment in the prevention of cultural-familial retardation. In D.A. Primrose, ed., *Proceedings of the 3rd Congress of the International Association for the Scientific Study of Mental Deficiency*, vol. 1. Warsaw: Polish Medical Publishers, 1975.

Heber, R., Garber, H., Harrington, S., Hoffman, C., and Falender, C. *Rehabilitation of families at risk for mental retardation: Progress report*. Madison, Wisc.: Rehabilitation Research and Training Center in Mental Retardation, University of Wisconsin, 1972.

Heber, R., and Kirk, S. Miracle in Milwaukee. In B.Z. Friedlander, G.M. Sterritt, and G.E. Kirk, eds., *Exceptional children. Vol. 3: Assessment and intervention*. New York: Brunner/Mazel, 1975

Heider, E.R. Universals in color naming and memory. *Journal of Experimental Psychology* 93 (1972):10-20.

Hellmuth, J. Compensatory education: A national debate. In J. Hellmuth, ed., *Disadvantaged child*, vol. 3. New York: Brunner/Mazel, 1970.

Hempel, W.E., and Fleishman, E.A. A factor analysis of physical and manipulative skill. *Journal of Applied Psychology* 39 (1955):12-16.

Henderson, R.W., Swanson, R., and Zimmerman, B.J. Training seriation responses in young children through televised modeling of hierarchically sequenced rule components. *American Educational Research Journal* 12 (1975):479-489.

Henry, G. *Teaching reading as concept development*. Newark, Del.: International Reading Association, 1974.

Hérorard, J. *Journal de Jean Hérorard sur l'enfance et la jeunesse de Louis XIII (1601-1628)*. E. Soulié and Ed. de Barthélemy, eds. Paris, 1868.

Herzog, E., Newcomb, C., and Cisin, I.H. But some are more poor than others: SES differences in a preschool program. Unpublished paper, Social Research Group of the George Washington University, June 1971.

Hess, R.D. Social class and ethnic influences on socialization. In P.H. Mussen, ed., *Carmichael's manual of child psychology*, 3rd ed., vol. 2. New York: Wiley, 1970.

Hess, R.D., and Shipman, V.C. Early experience and the socialization of cognitive modes in children. *Child Development* 36 (1965):869-886.

Henry, G. *Teaching reading as concept development*. Newark, Del.: International Reading Association, 1974.

Hicks, J.A. The acquisition of motor skill in young children. II: The influence of specific and of general practice on motor skill. *Child Development* 1 (1930):292-297.

Hicks, J.A., and Stewart, F.D. The learning of abstract concepts of size. *Child Development* 1 (1930):195-203.

Hildreth, G. *Teaching reading*. New York: Holt, Rinehart and Winston, 1958.

Hilgard, J.R. Learning and maturation in preschool children. *Journal of Genetic Psychology* 41 (1932):36-56.

Hilgard, J.R. The effect of early and delayed practice on memory and motor performances by the method of co-twin control. *Genetic Psychology Monographs* 14 (1933):493-567.

Hindley, C.B. The Griffiths scales of infant development: Scores and predictions from 3 to 18 months. *Journal of Child Psychology and Psychiatry* 1 (1960):99-112.

Hindley, C.B. The Griffiths mental development scale for testing babies from birth to two. In O.K. Buros, *Intelligence tests and reviews*. Highland Park, N.J.: Gryphon Press, 1975.

Hindley, C.B., Filliozat, A.M., Klackenberg, G., Nicolet-Meister, D., and Sand, E.A. Differences in age of walking in five European longitudinal samples. *Human Biology* 38 (1966):364-379.

Hirsch, N.D.M. An experimental study of the East Kentucky mountaineers: A study of heredity and environment. *Genetic Psychology Monographs* 3 (1928):188-244.

Hirst, G. An evaluation of evidence for innate sex differences in linguistic ability. *Journal of Psycholinguistic Research* 2 (1982):95-113.

Hissen, I. A new approach to music for young children. *Child Development* 4 (1933):308-317.

Hoffman, B. *The strange story of the quantum*. Harmondsworth, England: Penguin, 1963.

Hofstaetter, P.R. The changing composition of "intelligence:" A study in *t*-technique. *Journal of Genetic Psychology* 85 (1954):159-164.

Holbrook, B. *The stone monkey: An alternative Chinese scientific reality*. New York: Wiliam Morrow, 1981.

Holland, B. Among pros, more go Suzuki: Young American musicians get early start. *The New York Times*, Sunday, July 11, 1982.

Hollingworth, L.S. *Gifted children: Their nature and nurture*. New York: Macmillan, 1926.

Hollingworth, L.S. *Children above 180 IQ, Stanford Binet*. New York: World Book, 1942.

Honig, A.S., and Brill, S. A comparative analysis of the Piagetian development of twelve month old disadvantaged infants in an enrichment center with others not in such a center. Paper presented at the meeting of the American Psychological Association, Miami, September 1970.

Honig, A.S., Caldwell, B., and Tannenbaum, J. Patterns of information processing used by and with young children in a nursery school setting. *Child Development* 41 (1970):1045-1065.

Honzik, M.P., MacFarlane, J.W., and Allen, L. The stability of mental test performance betwen two and eighteen years. *Journal of Experimental Education* 17 (1948):309-324.

Horowitz, F.D., and Paden, L.Y. The effectiveness of environmental intervention programs. In B.M. Caldwell and H.N. Ricciuti, eds., *Review of child development research*, vol. 3. Chicago: University of Chicago Press, 1973.

Howells, W. *Back of history*. Garden City, N.Y.: Doubleday, 1954.

Howes, C. Peer play scale as an index of complexity of peer interaction. *Developmental Psychology* 16 (1980):371-372.

Huberty, C.J., and Swan, W.W. Preschool classroom experience and first-grade achievement. *Journal of Educational Research* 67 (1974):311-316.

Hudson, W. Pictorial depth preception in sub-cultural groups in Africa. *Journal of Social Psychology* 52 (1960):183-208.

Hughes, M. Egocentrism in preschool children. Unpublished Ph.D. dissertation, University of Edinburgh, 1975.

Huizinga, J. *The waning of the Middle Ages*. Garden City, N.Y.: Doubleday, 1954.

Hull, C.L. The concept of habit-family hierarchy and maze learning. *Psychological Review* 41 (1934):33-52, 134-152.

Hunt, D.E., and Sullivan, E.V. *Between psychology and education*. Hinsdale, Ill.: Dryden Press, 1974.

Hunt, J. McV. The effects of infant feeding-frustration upon adult hoarding in the Albino rat. *Journal of Abnormal and Social Psychology* 36 (1941):338-360.

Hunt, J. McV. *Intelligence and experience*. New York: Ronald, 1961.

Hunt, J. McV. *The challenge of incompetence and poverty: Papers on the role of early education*. Urbana: University of Illinois Press, 1969.

Hunt, J. McV. Reflections on a decade of early education. *Journal of Abnormal Child Psychology* 3 (1975):275-330.

Hunt, J. McV. Psychological development: Early experience. *Annual Review of Psychology* 30 (1979):103-143.

Hunt, J. McV., Mohandessi, K., Ghodssi, M., and Akiyama, M. The psychological development of orphanage-reared infants: Interventions with outcomes (Tehran). *Genetic Psychology Monographs* 94 (1976): 177-226.

Hunt, J. McV., Paraskevopoulos, J., Schickedanz, D., and Uzgiris, I. Variations in the mean ages of achieving object permanence under diverse conditions of rearing. In B.Z. Friedlander, G.M. Sterritt, and G.E. Kirk, eds., *Exceptional Infant: Vol. 3: Assessment and intervention.* New York: Brunner/Mazel, 1975.

Hymes, J.L., Jr. Early reading is very risky business. *Grade Teacher* 82 (1965):88-92.

Ignatev, E.I. Problems in the psychology and of the process of drawing. *Voprosy Psikhologicheskogo Analize Protsessa Risovania,* 25 (1950): 71-116.

Ilg, F.L., and Ames, L.B. Developmental trends in reading behavior. *Journal of Genetic Psychology* 76 (1950): 291-312.

Ilg, F.L., and Ames, L.B. Developmental trends in arithmetic. *Journal of Genetic Psychology* 79 (1951):3-28.

Ingram, D. Language development during the sensorimotor period. In N. Waterson and C. Snow, eds., *The development of communication.* New York: J. Wiley and Sons, 1978.

Inhelder, B. Cognitive schemes and their possible relations to language acquisition. In M. Piatelli-Palmarini, ed., *Language and learning: The debate between Jean Piaget and Noam Chomsky.* Cambridge, Mass.: Harvard University Press, 1980.

Inhelder, B., Sinclair, H., and Bovet, M. *Learning and the development of cognition.* Cambridge, Mass.: Harvard University Press, 1974.

Irvine, S.H. Contributions of ability and attainment testing in Africa to a general theory of intellect. In J.W. Berry and P.R. Dasen, eds., *Culture and cognition: Readings in cross-cultural psychology.* London: Methuen, 1974.

Irwin, O.C. Infant speech: Effect of systematic reading of stories. *Journal of Speech and Hearing Research* 3 (1960):187-190.

Isaacs, S. *Intellectual growth in young children.* London: Routledge and Kegan Paul, 1930.

Issawi, C. *An Arab philosophy of history.* London: John Murray, 1950.

Ives, S.W., and Gardner, H. Cultural influences on children's drawing. In A. Murwitz, ed., *Art education international.* University Park, Pa.: State University of Pennsylvania Press, 1980.

Jaffa, A.S. *The California preschool mental scale* (Form A). Berkeley: University of California Press, 1934.

Jakobson, R., and Halle, M. *Fundamentals of language.* The Hague: Mouton, 1956.

Jastrzembska, Z.S., ed. *The effects of blindness and other impairments on early development.* New York: American Foundation for the Blind, 1976.

Jeffrey, W.E., and Samuels, S.J. Effect of method of reading training on initial learning and transfer. *Journal of Verbal Learning and Verbal Behavior* 6 (1967):354-358.

Jenkins, M.D. Case studies of Negro children of Binet IQ 160 and above. *Journal of Negro Education* 12 (1943):159-166.

Jensen, A.R. How much can we boost IQ and scholastic achievement? *Harvard Educational Review* 39 (1969):1-123.

Jersild, A.T., and Bienstock, S.F. The influence of training on the vocal ability of three-year-old children. *Child Development* 2 (1931):272-291.

Jersild, A.T., and Bienstock, S.F. A study of the development of children's ability to sing. *Journal of Educational Psychology* 25 (1934):481-503.

Jersild, A.T., and Bienstock, S.F. Development of rhythm in young children. *Child Development Monographs* no. 22 (1935).

Johnson, O.G. *Tests and measurements in child development: Handbook II*, vols. 1 and 2. San Francisco: Jossey-Bass, 1976.

Jones, H.E. The environment and mental development. In L. Carmichael, ed., *Manual of child psychology*, 2nd ed. New York: J. Wiley and Sons, 1954.

Jones, H.E., and Jorgensen, A.P. Mental growth as related to nursery school attendance. In G.M. Whipple, ed., *Intelligence: Its nature and nurture. Yearbook of the National Society for the Study of Education* 39, (pt. 2), 1940.

Jordon, T.J., Deutsch, M., Deutsch, C.P., and Grallo, R. Long-term effects of early enrichment: A longitudinal study of persistence and change. Unpublished paper, Institute for Developmental Studies, New York University, n.d.

Kagan, J. What is intelligence? In A. Gartner, C. Greer, and F. Riessman, eds. *The new assault on equality*. New York: Harper & Row, 1974.

Kagan, J., Kearsley, R.B., and Zelazo, P.R. *Infancy: Its place in human development*. Cambridge, Mass.: Harvard University Press, 1978.

Kagan, J., Klein, R.E., Finley, G.E., Rogoff, B., and Nolan, E. A cross-cultural study of cognitive development. *Monographs of the Society for Research in Child Development* 44, Serial no. 180 (1979).

Kagan, J., and Kogan, N. Individual variation in cognitive processes. In P.H. Mussen, ed., *Carmichael's Manual of Child Psychology*, 3rd ed., Vol. 1. New York: Wiley, 1970.

Kagan, J., Moss, H.A., and Sigel, I.E. Psychological significance of styles of conceptualization. In J.C. Wright and J. Kagan, eds., *Basic cognitive processes in children. Monographs of the Society for Research in Child Development* 28, Serial no. 86 (1963).

Kagan, J., Rosman, B.L., Day, D., Albert, H., and Phillips, W. Information processing in the child: Significance of analytic and reflective attitudes. *Psychological Monographs* 78, Whole no. 578 (1964).

Kamin, L.J. *The science and politics of IQ*. Potomac, Md.: Lawrence Erlbaum, 1974.

Karnes, M.B. Conceptualization of GOAL (games oriented activities for learning) curriculum. In R.K. Parker and M.C. Day, eds., *The preschool in action*, 2nd ed. Boston: Allyn and Bacon, 1977.

Karnes, M.B., Hodgkins, A.S., and Teska, J.A. A follow-up of three of the five preschool programs. In M.B. Karnes, A.S. Hodkins, J.A. Teska, and S.A. Kirk, eds., *Research and development program on preschool disadvantaged children*. Final report to the U.S. Department of Health, Education and Welfare, vol. 1. Washington, D.C., 1969.

Karnes, M.B., Zehrback, R.R., and Teska, J.A. The Karnes' preschool program: Rationale, curricula offerings, and follow-up data. In S. Ryan, ed., *A report on longitudinal evaluations of preschool programs. Vol. 1: Longitudinal*. Washington, D.C.: Office of Child Development (DHEW), 1974. ERIC Document no. ED 093 500.

Kavanagh, J.F., and Mattingly, I.G., eds. *Language by ear and by eye: The relationship between speech and reading*. Cambridge, Mass.: MIT Press, 1972.

Kaye, K. Thickening thin data: The maternal role in developing communication and language. In M. Bullowa, ed., *Before speech: The beginning of interpersonal communication*. Cambridge, England: Cambridge University Press, 1979.

Kaye, K., and Marcus, J. Infant imitation: The sensory-motor agenda. *Developmental Psychology* 17 (1981):258-265.

Kearins, J.M. Visual spatial memory in Australian aboriginal children of desert regions. *Cognitive Psychology* 13 (1981):434-460.

Kearsley, R.B., and Sigel, I.E. *Infants at risk: Assessment of cognitive functioning*. Hillsdale, N.J.: Lawrence Erlbaum Associates, 1979.

Keary, F.C. *Indian education in ancient and later times*, 2nd ed. London: Oxford University Press, 1938.

Keister, B.V. Reading skills acquired by five-year-old children. *Elementary School Journal* 41 (1941):587-596.

Kellog, R. *Analyzing children's art*. Palo Alto, Calif.: National Press Books, 1969.

Kellog, R., and O'Dell, S. *The psychology of children's art*. San Diego, Calif.: Psychology Today, 1967.

Kendler, H.H., and Kendler, T.S. Vertical and horizontal processes in problem solving. *Psychological Review* 69 (1962):1-16.

Kennedy, W.A. A follow-up normative study of Negro intelligence and achievement. *Monographs of the Society for Research in Child Development* 34, Serial no. 126 (1969).

Kennistra, K., and Carnegie Council on Children. *All our children: The American family under pressure*. New York: Harcourt Brace Jovanovich, 1977.

Kent, M. Writing before reading. In R.C. Orem, ed., *Montessori: Her method and the movement*. New York: C.P. Putnam's Sons, 1974.

Kephart, N.C. Perceptual-motor aspects of learning disabilities. *Exceptional Children* 31 (1964):201-206.

Kershner, J.R. Relationship of motor development to visual-spatial cognitive growth. *Journal of Special Education* 8 (1974):90-102.

Kessen, W. *The child*. New York: Wiley, 1965.

Kessen, W., ed. *Childhood in China*. New Haven, Conn.: Yale University Press, 1975.

Keyserling, M.D. *Windows on day care: A report based on findings of the National Council of Jewish Women*. New York: National Council of Jewish Women, 1972.

King, E.M., and Friesen, D.T. Children who read in kindergarten. *Alberta Journal of Educational Research* 18 (1972):147-161.

King, J.A. Parameters relevant to determining the effect of early experience upon the adult behavior of animals. *Psychological Bulletin* 55 (1958): 46-51.

Klaus, R.A., and Gray, S.W. The early training project for disadvantaged children: A report after five years. *Monographs of the Society for Research in Child Development* 33, Serial no. 120 (1968).

Klein, G.S. Cognitive control and motivation. In G. Lindzey, ed., *Assessment of human motives*. New York: Rinehart, 1958.

Kleinfeld, J.S. Intellectual strengths in culturally different groups: An Eskimo illustration. *Review of Educational Research* 43 (1973):341-359.

Klineberg, O. A study of psychological differences between "racial" and national groups in Europe. *Archives of Psychology* no. 132 (1931).

Klineberg, O. Cultural factors in intelligence-test performance. *Journal of Negro Education* 3 (1934):478-483.

Klineberg, O. *Race differences*. New York: Harper, 1935.

Klineberg, O. Historical perspectives: cross-cultural psychology before 1960. In H.C. Triandis and J.W. Berry, eds., *Handbook of cross-cultural psychology. Vol. 1: Perspectives*. Boston: Allyn and Bacon, 1980.

Knobloch, H., and Pasamanick, B., eds. *Gesell and Amatruda's Developmental Diagnosis*, 3rd ed. New York: Harper & Row, 1974.

Kogan, N. *Cognitive styles in infancy and early childhood*. Hillsdale, N.J.: Lawrence Erlbaum Associates, 1976.

Kohen-Raz, R. Scalogram analysis of some developmental sequences of infant behavior as measured by the Bayley Infant Scale of Mental Development. *Genetic Psychology Monographs* 76 (1967):3-21.

Koluchová, J. A report on the further development of twins after severe and prolonged deprivation. In A.M. Clarke and A.D.B. Clarke, eds., *Early experience: Myth and evidence*. New York: Free Press, 1976.

Konner, M. Infancy among the Kalahari Desert Sun. In P.H. Leiderman, S.R. Tulkin, and A. Rosenfeld, eds., *Culture and infancy*. New York: Academic Press, 1977.

Koslowski, B., and Bruner, J.S. Learning to use a lever. *Child Development* 43 (1972):790-799.

Kounin, J. The effect of preschool attendance upon later school achievement. Unpublished master's thesis, University of Iowa, 1939.

Kraft, I., Fuschillo, J., and Herzog, E. *Prelude to school: An evaluation of an inner-city preschool program*. Children's Bureau Research Reports, no. 3. Washington, D.C.: U.S. Government Printing Office, 1968.

Kroeber, A.L. *Anthropology*, 2nd ed. New York: Harcourt, Brace, 1948.

Krutetski, V.A. An analysis of the individual structure of mathematical abilities in school children. In J. Kilpatrick and I. Wirszup, eds., *Soviet studies in the psychology of learning and teaching mathematics. Vol. 2: The structure of mathematical abilities*. Stanford, Calif.: School of Mathematics Study Group, 1969.

Labov, W. *Language in the inner city: Studies in the Black English vernacular*. Philadelphia: University of Pennsylvania Press, 1972.

Lado, R. Acquisition and learning in early reading. *Hispania* 60 (1977): 533-535.

Lally, J. *The family development research program: A proposal for prenatal, infant and early childhood enrichment*. Progress report, February 25, 1973. College of Human Development, Syracuse University, Syracuse, N.Y.

Lambie, D., Bond, J., and Weikart, D. *Home teaching with mothers and infants*. Ypsilanti, Mich.: High/Scope Educational Research Foundation, 1974.

Lane, H.L. *The Wild Boy of Avignon*. Cambridge, Mass.: Harvard University Press, 1976.

Langar, S.K. *Philosophy in a new key*, 3rd ed. Cambridge, Mass.: Harvard University Press, 1980.

Langer, W.L. Infanticide: A historical survey. *History of Childhood Quarterly* 1 (1974):353-365.

Lasky, E., and Klopp, K. Parent-child interactions in normal and language-disordered children. *Journal of Speech and Hearing Disorders* 47 (1982):7-18.

Lasry, J.C., and Laurendeau, M. Apprentissage empirique de la notion d'inclusion. *Human Development* 12 (1969):141-153.

Lawton, J.T., and Hooper, F.H. Piagetian theory and early childhood education: A critical analysis. In L.S. Siegel and C.J. Brainerd, eds., *Alternatives to Piaget*. New York: Academic Press, 1978.

Lawton, M.S. The development of analytic-integrative cognitive styles in young children. Unpublished Ph.D. dissertation, University of Toronto, 1977.

Lazar, I., and Darlington, R.B. *Lasting effects after preschool.* Final report, Consortium for Longitudinal Studies Grant no. 900-1311. Administration for Children, Youth and Families, Office of Human Development, U.S. Department of Health, Education and Welfare Publication. Washington, D.C.: U.S. Government Printing Office, 1978.

Lazar, I., and Darlington, R.B. *Lasting effects of early education.* A report, Consortium for Longitudinal Studies. *Monographs of the Society for Research in Child Development* 47, Serial no. 195 (1982).

Lazar, I., Hubbell, V.R., Murray, H., Rosche, M., and Rosche, J. *The persistence of preschool effects: A long-term follow-up of fourteen infant and preschool experiments.* Final report, Consortium on Developmental Continuity, Grant no. 18-76-07843. Administration on Children, Youth and Families, Office of Human Development Services, U.S. Department of Health, Education and Welfare. Washington, D.C.: U.S. Government Printing Office, 1977.

Lazar, I., and Rosenberg, M.E. Day care in America. In E.H. Grotberg, ed., *Day care: Resources for decisions.* Office of Economic Opportunity, Office of Planning, Research and Evaluation. Washington, D.C.: U.S. Government Printing Office, c. 1970, n.d.

Lazar, I., Snipper, A.S., Royce, J., and Darlington, R.B. Policy implications of preschool intervention research. In M.J. Begab, H.C. Haywood, and H.L. Garber, eds., *Psychosocial influences on retarded performance. Vol. 2: Strategies for improving performance.* Baltimore: University Park Press, 1981.

Leahy, A. Nature-nurture and intelligence. *Genetic Psychology Monographs* 17 (1935):236-308.

Lee, L.L. *Developmental sentence analysis: A grammatical assessment procedure for speech and language clinicians.* Evanston, Ill.: Northwestern University Press, 1974.

Lee, P. Early Chinese language stimulation of Chinese infants. Unpublished master's thesis, University of Toronto, 1978.

Lefebvre, M., and Pinard, A. Influence du niveau initial de sensibilité au conflit sur l'apprentissage de la conservation des quantités par une méthode de conflit cognitif. *Canadian Journal of Behavioral Science* 6 (1974):398-413.

Lehman, H.C. Young thinkers and great achievers. *Journal of Genetic Psychology* 74 (1949):245-271.

Lehman, H.C. *Age and achievement.* Princeton, N.J.: Princeton University Press, 1953.

Leiderman, P.H., Tulkins, S.R., and Rosenfeld, A., eds. *Culture and infancy.* New York: Academic Press, 1977.

Leighton, D., and Kluckohn, C. *Children of the people.* Cambridge, Mass.: Harvard University Press, 1947.

Leithwood, K.A. Complex gross motor learning and its influence on personal and social adjustment in four-year-old children. Unpublished Ph.D. dissertation, University of Toronto, 1969.

Leithwood, K.A., and Fowler, W. Complex motor learning in four year olds. *Child Development* 42 (1971):781-792.

Lenneberg, E. A biological perspective of language. In E. Lenneberg, ed., *New directions in the study of language.* Cambridge, Mass.: MIT Press, 1964.

Lenneberg, E. The natural history of language. In F. Smith and G. Miller, eds., *The genesis of language.* Cambridge, Mass.: MIT Press, 1966.

Leonard, L.B. Language impairment in children. *Merrill-Palmer Quarterly* 25 (1979):205-232.

Leontiev, A. Social and natural in semiotics. In J. Morton, ed., *Biological and social factors in psycholinguistics.* London: Logos Press, 1971.

Leopold, W.F. *Speech development of a bilingual child,* vols. 1-4. Evanston, Ill.: Northwestern University Press, 1947-1949.

Lesser, G.S., Fifer, G., and Clark, D.H. Mental abilities of children from different social-class and cultural groups. *Monographs of the Society for Research in Child Development* 30, Serial no. 102 (1965).

Levenstein, P. Cognitive growth in preschoolers through stimulation of verbal interaction with mothers. *American Journal of Orthopsychiatry* 40 (1970):426-432.

Levenstein, P. *Verbal interaction project: Aiding cognitive growth in disadvantaged preschoolers through the mother-child home program.* Final report to the Children's Bureau, Office of Child Development, U.S. Department of Health, Education and Welfare, 1971. Verbal Interaction Project, Family Service Association of Nassau County, Freeport, N.Y.

Levenstein, P. The mother-child home program. In M.C. Day and R.K. Parker, eds., *The preschool in action,* 2nd ed. Boston: Allyn and Bacon, 1977.

Levenstein, P., and Sunley, R. Stimulation of verbal interaction between disadvantaged mothers and children. *American Journal of Orthopsychiatry* 38 (1968):116-121.

Leventhal, A.S., and Lipsitt, L.P. Adaptation, pitch discrimination, and sound localization in the neonate. *Child Development* 35 (1964):759-767.

LeVine, R.A. Cross-cultural study in child psychology. In P.A. Mussen, ed., *Carmichael's manual of child psychology*, 3rd ed., vol. 2. New York: J. Wiley and Sons, 1970.

Levinson, B., and Reese, H.W. Patterns of discrimination learning set in preschool children, fifth-graders, college freshmen, and the aged. *Monographs of the Society for Research in Child Development* 32, Serial no. 115 (1967).

Lévi-Strauss, C. *The savage mind*. Chicago: University of Chicago Press, 1966.

Lévi-Strauss, C. *Triste tropiques*. New York: Atheneum, 1968.

Lewin, K. The conflict between Aristotelian and Galileian modes of thought in contemporary psychology. In K. Lewin, *A dynamic theory of personality*. New York: McGraw-Hill, 1935.

Lewin, K. *Principles of topological psychology*. New York: McGraw-Hill, 1936.

Liberman, I.Y., Mann, V.A. Shankweiler, D., and Werfelman, M. Children's memory for recurring linguistic and nonlinguistic material in relation to reading ability. Paper presented at the biennial meeting of the Society for Research in Child Development, Boston, Mass., April 1981.

Liberman, I.Y., and Shankweiler, D. Speech, the alphabet, and teaching to read. In L.B. Resnick and P.A. Weaver, eds., *Theory and practice of early reading*. Hillsdale, N.J.: Lawrence Erlbaum Associates, 1979.

Liberman, I.Y., Shankweiler, D., Fischer, F.W., and Carter, B. Explicit syllable and phoneme segmentation in the young child. *Journal of Experimental Child Psychology* 18 (1974):201-212.

Ling, B. Form discrimination as a learning cue in infants. *Comparative Psychology Monographs* 17, Whole no. 86 (1941).

Lipton, E.L., Steinschneider, A., and Richmond, J.B. Swaddling, a child care practice: Historical, cultural, and experimental observations. *Pediatrics* (Supplement) 35 (1965):521-567.

Lloyd, F., and Pidgeon, D.A. An investigation into the effects of coaching on non-verbal test material with European, Indian and African children. *British Journal of Educational Psychology* 31 (1961):145-151.

Lock, A. *The guided reinvention of language*. New York: Academic Press, 1980.

Lockwood, W.W. *The economic development of Japan: Growth and structural change, 1868-1938*. Princeton, N.J.: Princeton University Press, 1954.

Long, L. Conceptual relations in children: The concept of roundness. *Journal of Genetic Psychology* 57 (1940):289-315.

Long, L., and Welch, L. The development of the ability to discriminate and match numbers. *Journal of Genetic Psychology* 59 (1941):377-387.

Longstreth, L.E. Revisiting Skeels' final study: A critique. *Developmental Psychology* 17 (1981):620-629.

Lot, F. *The end of the ancient world and the beginnings of the Middle Ages.* New York: Harper & Row, 1961.

Lovell, K. Some recent studies in cognitive and language development. *Merrill-Palmer Quarterly* 14 (1968):123-138.

Low, S., and Spindler, P.G. *Child care arrangements of working mothers in the U.S.* U.S. Children's Bureau, Publication no. 461-1968. Washington, D.C.: U.S. Government Printing Office, 1968.

Lowie, R.H. *Indians of the Plains.* Garden City, N.Y.: The Natural History Press, 1963.

Lu, E.G. Early conditioning of perceptual preference. *Child Development* 38 (1967):415-424.

Lukacs, J. *The passing of the modern age.* New York: Harper & Row, 1970.

Lunzer, E.A., Dolan, T., and Wilkinson, J.E. The effectiveness of measures of operativity, language and short-term memory in the prediction of reading and mathematical understanding. *British Journal of Educational Psychology* 46 (1976):295-305.

Luria, A.R. *The role of speech in the regulation of normal and abnormal behavior.* New York: Liveright, 1961.

Luria, A.R. *Cognitive development: Its cultural and social foundations.* Cambridge, Mass.: Harvard University Press, 1976.

Luria, A.R., and Yudovich, F.I. *Speech and the development of mental processes in the child.* London: Staples Press, 1959.

Lytton, H. Parent-child interaction: *The socialization process observed in twin and singleton families.* New York: Plenum, 1980.

Maazel, M. What to do about the child prodigy. *Etude* 68, no. 8 (1950): 12-13, 60-61.

MacArthur, R.S. Assessing intellectual potential of native Canadian pupils: A summary. *Alberta Journal of Education Research* 14 (1968):115-122.

Macaulay, R.K.S. The myth of female superiority in language. *Journal of Child Language* 5 (1978):353-363.

Macfarlane, J.W. Studies in child guidance. I: Methodology of data collection and organization. *Monographs of the Society for Research in Child Development* 3, Serial no. 6 (1938).

Macnamara, J. Cognitive basis of language learning in infants. *Psychological Review* 79 (1972):1-13.

Macrae, J.W., and Herbert-Jackson, E. Are behavioral effects of infant day care programs specific) *Developmental Psychology* 12 (1976):269-270.

Madden, J., Levenstein, P., and Levenstein, S. Longitudinal IQ outcomes of the mother-child home program. *Child Development* 47 (1976): 1015-1025.

Makita, K. The rarity of reading disability in Japanese children. *American Journal of Orthopsychiatry* 38 (1968):599-614.

Malinowski, B. *Magic, science and religion*. Garden City, N.Y.: Doubleday, 1954.

Mallitskaya, M.K. K metodike ispol'zovaniya kartinok dlya razvitiya ponimaniya rechi u detei v kontse pervogo i na vtorom godu zhizni (A method for using pictures to develop speech comprehension in children at the end of the first and in the second year of life). *Voprosy Psikhologii* (Questions of Psychology) 3 (1960):122-126.

Malson, L. *Wolf children and the problem of human nature*. New York: Monthly Review Press, 1972.

Mann, V.A. Reading skill and language skill. Paper presented at the biennial meeting of the Society for Research in Child Development, Boston, April 1981.

Marge, M. The influence of selected home background variables on the development of oral communication skills in children. *Journal of Speech and Hearing Research* 8 (1965):291-309.

Mattingly, I.G. Reading, the linguistic process and linguistic awareness. In J.F. Kavanaugh and I.G. Mattingly, eds., *Language by ear and by eye: The relationships between speech and reading*. Cambridge, Mass.: MIT Press, 1972.

Mattson, M.L. The relation between the complexity of the habit to be acquired and the form of the learning curve in young children. *Genetic Psychology Monographs* 13 (1933):299-398.

Mayer, M. The prodigies. *Esquire* 61 (1964):106-107.

McCall, R.B., Appelbaum, M.I., and Hogarty, P.S. Developmental changes in mental performance. *Monographs of the Society for Research in Child Development* 38, Serial no. 150 (1973).

McCarthy, D. Language development in children. In L. Carmichael, ed., *Manual of child psychology*, 2nd ed. New York: Wiley, 1954.

McCarthy, D. *Manual for the McCarthy Scales of children's abilities*. New York: Psychological Corporation, 1972.

McCartney, K., Phillips, D., Grajek, S., Scarr, S., and Schwartz, J. Effects of day care. Paper presented at the Society for Research in Child Development, Boston, April 1981.

McCartney, K., Scarr, S., Phillips, D., and Grajek, S. Environmental differences among day care centers and their effects on children's levels of intellectual, language and social development. Paper presented at the Biennial Meeting of the Society for Research in Child Development, Boston, April 1981.

McCracken, R.A. A 2 year study of the achievement of children who were reading when they entered first grade. *Journal of Educational Research* 59 (1966):207-210.

McCune-Nicolich, L. The cognitive bases of relational words in the single word period. *Journal of Child Language* 8 (1981):15-34.

McCurdy, H.G. The childhood pattern of genius. *Journal of the Elisha Mitchell Society* 73 (1957):448-462.

McGarrigle, J., and Donaldson, M. Conservation accidents. *Cognition* 3 (1974):341-350.

McGarrigle, J., Grieve, R., and Hughes, M. Interpreting inclusion: A contribution to the study of the child's cognitive and linguistic development. Unpublished paper, University of Edinburgh, 1978.

McGraw, M.B. *Growth: A Study of Johnny and Jimmy.* New York: Appleton-Century-Crofts, 1935.

McGraw, M.B. Later development of children specially trained during infancy: Johnny and Jimmy at school age. *Child Development* 10 (1939): 1-19.

McGraw, M.B. *Growth: A study of Johnny and Jimmy, 1930-1942.* International Jubilee Congress of Sports Medicine, Moscow, 1958. McGraw film research collection. Film distributed by Motor Development Laboratory Film Collection, Department of Physical Education and Dance, University of Wisconsin-Madison, 1976.

McKee, P., Brzeinski, J.E., and Harrison, M.L. *The effectiveness of teaching reading in kindergarten.* Cooperative Research Project no. 5-0371. Denver Public Schools, Denver, Colo., 1966.

McLaughlin, B. Second-language learning in children. *Psychological Bulletin* 84 (1977):438-459.

McLaughlin, B. *Second-language acquisition in childhood.* Hillsdale, N.J.: Lawrence Erlbaum Associates, 1978.

McNeill, D. *The acquisition of language.* New York: Harper & Row, 1970. (a)

McNeill, D. The development of language. In P.A. Mussen, ed., *Carmichael's manual of child psychology*, 3rd. ed. New York: Wiley, 1970. (b)

McNeill, W.H. *The rise of the West.* Chicago: University of Chicago Press, 1963.

Meacham, J.A. The development of memory abilities in the individual and society. *Human development* 15 (1972):205-228.

Mead, M. *Coming of age in Samoa.* New York: William Morrow, 1928.

Mead, M. *Growing up in New Guinea.* New York: William Morrow, 1975.

Meeker, M.N. *The structure of intellect.* Columbus, Ohio: Charles E. Merrill, 1969.

Menninger, K. *Number words and number symbols: A cultural history of numbers.* Translated from the revised German edition by Paul Broneer. Cambridge, Mass.: MIT Press, 1969.

Menshinskaya, E.A. Fifty years of Soviet instructional psychology. *Soviet Pedagogy* (October 1967):126-142.

Menyuk, P. *Language and maturation*. Cambridge, Mass.: MIT Press, 1977.

Metzl, M.N. Teaching parents a strategy for enhancing infant development. *Child Development* 51 (1980):583-586.

Meyers, C.E., and Dingman, H.F. The structure of abilities at the preschool ages: Hypothesized domains. *Psychological Bulletin* 57 (1960): 514-532.

Miezitis, S. The Montessori method. Some recent research. *Interchange* 2 (1971):41-59.

Miles, C.C. Gifted children. In L. Carmichael, ed., *Manual of Child Psychology*, 2nd ed. New York: J. Wiley and Sons, 1954.

Miller, J. *Assessing language production in children*. Baltimore: University Park Press, 1981.

Miller, J., and Chapman, R. The relation between age and mean length of utterance in morphemes. *Journal of Speech and Hearing Research* 24 (1981):154-161.

Miller, L.B., and Dyer, J.L. Four preschool programs: Their dimensions and effects. *Monographs of the Society for Research in Child Development* 40, Serial no. 162 (1975).

Milner, E. A study of the relationship between reading readiness in grade one school children and patterns of parent-child interaction. *Child Development* 22 (1951):95-112.

Mirenva, A.N. Psychomotor education and the general development of preschool children: Experiments with twin controls. *Pedagogical Seminary and Journal of Genetic Psychology* 46 (1935):433-454.

Moerk, E. A Piagetian functional approach to early language development. Paper presented at the Society for Research in Child Development, San Francisco, March 1979. ERIC Document Reproduction Service no. ED 187-455.

Moerk, E. Relationships between parental input frequencies and children's language acquisition: A re-analysis of Brown's data. *Journal of Child Language* 7 (1980):105-118.

Monroe, M. The drawings and color preferences of young children. Unpublished Ph.D. dissertation, University of Chicago, 1929.

Montessori, M. *The Montessori method*. New York: Frederick A. Stokes, 1912.

Montessori, M. *The absorbent mind*. New York: Holt, Rinehart and Winston, 1967.

Moon, C., and Wells, G. The influence of home on learning to read. *Journal of Research in Reading* 2 (1979):53-62.

Moore, O.K. The preschool child learns to read and write. In Y. Brackbill and G.G. Thompson, eds., *Behavior in infancy and early childhood*. New York: Free Press, 1967.

Moore, R.S., and Moore, D.N. *Better late than early.* New York: Reader's Digest Press, distributed by E.P. Dutton, 1975.

Moore, T. Language and intelligence: A longitudinal study of the first eight years. Pt. 1: Patterns of development in boys and girls. *Human Development* 10 (1967):88-106.

Moore, T. Language and intelligence: A longitudinal study of the first eight years: Pt. 2: Environmental correlates of mental growth. *Human development* 11 (1968):1-24.

Morphett, M.V., and Washburne, C. When should children begin to read? *Elementary School Journal* 31 (1931):496-503.

Morrison, C., Harris, A.J., and Auerbach, I.T. The reading performance of disadvantaged early and non-early readers from grades one through three. *Journal of Educational Research* 65 (1971):23-26.

Morton, A.L. *A people's history of England.* London: Lawrence and Wishart, 1945.

Moskovitz, S. *Do preschoolers learning to sort prefer the help of Vygotsky or Piaget?*, 1972. ERIC Document Reproduction Service no. 075 094, PS 006 431.

Mott, S.M. Muscular activity an aid in concept formation. *Child Development* 16 (1945):97-109.

Mounard, P., and Bower, T.G.R. Conservation of weight in infants. *Cognition* 3 (1974):29-40.

Mowatt, F., and DeVisser, J. *This rock within the sea: A heritage lost.* Boston: Little, Brown, 1968.

Munn, N.L. Learning in children. In L. Carmichael, ed., *Manual of Child Psychology*, 2nd ed. New York: J. Wiley and Sons, 1954.

Murdock, G.P. *Social structure.* New York: Macmillan, 1949.

Murphy, G., and Kovach, J.K. *Historical introduction to modern psychology*, 3rd ed. New York: Harcourt Brace Jovanovich, 1972.

Murray, F.B., and Pikulski, J.J., eds. *The acquisition of reading: cognitive, linguistic and preceptual prerequisites.* Baltimore: University Park Press, 1978.

Nadel, S.F. Experiments on culture psychology. *Africa* 10 (1937):421-435. (a)

Nadel, S.F. A field experiment in racial psychology. *British Journal of Psychology* 28 (1937):195-211. (b)

Needham, J. *Science and civilisation in China. Vol. 2: History of scientific thought.* Cambridge, England: Cambridge University Press, 1969.

Nelson, K. Some evidence for the cognitive primacy of categorization and its functional basis. *Merrill-Palmer Quarterly* 19 (1973):21-39. (a)

Nelson, K. Structure and strategy in learning to talk. *Monographs of the Society for Research in Child Development* 38, Serial no. 149 (1973).

Nelson, K. Infants' short-term progress toward one component of object permanence. *Merrill-Palmer Quarterly* 20 (1974):3-8.

Nelson, K. Facilitating children's syntax acquisition. *Developmental Psychology* 13 (1977):101-107.

Nelson, K. Individual differences in language development: Implications for development and language. *Developmental Psychology* 17 (1981): 170-187.

Nelson, K. Carskaddon, G,. and Bonvilian, J. Syntax acquisition: Impact of environmental variation in adult verbal interaction with the child. *Child Development* 44 (1973):497-504.

Nelson, K., and Ross, G. The generalities and specifics of long-term memory in infants and young children. In M. Perlmutter, ed., *Children's memory. New directions in child development*, vol. 10. San Francisco: Jossey-Bass, 1980.

Nemec, T.F. I fish with my brother. The structure and behavior of Agnatic-based fishing crews in a Newfoundland Irish outport. In R. Anderson and C. Wadel, eds., *North Atlantic fisherman: Anthropological essays on modern fishing*. Newfoundland Social and Economic Paper no. 5, Institute of Social and Economic Research, Memorial University of Newfoundland, 1972.

Newell, A., Shaw, J.C., and Simon, H.A. Elements of a theory of human problem solving. *Psychological Review* 65 (1958):151-166.

Newland, T.E. *The gifted in socioeducational perspective*. Englewood Cliffs, N.J.: Prentice-Hall, 1976.

Newman, H.H. *Multiple human births: Twins, triplets, quadruplets and quintuplets*. Garden City, N.Y.: Doubleday, Doran, 1940.

Newman, H.H., Freeman, F.N., and Holzinger, K.J. *Twins: A study of heredity and environment*. Chicago: University of Chicago Press, 1937.

Newman, V.H. *Teaching an infant to swim*. New York: Harcourt Brace Jovanovich, 1967.

Oakes, M.E. Children's explanations of natural phenomena. *Teacher's College Contributions to Education* no. 926 (1946).

Oden, M.H. The fulfillment of promise: Forty-year follow-up of the Terman gifted group. *Genetic Psychology Monographs* 77 (1968):3-93.

Ogbu, J.U. Origins of human competence: A cultural-ecological perspective. *Child Development* 52 (1981):413-429.

Ogburn, W.F. *Social change*. New York: Viking, 1922.

Olson, D.R. Culture, technology and intellect. In L.B. Resnick, ed., *The nature of intelligence*. Hillsdale, N.J.: Lawrence Erlbaum Associates, 1976.

Orlansky, H. Infant care and personality. *Psychological Bulletin* 46 (1949): 1-48.

Osser, H., Wang, M.D., and Zaid, F. The young child's ability to imitate and comprehend speech: A comparison of two subcultural groups. *Child Development* 40 (1969):1063-1075.

Packe, M. St. J. *The life of John Stuart Mill.* New York: Macmillan, 1954.

Paget, K., and Bracken, B., eds., *The psychological assessment of preschool children.* New York: Grune and Stratton, 1982.

Painter, G. *Infant education.* San Rafael, Calif.: Dimensions, 1968.

Painter, G. The effect of a structured tutorial program on the cognitive and language development of culturally disadvantaged children. *Merrill-Palmer Quarterly* 15 (1969):279-296.

Painter, G. *Teach your baby.* New York: Simon and Schuster, 1971.

Palmer, F.H. Minimal intervention at age two and three and subsequent intellective changes. In R.K. Parker, ed., *The preschool in action.* Boston: Allyn and Bacon, 1972.

Palmer, F.H. The effects of early childhood intervention. In B. Brown, ed., *Found: Long-term gains from early intervention.* American Association for the Advancement of Science Selected Symposia Series, 1978.

Palmer, F.H., and Andersen, L.W. Long-term gains from early intervention. In E. Zigler and J. Valentine, eds., *Project Head Start: A legacy of the war on poverty.* New York: Free Press, 1979.

Palmer, F.H., and Andersen, L.W. Early intervention treatments that have been tried, documented, and assessed. In M.J. Begab, H.C. Haywood, and H.L. Garber, eds., *Psychosocial influences in retarded performance. Vol. 2: Strategies for improving competence.* Baltimore: University Park Press, 1981.

Palmer, F.H., Semlear, T., and Fischer, M.A. One-to-one: The Harlem Study. In M.J. Begab, H.C. Haywood, and H.L. Garber, eds., *Psychosocial influences in retarded performance. Vol. 2: Strategies for improving competence.* Baltimore: University Park Press, 1981.

Paraskevopoulos, J., and Hunt, J. McV. Object construction and imitation under differing conditions of rearing. *Journal of Genetic Psychology* 119 (1971):301-321.

Parisi, D., and Giannelli, W. Language and social environment at two years. *Merrill-Palmer Quarterly* 25 (1979):61-75.

Parker, R.K., ed. *The preschool in action.* Boston: Allyn and Bacon, 1972.

Partridge, G.E. *Genetic philosophy of education.* New York: Sturgis and Walton, 1912.

Pepitone, E.A. *Children in cooperation and competition.* Lexington, Mass.: Lexington Books, D.C. Heath, 1980.

Perani, J. Patronage and Nupe craft industries. *African Arts* 13 (1979-80): 71-75.

Perfetti, C.A., Beck, I., and Hughes, C. Phonemic knowledge and learning to read. Paper presented at the biennial meeting of the Society for Research in Child Development, Boston, Mass., April 1981.

Perlish, H.N. *Wordland workshop*. Philadelphia: Triangle, 1968.

Perlmutter, M., ed. Children's memory. *New Directions for Child Development* 10 (1980).

Peters, D.L. Early education: A limited view. *Contemporary Psychology* 26 (1981):379-380.

Peters, R.S., ed. *Brett's history of psychology*, rev. Cambridge, Mass.: MIT Press, 1962.

Phillips, J. Syntax and vocabulary of mother's speech to young children: Age and sex comparisons. *Child Development* 44 (1973):182-185.

Piaget, J. *The origins of intelligence in children*. New York: International Universities Press, 1952.

Piaget, J. *The child's conception of number*. London: Routledge and Kegan Paul, 1961.

Piaget, J. *Play, dreams and imitation in childhood*. New York: Norton, 1962.

Piaget, J. *Six psychological studies*. New York: Vintage Books, 1967.

Piaget, J. Several sections in M. Piatelli-Palmarini, ed., *Language and learning: The debate between Jean Piaget and Noam Chomsky*. Cambridge, Mass.: Harvard University Press, 1980.

Piaget, J., and Inhelder, B. *Memory and intelligence*. New York: Basic Books, 1973.

Pineo, P., and Porter, J. Occupational prestige in Canada. *Canadian Review of Sociology and Anthropology* 4 (1967):24-40.

Pines, M. What produces great skills? Specific pattern is discerned. *The New York Times*, March 30, 1982.

Pinneau, S.R. The infantile disorders of hospitalism and anaclitic depression. *Psychological Bulletin* 52 (1955):429-459.

Plato. *Collected dialogues*. E. Hamilton and H. Cairns, eds. Princeton: Princeton University Press, 1980.

Plessas, G.P., and Oake, C.P. Prereading experiences of selected early readers. *The Reading Teacher* 17 (1964):241-245.

Porteus, S.D. *The psychology of a primitive people*. New York: Longmans, Green, 1931.

Porteus, S.D. Racial group differences in mentality. *Tabulations of Biology, Haag* 18 (1939):66-75.

Porteus, S.D. *Porteus Maze test: Fifty years application*. Palo Alto, Calif.: Pacific Books, 1973.

Pressey, S.L. Concerning the nature and nurture of genius. *Scientific Monthly*, 81 (1955):123-129.

Preyer, W. *Mind of the Child*. H.W. Brown, trans. New York: Appleton, 1888-1889.

Pribram, K.H. A review of theory in physiological psychology. *Annual Review of Psychology* 11 (1960).

Pribram, K.H. *Languages of the brain: Experimental paradoxes and principles in neuropsychology*. Englewood Cliffs, N.J.: Prentice-Hall, 1971.

Price-Williams, D., Gordon, W., and Ramirez M., III. Skill and conservation: A study of pottery-making children. *Developmental Psychology* 1 (1969):769.

Provence, S. and Lipton, R.C. *Infants in institutions*. New York: International Universities Press, 1962.

Radin, P. *The trickster: A study in American Indian mythology*. New York: Schocken, 1972.

Ragsdale, C.E. Correlation between motor ability and verbal skills. In R.N. Singer, ed., *Readings in motor skill learning*. Philadelphia: Lea and Febiger, 1972.

Raine, J.W. *The land of saddle-bags*. Richmond, Va.: Presbyterian Committee of Publication, 1924.

Rambusch, N.M. *Learning how to learn*. Baltimore: Helicon, 1962.

Ramey, C.T., and Haskins, R. The modification of intelligence through early experience. Paper presented at the Society for Research in Child Development, March 1979.

Ramey, C.T., and Haskins, R. The causes and treatment of school failures: Insights from the Carolina Abecedarian Project. In M. Begab, ed., *Psychosocial influences in retarded performance. Vol. 2: Strategies for improving social competence*. Baltimore: University Park Press, 1981.

Ramey, C.T., and Smith, B. Assessing the intellectual consequences of early day care intervention with high risk infants. *American Journal of Mental Deficiency* 81 (1977):318-324.

Rapaport, D. Cognitive structures. In M.M. Gill, ed., *The collected papers of David Rapaport*. New York: Basic Books, 1967.

Rawson, H. Cognition and reading: An approach to instruction. In T.G. Waller, and G.E. MacKinnon, eds., *Reading research: Advances in theory and practice*, vol. 1. New York: Academic Press, 1979.

Raymont, T. *A history of the education of young children*. London: Longmans, Green, 1937.

Read, C. Preschool children's knowledge of English phonology. *Harvard Educational Review* 41 (1971):1-34.

Read, K.H. *The nursery school*, 6th ed. Philadelphia: W.B. Saunders, 1976.

Redfield, R. The folk society. *American Journal of Sociology* 52 (1947): 293-308.

Reese, H.W. The development of memory: Life-span perspectives. In H.W. Reese, ed., *Advances in child development and behavior*, vol. 11. New York: Academic Press, 1976.

Reisner, E.H. *The evolution of the common school.* New York: Macmillan, 1930.

Rescorla, L.A., and Zigler, E. The Yale Child Welfare Research Program: Implications for social policy. *Educational Evaluation and Policy Analysis* 3 (1981):5-14.

Resnick, L.B., Wang, M.C., and Rosner, J. Adaptive education for young children: The Primary Education Project. In M.C. Day and R.K. Parker, eds., *The preschool in action*, 2nd ed. Boston: Allyn and Bacon, 1977.

Resnick, L.B., and Weaver, P.A., eds. *Theory and practice of early reading*, vols. 1-3. Hillsdale, N.J.: Lawrence Erlbaum Associates, 1979.

Rheingold, H.L. The modification of social responsiveness in institutional babies. *Monographs of the Society for Research in Child Development* 21, serial no. 63 (1956).

Rheingold, H.L. Ethics as an integral part of research in child development. In R. Vasta, ed., *Strategies and techniques of child study.* New York: Academic Press, 1981.

Rheingold, H.L., and Bayley, N. The later effects of an experimental modification of mothering. *Child Development* 30 (1959):362-372.

Rheingold, H.L., Gewirtz, J.L., and Ross, H.W. Social conditioning of vocalization in the infant. *Journal of Comparative and Physiological Psychology* 52 (1959):68-73.

Ricciuti, H.N. Object grouping and selective ordering behavior in infants 12 to 24 months old. *Merrill-Palmer Quarterly* 11 (1965):129-148.

Richards, D.D., and Siegler, R.S. Very young children's acquisition of systematic problem-solving strategies. *Child Development* 52 (1981):1318-1321.

Richards, T..W. Mental test performance as a reflection of the child's current life situation. *Child Development* 22 (1951):221-223.

Richardson, H.M. The growth of adaptive behavior in infants: An experimental study of seven age levels. *Genetic Psychology Monographs* 12 (1932):195-359.

Richardson, H.M. The adaptive behavior of infants in the utilization of the level as a tool: A developmental and experimental study. *Journal of Genetic Psychology* 44 (1934):352-377.

Ridenour, M.V. *Motor development issues and applications.* Princeton, N.J.: Princeton Book Company, 1978.

Riesman, D., Glazer, N., and Denney, R. *The lonely crowd.* New Haven, Conn.: Yale University Press, 1950.

Riessman, F. *The culturally deprived child*. New York: Harper & Row, 1962.

Riessman, F. The overlooked positives of disadvantaged groups. *Journal of Negro Education* 33 (1964):225-231.

Riley, C.A., and Trabasso, T. Comparatives, logical structures, and encoding in a transitive inference task. *Journal of Experimental Child Psychology* 17 (1974):187-203.

Ringler, N. A longitudinal study of mothers' language. In N. Waterson and C. Snow, eds., *The development of communication*. New York: J. Wiley and Sons, 1978.

Roberts, G. Early experience and the development of cognitive competencies and language skills. Unpublished Ph.D. dissertation, University of Toronto, Department of Educational Theory, 1981.

Roberts, K.E. The ability of preschool children to solve problems in which a simple principle of relationship is kept constant. *Journal of Genetic Psychology* 40 (1932):118-135.

Robinson, H.B., Jackson, N.E., and Roedell, W.C. *Annual report to the Spencer Foundation: Identification and nurturance of extraordinarily precocious young children*. Seattle: Child Development Research Group, University of Washington, 1978. ERIC Document Reproduction Service no. ED 162 756.

Robinson, H.B., and Robinson, N.M. *International Monograph Series on early child care*. Vols. 1-12: *Early child care in Hungary, Sweden, the United States of America, Switzerland, Britain, France, Cuba, Poland, Yugoslavia, India, Israel, the Union of Soviet Socialist Republics*. London: Gordon and Breach, 1972.

Robinson, N.M., and Robinson, H.B. A cross-cultural view of early education. In I.J. Gordon, ed., *Early childhood education. Yearbook of the National Society for the Study of Education* 71, Pt. II. (1972).

Roderick, J.A. Cross cultural conversations about reading and young children. *Childhood Education* 55 (1979):286-289.

Root, W.T. A socio-psychological study of fifty-three supernormal children. *Psychological Monographs* 29, Whole no. 133 (1921).

Rosenstiel, A. The role of traditional games in the process of socialization among the Motu of Papua, New Guinea. In D.F. Lancy and B.A. Tindall, eds., *The anthropological study of play: Problems and prospects*. Proceedings of the First Annual Meeting of the Association for the Anthropological Study of Play. Cornwall, N.Y.: Leisure Press, 1976.

Rosental, T.L., and Zimmerman, B.J. Modeling by exemplification and instruction in training conservation. *Developmental Psychology* 6 (1972):392-401.

Rosner, J. Phonic analysis training and beginning reading skills. Unpublished manuscript, Learning Research and Development Center, University of Pittsburgh, 1971.

Rosner, J. *The development and validation of an individualized perceptual skills curriculum.* LRDC Publication no. 1972/7. Learning Research and Development Center, University of Pittsburgh, Pittsburgh, Pa., 1972. ERIC Document Reproduction Service no. ED 062 731.

Ross, G.S. Categorization in 1- to 2-year-olds. *Developmental Psychology* 16 (1980):391-396.

Rothenberg, B.B., and Orost, J.H. The training of conservation of number in young children. *Child Development* 40 (1969):707-726.

Rotter, J. Generalized expectancies for internal versus external control of reinforcement. *Psychological Monographs* 80, Whole no. 69 (1966).

Rowe, D.C. Environmental and genetic influences on dimensions of perceived parenting: A twin study. *Developmental Psychology* 17 (1981): 203-208.

Rozenthal, S., ed. *Niels Bohr.* Amsterdam: North Holland, 1968.

Rubenstein, J.L., and Howes, C. Caregiving and infant behavior in day care and in homes. *Developmental Psychology* 15 (1979):1-24.

Ruddy, M., and Bornstein, M. Cognitive correlates of infant attention and maternal stimulation over the first year of life. *Child Development* 53 (1982):183-188.

Ruderman, F.A. *Child care and working mothers.* New York: Child Welfare League of America, 1968.

Rudiger, D. Institutionalized "early reading" and its developmental effects. *Zeitschrift für Entwicklungspsychologie und Padagogische Psychologie* 3 (1971):195-211.

Rusk, R.R. *A history of infant education.* London: University of London Press, 1933.

Rusk, R.R. *A history of infant education,* 2nd ed. London: University of London Press, 1951.

Rutter, M. Maternal deprivation, 1972-1978: New findings, new concepts, new approaches. *Child Development* 50 (1979):283-305.

Ryan, S. *A report on longitudinal evaluations of preschool programs. Vol. I: Longitudinal evaluations.* DHEW Publication no. OHD 74-24-25. U.S. Department of Health, Education and Welfare, Washington, D.C., 1974. ERIC Document Reproduction Service no. ED 093 500, PS 007 392.

Ryan, T.J. *Promoting child development through a program of home visiting: Final report.* Ottawa: Carlton University, 1974.

Ryan, T.J., and Moffitt, A.R. Evaluation of preschool programs. *Canadian Psychologist* 15 (1974):205-219.

Ryan, W. *Blaming the victim*. New York: Vintage, 1971.

Ryckman, D. The relation of analytic-integrative cognitive styles to early competence. Unpublished master's thesis, University of Toronto, 1977.

Saggs, H.W.F. *Everyday life in Babylonia and Assyria*. London: Batsford, 1965.

Sakulina, N.P. The drawings of preschool children for literary works. *Doshkolnoie Vospitanie* 3 (1947):9-18.

Sarton, G. *A history of science*. Cambridge, Mass.: Harvard University Press, 1952.

Saxe, G.B. Body parts as numerals: A developmental analysis of numeration among Oksapmin in Papua, New Guinea. *Child Development* 52 (1981):306-316.

Saxe, G.B. Developing forms of arithmetical thought among the Oksapmin of Papua, New Guinea. *Developmental Psychology* 18 (1982):583-594.

Scaife, M., and Bruner, J. The capacity for joint visual attention in the infant. *Nature* 253 (1975):265-266.

Schaefer, E. The need for early and continuing education. In V. Denenberg, ed., *Infant education*. Stanford, Conn.: Sinauer Associates, 1970.

Schaefer, E., and Aaronson, M. Infant education research project: Implementation and implications of the home-tutoring program. In R. Parker, ed., *The preschool in action*. Boston: Allyn and Bacon, 1972.

Schacter, F.F., Marquis, R., Bundy, C., and McNair, J. Everyday speech acts of disadvantaged and advantaged mothers to their toddlers. Paper presented at the Biennial Meeting of the Society of Research in Child Development, April 1977.

Scheinfeld, A. *You and heredity*. New York: Frederick A. Stokes, 1939.

Scheinfeld, A. *Your heredity and environment*. Philadelphia: Lippincott, 1965.

Schlesinger, I. The role of cognitive development and linguistic input in language acquisition. *Journal of Child Language* 4 (1977):153-169.

Schwartz, M.M., and Scholnick, E.K. Scalogram analysis of logical and perceptual components of conservation of discontinuous quantity. *Child Development* 41 (1970):695-705.

Schweinhart, L.J., and Weikart, D.P. *Young children grow up: The effects of the Perry Preschool Program on youths through age 15*. Monographs of the High/Scope Educational Research Foundation. Ypsilanti, Mich.: High/Scope Press, 1980.

Schweinhart, L.J., and Weikart, D.P. Perry Preschool Project nine years later: What do they mean? In M.J. Begab, H.C. Haywood, and H.L. Garber, eds., *Psychosocial influences in retarded performance. Vol. 2: Strategies for improving competence*. Baltimore: University Park Press, 1981.

Science 81, Girls lose their lead. 2 (1981):6.

Scott, E., and Bryant, B. Social interactions of early and non-reading kindergarten students with high intellectual ability. *Catalogue of Selected Documents in Psychology (JSAS)* 8 (November 1978):1779.

Scott, J.P. *Early experience and the organization of behavior.* Belmont, Calif.: Brooks/Cole, 1968.

Scott, J.P. Early learning, critical periods in behavioral development. In R.N. Singer, ed., *Readings in Motor Skill Learning.* Philadelphia: Lea and Febiger, 1972.

Sée, H. Economic and social conditions in France during the eighteenth century. E.H. Zeydel, trans. New York: F.S. Crofts, 1931.

Sée, H. *Historie économique de la France.* Paris: A Colin, 1942.

Segall, M.H., Campbell, D.T., and Herskovits, M.J. *The influence of culture on visual perception.* Indianapolis, Ind.: Bobbs-Merrill, 1966.

Seitz, V., Apfel, N.H., and Rosenbaum, L.K. Projects Head Start and Follow Through: A longitudinal evaluation of adolescents. In M.J. Begab, H.C. Haywood, and H.L. Garber, eds., *Psychosocial influences in retarded performance. Vol. 2: Strategies for improving competence.* Baltimore: University Park Press, 1981.

Senn, M.J.E. Insights on the child development movement in the United States. *Monographs of the Society for Research in Child Development* 40, Serial no. 161 (1975).

Serafica, F.C., and Sigel, I.E. Styles of categorization and reading disability. *Journal of Reading Behavior* 2 (1970):105-115.

Shankweiler, D., and Liberman, I.Y. Exploring the relations between reading and speech. In R.M. Knights and D.J. Bakker, eds., *The neuropsychology of learning disorders: Theoretical approaches.* Baltimore: University Park Press, 1976.

Sharpe, P. The contributions of aspects of movement education to the cognitive development of infant school children. *Journal of Human Movement Studies* 5 (1979):125-140.

Shattuck, R. *The forbidden experiment: The story of the Wild Boy of Aveynon.* New York: Farrar, Straus and Giroux, 1980.

Sheldon, P.M. The families of highly gifted children. *Marriage and Family Living* 16 (1954):59-60, 67.

Sherman, M., and Key, C.B. The intelligence of isolated mountain children. *Child Development* 3 (1932):279-290.

Sherritt, H.S. Trainability and emotional reaction in the human infant. *Psychological Clinic* 14 (1922):106-110.

Shipman, V.C. *Disadvantaged children and their first school experiences.* Princeton, N.J.: Educational Testing Service, 1976.

Shirley, M.M. *The first two years*, vols. 1-3. Minneapolis: University of Minnesota Press, 1931-1933.

Siegel, L.S., and Brainerd, C.J. *Alternatives to Piaget*. New York: Academic Press, 1978.

Sigel, I.E. The relationship between parents' distancing strategies and child's cognitive behavior. In L. Laosa and I. Sigel, eds., *Families as learning environments for children*. New York: Plenum, 1982.

Sigel, I.E., Jarman, P. and Hanesian, H. Styles of categorization and their intellectual correlates in young children. *Human Development* 10 (1967): 1-17.

Silberman, C.E. *Crisis in the classroom*. New York: Random House, 1970.

Silva, P.A., and Ross, B. Gross motor development and delays in development in early childhood: Assessment and significance. *Journal of Human Movement Studies* 6 (1980):211-226.

Simoneau, K., and Decarie, T. Cognition and perception in the object concept. *Canadian Journal of Psychology* 33 (1979):396-407.

Sinclair, H. Sensorimotor action patterns as a condition for the acquisition of syntax. In R. Huxley and E. Ingram, eds., *Language acquisition: Models and methods*. New York: Academic Press, 1971.

Sinclair, H. Language acquisition and cognitive development. In T. Moore, ed., *Cognitive development and the acquisition of language*. New York: Academic Press, 1973.

Skeels, H.M. A study of the effects of differential stimulation on mentally retarded children: A follow-up report. *American Journal of Mental Deficiency* 46 (1942):340-350.

Skeels, H.M. Adult status of children with contrasting early life experiences. *Monographs of the Society for Research in Child Development* 31, Serial no. 105 (1966).

Skeels, H.M., and Dye, H.B. A study of the effects of differential stimulation on mentally retarded children. *Proceedings and Addresses of the American Association on Mental Deficiency* 44 (1939):114-136.

Skeels, H.M., Updegraff, R., Wellman, B.L., and Williams, H.M. A study of environmental stimulation: An orphanage preschool project. *University of Iowa Studies in Child Welfare* 15, Serial no. 4 (1938).

Skinner, B.F. *Verbal behavior*. New York: Appleton-Century-Crofts, 1957.

Skjelfjord, V.J. Different ways of viewing pupil readiness for learning to read. *Scandinavian Journal of Educational Research* 20 (1976): 105-121.

Skodak, M. Children in foster homes: A study of mental development. *University of Iowa Studies in Child Welfare* 16, no. 1 (1939).

Skodak, M., and Skeels, H.M. A follow-up study of children in adoptive homes. *Journal of Genetic Psychology* 66 (1945):21-58.

Skodak, M., and Skeels, H.M. A final follow-up study of one hundred adopted children. *Journal of Genetic Psychology* 75 (1949):85-125.

Smethurst, W. The nonprofessional teaching of beginning reading skills to young childen outside schools. Ed.D. dissertation, Harvard University Graduate School of Education, 1970.

Smethurst, W. *Teaching young children to read at home.* New York: McGraw-Hill, 1975.

Smilansky, M., and Smilansky, S. *The intellectual development of Kibbutz-born children of "Oriental" (Middle Eastern and North African) origin.* Research Report no. 120. Ruth Bressler Center for Education Research, Kiryat Menachem, Jerusalem, Israel, 1968.

Smilansky, S., and Boaz, T. Advancing language and cognitive performance of young children by means of earth-clay modeling. In M.L. Hanes, I.J. Gordon, and W.F. Breivogel, eds., *Update: The first ten years of life.* Gainesville, Fla.: Division of Continuing Education, University of Florida, 1976.

Smith, F. *A history of English elementary education, 1760-1902.* London: University of London Press, 1931.

Smith, J. A test of general information of preschool age. Unpublished Ph.D. dissertation, State University of Iowa, 1942.

Smith, M.E. Delayed recall of previously memorized material after twenty years. *Journal of Genetic Psychology* 47 (1935):477-481.

Smith, M.E. Delayed recall of previously memorized material after forty years. *Journal of Genetic Psychology* 79 (1951):377-378.

Smith, M.E. Delayed recall of previously memorized material after fifty years. *Journal of Genetic Psychology* 102 (1963):3-4.

Smith, M.G. Some aspects of social structure in the British Caribbean. *Social and Economic Studies*, 1, no. 4 (August 1953).

Smith, P. Soviet studies in language acquisition. *Alberta Journal of Educational Research* 19 (1973):109-118.

Smith, W.N. *Ancient education.* New York: Philosophical Library, 1955.

Snow, C. Mother's speech to children learning language. *Child Development* 43 (1975):549-565.

Snow, C.E., and Ferguson, C.A., eds. *Talking to children: Language input and acquisition.* Cambridge, England: Cambridge University Press, 1977.

Snow, C.E., and Hoefnagel-Höhle, M. The critical period for language acquisition: Evidence form second language learning. *Child Development* 49 (1978):1114-1128.

Snow, C.P. *The two cultures, and a second look.* Cambridge, England: Cambridge University Press, 1964.

Soar, R.S., and Soar, R.M. An empirical analysis of selected follow-through programs: An example of a process approach to evaluation. In I.J. Gordon, ed., *Early childhood education. Yearbook of the National Society for the Study of Education* 71, pt. 2 (1972).

Söderbergh, R. *Reading in early childhood: A linguistic study of a Swedish preschool child's gradual acquisition of reading ability.* Stockholm: Almquist and Wiksell, 1971.

Sorokin, P.A., Zimmerman, C.C., and Galpin, C.J. *A systematic source book in rural sociology.* Minneapolis: University of Minnesota Press, 1931.

Spangler, P.F, Smith, P.M., and Rosen, M. Symposium on structured teaching and training. I: The effects of a language training programme upon language deficient preschool age children. *British Journal of Mental Subnormality* 22 (1976):86-92.

Spaulding, R.L. *Educational intervention in early childhood: Final report of the Durham Education Improvement Program*, vols. 1-3. Durham: Durham Education Improvement Program, Duke University, n.d.

Speers, G. The mental development of children of feeble-minded and normal mothers. In G.M. Whipple, ed., Intelligence: Its nature and nurture. *Yearbook of the National Society for the Study of Education* 39, pt. 2 (1940):309-314.

Sprigle, H. Learning to learn program. In S. Ryan, ed., *A report on longitudinal evaluations of preschool programs: Vol. I: Longitudinal evaluations.* Washington, D.C.: Office of Child Development, U.S. Department of Health, Education and Welfare, 1974. ERIC Document Reproduction Service no. ED 093 500.

Staats, A. *Child learning, intelligence and personality.* New York: Harper & Row, 1971.

Staats, A. *Social behaviorism.* Homewood, Ill.: Dorsey Press, 1975.

Stanley, J.C., George, W.C., and Solano, C.H., eds. *The gifted and the creative: A fifty-year perspective.* Baltimore: Johns Hopkins University Press, 1977.

Stanley, J.C., Keating, D.P., and Fox, L., eds. Mathematical talent: Discovery, description and development ($MT:D^3$). Monograph no. 5. *Journal of Special Education* 9 (1975):29-103.

Starkey, D. The origins of concept formation: Object sorting and object preference in early infancy. *Child Development* 52 (1981):489-497.

Starr, R.H., Jr. Cognitive development in infancy: Assessment, acceleration and actualization. *Merrill-Palmer Quarterly* 17 (1971):153-186.

Steane, D.A. The effects of analytic-integrative cognitive styles in learning to read at an early age. Ph.D. dissertation, University of Toronto, in preparation.

Steinberg, D.D., and Steinberg, M.T. Reading before speaking. *Visible Language* 9 (1975):197-224.

Steinfels, M.O. *Who's minding the children? The history and politics of day care in America.* New York: Simon and Schuster, 1973.

Stemmer, N. Language acquisition: The product of innate capacities and linguistically relevant experiences. In B. Ketteman and R. St. Clair, eds., *New approaches to language acquisition*. Tubingen: Narr, 1980.

Stevenson, H.W. The teaching of reading and mathematics at the kindergarten level. *Ontario Journal of Educational Research* 7 (1964): 211-216

Stipek, D.J., Valentine, J., and Zigler, E. Project Head Start: A critique of theory and practice. In E. Zigler and J. Valentine, eds., *Project Head Start: A legacy of the war on poverty*. New York: Free Press, 1979.

Stodolsky, S.S., and Lesser, G. Learning patterns in the disadvantaged. *Harvard Educational Review* 37 (1967):546-593.

Stoner, W.S. *Natural education*. Indianapolis, Ind.: Bobbs-Merrill, 1914.

Strang, R. *Learning to read—insights for educators*. Toronto: Ontario Institute for Studies in Education, 1970.

Straus, M.A. Subcultural variation in Ceylonese mental ability: A study in national character. *Journal of Social Psychology* 39 (1954):129-141.

Strayer, L.C. Language and growth: The relative efficacy of early and deferred vocabulary training, studied by the method of co-twin control. *Genetic Psychology Monographs* 8 (1930):209-317.

Strickland, S. Can slum children learn? *American Educator* 7, no. 6 (1971).

Strickland, C.E., and Burgess, C., eds. *Health, growth, heredity: G. Stanley Hall on natural education*. New York: Teachers College Press, 1965.

Strodtbeck, F.L. *The reading readiness nursery: Short-term social intervention technique*. Progress report. Chicago: University of Chicago, 1964.

Sturtevant, W.C. Studies in ethnoscience. In J.W. Berry and P.R. Dasen, eds., *Culture and cognition: Readings in cross-cultural psychology*. London: Methuen, 1974.

Super, C.M. Environmental effects on motor development: the case of 'African infant precocity.' *Developmental Medicine and Child Neurology* 18 (1976):561-567.

Super, C.M. Behavioral development in infancy. In R.L. Munroe, R.H. Munroe, and B.B. Whiting, eds., *Handbook of cross-cultural human development*. New York: Garland Press, 1981.

Sutton-Smith, B., ed. *The games of the Americas*. New York: Arno, 1976.

Suzuki, S. *Nurtured by love: A new approach to education*. New York: Exposition Press, 1969.

Swenson, A. Long-term effects of infant language stimulation. Paper presented at the Society of Research in Child Development, Boston, April 1981.

Swenson, A. Parent-administered infant language stimulation: A comparison of two starting ages. Ph.D. dissertation, University of Toronto, Department of Educational Theory, in preparation.

Swenson, A., and Watson, A. The effects of an infant language stimulation program on phonology and syntax at two years of age. Paper presented at the Second International Congress for the Study of Child Language, University of British Columbia, August 1981.

Swift, J.W. Effect of early group experience: The nursery school and day nursery. In M.L. Hoffman and L.W. Hoffman, eds., *Review of child development research*, vol. 1. New York: Russell Sage Foundation, 1964.

Tawney, R.H. *Religion and the rise of capitalism*. New York: Harcourt, Brace, 1926.

Taylor, P.A.M. *The industrial revolution in Britain*. Boston: D.C. Heath, 1958.

Teale, W.H. Positive environments for learning to read: What studies of early readers tell us. *Language Arts* 55 (1978):922-932.

Terman, L.M. A study in precocity and prematuration. *American Journal of Psychology* 16 (1905):145-163.

Terman, L.M. The mental hygiene of exceptional children. *Pedagogical Seminary* 22 (1915):529-537.

Terman, L.M. The intelligence quotient of Francis Galton in childhood. *American Journal of Psychology*, 28 (1917):208-215.

Terman, L.M. An experiment in infant education. *Journal of Applied Psychology* 2 (1918):219-228.

Terman, L.M. *The intelligence of school children*. Boston: Houghton Mifflin, 1919.

Terman, L.M. *Mental and physical traits of a thousand gifted children. Genetic studies of genius*, vol. 1. Stanford, Calif.: Stanford University Press, 1925.

Terman, L.M., and Fenton, J.C. Preliminary report on a gifted juvenile author. *Journal of Applied Psychology* 5 (1921):163-178.

Terman, L.M., and Merrill, M. *Stanford-Binet intelligence scale*. Boston: Houghton Mifflin, 1972.

Terman, L.M., and Oden, M.H. *The gifted child grows up: Twenty-five years' follow-up of a superior group. Genetic Studies of Genius*, vol. 4. Stanford, Calif.: Stanford University Press, 1947.

Terman, L.M., and Oden, M.H. *The gifted group at midlife. Genetic studies of genius*, vol. 5. Stanford, Calif.: Stanford University Press, 1959.

Tetroe, J. A case study of the early experience of five eminent scientists. Unpublished manuscript, Ontario Institute for Studies in Education, Toronto, 1979.

Thoman, E. Changing views of the being and becoming of infants. In E. Thoman, ed., *Origins of the infant's social responsiveness*. Hillsdale, N.J.: Lawrence Erlbaum Associates, 1979.

Thomas, H. Psychological assessment instruments for use with human infants. *Merrill-Palmer Quarterly* 16 (1970):179-223.

Thompson, G.G. *Child psychology*. Boston: Houghton Mifflin, 1952.

Thompson, H. The modifiability of play behavior with special reference to additional characteristics. *Journal of Genetic Psychology* 62 (1943): 165-188.

Thompson, L., and Joseph, A. *The Hopi way*. Chicago: University of Chicago Press, 1947.

Thompson, W.R. Early environment: Its importance for later behavior. In P. Hoch and J. Zubin, eds., *Psychopathology of childhood*. New York: Grune and Stratton, 1955.

Thoreson, C.E. *Behavior modification in education. Yearbook of the National Society for the Study of Education* 72, pt. 1 (1973).

Thorndike, E.L. The influence of one mental function upon the efficiency of other functions. In R.F. Grose and R.C. Birney, eds., *Transfer of learning*. Princeton, N.J.: D. Van Nostrand, 1963.

Thurstone, L.L. Primary mental abilities. *Psychometric Monographs* Serial no. 4 (1944).

Timmermans, C. *How to teach your baby to swim*. New York: Stein and Day, 1975.

Tizard, B., Cooperman, O., Joseph, A., and Tizard, J. Environmental effects on language development: A study of young children in long-stay residential nurseries. *Child Development* 43 (1972):337-358.

Tolman, E.C. *Purposive behavior in animals and men*. New York: Century, 1932.

Tönnies, F. *Fundamental concepts of sociology*. Translated from *Gemeinschaft und Gesellschaft*, 1st ed., 1887. C.P. Loomis, trans. and ed. New York: American Book, 1940.

Travers, R.M.W., ed. *Second handbook of research on teaching*. Chicago: Rand McNally, 1973.

Treiman, R. The phonemic analysis ability of preschool children. Unpublished Ph.D. dissertation, University of Pennsylvania, 1980.

Treiman, R., and Baron, J. Phonemic analysis training with prereaders. Paper presented at the biennial meeting of the Society for Research in Child Development, Boston, April 4, 1981. (a)

Treiman, R., and Baron, J. segmental anlaysis ability: Development and relation to reading ability. In T.G. Waller and G.E. MacKinnon, eds., *Reading research: Advances in theory and practice*. Vol. 3. New York: Academic Press, 1981. (b)

Trevarthen, C. Communication and cooperation in early infancy. In M. Bullowa, ed., *Before speech: The beginning of interpersonal communication*. Cambridge, England: Cambridge University Press, 1979.

Trotter, R. Intensive intervention program prevents retardation. *APA Monitor* (September 1976):4-5, 19, 46.

Turner, G.H., and Penfold, D.J. The scholastic aptitude of Indian children of Caradoc Reserve. *Canadian Journal of Psychology* 6 (1952): 31-44.

Turvey, M., and Shaw, R. The primacy of perceiving: An ecological reformulation of perception for understanding memory. In L. Nilsson, ed., *Perspectives on memory research*. Hillsdale, N.J.: Lawrence Erlbaum Associates, 1979.

Turvey, M., Shaw, R., and Mace, W. Ecological laws of perceiving and acting: In reply to Fodor and Pylyshyn. *Cognition* 9 (1981):237-304.

Ulrich, R. *Three thousand years of educational wisdom*, 2nd ed. Cambridge, Mass.: Harvard University Press, 1954.

Ulrich, R. Personal communication. 1982.

Ulrich, R., Louisell, S.E., and Wolfe, M. The learning village: A behavioral approach to early education. *Educational Technology* 11 (1971):32-45.

Updegraff, R., Dawe, H.C., Fales, E.E., Stormes, B.E., and Oliver, M.G. *Practice in preschool education*. New York: McGraw-Hill, 1938.

Updegraff, R., Heiliger, L., and Learned, J. The effects of training upon the singing ability and musical interests of three, four, and five-year-old children. *University of Iowa Studies in Child Welfare*. 14 (1938):83-131.

Uphouse, L. Reevaluation of mechanisms that mediate brain differences between enriched and impoverished animals. *Psychological Bulletin* 88 (1980):215-232.

Uzgiris, I.C., ed. *Social interaction and communication during infancy*. San Francisco: Jossey-Bass, 1979.

Uzgiris, I.C., and Hunt, J. McV. *Assessment in infancy: Ordinal scales of psychological development*. Champaign: University of Illinois Press, 1975.

Vadhan, V.P. Induction of number and length conservation in preschool children by discrimination training. Unpublished Ph.D. dissertation, Syracuse University, 1974. *Dissertation Abstracts International* 10 (1976):5239-5240B. Order no. 76-7947.

Van Alstyne, D. The environment of three year old children: Factors related to intelligence and vocabulary tests. Columbia University, *Teachers College Contribution to Education* no. 366 (1929).

Van der Geest, T. *Some aspects of communicative competence and their implications for language acquisition.* Amsterdam: Van Gorcum, 1975.

Van De Riet, V., Van De Riet, H., and Resnick, M.B. *A sequential approach to early childhood and elementary education, Phase II.* Grant report to the Office of Child Development. Gainesville, Fla.: University of Florida, 1970.

Van der Spuy, H.I.J., Cunningham, C.E., Siegel, L.S., Elbard, H., Neilson, B., and Richards, J. The effects of classroom intervention on the language, cognitive, and behavioral development of specifically language delayed children. Paper presented at the International Conference of Psychology, Leipzig, 1980.

Vernon, P.E. Environmental handicaps and intellectual development. *British Journal of Educational Psychology* 35 (1965):1-22.

Vernon, P.E. *Intelligence and cultural environment.* London: Methuen, 1969.

Vernon, P.E., O'Gorman, M.B., and McLelland, A. A comparative study of educational attainment in England and Scotland. *British Journal of Educational Psychology* 25 (1955):195-203.

Victor, J., and Coller, A. *Early childhood inventories project.* New York: New York University, Institute for Developmental Studies, 1970.

Von Bertalanffy, L. *General systems theory.* New York: George Braziller, 1968.

Vygotsky, L. *Thought and language.* Cambridge, Mass.: MIT Press, 1962.

Wachs, T.D., and Cuccinotta, P. The effects of enriched neonatal experience upon later cognitive functioning. *Developmental Psychology* 5 (1971):542.

Wachs, T.D., Uzgiris, I., and Hunt, J. McV. Cognitive development in infants of different age levels from different environmental backgrounds. An explanatory investigation. *Merrill-Palmer Quarterly* 17 (1971):283-317.

Wagner, D.A. Memories of Morocco: The influence of age, schooling, and environment on memory. *Cognitive Psychology* 10 (1978):1-23.

Wagner, D.A., and Lofti, A. Traditional education in Morocco: Sociohistorical and psychological perspectives. *Comparative Education Review* 24 (1980):238-251. (a)

Wagner, D.A., and Lofti, A. Learning to read by "rote" in the Quranic schools of Yemen and Senegal. Expanded version of a paper presented in the symposium, Education, Literacy and Ethnicity: Traditional and Contemporary Interfaces, at the Annual Meetings of the American Anthropological Association, Washington, D.C., December 1980. (b)

Walberg, H.J., and Majoribanks, K. Family environment and cognitive development. *Review of Educational Research* 46 (1976):521-551.

Wale, D. A developmental measure of the analytic and integrative cognitive styles. Unpublished master's thesis, University of Toronto, 1972.

Wallace, E., and Hoebel, E.A. *The Commanches*. Norman, Okla.: University of Oklahoma Press, 1952.

Wallach, M.A., and Kogan, N. *Modes of thinking in young children*. New York: Holt, Rinehart and Winston, 1965.

Waller, T.G. Think first, read later! In F.B. Murray, ed., *Piagetian prerequisites for reading*. Newark, Del.: International Reading Association, 1977.

Walsh, R. *Towards an ecology of brain*. New York: S.P. Medical and Scientific Books, 1981.

Wang, M.C., Leinhardt, G., and Boston, M.E. *Individualized early learning program*. Pittsburgh, Pa.: Learning Research and Development Center, University of Pittsburgh, 1980.

Wang, M.C., Resnick, L.B., and Boozer, R.F. The sequence of development of some early mathematics behaviors. *Child Development* 42 (1971):1767-1778.

Warren, J. Motor precocity in African infants. *Developmental Medicine and Child Neurology* 12, no. 2 (1970).

Waterson, N., and Snow, C. *The development of communication*. New York: J. Wiley and Sons, 1978.

Watson, A. Reading—a problem solving task? In R. Levi, G. Forrest, A. Watson, and B. Bishop, eds., *Perspectives on reading: A literate community—whose responsibility?* Sydney: Ashton, 1977.

Watson, A. Thinking and reading: A cognitive developmental view of reading research and practice. Unpublished paper, Alexander Mackie College, Paddington, Australia, 1978.

Watson, A. The interrelationships among various language components in two year old children. Unpublished Ph.D. dissertation, University of Toronto, Department of Educational Theory, 1982.

Watson, R.I. *The great psychologists*. Philadelphia: Lippincott, 1968.

Watson-Gegeo, K. Hawaiian talk story. Paper presented at a Colloquium of the Reading and Language Department, Graduate School of Education, Harvard University, February 1981.

Weber, L. *The English infant school and informal education*. Englewood Cliffs, N.J.: Prentice-Hall, 1971.

Weber, M. The theory of social and economic organization. A.M. Henderson, and T. Parsons, trans. New York: Oxford University Press, 1947.

Wechsler, D. *Measurement of adult intelligence*, 4th ed. Baltimore: Williams and Wilkins, 1958.

Wechsler, D. *Manual for the Wechsler Intelligence Scale for Children—revised*. New York: Psychological Corporation, 1974.

Weikart, D.P., ed. *Preschool intervention: A preliminary report of the Perry Preschool Project.* Ann Arbor, Mich.: Campus Publishers, 1967.

Weikart, D.P. A comparative study of three preschool curricula. Paper presented at the biennial meeting of the Society for Research in Child Development, Santa Monica, Calif., March 1969.

Weikart, D.P. A traditional nursery school revisited. In R.K. Parker, ed., *The preschool in action.* Boston: Allyn and Bacon, 1972.

Weikart, D.P., Deloria, E.G., Lawser, S.A., and Wiegerink, R. *Longitudinal results of the Ypsilanti Perry Preschool Project.* Final report to the U.S. Department of Health, Education and Welfare, Office of Education, Bureau of Research, August 1970. ERIC Document Reproduction Service no. ED 044 536.

Weisberg, P. Social and nonsocial conditioning of infant vocalizations. *Child Development* 34 (1963):377-388.

Welch, L. The development of discrimination of form and area. *Journal of Psychology* 7 (1939):37-54. (a)

Welch, L. The development of size discrimination between the ages of 12 and 40 months. *Journal of Genetic Psychology* 55 (1939):243-268. (b)

Welch, L. The span of generalization below the two-year age level. *Journal of Genetic Psychology* 55 (1939):269-297. (c)

Welch, L. A preliminary investigation of some aspects of the hierarchical developmental of concepts. *Journal of Genetic Psychology* 22 (1940): 359-378. (a)

Welch, L. The genetic development of the associational structures of abstract thinking. *Journal of Genetic Psychology* 56 (1940):175-206. (b)

Welch, L. Recombination of ideas in creative thinking. *Journal of Applied Psychology* 30 (1946):638-643.

Welch, L. A behavioristic explanation of concept formation. *Journal of Genetic Psychology* 71 (1947):201-222. (a)

Welch, L. The transition from simple to complex forms of learning. *Journal of Genetic Psychology* 71 (1947):223-251. (b)

Welch, L. An integration of some fundamental principles of modern behaviorism and gestalt psychology. *Journal of Genetic Psychology* 39 (1948):175-190.

Welch, L., and Davis, H.I. The theory of abstractions and its applications. *Psyche* 15 (1935):138-145.

Wellman, B.L. Iowa studies on the effects of schooling. In G.M. Whipple, ed., *Intelligence: Its nature and nurture, Pt. II. Yearbook of the National Society for the Study of Education* 39 (1940).

Wellman, B.L. IQ changes of preschool and nonpreschool groups during the preschool years: A summary of the literature. *Journal of Psychology* 20 (1945):347-368.

Wellman, B.L., and Pegram, E.L. Binet IQ changes of orphanage pre-school children: A re-analysis. *Journal of Genetic Psychology* 65 (1944):239-263.

Wellman, B.L., Skeels, H.M., and Skodak, M. Review of McNemar's critical examination of Iowa studies. *Psychological Bulletin* 37 (1940): 93-111.

Wells, G. Describing children's linguistic development at home and at school. *British Educational Research Journal* 5 (1979):75-89.

Wells, G. Linguistic antecedents of educational attainment. Lecture presented at the Ontario Institute for Studies in Education, University of Toronto, March 12, 1981. (a)

Wells, G., ed. *Learning through interaction: The study of language development.* Cambridge, England: Cambridge University Press, 1981. (b)

Wells, H.G. *The outline of history.* Garden City, N.Y.: Garden City, 1920.

Werner, J.S., and Perlmutter, M. Development of visual memory in infants. In H.W. Reese and L.P. Lipsitt, eds., *Advances in child development and behavior,* vol. 14. New York: Academic Press, 1979.

Westinghouse Learning Corporation. *The impact of Head Start: An evaluation of the effects of Head Start on children's cognitive and affective development.* Executive summary. Ohio University report to the Office of Economic Opportunity. Washington, D.C.: Clearinghouse for Federal Scientific and Technical Information, June 1969. EDO36321.

Whipple, G.M., ed. Nature and nurture. *Yearbook of the National Society for the Study of Education* 27, pts. I and II (1928).

Whipple, G.M., ed. Intelligence: Its nature and nurture. *Yearbook of the National Society for the Study of Education* 39, pts. I and II (1940).

White, B.L., Castle, P., and Held, R. Observations on the development of visually-directed reading. *Child Development* 35 (1964):349-364.

White, B.L., and Held, R. Plasticity of sensorimotor development in the human infant. In J.F. Rosenblith and W. Allinsmith, eds., *The causes of behavior: Readings in child development and educational psychology,* 2nd ed. Boston: Allyn and Bacon, 1966.

White, B.L., Kaban, B.T., and Attanucci, J. *The origins of human competence: The final report of the Harvard Preschool Project.* Lexington, Mass.: Lexington Books, D.C. Heath, 1979.

White, B.L., Kaban, B.T., Attanucci, J., and Shapiro, B.B. *Experience and environment. Vol. 3: Major influences on the development of the young child.* Englewood Cliffs, N.J.: Prentice-Hall, 1978.

White, E.E. *Highland heritage.* New York: Friendship Press, 1937.

White, R.W. Motivation reconsidered: The concept of competence. *Psychological Review* 66 (1959):297-333.

White, S.H. Evidence for a hierarchical arrangement of learning processes. In L.P. Lipsitt and C.C. Spiker, eds., *Advances in child development and behavior*, vol. 2. New York: Academic Press, 1965.

White, S.H., Day, M.C., Freeman, P.K., Hantman, S.A., and Messenger, K.P. *Federal programs for young children. Vol. 2: Review of evaluation data for federally sponsored projects for children*. U.S. Department of Health, Education and Welfare, Publication no. (OS) 74-102. Washington, D.C.: U.S. Government Printing Office, 1973.

Whiting, H.T.A. *Concepts in skill learning*. London: Lepus, 1975.

Whyte, W.H., Jr. *The organization man*. New York: Simon and Schuster, 1956.

Wiener, N. *Ex-prodigy: My childhood and youth*. New York: Simon and Schuster, 1953.

Wiggin, K.D., and Smith, N.A. *Froebel's occupations*. Boston: Houghton, Mifflin, 1900.

Wilbert, J., ed. *Enculturation in Latin America*. Los Angeles: University of California at Los Angeles Latin American Center Publication, 1976. (a)

Wilbert, J. To become a maker of canoes: An essay in Warao enculturation. In J. Wilbert, ed., *Enculturation in Latin America*. Los Angeles: University of California at Los Angeles Latin American Center Publications, 1976. (b)

Wilcox, S., and Katz, S. The ecological approach to development: An alternative to cognitivism. *Journal of Experimental Child Psychology* 32 (1981):247-263.

Wilderspin, S. *The infant system*. London: James S. Hodson, 1840.

Williams, J. *Our rural heritage*. New York: Knopf, 1925.

Williams, J.P. Learning to read: A review of theories and models. *Reading Research Quarterly* 8 (1973):121-144.

Williams, J.R., and Scott, R.B. Growth and development of Negro infants. IV: Motor development and its relationship to child-rearing practices in two groups of Negro infants. *Child Development* 24 (1953):103-121.

Williams, M.A.J., and Hugues, F., eds. *The Sahara and the Nile*. Rotterdam: Balkema, 1980.

Wilson, F.T. Some special ability test scores of gifted children. *Journal of Genetic Psychology* 82 (1953):59-68.

Wiltshire, E.B., and Gray, J.E. Draw-a-man and Raven's progressive matrices (1938) intelligence test performance of Reserve Indian children. *Canadian Journal of the Behavioral Sciences* 1 (1969):119-122.

Winer, B.J. *Statistical procedures in experimental design*. New York: McGraw-Hill, 1962.

Winspear, A.D. *The genesis of Plato's thought* 2nd ed., rev. New York: Russell, 1956.

Wishart, J.G., and Bower, T.G.R. The development of number conservation in infancy. Unpublished paper, University of Edinburgh, 1976.

Witkin, H.A. Origins of cognitive style. In C. Sheener, ed., *Cognition: Theory, research, promise*. New York: Harper & Row, 1964.

Witkin, H.A. Congitive styles across cultures. In J.W. Berry and P.R. Dasen, eds., *Culture and cognition: Readings in cross-cultural psychology*. London: Methuen, 1974.

Witkin, H.A., Dyk, R.B., Faterson, H.F., Goodenough, D.R., and Karp, S.A. *Psychological differentiation*. New York: J. Wiley and Sons, 1962.

Witte, K. *The education of Karl Witte*. H.A. Bruce, ed., and L. Wiener, trans. New York: Crowell, 1914.

Witty, P.A. A study of one hundred gifted children. *University of Kansas Bulletin of Education* 2, Whole no. 7 (1930).

Witty, P.A. A genetic study of fifty gifted children. *Yearbook of the National Society for the Study of Education* 39, pt. II (1940):401-408.

Wober, M. Towards an understanding of the Kiganda concept of intelligence. In J.W. Berry and P.R. Dasen, eds., *Culture and cognition: Readings in cross-cultural psychology*. London: Methuen, 1974.

Wolfenstein, M. Trends in infant care. *American Journal of Orthopsychiatry* 23 (1953):120-130.

Wolff, J.L. Effect of subject-determined verbalization on discrimination learning in preschoolers. *Journal of Educational Psychology* 60 (1969): 261-266.

Wohlwill, J. A study of the development of the number concept by scalogram analysis. *Journal of Genetic Psychology* 97 (1960):345-377.

Woodcock, R.W., and Johnson, M.B. *Woodcock-Johnson Psycho-Education Battery*. Hingham, Mass.: Teaching Resources, 1977.

Woodworth, R.S. *Experimental psychology*. New York: Henry Holt, 1938.

Yarrow, L.J. Maternal deprivation: Toward an empirical and conceptual reevaluation. *Psychological Bulletin* 58 (1961):459-490.

Yarrow, L.J. Conceptualizing the early environment. In C.A. Chandler, R.S. Lourie, A.D. Peters, and L.L. Dittman, eds., *Early child care: The new perspectives*. New York: Atherton, 1968.

Yarrow, L.J., Rubenstein, J., and Pedersen, F. *Infant and environment: Early cognitive and motivational development*. New York: Halstead Press, 1975.

Yarrow, L.J., Rubenstein, J.L., Pedersen, F.A., and Jankowski, J.J. Dimensions of early stimulation and their differential effects on infant development. *Merrill-Palmer Quarterly* 18 (1972):205-218.

Yates, D.H. A study of twenty high school seniors of superior intelligence. *Journal of Educational Psychology* 11 (1920):264-274.

Yates, D.H. A study of high school seniors of superior intelligence. Bloomington, Ill.: Public School, 1922.

Zachry, W. Ordinality and interdependence of representation and language development in infancy. *Child Development* 49 (1978):681-687.

Zajonc, R.B., and Markus, G.B. Birth order and intellectual development. *Psychological Review* 82 (1975):74-88.

Zborowski, M. The place of book-learning in traditional Jewish culture. *Harvard Educational Review* 19 (1949):87-109.

Zborowski, M., and Herzog, E. *Life is with people.* New York: Schocken, 1952.

Zeitler, W.R. A study of observationai skill development in children of age three. *Science Education* 56 (1972):79-84.

Zelazo, P.R., Zelazo, N.A., and Kolb, S. Walking in the newborn. *Science* 176 (1972):314-315.

Zigler, E., and Valentine, J., eds. *Project Head Start: A legacy of the war on poverty.* New York: Free Press, 1979.

Zimilies, H. The development of conservation and differentiation of number. *Monographs of the Society for Research in Child Development* 31, Serial no. 108 (1966).

Zimilies, H. Has evaluation failed compensatory education? In J. Hellmuth, ed., *Disadvantaged Child, Vol. 3: Compensatory Education: A national debate.* New York: Brunner/Mazel, 1970.

Zimmerman, B.J., and Lanaro, P. Acquiring and retaining conservation of length through modeling and reversibility cues. *Merrill-Palmer Quarterly* 20 (1974):145-161.

Zukav, G. *The dancing Wu-Li masters: An overview of the new physics.* New York: Bantam Books, 1979.

Index

About the Author

William Fowler has been teaching and conducting research on early learning and cognitive development for many years. He has designed and developed a number of preschool and day-care programs, taught nursery school, conducted clinical evaluation and therapy with adults and children, and was principal of the University of Chicago Laboratory Nursery School. He has written numerous scholarly articles and monographs and is the author of *Infant and Child Care*, a textbook on early education. He has taught at Yale University, the Merrill-Palmer Institute, Yeshiva University, the University of Chicago, and the Ontario Institute for Studies in Education at the University of Toronto, where he was a professor in the Department of Applied Psychology for more than a decade. He received the B.A. from Dartmouth College in social science and international relations, the M.A. in clinical psychology from Harvard University and the Ph.D. in human development from the University of Chicago. He is currently a research scientist in the Department of Child Study at Tufts University.